# COVINGTON BILLIONAIRES

## BOOKS 7-9

## ERIN SWANN

WWW.ERINSWANN.COM

Copyright © 2019 by Swann Publications

Cover images licensed from Shutterstock.com, and depositphotos.com

Cover design by Swann Publications

ISBN-13 978-1692067090

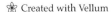 Created with Vellum

# CAUGHT BY THE BILLIONAIRE

# CHAPTER 1

*VINCENT*

THE MAN IN THE SUIT HAD FOLLOWED ME ALL THE WAY HERE FROM WORK THIS evening. It was the third time I'd noticed him in the last two weeks.

I stepped inside Holmby's Grill and peeked out the tinted window after the door closed. After a few seconds of not seeing the suited man, I found my way to my usual table in the corner. I mentally kicked myself for not getting a picture of him for our security team to check out.

Less than a minute later, *she* walked in atop her tall black heels with the self assurance of the runway model she'd once been. Her tits jiggled under the thin fabric of her low-cut dress—a dress that flaunted her ample braless cleavage and threatened to open just a bit too far.

Unfortunately for me, it never quite did.

Holmby's had been her choice tonight, and fine by me. Steak would be a welcome change, and the meat here was arguably Boston's finest.

Half the men in the restaurant stared as she greeted me with a warm, tight hug—and not the lean-forward-to-avoid-touching-your-tits-to-the-guy type, but a real hug. As we parted I breathed in the faint hint of jasmine perfume she'd applied to her neck.

No doubt the male onlookers wished they were me, and rightly so. Staci Baxter and I would be getting hot and heavy between the sheets before the night ended. She had a body to die for, and knew how to work it. A night with Staci never disappointed.

3

Her makeup was subtle and nicely done, accentuating the high cheekbones she was proud of.

"Vince," she purred as I pulled out her chair.

A quick peek down her dress before I rounded the table to my seat jolted my cock. Staci had no doubt gotten a million teenage boys off via her body-paint pictures in the *Sports Illustrated* swimsuit issue.

As I sat, I noticed her jaw showed an uncommon tenseness this evening.

"You okay? I asked.

She glanced down. "I'm a little nervous is all. I could use some wine."

I waved our waiter over. "That I can help with."

He arrived quickly.

"A bottle of Opus One Proprietary Red, please," I told him.

She managed a pasted-on smile after the waiter left and sipped her water—this was a definite off night for her.

I inquired about her sister, and that seemed to calm her while we waited for the wine.

When the bottle arrived, I approved it, and Staci guzzled down most of a glass.

She fiddled with her silverware. "I'm not sure I'm ready."

Since retiring from modeling, she had devoted all her time to her new clothing line. It was understandable that she felt apprehensive about tomorrow's meeting.

"Don't worry. The meeting with the bank will go just fine with the presentation you've got."

"Vince, you've been such a help. But I just don't know if it's good enough."

Asking for a two-million-dollar bank loan to expand her business would stress most anybody. But for a woman with the confidence to walk a runway nearly naked with cameras flashing, this should be a piece of cake.

"You've got this," I assured her.

Our waiter returned, and I ordered the gorgonzola truffle-crusted New York strip steak, while Staci chose the lamb chops.

"Would you like to go over it one last time?" I asked.

She smiled. "Please." She pulled the presentation folder from her oversized purse.

She placed it on the table and smiled. "Gentlemen…" She began the spiel I'd worked out with her.

The food arrived just as she finished her mock presentation.

I topped off our wine glasses and raised mine to hers. "Sounded damn good to me. You don't have anything to worry about."

An enticing blush rose in her cleavage.

I cut my first piece of steak. "Now, tell me more about how your little sister is getting on in New York."

She perked up and started in about how hard it had been for her sister to find a place to live in the city.

An hour later, we had finished dinner and decided against dessert.

We had long since left the topic of Staci's presentation tomorrow, but the undercurrent of nervousness in her demeanor hadn't dissipated. This was more than an off night for her.

"Staci, do you want to talk about what's really bothering you?"

She hesitated before retrieving her purse. After a moment of rummaging, she pulled out a piece of folded paper and extended it across the table with a shaky hand.

I opened it.

*Stay away from Vincent Benson unless you want to become collateral damage*, the note read.

My stomach turned over.

"What's going on, Vince?"

I sighed. Someone was messing with me and using her to do it.

"It's probably nothing... I can arrange some security for you, though."

"I live on the safest street in town. The chief of police lives next door. It looks like *you* should be the one watching out."

I took a picture of the note before grasping it with my napkin and folding it up. "Mind if I take this?"

She shook her head.

There might be nothing worthwhile on it, but I folded it inside the napkin and stuffed it in my pocket nonetheless.

I turned the conversation back to her clothing business while I mulled over who would be messing with me. No faces came to mind, except the nameless suit who'd followed me.

When we'd finished the last of the wine, I offered a very nice bottle of port I had at my place, just a few blocks away.

She wiped her lips with her napkin, but her eyes telegraphed the answer before the words arrived. "Not tonight, Vince. I've been stressing over this presentation all day, and I'm bushed. How 'bout a rain check?"

Begging off from our after-dinner gymnastics *was* unusual. This was a standing date we had pretty much every Monday night—no strings attached, just a good time.

Neither of us did commitments, so neither of us expected anything more than companionship and physical pleasure. "Casual intimacy with friendship on the side," she had once called it. She seemed to be the only woman in town who didn't want or expect anything more from me—except Barb, of course.

I had a more commercial situation with Barbara. Gifts changed hands, but never cash. She made attractive arm candy when I needed it and an enthusiastic bed partner when I wanted some variety, but the side of friendship I had with Staci wasn't there with Barb.

5

"I'll call you," Staci said when we made it to the door.

"Don't forget the LA trip is coming up," I reminded her.

I was counting on her for that, and it wasn't a trip I could make alone.

"Sure," she said in a less-than-enthusiastic tone.

I opened the door for her and waited while she hailed a cab. I checked up and down the street for the suited man. All clear, for now.

After Staci entered the cab, I checked again in the direction of my condo on Tremont Street. Its safety was not far away.

Before starting out, I felt in my pocket for the coin I always carried.

# CHAPTER 2

*ASHLEY*

"I'M GOING TO BEAT YOU OUT FOR THAT LA PROMOTION," MY OPPONENT, ELIZABETH Parsons, said as she stepped sideways on the mat, looking for an opening to attack me.

I slid to my left and dodged her first attempt. "Try all you want, Liz. But you know they only take blondes in California."

She sneered and lunged at me again, grabbing my hair.

It hurt like fuck, and I ended up on the mat.

I patted out ten seconds later. "That's against the rules. That one doesn't count."

She got off me. "Get over your rule hang-up; winning is what counts."

I got up, massaged my sore scalp, and tucked my ponytail down the back of my T-shirt.

She came for me again, ever the aggressor.

We tumbled to the ground, and she initially had the upper hand, but I had the leverage and weight advantage and pinned her fifteen seconds later.

She patted out.

"That makes three," I said.

"Best of seven?" she asked.

As the only women in our section of the FBI's Boston field office, we usually sparred against each other—and Liz hated losing.

I checked the wall clock in the gym. "Out of time today."

We had gone through Quantico together. At the Academy and every day

7

since, she had made up for her lack of stature with competitiveness and pure determination. She was shorter than me, and more buxom, which meant men often underestimated her. More than one bad guy had taken her for a pushover and ended up with a cracked skull thanks to her baton skills.

We grabbed our towels and headed to the locker room. We didn't have a lot of time before our eight am bullpen meeting.

~

Forty minutes later, we entered the bullpen upstairs on our floor of the Boston field office precisely at eight. Special Agent in Charge Randy White checked his watch. "You're late."

Liz started to complain. "But—"

"New rule: no less than three minutes early, understood?"

Anybody else would have accepted our arrival or told us five minutes early. Only SAC White would come up with something asinine like three minutes. He invented another stupid rule every few weeks—something my partner, John McNally, called Caesar moments. And I suppose he should know. John and Randy—excuse me, SAC White—had been partners previously.

"Yes, sir," Liz and I said in unison.

From across the room, John rolled his eyes just enough for me to see.

White had been promoted six months ago to the SAC position. Before that he'd been one of us in the bullpen, and only a little difficult to get along with. Now he was the boss, and beyond difficult. *Randy* was no longer allowed. *Sir* had replaced it. The running joke was that the next budget would have to have a remodeling line item for new doors his ego could fit through.

The special agents had started betting on how long this phase would last. My bet had been six months—that's how long it had taken SAC Sinella, the previous occupant of that office, to settle down. Sinella's transfer to Nashville had triggered White's promotion to Asshole Behind the Glass.

Liz and I both had to kiss up to him, because he would ultimately recommend one of us for the Los Angeles opening that was coming up.

White motioned for Liz to join him in his office. "Parsons, new assignment."

She followed him and closed the door.

I moved over next to John. "What the fuck's with the stupid three-minute rule?"

He shrugged. "He told us just before you two got here." He shook his head. "I'm changing my bet to nine months. The guy should be over his stupid Caesar routine by now, but he's definitely not."

I shrugged and settled at my desk, opening the first folder at the top of my stack.

"I'll call the agency," Liz said as she left White's office a few minutes later.

"Sweet undercover assignment," she mumbled as she passed my desk, trying to get a rise out of me.

I didn't take the bait. I wasn't letting her get to me today. My last undercover had netted me a month in a cockroach- and bedbug-infested cover apartment that still gave me the shivers when I thought about it. When your cover persona was down and out, the bureau went out of its way to make the entire experience realistic, and the latest budget cut had us going even further down-market in arranging cover locations.

Recently, Liz had been snagging the easier undercover assignments.

The men in the office seemed oblivious, but it was clear to me: White had gotten balls-deep into Liz during that ski weekend in New Hampshire last year before he'd been promoted.

She'd denied it when I confronted her about it, but the shift had been easy enough to see. Back when we were all in the bullpen together, she would walk in front of Randy's desk on her way to the coffee room, and although he tried to hide it, his eyes would follow her.

And now, although his eyes didn't follow like they used to, White had given Liz another plum assignment. It was mean of me, but I couldn't help hoping that when his wife found out, she had a sharp implement handy to fix him for good.

I closed my eyes and silently counted to ten. I had to let it slide—again. The Bureau didn't reward people who rocked the boat. If Liz was still seeing him on the side, it would be wrong on so many levels. But in this tight-knit family, back-stabbing wasn't allowed. An agent that snitched on another was a bigger problem than the one who'd committed the original error. The Bureau's anti-bodies would work to expel the offending snitch and keep the organization pure. I'd worked too hard at my career to let a little thing like the SAC's favoritism derail me.

Liz opened the folder on her desk. "Which cover should I use?" she mumbled rhetorically. She shook her head and kept reading.

I didn't answer.

She didn't expect one.

After a moment she picked up her purse. "I'm going out for a smoke."

"Those things are going to kill you," John said wearily, for the hundredth time at least, echoing my feelings.

"Not for a long time," she shot back over her shoulder. "And they keep the weight off."

Arguing with her wasn't worth the effort.

# CHAPTER 3

*Vincent*

My Tuesday morning started with fireworks.

This one had a temper. "Fired? You can't fire me. I quit," Marcy yelled.

The stapler she threw missed me and hit the wall with a bang. Security grabbed her arms and escorted her out.

It took Mason Parker, my number two, all of a minute to enter my office and close the door. "What the hell did you do this time?"

"Nothing," I insisted.

Nothing more than I ever did. I insisted on accuracy with my PAs, and that didn't suit Marcy very well. I needed diligent office help, not a personal assistant who thought the emphasis should be on *personal*.

He plopped down in the red chair he always chose. "At this rate, in a year there won't be anybody left in Boston willing to apply."

"Fuck you."

"What's got you in such a piss-poor mood this morning?"

I pulled up the picture of the note Staci had received and handed my phone to Mason. "Staci found that on her car yesterday."

He scanned it. "Somebody's messing with you."

"No shit, Sherlock. Now you tell me who."

He handed the phone back. "Fuck anybody's wife lately?"

"Fuck no, and you know that."

I had played the field, but married women were never my style. And after Marilyn went full-house psycho on me last year when I wouldn't call her back,

I'd limited myself to Barbara and Staci: the only two certified commitment-phobes I knew.

As long as they were provided with lavish dinners, shopping trips, and the occasional extravagant gift, those ladies were happy and supplied me with enjoyable interludes in the bedroom. The gifts were most often jewelry, but never ever would they expect a ring.

"Just checking," Mason responded. "You ought to give it to security."

"Already did."

He pointed a finger at me. "At least you have the advantage now."

"How so?"

"They've given up the element of surprise. You know somebody's coming at you."

I let Mason badger me for a few more minutes before I changed the subject. "We need to get back on the Semaphore deal right away."

"No, we don't. Let them stew a few days. We don't have to be so reactive."

"We need this. I don't want it to get away."

"If you really want it, get your dad's help."

I resisted reaching for my coin. My mission here in Boston was simple and clear: grow the eastern division of Covington to a billion in revenue. That's the target my father had set. Reach ten figures, he'd said, and I'd be ready to come back to LA, my hometown, and take over Benson Corp., our family business.

That was my ultimate career choice, but so far he wasn't ready to give me control. He'd said I wasn't seasoned enough, or experienced enough, nor did I have the right instincts—his list was a long one. But after I closed the Semaphore deal, that impression would change.

Mason shifted in his chair. "We can't seem too eager."

"I want this one. I'm not letting Gainsboro win."

"If you want it that bad, ask your dad for help," he said again.

"Not necessary."

We both knew the Semaphore deal was big enough to put us on the map and for me to reach my personal goal. But asking for Dad's help was out of the question.

"It's your show," Mason responded. "But it's like dating. Sometimes hard-to-get is the right approach. So put me down as wanting to wait."

*Noted.* But it was my show, and I wasn't waiting. "Meet back here at ten."

Mason left, shaking his head. He usually had balls, but for some reason, not with this deal.

*Wait, my ass.*

I called down to Nina in HR.

She had been expecting my call. "I'll have another candidate here tomorrow morning, Mr. Benson."

"Not soon enough. After lunch," I said.

Her response came quickly. "Yes, sir."

I returned to my spreadsheet on the Semaphore acquisition. I took out my coin and turned it over in my hand while reading.

An hour later, the numbers were swimming on the screen in front of me. I needed a break to clear my head.

Once I was on the treadmill downstairs, the hum of the machine and the pounding of my feet relaxed me. Exercise always cleared my slate mentally and allowed me to return to a problem with renewed focus.

When I dismounted, I pulled up the picture of the note on my phone again. The question remained: who was coming after me and why?

The *why* could only be answered by knowing the *who*, and only knowing the *who* would tell me how dangerous this foe would be, not to mention enabling me to counterattack. Sometimes the best defense was a counterpunch.

～

*ASHLEY*

JOHN AND I HAD SPENT THE MORNING INTERVIEWING NEIGHBORS OF JOHN SPINETTI, A suspect we were investigating in connection with a pair of bank robberies. He hadn't been back here to his home in two weeks, the same span of time as the robberies.

We didn't learn much from the group. This neighborhood in Brighton contained a lot of Russian émigrés, and although they interacted with one another, they didn't seem to have had much to do with Spinetti. It wasn't clear who had been avoiding whom, but not speaking Russian had made Spinetti a minority in this part of town.

My partner spoke just enough Russian that we'd landed the case as soon as White realized the suspect was from this area. Too bad his interviews in Russian hadn't offered anything better than mine in English.

We were now at the second to last house.

"What do we know about these people?" I asked.

John consulted his notes. "Oh, this should be fun. The Zubeks: Petra and Vanda both have petty theft priors for pickpocketing, so check your pockets on the way out; and Dorek, assault and burglary. Arrests, no convictions."

Petra answered the door and let us in when we said we were investigating Spinetti. The way her face wrinkled when she said his name made it clear she didn't like him.

Dorek descended the stairs and got in John's face. "Get out. No cops in heres." He was as tall as John, but much heavier.

John stood his ground and pointed to the three televisions on the floor against the wall. "We're not here about those. We just want to ask about your neighbor, John Spinetti."

"I makes it quick. We don't knows nothing," Dorek replied, taking a step back.

John stared at him for a moment. "Not good enough. Give us a few minutes, or we can start checking serial numbers. Your choice."

Dorek shrugged.

John took him back to the kitchen to start the interview.

From what I could hear, Dorek wouldn't even admit he knew the name of the cross-street.

John interviewed Petra second, with similar outcome, and finally went into the kitchen with the younger sister, Vanda.

After a minute, I could tell Vanda had started to open up.

I was in the front room keeping an eye on Petra and Dorek, who didn't look pleased with what his little sister was saying.

He stood and started for the back.

I moved to the doorway.

"Gets out of the way, little lady."

I moved one hand to my gun and pushed him back with the other. "Stand back."

"Or what? You gonna shoots me?"

I pushed him again. "Sit down."

He glared at me and instead of sitting, motioned for his sister to get up, which Petra did.

The big man grabbed for me.

I shifted back and gave him a swift kick in the balls.

He groaned and fell to the floor in a fetal position, moaning.

Still with a hand on my weapon, I pointed at Petra. "Sit down now."

Her face was red with anger, but after a quick glance at my gun, she sat.

"You okay out there?" John called.

"Yeah," I yelled.

"You too. Sit on the couch," I told Dorek.

He crawled over and climbed onto the sofa, cradling his groin.

A few minutes later, John finished with Vanda and returned to the front room. He eyed Dorek, who was still bent over, holding his crotch.

"What's his problem?"

I didn't answer until we had closed the front door behind us. "He wanted to check out my footwear."

"Ouch," John replied. We walked down the steps. "You know, with two of them you could have called me."

"Would you be saying that if I was a man?"

"It's not your gender; it's your size."

I dropped it. He was just looking out for me, as a partner should.

# CHAPTER 4

*Vincent*

After lunch, a knock came at my office door.

I checked my watch: half-past one. "Yes?"

Nina from HR popped in. "Sir, I've got your new PA candidate outside, if you're ready to meet her."

I closed the spreadsheet and rose.

The girl walked in with plenty of hip swivel and offered a firm handshake. Tall red heels, a short blue skirt, and an only partially buttoned pink top were meant to distract—and were having the desired effect.

She extended her resume. "Jacinda Wilder, sir."

Nina excused herself.

I accepted the resume and caught myself drawn to the well of her cleavage as she sat—definitely deep enough to get lost in. I glanced down at the resume and asked her about her experience.

She had an impressive list of prior jobs, but none had lasted very long.

"The nature of temporary work," she explained. "I often get called to fill in for maternity leaves or unexpected vacancies."

The way she smirked when she said *unexpected vacancies* made me guess she'd played the part of the revenge the boss brought in when his wife decided the old assistant had been too good looking.

"This position can be quite demanding," I told her.

She smiled. "Sir, I'm available any time of the day or night, as much time as you need, and whatever services you require."

The implication was naughty, but I wasn't interested.

I liked this girl. Her answers were all couched cautiously, not divulging very much information—exactly the kind of discretion we needed here. And, with a stint as a copy editor at the *Globe*, she'd likely be up to the task of my need for perfection as well.

~

ASHLEY

THAT AFTERNOON, JOHN AND I WERE SETTLED BACK IN AT THE OFFICE AFTER OUR Brighton interviews when Liz came back early from her first day undercover. She didn't look happy from what I could see through the glass of the boss's office.

I couldn't make out any of his words, but White was gesticulating in a menacing manner.

Abruptly, he stood and opened the door. "Newton, get in here."

I hustled over.

"You fucked up the top case on my desk," White said, pointing at Liz. "Getting blown in less than a day? What were you thinking, Parsons?"

Liz wisely didn't answer.

"This is way too important a case for you to screw up."

"It's not screwed, not yet," Liz argued. "They threw me out, but we can still get Ashley in, and I don't think they made me."

"What do you call getting caught in the subject's office on the first day and being walked out?"

"I got them thinking I worked freelance for a tabloid. The guy is a gossip magnet. They think I was looking for dirt to publish—nothing to connect me to here. That tabloid identity just has to be fully backstopped, and they'll stop looking. We're not blown yet."

Liz had thought ahead if she'd already worked that out. It sounded plausible enough to me.

White scratched his chin. "Tabloid could work. Get Frank to help you backstop that front."

"In the meantime," Liz continued, "we should send Ashley in right away. They have no way to connect the two of us."

White closed his eyes momentarily. "Newton, you're up, then." His eyes bored into mine. "And you better do a better job than Parsons here."

"Yes, sir," I answered.

White's reputation would suffer for a long time if he messed up a big case. Translation: I was cannon fodder, and if anything went wrong now, I'd take the blame. I'd fall on the boss's sword for him, or suffer the consequences—in Alaska.

"Newton, a word," he said, indicating Liz should leave, which she did. The door closed.

I took a seat.

"Parsons has better evals than you," he said. "We should have dinner and discuss how you could improve." The slight hint of a lecherous grin appeared.

I schooled my face to not show the anger I felt. In terms of my evaluations under Sinella, our previous boss, I knew the statement to be a lie. Liz and I had shared once, and our evals had been identical. This could only mean Liz's recent evals had been helped by her hide-the-salami sessions with our new SAC, and that wasn't fair. I wouldn't travel that road. I ignored the roiling in my stomach.

He took my silence as a no and continued. "This is DOJ's top priority, so I really want to get this guy. If you close this case quickly and solidly, I'll make sure you beat Parsons for the LA slot. But the loser heads to the parka store."

He'd hinted before that one of us was heading to LA and the other to Alaska, but never this directly.

"Thank you, sir" was all I said. We both knew he could swing the promotion whichever way he wanted it to go.

He tapped the closed folder in front of him. "DOJ has information that this guy is conspiring with organized crime on something related to gambling. The objective here is to cut off the head of the snake, not just a low-level minion. We want the top guy, the guy who can give us the mob side of the equation. Wiretap warrants have been turned down, so you're going undercover inside this guy's business so we can get him."

"In what capacity?" That connection took this case to the next level for me.

White opened the folder on his desk. "His secretary."

I nodded. This certainly beat out my last assignment; an executive assistant wouldn't require the crap cover motel with bed bugs.

"This won't be an easy undercover," he added. "Parsons isn't the first secretary he's fired this month, so you have to figure out how to last longer than the others did."

"Not a problem, sir."

"Good. I'm counting on you." He slid the folder across the desk.

"Our contact at the personnel agency is listed on the first page, and she'll be expecting your call. She'll see that you get sent over. It's up to you to get hired. Develop a cover and use John for whatever backup you need."

"Got it."

"We'll do dinner after this is over."

I ignored the dinner statement. "Is that all, sir?"

He went back to his screen and flicked his hand toward the door, shooing me away as if I were a fly. I didn't rate a verbal response.

After I closed the door behind me, I gritted my teeth and realized the faint odor in his office wasn't the new carpet. It was the stench of the swine inhabiting it.

My new boss was a much bigger pig than I'd thought possible yesterday, but I could only deal with the situation presented to me. Escape was imperative, and for that I had to nail this assignment and get the hell out of Dodge—away from him, and not by way of Anchorage. Taking down someone connected to organized crime would be the icing on the cake.

Back at my desk, I opened the file. The problem appeared on the second page: Our target was Vincent Benson.

Turning this assignment down wasn't an option. A few months ago, Ralph Turnbull had refused an assignment White gave him and was now in the Minot office chasing moose rustlers or something. Half the agents sent to North Dakota didn't make it to their second winter.

However…

Vincent Benson had taken me to our high school prom. I'd thought we had a future at one point, and I had just been assigned to nail his hide to the wall.

*I am so fucked.*

And I couldn't avoid it.

# CHAPTER 5

*Vincent*

I walked back toward my office after a second gym session. I'd needed it to work off steam after finding that Jacinda girl on my computer.

Why was good help so hard to find? All I wanted was someone who took the job seriously, did accurate work, was willing to work as hard as I did—and yeah, didn't poke her nose where it didn't belong. I paid ridiculously well, but I still wasn't getting what I wanted.

Mason had suggested I split the job in two—and it might come to that, but it shouldn't have to. Plus, that would mean finding two competent people, and so far I couldn't even find one.

Opening the door, I found Mason in my chair with his feet up on the desk.

He quickly pulled them down and stood.

"Checking it out?" I asked.

"Yeah, for the day Daddy pulls you back to LA."

I'd never hidden my longer-term goal, and he knew it better than anybody.

"You know who gets the job isn't up to me."

"I have confidence," he replied.

That was marketing bluster. I knew better. After a few beers, he was incapable of keeping anything from me, and he'd admitted one evening that he didn't expect Bill Covington to promote him to my office.

He changed the subject. "Where's that hottie Jacinda? She go home early?"

"I *sent* her home."

His brow creased. "Huh. If you didn't like her, you should've sent her my way. I could use a distraction like her sitting outside my office. If you don't need her tomorrow, I'll take her."

She had been distracting, for sure, and intentionally.

"You've got Anita," I reminded him.

"We could switch for a while," he offered.

He always joked about wanting a younger assistant, but if I called his bluff, he'd fold in a second. Anita provided him the organization he knew he needed, and all the talk aside, he was too smart to give her up.

"She's not coming back."

"Why the hell are you pissing everybody off? Is it that fucking note?"

I stood to look out the window behind me. "I fired her."

"Already? That has to be a record for you. Two in two days. Keep this up, and you know Nina is going to be right. Nobody's gonna take your job."

I turned to face him again. "I caught her at my computer."

That got Mason's attention. "And you think she was looking for something?"

"I don't know." I rubbed my temples. "After that note, I don't know what to think. But she had no business being on my computer."

"And you think this is related?" Mason asked.

"No idea, but let's have security check her out. If she's working for somebody, I want to know who it is. If they're sending people in to infiltrate us, this is a lot more serious than some prank note on a windshield. And, we're gonna have to take some precautions."

Mason got up to leave. "I'll get her particulars from HR and have security chase her down."

I leaned back in my chair and took a deep breath. "Tell them, whatever it takes. Budget is not an issue."

"You got it," he said as he departed.

After the door closed, I was alone with my worries. This had to be what paranoia felt like. Twice this morning I had noticed a car behind me, convinced it had been following me, only to have it turn off on a side street.

As they said, even the paranoid have enemies, and I had no doubt that was true. These coincidences couldn't be written off as random. Somebody had been following me, Staci had gotten the note, and this latest girl had been somewhere she had no right to be.

This unknown adversary was clearly dangerous. Jacinda could have been a random, clueless hire who didn't know any better than to poke around my computer, but if not, whoever it was wasn't wasting any time.

I turned in my chair and stared out the window again. Somewhere out there was my opponent, and his chief advantage was that he knew me, but I didn't know him. Yet. That needed to change.

I picked up the phone and dialed security.

Benjamin Murdoch, our director of security, picked up. "Hey, bossman, your idiot Mason is down here trying to give me orders."

"I'm just doing what he told me," I heard Mason complain in the background.

Ben knew how to press Mason's buttons and enjoyed doing it.

The team Murdoch had built was top notch, including several with government alphabet-soup backgrounds.

"Ben, do we know anything about that note yet?"

"The note's a dead end. No fingerprints but the girl's, and the paper is common. It won't get us anywhere."

I'd hoped for more, but expected this result. "Thanks, Ben. Now help Mason and me by tracking down what you can on that Jacinda Wilder girl. I want to know who she's working for and what their game is."

"Yes, sir."

"And Ben…"

"Yes, sir?" he asked.

"Be nice to Mason for a change."

"Sure thing, boss. We hadn't thought of using him for Taser practice, but that's a good suggestion."

"I heard that," Mason grumbled in the background.

"Call me when we have something on her. And one other thing—I'm going to have Nina run any more candidates by you if she deems them worthy to come upstairs. We won't hire anyone you haven't checked out thoroughly."

"Yes, sir. When will that start?"

"Right now." I hung up to let Mason and Ben sort out their differences.

One of these days I might get Mason back with some electric burn marks on him, but if anybody could track down Jacinda Wilder's pedigree, it was Ben and his team.

～

THE TEXT ARRIVED LATER THAT AFTERNOON.

STACI: Thank you so much 4 the help - I got the loan

I smiled as I composed my reply.

ME: It was all you - great news

She deserved to get the loan; her proposal had been solid.

STACI: Monday?

I didn't answer right away. I was in no mood to be pushed around by the anonymous note-writer, but Staci had been freaked out by the message and probably still was.

ME: Let you know later

# CHAPTER 6

*ASHLEY*

"WHAT'S THE PROBLEM?" JOHN ASKED.

I flicked my head toward the conference room. "We have a new assignment."

I stood and wended my way between desks to the smaller of our two conference rooms.

My partner grabbed a notepad and followed. He closed the door behind him, twisted the blinds closed, and took the seat across from me.

"The pressure's on because Liz was out in less than a day."

John didn't respond. He was smart enough to not voice his opinion of Liz.

"She broke procedure," I continued. "And now I'm in the crosshairs because she didn't follow the rules. If it goes south, White's gonna blame me."

"It's not always so black and white. Sometimes you have to operate in the gray and it's a matter of judgment."

"You defending her?" I shot back.

He raised his hands. "Hold on, I didn't say that."

I let it go, opened the folder, and slid it toward him. "I'm going in as a personal assistant," I said with confidence that didn't match the way I felt.

He perused it for a moment and slid it back. "Randy and I talked about this one a few days ago."

I suppressed an eye roll. Naturally they'd talked. They'd been partners before White's promotion. John still called him Randy and got away with it. His opinion would always carry more weight with White than any of the rest of ours. That was just the way it went with ex-partners. Those two had been involved in more than one shoot-out together—the kind of experiences that created a lasting bond.

"Any thoughts?" I asked.

"I've never seen him so wound up about a case. This is a big deal for him for some reason. Closing this is your best chance to get on his Christmas list."

I bit my lower lip. That last part I already knew.

"I've met this Benson guy," John said. "Had lunch with him at his fancy country club last year. With what's in this folder, he must be one slippery mother. You're going to need to build a careful cover. Companies like this have the resources to dig deep."

I took a breath before laying out our biggest problem, and maybe my one advantage. "He knows me."

John jerked back. "Fuck. Why didn't you tell Randy?"

I shook my head. "We haven't seen each other since high school. I left to go to Tufts, and he went to USC. Never saw each other after that. It's been a lot of years."

He settled into his chair. "And we're talking because you want to go in anyway?"

I didn't see any choice. "Yup. He'll trust me more than somebody new." Hell, he'd canned Liz in an afternoon. "I'll have an advantage we can't get with anybody else. I think it'll work."

My words made sense, but was I trying to convince him or myself? Vincent Benson had been my Kryptonite back then, but like I'd said, a lot of time had passed.

"He doesn't know you joined the Bureau?"

That was the sixty-four-thousand-dollar question. But I was pretty certain of the answer.

"Nope. We never had any contact after he left." I'd dredged through my memory and was confident I hadn't run into any of his friends or family since I left LA.

"You sure he doesn't know?" he asked.

It was John's responsibility to be sure I wasn't compromising the operation, but knowing that didn't make the accusation sting any less.

"Hundred percent. Outside of my family, only my roommate Hannah knew I was applying to the CIA. Everybody else thought I moved to Virginia to take a marketing job."

My original desire had been to work at the CIA, but my language skills hadn't cut it. The recruiter there had recommended me to the FBI, which turned out to be the best thing that ever happened to me. Here at the Bureau I'd developed skills, found a home, and made a difference taking bad guys off the street. At the CIA I would have been behind a desk analyzing intelligence and eating my way through bag after bag of Cheetos.

John scratched his chin. "You'll still have to clear this with the SAC." He was the responsible one, pointing out the obvious. "And no time like the present."

I gathered up the case folder and followed John back to the boss's office.

It was empty.

Frank informed us White had left for the courthouse and said he wouldn't be back this afternoon.

"Looks like you get the night to think it over," John told me. "But first thing in the morning, you better be sure you can handle it, or else pull the plug before going in. Once you're inside, it would be a career-ender to cry uncle because it's too hard."

I nodded. I had to do this. For so many reasons.

"Personally, I think you're stupid to try," John added. "I haven't done it myself, but the last guy who went under against somebody he knew said it was the hardest assignment he'd ever pulled."

I grabbed my laptop and turned for the conference room. "Let's get started on the prep."

I'd have this evening to think about it, but none of it would matter if we weren't ready.

John closed the door and put his laptop on the table. "What we need is something to make sure your resume floats to the top and gets you hired. You said he knows you. How well?"

I couldn't hide this from my partner; we trusted each other with our lives and our secrets. "He was my boyfriend for a while."

John sat back in his chair with his super-curious look, the one that meant at least a dozen questions were likely coming my way. He could pull a loose string until he'd unwound the entire ball.

"Go on."

"He took me to the prom."

"And now he's ex-boyfriend, right?"

I nodded. "We broke up in high school before leaving for college."

I could sense the next questions would be *who* and *why*.

John didn't disappoint. "And he broke up with you, or you broke up with him?"

"He broke it off."

"What caused that?" His question had been longer than *why*, but no less intrusive.

"A disagreement."

"Over what?" he asked.

"It doesn't matter."

"Hey, I'm not the enemy here. I understand it's sensitive, but your previous relationship affects the case. You know that."

"Look, he wanted to have sex, and I wasn't ready. Okay?"

That backed him off. "Sorry. I had to ask."

"You may not get it, but it was a big deal to me at the time."

"I get it, Ashley. Just one more thing—what do you think his reaction to seeing you again will be?"

I didn't have a good answer to that one. I'd thought about him a million times my freshman year at college. I'd fantasized about us meeting again, and how we would get back together. I'd wanted him to be my first. It hadn't worked out that way, but the memory of our time together had never left me, and never would.

"I don't know. It's been a long time, so I'm sure he's over it." Without so much as a call since then, he'd clearly been over me the day he left.

I'd seen pictures of him with a lot of different women. He might not even remember the girl who'd turned him down.

John and I spent hours devising my cover story. Liz had burned the cover we'd prepared months ago for any kind of office work, and we didn't have a second. Anyway, this one had to dovetail with my actual history to some extent.

It was late when we finally felt comfortable with what we had and left the field office.

Before opening his car door, John said, "Just be sure before you take this on. The time to back out is before you go in, not after."

OPENING THE DOOR TO MY SMALL APARTMENT THAT NIGHT, I TURNED ON THE LIGHT and removed my weapon. I locked it away in my gun safe. If I was going in as an executive assistant tomorrow, I wouldn't be armed. My creds went in the drawer. Opening my wallet, I purged business cards from the last case and my ammo discount card from Minuteman Arms. My wallet couldn't contain anything that linked me to law enforcement or guns.

Was I really doing this?

Was I ready to straight-up lie to Vincent Benson, and then turn around and slap the cuffs on him when I found the evidence?

I slid my work phone into the drawer with my credentials and gun safe, and removed the undercover phone for this op from my purse. John and I had loaded it with all the right history and contacts to match my story.

Pulling down a contact from the list, my fingers hovered over the call button before I eventually pressed it.

Australia was literally the other side of the world, and that meant it would be mid-afternoon there. Hopefully my sister would answer. She was spending a few months there working with a medical non-profit.

"Hello?" Rosemary said hesitantly when she answered.

"Rose, it's me."

She laughed. "Ashley, you know it's polite to tell people your name instead of just saying *it's me*."

"Sorry, maybe I'll get that right next time."

"Doubtful. But it's still good to hear your voice. It must be about midnight in Boston. Is everything okay?"

"I just needed to talk to my big sister."

"So that's a no. It's good you called today, because tomorrow we head into the bush for a while. No cell coverage where I'm going."

That was my sister, always volunteering to help in the most remote places on Earth, God bless her.

I sat on the couch and pulled my knees up. "It's an assignment."

"Normally you can't talk about those. What's different this time?"

"It's somebody you know."

"I'm listening," she said.

"My next assignment is undercover, and the target is…Vincent Benson."

"From high school? That Benson?"

"The same," I admitted.

"That's fucked up. Can't you get out of it?"

"Maybe, but I don't really get to choose my assignments."

I didn't bother to tell her the alternative was probably a transfer to Alaska—she wouldn't have believed me anyway. She'd never worked for a guy like White. I also didn't mention my boss's dinner invitation, which was clearly an invitation to more than dinner.

"Are you sure you're not doing this to get even?"

"You mean for our breakup?" I asked, knowing full well what she meant.

"Breakup makes it sound mutual. He dumped you because you wouldn't put out, and it messed you up for a whole year."

"I'm over it," I replied, although my words were more certain than I felt.

That was the part I couldn't sort out.

"So now you're telling me it didn't make you mad?"

I knew a lie wouldn't get past her. "I was mad; I admit that, but that's not why I'm taking the assignment."

"That's the reason you should seriously consider *not* doing it. Can you be unbiased when it comes to him?"

"I'm not biased," I objected.

"But can you stay that way?"

"You know I'm all about the rules. I'll follow the rules no matter what." I caught myself feeling the thin silver ring I wore on my right hand.

"You sound like you've already made up your mind to do this."

"I don't know," I told her, and that was the truth.

I didn't know how I felt about Vince. There was the period before he left and the period after. The period before was the happiest I'd ever been, and the period after had been the worst. I didn't know how to weigh the two against each other. And besides, I could have tried to contact him later, but I hadn't.

"So you called me so I could play devil's advocate?"

"I guess," I said.

This was our way of talking through problems. She seemed to know I needed her to explore the other side of the argument, and for the next fifteen minutes, she did.

"Did it help?" she asked when the grilling was done.

"A little."

But I was still confused. Tomorrow I would need to walk into the office in pants, carrying my weapon like any other day, and tell White I couldn't do an adequate job because the target knew me. Or I would go in without my gun, dressed for an office environment, and ready to tell White I was the perfect candidate for the assignment because I could easily get the target to trust me.

After hearing about Rose's next few weeks planned in the bush, I was happy my apartment had running water, a toilet, and a shower.

In that respect, Rosemary was tougher than I was.

I went to bed determined to fall asleep with nice dreams instead of nightmares, so I filled my head with memories of the night of the prom.

It worked.

# CHAPTER 7

*ASHLEY*

FIRST THING WEDNESDAY MORNING, JOHN AND I WERE OUTSIDE THE SAC'S OFFICE.
I was in a skirt.

"Is there a problem?" White asked after we closed the door.

We both took seats. I let John take the lead, as White's ex-partner.

"The target knows Ashley," John said, laying it out.

"Why the fuck didn't you say so?" White half yelled at me.

It didn't matter that he hadn't told me the target's name. I hadn't even
opened the folder while I was in his office.

"It can still work," I said. "We haven't seen each other in years. He has no
idea I work for the Bureau."

White rose up in his chair. "What's the first rule of undercover? The first
fucking rule is that you're not you; you're somebody else, goddamn it."

"Randy," John said calmly. "This could be good. Ashley doesn't have to gain
his confidence; she already has it. He has no reason to be suspicious of her, and
gaining the target's confidence is what it's all about. This could shave weeks or
months off the time frame."

White steepled his hands. "Well, we are under a real time crunch here. You're
sure he never knew you wanted to work for the Bureau?" he asked me.

I relaxed; it looked like John had convinced him. "Last he knew, I wanted to
teach high school."

White chuckled. To him, high school teacher was the perfect occupation for a
woman.

28

He fixed me with a stare. "Newton, you better be right about that. We are damned well taking Covington Industries and this Benson guy down. There's no room to fuck this one up. Do we understand each other?"

"Yes, sir. I'm positive."

"Okay then, keep me up to date," the boss said, returning to his computer.

After the door closed behind us, John whispered to me. "I don't get why he has such a hair up his ass, but your butt really is on the line. We need a clean bust that holds up."

"Yeah, that was loud and clear."

I had no idea why this was such a big deal either. But Vincent Benson was no longer the football jock I'd dated in high school. The folder made it clear that he and his company were conspiring with organized crime, and it was up to me to put an end to it.

By nine forty-five I was walking toward the Covington building downtown, going over the details of my cover background in my head. I had contacted the personnel agency shortly after five last evening. The Covington people had already called, requesting the replacement for Jacinda Wilder, Liz's cover identity. I was expected to report for an interview at ten this morning.

I shook my head thinking about her—out in less than half a day. Beating that wasn't a very high bar.

I checked my reflection in the glass before entering. I'd chosen conservative, professional: black pumps, a knee-length, gray skirt-and-jacket business suit with a white, long sleeve, collared blouse buttoned up demurely. Liz had chosen to dress provocatively, which could sometimes work but evidently had backfired on her yesterday.

Satisfied, I freshened my lipstick and pushed through the swinging glass doors into the lobby. I presented myself to the security desk at five minutes before ten. A call upstairs and I was quickly escorted to the third floor and the office of Nina Zaleski.

She perused my resume for a moment. "Assistant to the VP of marketing and then the CEO at Tenerife. That's quite impressive. I see that you have been out of work for the last year, though."

I nodded. "It was my aunt. She got sick, and I took time off to take care of her."

She smiled. "That's quite kind. How is she doing?"

I looked down and managed the beginning of a tear. "She passed two months ago."

This part of the cover was a pretty standard explanation for not having a recent reference to check. But I had no problem putting on a sad face. The facts of my aunt Michelle's death were even worse than the fiction we had concocted and backed up with a few changes to the records of the Middlesex County Medical Examiner's Office. I knew this part of my cover would stand up to scrutiny.

Her face fell as my answer had the desired effect. Now she would feel guilty asking much more about my background.

"I'm sorry. That was insensitive of me."

"It was cancer," I added.

The big C always threw a significant damper over the conversation as the questioner considered their own mortality and the randomness with which cancer took its victims.

"Breast cancer," I added.

If she had been a smoker, I would have chosen lung cancer, but her fingers and teeth were stain free.

Ms. Zaleski fidgeted and put down the paper. "I'm sorry to hear that."

I reached down and lifted my purse, pulling a tissue from the side pocket. I dabbed at the corner of my eye.

Ms. Zaleski folded her hands. "The position you're here to interview for is the personal assistant to the executive vice president of Covington Industries' east coast operations. The hours will be long. After your recent loss, are you sure you feel up to such a demanding position?"

I didn't hesitate. "Yes. That's exactly what I need right now, to throw myself back into work. The less time sitting at home thinking about my aunt the better."

"The man can be difficult and very demanding, and also quite gruff. You'll need to understand that going in."

Her description didn't sound anything like the Vincent Benson I'd known, but hell, people changed—or sometimes the job changed the person—and we'd only been teenagers before.

Anyway, I'd expected a warning along this line. We knew Vincent Benson had chewed through numerous assistants recently, so perhaps he *had* changed.

"After Mr. Honeycutt, anybody else would be a pussycat," I told her.

Honeycutt had been the CEO of Tenerife Inc. before he and his head marketing guy had been killed in a plane crash six months ago. The HR person at Tenerife was ready to field a reference call if they made one, and it was unlikely anybody would question my comment about Honeycutt. Dead men tell no tales.

She steepled her hands. "And you feel prepared for the pressure?"

"I have a friend who worked for the executive VP at Federated," I told her. "And she had pretty much the same experiences I did. It seems to go with the territory. High-stress jobs don't always bring out the best in people."

She nodded and seemed ready to agree on principle. She stood. "Very well. I'll take you up to interview with Mr. Benson while security runs your back-ground check. You won't start, however, until after security has completed their investigation."

I felt a slight chill. A background check had not been part of the plan. This morning all John and I had prepared for was a possible reference call to Tenerife, or a search about my aunt. We wouldn't be prepared for anything deeper for at least another day or two. It took time to assemble the necessary backstop information with people that only worked business hours.

If they got started quickly, my cover might be blown even faster than Liz's. *Poof*—everything would be up in smoke, including my career.

# CHAPTER 8

*Vincent*

Sitting in my office, I rubbed my tired eyes. Sleep hadn't come quickly last night. That fucking note, and then the girl messing with my computer had me worried—and I never worried. Dad had taught me to be the master of my destiny, not a victim of it, but today was different. An enemy I'd identified was easy to combat, but an unseen one? How did you counterpunch a shadow?

I pushed the intercom before I realized I didn't have an assistant outside my office to freshen my coffee this morning. Lifting the cup, I rounded my desk and started for the dining room. The lower floors had break rooms and a cafeteria. My floor had a small dining room for the executive staff when we wanted to eat in.

The two people in there left when I entered.

The touch screen on the expensive coffee machine took me a minute to figure out. Indecipherable icons instead of words didn't help. The first cup didn't come out right. I gave up when the second was worse.

I returned to my office, coffee-less, to find two women waiting: Nina Zaleski and another who had her back to me.

She turned. It was Ashley Newton, from high school.

"Ash?"

She was a vision from my past, and even more lovely than my memory.

Her emerald green eyes lit up as she recognized me. "Vince?"

Ashley had once been my very special Kitten, but that was a long time ago.

"You two know each other?" Nina asked.

"It's been a long time," Ashley said.

"Miss Newton is here about the PA opening," Nina informed me, as she handed me Ashley's resume.

"Is that so? Thank you, Nina. I'll take it from here."

Nina nodded as she turned to go.

I motioned to the office door. "Please."

Ashley entered, and I followed, trying hard to not stare at her ass.

"You look great," I told her.

Not my best line, but an understatement if anything. She filled out her gray business suit well, curves not hidden, but not shouting out. She'd been beautiful before, and she'd only grown more so. Her hair was up, which wasn't my favorite, but was suited to an office. She presented as the complete opposite of yesterday's girl.

"You don't look so bad yourself," she said. "But here? Boston?" She looked around the office. "I thought you were destined to run your family's company, not Covington."

That hit a sore spot. "Let's just say Dad didn't see it that way."

She pulled back. "Oh, I'm sorry."

I tried not to stare at the beautiful woman she had become. "No. This is better. Really. Out here away from headquarters, I get to call my own shots, and maybe someday…"

I didn't finish the sentence. Explaining what went on between Dad and me was not my favorite subject.

I felt for Dad's coin. I willed myself to not stare again, and failed.

∿

## ASHLEY

MY HEART HAD ALMOST STOPPED. THE SIGHT OF HIM TOOK MY BREATH AWAY. HE HAD certainly grown since high school. He had been the star tight-end on the football team, but now he was even taller. Judging by the way he filled out his suit, he'd grown more buff as well. His chiseled jawline seemed more pronounced.

"How many years has it been?" Vince asked with a smile that broadened by the second, accentuating his dimples.

I smiled, remembering prom night. He was a solid ten on anybody's scale. I mentally slapped myself for losing my concentration.

"Nine," I responded. *Hold it together, girl. This is an assignment, not a date. And you know nothing about who he is now.*

In 1934, Clyde Barrow had been a handsome rake, and where had falling for him gotten Bonnie? Shot full of holes. In the real world you couldn't tell the good guys from the bad by the color of their hats—or their looks.

Vince's eyes slowly traveled the length of me. "You look great, Ash," he said again with a hint of a twinkle in his eye—the same dangerous twinkle that had pulled me in nearly a decade ago.

I bit my lip. "Thank you."

John had warned me this would be hard, and it turned out he was right.

It was a large office, with a couch along one wall, a small conference table and a whiteboard at the close end, and Vince's desk on the far end with a pair of visitor chairs. Before I realized how inappropriate it was, I wondered how many women had shed their clothes on that couch. A dozen, maybe more?

He closed the door behind us.

I could see the harbor from here through the full-length windows. "Nice view." I took one of the chairs facing the desk.

"Thanks," he said as he took his seat. "I guess I don't take the time to appreciate it enough."

Zaleski had warned me he would be gruff, but so far his demeanor was anything but.

He took a slow breath. "Ashley, you look great."

"You already said that," I reminded him.

I felt the heat of a blush rise in my cheeks, signaling my unconscious reaction to his presence—the part of me my rational brain couldn't control.

I reminded myself I had a job to do, my career to secure. I touched my silver ring for just a second.

His eyes narrowed. "So what have you been doing with yourself? Last time I saw you, you planned on going pre-med."

That wasn't the whole story. The last time we'd seen each other, he'd left because I wasn't ready for sex yet. He'd decided to move on.

Before that decision, being Vincent Benson's girlfriend had been the high point of my life. But I'd promised my aunt I wouldn't take that step in high school, and I'd kept my promise, even when it meant losing Vince.

My aunt felt high school girls weren't old enough to make that choice. Most of my classmates disagreed and were eagerly sucking dick and spreading their legs in the backs of cars or wherever privacy was available.

When I'd made my limits known, I'd been the oddity—not quite the freak, but not one of the cool girls, that's for sure.

I'd seen the sideways glances and the conversations cut short as I approached. It was almost as if they had to be careful I didn't talk them out of a good time, not that I ever tried. Their choices were just that, *their* choices. I was comfortable with mine.

"Did you?" he asked.

I'd missed the question while playing my private way-back machine in my head. "Pardon?"

He glanced at the resume and put it down. "Did you like studying psychology at Tufts?"

This was where I had to be sure to stick to the script. "I did. After that, I got into this: executive assistant work."

"And you like it?"

The question had an undercurrent of disdain. He didn't think much of the position he was hiring me for. We had come from different worlds. Him the son of a powerful family with unimaginable wealth, and me, the girl who went on to become—at least in this cover—a secretary.

"Sure, and you know what they say about a psych degree: it qualifies you to work at Starbucks, and this beats that."

Too bad I couldn't tell him I was actually doing much more important work, work I could be proud of every day at a job he wouldn't dare look down on. I proudly carried the badge and gun of the premier law enforcement agency in the world, and I spent my days putting crooks away.

I took this moment to remind myself he was one of them.

His brow creased slightly. His degree had been in marketing, I'd learned, and it would have helped us bond if I could have claimed the same background. But undercover, it was best to make up as few lies as possible. Remembering the truth was always easiest.

"I like the interaction with people," I continued. "And in my last job, I worked for the CEO, which gave me a good overview of how the company operated. I look at this as future job training, for when I run my own operation."

A smile tugged at the corners of his mouth. That answer seemed to satisfy him more than the prior one. "That's quite perceptive."

"Thanks." Just that tiny compliment was better than anything I'd gotten from White in weeks, and it felt good.

"Where was that last job?" he asked. He didn't bother with the resume.

"Tenerife."

"So you worked for old man Honeycutt?"

"If he heard you call him *old man*, he'd hand you your ass in a sling and your balls in a cup."

I hadn't expected Vince to know anybody at Tenerife, but either way, we hadn't found a better choice when figuring out my cover resume last night.

He laughed. "I heard that about him."

He watched me with a slowly widening smile. His eyes bored into me, asking an indecipherable silent question. For a moment I was afraid he might have actually met Honeycutt's assistant, which would end this charade quickly.

I broke the silence. "Ms. Zaleski said you would want to interview me and another candidate as well."

"We'll see. At the moment I want to learn more about Ashley Newton." He checked his watch. "But first I have gym time. "We'll continue the interview after that."

If his time at the gym interrupted his work schedule in the middle of the morning, this guy had a serious issue.

"I can come back tomorrow, if that works better," I offered.

"Nonsense. Just make yourself at home here until I return. Won't be long." He winked and rose from his chair. In a few seconds he was gone, and I was alone in his office with the door closed.

I froze in place. Was this what had tripped up Liz? Had they left her alone in the office, and the temptation to begin a search had done her in?

He seemed sincere, but that could be my submerged feelings for the man talking.

I stood and walked to the window. The view was magnificent. The Covington building was one of the tallest in town, and nothing obstructed the view of the harbor or the old center of town. The lofty height of the office was a testament to the powerful position Vince commanded here.

But when it came to the law, position was immaterial. The mighty fell harder than the weak, but they ended up in the same place, behind the same bars. They had to eat the same food and obey the same rules in prison.

It was going to be quite a fall for Mr. Spit-and-Polish to trade his expensive business suit for prison garb. But that was the penalty for getting involved with the mob.

I returned to my seat. Liz hadn't explained exactly how she'd fucked up, just that she'd gotten caught in his office. I wouldn't chance it by making any move this early.

An executive assistant would probably be passing the time by checking her phone. I pulled out mine and looked up the weather. I pretended to check my email and send responses. The emails went to a dormant dummy address. As the time ticked by, I controlled the urge to follow in Liz's footsteps and possibly get caught.

At the Academy, it had been drilled into us that successful penetration of a criminal enterprise took time, and rushing things beyond their natural pace attracted unwanted attention. Blending in and seeming innocuous was the goal. I took a breath and slowly let it out.

# CHAPTER 9

*Vincent*

After twenty quick minutes on the weights, I returned from the gym and opened my office to find Ashley exactly as I had left her. "I'm back. We're going for a walk."

She stood. "What?"

"We'll continue the interview over lunch," I responded. "I told you we weren't done."

"Could I use the restroom first?" she asked.

I pointed down the hallway when she arrived at the door. "Down the hall, on the left."

I waited for her outside my office door. "Let's go," I said as she returned.

"Where to?" she asked.

I didn't respond. Downstairs I made a left turn at the street, and we started down the sidewalk.

"Where are we going?" she asked again.

"Is Italian okay?" She deserved better than just any old restaurant.

"Sure," she replied. After a moment she asked, "Why the gym in the middle of the day?"

"I'm training for a triathlon."

"That's heavy duty," she said.

"It's a goal of mine."

Three blocks later, without another word passing between us, I stopped and opened the door to Vitaliano's, where I ushered her inside. The crowd waiting to be seated was dense, befitting the restaurant's reputation as the best Italian dining in all of Boston.

We threaded our way between waiting guests up to the hostess station. Angelica was behind the desk, explaining over the phone that no, they didn't take reservations. She was dressed in her normal short, tight skirt and even tighter top.

I waited for her to get off the phone. "Hi, Angelica." That was all I needed to say.

She grabbed two menus. "This way, Mr. Benson." She escorted us through the packed dining room to a booth at the back.

I nodded as we passed a few guests I recognized. The lunch crowd was full of the usual movers and shakers.

I pressed a Benjamin to Angelica's palm before she left.

As Ashley slid into the booth, she said in a low voice, "I thought I heard her say they didn't take reservations."

I leaned forward to match her hushed tones. "They don't."

My normal waiter, Tony, arrived.

I knew the menu well enough to not need to open it. "Tony, would you choose us a nice Chianti, and we'll start with the calamari and the olive plate."

Tony nodded. "My pleasure, Mr. Benson."

Ashley's brow crinkled slightly. "So what's the story?" she asked, pointing a finger at the retreating waiter.

"Come again?"

She leaned forward slightly. "We waltzed right past the crowd out front to an open table, and the waiter wasn't wearing a nametag, but you know his name."

"I've been here a few times," I answered.

She lifted her water glass and pursed her lips. "And?"

As her lips parted and the word came out, I was tempted to reach a finger out to touch them, to feel the softness I knew they'd hold if I pulled her head all the way to mine.

I banished the thought. "And I loaned Carlo some money to get this place started."

That bought me priority seating whenever I came.

She smiled. "I guess, like they say, it's not what you know, but who you know."

"Something like that," I answered.

Ashley put her water down. "I thought this was an interview."

Evidently she wasn't interested in a social lunch. I took a cleansing breath. Getting her to relax was going to take some effort. "Yes, that's right."

She fiddled with her knife, as if it were a sword to keep me at bay, before finally putting it down.

Tony broke the awkward silence between us when he returned with the wine. He retreated after it had been tasted and poured.

"If you're going to work for me, I need to know all about you," I began.

But I wanted to know all about what had happened in her life, even if she didn't work for me. So much time had gone by since that fateful day I'd said goodbye, and I'd regretted being too proud to get in touch with her. Today I needed to fix what had happened between us.

Her eyes narrowed. "What do you need to know?"

I noted her use of the word *need* instead of *want.*

"I'd like to know what's happened since we last saw each other."

Her countenance darkened. "You mean since you broke up with me."

It wasn't a question, but a statement.

I nodded, avoiding words that might make the situation worse.

"Why does it matter?"

"It matters because…" I started. "Because I need somebody I can trust under me."

A second too late, I realized *under me* had not been the right choice of words.

"That's the problem right there," she countered. "Because I wasn't ready to be under you, you up and left. And without another word to me," she spat. "You treated me like shit."

"Can we call a truce on that subject?"

"Sure," she sneered, though she didn't convince me she meant it. She looked down and fidgeted with her napkin.

I broke the awkward silence. "I'm sorry for the way I acted. It was immature and selfish of me."

Those were the words I should have said back then. But years ago in school, I'd been too headstrong, too hurt, too…too a lot of things, and not man enough to admit my mistake.

Her eyes softened to the beautiful green I'd longed for back then.

"I'm sorry," I said again.

"You mean that?" she asked.

I offered a hand across the table. "I do."

She took my hand and squeezed. "Thank you. Truce accepted."

The electric feel of her touch brought me back to the nights we'd made out in my Mustang on secluded Poplar Avenue. Before I'd screwed it all up.

A*SHLEY*

I PULLED BACK MY HAND. THE FEELINGS HIS TOUCH BROUGHT TO THE SURFACE WERE not compatible with my mission. On a rational level, I understood he was the target, and I couldn't get involved emotionally. But keeping my rational brain in charge was going to be incredibly difficult if I allowed myself the luxury of his touch.

Just that short bit of hand-holding had reawakened feelings I thought I'd outgrown, urges I'd moved past, impulses I'd learned to control.

I'd made him think I was angry, and I had been, but anger didn't properly describe my current state of mind. I'd been hurt, but that touch told me how wrong I'd been to assume I was completely over him. John had been right that this would be hard.

Years ago, I would have died to hear that apology, to take Vince back and explore our future, but now I didn't have that option. Last night, I wasn't sure if I was going to be happy to nail his hide to the wall for payback, or sorry I had to be the one to bring him to justice. Today it was clear the end of this wouldn't be a happy day for either of us.

Sometimes in undercover work you had to challenge the target, put him on the defensive, and I'd accomplished that with my reaction. Now it was time to calm the discussion.

"Tufts was good. The weather here took some getting used to." This wasn't hard. The truth was always easier to remember than lies and made-up back-stories.

His eyes were on the tablecloth and his mind seemed somewhere else as I spoke.

"My freshman-year roommate was from Hawaii, and it was her first time away from home. She got so homesick, she didn't last past Thanksgiving, and I ended up with the room to myself for the rest of the year."

He twisted his spoon and looked ready to bend it in two.

"Classes were easy enough. But after AP English Lit with Mr. Peterson, anything would seem easy."

When I looked back at his spoon, he had bent it. Hearing about college wasn't why we were here. That was clear enough.

He put it down and sipped his wine with pained eyes.

"Vince, what's bothering you?" I feared I'd pushed too hard.

He put the wine down. "What?"

I motioned to the contorted spoon. "Do you always destroy your utensils?"

"No, no." He shook his head. "Just got carried away is all. Go ahead, I'm listening." His words were warm, but his eyes held something different. I couldn't tell whether it was anger or disgust, and I didn't know what I'd done to earn it.

With him wound so tight, I was loath to continue.

Our waiter returned, saving me for the moment. He brought calamari that smelled scrumptious and a plate of assorted olives.

I speared an olive and held it up. "Your turn. How was USC? That's where you went, right?"

Although I feigned uncertainty, I knew exactly where he'd gone to school.

And thanks to his sister, I knew which of the eighteen fraternities he had pledged. I'd even driven the length of West 28th, checking out the frat houses to locate his, although I would never in a million years admit that. We might have broken up, but for the better part of the next year, I'd regretted it, and I'd almost called him at least a dozen times.

"Your resume said you got a psychology degree," he stated, ignoring my question. "I thought you were planning to go pre-med?"

Becoming a doctor had been an aspiration, but I'd only mentioned pre-med once with him that I could recall. The fact that he remembered took me by surprise. With a memory for detail like that, I wasn't going to get by with any mistakes in this undercover.

I nodded. "Yup, that was the plan. I was a bio-chem major for the first year, but that only lasted two semesters."

"What happened?"

I speared a dark Kalamata olive. "I joined the Tufts Premedical Society, and in the spring we went on a field trip downtown to the med school."

He waited while I swallowed the olive.

"They were giving us a treat, letting us watch an actual surgery." I rolled my eyes. "I ended up passed out on the floor."

He chuckled. "The blood, huh?"

"That and the idea of dissecting dead people—I mean, real people? I barely managed the frogs in high school. Between the blood and cutting into somebody's dead grandmother, med school lost its appeal."

I didn't add that I'd had to learn to deal with blood from gunshot and stab wounds at my current job, so I could have tackled medical school now if I'd cared to.

"Why psychology, then?"

"After messing up the differences between sulfates, sulfites, and sulfamates a few times, I gave up on chemistry."

I forked a calamari ring, and just as it reached my mouth, Tony returned to take our orders. I flipped open the menu I'd ignored.

Vince chose the parmesan-crusted halibut for himself, and I decided on the spinach and ricotta ravioli.

As we waited for the main course to arrive, we talked more about college. Every time I shifted to asking Vince about his experiences, he turned the conversation back to my history.

Tony eventually brought our plates.

"How's your ravioli?" Vince asked after a bit.

I nodded. "Perfect."

I could bet this place charged exorbitant prices. This was the best ravioli I'd had yet, and Boston was the town to get good Italian food. "I always thought the hole-in-the-wall places had the best food, but this…" I circled my fork over the plate. "…is proving me wrong."

41

The corners of his mouth turned up. "I hoped you'd like it."

I asked the obvious question. "You take all your PAs here?"

He tilted his head as he finished chewing and pointed his fork. "You're the first."

I didn't need a mirror to tell me a four-alarm blush had risen in my cheeks.

"I brought you here because you're special to me still, and I wanted to apologize for my behavior."

I put up a hand. "Truce, remember? You don't need to say any more."

He shook his head. "No, I do. Apologies are not something I do well, so let me finish. I wanted to tell you I was sorry a hundred times, but I wasn't grown up enough to do it. I should have been man enough to accept your decision, but at the time I wasn't. I've been ashamed of that for a long time. The way I acted was childish, and what I put you through was mean. For that I'm sorry."

His words flowed over me in warm waves. I'd never had anyone give me such a sincere apology. "Apology accepted. And now you owe me one."

His dimples erupted with a smile that melted me. "One what? Never mind. Whatever it is, I owe you two at least."

I raised my wine glass. "Two will be fine. Two favors."

"Shoot. What can I do for you?"

"Later. I'll save them until I need them."

He raised his glass to me and sipped. "Like I should have said long ago, when you're ready."

I liked the sound of that. "Now will you tell me about USC?"

Now that he'd said his piece, the utensil torturing stopped, and I thought I understood this lunch.

We talked through the rest of our meal, dessert, and an hour beyond. It was the most relaxing time I'd had with a man in years.

I stopped him. "Vince, we need to do the interview. It's important. I need this job."

I hoped I'd built up enough goodwill that my desire for the position would carry weight.

"Can you type?" he asked.

"Naturally."

"Can I trust you?"

"Absolutely," I lied.

I'd practiced my innocent face in the mirror this morning before coming in, and it seemed to be working.

He pointed a finger at me. "Ash, you're hired."

"Just like that?" I'd expected a more rigorous interview.

The teenage me had been smitten with him. Hell, the whole class had been. When he'd asked me to the prom, I'd thought it was a prank. But the next day he brought me flowers, and I moved up a million notches in the social standing of our school. The star tight-end of the football team was asking me to the senior prom. It was a day out of Cinderella. Just remembering that feeling brought a smile to my face.

"Just like that," he said. "I need somebody I can trust, more than anything."

In the end, when justice was served and he was behind bars, he'd no doubt regret trusting me, or ever even meeting me. That would be a hard day, but the job wasn't meant to be easy. I'd taken an oath, and dirty guys like him had to be caught. Once I found the evidence we needed, I'd do the right thing, no matter my feelings. What happened to Vince after that was up to the system.

Even bank robbers could be good looking and pleasant dinner conversationalists. I had to remind myself that justice needed to remain blind. I couldn't apply one set of standards to friends and another to strangers.

The file on him was clear: he was conspiring with the head of the Alfonso crime family that was breaking the law on a large scale, hurting a lot of innocent citizens. Those citizens paid my salary so I could keep them safe from the likes of him—the sharks who preyed on the weak. In my book there was a special place in hell reserved for the mob and their enablers.

He picked up his phone and dialed. "Nina, please put Ashley on the payroll and forget the other interview… Yes, that's right. And tell Ben to scratch the background check. I know everything I need to about Ashley." He hung up.

I cocked my head. "No more questions about my work experience?" His instructions to call off the background check relieved me.

"We can finish your interview later."

He'd told me I was hired, and now he wanted to interview me more later? This guy had a seriously backward process, which might explain why he went through so many assistants. Hire first, interview second, fire third, and repeat.

He put up a finger. "Nina wouldn't have brought you up if she was concerned. Just one thing—you understand this isn't a nine-to-five job, right?"

I nodded. "I'm your beck-and-call girl. Whenever you need me, and for whatever." The words escaped before I realized how flirty they sounded. I had to control my inner Bonnie.

His mouth opened for a split second, followed by a fleeting hungry look that he quickly controlled. He'd caught the same unfortunate connotation of my comment, but decided against pursuing it.

I smiled. I was *in* now, and I couldn't let feelings of yesteryear interfere with the performance of my duties. If I wasn't careful, we might get pushed in an uncomfortable direction, given our history.

*You are going down, Mr. Bigshot.* Working with the mob was a one-way ticket to the slammer.

# CHAPTER 10

*VINCENT*

WHAT LUCK! JUST WHEN I NEEDED IT, I'D BUMPED INTO SOMEBODY FROM MY PAST who I could trust. Now things were going my way.

The walk back from lunch in the sunshine was a perfect cap to the day so far. Upstairs, I asked Anita to get her set up.

"We can catch up later," I said, backing away. "After Anita gets you situated." Anita didn't look amused.

I went back to my office and dialed the phone for the call I'd been avoiding since this morning.

"Vincent," my mother said as she answered. "Thanks for calling back."

"What's up?" I asked, although I already knew thanks to a heads-up from my brother Josh.

"It's about the barbecue. I just wanted to be sure you're still coming."

"Sure, Mom. I'll be there."

These barbecues were mandatory family events, even though I was now three thousand miles away. But that was only half the question.

"And will you be bringing anyone with you?" She dropped the rest of the inquiry.

"Mom, don't worry. She'll…she'll be coming along this time."

Mom sighed loudly. "Good, I'm looking forward to meeting this mystery woman."

I hadn't given Mom or Dad her name. I'd just told them I was seeing someone.

I had been expected to bring along a plus one and disappointed my mother too many times. Staci had agreed to do me this favor, and she would make a good impression. She knew how to play the part, even though we weren't really boyfriend and girlfriend.

"You promise now?"

"Promise, Mom. You're gonna love her."

"No excuses."

My visit to LA was my semiannual responsibility check with Dad. I had to come home to be grilled, quizzed, and inspected to see that I was being responsible. And arriving without a woman in tow would be unacceptable. At my age—second eldest in the family—I was expected to be married already. However, bringing a girl like Staci and pretending to be in a serious relationship would buy me some time. Not right, but close.

I would never be good enough for Dad without that final step, but fuck it. Today I didn't care. My older brother, Dennis, had given in to the emotional blackmail. He'd gotten married too early after giving in to Dad's view of morality. It had ended in a divorce. His ex-wife had seemed okay before the wedding bells and the altar, but after the ceremony she'd morphed pretty quickly into the bitch she was underneath. It had cost Dennis a sizable settlement, but the resulting pain was the worse price to pay.

His example had taught me pretty clearly the downside to getting married, especially to the wrong woman. I certainly had not met the right one yet—not that I was looking. Marriage was an institution that made sense once you were ready to have kids, but before then, what use was it?

Dad's seriousness about this whole thing became clear when he essentially forced my boss, Bill Covington, to get married—or at least commit to it—before he followed through on a promise to invest in Covington Industries. It had nothing to do with the economics of the situation; Bill's character was just a litmus test of sorts. A test like that didn't make any sense to me.

There was a knock at the door. "Great talking to ya, Mom. Gotta go."

She hung up only after complaining I was just like Dad, rushing her off the phone.

"Come in," I called.

Mason opened the door and checked the room before entering.

"Who you expecting?" I asked.

He closed the door behind him. "Nobody. I just heard you were busy."

I played dumb. "That never stopped you before."

"Anita introduced me to your new PA."

"Yeah, Ashley." I nodded.

"What happened to waiting on background checks after the last one?"

"No need on Ashley. I know her from way back. We went to the same high school."

"You're sure?"

"Like I said. I know her."

"Okay. If you say so. I reworked some of the Semaphore numbers. Want to go over them?"

I did, but suddenly I didn't feel like it just yet. "Later. I'm going to hit the treadmill first."

"Worried about the note?"

Mason had a knack for cutting through the bullshit, and he knew I ran when I needed to clear my mind.

"Yeah, a little."

He turned to go. "Fine. You go ruin your knees while I do some real work."

"In forty years when you can't get it up, you're going to wish you'd been exercising," I told him. "It's all about blood flow, you know."

He turned at the door and laughed. "In forty years, I'll have the little blue pill, and you, you're going to be on crutches and unable to catch even the slowest old lady."

"Get outta here."

I followed him out the door. The treadmill awaited.

~

AFTER A HALF HOUR OF POUNDING THE MOVING STRIP OF RUBBER, I'D BANISHED THE note from my brain, and it had been replaced by memories from years ago—memories of a wonderful dance and a not-so-wonderful aftermath.

The incline increased as the machine simulated a run through Central Park.

I'd asked Ashley to the senior prom, half because I'd been taken with her infectious laugh and always-present smile, and half to piss off Cynthia. Cynthia Powell had been after me forever, and we'd dated on and off senior year.

Cynthia had been easy on the eyes, and still was. In high school, she'd been easy in another way, and she'd been my first. When she assumed that meant I'd take her to the prom, I rebelled.

It had been my younger brother, Josh, who had the bright idea for me to invite Ashley instead, and it had worked.

Cynthia had blown a gasket, and I was rid of her, at least for a while.

Then I remembered the way I'd ruined everything with Ashley. After listening to all the guys in the locker room recount how they'd closed the deal with their dates at some point after the prom, I couldn't take it, and I'd pushed too hard.

She hadn't been ready, and I hadn't been patient enough. I'd said things I didn't mean. It hadn't gone well, and in my anger I'd hooked up with Cynthia again. As I'd admitted to Ashley, I hadn't been mature enough.

Only later, after I started at USC, did I realize how big a jerk I'd been. And then it had been too late. With me at college and Ashley still a senior in high school, I hadn't seen her again. Until today.

46

Until I'd taken the job out here in Boston with Covington, Cynthia had periodically reappeared in my life. All through college I'd been foolish enough to believe it was me she wanted. Only later did it become clear that if my last name had been Smith or Black—or almost anything else but Benson—she wouldn't have had the slightest interest in me. She hadn't gone to college for a BA or BS; she was just biding time until she could get her MRS degree, and only if it was attached to the right last name. In Cynthia's world, right depended on the number of zeros attached to your bank balance.

The treadmill took pity on me and leveled out for a flat virtual stretch through the park.

My lunch with Ashley had dredged up memories of good times and shameful ones. I'd treated her badly back then. Today, she needed a job, and I needed someone I could trust. It was a perfect fit.

~

ASHLEY

BEFORE HE DISAPPEARED INTO HIS OFFICE, VINCENT INTRODUCED ME TO ANITA Santos, the PA to his VP of Strategic Marketing, Mason Parker, and also to the marketing guy, Will Marston, who Anita explained handled divisional marketing.

I nodded, making a mental note to look up the terms later.

Anita was older than the other assistants here on executive row and clearly the alpha of the pack, based on the looks the others gave her as I was introduced around.

I would be joining Anita, Sophia, and Daphne in this area outside the executives' offices. Daphne and Sophia handled the other four executives. I was the only one on the floor assigned to just one person, Vince.

Anita caught me eyeing the romance novel in her drawer as she pulled it open to get her keys.

"I'm done with this one, if you haven't read it." She offered me the book.

I'd noticed a paperback on Daphne's desk with a bare-chested hunk on the cover, but hadn't caught the title before she covered it up.

I accepted the book. "Thanks, I haven't yet."

The title was *Secretary to the Bazillionaire*, and the cover featured a guy in a suit —more office-appropriate than Daphne's book.

"I think you'll like it," Anita said with a grin I couldn't decipher.

I deposited it in my purse to look at later. Fitting in to the environment was a key to successful undercover work. At Quantico, we'd been warned: if the subject drank wine, we didn't order a beer. I'd never had the time or inclination to read anything beyond the occasional detective mystery before—maybe three books a year. But this book would be my study material tonight. If this is what executive assistants read, it was going on my list.

After getting me through the process to get a badge, keycard for access, and keys to my boss's office as well as my desk, Anita sat me down at the computer to run me through the login procedures.

She quickly explained the file structure they used on the computer system before walking me to the end of the office area. She took me through a locked door on the end.

"This is the common file storage area we use for executive row," she explained. "The key to Mr. Benson's office will get you in here as well."

I nodded.

She tapped a row of tan file cabinets. "These four here are for Mr. Benson."

The rest of the room consisted of file storage for the other executives.

The final stop was back inside Vince's office at two locked file cabinets that held the most confidential materials.

"How do I file things in these?"

"You don't," she answered. "Mr. Benson is the only one with a key to these. He may unlock them and have you locate something for him or file it away, or he may not, depending on his mood. Remember, you don't touch them without his permission."

I nodded. "Got it."

Along the wall sat an old IBM Selectric typewriter. "What's the typewriter for?" I asked. "Does he collect antiques?"

These had gone out of use decades ago.

"On occasion, Mr. Benson or one of the others will need something confidential prepared and sent. If it is ultrasensitive, it will be typed. That way nobody can see a copy of it in a computer file."

This was an unforeseen complication.

"Interesting" was my only reply.

It was a security measure I hadn't seen implemented before, and a sensible one. It was also just the kind of subterfuge a criminal might think up—no electronic copies to be subpoenaed.

The logging and storage of email and text messages had made the bureau's job easier over the years. Electronic messages lived forever and were instantly searchable. If Vince was communicating with hard copies, the message had to be intercepted en route or risk being destroyed by the receiver and lost forever.

We had numerous tools to intercept electronic communication, and we could even surveil and record audio, but a written note passed between parties was the toughest thing to catch.

So far these two cabinets in Vince's office interested me most.

We passed a room with tables covered in white tablecloths. I stopped to look in.

"This is the executive dining room," Anita explained.

"Pretty posh."

"For those that get to eat in there," she added dryly.

Apparently, that didn't include us.

The room had space for about twenty, by my estimation, and a view of downtown that any restaurant owner would kill for. Whoever used this room had a treat in front of them. Even the place settings looked elegant.

An hour and more introductions than I could keep straight later, I was at my desk when Anita's boss, Mason, stopped by.

"How about dinner tonight?" His question immediately indicated where he was coming from. He probably came on to all the new assistants, and I was fresh meat.

"Sorry, I can't."

He didn't skip a beat. "Maybe tomorrow then?"

I paused thoughtfully. "That might work. I think my boyfriend is busy with SWAT training tomorrow. You know, kicking down doors and shooting people. I'll have to double-check and get back to you."

His face indicated that my boyfriend comment had gotten the point across.

"Let me get back to you instead," he said, retreating to his office.

I'd gotten the line from a TV show, and it had never failed me.

# CHAPTER 11

*ASHLEY*

FOR THE REST OF THE AFTERNOON, I HANDLED THE PHONES AND TRIED TO MANAGE the crowd outside Vince's office, as new people constantly arrived, demanding access to him. The job was apparently going to be part personal assistant and part traffic cop.

Vince had given me the task of pulling data out of some old annual and quarterly reports for a company to generate spreadsheets. The work was tedious, and after a while, the numbers started to run together. I took a break to get a cup of coffee to aid my concentration. Screwing this up wasn't part of the plan.

Just as I returned with my java, Vince buzzed me to get him another cup as well.

I did as requested and knocked at the door before walking it into his office.

The look in his eyes as I approached sent a tingle through me and heated my cheeks. I'd seen that look before, more than once. It was a look that undressed me as I walked, and the smile that went with it indicated he liked what he saw—as well as what he imagined.

I gave him a playful wink as I deposited the coffee on his desk.

He thanked me, and I left the room with an exaggerated hip motion. It was my turn to imagine what he looked like as he watched my ass from behind. As I closed the door, I snuck a peek in his direction. His grin was as full as I'd hoped it would be. As I took my seat, I realized that excited me more than it should have.

In a while, things would settle down and I would blend in enough at this job to start poking around. I wasn't eager to repeat Liz's mistake by being over-anxious.

As I opened the next quarterly report, I realized how unprofessional that thought had been. I was personalizing my relationship with the target, *who was being investigated as a criminal.* That would only lead to problems down the road, making what should be clear-cut decisions seem fuzzy and open to interpretation. I recalled John's admonition that this would be harder than I thought. I shook my head free of the concerns and started back on the spreadsheet.

AN HOUR LATER, ANOTHER MEETING IN VINCE'S OFFICE BROKE UP AND THE participants filed out.

"Getting settled in?" Mason asked, stopping in front of my desk.

I looked up. "Sure. Anita has been a big help."

He came around behind me to look at what I was working on. "We'll need annual rates of change for each of the quarters," he offered, pointing to the left-hand column on my screen.

I flipped to the next tab. "Already done. I moved all the rate comparisons to one sheet, where they would be easier to analyze."

I showed him where I'd moved the calculations he was asking about, careful to not appear as insulted as I felt. All these executive types thought they were smarter than the rest of us. Big paychecks led to big egos. Little did he know I could punch him in the throat and have him hog-tied in less than a minute, if I wanted.

"Good idea. I like it," he said.

Apparently I'd passed his test.

He turned to leave. "Good work."

I caught my new boss eyeing the exchange from his doorway with a smirk.

Vince approached. "He trying to give you instructions?"

I kept my irritation in check. "More like suggestions."

He looked at his watch. "I need that spreadsheet finished tonight."

I had more than a dozen more quarters to finish. "I can't get it all done this afternoon."

He put up his hand to stop me. "Remember, this isn't a nine-to-five job, right?"

"Yes, but…"

I couldn't tell him I'd scheduled a debriefing meeting with John after my first day. Keeping my partner up to date was imperative early in an undercover.

"Tonight," was all he said before walking off down the hallway.

*Anything you say, Mr. Bigshot.*

I grabbed my purse and headed to the ladies room. This was going to mess up my schedule big time.

51

Once safely in the end stall, I pulled out my white undercover phone and typed a message to John.

ME: Can't make tonight - working late

I turned off the phone, not waiting for a reply. I would have to be off the grid for the evening. My plan to go shopping this evening for skirts and dresses that fit this assignment was also going to be a lost cause.

Before I put my phone away, I heard two others enter from the hallway.

"She seems nice enough." It was Anita's voice.

"I guess," said Sophia, another of the assistants in the executive area. She worked for Mike, the sales VP, and the manufacturing guy whose name I'd already forgotten.

I stayed still and quiet.

"He knows her. She'll get the benefit of the doubt," Anita said.

"Knows her from where?"

From the sounds at the sink, they were rinsing out their coffee mugs.

"Back in LA before college, I think," Anita answered.

"I'm glad I didn't get sucked back into that job. The hours and the trips—I couldn't take it again."

Anita laughed. "He wouldn't do that to you."

"I guess," Sophia answered

"Bet she doesn't last the week," Sophia said as they walked toward the door. "Did you see how slow she types?"

"I'll give her two or three," Anita answered.

The door closed, and I stayed silent in the stall.

They had mentioned bad hours, and I'd expected that, but trips? That hadn't come up in the briefing materials, or with Ms. Zaleski.

And they were clearly betting I wouldn't last long enough in the job to complete my assignment. Nothing like a vote of confidence to give me a boost. I rolled my eyes.

I waited another few minutes before making my way back to my desk.

∾

*VINCENT*

ASHLEY HAD STAYED LATE WITHOUT COMPLAINT—A TEST MANY A NEW HIRE HAD failed.

I checked the time: seven thirty.

I opened the door to my office. "What kind of pizza do you like?" I asked her.

She looked up. "Anything, but no anchovies."

"Veggie, pepperoni, combo, all meat?"

"Combo sounds good," she replied.

"Me too," Mason called from his office.

I hadn't looked to see if he was still in, a mistake I didn't normally make. I had Ashley on the brain.

Retreating to my desk, I placed the order, and forty minutes later, the guard called from the lobby saying it was here.

"I'll go down and get it," Ashley offered.

I handed her cash, and she was off to the elevator.

Mason emerged from his office and sighed as we heard the elevator door close. "Just my luck."

"What?"

"She has a boyfriend, and he's a cop. He's on the SWAT team no less."

I walked back into my office and looked away to hide my reaction. "I don't hire them for you to date," I called.

I closed the door behind me and tried to breathe. I hadn't asked her; I'd merely assumed from the way she'd acted at lunch that there might still be a spark between us. I'd certainly felt it.

What Mason just said had knocked the wind out of me for no reason. I was tougher than this.

I didn't let women get to me this way. Letting one go to move onto the next had always been easy. Attachments were dangerous: it was the lesson I'd first learned from Ashley those many years ago. The pain of giving her up had been one I didn't care to repeat, and not caring was the one and only way to assure it.

I straightened my spine. This didn't change the fact that I'd hired her to do a job, and she was the one I could trust, the one I knew to be honest. And that was a damned sight better than a random girl off the street.

She returned with the pizza, and the three of us ate around the table in the small conference room. I was careful not to stare at her, but I had to face the feelings I'd had when Mason said she had a boyfriend. It had been a gut punch to think someone else had her heart, and that realization scared me. What did it say about me that this bothered me?

I was just being protective of an old friend, that's all. That made sense. Friends deserved protection.

At nine o'clock, when Ashley sent over the completed spreadsheet, I chased her and Mason out of the office for the evening.

I said goodnight to Ashley as if it were just another day and slunk back to my condo for a drink—or maybe three.

∾

*ASHLEY*

.  .  .

53

WHEN I GOT HOME, MY HEELS DIDN'T MAKE IT PAST THE ENTRY TO MY APARTMENT. I padded barefoot to the fridge for a bottle of hard apple cider. After taking off my clothes and hanging them neatly, I changed into sweats and a Tufts rugby shirt. The couch beckoned, and I plopped down with my bottle of cider and the book from my purse.

The book had several dog-eared pages. I turned to the first one.

*Holy shit.*

The heroine, Juliet, had gotten herself banged over the boss's desk—his name was Dalton—and this was only page sixty-eight. It went on for pages, with moaning, dirty talk, and orgasms in the office. By the end of the section, I was hot and bothered myself. I reread it again, substituting my name for Juliet, and Vince's for Dalton.

I was damp down below, with heat in my core as I closed my eyes and imagined the scene playing out between Vince and me—a dirty, passionate encounter with animal desires taking over. I found myself breathing heavily as I opened my eyes.

*If only, girl—get real.*

He's a real billionaire. And in bed with the mob.

Besides, I'm the one who turned him down and pushed him away, never to see him again.

We'd both moved on with our lives: him the rich kid with everything he wanted, and me. What was I? The FBI agent, make that special agent, trying to put him behind bars so I could get promoted out of Boston and away from my pig of a boss.

We fit together like a tuxedo and a baseball cap—or a special agent and a crook.

I went to the next dog-eared page. They had sex against the door, and the next was against the window—so far no in-the-bed scenes. Either that or Anita hadn't bothered to mark them.

Now I understood Anita's grin when she'd handed me the book.

Finally I got to a scene in bed, not to mention outdoors on the patio, in the shower, and on the kitchen table. These two were like bunnies—the very definition of fantasy.

*If only life could be like this.*

Instead of going to the next folded page, I started at the beginning to read the entire story.

At two thirty in the morning, I read the final words with a smile on my face and warmth in my heart. It had ended well for Juliet and Dalton.

They were on their well-deserved honeymoon, the bad guy was in the hospital after the gun he'd intended to shoot the heroine with exploded in his hands, and he was destined for jail when he recovered. The hero had even saved the bad guy's life by controlling the bleeding, because he was just that nice.

I would have rewritten that part. I wanted the villain dead for attacking poor Juliet, but that's just me.

I went to bed content, understanding for the first time what women saw in these books, and wanting to eventually have the time for another. But that wouldn't be for a while if they kept me up until three every night.

I closed my eyes and imagined myself as Juliet, saved by Vince, but only after I replayed the office scene over the desk in my head—page sixty-eight.

*My God, that would be hot.*

# CHAPTER 12

*A*SHLEY

IT WAS TEN O'CLOCK THURSDAY MORNING. I'D MADE IT TO THE OFFICE EARLY, BUT I still needed to set up the debriefing with John I'd had to skip last night.

I dialed the phone. "Hey, Donnie, is your mother home?" I asked the voice-mail box.

I continued the fake conversation for another half minute before hanging up. Anita looked over briefly, but neither Sophia nor Daphne paid me any heed.

We'd agreed on several scripts I could leave on the voicemail to communicate different messages back to the office. The phone number couldn't be traced to the Bureau, and the conversations would all sound innocuous to bystanders.

This particular script told John to meet me at the back of a small Chinese restaurant about ten blocks from here at lunchtime.

At eleven forty-five, I told Anita I was heading to lunch. I gathered my bag and made my way to the elevator. The door closed just as Vince emerged from his office.

I'd told Anita I would be out for an hour, but I'd avoided checking with Vince for fear of being overruled. Downstairs, I turned right for the walk to the meeting spot.

A block later I heard him.

"Ash, hold up a sec," Vince called from behind me.

I turned to find him jogging my direction.

*Shit.*

I hadn't escaped after all. I turned and smiled.

"Glad I caught you," he said reaching me. "I wanted to have lunch with you today."

I started walking again down the street. "Oh, I'm sorry. I made other plans. I'm meeting Maggie from school."

"Great, she can join us."

The guy was unreal. Was it not clear that my plans didn't include him?

"That won't work today. Maybe another time."

He stepped in front of me and forced me to stop. His smile was ear to ear. "Call her and suggest it. Or better yet, give me the phone and I'll convince her."

He seemed to have the billionaire disease. He was so used to people altering their schedules to accommodate him that he didn't understand the meaning of the word *no*.

I smiled up at him. "We can't join you, but maybe you'd like to join us. Maggie's been having heavy periods, and I mean really heavy—like, double-maxi-pad heavy." I sighed. "You can't imagine what that's like."

He backed up a few inches. It was starting to work. He wasn't turning green yet, but I was getting to him.

"Anyway, she has a gyno appointment scheduled, and I'm going in with her. The doctor's concerned she might have a uterine fibroid. You know how scary that can be—I mean the cramping and the bleeding. So she needs some serious hand holding. Actually, an extra pair of hands like yours could really help." I smiled innocently. "We shouldn't be there more than an hour."

The talk of periods and an hour in a gynecologist's waiting room had done the trick. It always did. Even asking most guys to go buy a box of tampons was like verbal kryptonite.

"Maybe we can have lunch tomorrow?" he offered.

"Tomorrow works for me, but I'll have to check with Maggie. She might still be cramping too much, ya know?"

He turned toward the Covington building. "Tomorrow then, but make it dinner instead of lunch." He waved as I continued my march down the sidewalk.

After a few more blocks, I looked back to be certain he hadn't changed his mind.

I breathed easier; it was all clear.

Once inside the restaurant, I wended my way through the tables to the back and down the restroom hallway. After checking behind me, I double-knocked on the storeroom door, and it opened.

Liz ushered me inside and quickly closed and locked the door.

Seeing her confused me. "Where's John?"

"He got sent to the New Haven office on some joint terrorism task force. Randy decided you get me instead."

I sighed. It was the SAC's call on replacing John, and I wasn't in any position to complain. I noticed she used the SAC's first name. She was getting careless, but it wasn't my place to tell her to hide her relationship better.

I eyed the two takeout bags sitting on the shelf. They smelled scrumptious. "Which one's mine?"

She pointed to the one on the left. "Got you the usual."

I nodded.

"Okay. You up to speed on the cover?" I asked.

"I looked at the folder. It seems pretty straightforward." She brought out her voice recorder and turned it on. "So what's the status so far?"

I gave several detailed minutes of dialog on the situation as it had developed over the last day. I left out any mention of my feelings, as they didn't pertain to the case, and I was sure I could keep things under control. My background reading last night was also not relevant.

She asked a few routine follow-up questions.

"The security is pretty tight, and I doubt it would be a good idea to try any interior surveillance," I said.

"We don't have a warrant for any of that yet," Liz said.

I continued speaking into the recorder. "It might blow the op. They do routine bug sweeps, and IT also runs virus checks on the computers. They're not haphazard in any way." Anita had made a point of explaining the routine virus checks IT ran.

Distress clouded Liz's face. She turned off the recorder. "What kind of software are they using?"

"I don't know, but everything about their security operation is top notch."

Her eyes widened. "We may have a problem."

"What?" I asked.

She stashed the recorder away. "We have to get the software off his computer."

"What software?"

"The keylogger we installed," she said in an almost hushed tone.

"When did we get a warrant for that?" I asked.

I could see panic in her eyes. "We didn't. That's the problem."

She was scared, and the reason was obvious now. The SAC wouldn't have authorized this—not ever.

I fixed her eyes with mine. "Who exactly is the *we* who installed the software?"

Her shame was apparent. "I put DarkGecko7 on his machine."

"Liz, that was stupid," I spat. "And illegal."

That could get her fired.

"Stop being so black and white. I thought I could get a lead that way and get it off before anybody noticed. It could've wrapped up the case in no time."

"It *is* black and white. It's illegal surveillance, and it torpedoes the case," I shot back.

"Not if nobody knows."

I tried in vain to calm myself. "That's not the point."

58

Her eyes pleaded with me. "If we take it off, nobody will ever know. Ashley, you gotta help."

"How could you be so dumb?" I grabbed my lunch, turned, and unlocked the door. I sighed and left without another word.

She followed me out to the street.

Her voice turned pleading. "Ashley, please."

She had just deposited a giant, stinking turd in my lap.

I turned back to her before walking off. "You're an idiot."

I left her there to contemplate her stupidity. This operation officially sucked now.

At a Starbucks on the way back, I snagged a coffee and sat outside, slowly picking at my Chinese lunch. I had to kill an hour, based on the story I'd given Vince.

Almost every bite tasted worse than the last as I contemplated my options. I had a terrible one, and even worse ones. I could go in and delete the software Liz had placed on Vince's computer and become complicit in her crime. That sucked.

I could tell the SAC how Liz had screwed up and let him deal with what to do, or even worse, I could clean up Liz's mess for White and then go tell him what she'd done. Crooks hated snitches, but cops might hate them even more.

If I finked on Liz, I'd pay the price. My career would be effectively over. I'd forever have *rat* tattooed on my forehead. Rats didn't have your back, and that was the kiss of death.

I forked some more rice into my mouth. It wouldn't be illegal for me to clean my boss's computer of the malware. But Liz had made me an accomplice after the fact the moment she told me, and that couldn't be undone. The conversation hadn't been recorded, but if asked, I wouldn't perjure myself by denying it. I couldn't leave it either. If it was discovered, Liz would have given any competent defense attorney grounds to sink the entire investigation.

The law was supposed to be clear: Black, white, right, wrong—not dark gray and darker gray. I needed a benchmark of right and wrong to measure against, but there wasn't one for this situation. There was no happily-ever-after solution available to me.

After clearing the table, I started back for the office, intent on treading the least-gray path available to me. Liz wasn't a close friend, but she was a fellow agent, and a female agent at that. I had to have her back and clean up her mess. If we didn't stick together, it would be harder for both of us in the future.

As I walked back to work, I went over past cases in my head, and it made sense now. Twice recently, she'd had a hunch about where the bad guy would be for his next meeting. Both times she'd been right. It could have been luck, but now it reeked of illicit knowledge she'd gathered without a warrant. This was a pattern with her, but that was a conversation for another day.

*She is such an ass.*

# CHAPTER 13

*VINCENT*

AFTER FAILING TO CONVINCE ASHLEY TO JOIN ME FOR LUNCH, I'D ORDERED A MEAL from Vitaliano's so I could work at my desk. I craved something that didn't come from Subway.

Over a chicken parmigiana sandwich, I contemplated the photo of that fucking note on my phone until a text arrived.

MURDOCH: Need to talk right away

I dialed Ben Murdoch, my security director, and told him now was as good a time as any.

I left the office to deposit my trash in the dining room. The smell would be distracting if I left it in my wastebasket.

Ashley was back from lunch. She instantly put a book down and busied herself on the computer.

"How'd it go with Maggie?" I asked.

She hesitated. "She'll be okay. She has a fibroid, but the doctor said it was minor, and she has a follow-up scheduled to deal with it. The good news is the doctor said it shouldn't cause any long-term problems."

"That is good." I continued to the dining room to dispose of my trash.

On the return trip, Ashley was away from her desk, so I stopped to check out the book she'd been reading. *Secretary to the Bazillionaire*. With dog-eared pages no less.

*Interesting.*

Back at my desk, I logged into Amazon and ordered a rush copy just before Ben Murdoch arrived at my door.

He'd brought along a skinny blond kid.

"Boss, I'd like you to meet Johan Tervo." He closed the door behind him.

We shook, and they took seats opposite my desk and waited for me to sit.

"Johan works with Gemini Insight Forensics. We brought him in to examine some malware we found on your computer."

I waited for the punchline.

Tervo fidgeted in his seat.

"Tell him what you found, Johan," Ben urged.

"The malware we identified is called DarkGecko7."

If it weren't so serious, I would have laughed at the names they gave these things. "And what's the risk from that? How much of my information has been compromised? Can you tell?"

"It's a keylogger only, which means it hasn't sent any of the data on your disk off site. But it has been transmitting your keystrokes, so passwords, email, memos, and the like would be at risk."

"It's not that bad, then?" I asked.

Ben urged Tervo to continue.

"Yes and no. If your passwords have been compromised, that can be quite dangerous. Our major concern, though, is the sophistication of the attack."

Ben decided to fill me in on this part. "This particular malware is very hard to detect and remove. It is state-level spycraft."

That chilled me to the bone. "International spying?"

"Possibly, but not necessarily," Tervo continued. "It was developed by the Russians, but it's now used by the CIA and several top corporate players."

"The tabloids?" I asked.

Ben shrugged and looked to Tervo for guidance.

"Not that we know of," he answered. "But it is possible. In the meantime, it has been disabled. As far as the other party knows, you've been off your computer. We can re-enable it, and you can use it for disinformation, if you want."

I contemplated the suggestion. "That might be useful if I knew who was spying on us. Is there any way to track this to the other end?"

Tervo shook his head. "No, sir. That might work in the movies, but in real life we can't do that."

I still didn't have any idea who the fuck was after me, except that his description made clear it was no Mickey Mouse outfit. "Any idea how it got on my computer?"

"No, sir. Any of the normal channels—email trojans, things like that—are possible."

"Mason and I have been working on the Semaphore transaction. Could our proposals have been compromised by this?"

"If you worked on it on your computer, absolutely," he responded. "But only what you typed, nothing more."

"And what about Mason's computer?"

"We've started daily automated sweeps," Ben said. "So far yours is the only one we've found compromised. And this wasn't picked up last month, so the infection is recent."

"It happened within the last couple of weeks?" I asked.

"Yes, sir," Ben answered.

I walked to the window and looked out over the city. Somewhere out there, somebody was stalking me. No names or faces came to mind as I scanned the cityscape.

"Come out in the open, you fucking coward," I mumbled to the window.

"Sir?" Ben asked.

"Sorry, just talking to myself. Thanks for the update. Any other steps you'd recommend?"

He hesitated.

"Out with it. What else?"

"Johan, could you excuse us, please?" Ben asked.

The kid left and closed the door behind him with only a slightly hurt look.

"Video, sir," Ben said.

"Explain."

"I understand it could be sensitive. But we could set up video surveillance of the executive offices. Because it's possible the software was installed by someone with physical access."

"One of our own?"

He nodded wordlessly.

The thought was chilling. A Covington employee? An inside job. I closed my eyes, breathed in through my nose and out slowly. There was only one possible answer to his suggestion. The fucking enemy had to be defeated, and if that meant finding a co-conspirator, no means were out of bounds.

"How soon can you set it up?"

"It's best that nobody else here know."

His suggestion was wise. I couldn't even let Mason in on it. We had to start without any preconceived notions of who it could be, and we couldn't risk a leak by widening the circle.

"Understood. Just you and me."

"I can do it over the weekend, when the offices are empty."

"Another thing, Ben. Video only, no audio. I don't want to be listening in on people's conversations." The undisclosed video was creepy enough.

"I was going to propose that."

I stood. "It's authorized then."

"One more thing. This office?"

I couldn't see excluding my space if we were going to be spying on everybody else. "Including this office, yes. Only, nobody reviews the footage of this office without my approval, and that includes you."

"Understood, sir."

# CHAPTER 14

*ASHLEY*

IT WAS FRIDAY MORNING, AND IT HAD NOW BEEN ALMOST TWENTY-FOUR HOURS SINCE Liz told me of her idiot move to put software on Vince's computer. I hadn't gotten an opening to go in and remove it yesterday afternoon, and Anita had said the IT guys checked the computers every few days. I didn't have long—if they hadn't found it already.

Vince had ordered in for lunch today, and it looked like I still might not get an opportunity to clean up Liz's mess.

A few minutes later, his meeting with the sales VP and the controller broke up. He stopped by my desk after seeing them off.

"I didn't get my morning run in. I'll be down in the gym if you need me."

"Sure," I replied.

"And dinner tonight at seven," he added.

I didn't object. "Oh, and where are the other quarterly reports when I need them?"

"Already?"

I nodded. I was now on to part two of my spreadsheet assignment, and I wasn't really ready for them yet, but I needed the excuse to enter his office while he was out.

"On the credenza," he said, backing toward the elevator.

I waved. "Have a nice run."

He smiled, waved, and turned for the elevator bank.

Ten minutes later, when I was certain he wouldn't return because he'd forgotten something, I waited for my opening. It came while Anita was in the copy room and Sophia and Daphne were also away from their desks. I slipped into Vince's office.

I closed the door behind me and quickly located the quarterlies I'd told him I needed. Then I took a seat at his desk. The computer's monitor was off. A tap of the power button brought the screen to life, and it showed he hadn't logged out.

My throat constricted, and I froze as I heard voices outside the door. I stood and waited silently.

Whoever it was walked away.

I sat back down and pulled up a window. The search for the innocuous file name DarkGecko7 hid under started slowly. I could feel my heart beating as the seconds ticked by. Staring at the window didn't speed it up. The search came back after half a minute, and seconds later I'd deleted it.

I closed the window and powered off the monitor. Placing the chair back where I'd found it, I grabbed the quarterly reports and returned to my desk.

Anita looked my way momentarily as I left Vince's office. "Ashley." She motioned for me to come over.

*Shit.*

A lump formed in my stomach, and my mouth dried. I forced a smile.

"Did you see where Mason went?" she asked as I approached.

I could breathe again. "No, isn't he in there?"

"That man is always forgetting to tell me where he's going," she complained.

I leaned forward to whisper, "They have these little tracking pendants for cats. You should get one for him."

She laughed. "I like the way you think."

I returned to my desk and sat down, taking a deep, relieved breath. I pulled a tissue from my purse and dabbed at my sweaty brow.

My heartbeat slowly returned to normal as I busied myself at my computer.

*Success.*

VINCENT

ON THE TREADMILL, I WONDERED IF I HAD DONE THE RIGHT THING IN AUTHORIZING the video surveillance yesterday. Eventually I decided it was the best counter-move, given the severity of the situation. By compromising my computer, whoever my fucking opponent was had taken off the gloves, and I needed to do the same.

I finished my run, and in the late afternoon Mason and I began working on the Semaphore acquisition again—with the door closed and locked. Ashley had instructions to keep the hordes at bay for the next two hours. Weird muffled versions of the occasional altercation outside came through the barricaded door. So far she had been more than a match for all the would-be visitors.

Semaphore had just informed us of another competing offer. The situation was getting completely out of hand. Every time we planned a move, Gainsboro seemed to see what we were going to do and made a countermove.

My cell dinged with a text. I ignored it, and we kept working.

Two minutes later it dinged again, and I checked the messages.

MURDOCH: I have something we need to talk about

MURDOCH: It's important

Security guys could get pretty alarmed about the simplest things, but that wasn't Ben Murdoch's style. If he said it was important, it generally was.

After his report yesterday, I wasn't about to put him off. I pulled up his number on my cell.

"Give me a second to check this, Mason," I said before I hit dial.

Ben picked up instantly. "Boss, I need to see you right away."

"Were pretty tied up right now…"

"I wouldn't bother you if it wasn't critical," he said in his *I'm serious* tone.

"Come on up, and tell Ashley I'm expecting you."

Mason and I tried to deal with the next line item before he arrived. We weren't successful.

It took less than two minutes before the insistent knock came.

Mason got up to let him in and locked the door after him.

"What's so important it can't wait?" I asked.

Ben looked warily at Mason. "It's about your last secretary."

"Mason is fine," I told him. "So what's the story, Ben?"

Ben sat and opened the folder he'd brought with him on my desk.

Mason shimmied his chair closer.

"You wanted us to dig into that Wilder girl."

I nodded. "Yeah, and?"

"Here are some surveillance photos you might find interesting," Ben said, pulling a picture out. "Look who she talked with yesterday."

My heart almost stopped. The picture showed Ashley on the sidewalk with that Jacinda Wilder bitch we had fired. Things were suddenly cloudy.

"That looks like the girl we caught in here messing with your computer," Mason said. "What's Ashley doing meeting with her?"

It was certainly a question I wanted to ask. I picked up my phone to buzz Ashley in to explain this.

"You might want to wait on that, boss. There's more," Ben said.

"Go ahead." I put the phone back in its cradle. *More* didn't sound good.

He pulled another photo from the folder. "We still don't know much about this Wilder lady, but we followed her." He placed the picture on the desk. "We followed her to Cambridge, and this is where she went." The picture showed her entering a red brick building I didn't recognize.

"Pat, you're killing us. Who owns the building?" Mason asked.

"The *Daily Inquisitor*," Ben said.

"So now we know which tabloid," Mason chimed in.

I put a hand up to silence him. "Is it confirmed, then, that she works for them?"

Ben nodded. "We called in to personnel and got it confirmed."

"Good thing you got rid of the bitch quickly," Mason said.

Ben picked up his pictures. "The note you got said collateral damage. What do we think they have planned?"

I could answer that easily enough. "Gossip and lies to boost circulation. Their whole business plan is lies—three-headed cows, visits by Martians, and the like."

"Do you want us to continue to follow her? Or perhaps talk to her, to find out what the plan was?" Ben asked.

I didn't know for sure what *talk to her* meant in Ben's lexicon, but it probably involved threats, which would be counterproductive. She'd hide behind the First Amendment and make us out to be the bad guys.

"No, let her go. She wasn't here long enough to get anything. With some luck, they'll get tired and move on to an easier target."

Mason spoke up. "If your new PA is friends with her, you can't keep her. She might even work with her. You know that, right?"

"I'll be the judge of that, thank you." If it were someone else, I might have agreed with him, but I knew Ashley.

He grimaced but said nothing further.

# CHAPTER 15

*ASHLEY*

AFTER TWENTY FOUR HOURS ON HIGH ALERT AFTER FINDING OUT ABOUT THE keylogger from Liz and then almost getting caught bailing her out of that jam, I needed to relax. It was just past seven in the evening. I located the sign halfway down the block and hurried. I was already late.

I pushed past the door into the darkened interior. I'd never been in Holmby's Grill, the kind of place the movers and shakers frequented. Sizzler was a better fit for my budget if I was looking for a steak. It took my eyes a moment to acclimate enough to spy Vince in a back booth, and I made my way over.

He checked his watch and rose as I took a seat across from him, but he smiled rather than berating me for being tardy. "You look lovely tonight."

"Thank you." I welcomed the compliment, but I was not sure what to make of it as I was wearing exactly what I'd had on earlier at work. "What's good here?"

He opened his menu. "I come here for the steak, but I understand the lamb chops and swordfish are both quite delicious."

I opened my menu as well. "Is that what your dates usually order?"

Our DOJ background folder on Vince contained tabloid stories about him and various women from about a year ago, plus a few more recent surveillance photos of him with two other women.

His glare had me regretting my words. "Are we really going there?"

"Sorry, I didn't mean—"

"I invited *you* to dine with me tonight. Nobody else."

I'd come across as a total bitch. "I'm sorry."

It had been too long since I'd spent time in polite company. My manners clearly needed refreshing.

Our waiter arrived.

"Any wine preference?" Vince asked me.

I pasted on my apologetic smile. "I'll defer to you."

"Stu, surprise me with your choice of a pinot. And we'll start with the garlic shrimp."

Once again, Vince was on a first name basis with the wait staff.

Stu vanished as quietly as he had arrived.

I could see why Boston's elite chose this place. The high-backed booths lent themselves to private conversations not meant to be overheard. The occasional yuppie had snagged a table to impress his date, but they were outnumbered by Boston's business leaders. Many of the men in expensive suits sat across from dates decked out in even more expensive jewelry, and the other half were accompanied by other businesspeople.

The wine and appetizer arrived, and we indulged in the shrimp and light conversation, reminiscing about high school.

Vince's dimples were in full bloom as he smiled and laughed and we traded our recollections of that time. The gravitational pull of his smile and the intensity of his eyes pushed all thoughts of him being a mob conspirator to the back of my mind. He became once again the prince charming that had chosen me for the prom.

That night had been magical, far and away the highlight of my years on the west coast— and actually since then as well.

As he spoke, the words floated past me. I imagined myself dancing in his arms again—a slow dance, swaying to the music, pressed up against him, lost in time and space with no cares, only hopes.

"Your thoughts?" he said, breaking me out of my reverie.

"Pardon?" I'd completely missed the question.

"You look so happy. I asked what you were thinking about."

The heat of a blush rose quickly. "Nothing," I lied.

"I can tell it's not nothing."

I looked down at the tablecloth. "It's silly."

"I want to know, Ash."

I decided on a quick lie. "It's just nice to have a boss take me to dinner. Mr. Honeycutt never did."

"Then he wasn't as smart as people said."

I gave myself a mental slap. Vince was the target of our investigation, and I had to keep my guard up and pay attention.

Our waiter, Stu, broke the conversation as he arrived carrying the steak Vince had ordered and the swordfish I'd chosen.

"Stu, can we please add a side of those wonderful parmesan truffle fries?"

He nodded. "Certainly, Mr. Benson. It will be only a few minutes."

"What's a truffle fry?" I asked after Stu left us.

Vince sipped his water. "French fries, but drizzled with truffle oil and parmesan cheese."

I cut a piece of swordfish and slipped it into my mouth. The mustard vinaigrette sauce on the succulent fish set a new standard for seafood in my book.

He finished chewing his bite of steak and put down his fork. "Did you know the girl that had the job right before you only lasted an afternoon?"

He was referring to Liz, of course.

I looked up. "I heard that." I picked up my wine glass and sipped.

"So, how do you know her?"

This innocent dinner had suddenly taken a serious turn.

I put down my wine, wondering what the question really was. "Know who?"

He cut another piece of meat before answering. He glanced up at me. "Jacinda."

My heart almost stopped, but I kept my cool. "Jacinda who?"

He put down his fork, and his stare froze me. "Ash, are we going to play this game?"

A shiver went through me, but I kept my game face on. We'd been taught to not give in to simple bluffs like this.

I giggled. "What game are we playing?"

He slid his hand inside his jacket and pulled out a photograph. "It's time for the truth." He laid the picture on the table for me to see.

My heart skipped a beat. It was a picture of Liz and me on the sidewalk after our meeting yesterday. "Oh… Yeah, I know her. But her name is Elizabeth, not Jacinda. I bumped into her after Maggie's appointment."

I put on my best innocently confused face. There was a possibility I could still get out of this without blowing my cover, but the options were narrowing.

He took another sip of his wine, staring at me.

I couldn't tell if my innocent face was working or not.

He looked down to cut another piece of steak. "We suspect she might work for one of those muckraking tabloids."

It seemed Liz's backup identity had worked.

"Really? She told me she was a freelance journalist."

He looked up at me as his fork stopped midway to his mouth. "Journalist, huh? Is that what they call themselves now?"

The fork completed its journey, and he held my eyes as he chewed slowly, a slight smile on his face.

I sensed I'd made a mistake offering those words. I remembered our dance together, and like magic, my best smile appeared again. I didn't know if it would be sufficient, but it was the best I had to offer my interrogator.

He put his fork down and pulled another picture from his coat. "I guess she had us both fooled then, huh?" He put the second photo down.

"And where is that?" I could feel the blood draining from my face, a reaction I couldn't control. The picture was Liz entering a brick building I didn't recognize.

He took a sip of his wine, silently daring me to say more, watching me struggle in my quicksand of lies.

There was nothing more for me to say, nothing to explain, nothing to ask. The next move was his.

"She actually works in that building," he said, "at the *Daily Inquisitor*."

I looked away and cut another bite of my fish. "Really?" When I looked back at him, he was staring again.

"You should know; she's your friend."

"Acquaintance," I shot back. "And if her name is Jacinda, she's messing with both of us. She and I met at yoga." I inserted the yoga reference, guessing that's what executive assistants did in their time off. "We had coffee once or twice back when I worked for Tenerife. Then I saw her on the sidewalk…" I pointed to the picture. "And she asked where I was working now."

His eyes narrowed as he considered my response.

Would he believe Liz's cover or not? And mine as well?

He resumed attacking his steak with knife and fork. "You can't have any more contact with her. Is that clear?"

I was careful not to show my relief. "Why not?"

He pointed at me with his fork. "Because I don't want to end up in one of their hit pieces, that's why."

The covers were going to stick.

He nodded his head toward the front door. "You might recognize Nancy at the table near the front. She works in the Channel 8 newsroom—the television station Covington owns, by the way. And her dinner partner tonight is her cameraman, Tony."

I glanced toward the door and noticed the striking blonde who had looked oddly familiar as I walked in. This was dangerous. Rule number one for under-cover work: never ever, under any circumstances, end up in the news.

"I didn't know if you worked with that Jacinda character, but in case you did, I had them come here to document the underhanded way that tabloid operates."

I froze in place.

"It would have been on the news for at least a week, maybe longer—catching the tabloids at their own game. A real ratings booster, not to mention a counter-punch that would keep them at bay for a while."

My throat was too dry to swallow. I grabbed for the water. "I barely know her. I certainly don't work with her."

∽

71

SITTING ACROSS THE TABLE, ASHLEY WAS INDIGNANT IN A PRETTY WAY.

"And I didn't tell her anything," she added. "I swear. What's with the paranoia?"

I finished chewing and pulled out my phone. After a few clicks, I slid it over to her. "This is what."

She looked at the screen and read the note. "When did you get this?"

She seemed even more shocked than Staci had been.

"A friend of mine found this on her windshield Monday."

"A friend?" she asked.

"A friend," I repeated.

The glint in her eye said she'd caught that Staci was more than an acquaintance. She studied my face. "Who would do something like this?"

She cut a bite of her fish, seeming calmer than she'd been a second ago.

"Somebody who has a beef with me, and I have no idea who."

"No jealous boyfriends...or husbands?"

"Why does everybody ask that? I haven't ever dated a married woman. And no, no jealous boyfriends either."

"That's not what the *Daily Inquisitor* said last year."

"That is exactly the problem," I hissed. I took a calming breath before continuing. "Those assholes print lies."

She reached a hand across to mine. "Sorry. It was a joke. You really have no idea who wrote it?"

I took another deep breath. Every time this note came up, it angered me. "I've wracked my brain, and I don't have a candidate."

She checked her watch. "I need to go soon."

"You can't leave yet. How's the swordfish?" I asked.

Her jaw relaxed slightly. "Very nice, thank you." She forced a semi-smile. "I'm your prisoner, is that it?"

I waited to finish chewing. "You're my dinner guest, and I have a proposal I hope you'll like."

"I'm here because I'm your employee," she stated.

I ignored her move back to argumentative. "I invited Ashley Newton to dinner, not my PA."

Her cheeks reddened.

I nodded toward the news crew. "I'm going to give you your fifteen seconds of fame—"

"No. You can't—"

"Let me finish," I said, cutting her off.

She bit her lip and quelled her tongue.

"You'll like it..."

72

She almost interrupted me again, but controlled herself. The tenseness in her jaw was apparent.

"I really can't," she said.

I scooted out of my side of the booth and moved to her side, trapping her. I wasn't taking no for an answer.

I waved over the news team, Nancy and Tony. "It won't take long."

# CHAPTER 16

*ASHLEY*

VINCE MOVED TO MY SIDE OF THE TABLE AND SLID OVER.

I needed to figure a way out of this, but I was drawing a blank. I couldn't tell him being on camera would ruin my undercover career.

He waved over Nancy Newslady, whose last name escaped me at the moment.

I panicked. "You can't."

His eyes narrowed. "Watch me."

I was trapped in the booth without any way to escape. No gun, no taser, no badge, no baton, no pepper spray, nothing.

Nancy patted her lips with her napkin and rose. Tony followed her with his camera in hand, but at least not on his shoulder yet.

I couldn't control my breathing, and my heart was speeding past its redline. "Vince, please don't do this."

He smiled toward the approaching newspeople and mumbled quietly, "Just calm down."

I pasted on a smile for the approaching duo and begged him. "Please, no."

As Nancy Newslady arrived at our table, Vince rose to greet them. "Nancy, Tony, how is the dinner?" He stood right by the edge of the bench, still blocking my exit.

Nancy took the lead. She was the anchor and certainly outranked Tony Cameraman in the television hierarchy. "Wonderful food. Thank you, Mr. Benson."

Tony nodded his agreement. "Yeah, great. Thanks."

Vince introduced me. "I wanted to introduce my dinner guest this evening. This is Ashley Newton, my new assistant."

I exchanged seated greetings with the pair.

Nancy's handshake was firm and confident, Tony's less so.

"Ashley and I knew each other growing up in California." Vince told them. "Nancy, I thought you could interview Ashley in a month or two and do a short character piece for some filler when you need it later."

Nancy nodded politely. She didn't seem thrilled to be assigned a fluff piece on the boss's assistant.

Vince continued. "Something along the lines of a woman coming up the ranks, learning from the bosses she's worked for, and finally being promoted into management training—a women's empowerment piece of sorts. Ashley here is about to get a big promotion."

I had no idea where Vince was going with this, but I smiled and nodded, playing along. Inside I was almost ready to upchuck my dinner.

Nancy looked at me, and her smile turned from forced to genuine. Vince's "women's empowerment" comment seemed to have done the trick.

"We'd love to."

As a woman working in a male-dominated field, I could see her relishing a piece about women succeeding in the workplace.

"Maybe you could get a five-second shot of us now?" Vince suggested. "You know, a mentoring session. Nothing much."

A few guests at a neighboring table were staring, probably having recognized Nancy.

Tony hefted the camera to his shoulder.

Vince was really going to do this.

"I'll have to check with the manager," Nancy said.

Vince shook his head. "Already cleared it."

"Yes, ma'am," our waiter, Stu, said. He had come up behind them and waited. "If we could just keep it brief, that would be appreciated."

Vince returned to his seat across from me.

This was my chance to escape, but before I could, the light from Tony's camera came on.

I kicked Vince under the table.

He winced, but recovered quickly.

"I'm not sure this is a good idea right now," I told him.

Vince had painted me into an inescapable corner.

He winked at me. "Sure it is. It will just take a second."

I couldn't stay, but I also couldn't run. I took a breath and tried to calm my racing heart.

"It will just be one question," Vince told Nancy.

"In, three, two, one, go," Nancy counted down.

Vince looked straight into my eyes, and those dimples reappeared as he smiled. "Ashley, will you accept the promotion?"

At least he hadn't ambushed me about Jacinda. I had no play here except the one he had maneuvered me into. "Thank you, Mr. Benson. I'd love to. But what if it doesn't turn out the way you expect?" He wouldn't understand my question until later.

He extended his hand across the table to shake. "Welcome to the team. I have every confidence in you. Things will work out just fine."

I took his hand, and we shook.

"Wrap," Nancy said.

Tony's camera light went off.

Nancy handed her card to me: *Nancy Sanchez*. "In a few months, then."

I lifted my wine glass. "Look forward to it." At least now I knew her last name.

Tony lowered the camera, and I took a big slug of wine. I needed it to calm my nerves. Actually, I needed something much stronger, and more than a single swallow.

"Enjoy the rest of your dinner," Vince told the news pair, who retreated to their table.

After they were out of earshot, I had to ask. "Promotion?"

He smirked. "We're buying a footwear division, and I need help. You'd be a natural."

"I've got no experience with anything like that."

He reached across to touch my hand.

The same electric shock hit me as at our previous dinner. A dangerous feeling of warmth crept up my arm.

"I have faith in you, Ashley."

I couldn't tell him his faith was misplaced, and that I'd be gone as soon as he was cuffed.

"That makes one of us."

He lifted a piece of steak. "The deal doesn't close for another three months. Plenty of time to get comfortable with the idea. Now, how much do you know about outdoor footwear?" He licked his lips before taking the meat into his mouth.

For just a second, I allowed myself to wonder if those lips tasted as good as they had those many years ago.

We talked through the rest of dinner about the shoe and boot business he was buying, as if nothing had happened tonight.

Before dessert arrived, I looked over. The news duo had left. This whole episode had illuminated another side to Vince. As puppetmaster he enjoyed pulling his various strings to get people to do what he wanted: Nancy Newslady to run a story he dreamed up, and me to take on a role I hadn't been hired for, just on a whim. He probably didn't see how his assistant getting promoted to run a division would be perceived. Come on, how common was that? Not that I would be around that long anyway…

Vince acted as if I were a prize employee, grooming me for greatness and completely unaware that I was instead the federal agent sent to investigate him and put him in jail.

And he still couldn't take no for an answer. Nonetheless, I found myself liking the charming man who explained my new job to me. Playing the part of happy employee at dinner with the boss was easier by the minute.

This reminded me of the Bond film *Casino Royale*. I had now bet all-in, and everything I had hoped to accomplish at the Bureau was riding on this: the bet that I could catch him, seal the case, and exit undetected.

But if I did win, what did I also lose? I could still hope the intel on him was false, and he really was the same Vince I'd known so long ago. That could be a win too.

Now the stakes felt ten times higher, but I was committed. It was all or nothing—game on.

"You're not listening," Vince said, catching me contemplating my fate.

"I'm sorry. It's late."

"What were you thinking about?"

"I was wishing I wasn't in this predicament."

He finished the wine in his glass. "Not me. For nine years I've wished I hadn't been a jerk. And now I have you back again. It's a miracle."

"You don't *have* me," I spat. I was *not* a plaything, or anybody's possession.

He put his hands up. "Sorry. Not what I meant. I just… Let me put it this way: seeing you come through my door on Wednesday made me happy."

His words mirrored my feelings, but I wouldn't admit that to him.

"So we're clear?" I asked.

His shame gave me the upper hand for the moment.

"Crystal," he replied.

His guilt could be my one piece of leverage over him, if I used it wisely. And now wasn't the time. "Thanks. I was glad to see you too."

We went back to discussing shoes and boots.

I wasn't going to fail like Liz had.

VINCENT

AFTER DINNER I WAS GREETED BY OUR DOORMAN, CARL, AS I WALKED THROUGH THE glass doors into the lobby of my building on Tremont Street.

Originally I'd chosen a house in a secluded section of Brookline past Boston

University, but I hadn't liked the extra time it cost me getting to the offices downtown.

Liam Quigley, my boss's brother, had encouraged me to look at an opening here when it came available, and now he and I had the two penthouse suites atop the building.

I entered the elevator and punched the button for the twenty-sixth floor.

Upstairs, I opened the condo door and was greeted by Rufus. There'd been a backyard at the house in Brookline, and maybe that was better for a dog his size, but here I had the services of a dog walker to take Rufus out, and the Common, our city's version of a downtown park, was just across the street. He had the black color and brains of his Labrador father, the size of his Great Dane mother, and the appetite of both combined.

I couldn't let him loose to run, but at least it had grass instead of concrete.

I shucked off my jacket and poured a tumbler of scotch before settling into the couch. Rufus put his head on my knee, and I gladly gave in to his demands to be petted. My dog loved me and didn't care if I was rich or poor, so long as I could afford to feed him.

The scotch slowly warmed my stomach as I drank. I pulled up the photo of that note again.

"Who the hell are you?" I asked the empty room. "You're a coward, ya know that?"

I was only half finished with my drink when I composed my message to Staci.

ME: I can't make it Monday - sorry

Staci would be glad to get the text and not have to make the decision herself. If the writer of the note was to be believed, even meeting me for dinner posed a risk.

I got up to refresh my tumbler with more of the amber liquid. I also threw a chew across the room for Rufus, who quickly located it and lay down, grasping it between his front paws, to start gnawing.

I put the phone back in my pocket. The note writer would reveal his identity sooner or later.

"Who do you think it is?" I asked Rufus.

My question didn't merit diverting his attention from the chew.

I leaned back into the couch and closed my eyes. The memory of tonight played against my eyelids. I'd fucked up my choice of words.

*"You don't have me,"* Ashley had snapped, and the defiance in her eyes had been unmistakable. She didn't feel the attraction anymore.

And she had a boyfriend. A boyfriend with a gun.

I'd lost Ashley once—been stupid enough to walk away. I was richer than sin, but the one thing I couldn't buy was a time machine to go back and make it right with her. I had learned from my mistake, but that had been a costly lesson. Discovering the woman she had grown up to be made me realize just *how* costly.

Whenever Ashley walked into my office, or I walked by her desk, the electricity in the air was palpable—at least to me. I could feel the pull.

But I had to face the fact that wishing for something didn't make it real.

I pulled my wallet out of my pocket and retrieved the photo hidden inside. I gazed at it for a minute.

*Wishing can't make it come true.*

Rufus interrupted my musing, nuzzling my hand to get a scratch behind his ears. No matter how much I screwed up, at least he was always glad to see me.

After scratching him for a minute, I sent him on his way. I replaced the picture safely behind my license, where I'd kept it all these years.

# CHAPTER 17

*ASHLEY*

It was seven o'clock Saturday morning, and I'd taken the MBTA train to Central Square and walked the few blocks to Waffle Castle. I'd chosen this as one of the alternative meeting sites because it was close to John's place—not that it mattered anymore with him sent to New Haven. This morning's debriefing had to be early because Vince expected me at work today. Again.

I pushed open the door and headed for the back.

Liz was waiting with a cup of coffee and scrolling through her phone. She put the phone away as I walked up.

"So?" she asked as soon as I sat.

Her question was obviously about her problem: the software she'd installed on Vince's computer. With Liz, everything was always about her.

I didn't have a chance to respond before the waitress arrived to take our order.

I chose the Belgian waffle, butter on the side.

Liz chose the strawberry-stuffed French toast. The picture of it in the menu looked absolutely scrumptious, like a thousand-calorie bomb even without the extra whipped cream Liz asked for.

After the waitress retreated, I gave my report. "I deleted the copy of Dark-Gecko7 on his computer."

Liz let out an audible breath and relaxed into her seat. "No problems?"

Of course there had been problems, but not ones I was going to tell her about.

My ongoing problem was that everything now relied on me keeping the Bureau in the dark about what Liz had forced me to do.

I took a breath. I was successfully ensconced undercover in the executive offices at Covington and was going to have access to everything we needed. That's all that was important.

"It wasn't easy, but I got it done," I told her. "You owe me." I fixed her with a grimace. "And I collect with interest." I had no intention of letting her forget this.

"Sure," she responded. "Anything, anytime." She sipped her water. "Why do we have to meet this early anyway?"

"And there's more. They already tracked you back to the *Daily Inquisitor*, so you better have that backstopped well. Their security department isn't full of mall cops."

She nodded. "No problem. It'll stand up."

"It better, because if it doesn't, I'm blown too. They got a picture of us meeting Thursday. I had to admit I'd met you before and say you were pumping me for information."

Liz looked nervously out the window. "You shouldn't have let them follow you."

I barely kept from shouting. "You shouldn't have gotten caught on the first day."

"If this blows up, it'll be because they followed you to the meet."

"If this blows up it'll be because you planted the keylogger, not because of me," I spat.

I wasn't taking the fall for her.

She pulled back. "I'll admit that wasn't my best moment."

I didn't comment again on how stupid she'd been. "I'm due at work this morning."

Her eyebrows went up. "Saturday?"

"He works weekends, and therefore so do I."

She shook her head. "Glad you got this assignment then, instead of me."

She'd already changed the history in her mind to omit the part where I was filling in because she blew the assignment and almost the whole case.

She set her voice recorder on the table and started it.

I gave a very quick description of the events of the last day and a half before our food arrived and I reached over to turn off the recorder.

Her breakfast looked even bigger than the photo in the menu had.

"I also had dinner with him last night," I added. I hadn't put that on the recorder.

She raised an eyebrow. "Anything to report there?"

I cut into my waffle. "Nothing of substance. We reminisced about old times, and I made solid progress gaining his trust."

It wasn't complete, but it was good enough for the Bureau.

"I didn't get invited to dinner."

"That's because you were stupid enough to get caught and thrown out in less than a day," I told her.

She wisely decided not to take up the argument.

One day, after this was all over and there was no danger of blowback, I'd let her know how badly she'd fucked up, and exactly how I felt about it. Today was not that day.

While we ate, Liz prattled on about another case she and her partner, Frank, had been assigned. She didn't like the paperwork involved.

Tough shit.

She devoured her massive plate in record time.

I needed to get to the Covington building, and she mentioned a yoga class. She picked up the bill, per protocol for these meetings. I couldn't have a receipt on my person linking me back to this location for someone to accidentally find.

Liz left first, and I followed a few minutes later.

I reached the Covington building after a quick ride on the MBTA Red Line back into town. I swiped in and found Vince's door open when I reached the top floor, but he wasn't in his office.

Even though I'd had coffee with Liz, I followed my usual routine of stopping by the coffee machine to make myself a cup before starting work. I had no idea who outside of Vince might be around, so I had to follow best practices. That included sticking to a routine, which for me meant coffee first thing in the morning.

Back at my desk, I was a half hour into the same massive spreadsheet as yesterday when footfalls approached.

"Ashley?"

I turned to find Mason, the strategic marketing VP, walking in with surprise written across his face.

"Uh, is Vince here?" he asked before poking his head in the office to check for himself.

"Door was open, but I haven't seen him yet."

A minute later, Vince's office line rang, and I answered it.

"Vincent Benson's office, may I help you?"

An exasperated breath came across the line. "Where is he? He's not answering his cell," the woman demanded.

"Sorry, he's not in the office at the moment. Can I give him a message?"

After a pause she said, "Just tell him Staci can't make the trip to LA to meet his family, and I'll talk to him later."

A knot formed in my stomach. "Certainly, Staci. Should I have him call you?"

Her tone calmed somewhat. "No. I'll call him later."

I wrote out the message and put it on Vince's desk.

Staci was obviously the girlfriend. Who else would he be taking to meet the family?

*VINCENT*

MY PHONE RANG TWICE ON THE SHELF BY THE WINDOW.

I ignored it and kept running. The treadmill screen registered eleven miles, only one more to go in my simulated two laps of the Central Park running loop.

I saw his reflection in the window before I heard him.

"Hey," Mason shouted over the noise of the treadmill in the otherwise empty gym. He stomped up to the front of my machine. "I saw Ashley upstairs."

I nodded. "Yeah." I kept my pace steady. I wasn't letting him cut my time short this morning.

"I thought you were going to get rid of her." His statement had an accusatory tone, like I hadn't carried out a duty I owed him.

"I said I'd *handle* it."

His eyes went wide. "Have you lost your mind?"

I kept running and ignored the insult.

"What are you thinking? We can't have her hanging around now that we know she has a connection to the *Inquisitor*."

"I'm keeping her." The distance remaining on my display slowly ticked down.

"But we agreed yesterday—"

I raised my hand to stop him and pulled the safety key out of the treadmill, stopping it. "We didn't agree on anything."

"But it's insanity to give her access to the top floor."

I stepped down. "I trust her."

The comment set him back. "I dunno… It doesn't matter. It's still stupid."

"I know her. She won't be a problem."

He laughed. "That's your dick talking."

I took two quick paces toward him. "I know what I'm doing, and it's my decision."

He stepped back. "I still think it's stupid."

The man didn't know when to quit.

I'd made it clear we weren't discussing this further, but his fatal flaw popped right out again. He always wanted to have the last word, and usually I didn't mind, but today was different.

"She stays, and that's not up for debate." I stepped into his space. "Is that clear, Mason?"

He swallowed. "Sure, crystal clear." He opened his mouth to continue the argument, but controlled himself and stayed silent for once.

I got back on the machine and started it up again.

He left, and I returned to running.

After the treadmill's display ticked over to twelve point two miles, I decided on another mile to make it half-marathon distance this morning. The extra time to cool off after Mason's attack would be good.

My phone chimed with a text, but I kept going. At the end of my run, I discovered two missed calls from Staci and a text.

Staci: I can't make the trip

I stepped off the machine and dialed her number.

She picked up after one ring, no doubt expecting my call. "Vince, I'm sorry. I can't—I can't go. I just can't."

"What's the problem?" I asked.

She hesitated. "I met someone."

Her statement surprised the hell out of me. "You know that doesn't bother me."

"But it would bother him," she said.

There was something off about the tone of her voice.

"I won't be doing any more Mondays either," she added.

So this is what it felt like, being dumped? I wasn't used to being the one told there wasn't going to be another meeting. I'd always been the one to end a relationship. Not that this was a relationship—clearly it wasn't—but it still stung.

"I hope he's a good guy. Staci, you deserve the best. You know that."

"He is. Thanks for understanding. He's flying me to Rome."

I wished her well again, and we hung up.

It didn't do any good to pry, but I didn't believe her. Staci had always been as anti-relationship as me. This was most likely due to that goddamned fucking note. The note writer was fucking up my life again.

I hadn't been looking forward to this trip back home, but it was necessary.


NOW, WITH STACI BACKING OUT, I WAS STUCK.

Barb, my other occasional companion, was a nonstarter. She wouldn't and couldn't act the part the way Staci could.

Coming without a girl on my arm was also not a viable plan. Everything about getting Dad's approval to come back to the company revolved around him judging me to be more mature.

In his antiquated view, being single was a mark of immaturity.

Now I was fucked.

What was I going to do?

On the way to the shower, my phone rang again. The screen showed my father's face.

Answering his call could wait until after lunch. It was never good to talk to him unprepared.

~

*ASHLEY*

A LITTLE WHILE LATER, MASON RETURNED FROM HIS VINCE HUNT. "HE'S IN THE GYM wearing out his knees. He'll be up in a while." His tone was curt, and he disappeared into his office without lingering.

My fake SWAT-team boyfriend had worked his magic a little too well. Mason had gone from flirtatious to downright cold.

Vince arrived before long, his hair wet from a shower.

"You run every morning?" I asked, already knowing the answer from Anita.

"Pretty much. Except when a customer meeting gets in the way. Bring your stuff tomorrow."

"Stuff?" I asked, leaving out the more obvious question about Sunday work.

"You ran cross country at Tufts. You must still have something you can run in. You can join me."

"Maybe."

He vanished into his office. He poked his head back out. "Please."

"Okay." It wasn't like it was a date or anything; it was just running together.

Sports hadn't come up in our dinner conversation. He had done some background research, or his security guy had told him.

Just before lunchtime, I entered the final set of numbers on the spreadsheet task he'd assigned and emailed the file to him.

"Ash, come in here," he called from his office.

I grabbed pen and paper and entered.

"This isn't right," he said. "I need all the quarterly detail."

"It's all there."

He took a breath. "This summary sheet is fine, but it's not enough."

I huffed and rounded the desk. "Let me show you."

He rolled his chair to the side.

When I grabbed the mouse to click on one of the detail tabs, my arm brushed his, and the sparks shot through me again. Proximity to him fogged my brain, and it took a second to focus on what I meant to say.

"The tabs down here each contain quarterly data that backs into the annual summaries on the front page."

"That's smart," he said, his delectable tone enveloping me like a warm breeze.

I stood and increased my distance from him. "They carry to hidden columns on the front sheet."

"Show me."

Leaning over again, I felt his eyes on me, heating me to the core. I flipped back to the front sheet and expanded the hidden columns. "Here."

He moved toward me, and I could feel his body heat.

"Where?" he asked.

I blinked a few times to clear my head. I moved the mouse to the columns and highlighted them.

He leaned in, and his shoulder met mine. The heat scorched my skin beneath the fabric and welded me to him, unable to move away. I could only wonder if he felt it too.

"I see," he said slowly before leaning back.

Instantly I missed the heat of his touch.

"That's really smart."

"You said that already." I let go of the mouse and stood.

His eyes held mine briefly with a flash of something feral. He pointed to the entrance. "Close the door."

I walked over and did as he asked. I waited by the door, unsure what was coming next.

"Come back over here."

As I walked back toward his desk, his eyes traveled the length of me, appraising me.

From the look in his eyes, I half expected, half hoped his next words would tell me to sit in his lap, or unbutton something, or bend over—anything that would show he felt this too.

Instead he said, "Take a seat," his tone businesslike, impersonal.

I sat and waited.

"This project..." He motioned to his computer. "The last one Sophia did took her twice as long."

Getting on the wrong side of the other assistants would be a bad move. "I'm sure the one she did was harder."

"Right," he said dismissively. "Good job, Ash."

I had to admit, his praise felt good. "What's next?"

He pointed to another two stacks on the credenza. "The left-hand one first."

I gathered up the top several inches of the stack, opened the door, and carried the papers to my desk. I was going to die of boredom if this was all he had me doing.

The moment between us had passed, and I still couldn't decipher if he'd felt it too.

# CHAPTER 18

*Vincent*

WHEN I RETURNED TO THE CONDO AT THE END OF THE DAY ON SATURDAY, RUFUS greeted me at the door.

"Want a go for a walk?" I asked.

His tail wagging accelerated. That was a yes, as always.

I put the Amazon box I'd picked up downstairs and my briefcase down on the table as I went to change and gather up his retractable leash.

Stopping at the door before we left, I changed my mind and opened the box, slipping the book that had arrived under my arm as we went out.

Across the street, it didn't take Rufus long to fill up my blue doggie bag, which I deposited in the trash.

I'd been watching, and today, as for the last several days now, there had been no sign of the suited man who'd followed me last week—a good omen.

Rufus and I walked on the grass so I could let out his leash for him to roam without tripping anybody. It was still light enough, so I began to read the book Ashley had been reading as Rufus sniffed here and there. I was soon caught up in Juliet and Dalton's story. Dalton was arrogant and sort of a jerk. It seemed that's how all of America saw rich people—so unfair.

Rufus and I made it back across Tremont to the building without him scaring anybody to death, which had happened before.

"Mr. Benson," Carl greeted me as we walked up. "Was he a good boy?"

"Always," I responded.

"Jimmy has been walking him regularly."

"Thanks, Carl."

I'd asked him to keep an eye out to see that Rufus was getting all the walks he was supposed to.

Upstairs, I locked the door, let Rufus off the leash, and prepared his dinner.

Checking the fridge and freezer, things were pretty sparse, and I hadn't stopped to pick up *my* dinner. "It looks like you're eating better than me tonight."

Rufus didn't stop eating to respond.

I moved on to the pantry and decided a can of baked beans and a can of Vienna sausages was the best I could do for tonight, unless I was going to subsist on only ice cream.

While the contents of the cans were warming, I opened the book again on page sixty-seven.

One page later, things got super interesting, and I took a seat at the table. If this is what Ashley was reading all the time, her boyfriend was in for a treat—she wasn't the demure wallflower I took her for.

I kept turning the addictive pages, until I noticed the smell.

"Fuck."

I raced to the stove and pulled the pan off the heat. Some of the beans had burned on the bottom. I spooned the edible top portion onto a plate and, with spoon and napkin in hand, returned to the table to read.

By the end of the evening, I'd gotten through the book. Dalton had saved Juliet, and they were on their happy honeymoon.

After taking Rufus downstairs to take care of business, I retreated to bed with my new book, and some tissue to clean up with.

I went to sleep after jerking off to the desk sex scene, envisioning myself pounding into Ashley again and again. I had page sixty-eight burned into my brain.

～

*ASHLEY*

TONIGHT I WAS HOME BEFORE DARK. AT LEAST SATURDAY WASN'T AS LATE A DAY AS during the week. Though I did have to go in tomorrow too, it seemed.

I gathered up my running things and shoes and put the packed gym bag by the door so I didn't forget it in the morning.

I decided to make a homemade dinner in my own kitchen for a change, and a glass of wine would be my reward.

As I began to cook, I thought back over my Saturday in the office. I'd managed to get a few minutes to access some of the file cabinet records after Mason had left. But so far nothing of interest had popped up.

The investigation of Vince's records was going to be slow-going, but being upstairs around him was anything but. The man was a dynamo, constantly active, and he had a team that worked well together. He engendered respect the old fashioned way—not through the occasional Caesar moments SAC White was always trying.

I hadn't had much direct interaction with Ben Murdoch in security, but he struck me as extremely competent, which was worrisome, especially if he dug harder into Liz's cover story, or mine.

My phone rang, startling me. The hot pouch of rice I'd pulled out of the microwave started sliding off the plate. I grabbed for it.

"Fucking shit." I pulled my hand back from the steaming bag before getting a serious burn.

A minute under the cold water of the sink and the burn subsided.

*I should know better.*

The phone had stopped ringing and sent the caller to voicemail.

Before I could get back to the phone, the oven timer went off, calling me to pull the filet of sole out. Once the oven was off and dinner was on a plate, I took the food and my phone to the table.

Dinner smelled fantastic, and I savored a bite of the fish with lemon-dill sauce before turning my attention to the phone.

My sister Rosemary had called, so I dialed her back and put the phone on speaker so I could continue to eat. I smiled. Talking to Rose was a treat.

"You back from the bush yet?" I asked when she picked up.

"One day back to civilization for a shower and some real food, then back where we belong."

It was odd to hear her say the bush was where she belonged. It had always seemed more her boyfriend's calling than hers.

"So what's up?"

"Just calling to see how my baby sister is doing. Haven't talked to you in almost a week. Shoot any bad guys lately?"

I finished chewing. "You know discharging my weapon is a bad thing, right?" The Bureau viewed *avoiding* a gun battle as an accomplishment.

"So have you caught your boyfriend yet?"

"One, he's an ex-boyfriend, and two, no, not yet. But I will."

She gasped. "I knew you were mad at him, but isn't this taking it a little far? I thought you were going to turn it down."

"I didn't start this. It came down from the DOJ."

"That's twisted. Can't you get out of it?"

I wasn't admitting the whole situation with White to anybody, not even Rose. "No, the other girl blew her chance, and I'm stuck with it."

"How are you coping? It's got to be fucked up trying to put away somebody you know, especially with your history."

She had that part right. The history made everything upside down.

I sighed. "It's okay so far. And they might even be wrong about Vince."

"Why investigate him if you're not sure he's a criminal?"

"We investigate to find out; that's why. Like I said, this came down from the DOJ. They're calling the shots."

"How will you handle it if he's dirty?"

I had an easy answer to that one. "I follow my oath and do my job."

It was the only possible answer. That choice was black and white—no possibility for gray.

"Maybe it won't come to that."

I took a sip of the wine I'd poured. "I hope not."

"You're still hot for the guy, aren't you? I can hear it in your voice."

"It's been nine years," I complained.

"My God, you are."

"Am not."

It wasn't a total lie. I felt an attraction, but I couldn't have the hots for a guy who didn't care about me, and who I might be destined to cuff.

"Are too. I don't have to see your face to know. Now you're really in a fucked-up situation."

"Yeah," I admitted.

She was right. This was going to be a battle of my hormones against my gray matter.

"If he's not dirty, do you have another chance with him?"

"Not a clue. He apologized for before—"

"Well, he should."

My sister had my back on that one.

"But," I continued, "he has a girlfriend, I think."

"Think or know?"

"I can't exactly ask him."

"Well, somebody there has to know," she said.

Asking around was the obvious answer, but wouldn't it seem odd with me working for him?

# CHAPTER 19

*Ashley*

Sunday morning I slapped my alarm clock so hard it landed on the floor, but at least it shut up. Rolling out of bed, I padded to the bathroom for a shower. The first time I'd showered here, the water had turned cold before I'd finished. I'd complained, and the manager had promised to upgrade the water heater when the budget allowed, but that hadn't happened yet. Now I managed by turning off the water while I shampooed and conditioned.

I hadn't slept well last night—Vince had dominated my thoughts. I couldn't get his face or his smile out of my head. Those dimples tormented me. But worst of all, my reaction to his touch scared me. Being unable to control my feelings could be dangerous. My oath required me to put my feelings aside and deal with the facts. In the end, the facts had to rule. I was all about rules. I could hold out hope that the DOJ source was wrong about Vince, but so far that's all it was: hope.

There had been dozens of virile young studs after me at Quantico, and none of them had engendered this kind of reaction. No boy in college ever had either. And there was the problem: they had all been *boys*, and Vince was the very definition of a man. It was as if he used aftershave of pure testosterone, or one of those poorly understood pheromones the magazines wrote about. That had to be it—a chemical that explained this and made it not my fault.

When I finished my shower, I dressed quickly, slung my gym bag over my shoulder, and left. On the way I picked up a breakfast sandwich and coffee at Starbucks.

Vince was already upstairs when I arrived. *Workaholic* was way too mild a description for him. The rest of the executive area was quiet and dark, as it should be on a Sunday morning.

It was lunchtime before Vince came out and ordered me to join him running. His wording didn't leave room for disagreement—not that I wanted to offer any.

We both got changed, and I followed him to the elevator.

When we arrived at the gym, it was immediately clear that, like everything else at Covington, this was a spare-no-expense facility.

He mounted a treadmill, clipped the safety key to his shorts, pressed a few buttons on the display, and the machine started whirring away.

I stopped watching his muscled legs and climbed up on the one next to him, but I was unable to figure out the controls. There were too many choices. I needed go and stop, nothing more complicated.

Vince paused his machine. "Let me help you get started. First you select the course here." He scrolled through some selections and ended on one that said *Boston Common Loop.* "Then we set the starting speed here."

A moment later the thing whirred to life, and I almost lost my footing, but I got caught up as Vince returned to his run. Just when I thought I had the hang of it, the machine changed angle. I stepped on the front cover, lost my balance, and it spit me out onto the floor behind it.

Vince jumped off his machine again. "You okay?" He rushed over. "Are you hurt?"

My ass was sore, but that seemed to be all. "Just my pride. This isn't running. I've done a lot of it, and this isn't it."

"You'll get the hang of it," he said, watching me get up.

I brushed off my butt. "No way. That thing doesn't like me, and the feeling's mutual."

This was obviously a killer robot masquerading as a piece of exercise equipment.

"What's wrong with running outside on solid ground anyway? At least outside you don't have a machine tripping you."

He gestured toward the door. "Okay. Outside then."

I followed him out of the gym and away from the malevolent robots.

Once on the street, he turned toward the Common, and I followed. The route required several stops at intersections, as well as dodging pedestrians who were looking down at their phones and not paying attention.

In short order we crossed Tremont at Park Street and got on the perimeter trail in the Common, where it was wide enough to run side by side.

"Done much running since school?" he asked.

I caught him looking over, checking out my boobs. I straightened up. "A short run in the morning on occasion is all I've had time for. And I chicken out when there's snow on the ground."

"That's the advantage of using an indoor treadmill."

"But then you have to breathe all that stale building air instead of being out here in the open," I replied. Outside was always better.

"You may have a point there," he said, looking over with a sly grin.

I made a show of watching a jogger going the other way, but really I was checking out Vince's powerful legs, and that nice ass. Thank God for short running shorts. There was no harm in looking, was there? If men could do it, why couldn't women?

A kid on a skateboard coming the other way decided he owned the middle of the path.

Vince dodged to the right, and the skateboarder went between us. "It's dangerous out here," he said.

"Sometimes you give way; sometimes they do. That's life."

We ran halfway around the Common.

He stopped at the hot dog vendor by the Charles Street gate. "How 'bout lunch?"

"I didn't bring any money," I countered.

"I'm buying."

He could certainly afford it, and I wasn't too proud to accept. "Sure, boss."

He ordered a polish dog, and I chose a simple hot dog.

A whiff of eucalyptus from his hair wafted my way as he leaned in front of me to pick out his water.

After adding condiments, he chose a nearby bench.

Sitting next to him, though not too close, reminded me of the time we'd spent down by Venice Beach a lifetime ago in LA.

"Has Mason hit on you yet?" he asked.

The question came out of the blue.

I couldn't stifle my giggle. "He tried, but I shut him down with my SWAT team boyfriend story."

His face lit up. "Story?"

I licked a bit of mustard that threatened to drip off the end of my hot dog. "I told him my boyfriend had SWAT training, kicking down doors and shooting people." I turned to give my shit-eating grin. "Dynamite couldn't have gotten him to leave faster."

He almost spit out his food laughing. "Not true?"

I shook my head. "No, but it works every time."

The smile that grew on his face brought out the dimples.

"Mustard," he said, wiping his finger on the corner of my mouth.

His touch was electric. "Thanks," I mumbled with my mouth full. Once I swallowed, I continued. "Once they hear about a boyfriend who carries a gun, they don't stick around long."

"That just means they lack self-confidence."

It had always seemed like more than a lack of confidence to me. "I guess."

I took a breath. "What about you?" I asked.

"Nothing serious," he said before sipping his water. "You shouldn't believe any of what you read in the tabloids."

My heart sped up. Perhaps I had a chance, if I dared. But there had been public pictures of him with a host of other women, all of them drop-dead gorgeous. And there was also the girl he'd mentioned who'd gotten the note.

After a moment I asked the question I really wanted to: "And the girlfriend who got the note? What about her?"

He didn't look at me. "I don't expect to be seeing her again."

"Scared, huh?"

"Seems that way. Staci Baxter is a friend. I was helping her prepare a presentation for a bank loan application when she got that note."

"Staci Baxter the model?" I asked with more than a hint of surprise.

He adjusted his grip on his polish dog. "Ex model. Now she's got a clothing line, and I was helping her line up financing to expand."

Her name landed on me like a stack of bricks. The Staci who had left the message yesterday was world famous. She'd been on the cover of *Sports Illustrated*. She was a twelve on every man's ten-point scale. How could any woman compare to her? Tall, perfect body, perfect teeth, perfect hair, perfect skin—perfect everything. I gulped a slug of water and caught another whiff of his eucalyptus scent as I put the bottle down.

My heart raced. "So you're unattached?" I asked outright.

"Relationships aren't my thing," he responded.

That deflated my balloon.

≈

VINCENT

I'D BEEN ENJOYING HER PERKY SMILE WHILE WE ATE, UNTIL HER SHOULDERS SLUMPED at my answer.

"Oh. Me neither," she said.

My spirit soared. I could sense the bullshit in her reply. I had a chance with her after all. *She doesn't have a boyfriend.*

She looked down at the pavement.

The run with Ashley had been half nirvana—even better than I'd imagined—and half torture as I'd tried to keep from staring at her tits while they bounced with every stride under that tight tank top. Now her legs drew my imagination. I wondered how they would feel wrapped around me.

I couldn't take back what I'd said about relationships, but I could try to fix it. "How about dinner tonight, say seven?" I asked.

Her face brightened, but confusion clouded it. "I thought you said—"

I stopped her. "Dinner? It's a simple question."

Her evil smirk appeared. "Is that an order?"

"No. I'm asking Ashley Newton, not my PA."

Her feistiness was one of her more endearing traits.

Her face gave away the answer before her mouth delivered the words. "I'd love to." She took the last of her hot dog in a big bite. And wiped her lips.

I followed suit, devouring my polish dog and trying to hide the smile I felt growing across my face. I leaned back and placed my arm along the bench behind her.

She relaxed, making contact with my arm—contact that sent sparks through my veins.

She slid just slightly toward me. "Have you ever wondered?"

She didn't finish the sentence. She didn't need to.

Knowing she'd had those same questions was a gift from heaven.

I slid my hand to her shoulder. "Hundreds of times," I said.

Would I finally get another chance with Ashley?

The look in her eyes as she turned to me answered my question and sent a jolt to my cock.

*She cares.*

I pulled my arm back and stood. "Ready?" I needed to get going before my condition got out of control and became obvious to everyone. I dumped my trash and carried the half-full water bottle.

Ashley made her trip to the trash and followed.

We resumed our run around the Common's outer path.

"You up for two laps?" I asked as we made the turn at the southern corner.

She pulled ahead. "If you can keep up."

I stayed back for a minute, enjoying the view and looking forward to having my hands on that ass. When I caught back up to her, I limited myself to the occasional glance to my side. Her tits called to me with each bounce.

When we made it back to the building, I considered it for a moment, but I controlled my tongue and didn't suggest a shower together.

She deserved to have me behave myself—at least for the moment.

The smile she sent my way as she entered the women's locker room convinced me she would have said yes.

Once in the shower, the thought of her in here with me had my cock at attention, begging to show her how I'd missed her. I turned the shower cold to deflate my erection. Going upstairs with an obvious hard-on wouldn't do.

# CHAPTER 20

*A*SHLEY

VINCE WAS ALREADY LOCKED BACK IN HIS OFFICE WHEN I GOT UPSTAIRS AFTER MY shower.

I spent the afternoon running through the spreadsheet work on autopilot while replaying our conversation in my head. No, he didn't have a serious girlfriend, and he'd asked about Mason hitting on me. That hadn't seemed to be coming from a protective-boss place.

That was all positive, but then he'd let slip that he didn't do relationships. He hadn't added the word *ever*, but he'd implied it.

If he didn't want a relationship, was dinner just a prelude to getting in my pants?

And what was wrong with that anyway?

I was all mixed up. It was my job to get as close to him as possible. The Bureau couldn't and wouldn't order me to sleep with a target. It was all wink-wink *whatever you're comfortable with*, and we won't ask, wink-wink.

Had I agreed to dinner as an FBI Special Agent, or as his ex-girlfriend? How could I separate the two?

My hormones were battling my brain cells, as I'd known they would. Did he ask me to get close to me to influence my investigation? It couldn't be that, because he didn't know. Right?

That wasn't my first question, but my training said it should have been.

His door opened.

"I'm going for another run," he said.

"Again?"

"I need more miles to be ready." He meant the triathlon.

"Have fun," I called as he headed to the elevator.

A few minutes after I heard the door close, I slid through his office door and closed it. With nobody else on the floor, I'd finally get a chance to check this space. He worked so many hours that these opportunities were going to be rare.

The file cabinet was locked, and I didn't have a pick set with me.

I checked his center desk drawer; some idiots left the keys in their desks. A check of the center and top side drawers proved Vince was no idiot. But it did yield one interesting item: a copy of *Secretary to the Bazillionaire*, and from the splaying of the pages, it seemed he'd read it.

*Anita?*

The question didn't merit my time.

I pulled a stack of papers from the bottom of the brass multi-level organizer on the corner of the desk. I leafed through them one by one, turning them face down into a new pile after scanning them, to keep the same order.

That pile was a bust, so I repeated the procedure with the stack on the middle shelf. Once again the papers were routine, nothing of investigatory value, except a few handwritten pages about a meeting. I snapped shots of those with my phone. The top level held only a few papers and nothing of interest.

The desk blotter had a smooth, green leather surface, and I recalled an instructor recalling how he'd raised the impression of something written from a surface like this.

I couldn't see anything from this angle, so I moved around to the other side so I wouldn't be between the window's light and the blotter. I leaned over the desk, and started to make something out. I leaned farther, resting my chest on the wide, wooden desk to glance along the blotter's surface toward the window. I could see an area of writing in the corner.

"What are you doing?" It was Vince from behind me.

I froze. I hadn't heard him open the door. "I was just…"

An explanation escaped me. I stood and turned. Just like Liz, I'd fucked up. The pounding of my runaway heart in my ears was like a freight train.

"This wood feels so good. I was just…" I had turned into a babbling mess.

A wicked grin replaced the surprise on his face. "Page sixty-eight?" he asked.

My jaw dropped at his mention of the book. I saw my one chance to get out of this and took it.

I smiled and nodded.

He closed the door behind him. "Do you want me, Juliet?"

It was Dalton's line from the book.

In the book, Juliet was speechless, so I acted the same.

"Do you?" he asked again.

"Yes. I have since the day I started here." I copied Juliet's line, and it was no lie.

"Will you obey me?"

So far he had all of Dalton's dialog down pat.

I nodded, and I didn't have to act the part to add the smile that came to my face.

"Tell me."

"Yes."

He moved toward me. The bulge in his jeans was obvious. He pulled me to him, and his mouth claimed mine.

My lips parted, and our tongues danced with lustful abandon. I laced my fingers through his hair, pulling myself up and closer. I needed more of this. It was better than high school. As we continued, I realized this is what I'd dreamed of last night.

One hand grasped my ass and pulled me against his hardness, and the other moved to my breast, tracing the underside, then moving over my hardened nipple.

He smelled like the woods, with a hint of eucalyptus, and he tasted like sex and pure lust. Moist heat pooled between my thighs. I clawed at his back to pull us closer, the closeness I'd missed all these years.

His hand found its way under my shirt to my bra strap and undid it with a flick. He moved his hand inside the loose bra cup to cradle my breast, his thumb circling the hardened pebble of my nipple. His pinch sent a shiver through me.

I broke the kiss. "I've wanted this since the first day." Juliet's line matched my feelings.

"And you're going to get it."

He undid my pants and pulled them down, turning me to face the desk. So far he was following the script.

I spread my legs as far as the pants around my ankles would allow and leaned over the desk.

He went around the side and retrieved a condom—from his briefcase of all places. The bulge in his pants was huge, and I was about to find out why.

In school, I'd gone so far as to rub Vince through his jeans, but that was all. I stayed in position while he moved behind me. I heard the tear of the packet and turned to see his pants off. I gasped at the size of the monster he was sheathing— the grande burrito.

He pulled my shirt and bra up to my shoulders and pushed me forward onto the desk. The wood was cool against my hot breasts.

He pulled one of my legs up, wrestled the shoe off, and pulled my foot free of my pants.

I spread my legs farther to give him better access and lowered my hips to the desk. I was about to find out if the words of ecstasy on the pages matched the experience.

He positioned his tip at my wet entrance and pushed in a little.

I winced. He was bigger than anyone I'd had before. "Fuck me, Dalton. Fuck me hard," I said as Juliet.

With that, he started easing into my soaked heat, just a little farther each time, pulling more lubrication onto his length.

Every movement sent heated sparks through me.

With a final push, he was fully in me, his hips flush with mine.

I yelped when he slapped my butt. The spot burned for a second.

His thrusting grew more rapid, and the added force built waves of pleasure that crashed over me.

"Fuck me harder. Harder. Yeah, harder." I'd never understood the line in the book, but now I did, as he granted my wish. My nerve endings were on fire as I climbed toward the peak of my climax.

My moaning matched Vince's grunting as the animal in him took over. The slapping of flesh against flesh grew louder. The rushing of the blood in my ears joined the cacophony of our moans.

He pulled my hips back from the edge of the desk, and his fingers found my clit.

That wasn't in the book.

The sudden pressure on my sensitive nub took me to a level I'd never experienced before as his fingers stroked me to match his thrusts.

He pounded into me again, filling me beyond full, and a tweak of my clit sent fire through my veins and pushed me over into a sea of bliss. Fireworks played against my clenched eyelids, my walls contracted around him, and the spasms shook me. I cried out his name—Vince this time, not Dalton.

My legs shook as he continued, and with a groan he pounded out his release within me.

I was a limp, boneless heap on the desk, perspiration sticking my skin to the wood.

He leaned over me, but spared me his entire weight. "You deserve better," he said.

That wasn't a Dalton line either.

"That was fantastic," I told him. "I mean it. It's what I wanted." I wanted to be certain he knew I wasn't reciting from the book. He needed to know.

The pulsing of his cock within me slowly ebbed. "I missed you, too."

His words sounded heartfelt and warmed me.

Before I could respond, the sound of a vacuum cleaner starting up outside the door filled the office.

He jerked up and pulled out, hurrying to dispose of the condom in tissues from the box on his desk.

I stood and hooked my bra again. "Do they vacuum in here?" I asked softly.

He was trying to fit his still-engorged cock in his underwear. "Yup."

I finished adjusting my bra and shimmied into my pants.

He pulled his shoes on while I located the one of mine that had hidden under the desk.

I got it back on and was fully clothed when he opened the door for me. "Dinner. Don't forget dinner."

"Right. Dinner," I echoed, still trying to get my brain back in gear.

He followed me out of the office. "I need to get more running in."

"I think I'll head home, if that's okay."

"Sure. Pick you up at seven."

The janitor and his vacuum moved from the open space between my desk and Anita's into Vince's office.

～

I MADE IT BACK TO MY APARTMENT WITH MY BRAIN STILL TRYING TO PROCESS THE afternoon's events. He'd caught me in his office, and I could have been on my way to Alaska, but somehow it had turned into an afternoon like none other—all due to Anita's book. I wasn't turning my nose up at romance novels ever again. This one had saved me.

The fire he'd ignited in me answered one question: I wanted Vincent Benson, even if only for a short time. I'd pushed him away before, but that wasn't happening again. No fucking way.

I set an alarm on my phone and slumped into the couch. When I closed my eyes, the prom played behind my eyelids. I hadn't dwelled on the event in years, and now I couldn't stop it from hijacking my brain.

What if he was taking advantage of me?

What if he wasn't?

What if I was taking advantage of him?

It didn't fucking matter.

# CHAPTER 21

*ASHLEY*

THE ALARM ON MY PHONE QUACKED THAT IT WAS TIME TO GET READY FOR DINNER—
not just dinner, a dinner *date*, and a special one at that.

Just like with Juliet and Dalton in the book, the sex had preceded the date, all backwards, but it had kept me from botching the assignment. I don't know what I would have done if Vince hadn't decided I was leaning on his desk fantasizing about that book.

I would have to find a way to thank Anita.

Vince hadn't mentioned where we were going, but based on the last two establishments we'd visited, I knew it wouldn't be Sizzler.

I chose my best little black dress. I had curves that could rock a nice, tight LBD, and this one had a neckline to get Vince salivating—low enough to show I was braless for the evening. If he was taking me someplace nice, I was going to make the most of it.

I'd worn this dress exactly once, and what a waste that had been. Monty what's-his-name had been a dud of a blind date, but at least he'd only spilled his wine on himself, not me or my dress.

I added my favorite necklace: a small sapphire pendant. The chain was too short, so I switched it out for one that hung the stone nice and low, drawing the eye toward my assets. I didn't own matching earrings, so I settled for simple hoops instead of the small studs I always wore for field work.

I was so out of practice it took forever to do a decent job on my makeup, and the buzzer rang as I was finishing my mascara. I touched up the right eye before rushing to the door.

When I opened it, Vince took my breath away.

The man could wear the hell out of a nice suit, but at the office he always took his jacket off and avoided a tie. The only time I'd seen a tie on him was the afternoon a customer had come in to meet, and the tie had disappeared as soon as the customer left the floor. But tonight, he had a tie in full effect.

I could tell my dress was working, and my necklace placement had also done the trick. He looked me up and down with ravenous eyes, and his gaze paused perceptibly at my chest.

"Wow," he said. The hunger on his face said even more. "You look gorgeous this evening."

"And you look pretty good yourself. I see I even rate a tie." I reached up to straighten it and received a gratifying smile in return.

"Only the best for you, Kitten."

His use of my nickname melted me. Back in high school, for a brief time I'd been his soft and cuddly kitten, and I'd purred in his embrace. The memories washed over me like a warm Hawaiian wave.

"Ready?" he asked.

I gathered my clutch, locked the door, and followed him downstairs.

The purse was a present from Rosemary that I hadn't been able to use until tonight. It wouldn't accommodate my Glock, which my job required me to carry at all times. But tonight was the exception since I was undercover with an identity that wouldn't be armed.

In high school, Vince had driven a pretty standard car for a teenager, a Mustang. Tonight, when he pressed the key fob, the sleek red Ferrari at the curb flashed its lights and unlocked.

"Nice wheels."

He held the door open for me. "I wanted to impress you, Kitten."

"It's working." I slid in, holding the hem of my short dress down.

When he started the engine, the sound was unlike anything I'd ever heard. Not only were the rich different, their cars weren't of this world either. The smell of leather upholstery and the surge of sudden acceleration as he punched the throttle completed the experience. I was not in Kansas anymore. Whether we were off to Oz or down the rabbit hole was yet to be seen, but tonight was destined to be unique.

"Where are we going?" I asked as he turned toward downtown.

"I know the owner at a nice Italian place," he said with a smirk.

The food at Vitaliano's had been superb; it would take a lot more than two dinners there to get bored with the place.

Driving through town, I could see necks crane to get a glimpse of our chariot. This was not your everyday conveyance, and eyeballs tracked us as we flew by. If only Rose could see me now.

When we arrived, the valet knew Vince's name.

*Naturally.*

Vince hustled around the car to open my door—a more gentlemanly act than I'd ever been afforded in this town. He guided me through the door with a light hand at the small of my back. The heat from that touch threatened to ignite my dress.

Once inside, we bypassed a crowd even bigger than the previous one at lunch to reach Angelica at the hostess desk.

She quickly showed us to a table.

I noticed something I hadn't paid attention to last time we were here: Vince's status in the community was evident by the several well-dressed businessmen who nodded their greeting to him as we passed. I was being escorted by a power player in this town.

After we ordered, all I could do was drink in the experience. This was all way above my GS-11 pay grade: exquisite food, expensive wine, and a ride in a car that cost more than many people's houses.

"How's the soup?"

Vince's simple question woke me. "Great. Even better than my aunt made." Aunt Michelle had made minestrone from scratch for us.

"How is your aunt, by the way?" It was an innocuous question. He couldn't have known about her death or the details.

I took a breath to calm myself. "She passed."

"Sorry to hear that. I liked her." He offered his hand across the table, and I took it. After this afternoon, the warmth of his touch threatened to fuse our hands together permanently. His eyes conveyed his sincerity.

"Thanks. She liked you too."

Aunt Michelle had not been happy to hear Vince and I had broken up, and it had been hard to lie to her about the particulars, but it wasn't anybody's business but mine.

He retrieved his hand to eat another bite of salad.

My brain didn't engage fast enough to stop the question that had haunted me since high school. "What happened with you and Cynthia?"

*How can I be such a jerk?*

His brow furrowed.

I regretted the words, but couldn't pull them back now. Maybe my subconscious was trying to screw things up with him.

Cynthia Powell had latched onto Vince after our breakup. Her reputation preceded her, and Vince probably got his fill from her of what I'd withheld.

"She tired of me after a while."

Thankfully he didn't elaborate. Knowing they hadn't lasted was all I needed, but it had been rude of me to ask. On reflection, I wished he'd said he'd tired of her instead.

Our waiter, Tony, interrupted the awkward silence to clear my soup and Vince's salad.

"Sorry," I said after the waiter left.

"No need. I don't have any secrets from you."

His words resonated in my heart. I certainly hoped that was true. With the way I felt this evening, it was going to be beyond hard to cuff him, if it came to that. I swatted that thought away. He was a good man; I'd always known that. I just had to fulfill my duty to investigate so I could return a clean report with a clear conscience. The Benson family was a solid one, and I had every reason to believe Vince was still the straight arrow he'd been when I knew him before.

Tony was back quickly with our main course: pollo al peperoncino for me and scallopine toscano for my date. The words rattled around my head for a moment, *my date*.

Just thinking of Vince as my date brightened my outlook. How many women in town, or in the state for that matter, could boast of being out with a man half as dashing, half as considerate, half as rich, and yes, half as virile as Vince looked tonight? Not many, for sure.

And tonight *I* was his date, not his employee.

I sat up straight with the confidence that thought brought me—a date I could honestly brag to my sister about. I was his *Kitten*.

"How is Rosemary?" he asked, shifting the conversation.

"She's doing well. She went into nursing."

"That's noble—a good calling."

I cut a piece of my chicken. "But long hours and worse conditions. She's working down in Australia right now with her boyfriend, helping Doctors Without Borders."

He finished chewing. "Like I said, noble. Nothing wrong with that."

"If you do it for the right reasons. I just want her to be happy."

"Maybe that's what makes her happy."

I nodded, not because I agreed, but because I couldn't tell where her drive ended and her boyfriend's expectations began.

We continued dinner, and I shifted the conversation to the Semaphore company he and Mason had been discussing.

Every time I looked at Vince, those dimples drew me in, and I saw something in his eyes, something from long ago that I'd missed terribly—a warmth that couldn't be faked. I was falling for him all over again, and in record time.

If I was honest with myself, he'd never left my heart. My feelings had merely been concealed by hurt and anger for a time, and then by distance and lack of contact.

When he laughed, I laughed. When he got serious, I listened intently. The man's magnetism was off the charts.

I'd spent a few minutes online earlier reading *Cosmo* articles on how to give head, something I'd never attempted. *Cosmo* said men really liked it. In college,

I'd been asked, almost forced, but I always got out of it with some vigorous sex instead. But tonight I was going to try on Vince, and I wouldn't allow myself to fail. I smiled at the thought.

"What's so funny?" he asked.

"Oh, nothing."

Vince went on. Between mouthfuls he explained how much of a feather in his cap it would be to get Semaphore under the Covington umbrella. It was clearly a top priority.

We finished our dinners, and Vince ordered key lime pie for us to split as a dessert. He'd remembered my favorite. So far his memory was infallible.

While we were waiting, an older man—slightly portly with thinning white hair and a matching mustache-and-goatee combination—walked up beside me and gave me an odd wink through his horn-rimmed glasses.

"Vincent. I knew I'd find you here," he boomed.

Vince's eyes went wide, and his face dropped momentarily before he jumped with a start and turned.

"Dad," he said, standing.

I stood as well.

I hadn't recognized his father, probably because I'd only been to Vince's house during the day back in high school, and his father had always been at work. A picture on the mantle had been as close as I'd come to this man.

# CHAPTER 22

*VINCENT*

DAD'S VOICE GAVE ME A HEART ATTACK.

I stood, and we shook hands vigorously.

"Well, aren't you going to introduce me?" he asked, turning to Ashley.

Ashley extended her hand. "Ashley Newton, Mr. Benson."

Dad took her hand gently, as he always did with women. "Pleasure, Ashley. Please call me Lloyd. Everybody does." He released her hand and pulled out a chair. "I'll just join you for a bit."

It was just like my father to invite himself. Tonight was going downhill quickly.

We retook our seats.

"Dad, I thought you were in London this week," I said.

Mom kept me abreast of his movements, and last I'd heard he wasn't due to leave London for a few more days.

"I was, but we wrapped up early, and I decided to come back home to see your mother. The pilot said the winds were too strong to make LA nonstop. So here I am. Thought I'd make it a surprise visit."

He'd succeeded in the surprise department. Dad was good at that—too good.

If I'd known he planned to stop by tonight, I would have arranged a late customer meeting, or something, anything to avoid a meeting with him. He and Mom were still expecting me at the barbecue with Staci on my arm, and with her unavailable, I'd planned to go alone with a story I hadn't yet concocted to explain.

"And I couldn't wait to meet your lady friend here," Dad said, smiling at Ashley.

"She…" My blood froze. Now I was caught. "She—"

Ashley cut me off. "Has been looking forward to meeting you too, Lloyd."

Dad beamed. "Well, that's very gracious of you."

The Ashley charm had overcome him as well.

"Would you like to order something?" Ashley offered.

My chest constricted when Dad looked ready to accept. A long conversation risked undoing everything.

"Thank you, but no," he finally said. "I need to be going in a minute, and I don't want to interrupt the intimate evening you two are sharing. The missus and I know how special those can be. I just wanted to stop by and say hi while the jet is being refueled."

He and I both knew it was more than that. It only took twenty minutes to top off the company jet, and it took a lot longer to get from Logan to here and back.

I'd dodged a bullet.

Dad cocked his head. "Ashley, have we met before?"

She shook her head. "No."

"Ashley and I dated for a bit in high school," I interjected.

Dad raised a finger in her direction. "That's it. Vincent showed me a picture of you two once. You were a beautiful couple then, and that hasn't changed one bit."

Ashley's face lit up.

Dad patted the table. "Well, I can't keep the pilot waiting forever. Very nice meeting you Ashley, and I look forward to seeing you at the barbecue."

Just a hint of confusion crossed her face. "It would be my pleasure, and it was very nice meeting you, Lloyd."

With that, Dad and I rose and shook hands, and he was off.

I felt a rush of gratitude toward Ashley as I returned to my seat. She had pulled my bacon out of the fire. She could have torpedoed this meeting with Dad, and I would've really been up a creek.

Now I owed her more than the favors I'd already promised.

"I take it the barbecue is the trip Staci was going to take with you?" Ashley asked.

I took a gulp of wine to calm myself. "Yes, but I hadn't told them who I was bringing."

She giggled. "And now he thinks it's me."

"You don't have to come. I'll make excuses for you."

She glared back at me. "Don't you dare. I told him I'd come, and I don't renege on commitments like that."

Somehow I'd dug myself a hole, and it wasn't getting any shallower. "These events can be pretty intimidating. I'm just saying you don't have to."

She put her glass down abruptly. "If you don't want me there, just say so."

I reached for her hand, and the warmth of it settled me. "Kitten, would you please come with me to California to attend my family's barbecue?"

"It would be my pleasure."

I let out a relieved breath.

The dessert arrived, and we split it by feeding each other a spoonful at a time —just as we'd done back in high school.

"Your father's very nice," she said between bites.

"In a social setting."

Her brow furrowed at my response, but she didn't pry. We could discuss my issues with him another time.

I dabbed some of the pie on her nose with my spoon, and her playful smile returned.

~

ASHLEY

VINCE DROVE ME BACK TO MY PLACE IN HIS RED ROCKET SHIP AND PULLED TO THE curb out front.

I'd been hoping he would take me back to his place, but I didn't push it.

"Would you like to come up?" I'd been thinking about what was to come the whole ride back, as evidenced by the dampness in my panties.

He turned off the engine. "Sure, for a bit."

The heat of his touch as he guided me to the stairs almost singed my skin. I licked my lips, wondering how he would taste.

I fumbled nervously with my keys at the door, but got it open and flicked on the lights.

He followed me into the kitchen.

"Would you like some wine?" I asked.

"Sure, whatever you're having." He went to the couch, sat, and turned on the DVR.

"White okay?"

"Sure." He was keying in a movie selection. He pulled off his tie and put it on the coffee table.

I brought over the glasses and sat next to him, the warmth of his thigh against mine had my motor revving as the movie started.

He accepted his glass and raised it. "To a do-over."

I clinked my glass against his and repeated, "A do-over." I wasn't sure which do-over he meant, but I didn't ask.

I hadn't seen the movie he chose, *Music and Lyrics*, although it had Drew Barrymore and Hugh Grant, so I was sure it would be good.

He slid his arm around me, and we snuggled.

He declined a second glass of wine.

As the movie progressed, I grew nervous that I would forget what I'd learned from those *Cosmo* articles and screw up my first blowjob. I snuggled closer, but his hand still hadn't left my shoulder.

What was I doing wrong? He hadn't made a move.

I slid my hand over to his thigh.

He removed it, and playfully, I went right back to his thigh. Was this some sort of game?

He took my hand off again. "Stop it."

I tried one more time.

"You said you'd obey. Now stop it." His tone wasn't playful.

I pulled my hand back. "That was this afternoon, and it was from the book."

"I didn't mean just this afternoon. Do you want to change your answer?"

"No, but what did I do wrong?"

He took my face in his hands and brought me in for the lightest of kisses.

I wanted more, but the look in his eyes told me to not complain.

"I told you, you deserve better. This afternoon we started things wrong. You deserve to be dated, to be courted, to be treated better."

So it had felt backwards to him too...

"I didn't complain."

"I know, Kitten. But we're starting again the *right* way. Tonight is just a date: dinner and a movie. I don't expect anything more from you."

I pulled his head to mine for another brief kiss. "Dinner and a movie."

I snuggled into this man who would deny himself what I had once denied him—and offered freely tonight—all because he wanted it to be *right*.

Before the movie finished, I got up to get a bowl of chocolate ice cream, his favorite. I handed him the bowl and spoon and lay down with my head in his lap.

He spooned bits for each of us as I lay there. I alternated between watching the screen and accepting small bites of ice cream.

He put the empty bowl down, and his hand moved to my ribs. His thumb traced the underside of my breast, challenging my self-control.

I could feel his erection under my head. The occasional twitches tormented me.

This had to be difficult for him as well.

I cried when the end of the movie came and Hugh and the singer sang the final song, "Way Back Into Love." I understood then why Vince had chosen this movie, and the song was going onto my phone tomorrow so I could listen to it again. It fit as our new song.

"Got to go," he said, lifting my head off his lap and standing.

The goodnight kiss I received wasn't chaste, but it also wasn't like this afternoon's.

Before he could leave, I pulled him back to me, pressing the heat of my breasts against his chest, my arms around his neck. I went up on my toes.

"Page one-twenty-seven," I whispered.

He squeezed me tight and whispered, "Another time, Kitten."

The gentleman left, and I was alone in my empty apartment with my damp panties.

I leaned against the door after it closed.

The man was impossible. We'd gone from the dirtiest, sexiest escapade of my life this afternoon to him leaving while I still had all my clothes on, even though I'd been ready to offer him something I'd never given anyone else.

# CHAPTER 23

*Vincent*

Leaving was what she deserved. For her, I could be a gentleman for once.

The door to her apartment closed behind me, and I walked down the hall. My cock ached. I could still smell the coconut scent of her hair.

"Page one-twenty-seven," she'd whispered. She was offering to blow me. *Fuck.*

My cock tried to rip through my zipper as the pages came to mind.

I paced back to her door and knocked.

The door opened instantly, and my irresistible Kitten was just as she had been, except with surprised, misty eyes.

I strode in and closed and locked the door behind me. I backed her against the wall, one arm on either side of her head, my lips inches from hers.

"Are you ready for our second date?"

She nodded, and a slow smile replaced the surprise on her face.

I moved my lips closer to hers.

She closed the distance, lifting up on her toes.

As our lips met, my need overrode my control, and I pressed her against the wall.

Her tongue sought mine.

She tasted like chocolate and desire. I knotted a hand in her hair as we traded breath and moans. One of her hands pulled at my hair and the other clawed my back.

I broke this kiss to nibble her earlobe and whisper, "Page one-forty-six." I was dying to have her lips on me, but tonight she was going to come for me—twice.

I moved to the side and slid my hand up the inside of her thigh, to a gasp of anticipation and a groan of pleasure. My fingers traced the damp fabric of her panties.

Her breathing hitched when I forced the panties down a few inches and my finger parted her slippery folds. She spread her legs to give me access.

I slid a finger inside and brought her slick wetness to her clit, circling.

She yanked my hair to get my lips back to hers and moaned into my mouth.

I continued pressing, releasing, stroking.

She broke the kiss and pushed at me to give her room to undo my shirt.

I pinned her to the wall with my thigh while my finger worked her little love button to increasing sighs and moans. I slid my finger back into her, and then a second.

Her trembling hands fumbled with my buttons. Exasperated, she yanked and the last one popped off and fell to the floor.

Her nails scratched my chest as I brought my fingers up and sucked her sweet juices off one and then the other.

Her eyes went wide. This was something new to her.

I slid my fingers down through her curls again to the sensitive flesh of her swollen clit.

She gasped as I pressed and circled.

I covered her mouth with mine.

She closed her lips to me, but relented after a moment and my tongue gave her a taste of herself, that sweetness I wanted to lap up. Next time.

Her hand slid down to stroke me through the fabric of my suit.

The sweet torture was too much. I let go of her hair and pulled that hand to my shoulder. If I let her continue, I was sure to burst and shoot my load in my pants.

Her legs trembled as I stroked and circled her tiny bundle of nerves. She was close, oh so close.

Her breathing became erratic, and her words came in staccato bursts.

"Oh God…Right there…More."

She arched up. "Oh shit…Don't stop…Oh my God…Yeah."

I kept it up.

She gasped. "Oh fuck."

I moved my other hand to pinch her nipple through her dress, and she tensed, unable to breathe. Finally she came to the end of her rope.

"Oh my God, Vince." She shook, and her hands clawed at me. "Holy fuck."

I pressed her clit one final time and slid my fingers inside her heat to feel her contract around me.

Her legs wobbled as she panted her way down from her high and rested her head against me.

My cock was about to explode. This holding-off shit was killing me.

Her hands went to my waist, and I pulled back to give her room.

I pulled my wallet out and fumbled for a condom.

She undid my belt and then the button and zipper of my trousers.

My pants dropped to the floor.

I tore the packet open with my teeth and pulled it on in record time as she leaned back against the wall, her face shifting from contentment to excitement at the sight of me rolling the latex down.

I pulled her panties to her ankles, and she stepped out of them. I hiked up her dress and lifted her.

She wrapped her legs around me as I pinned her back against the wall.

She pulled my head to hers, and her lips found mine.

I lowered her down and pressed my tip to her hot, wet entrance.

She gasped as I lowered her farther and started the thrusting—I couldn't hold off.

"Harder. Give me more."

I pounded her against the wall as I went in deeper—deeper and harder. I couldn't last like this. The anticipation had been too much.

*Holy shit.*

Her tightness was nirvana as electricity shot through my veins with every plunge into her pussy. I ground my pelvis against her clit as I pinned her to the wall each time.

She rocked her hips into the pressure and with a scream, she came undone again, shaking.

The pressure built behind my balls, and I lost it with one last push deep into her tight heat as her contractions milked me.

Panting, I held her against the wall. The pulses of my cock slowed, and she went limp in my arms. I lifted her up off me and shuffled—with my pants around my ankles—to her bedroom. I laid her on her bed.

Her fingers traced my hand as I shuffle-walked to take care of the condom.

On my return, a pout emerged as she noticed I'd pulled my pants back on. She patted the bed beside her. "Won't you stay?"

I shook my head and said the difficult words. "Can't. I have to let my dog out." I leaned over, kissed her, and left. It's what Dalton would have done.

Halfway down the hall, I pulled out my phone to review the message I'd gotten from Ben during dinner.

MURDOCH: The system we discussed is in place

I hoped he meant he'd just finished, but in any event, I'd given him explicit directions not to allow anyone besides me to view the footage of my office.

# CHAPTER 24

*Ashley(four days later)*

Vince had been in wall-to-wall meetings all week since our incredible Sunday. We'd barely had time to exchange pleasantries. I didn't want people at work to know about us, so I'd told him I'd have to wait until the weekend to see him again.

It was torture, but I'd set the rule.

Now it was Thursday, and I was starting the day with another early-morning update with Liz. Unfortunately John was still stuck in New Haven.

"A trip to see the family?" Liz asked across the table.

I nodded over my Waffle Castle breakfast.

"The file said he was dating some model chick."

"Staci Baxter," I answered.

"You mean *Sports Illustrated* Staci Baxter? That one?"

"The same, but that's old news."

Her eyes squinted. "You little slut. You're shagging him, aren't you?"

I brought another forkful of waffle to my mouth without answering.

"Fuck. If I hadn't gotten caught, I could be the one shacked up with the billionaire."

The thought of Liz with Vince made me lose my appetite. I returned my fork to my plate.

Liz started the recorder, and I made my report on the meetings and comings and goings I'd witnessed since my last report.

"And how far along are you on checking his files? Randy wants to know," she asked. Once again she'd slipped up, calling him Randy.

"Not halfway through yet."

She had to finish her French toast mouthful before commenting. "You should be going faster," she said, as if she was my boss and entitled to grade my performance.

I'd had enough. I reached for the recorder and clicked it off. "Look, the office is full of people almost all the time. They work crazy-long hours, and I don't often get an opportunity to poke around. If you hadn't fucked it up so quickly—"

"It was just dumb luck that they caught me."

I calmed myself before continuing. "If this is a level-one op, we both know accuracy is more important than speed. I'm being careful not to blow my cover, and that means it will take time."

"You probably want more time in the sack with the guy."

"Says the girl who almost screwed the whole op on the first day." I was tempted—mightily tempted—to throw her hookup with White in her face, but I decided against it.

My comeback had shut her up.

I turned the recorder back on and finished my report.

"Are you going to finish that waffle?" Liz asked.

I pushed the plate to the center of the table. "Be my guest."

A little while later, as I walked away from the Waffle Castle toward the MBTA station, I couldn't shake the sense that I was leaving something foreign with Liz and the Bureau, and moving back toward something normal in my undercover life with Vince.

It should have been the other way around. Undercover at Covington should be the unfamiliar world I had to be careful in—not the Bureau.

Turning the corner, I squinted into the early morning sun and walked past a vendor selling giant soft pretzels from a cart. The flavorful aroma drew me back. An exchange of cash and I had a warm, chewy one with cinnamon for my walk back to the train. The sun on my face and the sweet taste of the pretzel improved my mood with every step.

Or perhaps my mood was improving with every yard I came closer to Vince, or farther from Liz. Hard to tell—and immaterial this morning.

I was determined to not let her shit on my outlook.

When I checked my phone after arriving at the office, I found the annual reminder on it that still hurt. Today was the anniversary of my cousin Louise's death. I took a moment to silently ask her a question. My question was always the same: *Why?*

Why had she taken her own life?

Mid morning, Vince emerged from his office in his running clothes.

"Joining me?" he asked.

"Not today. Thanks."

In my mind, the head of the company running with his assistant wouldn't look right to the rest of the employees. I appreciated that he wanted to spend the time with me, but I'd said we needed to wait until the weekend to see each other, and that included running, as far as I was concerned.

Vince, on the other hand, seemed clueless about the appearance problem running together might present.

"Lightweight," he chided as he headed to the elevator.

And I had a second reason for not participating: I hadn't yet gotten access to some of the files in his office.

Vince had left his office door closed.

I continued working on the document he'd assigned me this morning while keeping an eye on the rest of the group on executive row.

The clock on the lower right-hand corner of my monitor eventually clicked over to ten fifteen.

Like clockwork, Anita rose from her desk. The rest of the assistants took their cues from her and also put aside what they were doing.

"Joining us?" Anita asked me.

"Thanks, but I've got to get this done," I said.

I'd joined them on occasion for their ritual coffee break downstairs, but not routinely. It seemed to be Anita's form of a staff meeting. Attending had been useful the first few times, to learn the general gossip running around the office, but otherwise they bored me.

I gave the assistants a minute after the elevator closed behind them. Then I lifted my phone from my purse, unlocked it, and opened the camera app, hoping I wouldn't need it to record anything damaging.

I slid inside Vince's office, closing the door silently behind me.

Taking a seat behind his desk, I surveyed the surface and noted the placement of everything with two clicks of the camera—one to the left and one to the right.

I started with the pile of folders on the left and opened them one by one, leafing through the papers. Everything in these looked quite innocuous. Many of them were things I'd prepared or had crossed my desk on their way into Vincent's: routine company business.

I moved on to the pile on the right. This dealt with the Semaphore acquisition. The spreadsheet printouts were familiar, but then I came across some discrepancies. There were three separate offer letters in the bottom folder. Each of them had been typed by an actual typewriter, not computer-generated and run on the laser printer.

These were obviously in the sensitive category Anita had mentioned my first day, typed rather than put on the computer so there were no records anybody could steal. It really was the perfect way to keep things confidential: never have a copy.

Vince had evidently typed them himself on the old IBM that sat off to the side.

I read each of them carefully. The terms changed slightly from one to the next, but other than that, the wording all appeared to be quite standard. I placed the offer letters back in the folder in the order I'd found them.

I opened my phone to review the pictures I'd taken of the desk before moving things. I repositioned the folders exactly where they'd been before my snooping.

Time was running short as I opened the drawers one by one. Only the lower left contained any papers worth checking.

As I pulled out the folder and opened it, a chill ran through me. I felt dirty looking at these. The folder contained correspondence with Vince's father, none of it recent. I skimmed the letters as quickly as I could, trying not to take in any more of the content than I needed to assure myself these weren't what I was looking for. And they weren't.

I closed the folder quickly and replaced it. Suddenly I felt like I needed a shower. I'd peeked into something private. It was my job to go through every-thing, but these made me feel dirty.

I shuddered and pushed back from the desk. I knelt on the floor and looked underneath, something they'd taught us at Quantico. I didn't find anything.

I reviewed my pictures once again to make sure the desk was at as it had been. It was, but I noticed one place I hadn't checked.

Rule number one: sometimes the best hiding place is right in front of you. I lifted the edge of the blotter from the desk.

A single-page memo laid underneath.

I took two paper clips from the drawer and used them like tweezers to slide it out. I shivered as I read it. It too had been typed on the old IBM.

I laid it on the blotter and positioned my phone over it, taking several pictures and checking them for clarity before replacing the agreement and putting the paperclips back.

I checked the time on my phone and hurriedly placed the chair back where it had been. The girls were due back upstairs from their coffee klatch any moment now. I had seconds to get out of the office. I sped to the door and listened for a moment.

Silence.

Heart racing, I exited the office, closed the door behind me, and hurried to my seat. I slid the mouse and reawakened my computer just as the door opened and the giggling coffee group returned. I typed gibberish into the next cell on the spreadsheet and hit return to look active.

After the chatter stopped and the others had settled in behind their desks again, I pulled my phone out to review the pictures of the evidence I'd found.

I felt nauseous as I reread the contract, dated two weeks ago. It confirmed that Vince had agreed to relinquish majority control of Semaphore to a Sonny Alfonso after he bought it, for two hundred million dollars. The DOJ's informant had been eerily accurate.

The one thing I hadn't wanted to happen had come about. I'd just found evidence that Vince was guilty as sin. With this, I would secure the LA promotion and Liz would be the one shopping for parkas.

The old me would've been ecstatic, but my feeling was the opposite.

I rushed to the bathroom and almost didn't make it in time. I knelt, but not fast enough. My breakfast came up. Some hit the toilet seat and splashed on my blouse.

Three more heaves followed.

I stumbled to the sink and turned on the water.

The door opened and Anita came in. "You all right?" she asked, surveying the mess I'd made. "You poor thing."

I splashed water into my mouth, rinsing the taste of bile away. It didn't wash away my feeling of dread.

Anita laid a gentle hand on my shoulder as I spit into the sink again. "You should go home and rest, dear."

I nodded, took another mouthful of water, and spit again. "I need to clean up first."

"Sure. I'll call you a taxi."

I wet a paper towel and wiped at my blouse. "Thank you."

She left, and I continued cleaning myself. Nothing special about this agent today.

Another heave overcame me without warning, but there was nothing left to come up. I hunched over the sink, and my stomach lining tried to make its way up my throat.

I dabbed and wiped, but the stain wouldn't come off my top. It was like rubbing at the guilt I felt. I couldn't make it go away. This was going to ruin everything.

# CHAPTER 25

*ASHLEY*

ANITA HAD PAID THE DRIVER IN ADVANCE, AND THE RIDE WAS QUICK, BUT uncomfortable. I dreaded vomiting again in the taxi.

We made it to my apartment building, and the driver offered to walk me up, but I declined.

How humiliating. A seasoned FBI special agent, and I'd puked after cracking a career-making case. As I unlocked the deadbolt, I decided the bathroom incident would not make it into my report.

Maybe I could stay in bed for two days and claim a stomach bug, but that wouldn't be honest. This needed to be reported. Omitting the inconsequential was allowed; sitting on the consequential was not.

I turned off my phone, locked the door behind me, and shucked off my clothes. I didn't have a super sensitive nose, but the lingering smell of my vomit threatened to make me heave again, so I stuffed everything except my shoes into a garbage bag and tied it closed before depositing the mess in the laundry hamper.

I shut myself in the shower and started the water. The hot spray washed over me, but didn't carry away the stink of failure. By succeeding at finding the evidence against Vince, I had once again failed somehow.

But that didn't make sense. My feelings had gotten intertwined with my duty, and it was screwing with my mind. My duty had to be clear. White was right, and black was wrong. The rules were the rules and had to be obeyed. Vince was dirty, and he had to pay the price for his choices. I twisted the silver ring on my finger.

My duty was to provide evidence for the courts to make the determination of guilt. That's how the system worked. I didn't have to like it; I just had to do it.

And, anyway, if Vince was guilty of this, he was definitely not the person he seemed to be.

I closed my eyes, braced my hands against the wall, and put my head under the spray. The water enveloped my head, running into my mouth and ears and down my body. I wished the sound of the water in my ears would drown out the self-doubt racing through my mind.

*What have I done?*

Wasn't our system predicated on being innocent until proven guilty? I couldn't be the judge and the jury, too. Vince was due the benefit of the presumption of innocence.

I lingered in the water until it started to cool.

After drying off, I slipped into sweats and wrapped a towel around my wet head. A bottle of rum in the cupboard called to me.

I poured half a glass of Coke from a can and added rum. Then I added more. This was no time for half measures. The glass only lasted a few minutes before I poured another.

I needed to forget today—the day my heart broke all over again. I grabbed a straw and slumped on the couch. Memory could be debilitating. My memories of the night of the breakup with Vince in high school had haunted me for a long time. I felt I'd made the right decision at the time, but I could never shake the doubts. What if I'd chosen differently?

The Robert Frost poem came to mind. What if I had chosen the other path? How would my life have turned out? Would I now be Mrs. Vincent Benson?

*Wish again, girl. Fairy tales are for fools. You'd be married to the mob.*

I took a long sip through the straw.

Had I done the right thing by accepting this case?

Wasn't the system I was part of interested in justice? The FBI was part of the Justice Department, after all.

Didn't the very name of the department mean guilt had to be proven beyond any shadow of a doubt?

In that moment, I realized Vince wasn't yet guilty.

I didn't have the logic or evidence to back it up, but in my bones, I could feel doubt about his guilt. If I felt doubt, didn't that constitute a shadow of a doubt?

I took another sip. I was talking myself in circles. I wasn't the jury, but I knew doubt abounded in this case.

Was I wishing for it because of my feelings for the man? Not just any man, I realized, but the man I wanted to call my own—provided he was the man I felt him to be. And who I so wanted to believe he was. I sipped long and hard, draining the rest of the glass.

I poured another and laid back into the couch. I closed my eyes and brought one of my favorite memories to mind.

The warm, gentle trade winds rustled the fronds of the palm trees. I was back in Hawaii, on Waikiki Beach. I'd been able to get there from LA only one time, but it had defined paradise for me. Sure, California had palm trees in some places and sunshine a lot of the year, yet the water didn't compare. Something about Hawaii's warm saltwater was soothing to the soul.

It was a place without cares. It was my mental escape pod. I shut my eyes, remembered swimming in the ocean, sitting by the pool, and lying on the beach watching tourists try to surf and kids splashed and played in the ocean.

The vision always brought me peace, transporting me to a carefree paradise for a short while. The refuge of sleep came quickly.

Pounding on the door woke me.

I pried my eyes open, and the room came slowly into focus. The half-empty rum bottle told its own story—it had started out almost full.

"Ash? Open up." Vince's voice came from the hallway.

I staggered to the door, and it came back to me. I'd been drinking to forget, but that had failed, and now I remembered it all: the memo, the puking. Oh my God, the puking. And now Vince was here. I was so totally fucked. I needed to sort this out, and not with him around.

"I'm worried about you," he called through the door.

"I'm fine," I lied.

"Anita said you got sick and she sent you home."

"I'll be okay," I responded, leaning my head against the door.

"Let me in to see for myself."

I let out a sigh. "I'm fine. Go away…please." I couldn't face him right now, not with what I'd found.

"I'm taking you to the emergency room to get checked out."

I couldn't allow that. "Not necessary. I'll be fine."

After a pause he said, "Last chance, Ash. Open up or I'm calling 9-1-1. Your choice."

What kind of choice was that? I gave in and unlocked the door.

He strode in past me.

I continued to hold the door open. "Why would you call 9-1-1? I'm fine. It's just some sort of bug. You can leave now."

He held his fingers to my forehead, taking my temperature, but then he spied the rum bottle. "Drinking our way to health this afternoon?" He put down his briefcase.

"I needed it to settle my stomach is all."

He closed the door and led me to the couch. "Sit and tell me what's bothering you."

I settled into the couch without arguing. "You should go."

He closed the door and sat as well. "After you tell me what the problem is." He put an arm around me and pulled me to his side.

I pulled away.

Obvious alarm wrote itself across his face. "What's the matter, Kitten? What did I do?"

I couldn't bear to confront him with what I'd found.

He put his arm around me. "I'm so sorry. Dancing might help your mood. Want to go dancing?"

"I need a drink."

"Drinking to forget, huh?" He rose and walked to the kitchen. "What's your poison today? Straight rum?"

I shook my head weakly. "And Coke."

He chuckled. "Really?" He checked the cabinets and found my meager liquor stash. "I still think dancing is a better idea, but if you're really intent on torturing yourself we could switch to Fireball."

I'd kept the remainder of a bottle Liz had brought over once and never touched it again. "No, thanks." That stuff had made me sicker than a skunk.

He opened the fridge and brought the remainder of my six-pack of Cokes over with a glass for himself. He split a can between our glasses and added rum to both. "If you really want to get wasted, I'm here to help." He handed me my glass.

I sipped.

He guzzled half his glass and shook his head. "That's not how you do it. Bottoms up. Time's a wasting if you want to get properly smashed."

I sipped again. "I don't want to get smashed."

"Bullcrap, Kitten."

His calling me Kitten made it that much harder.

"Drinking alone in the middle of the afternoon is the definition of wanting to get wasted," he continued. "Trust me, I know. Now drink up."

"You should go. I'll be fine tomorrow."

I couldn't face him until I'd processed this and figured out a plan. It should've been simple. I turned in the evidence, and the DOJ pieced it together to figure out what to do.

"No way. I'm here as your drinking buddy tonight."

"I don't need a drinking buddy."

"You sure as shit do, and I'm not leaving."

Short of pulling my gun, I didn't see a way to get rid of him—and pulling your gun after drinking was a no-no that had been drilled into us at the Academy. A drunk agent shooting somebody, even if they deserved it, was publicity the Bureau couldn't and wouldn't tolerate. There was probably a secret place in

Gitmo they spirited you off to and kept you forever, so the press could never get a hold of you.

Vince's phone dinged with a text. He checked it and put his phone away.

$$\sim$$

THE TEXT WAS FROM BARB.

BARB: How about dinner tonight?

I turned off my phone, put it away, and poured Ashley and me each another. A search of the fridge and freezer revealed a stash of frozen pizzas.

I held them up. "Pepperoni or four-cheese?" I turned on the oven.

"I'm not hungry," she said, predictably.

I shook my head. "Gotta eat. If you won't choose, I'm doing pepperoni."

She was guaranteed to feel even worse in the morning if she didn't eat something.

She sipped her rum and Coke without responding.

I put the four-cheese back in the freezer and located a baking sheet. "Pepperoni it is."

Pouring her another glass, I waited for the pizza to cook.

She sat silently on the couch, shoulders hunched.

I cut the pizza when it finished and brought it to the coffee table in front of her.

I turned on the DVR and located one of her favorite shows.

She had told me she liked *Castle*, even though they weren't putting out new episodes anymore. The female homicide detective was a character she felt she could relate to—a strong woman making her way in a man's world.

She tried unsuccessfully to hide her smile when the show started, a definite improvement.

Slowly, she relaxed as we ate and drank and watched her show.

I started another episode and poured another glass of her chosen poison when she returned from the bathroom.

Her eyelids were getting heavy, and she leaned into me. "Why won't you leave me alone?" she asked quietly.

"Drinking buddies can't leave, and you still haven't talked to me."

She giggled and sipped on the straw, draining the last of the glass.

I poured another.

"Yes, you can," she complained.

"You're the one who chose to get smashed instead of going dancing with me."

She sipped daintily on the straw as her eyes threatened to close. "Why do you have to be so nice?"

I put my arm around her and this time didn't get resistance. "Because you're my Kitten. And I'm here to listen," I added after a moment.

Half an hour and another glass later, I learned I'd failed.

She fell asleep leaning against me, and wasn't roused by me asking her again to talk to me.

# CHAPTER 26

*ASHLEY*

THE LIGHT WAS COMING IN AROUND THE SHADES WHEN I WOKE UP WITH MY BLADDER ready to burst. The pounding in my head as I got up told me the obvious: I'd had way, way too much to drink last night. Something was off as I waddled into the bathroom, and it wasn't just the vicious little woodpeckers trying to peck their way out of my skull.

I pried an eye open wide enough to see myself in the mirror.

I was wearing panties and a bra instead of my nightshirt.

As I sat down, I tried to remember, but couldn't. I must have been too wasted to get completely undressed.

After washing my hands, I flicked on the light and reached for the mouthwash. My tongue felt like it had grown fur. I ditched the bra and rubbed where the underwire had left its nasty mark.

I was getting too old for this crap.

*When had getting drunk become so bad the morning after?*

I desperately needed the Tylenol in my purse. I needed the whole damned bottle and then some, or I needed another drink. My stomach lurched at the thought.

*Veto that.*

I reached for the bathrobe I hung on the back of the door, but it was missing. Opening the bedroom door, I discovered why. The aromas of coffee and bacon flooded the doorway.

Vince was in my robe, at the stove, cooking. He turned. "Morning, Kitten. How do you feel? I like the outfit."

I retreated into my room and slipped a T-shirt over my head before venturing out again on my Tylenol quest.

"Morning," I said.

The woodpeckers were getting madder by the minute, now trying to escape through my eyeballs. There was nothing good about this morning. I searched my purse and found the bottle. When I removed the cap, only one tablet fell out.

"Shit," I yelled loud enough for the sound to punish me. I winced.

"That bad, huh?"

"Worse," I told him.

I'd forgotten I'd let Sophia use my Tylenol twice this week, and I hadn't checked the bottle.

"I've got Advil, if you'd like." He handed me a glass of orange juice.

"I'll take a dozen." I accepted the glass and washed down my lone pill while he fished an Advil bottle out of the briefcase he'd brought with him last night.

He handed me only two.

I gobbled down the pills and sat at the table, resting my head in my hands. I closed my eyes. The blaring noise of the blender startled me and infuriated the woodpeckers inside my skull.

"Hey, cut that out."

He slid a glass of something green in front of me and removed the orange juice. "Drink. It'll make you feel better."

"What's in it?"

"Celery and cockroaches. Now drink," he commanded.

I stared at it, cradling my aching head in my hands.

He glared at me. "Stop being obstinate. It tastes like shit, but it's good for hangovers. I should know."

I gave in and swallowed some of the green glop. He was right, it tasted like crap—or worse, like crap and wet sawdust.

He slid a steaming cup of coffee in front of me and a plate with strips of bacon. "Finish the drink, then eat."

"Stop being so bossy."

"Stop being obstinate."

"It's my apartment. I get to do what I want." I reached for the bacon.

He pulled the plate away. "After you drink your medicine."

I stuck my tongue out at him. It didn't do any good.

"Behave yourself, or I'll have to put you over my knee." His face echoed the threat.

Bacon was probably the only food that could overcome my nausea right now. I forced down the last of the green drain cleaner he'd handed me.

He rewarded me with a strip of bacon, and then the whole plate. It had been

126

way too long since I'd had bacon. Like French fries, bacon was one of my vices, and I couldn't stop once I started.

I held up the second bacon strip. "Where did this come from?"

"I went out to get it while you slept it off. Your fridge needed a serious restocking."

I was slowly putting it together. "What do you mean went out?" I chewed another piece of bacon. Why couldn't he have put bacon in the green glop? It would have made it taste better.

"You heard me. I got up and went to the store. You were out like a light."

I didn't remember a thing after drinking and starting *Castle* on the DVR, with pizza and more drinking, but he'd obviously slept over. "Oh."

"Hardest thing I ever did," he added, not making any sense.

The woodpeckers were crowding out any functioning neurons.

I finished another piece of greasy bacon and slurped my coffee. "What?"

"Lying next to you and not being able to touch you."

His words washed over me. He'd stayed, he'd put me to bed, and he'd watched over me, which explained my underwear this morning.

"You didn't need to stay," I chastised.

The way I felt right now was in complete opposition to my words.

"I told you I wasn't leaving until you talked to me, and I meant it."

How could he be so stubborn?

That brought me back to the source of my drinking.

Vince offered me the orange juice again. "I'm listening."

I couldn't tell him what I'd found, so I substituted a half-truth. "Yesterday was the anniversary of my cousin Louise's death. It always puts me in a funk."

He offered me his hand. "I'm sorry. I didn't know. Do you want to talk about it?"

"Maybe later. Right now I want to lie down and make this headache go away." The nausea was fading, but the headache continued. The fog of last night began lifting. I got up and went to lie on the couch.

He brought the rest of my orange juice to me. "It will help if you take a shower, but first finish this."

I took the juice with me to the shower and finished it before turning on the water. He was going to be arrested. There was no avoiding it.

The pain relievers slowly began to help, and a few of the woodpeckers stopped trying to crack my head open from the inside. The pain had diminished to a dull ache by the time I toweled off.

Vince was picking up his briefcase when I came out of the bathroom.

"I have to head in," he told me. He walked over and gave me a gentle kiss. "Come in when you feel better."

I nodded.

Despite everything, as soon as the door closed behind him, I missed him, and I wished we'd shared more than a simple kiss.

I turned on my phone, and it chimed with a text.

LIZ: Where are you? U R Late

Fuck me. I'd forgotten about our scheduled meeting this morning. I typed out a reply.

ME: Can't make it - explain later

# CHAPTER 27

*A*SHLEY

BY LATE MORNING, I FELT HUMAN AGAIN—NOT ONE HUNDRED PERCENT, BUT WELL enough to be out in public.

I got dressed to go into the Chelsea field office. It was time to turn in the evidence I'd uncovered.

I reminded myself I'd likely at least secured the California promotion.

Traffic was light, and I reached the FBI building quickly.

Upstairs, Liz's face showed her displeasure. "We were supposed to meet at Waffle Castle at seven. Do you have any idea how early I had to get up?"

As always, the world revolved around Princess Elizabeth.

"I couldn't make it."

"Is that why you look like shit?"

I collapsed into my chair. "Thanks for the compliment."

She pasted on a shit-eating grin. "Just calling it like it is."

She could be mean.

"I drank too much last night," I admitted.

"That's hardly an excuse to blow off an update."

"I couldn't make it."

"Regardless, maybe today you'll get a chance to find it and get back to real work." Her statement was nonsensical.

I cocked my head. "Find what?"

She laughed. "Oh yeah, this morning I was going to give you the intel we got from the DOJ contact about a memo."

*What?*

I sat down. "What intel, and what contact?"

"I don't know. Randy, I mean the SAC, told me to relay to you that the DOJ contact had gotten information. He said to tell you Benson had signed a contract with Sonny Alfonso and to check his office for it."

"What DOJ contact?"

"How would I know? You know they don't share squat with us."

The Department of Justice guys had always viewed themselves as superior to us simply because the director of the Bureau reported to the attorney general. While it was true they got to make the prosecutorial decisions, we did all the heavy lifting in the cases. If one went south, it was always because they fucked it up in the courts, not because we'd given them bad or insufficient evidence.

"Newton, my office," the SAC called as he strode into the far end of the bullpen, coffee cup in hand.

My phone chimed as a text arrived.

VINCE: When are you coming in - miss you want you need you

I stopped to re-read the text.

"Now, Newton," White repeated from his office door.

"Later," I told Liz as I left.

I pocketed the phone and shut White's door behind me.

"Parsons said you blew off your meeting this morning. What's up?"

I took a seat. "I couldn't make it," I said without elaborating.

His eyes narrowed. "And what are you doing in here instead of being on the assignment?"

"I'm due back in there later today."

"The DOJ tells us Benson signed a contract with Sonny Alfonso himself. You need to find it."

I noticed the hint of that same foul odor as before. His instructions to find the memo were off somehow.

"Liz only just told me. How do we know there's a contract, and what does it look like? How will I know I've found the right one?"

He rolled his eyes, obviously not happy with my questions. "DOJ's asset says it's a single page, Benson and Alfonso. It's in his office."

"Just one page—that may not be easy."

"I don't care if it's easy, just go find it, quickly, and check back in when you have it."

I pulled out my phone. The regs and my duty demanded I show him, so I woke up the device to show him I'd already found it. "I have…"

I paused, wincing at the thought of what my next action would cost Vince.

"You have what? I don't want to hear about cramps or some bullshit. Just get the job done."

*Pig.*

I clicked the screen off, pocketed the device, and closed the door behind me as I left.

The foul odor in the office was definitely the swine inhabiting it.

I returned to my desk, put my phone down, and went to get a cup of coffee to figure this out.

~

I RETURNED TO MY DESK WITH A MUG FULL OF COFFEE AND POWERED UP MY computer.

"If you want, you can dictate, and I'll enter it," Liz offered.

"No thanks. I've got time, and I want to go slow and get this right." This was one report I intended to type myself. I wasn't sure exactly what I was going to put in it yet, though.

SAC Randy D. White's parting words rang in my ears. Cramps, my ass. He was such a pig. How he had ever risen to his current position was beyond me. The process had to include a lot of ass kissing, ass licking, or something equally disgusting. His middle initial clearly stood for disgusting, or dick, or dipshit, or dickhead, or douchebag. Better yet, all of the above.

Since I wasn't traveling Liz's path into his good graces, the promotion out of this office took on even greater importance. Getting three thousand miles away from the douchebag was hardly far enough.

I logged into the computer and pulled up the software to log my report. The first few lines were easy. Then I got to the hard part. I had to explain my actions and observations since the last report.

Minimizing the window and pulling up the last report Liz had entered provided a respite as I got up to speed with where I'd left off. I reread the report several times before returning to the current one.

The first few days I needed to account for were easy. I found myself typing slowly though, not wanting to reach yesterday morning. I gulped down the last of my coffee. This was hard. I opened my phone again.

Liz walked by, and I closed it. Having it out in the open in the bullpen didn't seem like a good idea.

I grabbed the phone and headed for the restroom. I parked myself in a stall and opened the phone again. The pictures were in front of me in full color, the evidence of Vince's wrongdoing—or at least poor decision-making. It was up to the DOJ to figure out what it amounted to.

The regulations were clear: I was to make a full report—clear, concise, and without omissions. I closed the photo viewer and returned to reread my text message.

VINCE: When are you coming in - miss you want you need you

The message haunted me as I recalled the conversation where he'd told me somebody was out to get him and showed me the ominous note Staci had received.

White's words replayed in my head, *"DOJ's asset says it's a single page, Benson and Sonny Alfonso. It's in his office."* Since when did we get information that detailed, that specific, and with timing as convenient? The answer was never. And why was this so fucking high up on the priority list?

I went back to the pictures and expanded them. I flipped from one to the next, studying the text. The clue was in here somewhere, I knew.

I finally found it on the third line from the bottom.

In these days of computer printers, people forgot that sometimes typewriters could be traced the same way firearms could. Some of the letters might have slight imperfections that would be specific to a single typewriter.

I expanded the picture even further. The lowercase Z had a slight imperfection to it. This would tell me if Vince had typed the memo on his typewriter.

I had always logged my evidence and let the lab monkeys figure it out. Those were the rules, and I always followed the rules.

Until today.

I wasn't logging this. I'd found a piece of paper with some writing on it—just a piece of paper and nothing more. I closed my phone, left the restroom, and returned to my desk.

"Last night's bender still getting to you?" Liz asked as I sat.

I put my hand on my stomach. "Yeah, I'm still not a hundred percent."

I finished my report without mentioning my search of Vince's office. It would be consistent with my not having heard yet from either Liz or White to go look for the memo.

I finished the report and saved it. Packing up to leave, I told Liz, "I'll be in touch about the next meeting."

"Just don't make it early in the morning if you're not gonna show," she shot back.

"Sorry about that," I called as I left.

I'd broken a serious rule, and I'd officially gone over to the dark side. Down was now up, and everything was backwards. But I had to get a plan together, and fast.

I was one inch from getting fired, or arrested, or both.

# CHAPTER 28

*Vincent*

When I powered up my phone on the way in to work, the text I'd received last night popped up—along with another from this morning and two missed calls from her.

> BARB: How about dinner tonight?

> BARB: Call me

I ignored them and continued on. When I arrived upstairs at Covington, I closed the door to my office and dialed the florist.

"A dozen red roses," I told the lady. "No, make them white and two dozen, please." I gave them Ashley's name and our address here at the office.

"What would you like the card to say?"

It took me a second to come up with "Hope you feel better today."

"And how would you like it signed?"

"Uncle Benny," I told her.

Ashley didn't have an Uncle Benny, but I couldn't very well put my name on it.

I typed out the text I'd been mulling over, a text to Ashley.

> ME: When are you coming in - miss you want you need you

I sent it and waited.

Nothing.

I walked to the couch and laid down, closing my eyes. I hadn't drunk as much as she had last night, but I would still need some more Advil eventually.

The message arriving on my phone woke me. I sat up too quickly and felt faint for a moment.

ASHLEY: After lunch

I turned toward the window and smiled. My Kitten was out there somewhere, and she was headed my way. Checking my watch, I decided on an early lunch at Vitaliano's. A walk in the fresh air and good food was what I needed to get rid of this headache. That, and another few Advil.

～

I'd had an excellent meal and settled myself back in my office when Ashley arrived after lunch, just as she'd said she would.

A wide smile lit up her face when she saw the flowers. She read the card and her smiley face turned questioning.

I looked away.

"Those came while you were out," Anita announced, walking up. "Who are they from?" She could barely contain herself.

Daphne and Sophia joined her, crowding around to hear who had sent Ashley flowers.

Ashley looked down at the card. "My uncle…Benny."

Daphne sniffed the roses. "Man, I wish my uncle was that thoughtful. I don't even get a birthday card."

Sophia and Anita agreed.

I looked up and caught Ashley throwing a wicked stare my direction.

I smiled and cast a wave none of the others saw.

The gaggle dispersed after a few more *oohs* and *aahs*, and then Ashley marched into my office.

"You can't…" she said softly.

"I thought it was nice of Uncle Benny to try to cheer you up."

"But…" She stood there with her hands on her hips. "But…"

"I think your uncle Benny is a nice guy," I told her.

I ached to erase the distance between us and take her beautiful face in my hands—kiss the indignant attitude right out of her, lock the door, and introduce her naked skin to the leather of my couch.

But her rules forbade it, and I'd stupidly agreed to follow them.

"You can't." She huffed once more before turning on her heels and marching her cute ass out of reach.

134

Five minutes later, Ashley had located additional vases in the storage closet and split the flowers among the four assistants, which—based on the comments I heard—earned her points like crazy.

She walked back into my office and shut the door. "Thank you. But please don't do that again."

She'd calmed, but only marginally.

"Why not? It put a smile on your face, and that was kind of the idea."

"I can't have them knowing, that's why. I mean…Uncle Benny? Couldn't you have been more creative, *Mr. Benson*?"

"You're welcome, and how are you feeling?" I asked. "You really tied one on last night."

"Better… Now, at least. That green gunk helped. What was in that anyway?"

"Like I told you, celery and cockroaches." I smirked.

"Tasted like crap."

"The cost of overdrinking. You should have chosen dancing."

She took a seat. "We need to talk."

"Sure, but first, I'm sorry about your cousin, and I really am glad you're feeling better today."

Her eyes turned watery.

I got up and rounded the desk. She surprised me by standing and wrapping her arms around me, resting her head against my chest.

I rubbed her back. "It'll be okay. I'm here for you."

Yesterday had hit her harder than I'd realized—much harder.

"Just hold me," she mumbled into my shirt.

"I can do better than that. Wanna try the couch?"

"Stop that."

"I was being serious."

"That's the problem." She pushed away and tear-stained eyes looked into mine. "Can I trust you?"

Trust wasn't a question I'd anticipated.

I kissed her on the forehead. "You know you can, Kitten."

"You won't hurt me?"

I chuckled. "I could never do that." I pulled her back into a tight hug, and we rocked for a while as I soothed my hurting girl. I wished for the embrace to soak up all her pain, to slay her demons and give her peace. She deserved happiness.

"I got a call yesterday."

It was my turn to break the closeness so I could look into her eyes. "Go ahead."

"It was Jacinda. She said the paper had a tip that you did a deal with the mob."

I huffed. "They've got to be kidding."

She pulled away. "She wanted confirmation. I told her it wasn't true."

"Of course not."

"She said you met with Sonny Alfonso two weeks ago yesterday to ink a deal."

I urged her to sit, and I took the other chair. "You don't actually believe that shit, do you?"

"No, no, no." She shook her head. "But maybe I can help by telling her how wrong her source is. We can document where you were that day."

I thought for a moment and decided I could see how that might work.

She put a hand on my knee. "I think it would be easier to head it off at the pass than sue them after the fact."

I thought back for a moment to make sure I had the right day. "Two weeks ago yesterday, I got a call to meet my brother in Springfield. I drove there, but he didn't show."

"Which brother?" she asked.

"Dennis."

She cocked her head. "Does he do that often?"

I hadn't explained the whole situation. "I said I got a call to meet my brother. I didn't say I talked to him. There was a message left on my desk. It said to meet him at a restaurant by the interstate in Springfield. I drove over, but he wasn't there."

She nodded and waited for me to continue.

"When I called him, he claimed he hadn't called or left me a message. And I believe him. He may be a practical joker, but that's not his style."

"If he didn't do it, who left the message?" she asked.

"I have no idea. The message was taken by a girl who didn't last long: Marcy. At the time, I thought it was just another screw-up. But she claimed she'd gotten it right."

Ashley cocked her head. "Marcy?"

"Not the sharpest tool in the shed—the girl before that Jacinda bitch."

"I think that's enough for me to get her to back off for now."

"Fuck," I said. Now I could see the connection. "You said a deal with the mob, right?"

She nodded "Yeah."

"Now it's starting to make sense. It has to be Gainsboro behind all this."

"Why him?" she asked.

"Gainsboro is a company—the competition for the Semaphore acquisition."

She sat forward. "Why would they be out to smear you?"

"So far we've outbid them for Semaphore, and with more resources than they have, that isn't going to change. Among other things, Semaphore makes electronic gaming equipment for casinos. Mob involvement is a no-no for all of the gaming commissions, and making it look like I'm in bed with organized crime screws the deal for us and lets them get it."

"Casino machines is a big enough business for somebody to do this?"

"Several hundred million a year."

The number seemed to get her attention.

~

HE STOOD. "I DIDN'T GET MY RUN IN THIS MORNING."

"Why not?"

"I was worried about a certain assistant who wasn't feeling well," he said, giving me a light kiss.

"I'll bet you were a little hungover too."

He grinned. "Maybe."

I giggled. "Price of being a drinking buddy."

"It was worth it. I'll be down in the gym for an hour."

"Is it okay if I clean your office while you're gone?" I asked.

"It's all yours," he said as he left.

I followed him out, grabbed my purse, and then shut myself back in the massive room.

I pulled on latex gloves, removed the evidence bag from my purse, moved around behind his desk, and lifted the blotter. The memo was still there. Using paperclips, I shifted it into the evidence bag and sealed it up.

I'd called John on the way over, and he'd agreed to run this for me out of the New Haven office. It would take a few days, given the mail processing time, but I couldn't afford to drive it, and I certainly couldn't risk putting it through the Boston lab.

The fingerprint kit came next out of my purse, and I started on the desk, not expecting anything but hoping nonetheless. The results were as I'd feared: nothing but smudges.

Moving to the typewriter, I carefully dusted all the keys and other surfaces that were smooth enough to take a print. Using tape, I lifted the few possible partials that appeared.

Done with fingerprinting the typewriter, I inserted a page and typed the alphabet and numbers. Checking the paper, I was disappointed to find the same misshapen Z. The memo had been typed on this IBM.

That didn't mean for sure that Vince had typed it, and the fact that he'd been called out of town on exactly the day of the contract gave me hope that I could still exonerate him. *Innocent until proven guilty,* I told myself.

The chances of finding the culprit this way were probably low, but I had to pursue all the avenues. I glanced around the room for other surfaces to check. What came to mind was the edge of his door. People would sometimes pull the edge to close the door rather than the handle. Unfortunately, that area didn't yield anything.

I took a seat on the couch and looked around the room. Closing my eyes, I put myself in place of the culprit planting the memo. What would I do? How would I move around the room and what would I possibly touch?

The blotter.

Standing behind the desk, I carefully pulled the blotter toward me, hanging the first several inches of it off the edge of the wooden desk. Getting down on my knees and looking underneath, I found what I'd hoped I would—a smooth surface, one that could hold a print.

It was uncomfortable to work upside down, but I finally found what looked like a usable print on the right side of the back of the blotter.

After pulling the tape on that print, I scanned the room again. Nothing else seemed likely to help, so I went about cleaning the print dust off of the surfaces I'd checked.

A knock came at the door as I was finishing my cleanup.

I opened the door to find Anita.

"Oh, there you are," she said. "I have to go out to run an errand for Mason. Can you handle his phone? He's expecting some kind of important call."

"Sure. I'm just doing some cleaning in here. I'll be out in just a sec."

She closed the door behind her.

Confident I hadn't missed anything after scanning the room one more time, I went to my desk, pulled out an express mail envelope, and filled it out to get these things to John in the New Haven office tomorrow.

If ever there was a case that needed to be handled with flexibility, this was it.

This seemed like a well-done frame up. Vince had been called out for a few hours, so he was unable to prove he wasn't meeting Alfonso at the time. The memo had likely been planted on his desk, and the DOJ source had fed the Bureau detailed information to send me in to find that specific piece of paper. The Gainsboro guys were playing this well, but there was one hole in their plan. They had to have a person inside Covington. Who else could have gotten into Vince's office?

I had to find that person, and fast.

As I sealed the envelope, I felt as I might have sealed my career as well by going so far off the reservation. But what was done was done. I'd been forced to choose a side, and I'd chosen to believe Vince over SAC White's anonymous source. My gut told me this was the right call.

*Vince promised I could trust him.*

~

VINCENT

ANOTHER TEXT ARRIVED FROM BARB JUST AFTER I STARTED MY VIRTUAL RUN.

As my feet pounded out miles on the rubber strip, I thought back to last night. Why had I stayed? Why hadn't I left Ashley to her pity party and joined Barb for an enjoyable evening?

*Who am I?*

The old me would definitely have taken Barb's invitation. Staying in with Ashley to get drunk watching TV reruns and *not* getting my rocks off was completely out of character—my old character.

I hadn't responded to Barb precisely because she represented the old me.

The new me wanted one thing: Ashley. And I needed her to want me, warts and all. I wasn't going to let her get away again.

By mile seven on the treadmill, I'd decided on a plan of action. She was going to be mine—all mine.

After showering, I returned upstairs.

Ashley was at her desk, working on her computer.

I waved for her to follow me into my office.

Once she closed the door, I moved in close enough to smell the coconut of her shampoo. "Did you make that call to your acquaintance?"

"Sure did, and I think it will help."

That was a relief. If she could get the tabloid dogs off me for a bit, I could figure out how to combat Gainsboro.

I held out my hand. "Give me your apartment key."

She looked at me, stunned.

"I trust you," I told her. "Now, do you trust me?"

"Yes, but…"

I kept my hand out.

She relented and went to retrieve the key from her purse. "Are you making a copy?" she asked.

"Trust," I said.

She turned over the key, which I pocketed.

"We're going to dinner tonight," I told her firmly.

"I'm not sure—"

"Trust me," I repeated. I walked out of the office, leaving her behind.

I left the building, and when I reached her apartment, I let myself in.

I began my search.

When I was done, I dialed Anita.

# CHAPTER 29

*Vincent*

LATER THAT AFTERNOON, I CHECKED MY WATCH AND PACKED UP MY BRIEFCASE.

"Time to leave," I told Ashley after locking my office.

"But I'm not done."

"Yes, you are."

"But it's only four."

"It's a long trip to the restaurant."

She cocked her head at that, but held her tongue.

When we reached the street, the town car was waiting for us at the curb. I slid in after her.

"Just how far away is this restaurant?" she asked.

"You'll see."

She didn't appear happy with that non-answer, but she leaned back and watched the downtown scenery go by. It wasn't until we entered the Callahan Tunnel that she started up again.

"How much farther?"

I took her hand in mine. "It'll be a very special dinner, I promise."

My phone rang. It was Steven Covington.

"Any problems?" I asked, mentally crossing my fingers that he had come through with what I needed.

"None at all. Your contact will be a Mr. Cromartie. Just have them call him from the desk at the entrance. He has everything arranged for you."

"Thanks, Steven. I owe you."

"Just remember that when I call and need a favor."

I laughed, and we hung up. No doubt that call would come one day.

"Who was that?" Ashley asked.

"An old friend from California."

When we took the exit for the airport, her eyes widened. "I hate to break it to you, but airport food doesn't ring the special bell."

"Just wait. You won't be disappointed."

A few minutes later, we were buzzed through the gate at the private jet terminal and rolled up to my plane.

"You've got to be kidding," she said.

I opened the door and offered her a hand out. "Not in the least. It's faster than driving."

"How far?"

I went to the trunk and accepted our luggage from the driver. "New York, for the weekend."

"But I didn't pack anything," she complained.

"I went to your apartment and picked out a few things, and anything else you need, we can get there."

"Just like that? Pick up and go to New York?"

I carried the luggage to the back of the plane. "Yes, just like that. And you're going to love the dinner location, absolutely love it."

I handed our two bags to the crew member. The three gold stripes on his epaulets marked him as the copilot. He hefted the bags into the cargo compartment at the rear of the plane.

The sun reflected off the white of the jet's fuselage as we made our way to the forward door with the additional garment bag.

"Is this plane yours?" Ashley asked.

"Nope."

"Your father's?"

"After you." I motioned for her to start up the steps. "No, his is bigger. This is just a rental, sort of like a time share. I have partial use of it when I need it. Fractional ownership, it's called." I followed her inside. "My boss was against the idea of a jet, and a quarter share is all I could get him to agree to."

"I can take that," the flight attendant offered as I cleared the door.

I handed her the garment bag and followed Ashley.

"Wow," Ashley exclaimed, running her hand over the seats before selecting the forward-facing one on the right. "This is classy."

I took the seat opposite hers. "Buckle up; that rule is still the same."

I secured my belt, and she did as well.

The flight attendant returned with champagne, which Ashley accepted and I declined.

"This is what I call first class," Ashley commented. "And in real glass instead of plastic. You sure are spoiled."

It had been ages since I'd flown commercial, and her comment struck a chord with me. I'd become oblivious to the differences.

The copilot climbed in after us. "Mr. Benson, are we expecting any more passengers?"

"No. This is it."

He closed and secured the door. Moments later, an engine started, whirring to life.

"Flight time will be just over an hour, sir," he said before sliding into the cockpit.

I waved an acknowledgment. "Thanks."

The second engine started, and soon we were taxiing for takeoff.

Ashley quickly finished her glass of champagne and held it up for a refill.

Our flight attendant brought over the bottle, but I waved her off. "Maybe later."

The attendant didn't need to be told twice; she understood who the paying passenger was. She retreated to the rear, capping the bottle and placing it back in the refrigerator.

"But I need another," Ashley complained with a hurt look.

"Later."

"I need it to get through the flight."

"What you need is to realize that this is safer than driving."

She bit her lip. "Thirty thousand people a year die in traffic accidents, so that's not saying much." She fixed me with an angry stare. "It's not like if the engine light comes on they can just pull over to the side of the road."

"You don't need to worry. The engines are quite reliable."

She shook her head. "Yeah, until lightning strikes."

"The weather is fine today. No lightning."

"Or birds fly into the engine," she added.

I didn't respond. It was clear that logic was not going to prevail on this subject.

We turned onto the runway, and the engines spooled up to a mild roar. The jet swiftly accelerated.

Ashley's knuckles were white from her death grip on the armrests. I could see fear in her eyes.

"Close your eyes and take slow, deep breaths," I told her.

She didn't.

"Trust me," I insisted.

She finally did as I asked.

Seated facing backwards, I was pitched forward as the nose rose and we climbed away from terra firma. Whirring and clanks came from below us in the belly of the plane.

Her eyes popped open. "What was that?"

"Just the landing gear being retracted. It's perfectly normal."

She closed her eyes again.

"Slow, deep breaths," I repeated.

She kept her eyes closed, and slowly the color returned to her skin, her breathing steadied, and her grip on the armrests loosened.

I waved to our flight attendant, tipping my hand up to my mouth and pointing at Ashley.

The attendant smiled, understanding my signals, and brought over another glass of champagne.

"Now you're ready for the second glass," I told Ashley, tapping her on the knee.

Her eyes opened, and she accepted the champagne. "Thank you."

"Feel better?" I asked.

She sipped rather than guzzled the bubbly liquid as the attendant returned to her seat in the back.

"A little."

"Dad taught me that."

"You used to be scared of flying?"

"Deathly. My first trip in a plane didn't go well. There was lightning, thunder, and thousand-foot drops. I lost my lunch and refused to fly again."

"But you seem so calm now."

"Dad challenged me, as he often does. He said if I couldn't conquer my fear, I would never amount to anything. Anyway, he took me up every weekend for a while, taught me that exercise, and I got over it. Now it's no big deal."

"He sounds like a wise man."

"More like a bully. I was perfectly happy driving between LA and Vegas, but I couldn't let him get away with challenging me like that."

She took another sip and offered me the glass. "Want to share?"

I reached out to accept the champagne. "Thanks."

Encouraged by the increasing altitude of the plane, the bubbles tickled my nose as I sipped. I handed her back the remainder of the golden drink.

# CHAPTER 30

*ASHLEY*

I COULD HAVE DONE WITHOUT THE PLANE RIDE, BUT IF I HAD TO LEAVE THE GROUND, Vince's jet was certainly the way to do it.

His breathing technique had worked, at least somewhat, but I felt sort of stupid. I knew the statistics said flying was safe, but there was something about giving up control to the pilot and knowing we had miles to drop if something went wrong that paralyzed me in a plane.

The champagne helped, too, but Vince's understanding helped the most.

Sitting across from his entrancing gaze, I found his melodious voice soothing. Listening to him tell me about his childhood fear of flying and the way he'd overcome it brought a smile to my face—and I never smiled when I flew; I was always too worried.

Before I knew it, the plane pitched down and we were descending to land in New York. Once my feet reached solid ground, I felt better.

I didn't see skyscrapers anywhere. "This is New York?"

"No, silly. This is Teterboro Airport in New Jersey. Now we take another ride."

"Are you going to tell me which restaurant we're going to?"

"No. Surprise means surprise. But you will find it quite unique."

I would have been happy with a simple meal anywhere in Boston, but *simple* was not on Vince's radar this evening. I needed to sit back and enjoy the ride.

Instead of walking toward the terminal, however, the crew member was taking our bags to a helicopter—a fucking helicopter.

Vince waved me to come with him in that direction.

"Can't we just take a cab?" I asked.

"This is quicker."

I'd left my gun in my apartment in Boston, so I didn't see any way to dissuade him. "If I die in this, I'm going to come back and haunt you."

"You'll love it."

"Not a chance in hell," I shot back.

The helicopter shook, and it was so loud that we wore headphones to talk to one another, but the view as we crossed the Hudson and skimmed the skyline of Manhattan was breathtaking. That almost made up for it.

In what seemed like a matter of minutes, we were in the second town car of the evening on our way through Manhattan traffic, which seemed lighter than some of the congestion we'd had growing up in Los Angeles.

In short order, the car pulled to a stop in front of a hotel across from Central Park. The sign above the door read *Park Lane Hotel*. It was the tallest building on this end of Central Park.

At the registration desk, they summoned the manager as soon as they heard Vince's name.

The balding man and a bellboy escorted us up in the elevator to the forty-sixth floor, the highest button there was. With a flourish, he stepped out and opened the door that read *Park Lane Suite*.

The space was gargantuan, a hundred times more spacious than any hotel room I'd ever stayed in.

I walked to the window, overcome by the view of Central Park laid out in front of me.

"Isn't this a little overboard?" I asked Vince after they left us.

"Nothing but the best for my Kitten," he said, coming up behind me. He wrapped his arms around me and rested his chin on my head. "How do you like the view?"

The air was clear, and the green of the park magnificent. "Love it. Now tell me, do you book rooms like this every time you travel?"

"Every time I travel with you I will."

"How many women have you brought here?" I instantly regretted being so rude, so insecure.

His grip on me tightened as he lowered his mouth to my ear and whispered. "You're the first."

His words fogged my brain. I really was his Kitten, and I couldn't think of any better title I could aspire to. I snuggled back against his warmth and purred.

He cut the moment short by releasing me. "You have to get changed. We don't have a lot of time."

"Changed?"

He walked to the closet. "I got you something to wear tonight."

"What's wrong with this?" I had on a sophisticated outfit that would've gotten me in the door of any restaurant in town.

He unzipped the garment bag and pulled out a dress. "Tonight you need something more."

My jaw dropped. It wasn't just a dress, it was a Ferrari red dress that looked like it belonged on an actress at a movie premier—it definitely qualified as *more*.

He held the hanger up. "I had Anita pick it out." He laid that one on the bed and retrieved another from the bag. "If you don't like that one, maybe this will do."

I started to object, but he stopped me with a finger to my lips.

"Don't worry. I gave her your sizes, but she doesn't know who these are for."

I breathed a deep sigh of relief. But I didn't see how we were going to keep things under wraps if he continued like this.

The second dress was black, and equally stunning. It was almost floor length, with a dangerously deep V in front, a sheer back panel, and a hip-high slit on one side.

"My God, Vince. Why?" was all I could manage.

"Good, the black it is," he said. Naturally he chose the more provocative one.

"But I can't wear something like that without doing my face."

"Anita packed you some makeup. It's in the red suitcase."

I unzipped the bag and found a Lancôme makeup kit, as promised, along with an assortment of lipsticks. He'd thought of everything.

Underneath those I found a sheer teddy and held it up. "And this?"

"That's for breakfast."

I laughed and retreated to the bathroom to fix my face.

After blush, eye shadow, eye liner, and mascara, I considered a deep cherry lipstick, but chose a more muted peach in the end. I retrieved the dress and examined it.

It really wasn't a dress; this deserved the title of *gown*. The sheer back panel wouldn't allow a bra. I chose the highest-waisted of the undies he had packed and was relieved to find the slit didn't quite expose them. At least I wouldn't be going commando tonight.

I held up the hem as I came out. "Shoes?"

He'd changed into a tux, and the sight halted my breath for a moment. The man looked like he was straight out of a Bond movie.

"Check the bottom of the garment bag."

I shuffled over and discovered three choices of heels. I chose the bright red pair, and God bless Anita, they fit. With the heels on, the hem stopped comfortably off the floor.

"Ready?" Vince asked, checking his watch.

"Just need my lipstick."

When I returned from the bathroom, lipstick in hand, he held out a black leather clutch. It might have been small and simple, but the Gucci logo on it put it in the thousand-dollar price range. "You're spoiling me."

"That's the plan, Kitten."

We went downstairs to a waiting limo, which was soon going north on Madison Avenue—at least that's what the street signs said. Two dozen blocks and a few turns later, we stopped in front of the eight stone columns I would have recognized anywhere: the New York Metropolitan Museum, The Met.

"You remembered," I whispered to my handsome date.

I'd told him once in high school that it was my dream to visit the Met and the Empire State Building someday.

He smiled and squeezed my hand. "When it comes to you, I remember every moment."

He opened the door before I could tell him how romantically mushy he sounded.

He held my hand as we ascended the steps to the entrance.

With every step I took up the stairs, the slit opened wide, threatening to show everything and drawing a fair number of oglers.

*Chin up and smile, girl. They're just jealous.*

At the desk inside, Vince asked for a Mr. Cromartie, and either the James Bond outfit or the name got an immediate reaction, as the two employees at once started phoning to find the man.

Minutes later, a gray-haired man with an oddly askew bow tie rushed up and introduced himself. He turned out to be the director of the entire museum.

"Mr. Benson, Miss Newton, we have been expecting you," Cromartie said. "If you will please follow me, I hope you will find our arrangements acceptable."

We followed as he rattled off details about the exhibits we passed like a tour guide. Eventually he took us behind velvet ropes and held open a curtain as we passed into a room without any visitors. An elegantly set dinner table for two graced the middle of the room. The heavy curtain did a good job of muffling the sounds of the people shuffling through the museum beyond the velvet rope. Another curtain closed off the opposite opening.

"I thought the Vermeer room would be most appropriate for your dinner."

"Thank you," Vince replied.

Cromartie went back into tour guide mode. "This room contains six works by the esteemed Dutch artist Johannes Vermeer, more than any other museum in the world."

After a polite thank you from Vince, we were alone.

We took a moment to admire the paintings adorning the walls. One of them had a plaque indicating it had been donated by the Covington family.

"Is this why we're getting the royal treatment?" I asked.

Vince put his arm around me. "They donated several other priceless paintings as well, but being a Vermeer fan, this one in particular earned them points with

Cromartie. It lets him boast more Vermeers than even the Dutch National Museum."

Two waiters in waistcoats entered with bread, water, wine, and salads.

We took our seats.

Vince raised his glass. "To a wonderful weekend with a lovely lady."

I accepted the compliment, and we clinked glasses.

"Vince?"

He looked up from his salad. "Yes?"

"What is this all about?"

"You need a little cheering up. And that falls under my job description. So here we are."

This man was so over the top.

"You could have just bought me ice cream, and I would have loved it."

I would have been head over heels with a simple date at an ice cream parlor, especially after the flowers.

"Nonsense. You said you wanted to visit, and tonight is your night."

His thoughtfulness brought tears to my eyes.

"What's wrong?"

I dabbed at my eyes with my napkin. "Nothing. You just make me so happy." I sniffed.

"I try."

Those words meant so much. I twisted my silver ring absentmindedly.

"I notice you often touch that ring when you're nervous," he said.

I pulled my hands under the table.

"It's obviously important to you. What does it signify?"

I had to tell him the truth. "My aunt Michelle gave it to me. She called it my strength ring."

He waited quietly for me to continue.

"She was retired Navy, one of the fastest women to be promoted to captain. She told me to always wear it and remember that following rules to the letter made us strong. Nothing less was acceptable."

"Sounds like she cared a lot about you."

"She was wonderful."

I changed the subject to ask how he'd come to be at Covington.

A few minutes later, a giant grin took over his face.

"Close your eyes," he said. After a moment he continued. "Now you can open them."

As I did, I gasped.

He held a small red jewelry box out to me. "For you."

∾

VINCENT

. . .

SHE GASPED AT THE SIGHT OF THE BOX AND JERKED BACK.

"It's for you," I told her.

"But…"

I put the box down in front of her. "Go ahead," I urged.

She hesitated, wide eyed.

"You know it's rude to refuse a gift."

She moved her hand toward it. "I'm just surprised is all."

"Go ahead; open it."

She did.

"It's beautiful." She removed the emerald necklace from the box. "You shouldn't have. This is too much."

"Let me help." I rose and went behind her to fasten the necklace.

"How can I thank you?"

I returned to my seat, overcame my urge to offer a sophomoric sexual innuendo, and ignored the question.

"When I saw it, I knew it would complement your eyes," I said instead.

And my judgment was vindicated. She wore it beautifully, the emerald a perfect match to her eyes.

"It was supposed to be your graduation gift, but…" I stopped there. We didn't need to rehash the pain of what had transpired.

"You kept it…all this time?" she asked with a trembling lip.

"Well, I couldn't wear it. It's not my style."

"You could have given it to Roxy."

Roxy had been my freshman-year girlfriend at USC. "How do you know about Roxy?" I asked.

An immediate blush rose in her cheeks.

"You were stalking me?"

She looked down. "How's your salad."

"For how long?" I asked, not going for her attempted change of subject.

"I might have asked Serena about you once or twice," she confessed.

I'd obviously hurt her more than I realized if she'd been asking my sister about me.

"It was meant for you, Kitten, and you alone."

She reached across, and I took her hand. "Thank you, Vince. It's lovely."

The waiters returned, calling a halt to the awkwardness. They cleared the salad and brought the main course. Steak for me and salmon for her.

"Is it all you expected? The museum?" I asked as the waiters retreated behind the curtain.

She nodded. "And more. It's magnificent."

As we ate, we talked about the art class in California that had precipitated her desire to visit the museum, and the art history courses she took as electives in college.

Eventually, the waiters cleared our plates and dessert arrived. We were almost to the finale.

"Key lime pie? Again?" she asked.

The smile on her face was the thanks I'd hoped for.

A waiter stood in the corner, waiting for us to finish.

She ate her dessert slowly, savoring each bite—and torturing me as I envisioned her tongue on me instead of the spoon.

I finished mine quickly. The tension of the delay was killing me.

She sucked the last of the pie off her spoon with a seductive smile, and eyes that seemed to share the same hunger for nakedness I had.

She finally put down her spoon. "That was delicious."

I motioned to the waiter, and he pulled the curtain open to reveal the group arrayed in the next room.

Her eyes bulged.

# CHAPTER 31

*ASHLEY*

THE WAITER PULLED OPEN THE CURTAIN, AND MY JAW NEARLY DROPPED TO THE FLOOR.
*A band?*

Vince stood and offered me his hand. "May I have this dance?"

In a daze, I stood, and Vince pulled me to him. The heat of his body against mine jolted me. I'd imagined undressing him bit by bit all throughout dinner. The forced propriety of sitting across the table from him, looking as delectable as he did, had shifted my libido up a gear.

Several of those who'd been waiting on us pulled the table to the side of the room as the band began to play.

"I couldn't get the original Sugarloaf, so this will have to do," Vince said into my ear as we started to sway to the music.

They were playing "Green-Eyed Lady," the song he'd declared to be our song at the dance we'd attended in high school, in homage to my eye color.

We danced as the singer belted out the lyrics.

I wept tears of joy. This was unbelievable. We'd eaten a private meal in the middle of the Met, he'd given me a beautiful necklace he'd kept since high school, and now we were dancing as a band played our song, filling the museum with music. I sniffled.

Vince raised my chin with a finger. "You're crying."

"I'm just so happy; I can't help it."

I put my head back on his chest, and we swayed until the song stopped.

When it did, clapping erupted from behind the remaining curtains. The other patrons of the museum must have liked the impromptu performance.

A string quartet began playing next, classical music and much softer—much more in keeping with the decorum of the museum.

"Sorry, I could only get permission for the one pop song," Vince explained as we continued to sway in each other's arms.

My tears soaked his jacket.

"We can dance as long as you like," he said softly.

I didn't reply, just melted into his arms and took in the evening.

"Would you like to wander the museum until closing?"

"No," I said.

I squeezed him tighter. I wanted to stay in his strong arms, just the two of us —no crowds, no onlookers, just us.

He rubbed my back, igniting sparks with his touch. "What then?"

"I've wanted to rip that gorgeous tux off of you since the moment we sat down."

He lifted me and spun me around, setting me down after two turns. "And I've wanted to rip the slit of that dress right up to your shoulder since we got in the car."

I closed my eyes and pulled myself up for the kiss I'd been waiting for all night—the kiss that topped off the evening of a lifetime.

He didn't disappoint as he deepened our embrace, giving as good as he got. He pulled back and nibbled my lip lightly before his tongue traced my mouth. We traded breath and desire as we pulled each other close, attempting to breach the fabric between us and meld into one being, a couple.

The faint eucalyptus of his hair tickled my nose as he loosened his grip and we swayed again to the sounds of the string instruments.

At first I was self-conscious about the musicians as he grabbed my ass and caressed my breast. But as we traded the taste of the lime-flavored dessert and the smoothness of rich, red wine, I cared less and less. I kept my eyes closed, and we were dancing among the clouds—just me and my man. Time stood still, and all that mattered was the protective warmth he'd enveloped me in.

The music continued, and the scene playing behind my eyelids was that of our kiss that night so long ago.

"We'd better go before I lose control and rip that dress right off you," he breathed.

I nodded and took his hand as he led me out.

The quartet continued playing, and a sea of museumgoers parted, *oohing* and *aahing* as we passed through.

The ride back to the hotel seemed interminable as anticipation built within me. Our suite at the top of the hotel awaited. This had to be what a honeymoon was like.

# CHAPTER 32

*VINCENT*

SHE'D SAID SHE COULDN'T WAIT TO GET ME UNDRESSED, AND I WAS HAVING AN equally hard time—literally—keeping from ripping her thin dress to shreds to reach the hot flesh underneath. She was making me crazy. The obvious bounce of her breasts as she walked had driven me to distraction, and the slit in her dress had taunted me each time it revealed *all* of her long leg.

As soon as the door to the room closed, she was yanking at my tie, followed by my cummerbund. Then she stopped and pushed me back. "Page one-twenty-eight."

I worked my cufflinks loose and recalled the page: Juliet on her knees giving Dalton a blowjob. My cock throbbed at the mental image.

Ashley slipped off the dress. "I don't want it to get damaged."

She stepped out of it, the picture of elegant beauty: nothing but a high-waisted thong and black heels.

"No," I said. "Not one-twenty-eight."

That scene was too one-sided, and tonight was for her. I was dying for her mouth on me, but tonight it had to be something for her—something new, something unforgettable.

She cocked her head. "But I want to try."

The meaning almost escaped me, but I caught it just in time to clarify.

"You haven't...?" I didn't finish the sentence.

She cast her gaze down. "No. But I can try."

153

I closed the distance, tipped up her chin, and said the words I should have said to her many years ago. "Not tonight, and not until you're ready."

"But—"

I stopped her with a finger to her lips. "Page two-oh-two," I told her. "Get on the couch."

For a split second she looked ready to argue, but she seemed to change her mind. She walked to the couch and sat. She leaned over to undo the straps of her heels.

"Keep them on."

She let go of the strap and sat up again.

After freeing the second of the uncooperative cufflinks, I shed my shirt.

∼

ASHLEY

HE'D STUNNED ME BY REFUSING THE ORAL SEX I OFFERED. ACCORDING TO THE GIRLS I'd gone to college with, no guy ever refused a BJ—not ever. Then he'd turned the tables and changed to page two-oh-two. I couldn't quite remember what that was. There'd been three scenes involving the couch, or maybe four.

My sex clenched, and I shivered with anticipation as he strode toward me, shirtless. He pulled off his shoes one by one.

The heat between my legs grew unbearable as I yearned for his touch.

He pulled at my panties.

I lifted my ass to free them as he slid them to my ankles and picked up one foot then the other.

He spread my legs and licked his lips as his eyes raked over me.

The lights were still on. Feeling exposed, I tried to close my legs, but he wouldn't let me.

"You're gorgeous, Kitten."

I trembled as I finally remembered page two-oh-two.

He knelt between my legs and pulled me forward, my ass at the very edge of the couch.

I spread my legs wider and pulled my knees up, opening myself fully to him.

He blew on my wet lower lips and then traced a finger up one edge and down the other, avoiding my most sensitive flesh—teasing, tracing with just a feather-light touch.

"Give me a finger," I said, trying to remember Juliet's lines.

I trembled as his finger entered me, hooked, and stroked the tenderness inside of me.

"Deeper," I said.

He complied, keeping with the script.

As he moved his finger slowly in and out, stroking my walls, my anticipation built for what was to come. "Another," I begged, as Juliet had. My God Juliet had gotten it right.

The second finger joined the first, adding pressure.

I closed my eyes and tried to visualize Juliet's words. "Now my clit. I'm ready."

And I was as the heat grew, emanating from my core.

His other hand came to my clit, with surprising pressure, and held there.

"Now circle."

He did.

With the fingers inside me moving slowly, and him circling my little nub, the tingles were building.

"Lighter."

"Harder."

He did as I asked, and I began to understand the appeal of the page with every stroke. Juliet's words didn't matter anymore.

"Faster."

"Back and forth."

I pulled my knees up harder as the tension built in all my muscles, and more and more of my nerves became overloaded.

"Oh fuck. Harder."

"A little higher."

"Shit. Right there."

I let go of my knees and grabbed for his head.

He pulled back. That wasn't in the script. At least not yet.

I grasped my knees again.

"Circle...fuck yes." I could barely hear myself with the blood rushing in my ears.

"Lighter."

My breathing was coming faster every second. "Harder."

"Fuck, yeah. Faster."

"The other direction."

"Oh shit."

I arched my hips up into his pressure.

"Holy fuck."

"More."

He pressed harder, and the tremors started, sparks igniting all my nerve endings.

My walls constricted, and my clit exploded under his touch. I couldn't breathe, and my fingernails dug into my legs. "Holy shit," was all I could manage.

Slowly, the tremors receded, and I relaxed, letting go of my knees.

He pulled out his fingers and pushed his palm against the throbbing of my pussy, rubbing up and down with light pressure on the entire area.

I opened my eyes to the intense hunger in his and the monster smile written across his face. I'd have to remember this page for another day.

He stood and marched to his suitcase, returning with a tie. "Stand up."

I stretched out my hand, and he pulled me to my feet.

He spun me around and the tie covered my eyes.

"Page two-ninety-two?" I asked awkwardly. As tender as my pussy was, I wasn't sure I was ready for the spanking.

He cinched the tie tight and took my hand. "Guess again." He led me slowly forward.

I stepped gingerly, now blind to the room. I drew a blank trying to remember another blindfolded scene.

He lifted my hands, and they met the cold glass of the window.

Now I knew the page. "Three-fourteen."

He didn't answer me. "Stand there," he commanded.

I couldn't figure out if the blindfold made it easier or harder to stand naked in the window of a hotel room for anyone out there to see. Probably harder, as I imagined people on the street below pointing upward, guiding other eyes to take in the naked lady against the window. What if they snapped a picture with their cell phones? The thought chilled me.

I heard the tearing sound of the foil packet behind me.

Vince's hands started at my shoulders and traced my arms out to my hands as his cock settled against my back and the scent of eucalyptus invaded my nostrils. I trembled at the feel of his hot breath on the back of my neck.

His hands held mine against the glass. I flinched as his tongue grazed my earlobe.

"How many people do you imagine are down there watching us? A dozen? Maybe two dozen?" he whispered into my ear.

I cringed in fear. When Juliet had removed the blindfold, she'd found a dozen or more strangers gazing up at her.

"Keep your hands on the glass," he commanded. With his foot he urged mine apart. "Shift back a little."

I did.

Fingers traced a fiery trail down my arms and along my sides to under my ass, where they left me breathless and wanting more. I gasped as a single finger-nail scraped from my neck down my spine and back up again. The slow torture continued with barely-there fingertips tracing the insides of my legs from my ankles to my knees and then slowly farther north toward the destination I hoped for.

I spread my legs a bit more, but he stopped short. My pussy throbbed with the need to have him inside me.

"What do you want, Kitten?" His voice rumbled through me, extinguishing my inhibitions.

"You. I want you inside me." My words were only half as frantic as my need.

His cock teased between my thighs as his hands clamped down on my breasts. "First you have to come for the crowd."

A vision of people with their cell phones out flashed again in my brain. The danger only amplified the throbbing of my pulse in my soaked pussy.

His grip on one breast loosened to a light caress as a finger of the other hand slid slowly down my chest, over my bellybutton, and parted my folds to trace around my swollen clit in agonizingly slow circles.

He pushed me up against the glass. "You're going to come for me, Kitten."

The slow torment of his light touch was working its magic.

The glass was cold against one breast, with the other protected by the warmth of his hand.

I jerked as he pulled his finger away from my needy nub and brought it to my nose. The scent of me replaced the faint eucalyptus of him.

His finger pushed against my lips, and I opened for him, tasting myself for the second time.

"That's the taste of desire," he whispered into my ear.

I nodded.

"Imagine what our kiss will be like after I give you a tongue-lashing."

My pussy spasmed at the thought of his face between my legs, his stubble scratching my inner thighs.

His fingers returned to my crotch and the ministrations to my hypersensitive clit became strong and rhythmic.

"Faster," I urged him. "Yeah."

The words spilled out as he pressed me against the glass and continued to boil my blood with delicious torment.

"Oh, fuck…Yeah, more…Harder…Oh, shit."

With every movement, he sent me higher, closer to another, bigger climax.

"They're clapping for you," he groaned.

I didn't hear a thing through the thick glass, with the thrum of my own rapid heartbeat in my ears. Lightning bolts shot through my nerves.

He pinched my nipple. "Come for me, Kitten."

Another few strokes and the explosion came, hurtling me over the edge. My inner walls contracted around emptiness, longing to be filled by him.

He held me up as I wobbled in the high heels.

When I could breathe again, he pulled me back and spread my legs farther.

His tip found my slippery entrance, and he pushed in as I braced against the glass. I finally got the feeling of fullness I'd longed for.

His grip on my hips tightened as his thrusts became forceful and rapid.

My breasts swung forward and back with the movement.

His fingers tightened as the animal in him claimed me with more intensity.

He found his end with a final push and pulled me into him with a groan that was half roar.

As he held me against him, his cock throbbed inside me before he pulled out. He spun me around so fast I almost tripped. His mouth clamped over mine, and with his scent in my nostrils, his kiss said more than his words ever could. He pulled me close, erasing the space between us. I could feel the pounding of his heart against my breasts.

He broke the kiss. "Welcome to New York, Kitten."

I kissed him again.

He loosened the tie and pulled it off my head.

I blinked at the bright light in the room. As I turned toward the window, I realized there was no crowd. We faced the park, and we were more than forty floors up. At this angle, nobody could see a thing. I slapped his shoulder. "You lied."

He laughed. "I just followed the script."

In the book, Juliet had been naked in a second-story window.

This man had given me an incredible evening in a million ways.

# CHAPTER 33

*ASHLEY*

IT WAS SUNDAY AFTERNOON, AND OUR PLANE LEVELED OFF AT CRUISING ALTITUDE ON the flight back to Boston.

I rubbed the emerald on the necklace Vince had given me, the necklace he'd kept all these years. The necklace that marked me as his Kitten—a title I cherished.

The weekend had been nonstop fun. After a breakfast of Belgian waffles topped with strawberries and washed down with a mimosa, we'd spent Saturday exploring the Big Apple. We'd taken a rowboat from the Loeb Boathouse onto The Lake in Central Park. He'd taken me on a carriage ride. We'd visited the zoo, walked the stores of Fifth Avenue, and kissed on top of the Empire State Building.

We'd had burgers and fries for lunch at the original Shake Shack and dined for dinner at a rooftop restaurant in the garment district.

Vince crossed his legs, and the sight of his ankle crossed over his knee brought up the question that had been bothering me since Saturday morning. Without thinking, I blurted it out. "Who's Deb?" I'd seen her name tattooed on his ankle and I'd been jealous that it hadn't been mine. She must have been important to him.

He arched an eyebrow. "Pardon?"

It was too late to pull the question back. "Who's Deb, the girl's name you have tattooed on your ankle.

A frown replaced the quizzical look, and his eyes deadened.

Instantly, I regretted being so insecure.

He pulled down his sock. "You mean this?" He pointed to the small black letters: DEB. He took a deep breath. "It's so we never forget her. It's for Deborah Ellen Benson, my cousin. She died when I was nine. Debbie was five years old at the time. We all carry this tattoo, the whole family, so that we never forget her." The gesture was overwhelmingly sweet.

My stomach soured at how inconsiderate my assumption had been. "What happened?"

"She was kidnapped."

"Did you get…" I almost said *us*, but caught myself. "Did the FBI get involved?"

"Yes… Anyway, Uncle Seth paid the ransom, and the cops, FBI, whoever, followed the kidnapper, but it ended up in a gunfight. The guy died without ever telling us where she was. The cops looked. Dad and Uncle Seth paid for a search, but we never found her."

I couldn't tell him how it pained me that my Bureau had let him down. "I'm sorry."

"It was a long time ago. Like I said, it's so we don't forget." He pulled his sock back up and returned to his phone.

I sunk in my seat and stayed quiet, reflecting on how important the bond of family was to all of them. It was a lesson about the Benson's that I wouldn't forget.

Before long, the co-pilot called back to tell us it was time to buckle up for landing.

Now the weekend was over, and it was time to return to the real world—the world where bad guys at Covington's competitor were evidently trying to take Vince down, and I had no idea who the inside accomplice was. For a moment I contemplated whether it was time for me to start carrying my gun again. But I discarded the idea, intent on maintaining my cover.

I contemplated what steps I might take next and came up empty, save waiting for John's lab results on the note and fingerprints I'd mailed him before leaving for the weekend.

The time in New York had let me clear my mind of regrets for not yet turning in the evidence I'd found. After all, I'd become more and more convinced it wasn't evidence in Vince's case, but evidence in the case to be brought against the people trying to ruin him.

We'd both agreed to unplug from email and the internet for the weekend, but Vince was now catching up on his emails on the plane.

He looked up from his phone and smiled. "You seem to be doing better with the flying."

"I am, thanks. The breathing thing helps."

He went back to reading messages on his phone. A moment later he put the phone to his ear.

"Hey, Mason. What's up?... I told you I'd be out of touch for the weekend... And the Strongwood transaction?... How much more time do they want?... Tell them three weeks, then. It's only fair...You handle that one. Okay, yeah, I'll be in tomorrow..."

"I thought you gave them a deadline of this week?" I asked after he hung up.

"I did. But in the end, if both parties aren't happy signing the deal, the hard feelings will come back to cost us in the long run. What's a couple more weeks if it allows them peace of mind?"

As I watched and listened to him, I could sense Vince's innate goodness. He was not the criminal here; I knew that for certain. But now I had to figure out how to prove it before his enemy got the better of him.

Vince looked up again. "What's worrying you, Kitten?"

I loved it every time he called me that. It made me feel like cuddling up next to him and purring.

"I'm not sure what you should do next to find out who wrote that awful note," I said.

He shrugged. "I can worry about that tomorrow."

I nodded. He apparently thought the most important word in his sentence had been *tomorrow*, while I was focused on *worry*.

He had resources to throw at the problem. I was a team of one. I'd gone as far as I could by enlisting John's help on the evidence. I couldn't pull in any more Bureau help. *Dread* might have been an even more appropriate word than *worry*.

THE TOWN CAR PULLED TO THE CURB IN FRONT OF THE SLEEK STEEL-AND-GLASS building. The green of the Common lay to the left.

I unbuckled my seatbelt, but stayed obediently in my seat while Vince raced around to open my door. I'd made the mistake of not waiting twice in New York and had been properly scolded. If he wanted to spoil me, I was game.

On the curb, Vince handed me my roller bag, while he took the other and the garment bag.

The doorman held the door for us. "Welcome back, Mr. Benson. Did you have a pleasant trip?"

Vince stopped. "Carl, this is Ashley Newton. She is to have full access to the building."

"Very good, sir." The man bowed to me. "Very nice to make your acquaintance, Miss Ashley."

"You too, Carl," I replied as he ushered us through the quiet opulence of the building's lobby.

My ears popped on the way up to the twenty-sixth floor.

Vince unlocked the door, disarmed the security system, and rolled our bags out of the way.

I wasn't prepared for the sight. His place was immense and decorated tastefully with manly, black leather furniture, as well as the requisite monster flat screen on the wall. It was probably big enough that the football players looked almost life size on it. I walked to the full-length windows and admired his uninterrupted view over the Common and the rest of the city to the north and west. The people strolling on the paths of the Common were mere ants from up here.

"Like it?" he asked.

"Love it. You're spoiled. You know that, right?"

"Only because I have you."

"You don't have me," I shot back. Those words had always triggered me.

"I meant have you with me."

I controlled my temper and didn't argue. "I shouldn't have snapped."

His arms wrapped around me from behind and his chin rested on the top of my head. "Sorry. I have to go for a run. Want to come along?"

I curled my arms behind me to pull him tighter. "Nah, you go ahead."

"You'll get to see this view every morning now."

It took me a second to process his roundabout way of asking me to move in. "I can't."

"Sure, you can."

"No, I can't. I work for you. It wouldn't look right at the company."

"I could fire you. I'm always firing my assistants."

"You wouldn't dare."

He let go. "We can discuss this after dinner." He strode off to get changed.

I people-watched out the massive windows, wondering what it would be like to sleep with Vince every night, and wake to this sight every morning.

He returned, looking hot as ever in his running shorts. "Order a pizza in a half hour, and then I'll be back about when it arrives," he suggested. "Wallet's on the counter."

"You got it."

The door closed behind him, and I told Siri to set a timer for twenty minutes. The second door I tried was his office, and I started my search.

The timer went off before I finished. I called in the pizza order for half pepperoni and half deluxe before resuming my search.

Another fifteen minutes and I was confident that I could report there was nothing incriminating in Vince's home office.

Whoever was framing him hadn't planted anything here.

The doorbell surprised me. The pizza delivery was faster here than it was in my neighborhood. I scrambled to get Vince's wallet from the counter and raced to open the door.

The freckle-faced kid handed me the box and held his hand out expectantly.

Setting the warm box on the entryway table, I fumbled with Vince's wallet, opening it upside down. Everything spilled on the floor. I gathered up a few bills to pay the kid, along with a tip.

After the door closed, I knelt and started replacing the contents in the wallet. I picked up a photo and froze.

He had a wallet-size copy of our prom picture. He'd kept it all this time—a picture of us.

As I returned the last credit card, a tear came to my eye. Aside from two family photos of his parents and siblings, our prom picture was the only other one he carried. I put the wallet back on the counter with my heart thumping almost audibly.

*He has always cared.*

# CHAPTER 34

*ASHLEY*

THIS MORNING MARKED THE BEGINNING OF A NEW WEEK. ANOTHER BORING spreadsheet filled my computer screen when Vince left his office for downstairs.

It had been a wonderful weekend, though, topped off by the discovery I'd made in Vince's wallet last night. But I remained determined to not let people at work know about us. I'd won last night's argument about moving in with him. It hadn't been easy to go home to my dreary, empty apartment, but it was the right thing.

With nothing to distract me now, I was anxious to know about the lab results. Unfortunately, John hadn't answered his phone the first time I'd called.

This time was different. "Ashley, good to hear from you. How are things going up in Boston? You surviving without me?"

"Still wishing you hadn't left," I told him.

The bustle of the field office was audible in the background on his end. "Couldn't be helped. I go where they tell me, at least until they say Alaska. I might object to that one."

I got to the point. "Are the results in?"

"The doctor said nothing to worry about," he replied.

Clearly he couldn't speak frankly on his end—a situation I should have expected, but I didn't understand the code.

"Did the test results come in?"

He said something on the side to someone in the office, then returned to the line. "I'm putting the papers in the mail for you, don't worry."

"Can't I get them faster by fax?"

"Not to worry, just routine. And I think we can trust the mail."

It seemed he couldn't have the papers out in the open for others in New Haven to see. That made sense. He'd already gone out on a limb to help me keep this under the radar.

"I'll wait for the mail then," I told him.

"Yeah, they're keeping me busy here. Mostly because they're not as organized as we are."

I heard a complaint come from one of the Connecticut agents in the background. John was keeping the conversation real on his end. They would expect him to rib them if he talked to someone from the Boston office.

"Understood. Take care of yourself."

"You too, and don't neglect your range time. It's embarrassing when I beat you so bad."

I couldn't decipher what he meant by that. He never beat me at the shooting range… But we'd been on the line long enough. We couldn't risk this seeming like anything other than a short check-in.

After hanging up, I contemplated the possible meanings of his final comment, and all I came up with was "be careful." I couldn't carry my weapon on this assignment, and for some reason John's gut was telling him it could be dangerous. He always listened to his gut, and it had never steered him wrong.

Anita passed by me on her way into Vince's empty office.

The staccato sounds of the old IBM Selectric came through the door.

I went to the office door. "Do you need me to type something up?" It was the first time I'd seen anyone except Vince use the old typewriter.

She looked up. "No thanks, dear. Mason needs something typed. I got it." She went back to her work. Her fingers flew over the keys faster than I could have managed without the backspace key my computer afforded me.

Anita finished, and I wondered if her fingerprints would be the ones I'd lifted on the typewriter.

It wasn't long before Vince returned from his simulated run downstairs and closed himself away in his office.

Not long after, reception called up to me. "There are two agents from the FBI who would like to talk to Mr. Benson. The guard downstairs told me."

I froze for a second. It couldn't be. John wouldn't have turned over the memo I sent him—not without at least telling me.

"Just a moment. Let me check with him." I put the phone on hold and let myself into Vince's office.

He looked up and smiled.

I closed the door behind me, unsure how to handle this. "Reception called, and there are two agents from the FBI here to interview you."

"Send them up. I've got time."

I couldn't explain my real fear to him. "I'm not sure that's wise."

"Nonsense. I've got nothing to hide. Send them up, and see if they want coffee." He returned to signing the stack of papers in front of him.

"Just don't say anything to them."

He looked up, quizzically. "What's the problem?"

I had to come up with something fast. "The director of security at Tenerife. That was his advice. '*Remember Martha Stewart, and don't say anything.*' He told me that once."

"Thanks for the advice. I'll be fine."

That's what all the suspects who later got tricked into contradicting themselves said. Then they were charged with lying to the FBI.

There was nothing else I could say without blowing my cover.

"Go now," Vince urged. "Send them up."

I left with a chill and picked up the phone at my desk. "Have them sign in and escort them up," I told reception.

A few minutes later, the elevator dinged, and Randy White—the SAC himself, and Frank, Liz's partner, arrived.

This was totally out of the ordinary. We never sent an agent in anywhere near where we had someone planted undercover.

They introduced themselves to me as if we hadn't met.

I kept my cool. "Just a moment, gentlemen." I almost couldn't handle speaking the word *gentlemen* when referring to the SAC.

I opened the door. "The two agents are here."

# CHAPTER 35

*VINCENT*

ASHLEY BROUGHT IN THE TWO AGENTS. BOTH WORE OFF-THE-RACK SUITS THAT HAD seen better days.

The older man introduced them both. He was White, and the other was Dunbar.

I welcomed them and closed the door. "Please, have a seat."

White spoke first. "Thank you for seeing us, Mr. Benson."

"Certainly, Agent White. What can I do for you?"

"Special Agent," he corrected me.

I noted the irritation, but didn't respond.

White motioned to the window. "Very nice view."

"Thank you."

"This is quite an office. Are you in charge of this whole company?"

"No, not at all. I oversee the operations here on the east coast, but the true headquarters is located in Los Angeles. I'm sure you know that."

Dunbar smirked, giving it away. No way had they come in to talk to me without doing research ahead of time.

White's face remained unreadable. "But you're in charge of everything in this building?" he asked.

Ashley's warning came to mind.

"As I told you, I oversee a portion of the company. Now, what can I do for you?"

White scratched his jaw, then pulled a photo out of his jacket pocket and slid it across the desk to me. "Have you ever seen this man?"

The open-ended nature of his question had Ashley's admonition rattling around in my head all over again. "I don't know."

White's eyes narrowed. "You didn't even look at the picture, sir."

"I don't need to look to answer your question. I can't possibly remember everyone I have ever met, any more than you could. You asked if I had ever seen him. There's no way for me to know the answer to that question."

"Don't be smart," White said.

"I gave you a truthful answer. What else would you like to know?"

He picked up the picture. "This is Sonny Alfonso. Have you ever met him?"

"Not that I recall at this moment, but I could be wrong. I meet a lot of people and don't remember them all."

"So that's a no?" White said, trying to put words in my mouth.

I took a calming breath. "That's an I-don't-recall-meeting-him-but-I-could-be-wrong. I've met a lot of people in my life, and I don't remember them all."

Ashley had been right. Their game was to trip me up for some reason, and I had no idea why.

"Let's move on," White said.

So far, Dunbar hadn't spoken a word. He was clearly the junior of the two agents.

"Mr. Alfonso is one of the heads of organized crime in town," White said. "Very high up."

I didn't respond to that statement.

Ashley had mentioned that same name... The *Inquisitor* had been trying to tie me to him. It was a good thing she'd gotten that article killed, or at least delayed.

White shifted in his chair. "If he has contacted you, or were to contact you in the future, you would tell us, right?"

"Is that an official request?" I asked.

"Why wouldn't you want to cooperate with us?" White asked.

"I'm open to contacting you," I said.

White shook his head, probably upset that I'd seen his question for what it was. "We have information that he may be—make that *is*—looking for somebody to front for him."

I could guess where this was leading. "What does *front* mean in this context?"

White answered, "To front for the mob would be something like buying a business, which a company such as yours could do, and then selling an interest to somebody like Mr. Alfonso and his associates without disclosing that fact."

"I don't understand. Why wouldn't he just buy it himself if he wanted it?"

White shook his head like I was an idiot. I was getting to him. "Because there are numerous businesses he wouldn't be allowed to buy into."

"Such as?" I asked.

White huffed. "Such as anything to do with gambling."

"I see." And this confirmed where this was all coming from. Gainsboro had seeded the *Inquisitor* and now the FBI with the notion that I was in bed with organized crime in order to ruin my deal with Semaphore.

Gainsboro was taking playing dirty to a whole new level. They couldn't beat us legitimately, so this was their tactic? Get us kicked out of the bidding and leave the field open to them?

If I didn't do something, Semaphore would be yanked from my grasp, and proving the charges false after the deal had been sealed wouldn't help.

Those fucking Gainsboro assholes. At least the nature of my adversary was clear after this visit. There wasn't much they wouldn't stoop to.

"You're certain Mr. Alfonso hasn't contacted you yet?" White asked.

"I said I'd be open to contacting you if I hear from him in the future."

White fumed at my non-answer, but didn't say anything.

"Is there anything else, agents?" I carefully avoided adding *special*. The only thing special about White was his deviousness.

White shook his head. "No. That about wraps it up for today. Thank you for your time, Mr. Benson."

"My pleasure." I rose and escorted them out to the guard waiting behind Ashley's desk. "These gentlemen are done here," I told the guard.

I ignored Ashley's questioning look and returned to my office.

A minute later, she let herself in and closed the door.

She took the chair across from me. "So?"

"So, two things. First, you were right to give me that advice. The FBI is full of snakes. I don't see how they sleep at night."

Her brow knit.

"They tried several times to get me to agree to ambiguous statements, and to agree to have met, or claim to have never met, that Alfonso guy your friend from the *Inquisitor* was asking about."

"She's not my friend," Ashley corrected me.

"Acquaintance then. That underhanded Jacinda girl."

"What did you say?"

"I didn't agree to anything, and I didn't say anything except that I couldn't possibly know the answer to their open-ended questions. But before they left, they said Alfonso was going to approach me. All in all, I think it was a good meeting."

Ashley cocked her head. "How could that be good?"

"Now it's making sense. I can see what's going on. Gainsboro is behind this whole thing. They planted the same information with the feds as with the *Inquisitor*. They're out to paint me as being in bed with this Alfonso guy to screw the Semaphore deal."

"You think so?"

"The pieces fit. Their next step is probably to get the *Globe* to print an article that quotes anonymous sources within the FBI saying I'm under investigation for ties to the mob. Then they'll peddle that shit at Semaphore."

"Makes sense," she said.

～

LATER THAT MORNING, I ANSWERED DAD'S CALL.

"Vincent, how is that Semaphore transaction you've been telling me about coming along?"

I'd made the mistake of telling him this was underway, thinking it would earn me points. Instead it had led to him calling me every week for an update. He had become a constant backseat driver to the point of annoyance—not that I could tell him that. And anyway, instead of being a positive thing if I got the deal done, it was starting to look like it could only be a negative if I failed at it.

"Nothing much significant. The other potential buyer has made another counterproposal, and they want us to respond."

"And how do you feel about that?" he asked.

The question was pretty much the same every week.

"We haven't decided how to respond yet."

For a moment he didn't say anything. "Sometimes going slow is the best option," he said. "Seeming too eager can be a detriment at times."

His opinion mirrored Mason's on this.

"That's why we're taking our time," I told him.

"Good boy, Vincent. You know I'm available if you'd like to talk through some of your options."

He couldn't help reinforce that he wasn't sure I could handle this by myself—just as he had done my entire life.

"Thanks, Dad. I appreciate that."

I wasn't about to avail myself of the offer right now. I'd save that for some truly sticky situation he'd appreciate for its difficulty.

I took out my coin and wrapped it three times lightly on the desk. "Come in," I said off to the side. "Hey, Dad? I gotta go. Thanks for the call."

We hung up after perfunctory goodbyes.

I turned the coin over and read the inscription for the millionth time. *I have not yet begun to fight.*

Shortly before lunch, Ben, my head of security, called up to see if I was free. He joined me in my office five minutes later.

He closed the door behind him. "I've got some preliminary information for you." He opened a folder and turned it around on the desk for me to read.

"What am I looking at?"

"Remember we said somebody in the company could have planted that malware on your computer?"

"Yeah. But your guy said it was most likely through some email trojan or something."

He took a breath. "That was one theory. But now we know it was done from inside."

"How exactly?"

"Remember I told you we'd disabled it, but we hadn't removed it in case you wanted to use it to send misinformation?"

I nodded.

"Well, it disappeared off your computer. Which means somebody inside put it there, and then they removed it after we found it."

"Any way to tell who?" Mason and I had discussed the possibility of a mole on this floor after the keylogger had been found.

"I've been looking into the most likely candidates upstairs here, and these are the first results." He offered me a spreadsheet.

"You'll have to explain."

He pointed out a series of numbers that ran down the page. "This third column here is the monthly bank balance for Mason's secretary, Anita."

"Assistant," I corrected him.

"Sorry, I'm just a little old-fashioned. Mason's assistant, Anita."

There was a significant jump in the numbers near the end.

He pointed to the jump. "A lot of money came in recently. Unless you've given her a big bonus or something, we don't see anything that explains it."

His implication was ominous, and one I couldn't accept. Anita couldn't be involved.

"What do you mean, you can't explain it?" I asked.

"Exactly that. She didn't transfer any money from her brokerage account or anything like that. She hasn't sold her house, car, or anything else that could account for that amount of money. And it would have to be one hell of a car, anyway."

We hadn't given out bonuses recently, and certainly nothing of that magnitude. "You're implying she's a mole."

He sat back in his chair. "I'm not implying anything. I just bring you the data and let you make your own conclusions. She's come into some money, and I have no obvious way to explain it. That's all I'm saying."

I shook my head. It didn't make any sense. Anita had been with us forever, since even before I started. Liam had told me he'd trust her with his life, if it came to that.

*Not implying anything, my ass.* Ben was accusing Anita, pure and simple.

"You want me to talk to her?" he asked.

I shook my head. I was certain about that. "Not yet."

If I let Ben come at her, with his lack of tact, we'd be down one very capable assistant in a flash. Anita wasn't the sort to take that kind of accusation in stride.

Not any more than I was. It would be the ultimate insult to a long-term employee such as herself.

"Let me handle it," I told him.

He nodded. "A more direct route might be to review the video of your office. We haven't done that yet."

"Let me handle that. I'd rather do that myself." The last thing I needed was one of his guys reviewing footage of Ashley and me doing it over my desk.

"One or two of my guys could help, and it would go quicker."

"I said I'll do it myself."

"Yes, sir. I'll get you the equipment when you're ready. But be warned—it can be quite tedious."

"Got it. Another thing, Ben. I just had a meeting that makes it pretty clear to me that all this links back to the Gainsboro company."

"Anyone in particular there?" he asked.

"I don't have a name yet, but we should be looking for anybody here with links to anybody there as a suspect."

"That's a pretty wide net. I might have to pull in outside help to get it checked out."

"Whatever you need. Just keep it quiet."

"Yes, sir."

He stood and prepared to leave. "Like I said, I'm just giving you the data. It's nothing personal."

After the door closed, I looked down at the open folder on my desk, a folder filled with a nice, smelly turd. It couldn't be Anita.

The people who insisted shit always flowed downhill had never been in my position before. Sometimes the really shitty situations floated up for the boss to take care of.

I closed the folder and placed it in my drawer.

Not today.

# CHAPTER 36

*ASHLEY*

WHEN I GOT HOME FROM WORK ON MONDAY AND CHECKED MY APARTMENT MAILBOX, there it was. Just as John had promised.

The Express Mail envelope was rolled up and stuffed into my box. It almost didn't fit, and it took some careful pulling to get it out without ripping. My mail lady was the only one I knew who could truly stuff ten pounds of shit into a five-pound bag—or a tiny mailbox, in this case.

I carried the envelope under one arm as I opened the door and went to the kitchen for scissors to open my present. Once I'd unpacked, all the enclosed papers covered my table. A quick perusal showed he'd found nothing useful on the note itself, which had been returned in the plastic evidence bag.

The lack of any of Vince's prints, or even partials, settled it once and for all in my mind. This was a setup. There was no way to load paper into the old type-writer without at least partial prints unless you were wearing gloves while doing it. The case had officially, as far as I was concerned, shifted from determining if Vince was guilty or not into finding who was trying to frame him.

I would have to put it back where I'd found it for now.

Additionally, the fingerprints came back with two hits: Anita and Sophia on the typewriter keys. The one from the blotter was not complete enough for a match.

I'd hoped for something of a home run and had gotten a single at best. Tomorrow I would plan my next step.

I opened my purse to pull out my phone.

There was a note inside: *My place for dinner. Uncle Benny.*

I laughed at his corniness. He'd obviously slipped the note in there while I was away from my desk at some point.

During the Uber ride to Vince's place, I found my mind wandering. I was excited to be working this case to protect Vince now, rather than to convict him. It was all backwards, but felt right. For the longest time, the bullpen group in Chelsea had been my family, but things had changed there. Or maybe something had always been off. Either way, now I was essentially working against them.

In my heart I believed I was serving justice by working on Vince's side, not the Bureau's. The top of my ID read *Federal Bureau of Investigation*, but also *Department of Justice*, and I would be doing a disservice to both if I were the instrument of a frame job.

I couldn't prove it yet, but my gut feeling, and the lack of prints on the paper, was too strong to ignore. The note Staci had gotten was clearly from an adversary. Plus, the way the DOJ had been fed such specifics on the fake contract and I'd been told exactly where and when to find it all pointed to an elaborate setup. Paint Vince as fronting for the Alfonso family, and he was right, Semaphore and their gaming business would be out of his grasp—all so convenient for the competition.

The Uber came to a stop out front, and Carl waved me through as I entered Vince's Tremont building. I punched the button for the twenty-sixth floor and fingered the necklace I was wearing—the one Vince had given me in New York. I'd been doing that a lot.

At the door, I knocked.

Vince opened the door after a short wait. "Kitten, you're late."

He picked me up with a hug that threatened to flatten my breasts and let me down with a quick peck.

A black monster of a dog came up to sniff me. I crouched down to pet her. "Hi there, girl."

"Meet Rufus, my roommate. Call him a girl again, and I can't be responsible for the outcome."

I stood and the dog nudged his head under my hand, demanding more petting. "He's a cutie." After a series of scratches behind the ears, he walked to his master and demanded some more of the same.

"You hear that Rufus, you're cute. He's never been called that before. He scares most people."

" Not me. I love dogs." The aromas of what would undoubtedly be pizza wafted over me. "Pizza again?"

"Alexa, play 'Green-Eyed Lady' by Sugarloaf," he said loudly.

Alexa complied, and the music started.

"May I have this dance?"

I took his hand, and we began to sway. He sang some of the lyrics in my ear as we danced. My heart ached at his corny routine. Even if it was only frozen pizza for dinner, I could really get used to this treatment every time I got home—not that this was my home, but whenever I was with him, it felt like home.

The song ended, and he released me.

Rufus had retired to his bed.

"We need to talk," I told him.

It was time for me to level with him about my job and work openly with him to find out who was attempting to frame him.

He ignored me and continued to the kitchen. "Talk is overrated. First we feast." He opened the oven and surprised me by pulling out two pizza boxes. We weren't having frozen grocery store pizza after all. "We're splurging on Papa Luigi's tonight. I can afford it."

His use of the word *splurge* was odd. He could afford to buy the restaurant a hundred times over if he wanted.

"First I need to tell you something—"

"Second. I told you, first we feast on Papa Luigi's finest." An evil grin overtook his face. "Or I could feast on something even more delicious. You might like that."

His implication had me squeezing my thighs together. "Okay, pizza first, and maybe the other later."

He waggled his eyebrows. "I'm going to hold you to that."

"Have you been drinking?"

He opened the boxes on the counter. "Your choice of pepperoni, Hawaiian, veggie, or combo. We have half a pizza of each." This was way too much for the two of us, but like he'd said, he could afford it.

The pizzas smelled delicious, but I had a more immediate issue.

I followed him into the kitchen and hugged him from behind. "What's with the crazy routine?"

He was charismatic and fun this evening, but not my normal Vince.

He spun around in my arms and took my head in his hands, planting a quick kiss on my forehead. "Today started off so shitty—first the FBI visit, then the update I got from Ben—I decided tonight I was going to be happy no matter what."

"What did Ben have to say?"

"Later. Tonight I'm going to be happy."

I could smell it on his breath. "You have been drinking."

"A little," he admitted. He wiggled away and grabbed plates from the cupboard. "Did you make your choice, Kitten?" He pointed to the pizzas.

I wasn't letting him off so easily. "How many?" I asked.

He held up two fingers.

I cocked my head and fixed him with a stern stare.

He added a third finger. "You need to catch up." He picked up a glass of wine on the counter that I hadn't noticed before.

I relented and took the glass, sipping a bit.

"Well?"

"Pepperoni for me, please. And no jokes about my breath later."

He laughed. "Deal." He served two slices of pepperoni for me and chose Hawaiian for himself.

We set the table and made a game of feeding each other pizza and drinking our wine from interlocked arms. As I caught up to him in the wine department, our laughter filled the room.

It was a side of him I hadn't seen before. I'd seen the serious and businesslike Vince. I'd experienced the threatening Vince that night with the news team. The puppetmaster had reared his head, thinking he could tell me and everyone else what to do. I'd thoroughly enjoyed the romantic Vince he'd shown me in New York. This funny jokester, however, was also a nice addition.

My Vince had a way of transporting me away from the day to day to a special place. I'd never met anybody like him, and as I fingered my necklace one more time, I vowed to never let him go.

After dinner he wanted to watch a movie, and he chose *Top Gun* with Tom Cruise. It was more serious than I would've chosen. I never liked the part where Goose dies in the crash.

"You wanted to talk?" he said during a slow part.

"Another time."

The discussion I'd planned would go better when we weren't drinking, but mostly I didn't want to spoil the mood tonight. He'd had a shitty day, and he deserved a happy evening.

When we reached the singing at the piano scene in the bar, I repeated Meg Ryan's line, "Take me to bed, you big stud, or lose me forever."

I had to say it twice, louder the second time, for Vince to get my drift.

He flicked off the movie, sparing me the sad scene with Goose, and scooped me up from the couch.

He laughed as I repeated the line again, and he rushed me into the bedroom, without bothering with the lights or the dishes.

Our discussion could wait.

Tonight was happy night.

~

VINCENT

I KICKED THE DOOR CLOSED BEHIND ME AND PLOPPED ASHLEY DOWN ON THE BED.

She started removing her clothes, and I helped her wiggle out of them as quickly as I could.

I was hard as a rock. She'd been stroking my thigh as we watched the movie, revving my engine all night.

"You have no idea what you do to me, Kitten." I struggled out of the last of my clothes and moved to spread her legs. I was going to feast on her as I'd promised earlier.

She resisted, with her legs clamped together. "Hold me first."

I moved up alongside her and pulled her into my side, her head on my shoulder.

"Tell me what you want, Kitten."

She stroked my chest. "I want it to be special tonight."

"It's always special for me with you," I told her. "I'll give you a tongue-lashing you won't forget."

She was silent for a moment, her hand circling my nipple.

"I don't want…" She didn't finish her sentence.

"We can just snuggle then." It would be insanely hard to resist, but for her, I could be gentlemanly. At least I hoped so.

"No," she said slowly. "I want skin."

"You mean no…"

"Yeah, you inside me without a condom." She paused. "I'm on the pill, and I don't have anything."

"I'm clean too. But I might not last very long."

She rose up and straddled me. "Another thing, I want to be on top." She leaned over and playfully licked the tip of my nose.

I could go for that. "It's your night, Kitten." I palmed the weight of her marvelous breasts, soft mounds topped with those responsive pink peaks.

She rubbed her slippery slit over my length, slowing down as her clit ran over my tip. Each trip elicited a moan as she pleasured herself on me.

Her wetness had her gliding back and forth with heavy pressure, trying to milk my length and drawing shudders from me every time she rode over my sensitive tip.

It took all my concentration to resist the urge to lift her up and enter her. I let her guide her hips to her own rhythm while I attended to her breasts, holding their weight and circling her nipples with my thumbs, letting her murmurs be my guide. I looked up into her closed eyes as she vulva-fucked me, coming ever closer to the end of her rope.

She increased her tempo, and her breathing became the ragged little breaths that told me how close she was. Her hand went to mine, squeezing it against the warm softness of her breast.

Without warning, she lifted up, guided my cock with her hand, and slid down on me. She was so wet I slipped in easily, and she took me to the root, lifting up and sliding down first slowly, then more quickly. She arched her back and sat up, bracing her hands on my knees.

The sight of her breasts bouncing every time she came down on me was too much. I closed my eyes and concentrated on holding off long enough to satisfy her. Every stroke made it harder than the last as she lifted up to tease my tip at her entrance and then slid down fast to take my length. Each stroke sent a jolt all the way to my toes.

She reached around to tickle my balls, and they nearly exploded from her touch.

I retaliated by taking a thumb to her clit.

She ground forward and back against the pressure of my thumb as the words spilled out of her between quick breaths.

"Holy shit... Oh God...I'm gonna...come... Oh...my God... Holy crap...I can't."

And with the next rock of her pelvis, I rubbed her clit hard, and she crashed over the edge, tensing, shaking, and clawing my shoulders.

She shuddered and cried out my name—convulsing around me as she rode the wave down with several gyrations forward and back—and then collapsed on top of me, her breasts hot against my chest.

"My God," she said over and over again. "I had no idea."

She rolled off, panting to regain her breath. "Your turn." She put her head on the pillow and poked her butt up. "Ride me, cowboy."

I didn't need any more encouragement. I got behind her and let her position me with her hand before I pushed in—hard.

She moaned. "That all you got?" she asked with a giggle.

I grabbed her hips and dug my fingers in, pulling her to me, seating myself fully, and holding her there.

She wiggled her ass, and I started, pulling out and ramming home—all the way home. She was so fucking wet and so deliciously tight that I couldn't hold back.

"Harder," she urged.

I knew she said it for my sake, not hers, but I gave her harder. The sound of flesh slapping against flesh filled the room as I thrust again and again.

She'd been right, the sensations without the latex were to die for, and in no time, the pressure that had built behind my balls was too much to hold back. The strain finally snapped and I shot my load with a final thrust, tensing up and holding her hips tightly to me, welding my cock inside her. Slowly, the throbbing eased. I pushed her forward onto the bed and lay half off of her, sparing her my weight as I panted against her shoulder.

"That was fucking fantastic," I managed between breaths.

"Yeah," she replied, angling her head enough to give me a kiss.

After a minute I got up to wipe off and returned with a warm, wet washcloth for her.

I curled up behind her, cradling a breast with my hand. Our sweat mingled as I held my Kitten tight. She was mine, and I wasn't letting her go.

Her breaths eventually slowed to the rhythm of sleep.

Content, I soon joined her, my Kitten's warm back against my chest and her coconut scent in my nose.

# CHAPTER 37

*Vincent*

I WAS BUSY WITH THE LAST OF OUR BREAKFAST WAFFLES WHEN ASHLEY FINALLY emerged from the bedroom.

She was a sight to behold. She'd pulled on one of my button down shirts, but only bothered with the bottom two buttons. Her cleavage taunted me, and I wondered if she'd grabbed panties or not.

"Morning, Kitten. Sleep okay?"

She walked directly to the orange juice I'd placed on the table. "Like a baby." She popped pills in her mouth and took a long slug of the juice.

"Only two, remember? Don't try to go crazy like last time."

"I need four, but for you, I'm keeping it to two."

I turned back to the waffle iron. "I hope you like waffles."

She came over and wrapped her arms around me. Her hot breasts squeezed against my back.

I opened the waffle iron and forked the last sections onto the plate. "Careful there, or you might end up on page one-seventy-eight."

That one was her on the kitchen counter.

She let go. "We don't have time."

She was probably right.

"There's bacon staying warm in the oven," I told her.

She snagged a pot holder and pulled the plate out. "You spoil me."

I carried the waffles to the table. "It's in the job description."

We sat, and her eyes returned my loving feelings.

179

I moved waffles onto each of our plates.

She cut into one. "Chocolate chip. I should have guessed." She poured maple syrup over it and offered me the bottle.

I took the bottle but set it down without pouring any. "Chocolate makes everything better."

"No syrup?" she asked.

"Don't want it to cover up the taste." I forked a bite.

She took another bite. "You know we can't keep doing this."

"What, breakfast?"

"Me sleeping over during the week. Somebody's going to see us."

"Let them. I'm proud of you."

She put her fork down. "Stop joking around. It's not okay. They may not be judging you, but they sure as hell will be judging me, and I don't want to be seen as the office slut."

This was obviously a bigger concern to her than I'd realized.

"We still on for lunch?"

"Yes, but we have to cool it. No more weeknight sleepovers." She lifted the waffle to her mouth.

This was completely new territory for me, having to negotiate access to my woman. "I don't know if I'm going to last till Friday."

She shrugged, but I wasn't giving up. We were going to come back to this topic and soon.

She devoured breakfast and looked like a chipmunk with her cheeks stuffed full.

"I'll be in later," she said. "I have to go home to change." She took one last bite and rose from the table.

"You could leave some clothes here to make it easier," I offered.

"Stop it. I'm not sleeping over."

I thought it was worth one last try. "I could sleep at your place."

She laughed. "They have a rule against rich people in my neighborhood. And besides, you have to take care of Rufus."

She had a point there. Rufus trotted over at the sound of his name.

Ashley disappeared to get dressed, and I managed to drop a few bites of bacon on the floor for my dog.

～

AN HOUR OR SO LATER THE AIR SEEMED UNUSUALLY CLEAR AS I LOOKED OUT MY office window toward the north. The Gainsboro building was in that direction, and that's where the enemy was hiding.

Last night with Ashley had certainly lifted my mood after my shitty Monday, but I wasn't about to let this lie.

With some free time this morning, I decided to get busy locating the mole working with Gainsboro. And it had damned well better not turn out to be Anita.

I dialed Ben. "Hey, can you set me up to review that video in my office?" I asked when he answered.

"Sure thing. Give me a few minutes to put it together."

He appeared quickly and soon had the software set up on my computer. After showing me how to navigate the videos, he left me to it.

I told Ashley I didn't want to be disturbed at all this morning, and I soon discovered just how boring it was to go through the video. I started with the most recent date and decided to work backward. I had no idea if that was the smart way to do it, but I had to begin somewhere.

The software only let me speed it up so fast, and that meant it took a long time to go through the workday and even longer to cover the night. I got to the first overnight and almost fell asleep.

I jerked awake when there was a quick movement in the room and the lights came on. It turned out to be the janitor. I slowed it down and watched carefully. I couldn't miss anything.

Ben had been right that this was tedious in the extreme. When I got to a logical stopping point, I checked my watch and realized I was going to be late for lunch.

Ashley was still concerned with appearances, so she and I had agreed to meet, but not to walk out together.

She wasn't at her desk when I opened my door, so I grabbed my coat.

"Anita, I'll be at lunch for a while."

She smiled, nodded, and waved.

∾

ASHLEY

I STRODE CONFIDENTLY OUT OF THE DEPARTMENT STORE TOWARD MY LUNCH MEETING with Vince. I'd run short of office-appropriate skirts for my work at Covington. I checked my watch and picked up the pace to our rendezvous. We were having sushi today.

My hand went to my ever-present necklace as I thought back to last night and this morning. Nine years ago, as we'd parted without any kind words, I'd longed for an ending like this, but known it couldn't be. Back then I'd been too scared to give him what he wanted, too scared of how it would end.

Today I'd given him my trust without reservation. He'd earned it with every comment, every gesture, and every action. I finally understood the meaning of the word *love*. I would trust him with my heart, for he was my man.

I reached the restaurant a few minutes late. But a quick glance around showed that I'd still beaten Vince. The place was almost completely full, and the normal lunch rush was about to start. I asked for a table for two and was shown to one near the center of the floor.

Vince arrived before they had a chance to bring our tea.

"Sorry I'm late."

"I only just got here myself," I admitted.

He took the seat across the table from me, and I didn't get a chance for a kiss.

"Did I tell you how good you look today?" he asked.

My heart fluttered at the simple words, and heat rose in my cheeks. "Only three times this morning. But don't stop on my account."

His smile grew. "I'll control myself."

The waitress came and took our order.

I wasn't very adventurous, so I stuck to the simple things and avoided eel or octopus. If I was going to have seafood, it was going to swim, not hang out on the bottom.

Vince chose the octopus, and two kinds of rolls with more things in them than I could keep track of.

"You want to tell me what Ben had to say now?" I asked.

He took a sip of tea before responding. "He thinks it's Anita."

"Anita is what?"

He swirled the tea around in his cup before continuing. "I've had Ben looking into the people upstairs who might have had the access to plant malware on my computer."

"Malware?" I asked.

"Yeah. Ben found a keylogger installed on my computer, and it disappeared a few days later."

"What's a keylogger?" I asked, feigning ignorance and choking back my fear.

"A program that logs what you type and sends it off over the internet to whoever is spying on me."

"That's terrible."

He shook his head. "The kicker is that it appeared and then disappeared, and Ben tells me that means someone in the offices put it there and then deleted it. After looking at everyone on the floor, Anita is his suspect."

"I don't believe that," I said.

"Me either, but she came into a lot of money recently."

Our waiter interrupted us, delivering the food. At least mine was food; I wasn't prepared to put Vince's octopus in the same category.

With his chopsticks, he held a piece of his octopus with the gross suction cup thingies sticking up. "Did you know an octopus's blood is blue instead of red?"

"That's gross," I told him, making a face. "And another reason not to eat them. They were probably left behind when the Martians built the pyramids."

That got the desired chuckle out of him, just before he grossed me out by biting into the blue-blooded monstrosity.

I looked away to keep from turning green.

"It's the copper," he said. "It's copper in their blood to carry the oxygen. Unlike the iron we use, which makes our blood red."

I didn't need the scientific explanation. Being left here by the Martians was good enough for me. I kept my eyes down at my plate to avoid looking at the ugly octopus tentacle staring back at him.

"You sure you won't try it?"

I put my hand in front of my mouth to keep from upchucking. "No thanks," I said, still not looking up.

His phone dinged.

I looked up enough to see that he had taken the entire gross sushi piece and put it in his mouth. At least while he chewed, I wouldn't have to look at it. He checked his phone and a strange look came over his face.

"Something wrong?"

"It's nothing." He put the phone face down on the table and grabbed a piece of one of his rolls.

The phone dinged again with another message. This time he didn't check it. His brow furrowed.

"You sure nothing's wrong?"

"Sure," he said, not meeting my eyes.

The phone dinged again, and his eyes flashed to it.

I'd done enough interrogations to know a lie when I saw one, and this one wasn't hard to spot.

His phone dinged a fourth time. He checked it, put it on the table, and looked around the room, searching. His eyes came to a halt at the far corner, and recognition flashed in his eyes. Not in a good way, near as I could tell.

I turned the phone to face me while his gaze was averted. The text messages were the second thing to make me want to puke.

BARB: Is she why you won't call anymore?

BARB: Are we still on for this Saturday night?

BARB: We could do a threesome

BARB: Does she know you like anal?

His eyes flashed to the phone and his mouth dropped as he realized I'd read the messages.

I got up and threw my napkin on the table. "I've gotta go."

I was out the door five seconds later, gasping for air as I hit the sidewalk. I turned right toward the Covington building before I changed my mind and turned the other way, walking as fast as I could away from his office.

"Ash," he called from behind me.

I didn't stop. I didn't look back. I didn't know a thing about him after all. Barb Saturday night? A threesome? And that other thing?

His footfalls were loud as he ran up behind me and came alongside. "Stop and talk to me," he demanded.

"Nothing to talk about," I said, continuing on.

He kept pace with me without saying anything. Then suddenly, he grabbed my shoulder and turned me toward him.

"You can't just leave."

"Watch me. You can finish lunch with your girlfriend." I started off again down the street.

He jogged ahead and placed himself in my path, forcing me to stop. "She's not my girlfriend," he said firmly.

"So now total strangers are propositioning you for threesomes?"

He put a hand on my shoulder.

I pulled away.

"Her name is Barbara."

"That part I got," I spat.

"We used to see each other."

"She apparently thinks you still are."

"That's a lie. She's in the past."

"How long ago?" I asked. "I thought Staci was your girlfriend."

The look on his face told me I'd hit a home run with that one.

"No... Don't tell me you were seeing them at the same time?"

"I was completely open about it with both of them," he said, shuffling his feet.

"That doesn't make it right. You're a dickhead, you know that?"

"Barb's just a girl," he said, as if that made it okay. "She's just pissed I'm not interested anymore."

"You disgust me."

"I know it looks bad."

"Bad? This isn't in the same universe with bad. Who the hell sees two girls at once? Do you have a sex addiction or something? You need help." I tried to move to the side, but he matched my movement, blocking me still.

"The only thing I need is you. You're my girl."

I clenched my fists. "I need to go. Get out of my way or I'm going to scream my head off."

He moved aside, and I started walking again. I didn't know where I was going, but away was the right direction.

"We need to talk this out," he called.

"We just did," I yelled.

I hadn't missed the words. I'd been demoted from his Kitten to his girl, and it made me feel like shit.

# CHAPTER 38

*Vincent*

A car honked.

I jumped back onto the sidewalk.

I'd almost crossed the street in front of a speeding taxi. That could easily be a fatal mistake in this town.

Telling Barb to fuck off and blocking her number didn't go far enough; I needed to square this with Ashley. I needed her to understand. After our argument, I was a wreck.

The whole thing was my fault for not breaking it to her earlier, finding a way to explain what I'd been like before she'd come back into my life. She needed to know how she had changed me for the better—immeasurably better. I'd told her about Staci, but never mentioned Barb.

I made my way back to the Covington building and closed my door. There was nothing to do until she returned and I could talk to her.

The video setup was waiting at my desk, so I went back to it.

To fight the tedium, I ventured out to get myself a cup of coffee-flavored caffeine.

I locked the door behind me upon my return. Without Ashley to guard it, only the lock would give me the privacy I needed for this.

The pick-me-up seemed to be working as I sat back down and started the video rolling again. A lot of routine comings and goings, punctuated by a boring static image of my office, rolled by as my eyelids got heavier.

The knocking at my door woke me, and I jerked up.

The video had switched to nighttime.

*Fuck.* I'd fallen asleep in spite of the coffee.

The knocking sounded again, more insistent this time and accompanied by Mason's voice.

"I need a few minutes. It's important," he called.

I paused the video, rose from my chair, and walked to the door, rubbing my sore neck. The desk chair was fine for sitting, but it left something to be desired when it came to sleep.

I unlocked the door, and Mason rushed in.

He closed the door behind him. "It's Semaphore. They called. We're out of the running. They've decided to go with Gainsboro."

*Double fuck.*

"But we still had a week to respond," I said.

"The marketing guy told me—off the record, mind you—that it's because they heard we're being investigated for ties to organized crime, and they won't sully their reputation by talking to us any longer."

"Fucking FBI."

He stepped back. "What the fuck does the FBI have to do with this?"

I went back to my desk. "Have a seat. The FBI was here yesterday."

He took his seat. "Why didn't you tell me?"

"You were out all afternoon."

He shrugged.

"You know the rumors that were being fed to the *Daily Inquisitor?*"

"I thought we got that story squashed."

"Well, Gainsboro obviously peddled the same shit to the FBI, and they were here yesterday asking about it."

"They told you it was Gainsboro? That's great. That at least gives us something to work with to get back into it."

"No, they didn't, and they won't. But that's Gainsboro's play here. They feed rumors to the feds, then leak to Semaphore that the feds have been to talk to us, and we're instantly guilty by innuendo. It clears the field for them, like it just did."

"Those assholes."

His description was milder than my feelings right now. Gainsboro had outmaneuvered us so far.

Mason stood. "I think I can get us one more audience."

"Not yet. Ben and I are working on gathering evidence. When we have something concrete, that's the time to go in and talk to them and get Gainsboro knocked out—not before."

"So, what are you doing?"

"Ben and I are working on it."

His face dropped. He wasn't pleased about being left out of the mole hunt.

"I'll let you know when we have something."

He left without argument, and I relocked the door.
I would have to rewind quite a ways and restart my video search.
I would locate the mole, and Gainsboro was going down.

*ASHLEY*

AN HOUR OF WALKING LATER, I STILL COULDN'T GET THE TEXT MESSAGES OUT OF MY
head. He'd been seeing two women at once. Gross. That didn't match the Vince I
thought I knew at all. I pulled out my phone and typed a text to him.

ME: Have errands to run won't be back in this afternoon

I hailed an Uber to get me within walking distance of the field office.
Downstairs Joe let me pass without my ID.
Upstairs, the bullpen was oddly empty.
I went to my desk, located the file, sat, and opened it.
Amid the papers and pictures the DOJ had collected, I found it: a picture of
Vince at dinner with Barb. The picture was annotated with her name, Barbara
DeBecki, and also showed another girl whose name wasn't known. I noted that
the second woman was as pretty as Barb, before realizing how fucking jealous
my thoughts were. This was completely unprofessional.
I found another photo of him and Barb alone at dinner, interspersed with
pictures of him and the woman I now recognized as Staci Baxter.
Banging another girl at the same time as he'd had a *Sports Illustrated* swimsuit
model for a girlfriend? He was seriously fucked up. And threesomes?
Liz came around the corner from the bathrooms. "Hey, what are you doing in
here?"
"Afternoon off."
"I wish I got afternoons off, or evenings, for that matter."
I controlled my sneer. "It's just today."
My phone vibrated with a text message.

VINCE: Miss you

I ignored the text and the quizzical look I got from Liz.
She lifted a hefty file from her desk. "You can help me with this one in your
spare time." She set it in front of me. "I've got three others ahead of it."
I closed the Benson file. I would have complained, except I welcomed some-
thing to occupy me other than obsessing over Vince and his women friends.
What was I supposed to do with this information?

I took a deep breath and opened the tall file. It was a smuggling case running through Logan Airport. The transfer agent was suspected, but he dealt with multiple local companies, and finding the single end destination here was going to mean going through a ton of paperwork. A mind-numbing ton of paperwork —exactly what would force Vince out of my brain.

Another text arrived.

VINCE: Miss you Kitten

I turned my phone off. I didn't need any more of these messages.

By the end of the day, many of the agents had returned, and a few had left for the day.

Then I found it.

Gainsboro was one of the companies whose paperwork was included as suspect in Liz's smuggling case. This might give me leverage to investigate Vince's enemy.

I closed the file. "Liz, I'll work on this one in my spare time."

"Thanks."

I put the Benson file away, hefted the large smuggling file, and left the building.

I hailed an Uber to get me home.

The traffic was stop and go. I glanced out the window at the bus stop billboard. It advertised an exhibit at the Boston Museum of Fine Arts, and the image brought back memories of my evening at the Met with Vince.

My chest tightened. I closed my eyes and was transported back. I bit my lip. How could I have doubts about the man who had arranged such a magical evening for me? It was so much more than an elegant dinner. It had been special —he'd treated me as special—much more than special. I needed to listen to what he wanted to say about Barbara and whatever his dating life had been before me. I owed him that.

I'd had a completely petty reaction to the text messages. I needed to grow up. My fingernails dug into my leg. I was such an idiot.

# CHAPTER 39

*VINCENT*

THE TEXT ARRIVED BEFORE ONE O'CLOCK.

ASHLEY: Have errands to run won't be back in this afternoon

I called, but she didn't pick up.

I called Ben. "I'm not making any progress on this video here at the office. Can you set me up at the condo so I can go over it in the evenings?"

"Sure, we can do that, or I can have one of the guys screen it for you."

"No thanks. I got this. The condo would be better."

He agreed to bring it over this evening.

I went for a late-afternoon treadmill session downstairs and headed home early.

I hadn't heard from Ashley since the message after lunch, so I sent a text.

ME: Miss you

I checked my phone several times, but there was always the same blank screen. Willing it to show a message from her didn't work.

Ben arrived at my place shortly after I did. He must have instructed the lobby guy at Covington to tell him when I left so he could synchronize his visit. It didn't take him long to set everything up and be on his way. By eight o'clock, I'd gone through several more days of video without finding evidence of the mole removing the malware. But it had to be here, so I kept at it.

After ordering Chinese, I started back on the mind-numbing surveillance video.

The doorbell rang a half hour later.

I paused the video.

The tired-looking delivery guy got a twenty for a tip, which immediately improved his mood.

Opening the paper cartons filled the kitchen with mouth-watering aromas. I dispensed with my usual insistence on eating Chinese with chopsticks and started the video chewing my first forkful of kung pao chicken. The smell of the food got Rufus's attention, and I dropped some chicken on the floor for him before getting back to the video.

I texted Ashley again.

ME: Miss you Kitten

An hour later, I saw a girl enter my office.

My heart raced; I had her.

My first piece of good news.

Mike's assistant, Sophia, was at my desk. I couldn't make out what she did, but she'd definitely been in there alone.

Stopping and reversing, I played it over three times to be sure. She hadn't touched my computer, but she'd been right in front of it.

This wasn't quite good enough—not yet. I noted the time-stamp to be able to get back here.

I started the video again.

Ten minutes later, the doorbell rang.

~

ASHLEY

VINCE OPENED THE DOOR. BLOODSHOT EYES GREETED ME.

I pulled at the hem of my shirt. "I know I'm not supposed to be here."

"Nonsense."

Rufus came out to greet me and sniff my crotch.

I pushed the rude dog's nose aside.

"He has good taste," Vince said, opening the door wider.

I smirked and entered.

Once Vince closed the door, I wrapped my arms around him and buried my face in his shoulder.

His arms enveloped me, and he kissed the top of my head.

I waited for him to say something, but he didn't. We just rocked in each other's arms.

I looked up. "I want to use one of my favors."

He rubbed my back. "Name it."

"I want you to forgive me for acting like a bitch."

He loosened his grip and pulled my chin up with a finger. His eyes held mine with warmth and intensity. "No need. It's my fault. It's…never mind." He kissed my forehead. "Suffice it to say, I was a different person before you came back into my life, and I couldn't be more grateful for the changes you've led me to make. I could never be upset with you, Kitten." He released me.

Rufus sat expectantly in front of us.

Vince pulled a small chew from the bowl on the front table and threw it for him.

The dog chased it and carried the prize back to his bed.

Vince walked toward the kitchen. "Want a cider?"

I followed him. "Sure." I stopped at the table where he had video paused on a laptop. "Going through surveillance?"

"Yes," he called from the refrigerator. He pulled out two bottles and opened them.

"This looks like your office." It could get bad if he had Liz or me on tape.

"It is. Ben just put it in recently. I'm trying to find out who put that malware on my computer."

I steadied myself against the chair. "Find anything yet?" I mentally crossed my fingers that he hadn't found me at his computer deleting Liz's keylogger or rummaging through his office.

He brought the bottles over and handed me one. "Just one thing. I'll show you." He sat down and scrolled to a time-stamp he had written on a pad next to the laptop.

I stood behind him, watching the screen.

*This had better not be me.*

"Here." He started the video at normal speed. "Sophia went into my office here. She goes to the desk and messes around, but she doesn't touch the computer."

I saw something more than he did. Sophia lifted the blotter and looked underneath. She had checked for the planted memo. Now I had an opening.

He stopped it after she left the room. "So this doesn't say it was her that put on the keylogger, because she didn't touch my computer. But she had no reason to be in my office, so it's suspicious at least. I have a lot more to go through."

I couldn't tell him it proved Sophia was the mole, but it gave me an idea for tomorrow.

I rubbed his shoulders. "You're tight."

"Ooh, that feels good." He stretched.

A fear came over me. "Hey, are we on here?"

"Huh?"

"Page sixty-eight?"

"You want to watch it?"

I slapped his shoulder. "Get real. I just don't want it getting out on the internet."

He laughed. "I was kidding. I already deleted that day. Now, I need to get back to this."

That was the last thing I wanted. "Can't we just relax and watch a movie tonight?" I couldn't have him see me at his computer on that video.

He closed the laptop. "Sure, anything you want." He got up and led me to the couch. "Does the lady have a request?" He picked up the remote and took a seat.

I sat next to him and leaned in to snuggle. "Can we watch *Music and Lyrics* again?"

I'd liked the movie, but mostly I wanted to find a way back into a good place with my man.

"Coming right up." He worked the remote, and the movie began.

After about ten minutes, he asked, "Do you want to know about Barb?"

"No." I sighed.

I'd decided to be an adult about it, and what I didn't know couldn't hurt me, right? What he'd done before was ancient history, water under the bridge and all that. Only a middle-schooler would obsess over it.

His fingers traced lazy circles on my upper arm. Every once in a while, he'd squeeze me tighter for a moment.

I reveled in the safe warmth of his arm around me. It felt so natural to be leaning into him—my warm little cocoon of safety.

When I couldn't hold it in any longer, I asked, "Were you really going to see her Saturday?" Not all my worries had melted away.

His hand moved to scratch my head. "Of course not."

"But she said—"

"She was angry and trying to push your buttons."

I settled in for a second. "And you don't expect me to do a threesome?"

He laughed. "Of course not. I would never share you with anyone else, Kitten."

"And the other?" I couldn't bring myself to say the word *anal*.

"Not unless you're asking me to."

I snorted and shook my head.

There had to be a reason Barb was angry. I dreaded the answer, but it would eat at me if I didn't ask. "Did you care for her?"

He paused the movie and pushed me to sit up. He held my gaze and took my hand. "She was a girl I went out with, but it never progressed to the *friend* part of girlfriend. I'm not seeing her again. You're my woman—end of story. Can we drop her and focus on us?" His eyes conveyed even more conviction than his words.

I closed my eyes and nodded.

He took my face in his hands and pulled me closer for the lightest of kisses. "I told you she didn't matter. I trust you, and you should trust me." He brushed my nose with his.

"I do." I was his Kitten again.

He restarted the movie, I snuggled back into my cozy spot, my worries finally put to rest.

When the movie finished, I was even more teary-eyed than the first time. The hero had written a song just for the girl, and when she heard it, her heart melted. She learned he wasn't guilty of what she had imagined, and they were happy together. Just like me and Vince.

∾

*ASHLEY*

THE NEXT DAY, VINCE WAS OFF-SITE VISITING A CUSTOMER AND AFTER THAT WAS scheduled to spend the afternoon with his swim coach, working on his technique for the triathlon.

I needed him here to execute my plan, and I was getting antsy about the timing.

He returned to the office around five.

I closed the door behind me and found him standing by the window, looking out quietly. I rounded the desk to come up behind him.

"What do you see?" I asked.

"It's what I don't see yet: him."

"Who?"

"The asshole that's messing with me. He's out there somewhere."

"You'll figure it out."

He sighed. "Just don't know if it'll be in time."

I turned toward the desk. "So, Sophia was messing around at your desk..."

He turned back toward the desk as well. "But she didn't touch my computer."

I lifted up the blotter. "Didn't she... Oh my God." I lifted the blotter farther, and the planted memo showed itself. "Look."

Vince grabbed the paper before I could stop him. He started reading.

I watched helplessly as he added his fingerprints to the page.

I also grasped the corner of the paper. "What does it say?"

"This is exactly what that FBI ass was asking me about." He gave me the paper.

I took it, adding multiple sets of my prints to the sheet, and read. I couldn't let his prints be the only ones on the paper. I rubbed where I thought he'd grabbed it.

"That fucking bitch." He started for the door.

"Vince. Stop."

He did, and turned to me.

I lifted the corner of the blotter. "Did the video show her placing it here, or just looking?"

"Just lifting the blotter edge," he replied.

"Then you need to go farther back and find when she put it here, or see if there's a second person involved."

His brows knit. "A second?"

"It's possible."

"You're probably right. I'll start tonight."

"Can I help?"

"No. This is something I have to do alone."

# CHAPTER 40

*VINCENT*

I SWATTED THE ANNOYING ALARM AT FIVE O'CLOCK THE NEXT MORNING. LAST NIGHT I'd gotten tired after a few hours of the video search, and I'd set the alarm to get an early start on finishing today. This would be the day to confront Sophia, and possibly another, if Ashley was right.

After hours of video watching, the doorbell rang with my lunch delivery.

The pizza box warmed my hands as I juggled it and tipped the delivery guy.

Back at the screen, I punched go and pulled a steamy slice from the box.

*Oh so good.*

I loved the fare at Vitaliano's, but sometimes I needed the simple pleasure of finger food instead of elegant dining. For me it was a bit like getting back to my roots, when our ancestors had huddled around the fire and eaten with their fingers—not that they had Papa Luigi's, of course. But still, it held a visceral appeal for me.

I was focused on the screen when I pulled at the third slice to get it loose. The stringy cheese didn't want to release its grip on the rest of the pizza. Another yank, and instead of coming free, the whole box slid to the edge and over, off the table.

*Splat.*

Face down.

"Fuck," I yelled at the disobedient box.

*Just my fucking luck.*

I hadn't let go of the piece I was pulling loose, so I still had that, but the rest of my lunch, and tonight's dinner, was a goner.

I plopped the remaining slice on a napkin and went to retrieve a roll of paper towels from the kitchen.

When I returned Rufus had already nosed at the box and was scarfing down a piece of my intended lunch.

"Get out of there," I yelled as I shooed him away. "You know that's going to make you fart all day."

He didn't care, and I couldn't blame him. Ultimate Pepperoni was the best.

After cleaning up the mess, I returned to the table and my video hunt.

It was still running, and the door had just closed as I sat.

*Double fuck.*

That was a close one. One second longer cleaning pizza grease off the floor, and I might have missed it entirely.

Someone had just gone in and out of the office on the screen. Turning back the video, I reset it an amount I thought was far enough and watched again.

Sophia.

She entered, went to my desk, and slipped something under the blotter.

I slowed it down and watched two more times.

No doubt about it. I couldn't prove it was the same memo, but she'd definitely put a paper under my blotter.

I noted the time stamp and circled it.

Checking my watch, I dialed Ben.

"What's up, boss?" he asked.

"I found what I needed on the video."

"And who is it?"

"Sophia."

He laughed. "Really? I wouldn't have guessed she'd have the guts for it."

"I need you to put a tail on her night and day. Bug her phone—whatever you can. I need to know who she's working for."

"Sure, boss. Between my people and outside resources I can rustle up, we'll put a tight blanket on her. She won't be able to fart without us knowing."

"Let me know as soon as we find anything."

"You got it."

I finally had a string to pull to unravel the mystery of who was calling the shots.

~

ASHLEY

MY PHONE BEEPED A REMINDER AT ME.

*Shit.*

I had a check-in meeting with Liz scheduled, and I didn't feel like it. Besides, John was due back next week, and if I delayed, he would be my contact again. I pulled out my phone and composed a text message to her.

ME: Can't make meeting

I sent it.

Moments later, my phone rang. Checking the screen, I read, *Nurse Parsons*, my coded contact for Liz.

I ducked into the conference room to take the call. I answered the phone. "Yes?"

"Can't cancel. We need to talk," Liz said at a whisper.

This was a complete breach of protocol for the operation. "Why?"

"Big problem," she said softly.

"Explain."

"The op is not what it seems."

I knew the op wasn't what it seemed, but how did she know? More importantly, *what* did she know?

"How so?" I asked.

"Not over the phone."

That couldn't mean anything good.

"I can't make it," I told her.

"Alt three at two."

"Alt two is next on the rotation," I reminded her.

"Alt three, two sharp." She wasn't taking no for an answer.

"Alt three at two," I repeated.

"Be careful...very careful," she said before the line went dead.

Liz wasn't the most experienced agent, but she wasn't one to get rattled easily either, yet that's how her voice sounded today.

My stomach lurched. I shivered and stared at my phone. The call had taken less than thirty seconds, but already it had worsened my mood.

The call everyone dreaded during an undercover assignment was one telling us to get the hell out of Dodge, because our cover was blown and the bad guys could come for us at any moment. This call felt only one notch short of that.

She hadn't told me to abort; that would've been a fake phone call pretending to order pizza with extra anchovies. Telling me there was a problem just opened up nervousness on my end, without any resolution.

She'd insisted on alternate location three, the most desolate and out-of-the-way of our prearranged meeting spots. It was a small, empty warehouse that had given me the creeps when John and I had scoped it out.

Being abandoned, the building didn't have anybody around to observe us, but it also didn't have any utilities. The inside was dank, filthy, and dark, and that was before adding in the rats or the smell from the occasional homeless person using it as his personal outhouse.

I put away my phone, asked Anita to tell Vince I had an errand that could take a while, and left. There was nothing to be done until the meeting, and worrying wasn't going to get me anything more than heartburn.

～

I'd been walking in the general direction of the meeting for some time now.

Checking my watch, I realized I wasn't going to make it in time on foot, so I pulled out my phone again. I called up the Lyft app and put in an address about ten blocks from the warehouse. Proper protocol wouldn't allow a ride any closer than that. An electronic trail was bad operating procedure.

A few minutes later, a small yellow Hyundai pulled up, and I climbed into the backseat.

The driver tried to engage me in conversation, but I wasn't having any of it.

I wasn't about to break protocol any further or leave any inadvertent evidence about myself behind. Liz had said to be careful, so I would be.

To avoid panicking, I replayed the night at the Met in my head, and my hand went to the necklace again. How many girls got to experience a night like that? The man of their dreams takes them to the biggest museum in the country, arranges a candlelight dinner surrounded by priceless paintings, and then has a rock band serenade her? He'd remembered my favorite dessert, kept a photo of us from high school in his wallet all this time, and presented me with a necklace he'd bought years ago just for me.

Vince was a keeper if ever there was one. He was no longer the boy who'd left me abruptly in high school.

The third time the driver looked back toward me to start a conversation, he rear-ended the Chevy in front of him.

It was only a gentle bump, but I didn't bother telling the fucking idiot it was his fault.

He got out, and a shouting match between the two drivers ensued. Entertaining on any other day, but I was already running late—and so much for remaining inconspicuous.

It took ten minutes of cell phone pictures, pointing, yelling, and more yelling, before my driver slipped the other man some cash and we were on our way again.

*Boston drivers.*

The ride across the river to the warehouse district continued slowly in traffic, but he finally let me out at my chosen destination.

I punched up the app and gave him a two-star review, with no tip.

I started a fast walk toward the meeting place. Two blocks later, with the building numbers increasing, I realized my mistake. I'd gotten my directions mixed up and started walking the wrong direction.

Reversing course, I hustled as best I could in these shoes. It was already after two o'clock. I needed to know what had Liz so worried. None of this was like her at all.

My phone rang again as I neared the final turn. It was her.

"I'm almost there," I told her.

"Hurry. This will take a while to explain."

Her comment didn't make any sense. If she was out here to have a meeting with me, she could take as much time away from the office as she needed.

"Be there in a minute."

"I'm in the back," she said.

"Got it." I hung up the phone and made a left turn onto the street. The alt three building was just ahead.

A flash of light.

The noise was deafening.

An explosion blew out the front of the warehouse.

The brutal shockwave threw me back against the brick building on my side of the street.

Pain radiated through me as my head hit the wall, and a choking dust cloud rushed to envelop me.

I coughed, fell to the ground, and coughed some more.

The world went dark.

# CHAPTER 41

*Vincent*

Once back in the office, I went to do battle with the evil coffee machine.

Anita informed me that Ashley had gone to run an errand.

The cup started to fill, and my phone rang with Ashley's smiling face on the screen. It was a cute shot I'd taken of her over dinner.

"Kitten," I said as soon as I answered the call.

"Sir." A woman's voice came through the phone, but it wasn't Ashley. "Do you know an Ashley Newton?"

I felt stupid for the way I'd answered the phone, but I'd never heard a dumber question.

"Yes, who is this?"

"There's been an accident…"

The words stopped my heart. My chest tightened.

"I'm calling from Boston EMS because your number was in her phone as the last call received. Are you a relative, or do you know how I could reach one?"

"Yes, I am," I said without thinking. I couldn't have this woman hang up on me. "What kind of accident? Is she okay? Where is she?"

My mind was going a mile a minute with bad possibilities. I got up and grabbed my coat on the way to the door.

"Slow down, sir, please, and listen. She was near the site of an explosion on Burntwood Avenue. We've just brought her to Memorial Hospital, and she's being admitted now."

"Explosion? I don't understand." I pressed the down button on the elevator.

"Sir, I'm with the ambulance division. I don't know any more than that."

The elevator door opened. "Can I talk to her?" I frantically pushed the lobby button.

"She wasn't conscious when we brought her in, but her vitals are good."

"What's wrong with her?" I asked as the floors dinged by on the downward journey.

"You'll have to discuss that with the hospital staff."

"Thanks," I said, exiting the elevator and sprinting for the street.

I flagged down the first cab I found and told him to hot-foot it to the hospital. In the afternoon traffic, that didn't amount to much faster than if I'd jogged.

The ride to my Kitten was interminable as questions ran through my head. Why would Ashley go anywhere near Burntwood, and why would there be an explosion? And most importantly, how badly was she hurt?

When I reached the hospital, I couldn't get the attention of anybody who knew anything other than that she'd been admitted and was in the hospital computer.

I dialed Ryan Westerly. Ryan worked at Chameleon Therapeutics, one of my neighbor Liam Quigley's personal investments, and from our previous meetings, I knew his position gave him serious pull with this hospital.

"Ryan, I need your help. A friend of mine was in an accident and brought to the hospital, but I can't get answers out of anybody here," I told him after he picked up.

"A friend?"

"My girlfriend, actually."

"Where are you now?" he asked.

"The waiting room in Emergency."

"Vincent, wait there. If somebody doesn't find you in five minutes, call me back."

I thanked him and paced outside the waiting room, unable to sit still.

It took less than two minutes for a doctor to enter the small room and call my name. His name tag read Dr. Kulkarni.

"What's the name of the patient?" Kulkarni asked.

I followed him to the desk. "Ashley Newton."

He double checked the computer. "She regained consciousness here in Radiology, and she's about to be scanned. You can see her after we evaluate the results."

"What results?"

"In head trauma cases like hers where the patient has lost consciousness, a CT scan is called for. Just wait here, and I'll find you when they've completed her scan."

The words *head trauma* and *CT scan* made me shiver.

∼

"One, two, three," the nurse said as she and two others shifted me off the table and onto a rolling hospital bed.

My shoulder hurt with the movement, but not as much as my head.

They placed several blankets over me and pushed me out into and then down the hall.

I focused on the two IV bags suspended on a pole above me. *Drip, drip, drip.* Liz's time was fading away with each drip.

"FBI," I said to the nearest nurse. "You have to call the FBI."

"You have to get better first," he responded. "You can give your statement to the police when you feel better."

They maneuvered me into an elevator, and the door closed.

I squinted to read his nametag. "Nelson, I'm FBI. Call them now, or I'll come back here and shoot you."

He laughed. "Miss, you've had a pretty bad bump to the head. Last week we had the pope in here."

His joke garnered laughs from the other two nurses.

The elevator door opened after a moment. I grabbed his arm. The pull of the IV in my wrist hurt like hell.

"I'm not kidding," I hissed.

"Okay, already. I'll get the floor officer to your room right away."

They wheeled me around a corner and into a room.

After a minute of hooking me up to beeping instruments, I was alone, and cold.

But Nelson had gotten the message, and after a moment a Boston PD uniform entered my room.

"I understand you want to make a statement." He flipped open his note pad.

"My name is Ashley Newton. I'm a special agent with the FBI."

He cocked his head. "Sure. You have identification?"

I was wearing a hospital gown under this blanket. "No. Not on me."

"Right," he said as he closed his notebook.

"There was another agent in the building that blew up. You need to call the FBI field office in Chelsea right now."

"I'll talk to my sergeant about it."

I fixed him with my best evil glare. "If you don't call them this moment, so help me God I'll get you charged with a four-oh-seven," I hissed. "Failure to render aid to a federal officer in distress. That's good for ten to twenty. Your choice, officer..." I read his nametag. "Davenport."

The blood drained from his face, and he quickly keyed his radio. "Dispatch, place a call to the FBI field office. We have one of their agents down here at

Memorial, a victim in that gas explosion in the warehouse district, and there might be another agent still in the structure."

"Good choice," I told him as he left.

I'd made up the law that he had to help me or go to prison. There was no four-oh-seven, but it seemed like the kind of bluff that would get him off his ass.

Only minutes later, the cop was back at the door with SAC White.

White pressed his finger into Davenport's chest. "And I want a guard on this room twenty-four-seven, is that understood? Nobody comes in except doctors and nurses."

Davenport got back on his radio.

White came in and closed the door.

I lifted up a bit to speak. "Liz?"

"She's downstairs in surgery now. It's serious. That's all we know."

I sighed and relaxed into the mattress. She'd made it out.

"The cops on the scene called us when they found her creds while clearing the building."

I nodded.

"She was lucky," he said. "It looks like she took a cigarette break out back and wasn't inside when it blew."

I'd always been telling her the smokes would kill her, but instead a cigarette had saved her life.

"Gas explosion?" I asked.

"That's for the media. The gas to the building was off. This was a bomb." White paced. "And I'm going to get the bastard, so help me God."

"Who?"

"Benson, of course. Who else would have motive to attack you?" White apparently thought I was the target.

"It couldn't be him."

"Bullshit," he shot back. "Of course it's him. Attempted murder of a federal agent, for God's sake. That bastard is mine."

"I need to see her." It was Vince's voice, outside the room, arguing with the cop.

"You can't. FBI only," the cop yelled.

White opened the door and fell back as Vince shoved his way in.

Davenport grabbed Vince and pulled him back into the hallway.

White rushed out. "You're under arrest, Benson, for assault on a federal officer."

Vince got shoved against the wall, and I heard the click of the cuffs as they went on.

"It's not him," I yelled through the open door.

"Close that door," White ordered the cop, and I couldn't hear any more after that.

I yanked the leads off my chest and finger and rolled off the bed. Pushing through the pain, I dragged the IV pole behind me, opened the door, and yelled after White, who was leading my man away. "It's not him."

"I got this, Newton," White called back.

For the briefest second, I caught the pain in Vince's eyes as he looked back before White shoved him forward again.

The cop blocked my path. He and Nelson, the nurse, directed me back into my room and into bed again.

"You're a pain in the ass. You know that, agent?" Davenport said.

"Special agent," I shot back.

My side and hip hurt from the exertion, but not half as much as the pain of seeing Vince led away in cuffs.

At least Nelson called a female nurse in to reattach the leads to my chest.

# CHAPTER 42

*Vincent*

"*It's not him,*" Ashley had yelled, but the FBI asshole was having none of it.

After listening to a recitation of my rights, I was smart enough to not say a thing.

"FBI only," the cop had said.

"Assault on a federal officer," the FBI agent had said—the same fucker who'd accused me of working with the mob. He'd known Ashley's name, and been in her room.

FBI Agent Ashley Newton? It didn't make sense, but I didn't dare open my mouth.

I sat in the backseat as White and two other angry feds drove me away.

They took me through booking and told me I'd be arraigned on eighteen US code one-eleven, assault on a federal officer. The surprise came when I was informed it was three counts: one for shoving White's dumb ass, and two others.

At least I knew Ashley wasn't hurt that badly. She'd been able to make it to the hallway to yell out my innocence.

I was supposed to get to make a call, but that didn't happen right away.

Eventually, I got the phone call and chose my boss's brother and my neighbor, Liam Quigley. I considered calling in the big guns and dialing my father, but rejected it. This wasn't going to stay hidden from him, but right now I didn't need a lecture.

Liam answered, "Vincent, good to hear from you."

That opinion was about to change.

"Liam, I need your help. I've been arrested and booked, and they won't be letting me out tonight."

He morphed instantly into the get-it-done manager I knew him to be. "Don't say anything to them at all. Not a solitary word. I'll handle all the legal arrangements. Where are they holding you?"

"Suffolk County Jail," I responded.

"On what charge?"

"Assaulting a federal officer. But—"

He cut me off. "Don't say anything over this line, not a word. I'll arrange a lawyer."

"Thanks, Liam."

"It's what we do for family, and with the help your dad gave us, you Bensons are just like family."

I knew what family meant to them, and to us.

I hung up and was called in for questioning not long after.

It was that FBI douche White and the other agent who had visited my office, Dunbar.

"Why did you do it?"

"When did you pick the location?"

"When did you meet Ashley Newton?"

"Why did you go to the hospital?"

"How did you know Elizabeth Parsons?"

"Why target those two agents?"

The question about two agents raised a question for me, but I vowed to not say a word and kept my curiosity in check.

"When did you plant the bomb?"

"How did you detonate the bomb?"

"What did you do today?"

"What was your schedule today?"

"When did you get up today?"

"When did you get to work today?"

"When did you leave work today?"

"How long had you known Agent Newton was undercover?"

I controlled my reaction to the gut punch that question delivered. I looked down at the table and asked for water, which they denied. I asked again, churning the question over and over in my head.

How had I been so gullible? Ashley had lied to me. She was working for the FBI and trying to uncover some crime I didn't commit, all while claiming to love me. Mason's distrust of women suddenly looked prophetic. I'd let my cock override my intellect and hadn't questioned her arriving back in my life at the exact same time as that fucking note.

This had to confirm that Gainsboro had fed the FBI made-up dirt on me. That made sense. The bombing was another attempt to frame me. But why?

Semaphore was already theirs for the taking.

In the end, the interrogating officers got no information from me, but I got a few tidbits from them.

The other agent at the bombing was named Elizabeth Parsons.

And they'd confirmed that the Ashley I thought I knew now was not the Ashley I'd known back in high school. That sweet girl would never have done this to me. The woman she'd grown into had the morals of a pit viper.

Two guards led me to a holding cell after being told I was a high-priority prisoner. At least that got me my own bunk instead of sharing—who knows what kind of scum was also locked up here tonight.

I lay back on the hard bunk and thought long and hard about the day.

My enemy had tried to do one of two things, I decided. He was trying to frame me for the attack, which was the most likely with what little I knew. Or, he knew how I felt about Ashley and was attacking me by going after her.

That second one hurt the most, because it meant I might be the cause of Ashley and the other agent being hurt. It meant that if I hadn't hired her, none of this would have happened.

In here, I was completely cut off. I couldn't find out how Ashley was doing or demand to know how she rationalized what she'd done to me.

The questions haunted me all night.

Who could be framing me? And how could I have been so gullible with Ashley, the one woman I thought I could trust?

∼

ASHLEY

BY THE TIME DINNER ARRIVED, I'D ALREADY TRIED TO CHECK MYSELF OUT AND HAD been stopped by Officer Davenport at the door.

He seemed to relish the idea of keeping me restricted to my room—payback of sorts.

I finished what little I cared for of the hospital's offerings: meatloaf with the texture of cardboard and a taste to match, with a side of overdone green beans. Naturally, dessert was Jell-O.

The door opened, and SAC White let himself in with a folder and notepad in hand.

"Newton, how are you feeling?"

I doubted he really cared. "Fine. I'm ready to get out of here."

"Yeah. I hate hospitals too."

"Then tell little Napoleon at the door to let me by."

"He's there for your protection."

I noticed his shirtsleeve rolled up and a bandage on his arm. "What happened to you?"

He held up the injured arm. "Argument with a dog." He opened his notepad. "Let's go over a few things."

It was clear he was here for a debriefing rather than to see how I was doing. "First, how's Liz?" I asked.

His countenance clouded over. "She's alive, thanks to that cigarette break."

That sounded ominous.

Pain shot through my hip as I shifted up in bed.

"The doctors tell me the surgery went well. But…" He hesitated. "They've put her in an induced coma. She has some bleeding and maybe swelling of the brain, and they say that's the best way to safeguard her for now. We'll know more in a few days."

I felt a chill merely thinking about what she was going through.

"Her log shows the meeting was a scheduled check-in. Is that right?"

"Yes."

"Why that location?"

"It was one of the alternates, and Liz picked it."

He knew our procedure was to change up meeting locations.

"You didn't pick it?"

"No, she did."

He continued with a series of questions about my and Vince's whereabouts during the day.

I was sick of it. "He doesn't have a motive."

A grin appeared on White's face. "That's where you're wrong, Newton. We executed a search warrant at the office and his residence." He held up his bandaged arm again. "That's where I got this. Damned dog."

"What?" I felt like congratulating Rufus, but held my tongue.

He pulled the evidence bag out of the folder he'd carried in. "We found this. A memo that ties him to Sonny Alfonso—the one you couldn't locate. Two hundred million worth of ties."

I did my best to school my face and not give away the disappointment I felt.

"The DOJ's source was dead on. He had a deal with Alfonso involving a gaming equipment company. This gives him motive. He had to know you were close, and he tried to close the investigation on his terms. And no way are we letting this fucker get away with attacking the Bureau. We'll put him away forever."

I nodded, saying nothing. Answering White's questions had brought the biggest problem into focus for me: only an insider could have known when and where Liz and I were meeting. There was a mole at the Bureau, and a dangerous one. I needed to get the fuck out of here. The regs wouldn't let me work the case, at least not overtly, but I'd damn well work it from the fringes.

# CHAPTER 43

*ASHLEY*

WHITE HAD GONE, AND THEY'D CLEARED THE DELECTABLE DINNER OFFERING, WHEN the room phone next to my bed rang.

I answered it.

"Ashley, I know it's a dumb question, but how are you?" It was my partner, John.

"Okay, considering. I got my bell rung pretty good, but I'll be okay. However, I've got Boston PD posted at my door, and I can't even get to the Coke machine. I'm more worried about Liz."

"She's tough. She'll be okay. She's stable for now."

"How do you know that?" I asked.

"When one of our own is targeted, everybody in the Bureau knows everything."

I guess I shouldn't have been surprised. The only one who wasn't being kept in the loop was me. "I need your help on this. Any way you can get back here?"

"I already requested that, but Randy shot it down."

"That sucks. Well, with or without you, I'm on this as soon as I get out of here."

"You know they won't let you work your own case."

I knew all too well what the regs said, but I was not going to take a simple no.

"And anyway, you may not have much to do," John continued. "The scuttlebutt is they've already collared Benson for this."

"They've got the wrong guy."

"How can you know that?"

"Trust me, I just do. This wasn't him. The story's a lot bigger than it looks."

"Enlighten me."

I delayed for a second, considering my options. I decided I couldn't handle this on my own, and John was probably the one person in the Bureau I could trust to help me. "Do you have some time to talk?"

"For you, I've got all night, partner."

I started with today. "Liz insisted on this meeting. She had something to tell me about the op that had really upset her. She said things weren't at all what they seemed."

"And what does that mean?" he asked.

"Sensitive enough that she refused to discuss it on the phone."

"That's not good."

"It gets more complicated. Before that, White had called me into his office to give me specific instructions on finding a particular one-page document linking Benson and the mob."

"That paper you sent me to have the lab check?"

"The one and only, but there's more."

"Go on," he urged.

"When I met with White, I had just searched the office and found the exact document he was talking about. One problem though, it's a fake. It was planted in the office, and I was sent in to find it with more specific information than we've ever gotten from a source."

"You're sure it was a fake?" It was the obvious question.

"I'm sure," I said. "You saw it—there were no prints on it. How do you load an old-fashioned typewriter without touching the paper, much less sign the damned thing?"

I didn't have enough proof, but I believed Vince, and that made me sure enough.

"Did you tell the SAC you thought it was a fake?" John asked.

I put my career in John's hands with my next statement. "I didn't even tell him I'd found it."

The other end of the line was silent for a few moments as John processed what I'd said. "You better damn well be sure."

"I am," I responded, more with hope than knowledge. "I was sent in there as a tool to frame Vince."

"You know what you're saying?" he asked.

"Yeah. Somebody's dirty. I just have to figure out who."

"And you think Liz figured this out?"

"I don't know, but that's my working theory tonight."

John let out a long breath. "Are you saying the bomb was also an inside job?"

I swallowed hard. "That's what I'm saying. Only somebody with access to Liz's logs could have known the time and location of our meeting."

"And there's no way Benson could have known?"

I felt insulted, but I knew he didn't mean it that way. "*I* didn't even know until just before the meeting. Liz set the location. There was no way for him to know. The only person who knew both the time and location was Liz, or somebody in the office with access to her log file."

Laying out the evidence like this gave me a shiver. Before today, I would have trusted any one of my fellow agents with my life. Now, that wasn't a luxury I could afford.

"Then you better find out what it is Liz found."

"I know. But first I have to get the hell out of here."

"Any candidates come to mind?" he asked.

My answer wasn't going to please him. "The SAC had access to her log—"

He cut me off. "It can't be Randy. He's as straight as they come."

I continued. "He also was in here this evening asking odd questions. And he's the one that arrested Benson this afternoon. Now, how often have you heard of an arrest happening within an hour of the explosion? Before we even have forensics?"

He was silent.

"It's not conclusive, but you have to admit it looks odd," I said.

"Just like you insist it's not Benson, I'm convinced it's not Randy. I know the guy."

"Fair enough. But you're the one who asked if I had a thought."

"Better find another one quick. Accusing the SAC isn't something you can take back," he said. "I'll be up as soon as I can, and we can find the real perp."

I said goodbye, put the phone down, and settled back into my bed. The problem seemed intractable.

When Vince had first shown me a picture of the threatening note Staci got, I'd taken it for a joke, or a prank. The fake memo had upped my impression of his opponent, but today's events showed me I'd still underestimated whoever it was. Someone dangerous was playing for keeps. This was no street punk or pissed-off boyfriend. Bombings were rare—less than one a year on average—so this was a serious player. He was not going to be easy to track down. But the FBI specialized in the difficult.

When I closed my eyes, I couldn't get the vision of Vince handcuffed out of my head. What must he think of me? I hoped fervently that he had faith in me, as I had no idea what this must look like to him now.

As I tried to sleep, memories of him kept intruding. He couldn't be behind this; that was the one solid truth my heart knew.

# CHAPTER 44

*VINCENT*

THE NOISE STARTLED ME, AND I JERKED UPRIGHT. I MUST'VE FINALLY FALLEN ASLEEP IN the cold cell. The guard rapped his baton on the bars again to rouse me. I went to check my watch, but it wasn't on my wrist.

"Breakfast time," he said as he slid a tray through the slot.

I stumbled to the bars and grabbed it from him. The oatmeal was only lukewarm, but that didn't stop me from spooning it down. The long interrogation last night had meant no dinner. My stomach was ready for anything, even jail food.

I smeared jam on the two pieces of toast. A carton of orange juice wet my parched throat, and I followed it with part of the milk. I'd been afraid to drink from the faucet in the sink last night.

The guard arrived to unlock my cell door before I'd finished the second piece of toast.

"You've got an appointment," he told me.

I put the breakfast tray aside, and he led me down the hall to an interview room similar to the one I'd been in last night. This room smelled of vomit, though. It was empty, save a table and two chairs. I checked to see if one of them had better padding than the other—no such luck. I took a seat and waited.

The door opened and the guard escorted in a suited man with an ID badge hanging around his neck.

I recognized the name as soon as I read it.

"So we meet again, Mr. Benson," he said.

Assistant United States Attorney Kirk Willey was the walking definition of arrogance. He and I had only met once before, and it hadn't been under the best of circumstances. Liam and I had threatened to derail his campaign for attorney general of the Commonwealth—and it had worked.

I didn't stand, and neither of us offered the other a hand.

He took a seat and placed a voice recorder on the table, turning it on. "AUSA Willey interview of suspect Vincent Benson at seven-twenty AM. Please state your name for the record," he said.

"Vincent Benson."

His eyes were cold as ice.

He pulled out a plastic envelope with a piece of paper enclosed and pushed it my way. "Care to explain this?"

I silently read the paper. It was the fake contract Ashley and I had found. It purported to be an agreement between me and Sonny Alfonso arranging to sell him a stake in Semaphore for two hundred million dollars.

Willey smiled as I looked up. "We found this in your office, under the blotter on your desk. I've got you now on racketeering."

I kept quiet.

"Why did you attempt to kill two federal agents yesterday?"

I was done. "I have nothing to say without my lawyer present."

He leaned forward and spoke into the voice recorder. "Interview terminated at the request of the suspect." He clicked off the voice recorder.

I waited for him to say something or leave, but for the longest time he did neither. He just stared at me.

"It was a bad move on your part to threaten me last year."

I didn't respond. He was obviously trying to goad me into saying something.

"You probably thought I'd forget. I don't forget things like that, and I don't forgive. Your money can't save you now. I've got you, and all the years you spend in prison, you're going to regret ever having met me."

I held his stare and returned it in equal measure. One thing my father taught me: never flinch in the face of a bully. And Willey was a skunk in a suit, a bully with a capital B.

He stood to leave, done with me for today, apparently. He knocked on the door for the guard to let him out.

"Good talk," he said as he exited.

It *had* been a good talk. It told me what I needed to know about Gainsboro. They were playing for more than control of Semaphore. They were after me.

Willey departed, and all I had left were questions for Ashley. Why? Why had she lied to me? Why had she worked with them against me?

❧

ASHLEY

. . .

I WOKE THE NEXT MORNING STILL IN MY HOSPITAL BED. I WASN'T CUFFED TO THE BED railing, but it felt like it. I hadn't slept well. The triple problem of worrying about Liz and Vince at the same time as figuring out my plan of investigation had kept me up.

A nurse brought breakfast for me.

I shifted up in the bed as she rolled the table over with the tray. I winced at the soreness of my hip and shoulder. At least the pain told me I was alive; that was the good news.

Breakfast looked only slightly more appetizing than dinner last night: oatmeal and apple juice. But even this horrible hospital food was probably a step up from what Vince was enduring this morning.

"Any way I can get eggs and hash browns with this?" I asked.

"This is good for you. I can get you cream of wheat instead, if you like."

I interpreted her comment as a firm no. I likely hadn't been the first to complain about the food.

The doctor came around after I'd finished, and the exam began. The checking of my bandages, the stethoscope to the chest, the pen light in the eyes, and the balance test were followed by his version of twenty questions.

No, I wasn't nauseous. No, I didn't have a headache except when I touched the massive bump on my noggin. No, I wasn't dizzy, no, I didn't have blurry vision, and yes, I remembered the event and everything leading up to it clearly.

He said he wanted me to stay another day for observation, gave me a warning to take it easy, and told me to call a nurse if I developed any of the symptoms he'd asked me about.

Nurse Nelson from yesterday showed up five minutes later to check my vitals.

I wasn't staying. "I'm ready to leave. The doc says I'm good to go, but I didn't see my clothes in the closet."

"They took your clothes as evidence," he said.

"Figures."

"I apologize for doubting you yesterday. It's just—"

I raised a hand to cut him off. "No biggie. I get it."

He moved to the door. "Let me get you something to wear."

My clothes were probably a loss anyway, ripped, bloodied, and soiled from the blast.

He returned a few minutes later with blue hospital scrubs and a pair of tennis shoes. "Will a size nine and half work? I borrowed these from Susie."

"Thanks. Close enough." I accepted the shoes and clothes.

He left, giving me privacy to dress.

I winced as I sat to pull on the pair of men's cotton briefs he'd supplied—they were better than nothing—followed by the scrub pants. There wasn't a bra in the pile.

"Back up, sir. Nobody is allowed in this room." Davenport's voice came from outside my door.

"I'm FBI, son. Stand aside before I charge you with obstruction," John's welcome voice sounded from the hallway.

I pulled on the top just before John opened the door.

"Morning, Newton," he announced.

I cinched up the drawstring on the pants and prepared to reclaim my life. "Doc says I'm fine. Let's go."

He closed the door behind him. "First, I know everybody's asking, but how are you?"

"Pretty sore, but good enough to get the hell out of here." I grimaced as I leaned over to pull on the shoes. "Last night you said you weren't coming."

"No, last night I said Randy wouldn't pull me back. But as soon as I told the SAC in New Haven you were my partner, he couldn't release me fast enough. So here I am."

I pulled on the second shoe and tightened it up. "I'm glad you came."

Now it was two of us against the system.

"Have you thought about a plan?" John asked as he opened the door for my escape.

"First stop, my place for some clothes," I told him.

Davenport stopped us. "She can't leave. Orders."

John's hand moved to the butt of his gun. "You're relieved of responsibility for her, son. The FBI has her now."

John didn't lose stare-downs like this, and after a few seconds, the cop relented.

We started down the hallway as the poor officer got on his radio to tell dispatch overwhelming force had arrived to spring me from lockup.

Our first stop was the ICU, where John's badge got us entrance.

Another Boston cop was stationed outside Liz's room. His badge read *O'Mara*.

We introduced ourselves. After hearing John's last name was McNally, the two Irishmen bonded, and we were allowed in to see her.

I moved around the bed and gently took the hand that wasn't hooked to an IV. "Liz, I'm here with John. We're going to find the bastard who did this."

I didn't expect her to respond, but I hoped her subconscious could hear us. A bandage worthy of the movies covered most of her head, and a tube ran from under it to a bloody collection bag hanging below the bed.

We spent a few minutes telling her to be strong, that John and I were on the case, and that the bastard would pay. Then reluctantly, I let go of her hand and we left. As annoying as she had sometimes been, she was a fellow agent above all else, and John was right, an attack on one of us was an attack on all.

"She certainly got hit worse than you," John observed on the way out.

"They told me she only survived because she'd snuck out back for a smoke."

John cocked his head. "And to think I always told her the smokes would kill her."

I nodded. I'd already had the same thought.

~

LIAM HAD ARRANGED FOR MY LAWYER.

David Perlman seemed like a nice enough guy when I met him this morning a few minutes before entering the courtroom.

"What is Ashley's condition?" I asked him.

He ignored the question and gave me simple instructions at the door. "The purpose of this hearing is to enter your not-guilty plea and to set bail, nothing more. Don't say anything at all in there, except if the judge asks you if the plea is correct. And if you answer the judge, don't forget to address him as *your honor*. No matter what, don't allow the prosecutor to push your buttons. That can only hurt us with the judge."

I nodded. "Okay."

Liam and Ryan Westerly were both in the public section of the courtroom when Perlman and I entered.

I exchanged nods with them.

At nine o'clock sharp, the court was called into session, and my case was first on the docket.

Perlman slid over the charging paperwork. It said I had assaulted a federal officer during the performance of his duties while investigating a bombing targeting federal agents.

I turned to the second page, which contained pictures of the blast site and the two agents. One was a federal ID picture of Ashley.

The second was Jacinda. She'd been an FBI plant as well, and Ashley had lied to me again about her being only an acquaintance.

Kirk Willey himself was at the prosecutor's table. His summary of the charges against me made me sound worse than Al Capone, and possibly worse than Osama bin Laden. According to him, I'd personally attacked the entire country by conspiring with organized crime, yada yada, yada, racketeering and conspiracy were the charges, along with one of assaulting a federal officer. And he intended to add the attempted murder of two federal agents.

The judge lost patience and cut him off mid-sentence. "We're only here to discuss today's charges. I'm sure you're aware of that, Mr. Willey."

Perlman entered my not-guilty plea and pointed out that I was a respected member of the community with no prior record. He started to go on, but the judge cut him off as well.

216

"What bail is the government proposing?" the judge asked Willey.

"One hundred million," he said coldly. "The crimes are serious. The defendant is a man of means and poses a significant flight risk."

Perlman objected to the amount, pointing out that there was no evidence tying me to any crime and suggested no bail.

"Bail is set at twenty million," the judge said. He didn't rap the gavel as they did on TV.

I let out the breath I'd been holding. That amount I could handle.

Willey stood. "Your honor, because of the obvious flight risk the defendant poses, we would ask that electronic monitoring be included."

Perlman complained that I wasn't a flight risk in the least, but the judge wasn't swayed.

"Electronic monitoring is ordered. The defendant will be confined to his residence." Then he rapped his gavel. "Next case."

I was led out the way I had come in and returned to the deputies. The whole event was over in minutes.

Once out of the courtroom, Perlman and I were escorted to the small conference room.

"I need to know how Ashley is," I told my lawyer.

Once the door had closed, he opened his mouth.

"Mr. Benson, have a seat. The first rule is we don't talk except in private. Do you understand?"

"Got it." I sat, and so did he.

"Who is Ashley?" he asked.

"Ashley Newton is my girlfriend and was injured in the explosion. She was taken to Memorial yesterday. They arrested me before I could see her."

"You must be confused, Mr. Benson. The only injuries were to two FBI agents."

"That's right, and she was one of them."

His brow creased. "You mean to tell me your girlfriend is one of the FBI agents?"

"I didn't know that until yesterday, but yes. Exactly."

He steepled his hands before going on.

"I'll check in with the hospital, but this presents a problem. You mustn't have any contact with her. She's on the prosecution's team and most certainly a witness. The court won't allow it, and her bosses at the Bureau won't allow her to have contact with a defendant. It's out of the question."

He paused for a moment. "Now, about bail," he said.

"If you call Mason Parker at Covington Industries, he can raise it."

"No need. Mr. Quigley told me last night that anything up to twenty-five million, he would take care of."

With Liam, at least I had one person on my side in this town.

Perlman rose and handed me his card. "We'll talk later. The deputies will take you back to the jail until bail is arranged. And one more thing."

I waited.

"The ankle monitor is not a joke. You mess with it, and bail is revoked. You'll end up back in lockup until the trial. You go outside of the radius you're allowed, and the same thing happens. There are no second chances. None."

∿

ASHLEY

John drove me home to pick up clothes, my weapon, and my credentials.

I added Liz's smuggling case file to the pile I carried out.

"Which safe house you figure is best?" I asked after locking up.

"Neither. If somebody on the inside is involved, those will be compromised. You're going to stay with Ivy."

I'd met his sister once, and the prospect of a day with her didn't excite me. "I'd rather stay with you."

"Too obvious. Don't worry, you two will get along just fine."

"Yeah. She's dangerous, but I'm armed."

He laughed. "She's not that bad."

"I need to call Vince," I blurted.

John pulled the car to the side of the road and stopped. "Vince, huh? I warned you about going under with someone you had a history with. Talking to him is the one thing you can't do. I'll pass a message to him that you're worried and explain that you can't contact him, and that's the best we can do."

On the way to Ivy's, John made several changes of direction and reversals. In the end, we were fairly confident no one was tailing us as he drove south.

"She takes some getting used to," John said.

This was obviously his attempt to prepare me to meet Ivy again.

I'd thought she was pretty out there when I'd met her at John's barbecue, but that was after at least three beers more than she should have had.

She and her boyfriend had been in the pool doing chicken fights with Liz and her boyfriend. And Ivy had had the bright idea to pull at the bow holding Liz's top up. It only took another minute before Liz retaliated and they were both topless. Of course all the guys were having a great time, and I got several invitations to form a team and join the pool shenanigans. But I worked with those guys, and no way was I losing my top.

John called ahead. "Ivy, I need your help. My partner needs a place to crash for a while... Yeah, we just got her out of the hospital... Thanks, sis."

After a while, John turned left and pulled up in front of a little green house.

This was so different from where I lived. A wide, tree-lined street with plenty of space to park and cute houses with well-kept front yards—unlike the hardscrabble apartment buildings in my section of town.

Ivy opened the door as we approached the porch and greeted John with a hug, followed by me.

"It's going to be nice to have a girl around here to talk to," she noted as we moved inside with my luggage. One of her arms had an ivy vine tattooed on it.

"Yeah," I replied, although I felt less than enthusiastic about adding girl talk to my agenda.

Her tight tank top read *Polite as Fuck* in giant black letters on the light blue fabric—not something I would be caught wearing.

She saw me staring. "Never mind the shirt; it's work clothes."

"Work?"

"I tend bar, and a few things make for better tips: strong drinks, a low-cut top, and something that gets them to stare. After you catch them, they feel obligated to tip well."

This lady had a smart business head on her shoulders.

"Oh, and the third thing, walk with a bounce in your step, if you know what I mean."

I knew the boob-jiggle walk well.

John shook his head. "And she gave up acting classes to do this."

"It pays better," Ivy countered.

"I'll be on your case, and I'll let you know what we find. Remember, you can only work this from the fringes. Randy won't let you in on it." John excused himself toward the door. "Keep her safe, Ivy. I have to get back to work."

"She's the one with the gun," Ivy said.

After John left, Ivy showed me to her spare room. "It's not much."

"It'll be fine, thanks. I don't need much space."

"I need to go to work. You want to come along? We could talk," she suggested.

"No, thanks. I think I'll rest."

"We can talk when I get back, then."

I wasn't really in the mood. "I might just go to bed early."

She pointed a finger at me. "Look, girl, I read people for a living. You almost got your ass blowed up. You need to talk; I can tell."

"Maybe so," I admitted.

After she left, I dialed my sister. She was the one I needed to talk to.

There was no answer.

I was alone.

# CHAPTER 45

*ASHLEY*

THAT AFTERNOON, I LAY ON THE COUCH IN IVY'S HOUSE WILLING THE PAIN IN MY shoulder to recede—it wasn't working. Thirst forced me to get up to find another bottled water.

My hand went instinctively to the gun on my hip with the sound of a key turning in the deadbolt. I resisted the urge to draw.

Ivy came through the door, shopping bags in her arms. She kicked the door closed behind her.

"I appreciate you being protective of my house, but if you draw your gun on me, we're going to have a problem."

I pulled my hand away. "Sorry, just a habit."

She dropped the subject. "Want to help with dinner?"

"Sure," I said, coming over and taking one of the bags from her. "What's on the menu?"

"You heard of three-alarm chili? Well, tonight were makin' my six-alarm chili. Helps you to forget all your troubles. After a dozen bites, you can't think about anything except dunking your head in a bucket of ice water." She laughed.

It sounded like just the ticket. "Game on, then."

We unloaded the bags together, and she started to grill the ground beef while I chopped celery.

Ivy looked away from the skillet for a moment. "Tell me about it."

"What?"

She waved her spatula in my direction. "Girl, I'm a bartender. You got that face, like you're struggling with a decision and you gotta talk about it."

"Shows, huh? It's my boyfriend." Just saying I had a boyfriend calmed me.

She went back to stirring the meat. "I'm listening."

"Did you hear about the blast out in the warehouse district?"

"John told me about it. He said you were outside, and I'm guessing that's what those are about," she said, pointing to the butterfly bandages on my face. She stopped stirring. "Gas explosion, the news said, but John told me the truth. Oh, and we'll need that red onion chopped up in a sec, to go in with the meat."

"Sure." I put the celery to the side to peel and chop the red onion. "You want the white too?"

"You can do that next. The white goes in with the beans. Only the red one sautés with the meat."

I followed her instructions. "Yeah, it was a bomb, and another agent got hurt. Worse than me."

She turned around. "Like a take-you-out kinda bomb?"

I shrugged. "Liz, that's the other agent, and I were supposed to meet there. I was running late. Otherwise…" I could feel the bile rise in my throat just thinking of what would have happened if my Lyft driver hadn't gotten in that accident. If I ever got that driver again, he was getting a monster tip. Exchanging gunfire was one thing, because you could take cover, you could shoot back, but a bomb, you were helpless, completely at the mercy of the bomber.

"That's serious shit."

I didn't answer. Instead I opened the two cans of white kidney beans she'd put on the counter.

"Do you know who did it?"

I added the cans of beans to the red ones already in the pot. "Not yet. That's the scary part."

She sighed. "So that's why you're hiding out here." She stirred the pan. "And John doesn't know either?"

"Not a clue, at least not yet."

After the beef and onion had browned, she poured them into the pot.

"Now six strips of bacon, if you please."

I located the bacon in the fridge, and the strips sizzled as they hit the hot pan.

"What's this have to do with your boyfriend?" she asked.

Red, green, and yellow peppers were next on the cutting board. "I need to talk to him, but the Bureau won't allow it."

"They can't tell you that shit."

The bacon aroma filling the kitchen had my mouth watering. "They can, and they have. I'm a witness against him in a case we're working."

Ivy pushed the bacon around. "You're in the FBI and you want a criminal as a boyfriend? You got a few screws loose, if you ask me."

I slid the chopped peppers into the pot. "That's the thing; he's being framed."

"One bunch of cilantro as well when you're done with the carrots," she said.

Her chili certainly had a lot more ingredients than mine, which was mostly chicken, tomato sauce, kidney beans, and spices.

"And you can prove that?"

I started on the carrots. "Not yet, and not being able to talk to him makes it harder."

She turned the bacon. "Then talk to him. It's the right thing to do."

"I can't."

"You mean won't," she shot back.

"The rules are pretty clear." I appreciated her argument, but the rules were unambiguous. "Your brother's going to get him a message from me."

After the bacon crisped up, I chopped it while Ivy added so many spices, I couldn't keep track.

When she got to the chili powder, she spooned it rather than shaking it in. This was going to be as hot as advertised. "I say you should still talk to him."

I stirred the concoction while she tasted and added even more spices to the aromatic pot.

"After three bites of this, all your cares will melt away. I guarantee it," she said.

I kept stirring, hoping she was right. I could use a carefree evening. Even the preparation had taken my mind off the soreness of my shoulder and hip. My head only hurt when I touched it, but the bruises constantly reminded me of their presence. I put the wooden spoon down and retrieved some Advil from my purse. It had been four hours, and I was allowed another dose.

"Still hurts?" she asked, spying the pills in my hand.

"Yeah," I admitted.

"Then I've got just the thing for you," she said. She moved quickly to open a cabinet full of liquor. She poured from various bottles before adding ice and handing it to me.

"And this is?" I asked.

"A zombie, pretty much the strongest mixed drink on the menu. Guaranteed to take the edge off." She pulled a beer out of the fridge for herself.

I sipped the drink and could instantly tell she wasn't joking about its potency. I took a slug to swallow my Advil, then sipped some more.

She put a lid on the pot and turned down the stove. "Let's give dinner a while to simmer."

We parked our butts on the couch, and I could feel the drink getting to me, just a little.

"The right thing to do is talk to him," she said, without prompting.

I'd been considering it all day, but recoiled at the implications of breaking this rule. If I got caught, it could be bad for Vince as well. Asshole that he was, White would probably try to add witness tampering to the charges.

"I told you, I can't get approval."

"I didn't say ask. Just do it. Don't tell your boss—what he doesn't know won't hurt him. It's like stopping at a red light in the middle of the night. You go through it when nobody's around. No harm, no foul."

I slurped another sip of the zombie.

She lifted her beer bottle. "Your choice, but I think you sometimes gotta bend the rules to do what's right. And not talking to your man? That's not right. Now you're breaking the girlfriend rules." She knocked back a slug.

I pondered her argument over the remainder of my drink.

"Just do it so you don't get caught," she said.

I didn't know if it was her encouragement, or the effects of the zombie, but I picked up my burner phone and closed myself in her guest room.

Five minutes later, I'd made a call and gotten an agreement to help me with my plan. I returned to the couch.

"Chili's ready, if you're up to the challenge," Ivy called from the kitchen.

I felt the drink's effect as I stood. I brought my glass and deposited it in the sink. "I think I'll stick to beer for the rest of the night."

"Good choice. Two of those will put you on your butt faster than you can spell Massachusetts."

I changed my mind and poured myself a water from the fridge while she ladled the chili into bowls.

She carried them to the table. "First one to finish wins. You up for this?"

"Like I said, game on."

～

## Vincent

It had taken three hours to be escorted from the county lockup back to my Tremont Street condo with the uncomfortable electronic monitor fastened around my ankle.

Rufus was even more excited than usual to see me and got a quick breakfast.

My condo was now my cage, but at least the fridge held beer.

After a beer, I found my checkbook and a pen. That Willey guy was such an asshole. He'd demanded an ankle monitor like I was a common criminal. I didn't have the federal government behind me, but I did have a checkbook, and he'd pissed me off. A one-million-dollar check made out to his opponent's campaign committee in the election for attorney general was a terrific way to retaliate. Fuck you, Kirk Willey. It might not be the best idea I'd had, but it made me feel better to strike a blow against the arrogant ass.

*Let's see how a little payback feels, you asshole.*

It felt so good, I decided I might write an additional check to start off each day for a while.

"Rufus, what do you think? Should I write another check every day for a week?"

Rufus lumbered over to me, tail wagging.

"I'll take that as a yes." I threw him a chew.

Rufus's ears perked up when my phone rang. The caller ID showed a blocked number. I ignored it, but it rang again and I answered, ready for another annoying marketing call.

"Mr. Benson, I'm calling for Ashley. If you are not alone, hang up and I'll call back later." The words were ominous.

"I'm alone."

"Please listen. My name is John McNally. I'm Ashley Newton's partner at the Bureau."

"How is she?"

"She'll be fine—a little banged up right now, but nothing that won't heal."

"Thank God. They wouldn't let me see her."

"I know. She wanted to know how you are. The problem is that Bureau regulations will not allow her to have any contact with you until this matter is resolved."

The "matter" was obviously the trumped-up charges the FBI had leveled against me.

"I'm okay." I didn't add how pissed I was that she'd lied to me.

"She and I are going to be working from this end to untangle this mess."

He made it sound like we were mopping up a kitchen spill instead of dealing with potential prison time for crimes I hadn't committed.

"I have to go now. And, another thing…"

"Yeah?"

"We never had this conversation." He hung up.

Rufus looked over at me.

"Sorry, boy. I'm not allowed to take you for a walk." It sucked that I couldn't even go across the street with my dog.

I sat down to wallow a bit in my feelings of betrayal. I'd so wanted to believe Ashley was the one, but she'd proved I didn't know her after all. I'd trusted her, I'd cared, I'd thought she cared, but she'd lied to me and been a part of the setup the whole time. None of it made any sense.

I kicked the other chair.

*Fuck.*

How could I have been so blind?

I retrieved my phone, wandered out to the patio, closed the door, and dialed Ben.

"How you doin', boss?" Ben asked.

"I've been better. What do we have on Sophia so far?"

"Nothing yet."

It was time to let the dogs loose. "We can't afford to wait any longer. I want you to interview her. Scare the living crap out of her. Tell her we've got her on tape and get a confession. That's what I need. And I want it right away, before this thing gets any more out of hand."

"No problem, between me and Mickie, we got scary down to an art," he said.

Mickie was three hundred pounds minimum, and with the tats that showed above his collar, he would be scary reciting a nursery rhyme.

"I want to know who put her up to it," I added. "Most of all, I want proof that the memo's a fake, a plant."

"Got it. I'll call you when it's done."

"Thanks, Ben."

I hung up, wishing I could be a fly on the wall when he and Mickie confronted her.

I wandered the rooftop patio, circling the perimeter like a caged animal.

Rufus gave up after a few laps and lay down, watching me wear out my shoes.

How I could have been so stupid as to believe Ashley cared after all these years. She hadn't tried a single time to contact me since that day we'd parted ways—not even a Christmas card, just complete radio silence. That wasn't the behavior of a woman who'd been pining over me for nine years.

I'd bypassed my own procedures, hiring her without a background check. Her beautiful green eyes had short-circuited my brain and blinded me to the fact that after nine long years, I couldn't possibly know who she'd grown up to be.

The next minute, the thought of those gorgeous eyes and the way the necklace I'd given her matched them brought me back to our weekend in the Big Apple. Nothing had ever brought me more joy than the feel of her in my arms and the look on her face as we danced to our song in the museum. It had been the first weekend since I started at Covington that I hadn't done one iota of work. And I hadn't even wanted to while I was by her side.

She'd looked equally happy. How could that have been an act? Was anyone that good an actress? I could normally spot a bullshitter in seconds, and I'd gotten none of the warning signs with her, not a one. Every feeling of love I gave her, she returned in kind. Her eyes couldn't lie that well. I couldn't lie that well— I'd fallen for her, and she for me.

My feelings ping-ponged from one extreme to the other every few laps of my personal prison exercise yard. The only truth that remained was that she'd lied to me, and since I hadn't detected it, I had no idea how I could trust anything she said in the future. She'd been working against me, hadn't she? For the very FBI that was complicit in this scheme of Gainsboro's to take me down.

As evening came, I went inside and powered on the TV. Scrolling through the options, I decided to watch her favorite, *Castle*.

I was less than ten minutes in when the doorbell rang.

Opening the door, I found Amy, Liam's wife. She held a package.

I opened the door wider. "Amy, come on in. How are you?"

She entered and didn't utter a word until I'd closed the door. "Just fine, Vincent, thank you," she said, putting a finger to her lips. "I'd love a glass of water and some fresh air." She pointed at the door leading to my patio overlooking the Common.

"Sure, one glass of water coming up. Still or sparkling?"

"Sparkling, if you have it."

I poured us each a glass of Pellegrino.

She opened the door to the patio, and I followed, closing the door behind us. She accepted the glass, but didn't speak until we reached the edge, overlooking Tremont Street below. "This is for you, from Ashley," she said in hushed tones.

I took the package she offered, unclear about her odd statement.

"How is she?" I asked.

I couldn't trust Ashley, but I could still care about her.

"Okay. A bump on the head and scratches and bruises. Mostly she's scared for you and also herself after the bombing, but she can tell you that." She tapped the padded envelope. "That's what this is for."

I tore open the package and carefully removed a flip phone, a charger, and a slip of paper with a phone number on it.

A smile came to my lips. "A Batphone?"

Amy put a warm hand on mine. "She said not to answer it in the condo, or when anyone else is around."

"Got it. No eavesdroppers." I hadn't considered that they might be bugging my condo, but it was the government, and there wasn't much I would put past the fucking FBI at this point.

"She said she'll call when she can and that it might not be right away." She took a swig of her water and leaned over the railing. "Also, Liam said to remind you that of course whatever help we can provide, we will."

"Thanks. You've been a great help already."

She appraised me with caring eyes. "I can't imagine how hard it is."

I shook my head. "I'll survive." I decided against telling her anything about the Gainsboro asshole after me.

Amy left after finishing her water, and I was alone again.

Even if Ashley called, how could she explain herself?

After pulling another water from the fridge, I opened my wallet, took out the photo from behind my license, and asked out loud how she could have done this to me. The photo landed on the kitchen counter.

I knew Ashley was all right, and for the moment, that's what mattered. I shifted my focus from her to my foe. I needed to locate the mole.

I put the water to my lips and tried to piece together all that I knew about the problem.

LATER IN THE EVENING, I CLOSED THE DOOR TO THE GUEST ROOM AND PICKED UP ONE of my burners. I called the number of the phone Amy had told me she'd bought for him.

"How are you?" Vince asked.

Just the sound of his voice eased my pain.

"I'll heal, but it's you I'm worried about."

"How is Elizabeth?"

His mention of Liz surprised me, though it probably shouldn't have. "She's not out of the woods yet, but we think she'll be okay."

"That's good. I didn't do this. I want you to know that."

How could he think I suspected him? "Of course not. I know that."

He took a long breath. "Ashley, how could you?"

His question hit hard. It was so open-ended, and his reversion to my name was a bad sign.

I only had one place to begin. "It started as my job."

"Your job is to lie to people and pretend to care about them?"

"I wasn't pretending. I love you, Vince."

It was the first time I'd uttered the words to him, but they were true, if only he could believe me.

"Sure. I can't believe a single thing out of your mouth. Everything you told me about yourself was a lie. Your entire job is lying."

I pleaded with him, "I'm serious, Vince."

"Serious and truthful are two different things. You should learn that."

"But I mean it."

"Just like when you told me Jacinda was an acquaintance?"

His accusation stopped me cold. I'd been caught in another lie.

"Goodbye, Ashley. At least I can be honest when I say I'm glad you're okay."

"But..."

He had already hung up.

I redialed.

He didn't answer, and he didn't pick up when I tried again either.

I turned off the phone.

# CHAPTER 46

*ASHLEY*

THE NEXT MORNING, I WOKE TO THE QUACKING OF MY PHONE'S ALARM.

Stretching the directions on Advil usage and adding a bottle of beer had allowed some sleep, but my Vince problem kept intruding.

My biggest failure was that I hadn't leveled with Vince on my terms, when I could have explained how I was bending the rules to help him, not hurt him. I'd meant to tell him at dinner, then at lunch.

*If only I had.*

How could I repair his trust in me? Only one possible path remained: find his enemy. It damned well wasn't Sophia. This was beyond her. She was a pawn doing someone else's bidding.

And I had a second task as well. I had to find whoever had attacked Liz and me, because it damned well wasn't Vince. Liz had wanted to warn me about something, and I had to find out what.

After a sponge bath and dry shampoo, I ventured out to find Ivy cooking a delicious-smelling breakfast.

"Sleep okay?" she asked as she turned. Her shirt today read *Drink the Fuck Up*, probably another crowd pleaser at work.

"A little. Thanks." I put a pod in the coffee maker and pressed the button.

"Did you call him?"

I nodded.

"And?"

"It didn't go well. He's mad I lied to him."

"Wouldn't you be if the roles were reversed?"

"I guess."

She pulled out a frying pan. "We got sausage and eggs, or we have leftover chili, if you want that."

I opted for eggs.

"Chicken," she chided me.

She'd won the chili contest last night by a mile.

After breakfast, John arrived right on time and drove me to get my car after I insisted I was well enough to drive myself to work.

I didn't dare tell him I'd ignored his advice and called Vince. It risked putting him in danger as an accessory. After I started my car, he followed me all the way to Quincy.

I stopped off downstairs at logistics to get a new smartphone to replace the one White had locked away as evidence—no telling when I would get that back.

Upstairs, the bullpen seemed familiar, yet oddly foreign. I'd only set foot in the field office twice since this episode had started, and somehow the Covington offices seemed more like home to me.

It took almost an hour for the well-wishers to disperse after I finished assuring everyone I was ready to get back to work. It was Liz we all needed to worry about. I called the hospital, reached the ICU desk, and after getting the initial runaround, asked to talk to Officer O'Mara. He quickly told the nurses to add me to the list of people they could release details to. Before me, the list had only included the SAC and Liz's partner, Frank.

The update itself was anticlimactic: no change. But that was a good thing, and the tube in her skull continued to drain properly, keeping the pressure at bay. The nurse told me that was the doctor's chief concern.

I thanked her and promised to call in regularly.

White appeared mid-morning, bitching about having to drive downtown first thing to meet with the DOJ at the courthouse. The man hated rush-hour traffic.

"Newton, my office," he said with his usual charm.

I followed him and shut the door before taking a seat.

"Shouldn't you still be in the hospital?" he asked.

I sat up. I wasn't going to let him intimidate me. "I'm a little sore, but I'm ready for duty. And I owe it to Liz to find out who did this."

He waved his hand. "You're a victim. You can't be involved." He'd clearly shut the door on any way for me to join the investigation. "Besides, you know the drill. You're on a desk until the Bureau doc clears you for field duty."

"I could help Frank with Liz's workload while she's still laid up."

"Yeah, whatever. That probably makes sense."

He didn't realize he'd just given me the opening to work the case from the inside. Hopefully I could locate what it was Liz had wanted to tell me.

"Yes, sir. I'll book an appointment with the doc."

"Besides, we need you to help nail this Benson bastard. Like I said before, this is a top priority, so what do you have on him that we can add to the file?"

"I can't think of anything right now."

"Does he beat his wife?"

"He's not married," I said flatly.

"Well then, does he beat his girlfriend? Take some time and write down what you know. You've been there a while. There's gotta be some dirt you've seen or heard. The lawyers will want whatever you've got. These scumbags always have skeletons hiding somewhere."

"I understand."

I knew what he wanted, but I didn't like the way it smelled. This is not what we did.

He turned to look at his computer monitor, his habit for nonverbally telling us the meeting was over.

I rose.

"Newton," he said, before I escaped.

"Yes, sir?"

"Dirt on this guy, that's what we need."

"Understood." I closed the door behind me, locking the pig in his pen.

The exercise was obviously biased. Thinking back, I couldn't come up with a single other case where the request had been made, an order given to find dirt on a suspect unrelated to the crime we were referring for prosecution. That practice had gone out with J. Edgar Hoover.

*This officially stinks.*

WHEN I CHECKED IN WITH FRANK, LIZ'S PARTNER, I HELD UP THE SMUGGLING CASE file I'd brought from home. "Mind if I work on this at Liz's desk?"

"Be my guest."

It took a few minutes to organize a bit of open space in the heap of papers Liz called her desk. I opened the folder and went through the motions, reviewing what had already been checked on and figuring out what was left to do. She'd been right that this case was a lot of boring paperwork.

I kept busy until lunchtime, when pretty much the entire gang decided to head out for pizza.

"You coming, Newton?" Frank asked.

I patted my stomach. "No, thanks. Something they gave me at the hospital seems to have interfered with my digestion. Next time, though."

He didn't argue, probably happy to not sit next to somebody farting all afternoon.

I took my mug to the coffee room, filled it, and returned, double checking that our floor of the office was empty for a while.

One by one, I opened the drawers to Liz's desk and started my search. It wasn't likely that I would find anything, but I had to be methodical about this. I wouldn't get very many opportunities to rummage through her desk. In the bottom drawer, I found three envelopes. They were addressed to the Inspector General—none sealed.

The only other thing of interest I found was her handheld voice recorder.

I checked it for recent recordings and found only two. After listening to them both, I deemed them unrelated and put the recorder back where I'd found it. My watch told me I still had plenty of time before the group returned, but the hairs on the back of my neck were standing up with an uneasy feeling. Closing the center drawer, I had the odd feeling I'd missed something obvious.

I reopened the drawer and reviewed the items one by one. That's when I realized the silver pen was not what it seemed to be. Liz had been into buying Bond-like gadgets off the internet, and this was a pen with a built-in voice recorder she'd shown me once. I placed it in my purse to check later. I'd have to research how to access it on the internet back at Ivy's.

I turned on her computer, which is when I hit the roadblock. I knew Liz had started with her badge number as her password, but when I tried that, it didn't work. Now it was going to be a matter of guessing.

I tried the standard things like her birthday, her sister's name, her favorite rock band.

I tried a few more combinations, and to my surprise, 'Garfield' opened the computer. Who names a cat Garfield anyway? A quick review of the file structure didn't show anything that leaped out at me. I started a search for files that had been created or modified in the last few days.

The sound of the elevator door opening almost tripped my heart. I killed the search window, started the shut down, and turned off the monitor. I was back to reviewing the paperwork on Liz's boring smuggling case by the time they rounded the corner into the bullpen.

It was two agents I didn't recognize.

"Where is everybody?" the tall one asked.

"They went out to get pizza."

"Pizza sounds good," the short one said.

Based on their accents, they must've been on loan from the New York office.

"Any idea where they went?" the tall one asked.

"They didn't say exactly, but Pizza Hut is the usual destination." I tried not to sound as nervous as I felt.

"Sounds like a good plan to me," the short one said. "You want us to bring anything back?"

I touched my stomach again. "No thanks. Stomach issues today."

After dropping off backpacks in the conference room they disappeared around the corner, and after a moment I heard the sound of the elevator door closing.

I was alone again.

It took another minute before my heartbeat returned to normal. Trying to go through Liz's things while people were at lunch wasn't a winning plan. Coming back late at night after everybody had gone made a lot more sense. Checking her computer was not going to be a five-minute task.

I resigned myself to spending the afternoon working through Liz's boring folder of paperwork. The idea of making an appointment with the Bureau doctor was looking better by the minute. I looked up the number and called. A time slot was available tomorrow morning, and I took it.

After a half hour I couldn't keep my curiosity at bay and looked inside the first of the three mysterious envelopes addressed to the Inspector General. It was a sexual harassment complaint against the SAC from before he was promoted—the weekend in New Hampshire. The other two were similar, but with different events and later dates.

Now I saw the connection: Instead of offering herself to White to get the good assignments and preference for the California promotion, Liz had been holding this over him.

The envelopes went back in the drawer, and I sat back. I didn't know whether to be proud of Liz for resisting him, or pissed that she hadn't filed them, because White deserved to be investigated. I settled on both.

By the end of the day, I hadn't found anything that gave me a hint of what Liz had wanted to talk about, unless it was the three envelopes.

John had been out in the field all day with Frank on the bombing, and he hadn't returned by the time I was ready to call it quits.

# CHAPTER 47

*ASHLEY*

I OPENED THE DOOR TO IVY'S HOUSE AND WAS ONCE AGAIN GREETED WITH DELICIOUS aromas emanating from the kitchen. "Smells wonderful. What's cooking?"

"Chicken scaloppini with hot dogs on the side."

It was the wackiest menu I'd ever heard of. "Hot dogs? What's with that?"

"I figured since you're flunking girlfriend one-oh-one, we should go back to basics and practice sucking the wiener."

I laughed. "I don't need a lesson, thank you very much."

Maybe I did, but I planned on having my man teach me. I dumped my purse on the front table and headed to the kitchen. I didn't see a hot dog anywhere.

"Ha ha."

"Just thought I'd offer, if you need a few pointers."

I ignored her and went to the guest room to change. Was I really flunking as a girlfriend? The thought hurt. I was protecting him.

When I returned, Ivy was serving dinner. That's when I noticed the small letters on her tank top that I'd missed earlier. It read *Learn speed-reading, dumbshit. You're staring too long.*

As we ate, she asked how work had gone, and I had to explain how boring my paperwork day had been. I didn't recount the scary episode of almost getting caught searching Liz's desk. My poking around needed to stay between John and me.

Ivy seemed actually interested in my musings and asked probing questions for an outsider to our investigations. It was no wonder she earned good tips as a bartender; she had a knack for making people feel listened to.

Mentally I shifted Ivy from the weird-keep-at-a-distance column to the interesting-friend column. Being sassy was just her style. Her poking at me about my relationship with Vince had been her way of helping, while keeping it light. I had to remember that through the ages, barkeeps had been the first psychologists, parceling out advice over mugs of ale or shots of whiskey. She would make a fun drinking buddy when I had the time.

"I make a wicked martini," she offered.

"Not tonight, thanks." I had to keep a clear head for work tonight.

"A zombie, then?"

I shook my head. "Double no on the zombie."

"Lightweight," she said. After a moment she added, "Go ahead, make the call."

"What?" I asked feigning ignorance.

"Your boyfriend, of course. I know you're dying to talk to him. At least I would be if I was in your position."

I leveled with her. "He won't talk to me. Because I lied to him."

"He wanted to know if you were okay?"

"Sure, but—"

"No buts. That's a man who still cares for you deep down. Sure he's pissed and he's hurt. But that's not a man who hates you."

I thought through her logic, and liked it. "Thanks."

"But you still got a ton of groveling to do, girl. And that's something you gotta do in person."

That deflated me, but a spark of hope was better than none at all.

We ate for a few minutes, and Ivy suddenly asked, "When are you going to sneak over there and see him?"

I didn't know how to respond. "I can't," I said. "The rules don't allow it."

"I say your rules suck," she said between bites.

"I agree, but that doesn't change 'em."

She took another gulp of beer. "You suck at the girlfriend thing."

"He won't even take my calls." My words were more polite than my attitude. If I hadn't been a guest here, I would have told her to fuck off.

She pointed her fork at me. "No offense, but if he were my boyfriend, I'd be there to support him, no matter what. But that's just me, what do I know?"

Her words slammed into me. How was I being a bad girlfriend by protecting him from another possible criminal charge? I stuffed a forkful of chicken in my mouth to keep from saying anything I would regret.

The more I thought through her words, the worse I felt. I was caught between two impossible choices, and she was right. I didn't know how to do this girlfriend thing. I had to figure out how to regain his trust.

"You said he was training for a triathlon?" she asked, changing the subject.

I nodded with my mouth full, and mumbled, "Mm-hmm."

She lifted a folded shirt from the chair next to her and handed it to me. "For when you decide to go over."

I put down my fork and unfolded the tank top. It read *I don't do triathlons. I do a triathlete.* I laughed. "I like it."

"For when you go over," she repeated.

She'd said *when*, and not *if*.

After dinner, it took me a few minutes of internet searching to find the online user manual for Liz's audio recording pen. I took off the cap to locate the micro-USB connector to download it.

Before I could hook it up, my phone rang. The number was the Covington offices.

"Hello?"

"Agent Newton, this is Ben Murdoch, head of security at Covington. Are you alone, and do you have a moment?"

I was intrigued. "Sure, Ben. What can I do for you?"

"Agent Newton—"

"Ashley, please."

"Ashley, I have some information I think you need to hear right away."

That got my attention. Murdoch hadn't seemed like the excitable type.

"What kind of information?" I asked.

"Information that proves my boss was set up, and by whom."

"I can put you in touch with my partner who's on the case."

"Ashley, it has to be you. The boss said not to trust anybody but you with this."

My heart leaped at his words. "He said that?"

"Exactly."

*Vince told him he trusted me?*

"How is he?"

"Worried—for himself and for you."

Ivy had been right in her assessment after all.

I told Ben where and when I wanted to meet.

A LITTLE WHILE LATER, I SAT ON THE BENCH AT THE EDGE OF THE RED-BRICK CIRCULAR walkway surrounding the Parkman Bandstand, with the closed Earl of Sandwich sub shop to my left and the tennis courts behind me. The area was quite open, with yards of empty grass in all directions. There was no way for anyone to get close enough to hear without me seeing them. I didn't care about being seen with Ben Murdoch; I merely needed the conversation to be private, and this was much better than trying hushed tones over the table of a diner.

Ben approached from around the far side of the bandstand. He'd obviously had training, judging by the way he surveyed the area as he came.

I didn't stand to shake his hand.

He took a seat beside me. He handed me a voice recorder with earbuds. "I think you'll find this very interesting."

I put the earbuds in and started the playback.

The voice was Sophia's, by my estimation, and it was laced with fear.

I stopped it. "You edited this."

"We also have a full recording of the session. This one is just her confession."

He didn't say it, but I was guessing the other tape contained a fair amount of coercion or threats based on the sobbing I'd heard.

I restarted the recording.

"Sophia, did you type this memo?" Ben asked.

A sob, followed by, "Yes, I did."

"Did Mr. Benson ask you to type this?" Ben asked.

"No, sir."

"Who asked you to type this?"

Sophia's answer. "Mr. Paisley."

"And did Mr. Paisley give you the wording?"

"Like I said, yes,"

"And did Mr. Benson sign this?" Ben asked.

Another sob. "No, I copied it."

"Copied what?"

"I copied his signature. I have it on lots of papers. I practiced it."

"And what did you do with the paper after you signed it?"

"I put it in Mr. Benson's office under the blotter."

"Why?" Ben asked.

"That's where Mr. Paisley told me to put it."

"When?"

"The middle of last week."

"So this contract was dictated by Mr. Paisley and signed by you and placed by you in Mr. Benson's office, is that correct?"

Another sob. "Yes. I told you. Yes. Can I go now?"

The recording stopped there.

"Can I keep this?" I asked him.

He nodded. "I've got a copy."

Of course he did; he was a professional. I'd never checked, but he'd probably been government trained.

I pulled out the earbuds and handed them back to him before slipping the recorder itself into my jacket pocket.

"I don't get it. Why?" I asked.

He smiled. "We got that, too. I just didn't think it was necessary on the confession. It's on the second file."

I waited for the explanation.

"Her sister was in a jam with the law. Paisley said he could get her off if Sophia did this favor for him. And I guess he has the pull he claimed, because the charges against her sister were dropped this morning."

"And what does this Paisley get out of this? Why does he have a beef with Vince, I mean Mr. Benson?"

Ben chuckled. "Simple greed. He works for Gainsboro."

So Vince's first instinct had been right after all. Covington's competitor, Gainsboro, had been behind this the whole time.

"I'm going to need to talk to her," I told him.

Actually John would need to talk to her, but I didn't need to go into that with Ben.

He pulled a piece of paper out of his pocket and handed it to me. "I figured that. Here's her home address, and you know where to find her at work."

I opened the paper, looked at it, and pocketed it as well.

"I'll be on my way, if you don't have anything else, Ashley," he said.

"This is good. Thank you for this."

"Anything to help Mr. Benson," he said as he stood. "Have a nice evening."

He turned to walk back the way he'd come.

"Oh, and Ben? Tell him I'm sorry about all this."

He nodded and left.

We were almost there. I wrapped my hand around the recorder with the key to releasing Vince from the nightmare that held him right now. This could all be wrapped up in a day or two.

John would need to bring Sophia in for a proper interview and a signed confession. It shouldn't be too hard with this recording.

My task would be to get to Paisley, and I recalled seeing his name on some of the paperwork I had from Liz's smuggling case. Interviewing him tomorrow would be my task.

I'd ask him if he knew Sophia, and if he denied it, I'd have him. He wouldn't know we had Sophia's confession yet, and once he'd made a false statement, the trap would spring shut. Proving that Gainsboro was behind this would be good enough to clear Vince, at least of the racketeering charge. And there was no way they had any evidence tying him to the bomb.

Ben had disappeared around the other side of the bandstand.

I got up to leave and turned down the red-brick path.

Ivy's words haunted me as I strode back to my car. "*You're failing girlfriend one-oh-one.*"

# CHAPTER 48

*ASHLEY*

I knocked on the large, solid door.

Nothing.

I rang the bell.

The door opened.

Vince.

I tried to read his expression—a mixture of surprise and, could it be, happiness? His visage faded to stern.

"You shouldn't be here."

He was right; he was always right.

"I don't care. I've been breaking a lot of rules recently, and we need to talk."

He blocked the doorway, clad in jeans and a USC T-shirt instead of the suit he always wore to work. "You need to go."

I pushed aside the hurt of his words. "Not until we talk."

He moved to let me in. "And then you go."

I passed through the doorway.

He pulled away when I moved to put an arm around him.

I followed him toward the kitchen. "Do you have anything to drink?"

He opened the large refrigerator door, pulled out a hard cider, and offered it to me.

"Thanks."

He removed a cider for himself as well.

"You converted to cider now?"

He took a sip. "No. I got them for you."

I smiled. "Thank you."

"Should we talk outside?" he asked, cocking his head toward the door leading to his rooftop patio.

I'd learned from John that there wasn't surveillance on his condo. "No. Inside's fine."

As I turned, I noticed the old, worn photo on the counter.

It was our prom picture. The one I'd found in his wallet. I'd been worried he'd moved on to greener pastures, easier girls, and forgotten about me.

I averted my gaze before he caught me staring, and wandered toward the full-length windows overlooking the Common and the city beyond. He'd brought me here after our New York weekend only a few days ago. I hadn't taken in the full grandeur of his place that night.

"Paisley's out there somewhere."

Vince joined me by the wall of windows. "I don't want to talk about him."

I winced when he touched my left shoulder. "Ow."

He yanked his hand back. "Sorry."

I turned to him. "I'm a little sore from the blast."

"Tell me what happened. I was worried about you," he said as he moved away from the window.

I followed and took a seat on the couch. "First I want to explain."

Instead of sitting with me as I'd expected, he sat in the old leather wingback chair.

"You should have told me who you worked for," he said curtly.

"I couldn't."

"Yes, you could."

"No, I couldn't. That's the job."

"So I was just a job?"

I huffed. "Stop it. You know better than that." I took a breath and lowered my voice. "I meant to tell you after things had progressed between us, but I didn't get the chance."

"You could have refused the job," he shot back.

"No, I couldn't. And if I had, you'd be in even worse shape now."

"Bull."

I sat up. "You owe me another favor."

"I said that when I thought I could trust you."

"Are you going back on your word?"

That stopped him. "No. Of course not."

"You need to know the whole story, and I just want you to listen to me. Can you do that?"

He nodded. "I guess."

"I've been trying to find out who did this to you."

"I should have shredded that letter when you found it."

"What happened to listening to the whole story?" I reminded him.

He shrugged.

I pulled out my phone. "Look at this." I pulled up the memo photo and handed it to him.

He looked at it briefly. "So?"

"Look at the date on the snapshot. I found this eight days ago. I didn't turn it in to the FBI like I was supposed to. Instead I sent it out to a friend for analysis to prove you didn't write it."

He cast me a wary glance before checking the phone again. "If you knew it was planted, why am I in this mess?"

I moved closer to him. "I have to have evidence. I tried, but I couldn't identify who wrote it. I put my job on the line for you by not turning it in when I found it. If any other agent had been assigned to this case, it'd be game over for you right now. And if the Bureau finds out I held that back, I could get fired."

His eyes softened. "I didn't know that."

I shifted forward on the couch. "I believe in you, Vince. I know it's a forgery, but we have to prove that."

"Since when do I have to prove I'm innocent? What about Sophia's confession?"

"It's part of the solution, but not good enough on its own. You and Ben don't understand how the system works."

"If a confession that the evidence was planted isn't enough, I don't care for your system."

I straightened up. "I get that you're pissed, but the justice system is what I know. I've had to work really hard to get where I am, and I'm damned proud of it. I carry a gun every day and face real bad guys. You need to trust me on how to handle this."

He waited for me to continue.

"Look, the cards have been stacked against you from the beginning. Paisley planned this really well. He had Sophia plant that contract, and he fed information to the DOJ that got them to assign us to investigate you. After I was in place, I was given very specific instructions about how to find that memo. We only caught Sophia because I didn't turn it in. What we need now is to have my partner, John, get a signed confession from Sophia. The recording won't cut it. Then I'm going to pay Paisley a visit. If it goes as I expect, he'll deny knowing Sophia. That should get us the leverage we need. Lying to the FBI is a serious crime."

Vince moved to the couch and put his arm around me.

"I'm sorry I doubted you," he said softly.

I wrapped my arms around him, and we hugged each other tightly.

"I have to go."

He took me into one of his intense kisses, the kisses that drowned out the sound of the outside world and all my fears.

He nibbled my earlobe and whispered, "You should stay."

"I can't. Tomorrow is too important."

After another intense kiss meant to change my mind, I pushed away and stood. "With John's help, we should be in a better position by tomorrow night. Now I really have to go."

～

WHEN I GOT BACK TO IVY'S, THE RECORDING PEN STILL SAT NEXT TO MY LAPTOP. Curiosity beat out my desire for sleep.

Three minutes later, I had it downloaded and was listening to Liz and White discussing her progress on two cases she'd been assigned. The kicker came a few minutes later.

"What makes the Benson case so hot?" Liz asked.

White answered. "I got no fucking idea, but AUSA Willey is all over my ass. If Newton fucks this up, he's going to be royally pissed, and my neck will be on the chopping block."

After that, the rest of the conversation was mundane, and then the recording stopped. A moment later I replayed it to confirm one more thing: In private, Liz wasn't calling him Randy. She was sticking to *sir*. Interesting.

# CHAPTER 49

*ASHLEY*

THE NEXT MORNING, WITH BEN'S VOICE RECORDER SAFELY IN MY HAND, I RODE THE elevator up to our floor in the FBI field office. It felt good to have a weapon on my hip again—the hip that didn't hurt. I found John upstairs at his desk, and I nodded to have him follow me into the conference room.

He closed the door behind us. "What's up?"

I played the confession from the voice recorder.

He waited until it was over before speaking. "Where'd this come from?"

"The security guy at Covington got this out of a girl that works upstairs. Her name is Sophia Nazarian."

"But how did you get it?" he asked.

"Vince found her on the video surveillance of his office."

He stopped me. "Then why didn't he tell us so we could check it out?"

"Because he thinks somebody here is out to get him, that's why."

"That's bullshit."

"You tell him that. When he found the footage that showed her planting the evidence, he had his security guy interrogate her."

John shook his head. "And he gave it to you, right? You know this isn't how we're supposed to be doing this. You can't be handling evidence on this case."

"How could I know he was gonna give it to me?" I handed him the recorder. "Now you need to bring her in and make it legit. Get her to sign a statement. Tell them Benson called you last night and turned this over to you."

He sighed. "Name and address?"

I fished the piece of paper from my pocket and handed it over. "Just keep my name out of it."

John shook his head. "This better not blow up in my face."

"Right," I agreed.

"Who's this Paisley character, anyway, and how is he tied to this?"

"That's what I'm going to go find out."

"You can't interview him about the Benson case."

I nodded. "I'm not going to. He's involved in one of Liz's cases that I'm working. I just might happen to ask him if he knows who Sophia Nazarian is, that's all. Her name is on one of Liz's papers. He'll deny it, and then when you get her signed statement, we got him. Perfectly neat and by the book."

"This *has* to be by the book," he cautioned me.

I nodded again, but John was still shaking his head as we left the conference room.

I sat at Liz's desk and gathered up the papers I needed for the interview with Paisley. Before I left, I took a pen in my left hand and scribbled Sophia Nazarian at the bottom of one of the sheets. Writing with the wrong hand was a lot harder than it looked. Satisfied that it didn't look anything like my normal handwriting, I put it in the middle of the stack and closed the folder.

I called the hospital to check on Liz again. The nurses knew me by now and were chattier than the first time I'd called. Liz was doing well, in their opinion. The pressure inside her skull was controlled, she didn't have a fever, and the doctors were saying encouraging things—all good news.

A background search on Thomas Paisley didn't show anything out of the ordinary: VP of software engineering with a degree from Berkeley. Multiple years at some southern California software companies, and hired at Gainsboro a few months ago. Nothing criminal to suggest this was a pattern with him.

After gathering my files, I told Frank where I was going and escaped without running into the SAC.

∽

VINCENT

THE BATPHONE RANG IN THE LIVING ROOM AT LUNCHTIME. I RUSHED TO ANSWER IT.

"We got him. I got Paisley," Ashley said in an excited voice.

"He confessed?"

"No way. He denied knowing the name Sophia Nazarian, and I have him on tape. My partner should be getting Sophia's statement right about now. That will be the nail in his coffin. We'll be able to play the two against each other to get him. And regardless, Sophia's admission that she planted the memo is going to get you off the hook on the racketeering charge."

I soaked in her words. "That's terrific."

"I'll call you later. Right now I have to get this back to the office."

"Miss you, Kitten," I said as we ended the call.

After I put the phone back on the coffee table, I took my coffee out on the patio and surveyed the scene: people walking the Common, free to go wherever they pleased. Soon I'd be joining them, thanks to Ashley. Once we signed the paperwork on Semaphore, and Gainsboro was officially beaten, this would all be over. Paisley and Sophia would get whatever the penalty was for planting evidence like that, and they wouldn't be a threat any longer.

I sat back in the lounge chair, and the sun warmed my face, improving my mood even more.

*It's about fucking time.*

# CHAPTER 50

*Ashley*

Letting Vince know he was soon going to be in the clear had lightened my mood. This didn't solve finding who had attacked Liz and me, but one problem down, and now on to the next.

I finished my Whopper and started the recording one more time with an earbud in one ear. I could hear the hitch in his breathing when we came to the sensitive part.

"This document is authentic as well," Paisley said.

My voice followed. "Do you recognize the name written there on the bottom? Sophia Nazarian?"

"No, I don't. Should I?" was his clear response.

*Gotcha.*

I had him on a ten-oh-four violation at least, lying to the FBI. Along with Sophia's confession, it would provide the leverage to get them both.

I took the last onion ring in my mouth and rewound the recording to listen to it again.

I smiled as I left the Burger King, vanilla shake in hand.

An elderly man recoiled from the door at the sight of the gun on my hip.

I was used to it. Something about a woman strapped with a weapon seemed odd to many men.

"Government agent," I said as I held the door open for him.

He passed through. "Thank you."

While I drove back to the Chelsea field office, I realized it wasn't just the

Paisley recording that had lifted my mood, it was last night as well. Ivy had been right about me failing as a girlfriend, and I'd underestimated how important that was. Going to see Vince had been a violation of all the rules, but it had been the right thing to do.

Rounding the corner into the bullpen, I caught sight of John, and he nodded toward the conference room.

I put my files down and joined him there.

John's expression telegraphed bad news. "We're fucked. She skipped town," he said.

My heart sank. "Sophia?"

"She and her sister boarded a flight at Logan this morning."

*Shit.*

They were probably on their way back home to Armenia, out of our reach.

"What did you get out of Paisley?" he asked.

"Nothing. He denied knowing her." That would have been more than enough with Sophia's signed confession, but without it, my recording was useless. I paced the small room, racking my brain for a next step. "Maybe I can find a financial trail that links them."

"Not likely," John said. "The recording said dropping the sister's charge was the payoff."

I started pacing again, trying for another angle.

"I know this is important to you," John said. "But I have to get back on the bombing. Forensics came back and matched the explosive to that Russian mob car bomb we had last year. They're sure it's the same bomb maker, Yuri Meledev."

We had worked the case with ATF and nabbed Yuri and the stash of bombs he'd been about to sell last year. Things had just taken a twist.

"What do you think that means?" I asked.

"No idea. Larry and I are going to roust Yuri in lockup and see what he knows. In the meantime, the forensics guys are chasing down the extra bombs to verify the detonation mechanism. Our evidence room says Boston PD has them, and they say ATF has them, and ATF is pointing at us. A regular circle jerk. Somebody has to have them."

I shook my head and went back to Liz's desk. I was looking through the smuggling file when the SAC burst out of his office.

"Newton, in here now," he yelled.

I put the file down and followed him into the glass-enclosed pigpen.

He held out his hand. "Your badge and your gun," he demanded.

My chest tightened. "What?" I squeaked.

"Now, Newton. You violated Bureau policy and my direct orders. You interviewed a man today, scrounging around for information on the Benson case."

*How could he possibly know?*

"But, sir…"

His hand stayed out, demanding my weapon and badge. "Now."

If he were a cartoon, steam would have been coming out of his ears.

I handed him my credentials, pulled my weapon from my hip, released the magazine, ejected the chambered round, and examined it to be sure the chamber was empty. Then I placed the gun, bullet, and mag on his desk. I could barely breathe.

"Newton, you're suspended. And if I get my way, terminated. Now get the hell out of my sight and out of my building."

There was no point in arguing; the sentence had been handed down. I was temporarily—and maybe permanently—out of the Bureau.

All eyes were on me as I left the stinky office with my heart pounding. They'd obviously seen and heard it all.

My knees were weak as I shuffled to Liz's desk to collect my things.

They could all see what had happened through the glass, and probably heard it as well.

I was no longer one of them. I was persona non grata. I might as well have had a red letter painted on my forehead.

As special agents, we were a tight-knit family. Now out of that circle, I was a nobody.

In my current mood, I didn't give a shit about the Bureau rules on contacting Vince; I needed him. Even worse, I had to tell him the evidence we thought we'd had an hour ago had gone up in a puff of smoke.

But first, I turned my car toward the hospital to check in on Liz. At least unconscious, she wouldn't reject me.

How had everything turned so utterly to shit?

*How can I explain this to Vince?*

I dialed his number. He needed to hear the bad news right away, and from me.

## VINCE

I WAS OUT ON THE PATIO WITH RUFUS WHEN THE BATPHONE RANG FOR THE SECOND time today. I rushed inside. By now they probably had Sophia's signed confession, and I could start counting down the hours until this whole thing was over.

"Hi, Kitten. Such a treat to hear your sexy voice again."

She sobbed. "It's not good news, Vince."

"Tell me. What's wrong?"

She sobbed again, and the background noise told me she was driving. "Sophia's gone, left town. And my boss suspended me."

"What? Why? That's not right."

She took a loud breath. "He found out I interviewed Paisley somehow."

I leaned against the couch to steady myself. The world was collapsing around us. "Where are you now?"

"On the way to the hospital. I need to visit Liz."

I ran a hand through my hair. "Okay. Come over when you're done, Kitten. I'm here for you."

"Vince, I'm so sorry. I let you down."

"Stop that talk. No, you didn't. This is Sophia's fault, and Paisley's fault, not yours. Come home after your visit."

She sniffed. "I will. I love you."

"Love you too. Drive safe."

After hanging up, I was ready to kill that fucking Paisley guy, whoever he was.

I grabbed the nearest thing, the TV remote, and heaved it blindly against the wall. It hit the picture, the glass shattered, and the picture fell to the floor.

Rufus escaped out the open door to the patio.

"Come back here," I yelled after him. "It's not you."

He didn't believe me.

I went to the liquor cabinet and pulled out my best bottle of Macallan. I poured a hefty glass and put it to my lips.

Ashley would be on her way soon.

I didn't drink it. I poured it down the sink.

She needed me, and I wouldn't be drunk when she came.

I paced between the patio and the great room, looking out the window and over the edge of the railing at all the free people outside. I needed to hold Ashley and apologize for getting her involved in this. If I hadn't hired her, none of this would have happened to her.

Finally Rufus felt safe enough to follow me again.

My regular phone rang. This time it was Perlman, my lawyer, who wanted to visit.

I wasn't in the mood, but since he was already downstairs, there wasn't any way to put it off.

When I opened the door, he had what amounted to a broad smile for him. "I have some good news, Mr. Benson."

"I sure could use some about now."

Rufus approached.

"Oh, my." Perlman backed away.

"Don't worry; he's harmless," I assured him.

He came in tentatively, walking around Rufus, and I offered him a seat at the dining table.

We sat, and he opened his worn leather briefcase. It seemed an odd truism that the successful lawyers relished carrying old, worn briefcases, whereas the young, unaccomplished ones carried shiny, new bags.

"I—we—have received an offer from the other side."

The other side seemed to be a polite way of not referring to them as *prosecutors*, which in this case meant *persecutors*.

"Already?"

"Yes, we're quite lucky in that regard. It often takes much longer for them to consider things."

That sounded ominous.

"I'm listening."

He pulled out a two-page document and began to review the details with me. Nausea rolled over me at the mention of jail.

"Only three months. That's quite generous," he said.

Three months was ninety days longer than it should've been, in my book. I hadn't done anything wrong. Not a single damned thing. It was the Gainsboro creep Paisley who should be going to jail.

"Let me go over it again to make sure it's clear," Perlman said.

I nodded and listened as he explained each of the points in detail a second time.

"You should think this over carefully, Mr. Benson, before responding. Talk with your family."

That last part I didn't relish.

I rose. "I will."

He left me the papers and gathered up his briefcase.

"However, the clock is ticking," he added as I walked him to the door. "We don't have forever."

"I'll get back to you," I told him as I let him out of the condo.

The door closed behind him, and I was alone again with Rufus, and a decision to make.

*Trapped.*

# CHAPTER 51

*ASHLEY*

OFFICER O'MARA LET ME PASS. LIZ LOOKED VERY MUCH AS SHE HAD YESTERDAY—peaceful, despite the beeping of the hospital equipment around her.

I'd checked in with the nurses at the desk on the way in, and they'd assured me she was doing better. The volume of excess cerebrospinal fluid was down considerably. They said that was a good sign.

Rounding the bed, I sat beside her and took her hand. "Well, it looks like you're gonna beat me out on that California promotion. I got myself suspended today."

She would normally have laughed at me.

"John and the guys are working hard to run down who did this to you. All we know so far is the explosive was the same as the others made by that guy Yuri we collared last year. So the thinking is, he must've sold one of his bombs before we got to him."

For the longest time I'd been wrong about Liz. I'd thought she was sleeping with White to get better assignments and evaluations. Instead, she'd held the threat of those envelopes over him. And, she'd been trying to warn me about something when she ended up here in the process. As much as she'd annoyed me at times, we were sisters in the same FBI family, and we had to stick together. She'd had my back, and now I had to have hers.

I squeezed her hand, hoping for a responsive squeeze back, but I didn't get one. A tear clouded my eye.

"I wish you had given me a clue—a clue about what you wanted to talk about that day. It would really help our search."

Her hand closed imperceptibly around mine.

Or had I just imagined it? Was she trying to communicate?

"Is it somebody in our office?" I asked.

I waited carefully and watched. There wasn't any response from her hand or any indication in her eyelids that she could hear me. I'd just imagined it.

I stroked her hand. "I'll be by again tomorrow. You can count on it, because I have lots of time on my hands now. A suspension will do that." I tried to laugh but couldn't.

One of the nurses came in, checked the monitors, and felt Liz's skin on her arm, her leg, and her cheek. "I think she needs another blanket."

"I think I felt her squeeze my hand," I told the nurse.

She smiled at me. "That's not possible, dear." She opened the closet door and retrieved a blanket that she spread over Liz.

On the floor of the closet lay a clear plastic bag with bloody clothes inside.

I pointed to the bag. "Are those hers?"

She turned to look. "Yes. They were cut off of her down in the OR, so the police missed them when they were picking everything up. I've been meaning to call."

"I'll take them in," I told her.

After she left the room, I pulled out the bag and searched through it.

In the pocket of the pants I found something—house keys…and…

A thumb drive.

I pocketed the little treasure. "Thank you, Liz. I hope this is it."

*I might finally have a clue.*

## Vincent

PLEAD GUILTY TO SOMETHING I DIDN'T DO AND SPEND THREE MONTHS IN JAIL. Perlman thought the deal was a sweet one I should jump at, but I'd learned long ago to sleep on big decisions.

Between Ashley's call and Perlman's visit, this was shaping up to be one super shitty day. And it would only be worse once I told my Kitten what was on the table.

I paced back and forth.

Jail time. Had it really come to that?

They'd planted the memo.

I had proof, but it wouldn't be admissible in court. They'd claim I'd paid an actress, anybody, to record the confession, and that I'd paid Sophia to disappear.

251

The Semaphore purchase was hosed no matter what. And my job back at Benson? Fat chance of that. I was either the admitted felon or the one everybody knew was guilty but had been rich enough to get off. Either way, I was screwed. No amount of money could rehabilitate a ruined reputation.

And Ashley sticking with me while I fought this was sure to ruin any future law enforcement career for her. Hanging out with even an accused felon would be poisonous to her ambitions.

I made another circuit out to the fresh air of the patio and back to the couch with Rufus following.

The picture on the floor taunted me—broken, just like my future.

I picked it up off the floor to rehang. At least I could fix one thing. I pulled the remaining shards of glass carefully out of the frame. The painting itself was unhurt, just without the protective glass. I gently hung it back on the wall, finding it even more impressive now that it was naked to the room.

The picture was a special gift from Dad: an oil copy of Richard Willis' painting of the battle off Flamborough Head in the Revolutionary War. It had been one of Dad's prized possessions, and he'd sent it with me when I moved out here. It depicted the battle between the Bon Homme Richard and HMS Serapis—the battle that had made John Paul Jones the hero of the American Navy.

The painting went along with the John Paul Jones coin Dad had given me. He'd said there was a lot I could learn from studying John Paul Jones. Some Christians approached a decision with the saying "What would Jesus do?" But a naval captain was expected to approach his decisions with "What would John Paul Jones do?"

"Surrender? I have not yet begun to fight," Jones had said more than two hundred years ago.

That paperwork Perlman had brought me was asking me to surrender.
*FUCK THAT.*

I wasn't Navy, but I was damned well going to fight this fucking battle to the end.

Fuck you, Paisley. Fuck you, Willey.

Before Ashley arrived, I needed to make the one call I dreaded most.
I dialed.

"Hi, Vincent. It's good to hear your voice," my father said across the wires.

"You too." I swallowed hard. "I need help."

"Okay."

"I assume you've heard about the situation out here." Calling it a *situation* sounded better than my problem, better than my arrest.

"Yes, I have."

I felt the urge to clear up one thing. "I didn't do it." He needed to know—to hear it from me.

"You don't need to tell me that. I know you didn't. You couldn't. You forget I know you."

I wanted to thank him for the confidence, but didn't. "I need to know what to do."

"You just did it, Vincent," he replied.

I had missed something. "What?"

"You needed to ask for help. That's all. It's your Achilles heel. You take on too much alone. You need to use the resources around you. John Paul Jones didn't defeat the Serapis alone; he needed his whole crew to accomplish that."

I realized this was another of Dad's John Paul Jones teaching moments.

"I'm in China today, and it will take me a couple shakes to get back," he continued. "Call Dennis, if you think he can help, but I'd start with your Boston neighbor, Liam Quigley. Those Covington boys know a thing or two about fighting problems, and their uncle can be quite resourceful as well. But first, do you know who's behind these shenanigans?"

"I'm pretty sure it's a guy at our competitor, Gainsboro, and maybe a federal prosecutor out here named Willey."

He took a loud breath. "A federal prosecutor? You sure know how to pick your enemies. Well, start playing offense. Take the fight to them, I say. Damned lawyers are all pussies anyway."

"That's what I intend to do."

"I'll back you one hundred percent in any way I can."

"Thanks, Dad."

"You don't need to thank me. It's what family does."

I nodded. That was one truth every member of our family knew. "I remember."

"Well, don't waste time on the phone with me. Make a plan and kick those sons-of-bitches so hard they know never to mess with a Benson again."

I laughed. "I will, Dad. I will."

Those fuckers. Paisley wasn't going to know what hit him.

I hung up and closed my eyes to think for a few minutes.

In order for Paisley to be able to promise to get Sophia's sister's charges dropped—and then deliver—someone in the prosecutor's office had to be involved.

*"You're going to wish you'd never met me,"* Willey had said.

It could be him, or it could be someone else in the office. If I went after the wrong target, I'd be kicking a hornet's nest.

This was suddenly more complicated than it had seemed a minute ago.

It was time for all hands on deck. I located my phone and dialed Liam.

# CHAPTER 52

*VINCENT*

WHEN I OPENED THE DOOR, ASHLEY RUSHED IN TO HUG ME.

After yesterday, I was careful about returning the embrace. Those bruises on her side and shoulder still looked awful.

She broke the hug, but looked up at me with a smile a mile wide—not what I expected from a woman who'd just been suspended.

"I might have something," she said in a giddy tone.

She held up a thumb drive.

"What? What is it?"

"I need to use your computer. The agents missed this. It was in her pocket, Liz's pocket."

I pointed down the hall. "The laptop's in the office."

She rushed off in that direction.

I followed her and typed in the password when the machine booted up.

She inserted the thumb drive, and surprise came across her face when the directory window opened.

"These are keylogger files," she told me, pointing at the screen.

I didn't understand the significance of her statement. "And?"

The doorbell rang.

I started toward the door. "We have dinner guests coming over."

"I'll be there in a minute. I have to check these first," she said.

I closed the door to the office to give her some privacy. She was obviously on a mission.

I opened the condo door to find Liam and his wife.

"Dinner is here," Amy said as she strolled in with two bags that smelled scrumptious.

I gave her a peck on the cheek as she passed.

Liam shook my hand. "We're here to help."

"After dinner," Amy corrected him. "We don't want this to get cold."

"Give me minute to pry Ashley away from the computer," I told them.

Amy began unpacking the dinner she'd brought.

I found Ashley still glued to the computer screen.

"I'm almost there," she told me.

"You can get back to this after dinner."

"Give me five or ten minutes; that's all I need, I swear."

I returned to my guests, without Ashley. "She's found something she needs a few minutes to analyze."

"Does it have to do with this whole problem?" Liam asked.

I pulled the plates down from the cupboard. "She seems to think so."

"Then this will keep," Amy said.

I opened the wine fridge. "White or red?"

"White," Amy answered. "Red sometimes gives me headaches."

Liam shrugged his acceptance.

I retrieved a nice bottle of pinot grigio and poured four glasses, handing two to my guests.

"Tell me about this plea offer you got today," Liam said.

I explained the offer fully, and he had several questions about sentencing guidelines for the individual charges.

"You've got 'em on the ropes, if you ask me," he said after I finished. "There's no way they'd offer something like that this early unless there's time pressure for some reason, or they don't have anything and they want you to cave before going to trial. No way."

I knew they didn't have anything real, just the fake memo, but it was comforting to hear his analysis of the situation.

The office door opened, and Ashley emerged carrying a few sheets of paper with a Cheshire Cat grin on her face.

"Liam and Amy, I'd like to introduce Ashley Newton."

Ashley exchanged greetings with Amy first.

Then Liam took Ashley's hand. "Ashley, that is such a beautiful name, from the old English words for *ash* and *meadow*, I believe. I like it—a beautiful name for a beautiful lady."

My woman beamed with pride at the compliment.

"Ashley, why don't you and I gather up the food while the men set the table," Amy suggested.

Liam and I did as instructed, and in no time we were seated with veal parmigiana, chicken piccata, fettuccine marinara, and garlic bread to fill our plates.

We'd started to serve ourselves when Liam said, "Why don't you start at the beginning and tell us—"

His wife interrupted him. "First, Ashley, how are you feeling? That explosion must have been an awful experience."

Ashley moved her hand to the bump on her head. "I'm still a little sore, but that'll pass. My friend Liz—she was the other agent at the scene—she got the worst of it. She's still in the ICU."

"We hope she gets better soon," Liam added.

Ashley nodded. "Thank you. She's getting better day by day. She's tough. She'll make it."

I cut into the veal on my plate.

Ashley held up the papers she'd brought out from the office. "Want to guess what I found?"

I waited, unwilling to play a guessing game tonight.

Ashley handed me the papers. "Sneaky Liz had a keylogger on the AUSA's computer. And guess who told Paisley what the memo should say and where to hide it?"

"Willey?" I asked.

Ashley nodded enthusiastically. "And, I think Willey is behind this—"

"Stop," Liam interrupted. "Would that be Kirk Willey and Thomas G. Paisley?"

"Tom Paisley," Ashley answered. "Don't know about the middle initial."

Liam shook his head. "Those fuckers. Kirk Willey is Monica Paisley's brother. She's the wacko that's doing prison time for attacking my sister, and Thomas Paisley is her husband, Willey's brother-in-law. I thought he was still in California." The hatred in his face was obvious.

Amy leaned over to rub her husband's shoulder.

"Well, that explains a lot," Ashley said. "Vince thought Willey might be involved, but we couldn't see a connection."

"I told you it was him," I added.

Liam raised his glass. "Here's to bringing down the Willey family…again."

The rest of us joined the toast.

Liam put his glass down. "If we're going to stick it to those two, I can't wait to hear the plan."

"That's where I need some help. I don't really have a plan yet," I admitted.

Over the next two hours, the four of us devised what I thought was a workable approach.

"Will your partner help out with this, or are we on our own?" I asked Ashley.

"I'll have to check. But either way, this will only work if we move on it tomorrow," she responded.

# CHAPTER 53

*ASHLEY*

JOHN HAD AGREED TO HELP, AND THE NEXT MORNING HE PULLED A HALF DOZEN encrypted radios from the field office. An urgent operation with Boston PD, he'd told them.

Ivy and I were in the middle of the Common, ready to make the call. For once she wasn't wearing a shirt with some outrageous saying printed on it.

Liam and Amy were fifty yards to the north on a bench.

Vince and John were atop his condo with binoculars, waiting on the call.

"They got his phone," John said over the radio. That was something we'd needed to go right. John had promised Petra and Vanda to get the latest charges dropped against their brother Dorek if they lifted Paisley's phone off him this morning.

I turned the radio volume down. We were ready to drop the hook in the water.

"Okay, you're up. You ready for this?" I asked Ivy.

"Yup."

Ivy dialed the phone and held it so we could both listen.

"Willey here," came the answer from the other end.

"Mr. Willey, this is Sophia Nazarian."

He paused before answering. "You must have the wrong number."

"Mr. Willey, I have to get out of town after what I did for you and Mr. Paisley."

"I don't know who you are or what you're talking about," Willey said.

257

"The paper I put in Mr. Benson's office for you. They know it was me, and I have to leave and go back to Armenia. It's not safe here."

"I don't see what I can do for you."

He'd stopped insisting he didn't know who she was. His answers so far meant we'd guessed right that he didn't know Sophia's voice, and this was going to work.

"The security man from the company, Mr. Murdoch, he has a video of me putting the paper under the blotter in the office."

We'd put the mention of the exact placement of the memo in the office into Ivy's script to convince him she was Sophia. That fact would be in the file he had on the case, and only Sophia and the agents involved should have known it.

"I still don't see what that has to do with me."

Ivy gave him the punch line. "I need money for me and my sister to go back home."

"Your sister got out of jail; that should be good enough."

We had his attention.

"He said he was going to call the FBI. I can't go to jail. We need money to go home to Armenia. We need five thousand dollars."

We'd picked an amount he should be able to get quickly.

"I'm not a goddamned travel agency." Now he was riled.

"Today," she added. "I don't have anywhere to go that they won't find me."

"I'll need time to get the money, and I have a conference at the courthouse at one this afternoon. I'll call you after that."

"Okay," Ivy said and hung up the phone.

I turned up the radio volume again. "The fish took the bait. We land him this afternoon. We're done till after lunch. Amy, he has a court appointment at one, so you can stake out the courthouse then and let us know when he leaves."

"I'll be there," Amy said over the radio.

"In the meantime, we can all do lunch up here," Vince's voice added.

I checked my pocket to confirm I had Nancy Sanchez's card for later.

*ASHLEY*

AFTER LUNCH, AMY LEFT FOR THE COURTHOUSE.

John called the Sheriff's office to tell them he'd be taking Vince for questioning for a while, so Vince would be off his electronic tether and could join us.

And then we waited.

The call came around two.

Ivy picked up the burner phone I'd given her and answered. "Hello?"

258

I huddled next to her to listen.

The others were quiet.

"I've got the money," Willey said.

I gave the group a thumbs up.

"Good. Meet me by the bandstand on the Common in an hour," Ivy told him.

His response was cold. "No, I set the place. 401 Morninglight Ave. in an hour."

I shook my head at Ivy. We needed the meet to be in the open.

"No, the Common. I don't know where that is."

"Google it," he said, and hung up.

I double checked that the call had terminated before talking. "He moved it to 401 Morninglight." I didn't recognize the street name.

John was the first to speak. "That's an industrial area halfway to Roxbury. I don't like it. The meeting needs to be in the open so we can see Ivy."

"I'll be fine," Ivy assured him. "Besides, I didn't have a choice. This Sophia girl has to be scared and desperate. It would be out of character for her to refuse."

I put a hand on Ivy's shoulder. "I'll go in the building with her and be able to be closer than if we were on the Common. We don't have a choice."

John shook his head. "I still don't like changing the plan."

Vince spoke into his radio. "Amy, has he left yet?"

"Not yet," she replied.

"The meeting spot's changed to farther out of town. He should take Harrison or Albany over the Turnpike. If you can follow him to there, we'll pick up the tail on the south side."

"No problem," she said.

I pulled my backup weapon, ejected the magazine, and verified the load before slamming it home again. "Ivy and I better leave now so we can get the cameras set up."

"Take care of my sister," John said.

I patted my holster and nodded.

The guys gathered up their things, and we all left the condo.

~

IVY AND I ARRIVED AT THE LOCATION PLENTY EARLY, AND I PARKED IN THE BACK behind the cinderblock-enclosed dumpster. Just before we arrived, Amy had announced that Willey was on the move.

It was a smaller building adjacent to a larger industrial building. The door in the front was oddly unlocked.

Going inside, the putrid smell of disuse permeated the air. The light switch inside the door was unresponsive, but enough light filtered in through the dirty upper windows in back to allow the filming we needed to do.

Ivy coughed. "This place stinks."

I turned on my cell phone's light. "Careful where you step. The homeless sometimes take a crap in empty buildings like this."

Ivy stopped in her tracks. "Eww." She switched on her phone's light before proceeding.

A few crates and cardboard boxes near the back wall were the only contents of the room. I went to the back door, unlocked the deadbolt, and ventured outside into the clearer air and bright afternoon light. After retrieving the camera gear from the trunk, I returned to the dim interior.

Ivy leaned against one of the crates, scrolling through her phone and muttering about how disgusting the place smelled.

After surveying the space, it was clear concealment would be an issue. I picked up a small cardboard box. The dust I shook off it floated in the air, lit by the sunlight coming in the windows above and behind us. Folding the top panels inward, I placed it on its side in the front left corner, with the camera hidden inside facing the center of the room.

Another cloud of dust rose as I prepared a box for the second camera, which I placed on one of the crates facing the door. I walked from the door to the crates and assured myself that the shadows of the boxes' interior kept the cameras hidden. I started both cameras.

"Remember your lines?" I asked Ivy.

"Sure do."

"And remember to get the money from him."

"Duh," she replied.

I cringed. "Sorry. It's just that things can be missed when you get nervous."

"I handle drunk bikers for a living. A paper-pushing lawyer will be no problem."

I realized I didn't appreciate the occasional difficulty of her chosen profession.

The radio calls told us Amy had stopped following, and the guys were now tailing Willey here.

I didn't relish kneeling behind the crates any longer than I had to. "Let us know when he's close," I told the guys.

"Roger that," Vince said.

"Now we wait," I told Ivy.

She continued scrolling through her phone.

❧

VINCENT

AMY HAD RADIOED THAT WILLEY WAS ON THE WAY IN HIS BRIGHT RED MASERATI.

We waited in my Escalade on the south side of the Turnpike.

"He's on Harrison now," Amy said over the walkie-talkie.

I repositioned the car one block up to be ready to turn right on Harrison to follow him.

"He's about to go over the Pike. I'm turning off now," Amy announced.

John started counting down. "Ten, nine, eight…" Just after he reached one, the metallic red sports car passed across the intersection. "Give him space… Now."

I pulled away from the curb and turned right to follow him. From our perch in the tall SUV, picking out the bright red car among the string of dull whites, tans, blues, and blacks was easy.

"This distance is good. Don't get any closer," John said.

The Maserati crossed an intersection on the yellow, and we got stopped.

I thrummed my fingers on the wheel with impatience.

"Don't worry. We know where he's going," John assured me.

Two streets later, we stopped four cars behind him at another light.

I wiped my sweaty palms on my pants. We were about to nab my nemesis in the act of paying off the girl he thought had planted evidence for him. I should have been giddy at the prospect. I didn't have a specific fear, but something about this bugged me. It was probably that it had been so long in coming.

A few blocks later, he turned, and we followed him.

"With less traffic here, you want to fall back and give him more space."

I slowed as John suggested. We would be there soon, and this nightmare would be over.

Two blocks from the destination, Willey suddenly pulled to the side and stopped.

"Pull over," John said abruptly.

I stopped by the curb and checked my watch—five minutes to the meeting time. "What's he doing?"

"I don't know." John keyed the radio. "The target has stopped and parked two blocks short."

"Roger," Ashley replied.

~

A*shley*

"R*oger*," I *said*. I *checked the time: five minutes before the hour.*

"Why would he stop?" Ivy asked when I finished talking into the radio.

"No idea."

The phone in Ivy's pocket rang.

I stood up. "Answer it. Maybe we're about to find out. Remember, you're scared."

"Hello?" Ivy said tentatively as she accepted the call.

"Are you there yet?" Willey asked.

The tone of his voice raised the hairs on the back of my neck. I grabbed Ivy's shoulder and shook my head vigorously, mouthing the word *no*.

"Not quite," she said.

"How much longer?" he asked.

Ivy looked to me for guidance.

I held up two fingers.

"Two minutes or so," Ivy answered.

"Good. I'll be there right at three," he said, and the call ended.

I quashed the temptation to check with John to see if he'd made a move yet.

"Not much longer now." I got down behind the crates.

Ivy paced back and forth. "I hate people who are late."

I didn't tell her I had a hundred other reasons to hate this guy.

I checked my watch again. One minute before three.

VINCENT


WE WAITED FOR SEVERAL AGONIZING MINUTES.

"Maybe he wants to walk the rest of the way," I offered.

"Or he wants to be late. Either way, we wait."

The top of the red car was visible, but other parked cars blocked our view of the interior.

Willey didn't get out of the car, and he didn't drive the rest of the distance.

I checked my watch again. Two minutes past three.

He was now late.

A FLASH.

The shockwave of the explosion shook the car.

Debris and a dust cloud spewed from the building two blocks ahead.

"Ivy," John yelled into the radio. "Ashley."

I yanked the car into drive and floored it.

# CHAPTER 54

*VINCENT*

I ROARED PAST WILLEY'S CAR AND THROUGH THE NEXT INTERSECTION WITHOUT EVEN bothering to slow down.

"We're okay. Get the bastard," Ashley yelled over the radio.

I hit the brakes hard and spun the car around in the wide street.

Willey was pulling slowly away from the curb.

"Don't let him get away. He'll outrun this tank," John yelled.

Willey turned in the middle of the street to head back the other direction.

I floored the big V-8 and aimed for the shiny red target. "Brace yourself."

Willey's car spewed smoke from the rear tires.

Metal and glass crunched as we rammed the rear quarter of his car and spun him around.

The airbag exploded in my face and dazed me, and I fought to punch it down and open the door.

John was already out the other side with his gun drawn. "Show me your hands," he yelled. "Show me your hands."

The tank had done its job. The rear of Willey's Italian speedster was twisted and crumpled metal and rubber. It had been no match for the three tons of American steel I drove.

Willey struggled to get out of his car.

"You're under arrest, asshole. Interlace your fingers. You know the drill."

"I'm a US attorney; you can't arrest me," Willey hissed.

263

John kicked the back of Willey's knee. The man's legs folded, and in seconds John had him facedown on the ground and cuffed.

"Save it for the judge."

Willey stopped struggling.

The smell of gasoline filled the air. I turned to find gas streaming from the rear of the crumpled red car.

"It's going to blow," I warned John, pointing to the growing puddle of gas.

John pulled Willey roughly to his feet. "Get this piece of shit to the sidewalk."

I grabbed Willey and yanked his ass toward the curb as instructed. All I needed was one excuse to kick this asshole into the next county.

John did the unthinkable: he rushed toward the car that was about to go up in flames.

I pulled myself and Willey behind a parked car.

~

ASHLEY

MY KNEES HAD HURT FROM THE CEMENT FLOOR. I HAD CHECKED MY WATCH incessantly while we waited for Willey.

When it was one minute past three, I'd put it together. John said Willey had parked, and his voice had been tinged with annoyance when Ivy told him we weren't in the building yet.

I'd jumped up and grabbed Ivy. "Out. Get out now."

"Why?" she'd complained as I'd pulled her through the back door.

I'd hustled us into the cinderblock dumpster enclosure and pushed her to the ground just in time.

The explosion threw me against the wall, on my good side, and my head hit the cinderblock. Glass and bits of building had rained down on us amid the suffocating dust cloud.

My ears rang, and the dust had made it impossible to see.

That fucker Willey had been behind the explosion that put Liz in the hospital.

Ivy coughed from the dust.

I'd pulled my shirt up to my mouth to breathe through and yelled into the radio, "We're okay. Get the bastard."

As the dust started to clear, I still couldn't hear, but I pulled Ivy to her feet, and we started around the building.

Reaching the street, I keyed the radio again. "Did you get him?"

A fireball erupted several blocks to our left.

Ivy took off in that direction. "John," she yelled.

I hobbled after her, unable to keep up with my injured leg. My head hurt, and my hand came back bloody after I felt my hair.

When I made it to the scene, both cars were engulfed in flames. Ivy was hugging John on the far sidewalk, and Vince had Willey on his knees—at just the right height for me to kick his teeth in.

John was on the phone, and sirens wailed in the distance.

Vince grabbed me into a tight hug as I reached him. "I was so scared you were in there."

I didn't care about the hurt of his squeeze; I hugged him back with all my might.

"I figured it out just in time."

John held up a controller from a radio-control car. "Look what I found in this dirtbag's car."

Willey sneered.

"Ashley pulled me out just before the bomb," Ivy told her brother.

John nodded his appreciation to me. "Thanks."

"I should have figured it out sooner," I told him.

In retrospect, it was so obvious. The Russian bombs that had gone missing from evidence used the same radio-controlled car detonation mechanism the Marathon bombers had employed. That meant the radio-control transmitter had to be within a few blocks to set off the bomb. That's why Willey had stopped where he did, and why he'd wanted to know when we would be in the building.

Vince released me. "You're bleeding." Alarm clouded his voice.

"Good," Willey said.

I kicked his leg.

He screamed.

"Oops."

If his head had been on the ground, that would have been my target.

"You have the right to remain silent," John began reciting Willey's Miranda rights.

Willey didn't say anything. He was a smart enough lawyer to clam up at this point.

Two fire trucks were the first to arrive. One stopped to work on the car fire. The other proceeded to the explosion site.

Vince called one of the firemen over to look at my head wound.

I felt woozy and sat on the curb.

Vince joined me.

The fireman looked at my head and radioed for an ambulance pickup.

Boston PD rolled up just after that and argued with John for a moment about jurisdiction. But John's charge of attempted murder of a federal officer trumped anything they could come up with.

Willey was going to get a taste of the other side of the bars.

After they loaded me into the ambulance, I blew Vince a kiss.

"Love you, Kitten," he called as they shut me in.

I pulled the business card from my pocket and dialed Nancy Sanchez.

# CHAPTER 55

*ASHLEY*

THE ROOM WAS BRIGHT, AND THE BEEPING OF THE HOSPITAL MONITORS WAS annoying.

My head sported a second bump to match the original one on the other side, as well as bruising on my right side to go with the purple marks healing on my left.

Vince pulled his chair next to mine and took my hand—about the only part of me that didn't hurt.

It had been two days since Willey's arrest.

The charges against Vince had been dropped the same day. One inquisitive call to Willey's boss, the US Attorney, from Nancy Sanchez at Channel 8 had done the trick. News coverage of the details was the last thing the government wanted. Nancy hadn't wanted to sit on her scoop, but she seemed to understand how much cooperating could pay off for her career in the end.

I'd been carefully examined after the second bump to my head but cleared to leave yesterday. Vince and I now sat in Liz's room, waiting for her to wake up.

The tube in her head had been removed, and they had stopped administering the barbiturates that had kept her unconscious. The doctor expected her to wake up any time this morning and allowed us to stay, with the proviso that we have the nurse call him as soon as she woke.

Liz's eyes fluttered and then opened into slits.

"Hi, sleepyhead," I said softly, taking her hand and squeezing it.

"What happened?"

I took a breath. "A guy tried to kill us both with a bomb."

"Is that why I feel like I'm gonna throw up?"

I pressed the nurse call button.

"A bomb?" she asked. "Is that why you look like shit?" She laughed weakly and winced.

The nurse arrived, pulled her phone, and summoned the doctor.

"AUSA Willey planted a bomb at the alt-three meeting place," I told her.

"Fucker. I was going to tell you he was a problem. I found—"

"I know. I found the thumb drive."

The doctor walked in and asked us to leave.

"No, I want them to stay," Liz objected.

The doctor relented and started his exam. It was similar to what I had gotten twice now, but longer and more thorough.

"You seem to be in fine shape," the doctor told Liz as he moved to leave.

"Then why do I feel like crap?"

He stopped. "I meant mentally. You have two cracked ribs, and the deep bruising will also take time to heal. We'd like to get you up and walking right away, though. I'll send a nurse in to assist you."

"Make sure he's a cute one," she countered.

The old Liz was back.

"And I need a smoke."

The doctor crossed his arms. "Absolutely not."

After the doctor left, Vince offered Liz a paper bag. "Nicotine patches."

I'd mentioned Liz's habit, and he'd come prepared.

"Thanks," she said, accepting the bag. "Maybe we could go out for dinner after all this."

I couldn't believe Liz was making such a brazen play for my man.

"Sorry, Jacinda," he said, putting his arm around me. "I'm taken."

And I wasn't giving him up.

I planted a kiss on my man hot enough that even Liz blushed.

"By the way, those envelopes you forgot to mail? I put the postage on them and sent them to the IG's office."

Her mouth gaped open. "You what?"

I met her stare. "It was the right thing to do, and you know it."

Her frown indicated her preference would have been to keep holding them over the SAC.

"You think he's a pig, and I agree. He needed to be turned in."

She shrugged. "Yeah."

Changing the subject, I pulled out my phone. "I've got someone who wants to talk to you," I told her.

"Huh?"

I hit the special speed dial I'd programmed.

She cocked her head "Who?"

I held up a finger to hold her off.

"Director Kelly's line," the person on the phone answered.

"She's awake," I told the FBI director's assistant.

"Just one moment," she said.

I handed the phone to Liz.

"Who is it?" she asked.

"The director."

"Fuck no," she protested. "Oh no, not you, sir," Liz said into the phone. "Sorry, that was somebody else here trying to poke me with a needle…"

When the director finished wishing Liz a speedy recovery, I took back the phone and made sure the call had been ended before I spoke.

"We nailed AUSA Willey, and he's being held on attempted murder and conspiracy. That gives the director quite a bit of leverage on his boss, so you and I get postings wherever we want."

Director Kelly had been rumored to be on thin ice with the Attorney General, but our arrest had changed the power dynamic in DC in favor of the Bureau. We were now on the director's Christmas card list.

"We?"

"I told him it was your intel that allowed us to trap him."

"What does *trap him* mean?"

"I'll let John fill you in later. My part in the thing only amounted to getting my ass blown up for the second time."

Her face clouded over with concern. "You didn't tell the director about the…" She glanced nervously toward Vince. "You know what?"

"I had to. But for the official report, you overheard a conversation outside his office. That software is something we'll never talk about again."

Relief washed over her face.

"He also told me to warn you that if you mention a word about this, or ever do it again, he will personally see to it that you are collecting your social security behind bars."

She shivered visibly.

"Do you understand?" I asked.

Liz made a zipping-her-lips-shut motion. "Got it. I've got no idea what you're talking about."

Her nurse reappeared. "Time for you to take a few laps up and down the hall, young lady."

Vince stood, and I followed.

"You'll get the rest of the details later," I told her. "Until then, best not to talk about this."

The nurse started unhooking Liz from the monitors.

"Thanks, Ashley," Liz said with more conviction than I'd ever heard from her.

# EPILOGUE

## "THE BEST AND MOST BEAUTIFUL THINGS IN THIS WORLD CANNOT BE SEEN OR EVEN HEARD, BUT MUST BE FELT WITH THE HEART." – HELEN KELLER

*ASHLEY*

I WOKE EARLY AND LISTENED TO MY MAN SNORING LIGHTLY BEHIND ME.

Vince did that sometimes when he lay on his back, which was one of the reasons I enjoyed spooning so much.

Today was the big day. We'd spent a week preparing for this afternoon's barbecue, and Vince tried not to show it, but he was nervous.

His father was coming out to join us.

My attempts at getting Vince to even acknowledge his nervousness, much less talk about it, had been an exercise in futility. It wasn't up for discussion.

Still, I had an idea to help him relax.

I reached over to the nightstand and brought the lube under my pillow. I started without him. With my legs spread, my finger slid through my curly hair to part my slit and circle and rub my most sensitive flesh. I rubbed myself slowly then faster, all the while imagining Vince's fingers doing the work—teasing, darting, pressing, and tweaking. It didn't take long to have my engine humming and my juices flowing.

I slipped my head under the covers to execute my plan.

A gentle lick to the tip of his cock, and I got his attention.

"Morning, Kitten," he said groggily from above the covers.

The skin of his engorged shaft felt silky smooth under my fingertips. It gave a slight jump with my every touch. I positioned my mouth above his tip and licked it with every jump upward. The magazines were right, and his hardness proved it—a man's testosterone level was highest in the morning.

269

One hand found my scalp and started the fingernail massage I loved.

"Keep that up," I urged him.

The other hand cupped my breast to begin the massage that turned him on as much as it did me.

I'd learned that the feel of my breasts in his hands was something he couldn't get enough of. When we watched TV or a movie on the couch, his hand would automatically take up gentle bra duty.

I cupped his balls and pulled lightly, then teased his tip with my tongue.

His fingers knotted in my hair—a warning to be careful.

I eased up, rolling his balls lightly with my fingers and taking the crown of his cock in my mouth. The exquisite moan I elicited as I worked my tongue over and around him was music to my ears. I gave him a playful rasp of my teeth.

"Careful there," he warned me.

I might be a beginner at this, but his moans, and watching the tension of his legs and abs, had proven a good guide to what turned him on.

He tried, but I shifted position so he couldn't reach my soaked lady bits. This morning was my turn to call the shots.

"What's your pleasure, Kitten?"

I paused for a moment, tracing the sensitive underside of his cock with my tongue. "Page two-twelve."

"You dirty vixen, you." He threw off the covers.

Quickly I straddled him. Reaching down to guide him inside me, I couldn't help but gasp as he filled me to the brim. Every time with Vince was a rapturous new experience. His cock never disappointed.

His legs tensed, and his breath faltered as I started to rock back and forth. His hand held my hips firmly down against him. Then he brought his thumb to my clit, and every push forward sent electric jolts up my spine.

On the page I'd chosen, he wasn't allowed to touch my breasts—torture for both of us. I followed the script by grinding into him and his thumb, quickly finding my rhythm. Every rocking motion forward pushed my tiny nub into him and sent arrows of heat racing through me. Every movement back pushed me farther up the hill of building pleasure as the tension within me grew nearly intolerable in no time.

He cheated by pulling my neck down and my breasts to meet his chest.

My nipples scraped across his skin. I rocked into his thumb again as my orgasm erupted. I screamed out my pleasure as the fireworks played against my closed eyelids, and I fisted the sheets. My toes curled, and the shaking took over as my body clenched around him.

Vince pulled me close and I melted onto his chest, breathless and spent. I shifted my legs down to his.

In a simple move he rolled us over, pulled out, and straddled me.

I found the lube under the pillow and filled my palm. The cold gel quickly heated as I stroked his length with slippery hands. A double-handed motion, running my slippery fingers up and over the tip and down again, had him shaking as he held back.

His breathing became labored.

I started slow, then quickened the pace. I loosened my grip on the down stroke and tightened on the pull upward.

His hands went to my breasts as they always did, and his eyes slammed shut. In no time, first his legs then his torso tensed. Finally the guttural groan of his orgasm came as the spurt landed on my chest. It was followed by another and another of the sticky liquid as my man marked me as his.

The contented smile on his face as he tried to catch his breath was the reward I needed this morning.

"You dirty vixen, you," he repeated.

I'd chosen this scene just for him. "Relaxed now?"

"You have no idea." He got up and brought me a washcloth to clean up, but the warm, wet cloth did nothing to wipe away the warmth I'd felt as his seed covered my heart.

Vince was out on the patio grilling the burgers and dogs. He wanted this to be a version of the family barbecue we'd missed when I'd been in the hospital after the second bomb blast. Simple, with burgers and hot dogs, was the order of the day.

The doorbell rang for the tenth time, and I opened it.

"Ash." Rosemary stood in front of me.

She rushed in, and we hugged for what seemed like an eternity.

"How'd you get here?" I asked when she released me. "I thought you were still in the bush."

"*Was* is the operative word. Didn't Vince tell you?"

So *she* was the surprise Vince had hinted at.

"No, that rat didn't." I looked through the open door, confused. "Where's Jeremy?"

"He's out in the bush again," she said.

"Is there something you want to tell me?"

"He promised it would be over by now, but he can't give it up. And I can't keep going weeks without a shower, so here I am. I hear this state needs nurses."

I gave her a comforting hug. "I'm sorry."

"I'm not. It's good to be back to civilization."

I ushered her out back, and we made a round of introductions.

Vince's father, Lloyd, was in some debate with the FBI crowd I'd invited.

Anita joined them. Vince had been relieved to find out that Ben's suspicions of Anita had been unfounded. The extra money she'd come into had been a small inheritance from an uncle in Australia who'd passed away.

271

John was throwing back a beer with Vince.

Those two had become fast friends when we learned it was John's note to Staci that had gotten Vince concerned enough to put in the video surveillance that eventually led us to Paisley and Willey. Staci Baxter, it turned out, was John's cousin, and he'd felt he had to warn her when he saw her picture in the file the DOJ sent over.

"And Paisley folded like a wet noodle when we started listing the charges," John told us. "Turns out the whole scheme had been concocted by Willey to enable Gainsboro to buy Semaphore. And you'll never guess why."

Neither of us ventured a guess.

"For Paisley to be able to rig the voting machine software to ensure Willey won the election for attorney general."

Vince's face screwed into a sneer. "That slimy fucker. I hope he gets a million years."

John nodded. "With the extra bomb we found in his garage, it's a pretty sure thing the sentence will be stiff."

Willey was as low as they came.

When John wandered off, I gave Vince a nice, hard spank on the butt.

"Hey, what's that for?" he complained.

I elbowed him. "You didn't tell me you were bringing Rosemary out here."

"What kind of surprise would it have been if I told you? I thought you'd like to see her."

"But you didn't give me any warning to find her a place to stay."

He spanked me back, but not as hard as I'd gotten him.

"Fine sister you are. I invited her to stay with us for a while."

Once again, Vince surprised me with his generosity.

When I went back inside, Rose was talking with a group from Covington.

I joined Liam, Amy, Lloyd, Liam's uncle Garth, Liz, and John at the dining room table.

I pulled Liz aside. "I like your hair, by the way."

She'd come today as a honey blonde, and I hadn't been the first one to comment on it.

She smiled and played with the ends of her locks. "Thanks. Do you think I'll fit in now?"

"Sure. They'll love you."

Liz had taken the director up on his offer and had selected Los Angeles as her new posting.

She winked. "I know why you're staying. And I don't blame you."

I'd decided to remain in Boston for now and see how things worked out with Vince.

White had resigned after being called down to the Inspector General's office in DC, and John had just been announced as the new SAC in Boston. Things in our office would be looking up.

I located Vince and headed his direction.

He was turning the last of the burgers on the grill and talking with his father when I walked up.

"You sure about that?" Lloyd asked Vince.

Vince smiled at me. "Absolutely. Thanks for the offer, Dad, but I'm happy right here."

Lloyd stepped back from the smoke of the grill. "I thought it was what you wanted."

"So did I," Vince replied. His arm encircled me. "But things have changed."

"Let me know if you reconsider."

After his father left, I had to ask, "What was that about?"

"He offered me the job of running Benson Corp. back in LA."

"But haven't you been working toward that? Isn't that why Semaphore was so important?"

He took my face in his hands. "Not nearly as important as what I have here with you." His words made my heart melt and my head spin. "I love you, Kitten."

"Hey, are they done yet?" Mason complained from behind Vince.

"Take over for me." Vince handed him the spatula and focused his attention on me. "What's your favorite restaurant in Hawaii?"

I struggled to get my voice back. "Duke's."

"We'll have dinner there tomorrow. We fly out in the morning."

"I can't—"

"You have the week off," he informed me.

"No, I don't."

He gave me a sweet kiss on the forehead. "Yes, you do. It's all arranged."

*Ashley*

I CLOSED MY EYES, LISTENING TO THE RHYTHMIC SOUND OF THE SURF. WE'D HAD TO leave early to make it to Honolulu with the sun still shining, given the six-hour time difference. I hadn't been thrilled about waking up before dawn, but Vince had insisted.

I'd taken a quick nap after we arrived, and Vince had chosen a walk.

Now the sun was low over the ocean as I leaned on the lanai railing. Warm trade winds rustled the fronds of the palm trees lining the beach. Beyond them lay dozens of pink umbrellas on Waikiki Beach in front of the historic Royal Hawaiian hotel.

When I tore myself away and opened my suitcase to unpack, I found books inside. I held them up. "Look what I found."

Vince chuckled from the mahogany dining table of the Ali'i suite he'd booked for us. "Vacation reading."

He'd packed two copies of a new book: *Seducing the Bazillionaire*.

"We can read to each other."

I didn't complain. We were going to have some exciting new pages to quote.

"Ready?" he asked.

I turned to see my man smiling in my direction. He closed the laptop in front of him.

"Sure, whenever you are."

I still couldn't believe my life. Vince had given up his dream of running his father's company to stay in Boston with me, and he'd asked me to move in with him.

Duke's Waikiki had been my favorite restaurant the one time I'd been lucky enough to come to the fiftieth state before. It was named after Hawaii's hero, Duke Kahanamoku.

We walked in past the posters and articles devoted to Duke. Descended from Hawaiian royalty, he'd won multiple Olympic medals in swimming and water polo across a staggering twenty-year span, but was even better known for bringing the Hawaiian sport of surfing to the mainland United States. A sportsman and goodwill ambassador for Hawaii, Duke had been loved on the islands, and a statue of him welcomed tourists to Waikiki.

After a whispered conversation between the hostess and Vince, accompanied by a bill pressed to her hand, we were led to a table by the railing. We had a clear view over the bar deck to the beach and ocean beyond. A band played on the deck below us.

After perusing the menu, Vince went for the sesame-ginger ono, and after waffling, I chose the macadamia-and-herb-crusted mahi-mahi.

The view and the meal brought me back to the second happiest time of my life, the week I'd spent here on the beach and in the warm Pacific waters.

"Tell me about it," Vince urged.

"What?"

"You're thinking back to the time you were here before." He pulled my hand to his lips and kissed it. "Aren't you?"

"Guilty as charged. It was summer like this, and my aunt Michelle brought the three of us here: Louise, Rose, and me. That week of walking, sunshine, and swimming will always define this place for me." It had been my third happiest time, after the night I'd danced away with Vince in high school and the night he'd arranged at the Met.

"You can always make new memories here."

Those entrancing dimples made another appearance to go with his heartfelt smile.

"I guess." It was hard to see how anything could compare to that week with my family.

The sun threw gorgeous yellow, pink, and orange hues on the clouds as sunset approached.

A little while later, our dinner had been cleared, and I enjoyed the colorful sky with my second blue Hawaii drink.

Vince raised his coconut mojito to my glass. "To making memories."

"I can drink to that." My bruises had healed, and I was looking forward to basting myself with sunscreen and laying by the pool.

"I'm ordering dessert," he announced.

I'd already told him I was stuffed. "I'll pass." I held up my tall blue glass of liquid happiness. "I'm drinking my dessert."

The band playing on the lower deck started a new song "Sweet Home Alabama," and the crowd sang along.

Vince waved over our waitress.

The girl looked on expectantly while Vince perused the dessert menu one last time. "I'd like the hula pie, and the lady would like the ke komo lima chocolate cake."

"No, nothing for me," I objected.

"Yes, you will," Vince insisted with a firm glare.

Then the waitress got in the middle of it. "I think you'll really like the cake," she told me. "It's to die for."

I gave up and rolled my eyes. "Okay."

He could order it, but I didn't have to eat it.

The sunset colors burst against the horizon as dessert arrived—Vince's a monster piece of hula pie large enough to feed a soccer team, and mine in a pink cardboard box.

He dug into his dessert, with a watchful eye on me.

I set mine to the side. "Perfect. It's already in a box. I'll take it back to the room for tomorrow."

"At least try a little of the frosting," Vince encouraged. "It's chocolate. You can tell me if I made a mistake getting this hula pie instead." Vince raised his hand high and waved down to the band.

They interrupted their song. "By special request," came over the speakers, and they started our song, "Green-eyed Lady."

"You didn't?" I accused.

"It's amazing what a hundred dollar tip can get you." He pushed the box toward me. "Just a taste."

A photographer who had been wandering the floor stood nearby and aimed his camera in our direction.

I ignored him and opened the box.

I gasped.

It was gorgeous.

The photographer's camera flashed.

"Ashley Lindsay Newton, will you marry me?" Vince asked, loud enough for the neighboring tables to hear.

The photographer's flash went off again.

The nearby guests were staring.

I stood to round the table, and Vince did the same. I wrapped my arms around him, and his mouth clamped over mine as he squeezed the breath out of me. The kiss he devoured me with claimed me as his Kitten, and soon to be his wife.

"The question demands an answer," he said as he pulled away.

The area had gone quiet as the surrounding diners looked on.

"Hell yes," I answered.

He lifted me off my feet and swung me around with the crowd clapping and the camera flashing. When he let me down, we retook our seats.

The crowd went back to their meals, and I pulled the sparkling diamond ring from the cake and licked the frosting off. "Ke komo lima?"

"Hawaiian for engagement ring."

The gorgeous ring fit on my finger tightly enough to not slip off. The day I'd dreamed of since I was a little girl had come, and in a totally surprising way.

Vince's eyes conveyed the warm love I'd felt flowing through his touch as he'd held my hand on the walk here.

"Do you like it?" he asked.

"I love it. I love everything you give me." He'd given me his heart, and now offered me his name, and I couldn't wish for anything more.

The camera flashed one more time. "A photographer?" I asked.

"I'm going to add one of tonight to my wallet."

I smiled as I remembered the picture he'd carried with him all these years.

Tomorrow was a new day, and I gazed into the loving eyes of the man who was my future.

Bending and breaking a few rules had made my dreams come true.

Vince had been right; a new memory would now define this place for me: ke komo lima chocolate cake at sunset across from my man.

THE END

# THE DRIVEN BILLIONAIRE

# CHAPTER 1

*BRITTNEY*

I didn't dare open the intimidating gray envelope. Instead I slipped it under the orange folder, grabbed my keys, and departed for my date. This was the only night of the week I didn't work and could fit in a social activity.

I arrived five minutes late after intentionally parking three blocks away, behind the restaurant. My date for the evening, Jeffrey, was already here. I passed his BMW out front as I hurried up the walk to the Tres Pinos entrance.

He'd suggested this place after our first meeting last week over coffee, and I didn't want to jinx anything by objecting to his choice, so I told him I'd love to try it. The food here was great, and the prices were reasonable. As an added bonus, the bowl of chips would occupy me enough to not fidget, and maybe keep my mouth full enough to prevent me from saying something stupid— at least I could hope.

Jeffrey smiled from beside the ficus tree as I pulled open the door. He kindly didn't check his watch. "I was hoping I didn't get the time wrong."

I smiled. His button down shirt and blazer were more formal than average for this area, but I attributed that to him working in marketing.

"No. I'm just running late. Traffic on Pico."

His hand at my waist guided me to the hostess station, where he whispered something to the cute young thing.

His touch reminded me this was a date. I fingered the heart-shaped gold medallion around my neck. It had been long enough since Todd, hadn't it?

Cute Young Thing beamed a smile back. She showed us to one of the primo tables by the front window. "Will this one do?"

Jeffrey nodded. "*Perfecto, señorita.*" He slipped a bill into her hand and pulled out a chair for me.

"*Hablas español*, Jeffrey?" I asked after the hostess left.

"No. You just heard it all, if you don't count asking for a Dos Equis. I had Spanish in middle school, but these days I couldn't even ask where the bathroom is."

"*Dónde está el baño*," I told him.

"I'll take your word for it." He arched an eyebrow. "And, what did I do wrong to be demoted to Jeffrey?"

His correction caught me off guard. "Sorry, Jeff. Nothing at all."

His smile told me he was letting me off easy.

It had only been a week, but I shouldn't have made such an obvious mistake. Benji's harassment was screwing with my concentration.

So far I was finding Jeff's modesty refreshing after all the braggarts I'd met on the SuperSingles dating site—not that I'd had many dates. Somehow dating brought out the need to show off in men, which often translated into exaggerating everything in their lives. I was over having men try to impress me with the car they drove, their expensive taste in wine, or the latest concert tickets they'd snagged.

Jeff had showed up in a BMW, a million steps above the Accord I drove, but he hadn't mentioned it once on our previous coffee date—ten points for him.

Our waitress arrived with chips and salsa, both hot and medium. They didn't serve mild here.

Eager to get past my embarrassment, I ordered a margarita on the rocks, no salt. I couldn't tell if Jeff was following my lead, or we merely liked the same adult beverage, when he copied my order.

"So, what do you think's good here?" he asked, ladling the milder of the two salsas onto his chip.

I chose the hotter salsa. "Pretty much everything."

"So you've been here?"

I maneuvered to escape my mistake. "No. But my friend Lillian eats here all the time, and she raves about it." That was a close one.

He switched to the hot salsa for his next chip. "I'm liking the looks of the burritos. What about you?"

I perused the menu slowly before answering. "I think I'll try the fajitas." That was my go-to order here when I didn't feel like an enchilada.

"Then maybe I'll try that too."

I inquired about his work, and he told me about some of his recent customer visits. At least he got to talk to his customers.

"I guess your clients don't talk much," he noted.

I laughed. "The jabs and scrapes of my instruments against their teeth keep their responses to mumbles when they aren't shrinking away."

I didn't drill teeth, but patients still cowered at the sight of curettes, scrapers, scalers, and probes. If a root canal was on someone's most-hated list, a visit to my chair was not far behind. Nobody ever moved a cleaning appointment up because they were looking forward to the experience.

He grimaced. "Ouch." A bead of sweat appeared on his forehead after another chip with the hot salsa. The hot stuff here was scorching hot.

I took pity on him and switched to the milder salsa.

The waitress interrupted us to take our orders, and once again I went first. Jeff copied my order of fajitas, even down to choosing chicken and no sour cream.

I raised my margarita. "I'm used to it. Nobody puts a visit to get their teeth cleaned at the top of their wish list."

He joined me with a sip of his drink, and his next chip went into the milder salsa.

"My dentist only works four days a week. Does that mean you get a lot of time off as a hygienist?"

"More than you might think. My dentist has us all under twenty hours a week so she doesn't have to provide benefits."

He grimaced in sympathy. "That's not fair."

"*Fair* isn't in Dr. Call's vocabulary. It is what it is."

Jeff finished the chip he was chewing. "Can you fill in with another dentist?"

"I wish, but she keeps moving our days around, so that makes it hard."

"That's tough."

I smiled. Jeff was the first of my dates to understand the unfairness of the way she treated us. "I fill in my other hours tending bar."

"Very ambitious of you."

I smiled and sucked down more of my margarita. "A girl does what she has to do to make ends meet."

"That must keep you pretty busy."

"Busy girl, that's me. What about you? I hear startup hours can also be on the brutal side."

He was detailing his most recent few days when our food arrived.

As always, the fajitas were served still sizzling on hot cast-iron plates.

Mine was as tasty as always, and Jeff seemed impressed with his.

"You said you had a sister?" he asked.

I had to finish chewing before I could answer. "And a twin brother, Doug. Samantha is two years younger and getting her MBA at Wharton. Doug is in the Marines."

Just then my heart skipped a beat as I caught sight of a gray Charger driving by, which looked like it could have been Benji's.

Every time I saw one, my skin crawled as I wondered if it could be him.

I crossed mental fingers that Benji wasn't prowling for me.

Jeff's brow creased. "Something wrong?"

I willed a fake smile onto my face. "Oh no," I lied. "Just trying to remember when her tuition is due." Picking up my drink, I tried to be casual about looking out the window in the direction Benji had disappeared.

"You're paying? That's an expensive school, I imagine."

I knew that better than anyone. Putting my younger sister through school had fallen to me and Doug, and he couldn't help much with the debts he was still paying off. Providing for Sam's education kept my bank balance hovering near zero, and sometimes below, even with all the overtime I pulled down at the Pink Pig.

"My mom passed away two years ago," I told him. My father's departure years before didn't warrant a mention. "It's my responsibility now to get her through school."

There were months I wouldn't have been able to feed myself if it weren't for credit cards.

"She's a grownup. She should take care of herself," he remarked.

That was a common feeling, I'd learned.

"It's not how I was raised. The older ones look out for the younger ones."

He nodded and smiled without offering an opinion of my family values.

I scooped veggies and chicken inside a tortilla and asked about his family.

That steered the conversation away from my plight, and had me longing for the simple situation he enjoyed.

All through dinner I kept a cautious eye out the window for Benji—without any sightings.

I finished the last of my fajitas, save the green bell peppers I never ate.

Jeff checked his watch again—the third time in the last few minutes.

This dinner was coming to a close soon. If the third date didn't improve from this, there likely wouldn't be a fourth.

I wasn't heartbroken about it. Jeff seemed nice, stable, almost normal—unlikely to be an axe murderer—but there was no spark. He was about as exciting as cream of wheat. I'd nearly nodded off listening to his description of his sister's latest venture—she was apparently the Waikiki hamburger queen—when I caught it.

Jeff lived with his parents. Though, at least, he probably didn't live in the basement, since almost no houses in California had basements.

Five minutes later, we'd both declined our waitress's dessert query, and I followed him out the front door into the warm evening air.

Jeff stopped at his car and unlocked it with his key fob. "Next week, would you prefer sushi, or perhaps a movie instead?"

The marketing guy was on his game. His question presumed a third date.

I considered my choices.

"Hey, get away from my girl." The yell came from down the sidewalk as Benji approached at a fast clip.

He'd been behind the hedge, probably for a long time. Sneaking around was his style.

Jeff backed up, looked first at Benji, then at me. Fear marked his face.

Benji's version of crazy could do that.

"Get out of here, Benji, and leave us alone," I yelled. I put my hand in my purse, feeling for my pepper spray, just in case.

Jeff disappeared around his car and climbed in. He didn't have any interest in an altercation with my crazy ex.

My heart galloped a mile a minute, but I stood my ground and pulled out my phone.

Jeff burned rubber pulling away from the curb.

Benji gave him the finger along with a "fuck you."

"Benji, get the hell out of here before I call the cops," I yelled.

He stopped.

I pulled out my phone.

An older couple that had just come out of the restaurant retreated back inside.

"You can't go out with him," Benji yelled.

The guy didn't get it. We weren't an item any more, and weren't ever going to be again. Not ever.

I lifted my phone with my finger poised over the emergency button. "I'm calling the cops in three… two… one."

Benji turned and ran back the way he'd come.

I couldn't take this shit.

As soon as he turned the corner, I left in the opposite direction, struggling to get my breathing back under control.

He got crazier every time.

ZACK

A SALTY BEAD OF SWEAT TRICKLED INTO MY EYE. WIPING IT AWAY WITH MY GLOVED hand made it worse when a fleck of sawdust joined it.

"Shit."

Standing up and removing the glove, I blinked like crazy and coaxed the irritating particle out of the corner of my eye with a fingernail.

With two functioning eyes again, I located the last cold can of ginger ale, popped it open, and took a few long, stinging gulps. I reversed the towel that had covered the can to find a clean section. I wiped my brow and surveyed the dusty room.

After two evenings of work, I was only a quarter done with this room. I refolded the rag, dirty side out.

What idiot would glue crappy fake laminate like this over the marvelous oak flooring the house was built with? And the second layer glued down without removing the first was double sacrilege against this fine old mansion.

It would take a lot of work, but I could already envision walking on the warm golden strips of oak, dotted with tasteful area rugs, instead of the half-plastic crap the last two owners had glued down.

I gulped the rest of the can before tossing it in the corner garbage bag and kneeling down with my pry bar to attack the offending laminate again.

Three small sections later, the music started up next door.

*Fucking punks.*

I rose, brushed a layer of dust from my jeans, and walked back to the kitchen—one of the only two semi-clean rooms downstairs during this project of mine.

I wiped down my hair and torso with a clean towel and pulled on a T-shirt. The snub-nose pistol went into my waistband at the small of my back, and I grabbed a flashlight from the counter.

Neighborhood kids had taken to using the abandoned house next door as their occasional nighttime party spot, and I was sick of it.

Twice I'd tried calling the cops. But the cops had rolled up an hour later, turned on their flashing lights, and the kids dispersed out the back, only to return a few days later. The officers viewed scaring them off as the easy way to deal with it, and they never attempted to catch any of the buggers.

The moon lit the way as I moved toward the back porch door I knew to be open. One of the delinquents had broken the lock on the doorknob and removed the deadbolt for easy access. Tomorrow morning I'd get a replacement deadbolt on the way to work and be able to put an end to their parties.

God-awful music blared out of an open window. How they could even call that music was beyond me.

The back door was ajar. The squeak of its rusty hinges as I entered was drowned out by the cacophony coming from the boom box toward the front.

I passed through the old dining room to the front parlor. The kids had laid down their cell phones with the lights pointing to the ceiling for illumination. They were so busy dancing, none of them noticed as I approached.

A solid kick from my work boot, and the plastic boom box went quiet as it shattered against the wall. Simultaneous protests from the three couples replaced the music.

The tallest of the boys started toward me. "What the fuck, asshole?"

I pointed the pistol.

The click as I cocked the hammer was loud in the instantly quiet room. "What did you call me?"

The boy backed up and the front of his jeans went dark with piss. "I didn't mean…"

The others grouped together and backed toward the wall. Piss Boy didn't have any rescuers in this group.

"I catch you creeps in here again, and there'll be hell to pay. Do you understand me?"

Piss Boy nodded and backed toward the others.

One of the others stooped to pick up a phone.

"Leave it," I yelled.

The girl dropped the phone.

I rounded the room toward the door. "The phones stay on the floor. Now, get over there." I motioned toward the corner with the gun.

The group shuffled toward the corner.

I counted and only saw five phones. "I said all the phones." I waved the gun at the group.

A girl in the back slid the missing phone to the middle of the room.

"Listen carefully. This is how this is going to go. You can come to my house next door after dinner time tomorrow…" I pointed toward my house. "…with a letter of apology, and I'll give you back your phones. Do you understand?"

The group nodded, even Piss Boy.

I unlocked the deadbolt of the front door and backed away from it. "Now out." I raised the pistol toward the ceiling and fired.

The loud report of the gun reverberated in the room as Piss Boy made it to the door first, with the rest of the pack only seconds behind.

It was only a starter pistol loaded with blanks, but it got the point across. Piss Boy and his crew wouldn't be back.

I locked the front door after them, gathered up the phones, and exited through the back. Tomorrow when they came back to retrieve their phones, they'd get another reminder not to return. Back inside my house, I locked my doors, set the alarm, and replaced my starter pistol in the drawer.

If I knew teenagers, the word would spread, keeping them from destroying the majestic house next door any further.

*Fucking juvenile delinquents.*

# CHAPTER 2

*BRITTNEY*

I TURNED IN TO MY ASSIGNED PARKING SPACE BETWEEN THE TWO PICKUPS AND noticed it just in time. I hit the brakes, got out, and pocketed the nail—placed conveniently on end where my tires normally rolled—before getting back in to finish parking.

Fucking Benji.

He'd told me two weeks ago, *"What if you get a flat tire? You'll need me then."*

This was the third time I'd found a nail or screw in my parking spot since.

Safely upstairs in my apartment, I locked the door behind me. The orange folder on my desk taunted me.

I opened it to the printout of the last email from Detective Swenson I'd read and printed out. It suggested one more time that I'd be safer if I could remember what had happened to the key—the key I had no idea about. My sister, Samantha, had convinced me to stop checking the secret gmail account, and I hadn't since this had arrived nine months ago. Every previous message had only turned into an hour-long crying session with her over the issue. I couldn't remember something I never knew.

*Would I ever really be safe?*

I opened my laptop to log in and tell him one last time to leave me alone, so I could put the reminders of my plight behind me.

But I chickened out and closed the laptop's lid. He didn't need a message from me. Samantha's solution was simpler. I tossed the whole ugly folder back in the bottom drawer where it belonged—out of sight out of mind. What I didn't read couldn't bother me.

But when I did that, I was faced with the fucking gray envelope again. The envelope that detailed my real problem. Hovering over it for a few seconds, I resisted and stuffed it in my purse. It needed to be dealt with, but it was going to wait.

Saving me from my dilemma, my phone rang, with Samantha's pretty face on the screen.

"How'd your date go, Brit?" she asked.

Her saying the word *date* sent my fingers nervously to my medallion. I winced as the scene with Benji replayed in my head.

"Okay," I said.

Technically, the date had been okay; it was the ending that got all fucked up.

"Tell me about him. I think Jeffrey is an okay name, but not a leader."

She thought a lot of names were cool, as if you could judge a guy's character by what his parents had named him when he was mere hours old. Although she'd thought Derrick was a creepy name, and her theory had been borne out, and same with Norman before him.

But after watching Hitchcock's *Psycho*, I should have known better than to go out with anyone named Norman.

"We went to Tres Pinos," I told her as I sank into the couch.

"I bet he had the fajitas and a margarita on the rocks," she guessed. Some of these guesses were her superpower.

"What makes you say that?"

She laughed. "Simple. Jeffrey is a follower name. Like I said, not a leader, and you always get a margarita on the rocks and the chicken fajitas."

She knew me too well.

"Sam, that was just a lucky guess."

"Was not. Bet it ended without a kiss. Jeffreys move slow."

She had guessed right again, but not for the reason she thought.

"Well, am I right?"

"No kiss," I confirmed.

"I knew it. Boring, huh? Brit, you deserve better. You deserve hot. You deserve tall, dark, and studly."

"He was okay."

"But no third date, right?"

She was likely right once again.

"I'm pretty sure that's not happening."

"I hear it in your voice. Spill, big sister. What happened?"

I sighed, caught again. I swear she must have hidden a webcam in my apartment last time she was here. "Nothing. I just don't think he'll be calling."

"Stop holding out."

"It was Benji. He accosted us outside the restaurant."

She gasped. "Worse than last time?"

"Yeah, a little."

I underplayed how I'd felt for my sister's benefit. She needed to concentrate on school instead of worrying about the drama in my life.

"That idiot's a dozen crayons short of a box. You better get a gun."

"That's one thing I'm not doing."

"He's dangerous, if you ask me," she retorted.

"He's got no balls. I know how to handle him. He'll get over it sooner or later."

My words were more confident than my feelings.

"He doesn't need balls to be dangerous. He can poison your cat, or burn down your house without having the guts to face you."

"I don't have a cat."

"Very funny. You know what I mean. Benjamin is a back-stabber's name. Better be careful."

She had warned me against Benji from day one. It was my fault for not listening to her. "He'll get tired of it sooner or later."

So far all my predictions of that had been premature. Sooner wasn't looking likely.

"You know Grams's house is empty, and it's half yours now."

Our grandmother had passed on last year and left Doug the tiny lake cabin and my sister and me her house in west LA. Doug had rented the cabin, so that wasn't an option—not that commuting from the mountains would work anyway. The thought of living at Grams's house would be tempting if it wasn't in LA, and also if she hadn't died in the house.

I dodged the suggestion. "Dealing with ghosts is not on my agenda."

"The house is just waiting for you. And you could save on rent."

Her mention of rent brought my gaze back to the gray envelope.

I'd never shared with her how hard it was keeping my nose above water financially with her tuition. If I could just handle it another two semesters, she'd be done and launched into a life with loads of potential. She deserved that.

But move back to LA? I didn't intend to ever go back.

"I like it better up here."

"Right. Well, keep the house in mind and don't turn your back on Benji. I don't trust him."

I changed the subject. "What classes are you signing up for?"

As she started to talk, I glanced across the room. The clock I kept on the counter was facing toward the kitchen instead of its normal orientation toward me on the couch.

After ten minutes discussing her upcoming semester and another ten on her non-existent dating life, we hung up.

I got up, repositioned the errant clock, and settled in for a little television.

# CHAPTER 3

*Zack*

Tuesday morning, I took a deep breath as the red digits increased one by one, with a ding at each floor. The elevator doors finally opened on the top floor of Benson Corp.—Galactic HQ, as I liked to call it—where my father reigned supreme over all he surveyed.

I cinched up my tie and turned right toward marketing.

My ever-cheery assistant, Wendy, was at her desk ahead of me, as always.

"Good morning, Mr. Benson. Make much progress last night?"

Wendy understood my passion to get my old house restored to its former glory. There was something majestic about an old Victorian—the craftsmanship of the woodwork and the unique personality of each one. They'd been built in a time before cookie-cutter designs and mass production became popular. They were built lovingly by hand and exuded a warmth missing in the square McMansions of today.

"Slow and steady. Still arguing with the laminate those two idiots laid down. Any emergencies this morning?"

"Just the usual."

"Let me guess. Stanton from the London office?"

He needed something pretty much every morning, and the issues were almost always minor. He had the mistaken impression that phone time with me, just because my last name was Benson, would accelerate his career. He didn't get how Dad operated.

"One point for you. And your father wants to see you."

289

I schooled my face to not show the irritation I felt, but the cock of her eyebrow revealed I'd been unsuccessful. Wendy knew how much I enjoyed my father's interruptions.

*Not.*

Yesterday's breeze had cleared out the smog, and I took a moment to enjoy the view of the Pacific Ocean out my office window.

"Anything special?" I asked Wendy as I picked her coffee cup up off the desk and headed to the break room with mine in the other hand.

"The usual will be fine, thanks." She enjoyed a mocha with non-dairy creamer most mornings. On occasion, she'd change it up and ask for decaf.

My first and only argument with Wendy had been my insistence that it wasn't in her job description to get me coffee the way she had for Walt before me. Walt was old school in that respect.

I'd insisted on changing that dynamic, and it was my routine to make and bring coffee for each of us—black for me and mocha for Wendy. It seemed like the civilized thing, and Wendy wasn't wrong when she suggested I did it to be different. Different was good.

After a sip of the hot brew, I took off my coat, threw my keys on the desk, and settled in for the inevitably boring call with Stanton. I opened my cell phone to the timer screen and hit speed dial on my desk phone to Stanton's London office number. Dad insisted we use the landlines when communicating between offices to avoid interception of calls.

Stanton picked up after a few rings, and I started the timer on my cell. He wanted to review some customer quotes he'd emailed.

I pulled the messages up, and we went through them one at a time. Predictably, half of them were within his pricing authority and didn't require a call to get my authorization. I glanced at Vince Lombardi's face on the coin attached to my keyring. I considered giving Stanton one of Lombardi's quotes —"*The only place success comes before work is in the dictionary.*"—but decided he wouldn't get it.

We finished the last quote with two minutes to spare on my timer. I'd warned him often enough to keep the calls below fifteen minutes so I had time to call the Rome office before they went home for the day.

After a short call to Lucio in Rome, it was time to see the old man. I gathered my keys and a notepad before making my way to Dad's office on the other end of the floor.

My father was on the phone, but he waved me in as he finished up his call. "Zachary, how are you this morning?"

"No complaints."

"Great. I wanted to congratulate you on the Swankstead deal. That's another first-rate piece of business."

"Thanks, Dad, but it was mostly Franciscovich."

Swankstead had taken a month and seven trips to their headquarters to put together, but hundred-million-dollar equipment sales didn't happen overnight. Franciscovich, the sales guy, had done most of the legwork.

"He'll get a fat commission check for this one. But either way, you handled that admirably."

I nodded.

"So well, in fact, that I think you're ready for your next challenge."

I knew exactly what he meant, and I didn't like the sound of it. "I'd like to spend more time in marketing before moving on."

"Nonsense, Zachary. A position is opening up in finance at the London office before long."

"London?"

"Sure. It's a great little town."

Only Dad could call London a *little town*.

"Why not here?"

"You'll have to get used to warm beer, and don't eat the mushy peas. Those mushy peas are awful."

Apparently, he'd already decided I was moving to my next rotation. All that remained in his mind was to set the date.

"I'll think about it," I told him.

"I think you could learn what you need to in less than two years there."

He evidently hadn't heard me.

"I said I think I need more time in marketing first."

My words finally registered, and the effect wasn't pretty. His brow furrowed, and his eyes bored into me.

I returned his glare in equal measure.

"Nonsense. Finance is next up for you. "

This conversation was reminiscent of the one we'd had three years ago when I'd agreed to take my current marketing position at the company. That time I'd folded quickly and agreed to move when he wanted. The departmental rotations were mandatory for family members, but I was trying to have some input on the timing, and not making a lot of progress.

He meant well. He was doing his best to train me, and all of us, for the futures he envisioned for us.

I was committed to supporting the family company, and I'd known what that entailed when I joined.

"Review it with Harold in finance," he said. "He has all the particulars. We'll talk about timing later."

"I will," I said as I stood to leave.

I felt in my pocket for the keyring Dad had given me. Family obligations came above all else—but London?

"Congratulations again on Swankstead. I mean that."

"Thanks, Dad," I replied as I departed his office.

*Why London?*

# CHAPTER 4

*BRITTNEY*

I HADN'T SLEPT WELL, WORRYING ABOUT SAMANTHA'S BENJI WARNINGS. IT WAS THE first time she'd been so adamant about him being dangerous.

I'd written him off as obsessive, but last night's encounter had been worse than anything yet. Still, sooner or later, he'd get tired of chasing me. He had to. Didn't he?

My ponytail didn't look quite right on the first try, so I redid it. Dr. Call was picky about her hygienists' appearance.

I opened the door and saw it immediately. The chill went all the way to my toes.

*SLUT* in big red letters, spray-painted on my apartment door.

Fucking Benji had gone too far—way too far.

I looked both ways down the hall before closing the door behind me and locking the deadbolt.

The nasty word was also painted on the wall next to my door, with the drips from the letters making it look like the letters were bleeding.

Mrs. Butterman exited her unit. Her mouth gaped, and she shook her head before scurrying for the stairs.

I waited a moment before following.

MY FIRST PATIENT WAS MR. SNODDER. HIS CHART SAID HE HADN'T BEEN IN SINCE last year, and the tartar he'd accumulated took especially long to remove.

"I can tell you haven't been flossing as often as you should," I told him.

"Probably right."

"And you really should have a cleaning every six months," I encouraged.

"I come in as often as I can afford to," he said.

Dr. Call came in shortly after and told him the same things, and got the same responses.

"Your insurance covers it," she told him.

"Really?" he said, faking surprise.

A visit to our office was just something he wanted to avoid.

The rest of my appointments for the morning were pretty ordinary. I put my fingers and instruments in patient's mouths, and tried to avoid getting bitten. I was used to it: staring down at teeth and bleeding gums, and dealing with the occasional dose of bad breath. It wasn't glamorous, but the pay was good on an hourly basis. If I could get more hours, things might actually be manageable, but with Dr. Call, that wasn't likely.

I was in the middle of my last patient before my lunch break when I heard him.

"I'm here to take Brittney to lunch." It was Benji's loud voice coming from reception.

"You need to leave, sir," Rosa at the front desk told him.

"No. I'm not leaving without Brittney," Benji said, even louder.

Dr. Call came to my station. "You need to take care of this."

I got up and excused myself from my patient. I could feel the heat of the doctor's glare as I walked up front.

"Benji, you need to leave," I told him as I reached reception.

His eyes were wide and bloodshot. "Not without you."

Rosa rolled her eyes.

The two patients in the waiting area looked on apprehensively.

"I'm not going to lunch with you."

Benji kicked the reception partition. "Yes, you are," he said angrily.

One of the waiting patients got up and left.

"Call 9-1-1," Dr. Call said from behind me.

Rosa dialed.

I pointed to the door. "Get out of here, now."

He didn't move, but the remaining patient did.

Dr. Call followed him. "Mr. Carson, don't go."

It was a standoff for a half minute or so, with him pacing the waiting room and me demanding that he leave.

The wail of a police siren sounded outside and Benji bolted for the door.

Dr. Call poked her head in the door from outside and motioned for me to join her.

Once I'd stepped outside, she said, "Brittney, it's not acceptable for your boyfriend to impact the practice and scare patients, not to mention the rest of us."

"He's not my boyfriend," I explained.

Her countenance didn't soften. "I'm canceling your shifts for now."

My stomach clenched. "But..."

"Collect your things, and call me when you have your situation sorted out."

"Now?" This couldn't be happening.

"Right now."

The police cruiser pulled up in front, and Dr. Call went to talk to them while I walked back inside, stunned.

As I left, Dr. Call whispered to Rosa, who gave me the side eye.

When I stepped back outside, the police car was gone, and my life was a shambles. The gray envelope with Samantha's tuition bill loomed as an even bigger problem than it had been yesterday.

I drove back to my apartment in a funk. I'd have to start checking with other dentists for a hygienist opening right away.

Maybe I could explain that I needed more days than Dr. Call was willing to schedule me, but that was tenuous. If they called her, the truth would sink me.

Benji had fucked my life big time.

I must have looked odd to the other drivers on the road. I spent the drive home yelling at the windshield, telling Benji to fuck off a hundred times.

Upstairs, the paint had been removed from the door, and the wall had been repainted, with a wet paint sign taped up.

I let myself in and collapsed on the couch.

I'd barely caught my breath before the knock sounded on the door.

I braced myself for a confrontation with Benji through the closed door. It would be just his style to show up now to apologize and ask to be forgiven.

*Fat chance.*

The view through the peephole, though, showed Mrs. Honeycutt, the manager's wife.

I opened the door. "I'm sorry about Benji," I started.

She forced a folded up paper in my direction. "And I'm sorry about this. But we run a quiet, respectable complex here."

I opened the paper.

**THREE DAY NOTICE TO QUIT.**

I was being evicted. "But, I can't possibly find a place—"

"Three days. You can call later about where to send your deposit, if any is left," she said before she turned and walked away.

I couldn't breathe as I closed the door and let the ugly paper fall to the floor.

The first tears rolled down my cheeks.

A knot of dread formed in my stomach.

Find a place to live and a new job at the same time?

*How?*

What would I tell Samantha?

This was impossible.

I had to pull myself together. I tore open the gray envelope from the Wharton School of Business and took in the total. It didn't include books, and it was way too big for me to handle now.

I logged onto my bank account. The meager total almost made me sick.

I could ask for extra shifts at the Pink Pig, but the number was still insurmountable. And even if I could find a place in three days, Sam's tuition, plus first, last, and a security deposit was out of reach anywhere in this town.

*"You know Grams's house is empty, and it's half yours now,"* Samantha had said.

But when I'd left, I'd told myself I would never go back to LA.

Now it was either that, or call Sam and tell her she couldn't finish her degree this year.

Getting help from Doug was out of the question. We'd talked last week, and he'd already maxed out his credit card sending me what he could.

I pulled a pen from my purse and started working numbers. If I got my job back at the Rusty Bucket in LA, and also managed to get a few shifts as a hygienist down there, it could work.

And, moving would provide a workable explanation for leaving Dr. Call's practice. Dr. Fosback might even have some open shifts. He'd take me back in a minute; I was sure of it.

LA was looking more and more like the solution to my money problems.

My phone said two in the afternoon. I pulled up Dr. Fosback's number and dialed.

Fifteen minutes later, I fist-pumped the air as I hung up.

He said he could get me up to eighteen hours a week in his practice, and maybe more later.

I could do this. I had to do this.

My clothes went into garbage bags as fast as I could fill them. In an hour, my car was filled to the brim. Not everything would fit, so I left some winter things in the closet.

I swept the jewelry on my bathroom counter into a plastic bag to keep from losing any of it. Then I remembered the heart-shaped, solid gold pendant my ex-boyfriend, Todd, had given me before he'd disappeared.

After Benji, I'd gone back to wearing it on occasion. It was pretty, but stupid, with a Klingon love quote on the back. It was heavy, so I planned to melt it down and make a proper gold ring and a pair of earrings, maybe two, when I got the chance. If I had to, I could sell it for the gold. I laughed to myself—my financial life preserver of last resort. I added the pendant to my makeshift jewelry bag and toted it, along with my bathroom items, to the car.

I put my key under the mat and pointed the car south on the freeway. My legs were jittery as I dialed my bartending buddy Lillian.

"Hey, what's up?" she answered.

"Lil, I've gotta leave town. You can have my shifts, if you want them."

"Sure, I could use the hours. How long will you be gone?"

I spit out the truth. "A long time."

"Why?"

I ignored the question for the moment. "I'll call Tony and tell him I can't come back, but I'm also calling about my place. You were interested in my couch last time you were over."

"Yeah."

"The key's under the mat. Take the couch and any of the other furniture you want. Could you do me a big favor and box up and send me the clothes that are left in the closet? But you gotta do it in the next three days, and you can't tell anyone where I went."

"Brittney, what's going on?"

"I'm getting kicked out of my apartment because of Benji, so I'm getting as far away as I can. And I don't want him finding me."

"I'm sorry about the apartment. Randy and I can go over Thursday night and get your stuff. Is that soon enough?"

"That's great. Thanks, Lil."

"Are you sure you're doing the right thing? I mean, just up and leaving?"

"It's the only thing I *can* do."

"What about a restraining order or something?"

She meant well, bringing up alternatives.

"That would cost money, and I don't think it would work with him. He's just crazy." I was too embarrassed to admit I'd also lost my job because of him.

"Where are you going?"

I kept my answer vague. "LA."

"Call when you get settled and let me know you're okay. I need an address to send your stuff anyway."

"I will, and thanks," I answered.

A bit later, I turned onto route 152 toward Interstate 5, which would get me into the LA basin in six hours, give or take.

Heading south on the interstate, I couldn't get past the feeling I'd forgotten something. When I finally figured it out, it was too late to turn around.

I redialed Lillian and asked her to add the contents of my desk to the care package she was sending me.

# CHAPTER 5

*Zack*

ALL DAY AT WORK, I'D ONLY WANTED TO GET BACK TO MY PROJECT.

This restoration kept me grounded. I was expending real sweat, creating something that would last. Working with Dad, nothing lasted. Each price negotiation gave way to the next, and would be forgotten a week later. No PR plan had any lasting impact. I couldn't point to a single lasting thing I'd done in the past year at Benson Corp.—nothing that was visible now. Nothing I'd accomplished withstood the tyranny of time. Swankstead was a win this week but would be forgotten with next week's impending deal.

I wanted something solid, something I could point to and say I fucking *did* that. I fucking *made* that.

"Fuck," I hissed as the section of floor I pried up splintered and hit me on the forehead. My safety glasses protected my eyes, and at least my glove came back without blood on it as I wiped my brow. Even more care was required on this section, with particularly difficult glue holding the stupid laminate to the beautiful oak below.

A glint of light caught my eye from next door. After a look out the window showed the neighboring house still shrouded in darkness, I refocused on the flooring.

A minute later I saw it again, upstairs this time.

Those good-for-nothing kids were back. Four of them had come by with apology letters to retrieve their phones earlier this evening—the three girls and one of the boys. The girls had come by in a group, likely too scared to approach the crazy man alone.

I stretched my legs after getting up and unclipped my knee pads. With my flashlight, I went out my back door and slid sideways through the hole in the fence and up to the back door of the old Victorian next to mine.

There wasn't any music tonight to mask my approach, so I climbed the stairs slowly. This might have been avoided if I'd stopped at Home Depot after work to get a new deadbolt for the door as I'd originally planned. Unfortunately, my father's words had rattled around in my head all day, crowding out my rational plans. In short, I'd forgotten.

I'd also neglected to put fresh batteries in the flashlight, and it was almost useless, emitting only a dim yellow glow.

The back door to the abandoned house opened with a squeak. I paused. Foot-falls came from the second floor. Walking softly, I made my way to the stairs and started up.

"I warned you," I called.

The sound of scurrying came from above, but no voice accompanied it.

If this was Piss Boy again, I was going to drop-kick him across the street.

At the top of the stairs, I stepped over a garbage bag on the landing. I turned right down the hallway.

Then it happened.

The kid came from behind a door, kicked me in the shins, and sprayed me with pepper spray. My lips burned and my nose stung, but the safety glasses I still wore protected my eyes. I dropped the flashlight as I grabbed my injured leg.

He came at me again in the darkness.

I grabbed his hand and twisted it, wrenching the can loose from his grasp. I pointed it back at my attacker, giving him a long spray in the face.

He fell back, hands to his face, and let out a blood-curdling scream.

A woman's scream.

I picked up the flashlight. It was a woman all right, and not one of those teenagers.

She moaned and writhed on the floor.

I dodged a kick.

"Get the fuck out before I call the cops," I yelled. My lungs burned from the acrid mist.

"*You* get the fuck out. This is my house." The voice was oddly familiar. She moaned and rubbed at her closed eyes.

"Brittney?" I asked incredulously.

It was Brittney Spear, a vision from my past.

~

*BRITTNEY*

MY EYES CLAMPED SHUT WITH THE SEARING PAIN. IT WAS LIKE GETTING A HUNDRED bee stings on my eyeballs. I rubbed them with my fists, but it did nothing to relieve the excruciating burning.

"Brittney?" the asshole asked, no longer yelling.

I kicked at him but missed.

"Stop that. It's Zack…Zack Benson."

I struggled to my knees. The voice came back to me in a rush. I couldn't believe it. Zack Benson, of all people. I tried for a deep breath and the burn made me regret it.

He pulled me up to standing. "I have to get you next door."

He wasn't making any sense. None of this made any sense.

Even shallow breathing stung. "I'm not leaving."

"Bullshit. The quicker we get this crap off you, the better." He picked me up, and I was over his shoulder the next second.

My eyes were on fire, and I couldn't open them. I beat on his back with no effect. "Put me down."

I bounced on his shoulder as he must have been carrying me downstairs. Every step hurt my stomach. I kept pounding on him.

"Put me down," I screeched again.

"Stop your bitching, for once."

"I can walk," I insisted, even though my lungs burned and I couldn't pry my eyes open one bit.

"Shut up. This is safer."

I gave in and stopped fighting. I heard the door opening, and the next second we were going down what must have been the front steps, then after a moment up another set of stairs before he stopped to open a door.

Finally, I could breathe without each inhale bringing flaming pain to my lungs.

A few moments later he set me down.

I tried to pry open my eyes, but they stung too much. I clung to his arm to steady myself.

"Give me your phone," he demanded.

I didn't have it. "I dropped it."

"Arms up so I can get your shirt off."

I'd wished to hear those words from him years ago, but not now. "No way."

"Stop being a baby. You're going into the shower clothed or not. Your choice."

I lifted my arms, and he pulled my shirt over my head. He guided my hand to what felt like tile.

"Hold on to the counter. Don't move. I'm going to untie your shoes."

He finished one shoe, urged my foot up, and slipped the sneaker off, followed by the other.

My eyes still burned and remained welded shut. Being undressed like this without being able to see was the oddest feeling.

He pulled down my jeans, but thankfully left my underwear and bra.

I heard the water start.

"It's a tub shower. Step up and over." He held my forearm and guided my foot into place.

I completed the rest of the climb into the tub and braced myself against the far wall.

The showerhead started to spit, and the warm spray hit me.

"Get it off your face and out of your hair first," he commanded.

Inching closer to the shower, I let the water cascade over me. The acrid taste and smell around me slowly dissipated.

"Hold out your hand. Here's some shampoo."

I did, and I felt the cool gel fill my palm.

"Make sure to wash your hands as well. You don't want to rub your eyes and get it back in there."

I worked the shampoo into my hair, rinsed, and then blinked into the spraying water, slowly ridding my eyeballs of the vicious chemical.

"I'm putting your clothes in the wash. I'll be right back."

Slowly, the water cleared my eyes, and I could see enough to clean myself off. The shower curtain was closed. I pulled it aside and peeked around an old bathroom with a pink pedestal sink and pink tile halfway up the wall—very un-Zack. None of this made any sense. The door started to open, and I ducked behind the curtain again.

"Clean clothes are on the sink. I need to rinse off, too, so hurry up, unless you want me to join you."

I heard the door close. Turning off the water, I stripped off my wet underwear. After toweling off, I stepped into the hip-hugger panties he'd provided. They fit, but the bra was more than a cup size too big, so I skipped it and donned the sweatpants and sweatshirt in the pile.

"You stock women's underwear?" I yelled.

"Don't ask," came back from the hallway.

I didn't ask anything further. I probably didn't want to know how many drunken women had left parts of their wardrobe here after a night with Zack. I'd missed a sock after one night out, but never lost track of my panties.

I grabbed the brush beside the sink.

As I opened the door, he said, "Wait in the room across the hall while I rinse off. Then we can talk."

I went across the hall and sat on the bed. I should have closed the door.

He walked past and into the bathroom—buck naked.

When I saw him, I couldn't look away, or I didn't want to. The sight of him after all these years halted my breathing.

The man was even more muscled than when I'd known him before, and in high school I'd thought he was the epitome of buff. His shoulders were even broader now, and I couldn't help noticing the back muscles that tapered down to that tight ass and powerful legs. Also, his dangly parts were on full display. The man was Adonis in the flesh, and I couldn't help but look—stare, really.

I shook my head and closed my eyes tight. It was a sight I wasn't going to unsee anytime soon. All the memories of afternoons with him and my brother, Doug, came rushing back. I'd hung out with my brother a lot, just to be near Zack—just to hear him talk, and to imagine what it would be like if he noticed me as a girl instead of merely Doug's twin sister.

The door closed, and the shower started.

I pulled the brush through my hair.

This evening had been such an emotional roller-coaster. When I first drove up, I was elated to see Grams's house again. But when I located the hidden key in the planter and opened the front door, I found the lights didn't work. It made total sense, in retrospect, that the utilities would be turned off after her death, but it hadn't occurred to me on the drive here.

*I'm such an imbecile. Of course the house isn't as I remember it.*

When I'd heard the intruder, I'd prepared to defend myself and thought my day couldn't get any worse. But having the pepper spray turned on me had proven that thought false and become the new low point of a completely shitty day.

Now I was sitting on a bed, having just seen my teenage dreamboat naked, waiting to talk to him after all these years. Zack Benson—I mean, how lucky could a girl get? I should have taken him up on his offer to join me in the shower. How sexy would that be?

*Get real, girl.*

He wasn't into me then, and it could only be worse now. I'd just kicked him and pepper-sprayed him.

I kept brushing my hair.

The water stopped, and a minute later Zack emerged from the bathroom with a towel around his waist. He ran a hand through the mane of sandy blond hair that was now darker for being wet. The slight bulge in the front of his towel had me imagining the magnificent man parts I'd seen minutes earlier.

I looked up, and his smirk indicated he'd caught me staring. I looked away, but couldn't control the heat in my cheeks. I heard him pad off down the hall, followed by the closing of a door.

A minute later he returned in a pair of jeans and T-shirt. He took a seat in the chair across from the bed. His deep blue eyes bored into me.

I handed him the brush.

He ran it over his scalp. "Thanks."

I couldn't help but admire his arms as he pulled the brush through his hair.

He handed it back to me. "Now you can tell me what you were doing sneaking around that old place." His words came out cold and accusatory.

"I told you, it's my place—well, me and Samantha. We own it now."

"Bull," was his one-word answer.

"Our grandmother left it to us when she died last year."

Surprise wrote itself across his face. "Wilma Gossnet was your grandmother?"

"Duh."

His voice hitched. "I'm sorry to hear that. I had no idea. When I bought this place six months ago, they told me she lived in Seattle. I've been chasing kids out of there lately trying to keep them from destroying it."

"You could have said who you were."

"I didn't hear you announce yourself," he shot back. "And I'm the one who's been keeping the place from getting any more trashed than it already is."

I stood. "I need to unload my car and get my stuff in the house. I've got work tomorrow."

"No," he said curtly.

"I beg your pardon."

He blocked my path to the door. "Is your car the gray one out front?"

I nodded. "Yeah."

He pulled my car keys from his pocket. He'd obviously gotten them from my pants. "Stay here, and I'll bring your stuff up."

"No way." I was unsuccessful in grabbing for my keys. "I'm staying in my own house, thank you very much."

He stepped toward me. "No. You're not. It's not safe. No electricity, no water, and no locks. You're staying here with me until it gets fixed up, and no arguments."

I hated the news, but his concern for my wellbeing warmed me.

"Bossy much?" I complained, although the thought of not having any water or a working toilet in the house had me happy to accept his offer to stay—at least until I got the utilities turned on.

"No. Just practical. Doug would kill me if I let anything happen to you."

He was probably right about that. He'd phrased it as though he was doing this for Doug, but his look gave me hope—for the first time ever—that he was doing it for me.

He pulled out a set of keys and worked one off the ring. "Here's a key to this house. You're staying here for now."

I took the key. "My purse is in the other house, in the kitchen." I followed him to the door.

He left down the hallway. "Stay here, Sunshine. I'll get it."

It was the first time I'd heard that name in years. I couldn't help but smile. Watching his tight ass walk away down the hall, I couldn't believe this turn of events. I'd crushed on Zack forever growing up, but he'd never noticed. He'd never asked me out, or given any indication that he cared to.

But tonight, that nickname gave me hope.

# CHAPTER 6

*Zack*

I BOUNDED DOWN THE STAIRS AND OVER TO THE HOUSE I WOULD NOW HAVE TO THINK of as Brittney's. Seeing her again had been a surprise of the tenth order. She'd moved out of state, and then to San Jose, and to hear Doug tell it, she was *never, ever* coming back.

The odor of the pepper spray in her house wasn't as obnoxious as it had been, but was still noticeable. I located her purse and, using my phone's flashlight, looked around for anything else she might have left. Finding nothing, I locked up and started carrying bags of things from her car to my house.

I noticed Piss Boy walking down the other side of the street. He watched as I pulled a bag of Brittney's belongings from her car.

Each trip back up the stairs with bags, to the room I'd put her in, brought back memories.

She smiled as I deposited another load. "Zack, you don't have to bring them all in."

Her smile now was even more gorgeous than when I'd first given her the Sunshine moniker in middle school. With every trip, I noticed the curves under the sweatshirt that covered her delectable body. She'd had perky tits back then, and they looked even fuller now, begging to be held, fondled, and sucked.

The memory of her soft skin, and the mounds of her tits spilling out over the top of her bra as I'd undressed her in the bathroom a short time ago tortured me. It had taken monumental willpower to not unclasp the bra, pull down the panties, and take in the full sight of her. The girl had become a woman with true beauty.

"You don't have to," she repeated.

"Yes, I do—no telling what would happen to them if I didn't. This isn't the best neighborhood."

I didn't trust Piss Boy to leave the car alone overnight. But why bother her with details of our prior altercation? I headed downstairs for another load.

As kids, Doug and I had hung out together. And almost no matter what Doug and I had going on, Brittney would tag along. She had been a constant source of temptation, a lure I had to avoid. Rule Number One: you don't touch your best friend's sister. Rule Number Two: leave the country if you already broke Rule Number One. Neither of the rules said I couldn't think about touching her, though, and I'd done a lot of that in the past.

I'd spent many a night envisioning a lot more than touching her. I'd planned how I would kiss her, and yes, how we would do all the dirty things boys and girls did together. But all that was just mental exercise—most often while pumping my dick in the shower and releasing my pent-up frustration at the rules.

Doug never had any idea of my lurid thoughts about his twin sister, and good thing, because he would have beaten me to a pulp, or we would have bloodied each other up while he tried. I had two inches on him back then, but it probably wouldn't have made up for the fierceness he'd have brought against anybody who messed with Brittney—even me. Probably especially me.

I brought another bag up the stairs to her room, along with her lone suitcase. "I left some of it downstairs until you get this put away."

"I won't be putting it away." She turned and piled the last bag on top of the others. "I'll get the utilities turned on and move in tomorrow."

The bag fell, and she leaned down to pick it up, poking her ass out—one of the positions I'd always imagined for us.

I blinked back that image, went to her, and turned her around. That was a mistake. The electric shock of touching her, even clothed, was more than I'd bargained for. I wasn't ready for the heat of that touch.

"What?" she asked.

I backed away. "Not until I get a chance to fix the locks. You said you have work tomorrow. What time?"

"Eight."

I backed into the hallway. "I have work tomorrow as well. We'll talk about a plan tomorrow evening, then. You're staying here until the house is safe and the utilities are on."

A slight smile appeared. "How can I thank you, Zack?"

"I'll think of something." The words escaped before I realized the innuendo involved.

Her grin grew. She hadn't missed it.

304

"See you in the morning, Sunshine." I escaped to the stairs to move the laundry to the dryer before heading to bed.

"Good night, Zack" she called.

It had been a good night—not the pepper-spray incident, but what had followed. That hadn't been the way I would have imagined me undressing her, but the sight of her almost naked had been burned into my brain. I wasn't letting go anytime soon. For a sight like that, I had a photographic memory.

Downstairs, I moved the wet clothes to the dryer and started it. Closing my eyes for a moment, my skin heated and my cock surged. I saw her in front of me again…felt her skin as I raised the shirt over her head, putting me face-to-face with her cleavage—cleavage I wanted to nestle my face in.

I repositioned my swollen dick in my pants and took a deep breath before heading back upstairs.

Inviting her to stay here had been the right thing to do—the only thing, under the circumstances. But life would be a whole lot more complicated after tonight.

Living next to Brittney was going to be pleasure and torture all wrapped together. A constant temptation, but one I could manage. I could envision Friday night pizza and a movie with her—no, make that Thursday night, just like we'd done as teenagers, the three of us.

Only now it would be just the two of us, without Doug to keep us apart.

Complicated *is not nearly a strong enough word.*

# CHAPTER 7

*BRITTNEY*

I woke up early Wednesday morning. More correctly, I re-woke for the umpteenth time since trying to fall asleep. The sky had started to brighten outside, and the sheer curtains wouldn't allow even an attempt at further sleep with the sun up. Between memories of Benji's harassment, thoughts of Zack's kindness had bounced my emotions from one extreme to the other, so sleep had come in fits and starts.

Rolling out of bed, I slipped into the sweats Zack had provided last night and a pair of black work shoes from my suitcase.

The house was quiet as I descended the stairs.

Last night, I hadn't seen anything of the downstairs, and I was surprised to find the first two rooms with construction debris and torn-up floors. One of the rooms had a wall out down to the studs. This place was a disaster zone. Passing through plastic sheeting covering a doorway, I found two rooms in back without any of the destruction of the other rooms: a room with a TV and the kitchen. A check of the fridge yielded the normal bachelor-living-alone situation: no veggies, a package of hot dogs, some containers that looked like leftover Chinese, beer and soda cans, bottles of wine, and an egg carton with one egg in it, but no milk.

I closed the fridge and checked the small pantry. Nothing worthwhile for breakfast in there except some protein bars and coffee.

After a return trip upstairs to grab my purse, I let myself out the front door.

I'd passed a grocery store a few blocks from here, so I climbed into my trusty little car for a quick shopping trip.

My first order of business was the restroom in the store. I hadn't wanted to wake Zack at this ungodly hour by flushing in his house. Although Doug hadn't minded peeing and not flushing, it wasn't my style.

With that out of the way, I started filling my hand-held basket with real food. Dodging the early-morning employees restocking shelves, I needed a while to find everything in the unfamiliar layout.

At the checkout lane, I added an energy drink for later.

The elderly lady in front of me was counting out coins to pay for her apple, a dozen eggs, and three cans of cat food.

The cashier looked on nervously as she fumbled in her coin purse to come up with enough.

After pushing the coins around on the counter she glanced back at the screen and her face dropped even further as she recounted her coins. "Maybe if we take off one of the cans," she suggested to the cashier.

My stomach clenched for her. I fished two quarters out of my purse and placed them on the counter. "Please, allow me."

She turned to me with teary eyes. "I'm sure I've got it in here somewhere." She fumbled through her purse again.

"I insist," I said, pushing the coins forward. "I know how much our cats mean to us. I have one too."

I'd never had a cat. But I'd known people who had, and that was close enough.

She blinked back tears. "Thank you so much, dear."

The cashier swept up the coins and returned a nickel to her.

When it was my turn to pay, a few measly fives and a twenty stared back at me from my wallet, so I used my Visa. As I exited the store with my bag, the sunrise lifted my mood. Today was a new day, a new beginning. Benji and San Jose were behind me. LA and my new neighbor Zack, of all people, were ahead of me.

The thought made me grin—my neighbor Zack. I'd noticed the kitchen windows of the houses faced each other. With some luck, I'd get a glimpse of him eating his Wheaties or whatever every morning. I envisioned myself waving to him through the glass, and him smiling when he noticed me and waving back.

After closing the car door, I pulled mascara out of my purse and used the visor mirror. A few strokes before starting back to Zack's place wouldn't hurt.

~

ZACK

. . .

I LISTENED FOR A MOMENT BEFORE ROLLING OUT OF BED. NO NOISES INDICATED THAT Brittney had woken yet.

Downstairs though, I realized I'd been wrong. The aroma of bacon was unmistakable as I neared the kitchen.

The sight of her brightened my morning. Brittney was busy at the stove with her back to me. She hadn't noticed me enter as she swayed to music in her earbuds.

I noisily pulled a chair out at the table and sat.

"Breakfast is almost ready," she said as she turned to see me.

"My breakfast is just a protein bar or a Hot Pocket."

"No way." She waved the spatula at me. "Breakfast is the most important meal of the day." She turned back to the stove. "I didn't know what you liked, so I kept it simple. I've got French toast and bacon."

"Just a breakfast bar is fine."

She ignored my comment. "If you don't like the French toast, I can scramble some eggs."

I went to the pantry and pulled out two bars, tore off paper towel sections for napkins, and returned to the table.

Brittney arrived with two aromatic plates of breakfast, added bowls of raspberries, and took a seat across from me.

I lifted a bar, ready to open it.

She fixed me with a glare. "Don't you dare insult the cook."

I stopped. "Now who's being bossy?"

"You provided the roof. I'm providing the food. Now grow up, eat it, and stop complaining."

This sassiness was an adorable new side of Brittney.

I put the bar down, trying not to show a grin, and bit off a piece of bacon. The taste was perfect.

"Thank you. You didn't have to."

The warm smile she offered was as contagious as I remembered from before.

"You're welcome. I wanted to. And from the look of your refrigerator, I could tell you needed a regular meal."

I drizzled a little maple syrup over the French toast. "I eat out a lot."

"That's not healthy."

"Who are you? My mother?" I asked, suddenly annoyed.

She stared at me as I cut into my French toast. The corner of her mouth turned up ever so slightly. She thought she'd won.

The French toast melted in my mouth. "This is good," I mumbled, chewing.

She started in on hers.

"Long drive down from San Jose?" I asked between bites.

She rolled her eyes. "I've never seen so many trucks on the road, and there was an accident with a car fire on the Grapevine that took forever to get past."

I took a guess. "You must have started late."

She finished chewing before her answer. "A little after three, I guess."

"Had to skip dinner?"

"Yeah, I wanted to get here before it was too late."

"Why didn't you start earlier?"

She looked down at her plate and shrugged. Instead of answering, she filled her mouth with berries.

I didn't pursue it, but finished my bacon and French toast in silence. I glanced up at her after my last forkful, and for just a second imagined how those pouty lips would taste. Would I be able to separate the taste of her from the maple syrup and bacon? I settled on yes.

"What are you smirking about?" she challenged with a creased brow.

"Nothing."

Her fork came up and pointed at me.

"You suck as a liar, Zachary Benson."

I got up to leave before I painted myself into an inescapable corner. "I was just admiring...what a good cook you are."

Honesty was not the best policy here.

"You didn't eat your berries."

I took my plate to the sink, unable to look at her for fear she'd see right through me.

"I'm not a big fruit person." At least we'd changed the subject.

"You need fruit. Sit down and eat or I'll be insulted."

I took my seat again. "Well, we can't have that." I didn't dislike all fruit. Apples were okay. I spooned some of the tart, red berries into my mouth.

"I forgot to ask, where are you working?"

I forced another spoonful before answering, but the real reason for my delay was that smile.

"I'm part of the Benson Corp. team."

"How is working for your dad?"

I glanced at my watch and stood. "I'll take the first shower, if that's okay. I have to get to the office. Call me if you need anything."

"Not until you finish those berries."

"I've had enough." In my terms, three spoonfuls had been two too many.

"Don't be a baby."

I didn't sit, but I did force another spoonful.

"To call you, I'll need your number."

I held out my hand. "Give me your phone."

She handed it over.

I added myself as a contact and sent myself a text, so I'd have her number as well.

She followed me to the sink with her plate and bowl.

I felt that same electric shock as her arm brushed against mine, and I pulled away. Distance from temptation is what I needed.

She was rinsing the dishes when I looked back before exiting the kitchen. Her ass from this perspective was perfect, too perfect.

"Don't use all the hot water," she called as I mounted the stairs.

## BRITTNEY

HE'D GIVEN IN PRETTY QUICKLY FOR A MAN WHO CLAIMED HE DIDN'T EAT FRUIT. Whatever his problem was, I intended to fix it. Good nutrition was the bedrock of good health. Everybody knew that. Even if the seeds were hard to get out from between your teeth.

Cleaning the dishes, I mulled over my plan for the day. Dr. Fosback was first on my to-do list. Getting on his schedule quickly was imperative, and Dr. Fosback had always been good to work for. With some coaxing I might even get a few extra days out of him.

Back upstairs, I took my turn in the bathroom once Zack had finished.

Last night I hadn't realized how quaintly cute it was with the pink tile and vintage world-map wallpaper above that. The freestanding linen cabinet, dressing chair, and antique brass fixtures gave the room real character, like the grand old lady this house had once been.

I pulled out a cleaning wipe and removed my mascara—Dr. Fosback didn't allow hygienists to wear makeup—allergy avoidance, he'd once explained. Stepping into the tub, I pulled the curtain, adjusted the water, and smiled to myself— Zack liked my cooking.

MY FAVORITE PARKING SPOT IN THE FAR CORNER BEHIND DR. FOSBACK'S PRACTICE WAS empty when I arrived. I checked my ponytail in the mirror. It didn't look tight enough, so I redid it—professional job, professional appearance.

Inside, Martha was at reception, just as she'd always been. "Brittney, it's so great to see you. How have you been?'

"Good, thanks."

"I couldn't believe it yesterday when Darren said you were coming back. I thought you'd left us for good."

She had worked with Dr. Fosback forever and was the only one who got away with calling him by his first name.

"I've had enough of San Jose. Is he in yet?"

"Yeah, you know the way."

I let myself in past waiting and found Dr. Fosback all the way in the back.

"Brittney Spear, look at you, pretty as ever." He greeted me with the same firm handshake he always had.

"It's Clark now," I corrected him.

"Married? Good for you."

"Not anymore, but I'm keeping the name. It was difficult always getting mistaken for the pop princess."

The marriage assumption was a common one. I hadn't gotten married, or divorced, but nobody here needed to know the real reason for my name change. Anonymity meant safety.

"Sorry to hear that. Anyway, I wasn't expecting you so soon."

"I left as soon as we got off the phone."

His brow dropped slightly. "Well, when I said I could fit you in a few days a week, I didn't mean this week. I was thinking more when Sandy goes out on maternity."

I forced as much of a smile as I could muster. "Oh. Well then... In the meantime, I'm available to fill in if any of the girls needs to take a day off."

This was bad news for my bank account, and it wasn't the sense I'd gotten from him on the phone yesterday.

"Sure thing. Why don't you get the paperwork started with Martha, and we'll be in touch as soon as anything opens up."

"It's great to see you again, Doctor," I said as I backed toward reception.

He nodded. "You too, Brittney." He went back to the patient record he'd been reviewing.

I found Martha out front and took the spare seat. "Dr. Fosback said to do paperwork with you."

She pulled a file folder from under some others. "I made this up yesterday. Did you bring your hygienist license?"

"Sure." I retrieved the folded paper from my purse and handed it over.

She read the name, and then eyed my ring finger before taking the paper back to the copier.

The first form in the folder was an I-9 for me to fill out, followed by a W-4. I handed over my driver's license.

Martha copied my ID. "Name change, I see," she said, glancing up.

"It didn't work out." I didn't say any more. She could work out the implication without me having to lie.

"Good for you. Better to cut your losses soon if it isn't going to work in the long run. I learned that the hard way."

I nodded.

"The government needs a second form of ID these days as well."

I mentally kicked myself for leaving everything behind. "My papers are with the things being shipped. Can it wait a few days?"

"Sure, bring it in when your things arrive. You'll need your marriage license too for the name change." She handed me an employment application.

. "Do I really need to do this one?" I took the application and didn't correct her about the marriage license. I had the Arkansas court order for my name change coming.

"Yeah, you never know. You might have been convicted of a felony or something since you last worked here." She laughed.

"Goodness, no," I said.

I worked through the forms slowly and tried not to show my concern. I pulled up the address and phone number for Dr. Call's practice on my phone as I filled out the employment history. It was a complication I hadn't anticipated. I hadn't broached the subject of my suspension with Dr. Fosback on the phone yesterday. I hadn't thought it would come up. I was moving back into town, and I'd had to leave Dr. Call's practice—it should be as simple as that. My hand shook as I wrote *moving* in the column labeled *reason for leaving*. I did the same for the Pink Pig entry.

As I continued through the form, my phone vibrated with an incoming call.

"Do you need to take that?" she asked.

Seeing Benji's name on the screen made for an easy decision. "Nah. It can wait." I sent the call to voicemail, then turned it off. I had no desire to be interrupted again by Benji, and that's exactly what he would do—call three times in a row before giving up.

"Dr. Fosback mentioned that Sandy would be going on maternity leave soon," I said.

Martha looked up. "She should be taking it easy, if you ask me. Girls these days seem to want to work right up until the end, without any thought of the baby. Becoming a mother is a job in itself."

"I agree. Sooner is better. She should think about the baby. Is it a boy or a girl?"

"Twins, one of each, I think. You're a twin, aren't you?"

I knew the situation well. "That's right. Mom said we were hell on wheels for a few years."

"Don't tell her that. She's nervous enough as it is."

I laughed. "Got it. Growing up a twin was a great experience. You can tell her that."

"I will. At least she'll have an easier delivery. My first was nine pounds twelve ounces."

I didn't want to get into the difficult delivery discussion she'd had with me more than once. "When is she due to go out?"

Martha checked her calendar. "In about two."

"Two weeks? She is getting close."

"No, dear. Two months."

I couldn't keep my shoulders from slumping. That wasn't the news I'd expected.

Back in my car, I leaned my head against the steering wheel and tried not to cry. I had to be strong for Samantha and power through this rough patch. Two months, though, was more than a rough patch. I pulled out my ponytail, started the car, and turned it toward home. My grandmother's dark house was now my home, my only place to call home.

The low fuel light came on, and I turned into the gas station two blocks down. A twenty and two fives stared back at me from my wallet. I marched one of the small bills into the mini-mart and handed it to the cashier. "Five on three please."

She nodded without a word, and I pumped the tiny amount of fuel into my tank.

Two months would be an eternity to go without hygienist pay. Hopefully the Rusty Bucket would come through with lots of hours.

After the short drive back to Zack's house, I let myself in with the key he'd provided and pulled a Pepsi from the fridge. I'd have to add diet to my shopping list for next time.

It took a moment to locate the number for LA's department of water and power, but the nice lady there was happy to take my credit card number for the turn-on deposit. She told me to expect technicians for the water and electric by the end of the day. Unfortunately, without any time frame, I was stuck here until they came.

That meant no visit to the Rusty Bucket this afternoon to talk to Max about getting my old job back. But first things first, I needed the utilities turned on as quickly as possible.

I hadn't shopped for lunch fixings, so I set about frying eggs and toasting English muffins for an early lunch.

After eating, I started pulling things out of the pantry and putting them on the table to restock in a proper order. The box of protein bars fell over and knocked my purse to the floor.

I knelt, and the second thing I picked up was my pink penance envelope—the one with the reminder of the worst stage of my life, the reminder to be a better person in the future and not let others down. I replaced it in my purse without opening it to read again.

One by one, I replaced the pantry items in a sensible order.

When I turned, the pink envelope still peeked out of my purse. I pushed it to the bottom. Things were shitty enough. I didn't need to torture myself that way today.

# CHAPTER 8

*Zack*

With every ding and ratchet upward of the red numerals, I moved farther from where I wanted to be.

The elevator door opened, and I straightened my mandatory tie.

Wendy checked her watch as I approached.

"Let me guess. Stanton again? Did you give him my message?" I asked.

I'd instructed her last night to tell him I didn't want to discuss irrelevant items going forward.

"Yes, yes, and he assured me these were important."

"Yeah, right."

It was getting late in London, at least by Stanton's standards, but I still went to fetch coffee for Wendy and me. "Decaf?"

"Regular," she responded.

Returning, I put the mocha down on the coaster she used to protect the elegant mahogany of her desk—the perk of being an executive's PA.

She pulled out a sweetener packet from her drawer. She insisted on Stevia, which wasn't stocked at the coffee machine. "Thank you."

"If Brittney Spear calls at any time, put her right through, or hunt me down if I'm out and about."

"The singer?"

"No, just Spear—no S on the end."

"Brittney, huh?" Her eyebrow arched with an unasked question.

"It's just in case she calls, but she probably won't. She moved back to town, and I promised her brother, I'd help her if she needed it."

"Right." She stirred her coffee with a smirk. "Hunt you down. I'll definitely do that."

I had just dispensed with London and Rome when Wendy popped her head in. "Harold is here to see you."

"Sure," I responded.

Harold Synderman, our company CFO, let himself in and closed the door. "I guess it's my turn now."

"I guess." We'd previously discussed my father's view that we Benson children should be rotated through several departments in the company to *broaden* our exposure.

Harold understood that his role in this was to provide a position and training at the appointed time, whether he needed us or not.

He unbuttoned his coat and sat. "I know finance is not anybody's first choice."

"I'm not sure it's the right time."

Harold thought the rotations were a good idea, and he seemed to view it as his place to encourage the reluctant among us to see the light. But I wasn't in the mood to discuss it this morning. Many people in the company would relent quickly in an argument with me, but not Harold. He was confident enough in his position and his relationship with my father that the family name didn't sway him. For that, I was grateful—on occasion. It allowed me to bounce ideas off him with a rigorous testing of my position, but not this morning.

"You know the opportunity Lloyd is providing for you is one of a kind." He lowered his voice. "The experience will be valuable. On top of that, London is an exciting city."

"Like I said, the timing might not be right. I'll need to give it some thought."

He rose. "Well, you do that. Decisions like this are important, but you know he'll expect an answer soon." He buttoned his coat.

"I know."

After he left, I turned toward the window to think. I took out my keys and fingered the attached coin he'd given me.

Dad wanted me—no, expected me—to take the London assignment, then come back here to take on his next lesson. Such was my family obligation. Obligation with a capital O.

Harold had been right; the management training aspect of it was invaluable.

I turned back to my desk and got busy on tomorrow's customer presentation. Deciding later meant exactly that, *later*.

As the day progressed, the occasional call from a US-based sales guy brought my desk phone to life, but my cell stayed silent.

I double-checked that it was on and charged.

Wishing didn't make things happen.

~

*BRITTNEY*

MY PHONE RANG AS I BEGAN COLLECTING MY BAGS OF CLOTHES IN THE ROOM
upstairs at Zack's place. The screen said Darth Vader, and I had no idea who that
was. I sent it to voicemail, but it rang again, and I gave in.

"Hello?"

"Wanna have lunch?" Zack asked.

The mere sound of his voice lightened my mood. He must have named
himself Darth Vader when he'd put in his contact information this morning.

"Sorry, I already made myself something, and I have to wait for the DWP
guys anyway to get the water and power back on. They wouldn't give me
anything more definite than sometime today."

"Oh...then dinner."

"I can take care of myself, you know."

"If you're going to be snotty about it, forget it." He hung up on me.

He was right. I needed to control my urge to talk back. Today he was the one
friendly face in town, and I'd just been bitchy to him.

I returned his call. "I'm sorry. I'd love to have dinner with you."

"Great. I'll get off early. How does Cardinelli's sound to you?"

"Way too expensive. I can't afford that. Taco Bell is even stretching it on my
budget these days."

"Forget that. I'm paying, and no complaints. I'll be back around five."

"I can't let you do that. Taco Bell, and I'm paying my share."

He chuckled. "You argue with me one more time, and I'm gonna have to take
you over my knee."

He had no idea what that threat did to me. I couldn't count the number of
times I'd envisioned his hand on my bare bottom, and if I had to go over his knee
to get it, fine.

I swallowed. "I'll be good, but just this once."

"What are you doing to stay busy this afternoon?"

"Just doing my nails and watching a few soaps." I hung up before he had a
chance to say anything.

The phone rang again, as if on cue.

"Can't you be serious for a change?"

"Well, you deserve it. You called me snotty."

We both hung on the line in silence, daring the other to say something.

I broke down first. "I'm actually going to take my things over to the house
while I wait for the DWP guys to show up."

"I'd be careful about that, if I were you."

"Why? It's my house now."

"I'm just worried for you."

The sentiment warmed me. I'd always wished he'd care about me, and worry was close enough for today.

"I can handle a few bags of clothes."

"It's not the bags I'm worried about."

"What then?"

"The spiders," he said in a low tone.

I shivered at the word.

He knew I'd had severe arachnophobia ever since the bite I got in the fourth grade. It had been a black widow—a female, the kind that ate her mate after sex. Although I'd survived it, the experience had left me jumping at the sight of a spider, regardless of the type. There was no such thing as a *good* spider. I didn't trust any of them.

"You're just saying that," I shot back with false confidence.

"Take your chances, if you want. Or wait for me to get home and help you."

He was trying to scare me needlessly. That had to be it.

"Thanks. I'll manage."

"Also, the back kitchen door doesn't lock. That's how the kids got in, so I wouldn't take anything over you're not willing to lose."

Great. Now I had another thing to pay for. "Who do I call to get that fixed?"

"Nobody. I'll handle it for you."

We hung up after he admonished me again to be careful.

He didn't run my life. Nobody did.

With a purse and two bags in hand, I headed next door. I wasn't going to be scared out of making progress, but the bags I brought didn't have anything I needed for work.

I opened the door to my new *old* house with the key I'd retrieved from the planter yesterday. In the afternoon light, it looked dirtier than it had last night. Dust hung in the air, highlighted by the streams of light sneaking around curtains that were not quite closed. The onion-like odor of the pepper spray lingered, and my airway tightened with the memory of not being able to breathe last night.

I put the bags of clothes outside on the porch and returned to open the curtains. The situation looked way worse with more light.

Cleanup would have to come first.

Three hours, three buckets of water carried from Zack's house, and four rolls of paper towels later, I was done for the day. I'd wiped down the walls and floor upstairs—which had taken the brunt of the pepper spray—worked on the stairs, and swept lightly downstairs.

Every stitch of furniture in the house needed heavy-duty cleaning. Grams hadn't been up to it in her later years, and wouldn't hear of letting a stranger in the house to touch her things.

I put away four bags of clothes upstairs and re-purposed the bags to hold the

317

miscellaneous trash that had been left around, mostly fast-food wrappers, beer cans, and the like. A receipt from a Burger King bag showed it hadn't taken the local kids long to start occupying the house after Grams died.

The pantry still had miscellaneous spices and canned foods. I added the few things that were obviously too old to the trash bags. The safe was on the floor of the pantry where it had always been. Gramps had said this was the last place a thief would never think to look. The pepper spray can found a new home next to the safe. I was probably safer without it in my purse.

The bathrooms and toilets were a disgusting hazmat situation, and not getting any better until the water was back on. The rugs were going to need a good vacuuming, and probably a proper cleaning when I could afford it. I was sure they had looked quite nice in their prime, but today they were terrible. The furniture was old, really old, but solid and in good condition.

The surprise had been the two hypodermics I found in the corner behind the loveseat. They had to have been from after Grams died, so at least they weren't from any of my victims.

Just the thought of that made me cringe. The nightmares had only recently stopped, and I hoped this wouldn't bring them back.

I went to the front door to answer a knock.

Two guys in brown LADWP shirts were at the door. "Miss Clark?"

"Yup." I went out to greet them and get things started.

They each had a white DWP truck on the street.

I went with Jerald, the electric guy, first, and turning on the juice to the house was done in ten minutes. I thanked him and approached Ernesto, the water guy, who wore a worried expression.

He was messing around on the front lawn, looking into what must have been the water meter box.

"Something's wrong," he said.

"Like what?"

He twisted a long-handled rod. "I have to keep you shut off until you fix the leak."

"What leak?"

"No idea. You'll have to have your plumber figure that out, but your pipes aren't filling up like they should. I had the water running full blast for a good five minutes. You're not running any sprinklers that I can see, so you have some monster leak in the house. I can't turn you on until you get it fixed. Those are the rules."

I kicked the dirt. "Damn," I said. It took all my strength not to swear up a storm.

"Look, it's just the rules."

"Sorry. I didn't mean you. It's just the damned situation."

He slid the concrete cover back over the box. "When your plumber fixes the problem, call the installation number, and I'll be right back here in a flash."

"Thanks." I didn't have a plumber, and if I did, I couldn't afford to pay him.

He picked up his things and left, probably anxious to get away from the angry lady.

I trudged back up the steps and into the house. I flipped on the light switch inside the door.

Nothing.

*Fuck.*

I tried lights on the stairs, and in the kitchen—still nothing.

Why did everything have to go wrong? Now with bills from an electrician, as well as a plumber, and with no hygienist job, I was in even worse shape than I'd been in San Jose.

*Double fuck.*

I locked up and went back next door to get cleaned up. I wasn't going to dinner with Zack with this layer of dirt on me and my clothes. I sniffed the shoulder of my shirt—or this BO.

After cleaning up and dressing in clean clothes, I looked semi-presentable. I decided on a little mascara tonight.

# CHAPTER 9

*Zack*

THE WEEKLY ADVERTISING REVIEW WAS RUNNING LONG. I CHECKED MY WATCH: TEN till five. "Hey guys. We're cutting this short. That's all for today."

With the exception of Stan, who hadn't gotten a chance to present yet, I didn't see any disappointment around the table.

"Stan, we'll start with you next week."

He perked up and nodded.

The group gathered their papers, and the room emptied quickly.

"You're done early," Wendy noted as I returned.

I parked the papers on my desk, grabbed my coat and briefcase, and locked up. "Have a dinner meeting I have to get to."

Wendy flipped her calendar back and forth. "Sorry, I must have missed it."

I smiled. "I forgot to put it on the schedule."

She cocked an eyebrow. "Give her my regards."

I walked away without answering and waved over my shoulder.

She didn't miss a thing.

THE DRIVE HOME HAD BEEN SLOWER THAN NORMAL WITH ALL THE TRAFFIC ON THE roads that I normally missed. Pulling up, I parked out front instead of turning into the driveway alongside the house, which led to the garage in back. I wandered past the front room into the kitchen and found Brittney at the table, head in her hands.

"Hey, Sunshine. Ready for dinner?"

She closed her eyes and mumbled, "The house is all screwed up."

I set my briefcase down. "Come on, we're burning daylight here. I'm buying you a good meal, and you can tell me all about it. I'm a great house fixer and an even better listener."

That got a hint of a smile out of her. "But it's so bad."

"What did I tell you about causing trouble earlier? No moping allowed in this house." I rounded the table, grabbed her arm, and pulled her up.

"Hey," she complained.

"No moping, no complaining. Dinner first. After that, I'll go over and look at the house with you, and we'll make a plan."

She huffed. "But I can't afford to fix it."

"What did I just say about complaining? You can tell me all about it over dinner." I motioned to the front. "Your chariot awaits."

She stopped her mumbling, and I followed her to the front. I locked up before descending the steps.

"Which car is yours?"

"The blue one." The car still had its original Acapulco blue paint. "I call her the Snake."

She walked toward it, and her mouth dropped open as she went to the back to check out the name plate.

"You drive a Shelby?"

"They don't make 'em like this anymore."

That was an understatement. A '67 Shelby GT500 was the pinnacle of the early Mustangs, the ultimate big-block muscle car from that era—all engine and little refinement. This wasn't a sissy car with leather seats, cup holders, a million-watt stereo, and a moonroof. It was a car that took off in a squealing cloud of tire smoke if you had a heavy foot. And, I had upgraded it to Super Snake specs.

"Does Doug know you have this?" she asked.

"I got it after he left. It'll be a surprise next time he's back."

She put her hand on the roof and looked inside. "He'd kill for a car like this."

She had that right, any car nut would.

I had debated getting a Cobra roadster, but chose the GT500 with a roof and real roll bar as being more practical.

"He'll be jealous when he hears you got to ride in it before him." The car was ten-percent practical and ninety percent chick-magnet. Make that ninety-nine percent chick magnet.

Piss Boy was walking down the other side of the street, his eyes glued on either my car or my date, I couldn't tell which.

"I still need that letter if you want your phone back," I shouted.

He gave me the finger, looked away, and kept walking.

"What's that about?" Brittney asked.

"Tell you at dinner."

She tilted her head and frowned, no happier about delayed gratification than she had been growing up.

I opened the door for her. "Climb in."

I hurried around and got in myself, taking a quick glance at Piss Boy up ahead.

He looked back in our direction again, walking slowly away.

"I can't figure out how to work this seatbelt," Brittney complained.

"Here, like this." I showed her how to fasten the twin shoulder belts that went with this car—another racing heritage setup.

Since the engine was warm, the car started easily. The big V-8 roared to life and settled into a rough, burbling idle. I pulled out and headed north.

Piss Boy threw us another middle-finger salute as we passed him.

"Are you going to tell me what his problem is?"

She hadn't changed; waiting didn't suit her.

I shifted into third. "He was one of a group of kids I rousted from your house two nights ago. I took all their phones and told them they would only get them back when they brought me apology letters for breaking into your house."

Brittney laughed. "Let me guess. He's too proud?"

"More like too stupid. Anyway, I still have his phone, waiting for the punk to wise up."

She watched the road silently as we wended our way north. "Thank you."

"For what?"

"Guarding the house for me."

"The least I could do for the neighborhood. Next thing you know they'd be too drunk one night and break into my house by mistake."

I was only half joking. Letting them get away with partying in an abandoned house would only escalate to worse things later.

# CHAPTER 10

*BRITTNEY*

ZACK PULLED TO THE CURB IN FRONT OF THE RESTAURANT: CARDINELLI'S IN Westwood.

The young valet opened the door for me.

Zack traded him the keys for a stub.

"You sure you trust him with your car? He looks a little young," I noted.

I guessed him to still be in high school.

"Tony will be careful. He knows what will happen if he dings any of the cars, and mine in particular."

"You must eat here often."

Zack guided me toward the door with a hand at the small of my back. It scorched my skin through the fabric.

My reaction to the touch surprised me.

He must've felt the heat too, as he quickly removed his hand. "Often enough."

I slowed my walk, yearning for that touch again, but he didn't provide it. I followed the couple ahead of us toward the entrance.

"This seems a little fancy. Are you sure I'm dressed well enough?"

The man ahead wore an expensive suit, and his date wore an equally elegant dress. Make that his wife, judging by the wedding band and monster diamond on her finger.

"Trust me," he said. "Your beauty will put the rest of the women in here to shame."

A blush rose in my cheeks, and I gave him a light punch to the shoulder. "Stop that. You're embarrassing me."

"The truth, the whole truth, and nothing but the truth."

My blush rose to three alarms, but I managed to hold my tongue.

"You remember Bill Covington from Brentmoor?"

It only took a second to come back to me. The Benson boys and the Covingtons had often hung out together. "Yeah, vaguely."

"He's a part owner of this place. He and Marco Cardinelli started it after school."

Naturally the rich families owned restaurants to dabble in. "Does that mean you get a discount?"

"No, but I do get a good table."

The well-dressed couple ahead of us gave the hostess their name and were told they would have to wait.

"Mr. Benson," the hostess said as we approached the stand.

Zack's status as a VIP customer was evident when she picked up menus and ushered us in without even bothering to look at her reservation list.

Mr. Expensive Suit checked his watch with a scowl.

The ceilings were high, lending the room a spacious atmosphere. White tablecloths and waiters in matching vests and trousers set this apart from any place I could afford to frequent.

As he'd predicted, the hostess stopped at a table by the window with a view up the hill. The perks of being rich.

Zack pulled my chair out for me—we were going first-class tonight—almost as if I were a girlfriend.

"Nice place."

"You deserve it, Brit."

I basked in the warmth of his smile and opened the menu. The writing was in Italian, naturally, but it was close enough to Spanish that it was possible to pick out what I wanted.

Our waiter, Vinny, arrived with bread and an olive oil-vinegar dipping plate.

Zack put down the wine menu. "Prosecco okay?"

"Sure," I said. When in Rome and all.

Zack ordered a bottle for us and bruschetta to start.

I watched his lips as he spoke, wondering what they tasted like, and what they felt like. The impure thoughts made my pulse race.

Zack set his menu down and looked at me oddly. "The house. You were going to tell me about the house."

I must have missed the question. Just the thought of the problems threatened to give me a headache. "I spent the afternoon cleaning, and I pretty much got the pepper spray cleaned off everything. Then the DWP guys showed up, and the electric guy turned on the power, but none of the lights I tried worked."

"Did you check the fuses?"

"I wouldn't even know where to start."

"No matter. I do."

Vinny interrupted us with the prosecco bottle, which he uncorked with a loud pop.

I perused the menu again while Zack approved the wine. I settled on the *ravioli alla lucana* for dinner.

Zack lifted his glass. "To getting into your new house."

I clinked my glass to his and sipped. The sentiment was nice, if a little out of reach.

Zack set his glass down. "It's probably the fuses. I can check for you when we get back. Mine have blown on occasion. These old houses weren't built with very hefty circuits."

"Thanks, but that's just the beginning." I broke off a piece of bread.

"How so?" he asked.

I dipped my bread in the oil and vinegar plate. "The water guy wouldn't turn the water on. He said there was a big leak somewhere."

Zack took some bread as well. "Did you see a leak, or hear anything?"

I had to finish chewing. "No, but I wasn't inside when he was doing it. I went through the house when I closed up and didn't see any water, but I didn't check upstairs either."

"A water leak is not good. You wouldn't want standing water on those nice floors. That's for sure something we should look at when we get back."

A knot formed in my gut at the thought that my Grams's nice house might be getting damaged as we sat here. "Is it something we should go back and check on right now?"

He waved his piece of bread. "No. It's a question of days, not minutes. We can check when we get back." He dipped his bread in the oil plate.

"But he said I have to have a plumber fix it."

He sipped his glass of bubbly. "I'm your plumber."

"But I can't—"

"We got this," he said, interrupting me. "Let's catch up over a nice meal and worry about the plumbing when we get back. What you can't do..." He pointed his finger at me. "...is obsess about it. You know I'm right."

I let out a breath. "I guess."

Vinny reappeared and took our orders.

After the waiter left, Zack leaned back in his chair. "So catch me up. What have you been up to?"

I wasn't really sure where to start, the question was so open-ended. "Nothing much. I've been up in San Jose for a few years."

He leaned forward. "And?"

"Not much, just tending bar and doing hygienist work during the day. That is, when I can get the days, the hours."

He spun his glass a bit. "Is that a problem? Getting work?"

"It was with the practice I joined. Our dentist, Dr. Call, didn't... Well, she hired enough hygienists that none of us ever got very many days. We were always trading off with one another, so I averaged two days a week, sometimes three, when what I really wanted was a full four."

"That sucks."

My feelings exactly.

"Is that why you're back down here?" he asked.

I debated giving the full answer, but chickened out. Rattling the words around in my head, they sounded pathetic, even to me. "Yeah. I want to get back to working with Dr. Fosback here in LA."

"That sounds like a good plan. That practice will give you the hours you want, right?"

"Yeah, I think. Sooner or later." I shrank down in my seat.

His eyes widened a bit, apparently sensing the deception in my answer. "You checked with them before coming back, right?"

At least my answer could be truthful. "Yeah, I called them."

"You said you had to go to his office today. How did that go? When do you start?"

Vinnie came back to the table with our salads—Caesar for him, house for me—sparing me an immediate answer.

"Doug tells me your little sister is going to business school."

Mercifully he'd changed the line of questioning.

"You two keeping in touch?" I asked, although I knew the answer.

"Yeah, we keep up." He forked a bite of salad into his mouth.

I did the same.

We were like a couple of prizefighters circling each other, cautiously looking for an opening. He was trying to get up to speed on my history, and I was trying desperately to withhold it.

"He told me you broke up with a guy that was an idiot," he said, peering over his wine glass at me.

There it was, a question about Benji. "My ex an idiot? That's the nice way to put it." Actually he was much worse.

"He's still hassling you, then?" Zack asked before taking another bite of the salad.

"What do you mean?" I asked, feigning ignorance. With a little luck I could get out of this without a full data dump.

"Doug said he was turning into a stalker." Zack took a sip of his prosecco, not taking his eyes off of me for a moment.

I regretted having opened up to Doug about that now. "A little. He's a creep."

If I'd given Doug the whole story, Benji would probably be in pieces in a landfill by now.

"You could've called me, you know."

That was the suggestion Doug had made when I told him about it.

326

"You were too far away." I looked down, avoiding his eyes.

"Using Dad's jet, it's only an hour. You should've called."

I looked up and appraised him.

He looked as if he meant what he'd said. He would've protected me in a heartbeat.

"One visit is all it would've taken," he said. "You should have called."

"I guess." I took another bite of salad to keep from having to say any more.

"I bet it'll be good to get back to your hygienist job right away. Doug told me how hard it's been for you to put Samantha through Wharton."

He seemed to have gotten much more detail about our lives from Doug than I'd guessed.

Vinny arrived with our dinner plates.

Mine smelled and looked as scrumptious as the menu description. The first bite was even better than the aroma.

"Like it?"

"Delicious, absolutely delicious."

I didn't have the words I needed to describe how good this was. I should have known Zack wouldn't choose anything but the best.

"Marco—that's Bill's partner here—really does a good job."

I decided the best defense was a good offense. "You haven't told me what you've been doing."

"Same old, same old. I'm working in marketing now." He didn't elaborate further.

∾

ZACK

"Do you have a picture of this jerk?" I asked.

"Why?" Brittney eyed me skeptically.

I put my fork down. "Do you?"

She took another bite of ravioli and shrugged.

I held my hand out. "Just give me your phone."

She cocked her head. "Yes, I have a picture. Why? Are you going to smack the picture or something?"

I kept my hand out. "I want to be able to recognize him if he shows up. That's why."

She seemed to deem that reasonable enough and handed her phone over after scrolling through pictures.

The guy didn't look like much, but at least now I knew who to pound if he came by. "Thanks." I put the phone down and slid it to her. "What's his name?"

She frowned. "Ex."

I waited, but didn't get anything more out of her.

She swallowed the wine she'd sipped. "Thank you." She licked her lips.

That simple gesture had me wondering how they would taste, and how they would feel, if the time ever came.

I shook off the thought. "For what?"

"For being concerned. I'm used to looking out for myself."

"I'll protect you," I offered. It sounded lame after I said it. "I promised Doug," I added, which didn't sound any better.

"I have pepper spray, if I need it."

I laughed. "And we saw how well that went for you."

"I didn't do very well, did I?"

"Nope. You should take that out of your purse before you hurt yourself."

She giggled. "I already did."

I grinned. Seeing her giggle was a treat. She needed to do it more often, and somehow that task was going to fall to me.

"What are you smirking about?" she asked.

"Nothing."

"Really? You're going to try that on me?"

"I was grinning, not smirking, and it was because I enjoy seeing you happy for a change. It's a good look on you."

She blushed. "Oh."

The blush was also a good look on her, and another thing I would have to encourage. She dug back into her food.

To change the subject, I asked about Samantha's situation and how things were going for her.

Brittney was very proud of her sister. That came through clearly.

I ate as Brittney talked, and admired the pale blue of her eyes, the way they sparkled when she was enthusiastic or giddy. I watched her lips as she spoke and couldn't help but want to touch them with mine—explore them, or have them explore me.

Before long, the meal had come to an end, and it had been quite enjoyable. Brittney had grown into a beautiful woman. She just needed to control her impulse to argue, although she was adorable when she got worked up.

Vinny took our plates and brought the dessert menu.

I had it memorized.

She looked it over briefly. "It all looks like too much for me, and you've already spent so much this evening."

"Nonsense. No amount is too much for you." It sounded sappy, but it was the way I felt.

She shook her head. "These are too fancy for me."

"I've got simple ice cream at home," I offered.

"I don't need anything."

"I'll be insulted if you refuse my dessert invitation."

"Okay then. I'd love a simple bowl of ice cream."

I settled the bill and helped her to the door. When my hand touched the small of her back, I felt another jolt up my arm. I pulled it away and opened the restaurant door for her.

The gesture earned me a sultry *Thank you*.

I walked beside her out toward the valet stand.

She stopped. "Just a sec."

I looked back to find her looking down into her purse.

She tripped and came flying my way.

I stepped toward her and grabbed her to prevent a face plant.

"Careful." My arms came around her and she ended up against me, chest to chest.

She grasped me and steadied herself, looking up, her chest hot and soft against mine. "Sorry."

I kept her close. "Don't be."

Those were the only words that came to me. The sudden warmth of her body obliterated rational thought for a moment. Time stood still as I stared back into those eyes, the pale blue eyes that drew me in, that begged me to pull her closer yet, to fist her hair and pull her mouth to mine. I lifted a lock of her hair to my nose and breathed in the scent. "Vanilla?"

"Like it?"

I nodded, relishing the feel of her tits against me. My cock pushed against my zipper, taking more than a casual interest in her.

"You can borrow it if you want," she said, her fingers stroking my chest lightly.

I let her go and she stepped back, just far enough away that I longed to feel her body heat again, yet close enough that I could still detect the vanilla.

I turned back toward the street and was surprised when she took my hand in hers. I didn't resist as I should have. This was dangerously close to PDA.

Tony raced off to retrieve my car. He didn't need the chit to know which one was mine.

Remember Rule Number One, I mentally chanted to myself.

I pulled my hand away to retrieve cash from my wallet to tip Tony. I could have waited until he got back. I should have waited, but it was too late. The moment had passed.

Why was I conflicted? I should have been relieved to avoid the temptation—she was becoming my Kryptonite. Actually, that's what she'd always been. Without Doug to remind me of the rules, I was becoming weak. I was becoming a pathetic excuse of a friend. Doug deserved better from me.

Tony brought the car up, breaking the awkwardness.

I opened the door for Brittney.

She smiled at me as she scooted in—a smile that seemed to say more than merely thank you. Had she felt it too?

I climbed in the driver's side, buckled in, and we were off. Motoring toward my street, I reviewed my to-do list. Fix her fuse-box issue, turn off the water to her leaky faucet or whatever, fix the back door deadbolt, and she would become my neighbor instead of my guest. *Roommate* was too dangerous a word. It implied cohabitating, sharing the television, the kitchen, and let's not forget the bathroom. It implied glimpses of her in a towel, or hearing her through the wall as she undressed, picturing the scene in my mind. It implied a treacherous closeness that could involve accidental touching. Touching that threatened to erode my discipline.

It also would mean marshaling the self-control to keep from knocking on her door in the middle of the night to join her in bed. In the end, those urges would tear me apart. Just having her in the seat next to me was difficult. A whiff of the vanilla in her hair drifted my way and brought back the feel of her against me, along with the desire to feel that again, without the clothes separating us.

I shook my head in an effort to rid myself of the thoughts, the temptations.

"What's wrong?" she asked, her voice a reminder of her closeness.

I clenched my teeth. "Nothing."

She wasn't the problem. I was.

Being a neighbor was better, safer, a more controlled situation, one with less temptation.

I would still be able to see into her kitchen from mine in the morning. I could wave through the glass. I could invite her over to share Hot Pockets, maybe even fruit, if she insisted. That would be the ticket—fresh blueberries and a Hot Pocket for breakfast across from Brittney, the perfect start to the day. I could stomach berries for her company, and the table between us would provide enough distance for safety.

I stopped at a red light.

"What are you brooding about?" she asked.

"I'm not brooding."

"You haven't said a word since we left the restaurant. That's brooding."

"You haven't either," I reminded her.

"I was waiting for you," she complained.

"And I was trying not to talk your ear off."

She just stared at me. "Bullshit."

"Okay. I was thinking about fixing your house." At least my answer was partly truthful.

"Oh... Do you think it will be hard?"

"I doubt it, but we won't know till we look. If it's just a fuse or two, Home Depot is open until ten, and we'll get the lights on for you this evening."

She played with her hair. "That sounds good."

I looked over, and her smile had turned down for some reason. "What's wrong?"

"How much do fuses cost?"

"I don't know. Maybe a few bucks a piece."

The answer seemed to relieve her.

"Don't worry about the money. I'll take care of it."

She turned toward me. "No, I'll pay. I can't accept any charity."

I pulled the car quickly to the curb. "We're going to settle this right now. I'm paying to fix your house so it's safe, and that's that."

She huffed. "I pay my own bills."

"You aren't this time. I told you what's happening. I'm taking care of it, end of discussion."

She glared at me. "I'm paying you back."

"No. You're Doug's sister, and I'm keeping you safe. I'm taking care of it, I told you."

"That's the problem. You only see me as Doug's sister. But I'm me, and I get to make my own decisions. I'm paying you back."

She had hit the nail on the head. She was Doug's sister, and that changed everything. All the rules were different. And it wasn't something that could be undone.

"Fine. If you want to pay me back, you can make me breakfast every morning."

"Make you breakfast? No way." Her temper was getting the better of her now.

"What, you don't know how?"

"Of course I do. And a lot better than you too."

"Since when did you become so obstinate? That's the deal. Take it or leave it. Unless you want to fix the house yourself."

"Who put you in charge?"

"I did."

"You're impossible."

"I'm practical." I moved my hand to the shift lever, ready to leave. "So, do we have a deal?"

"I guess." Her hands clenched. "You're bossy, you know that?"

I pulled back into traffic before answering. "And you're being irrational." I could live with the bossy description if it meant I could keep her safe.

"Why, because I'm a girl?" she spat.

I knew enough not to respond to such a loaded question. "Because you're getting mad at me for trying to do something nice for you."

"I still say you're bossy."

I let it go. No matter what, she was going to insist on having the last word.

# CHAPTER 11

*BRITTNEY*

THE ENGINE ROARED AS WE PULLED AWAY FROM THE CURB TO RESUME THE TRIP BACK to my new home.

*Make him breakfast, my ass. And me irrational?*

The first chance I got, we were going to see how much hot sauce he could stomach in his eggs. Or maybe salt and pepper on his berries. He'd be begging to do his own breakfast again.

How had the ride back from the restaurant become such a study in contra-dictions?

First there had been my stumble into him as we walked to the car. I'd been tempted to kiss him when he caught me and held me in his arms. I'd never felt so mesmerized by a man's embrace. I hadn't known what to do, and like a dummy, I'd waited for him to make the first move. The way he'd sniffed my hair had been a ten Richter-scale shock to my libido—a move straight out of a movie, or at least a movie I wanted to be in. My breasts ached to be pressed up to his hard chest again.

But then I'd said something lame about letting him borrow my shampoo, and the moment had passed.

I should have offered to let him wash my hair. No, I should have asked him to join me in the shower so I could wash his hair, or he could watch me wash mine, or something. Anything about getting in the shower together would have been better than what I'd said.

Or maybe I should have just kissed him, or closed my eyes and moved closer, offering my lips. I could have rubbed up against his crotch—that might have gotten the message across.

Fuck it, I was so confused. All I knew was I'd blown it somehow, and we'd ended up arguing about paying to fix up the house.

Now I was a fucking breakfast cook.

"Now what are *you* brooding about?" he asked.

"Just worried about getting things fixed at the house." I couldn't possibly be straight with him about my daydreaming.

He turned onto our street: Snakewood. "Don't worry, I'm sure it's minor."

Now this was home; it was where I belonged. Belonging next to him just seemed right.

He pulled into his drive and drove toward the garage. The door rolled up after he pressed a remote, and the car slid in. It was quiet for a second after he turned off the rumbling motor.

"And I'm not bossy. I just want what's right."

I gave up on arguing with him, for tonight at least. It wouldn't have gotten me anywhere. "Yeah, right." I pulled the door handle.

"Stop. Stay there."

Mr. Bossy was back. He got out and jogged around the car to open the door for me.

I hadn't realized I'd broken one of his rules, but the gesture was cute.

"A gentleman opens the door for a lady," he explained as he pulled the door open.

"I'm not always a lady," I replied.

"You are in my book—except when you argue."

I stifled the comeback that started up my throat and let the compliment he meant it to be flow over me.

We walked in silence back to the street and up to my house.

Something was wrong with me tonight. I couldn't manage to go more than a few minutes without saying something that ended in a fight.

We ascended the stairs to the porch, and I let us in.

He tried the light switch, resulting in the same disappointing lack of response I'd gotten earlier. He tried each of the switches we came across without any success.

"Time to check the fuse panel." He led me out the back door. "I need to fix that deadbolt for you tonight as well."

Until he mentioned it, I hadn't noticed that it had a handle, but the mechanism had been taken out.

We went around to the back wall, and he opened a metal panel.

He turned on the flashlight of his phone and looked around inside it. "I'll need my ohm-meter to check the main fuses, but all the branch ones look fine."

"Is that good or bad?"

"Don't know yet. Let's look around for that water leak."

We went back inside and after checking all the rooms found nothing indicating a leak.

"That only leaves the basement," he said as we finished in the last bathroom upstairs.

"I didn't see any stairs. Are you sure there's a basement?" I'd been everywhere in the house, and I should have seen them if there were any.

"You get to it from the back," he told me as he ushered me toward the kitchen.

Outside, he pulled up a slanted storm-cellar door, like out of an old movie. "They built these in the old style. You couldn't reach them from inside the house."

I made my way down the creaky stairs after him and heard the splash of water. I quickly stepped back up onto the step. In the light of his flashlight it was now obvious where the DWP guy's water had gone. An inch of water covered the floor.

He walked through the area, shining his light up toward the floor above us and across to the walls. "Fucking punks."

"What?"

"Go back outside." Bossy was back again.

I climbed the stairs to the backyard and waited.

He slammed the cellar door closed after coming back up. "Fucking thieves." He kicked the door threshold. "I'm such a fucking idiot." He kicked it again, harder.

I backed up. He was one pissed-off dude—scary pissed off. "What? What is it?"

He kicked at the wood again. "Fucking copper thieves."

He wasn't making any sense as he kicked it again.

"Copper?" I pulled at his arm to get him away from the door before he broke his foot.

"Yeah, fucking copper. It's expensive, and since the construction sites started adding security, they've been hitting abandoned houses. They yank out wiring and piping and sell it for scrap."

"And my house?"

He took a deep breath and blew it out slowly. "They ripped out a bunch of water piping and wiring from under the house. I'm sorry, but it's going to take a lot more than one evening of work to make your house livable again."

I almost fainted. I stumbled to the back steps and sat. "This can't be happening," I moaned into my hands as the tears started. "I can't afford this." I felt the warmth of a shoulder against mine as Zack sat next to me.

He laced his arm behind me and pulled me toward him. "I've got you, Brit. You're staying with me. You're my roommate until we can get this fixed up." His words soothed me.

"But I told you I can't afford to have work like this done."

334

"I can, and I'm going to fix it for you."

"But—"

"Stop, dammit," he said, releasing his hold on me and standing. "What is wrong with you, woman? I'm not having this argument again."

He walked two paces and turned. "You sit here and feel sorry for yourself all you want. When you're ready to face the situation and get on with fixing your life, you can come in and join me for dessert. You just have to agree to stop complaining. We all have choices to make, so make yours." He walked off.

My life had completely imploded, and all he could think about was his stomach? The man was impossible.

Slowly, my tears dried, and I shivered as the cool evening air chilled me. I was trapped with nowhere to go. I stood and hesitated before starting my inevitable walk to his door in the failing light. I could sit on the steps all night and freeze, go inside my house with no lights, no water, and hazmat traps for toilets, or join him for ice cream and chocolate sauce in a house with working toilets and a bed with clean sheets. Some choice.

I went back through my house, locked it, and took the sidewalk to his front door.

Watching the kid in the hoodie on the other side of the street, I completely missed the raised crack in the concrete sidewalk and tripped, falling forward.

My palms stung, but it was my right knee that took the brunt of the fall and hurt like a mother. I grabbed it as I struggled back to my feet.

My hand came back with a spot of blood.

# CHAPTER 12

*BRITTNEY*

I LIMPED UP THE STAIRS TO ZACH'S DOOR AND LET MYSELF IN. I FOUND HIM IN THE kitchen.

"What did you decide?" he asked as he turned to open the freezer.

I swallowed as if my pride had clogged my throat. "I'd like to stay with you."

He pulled out a gallon of vanilla ice cream and a squeeze bottle of Hershey's chocolate syrup. "And?" he asked, facing the cabinets.

The cobwebs of my brain were not giving up whatever it was I'd forgotten.

He collected bowls from the lower shelf. "And?" he repeated.

Replaying his words in my mind, it dawned on me what he was fishing for. I gave in.

"*And* I'll stop complaining."

There, I'd said it.

With his back still to me, he scooped ice cream into the bowls. He added spoons and turned to bring them to the table.

He looked at me and quickly put them back down. "What happened?" He pulled a paper towel off the spool and rushed to press it to my knee. "Sit." He ushered me to a chair.

I steadied myself with the table as I sat.

He lifted my leg on to the other chair and put my hand over the paper towel. "Hold this in place." He rushed off and returned with a first aid kit. "Did you fall?"

"Duh."

He wetted cotton gauze with alcohol. "Where?" He pulled the paper towel away and dabbed at the wound through the rip in my jeans. "This may sting."

I cringed. Sting was an understatement. "Out front on your stupid sidewalk."

He took scissors to the leg of my jeans and started cutting. "My sidewalk?"

"Hey. These are almost new."

He kept cutting. "Not anymore. What are you going to do? Mend them?"

"Ripped jeans are in. Don't you know that?"

"Now you can turn them into cutoffs." He cleared away the bottom half of my jeans leg and cleaned the wound with stinging, alcohol-soaked gauze. "I'm going to use a styptic pencil on this."

He held up two fingers in front of me. "How many?"

"Duh, two."

"Did you hit your head?"

"What's with the twenty questions?"

"Did you?"

"No," I said emphatically.

The styptic whatever made my wound hurt even worse.

"Why'd you fall? We have street lights."

"I was worried about this kid across the street. So I guess I wasn't looking."

He fussed over me for a few more minutes before putting away his supplies and offering me Advil.

I swallowed the pills. "Thanks."

"In the meantime, you're not going out at night by yourself."

"You can't say that."

"I just did. I'll keep you safe, and you can watch where you're putting your feet without having to worry about the local kids. This isn't the greatest neighborhood."

I took a breath. I wasn't going to win this one. "I don't mean to argue with you. I just want this string of bad luck to be over."

"So you'll stop complaining when I offer to help?"

I nodded.

"Good. Working on the future is always preferable to dwelling on the past."

That was easy for him to say. With his money, his future was always guaranteed to be bright. He brought over the Hershey's syrup and drizzled some on his bowl before offering it to me.

I took it and added some to my ice cream, but not as much as he had.

He sat and prepared to dig in.

"Stop," I almost shouted.

His spoon froze in place, and his head jerked up. "What?"

I stood and went to the fridge. "If I'm living here, and cooking for you…" I pulled the strawberry container from its shelf. "You're going to eat healthy, and that means fruit." I found a knife and sliced a few of the berries over his bowl. "There. Now it's ready."

He feigned a scowl, but a smirk grew from behind it. "If I have to."

I'd won a round for a change. I added berries to my bowl as well and re-took my seat.

He lifted his spoon of ice cream toward me. "To living together."

I filled my spoon and raised it to his toast. "With fruit at every meal."

It wasn't what I would have pictured years ago when I dreamed of being with Zack, but I was living with him for real now. There was no going back. I glanced up to see him smiling at me.

As much as he'd complained, he wanted me here, and that was the most comforting thing I could have asked for.

The thought rattled around my brain, sending an odd warmth through me. I took another spoonful and decided this was the best dessert I'd had in quite a while, and it was all due to the man I sat across from. He'd vowed to take care of me. It wasn't something I'd ever sought out, but from Zack, it seemed to fit naturally. Accepting help from him was the right thing to do.

"Thank you," I said.

"For what?"

"For caring."

His brow creased, and he went back to eating. Compliments were obviously not his thing.

I looked around the kitchen. If I had to live here with him and cook for a while, this was my kitchen, and I was reorganizing it.

Take that, Mr. Control Freak.

He rose suddenly. "I have to fix that lock on your back door."

"Can I help?"

"No, I got it."

"To proud to accept help from a girl?"

He took a deep breath, and his expression said I'd almost pushed too far.

"Sure," he huffed. "If you're up to it."

I followed him as he picked up a Home Depot box, a screwdriver, and a hammer.

Once on my back porch, he handed me his phone. "You can hold the light."

"I want to do more to help."

He handed me the box and took back the phone. "Okay, you do it, and I'll hold the light."

How hard could it be?

I struggled to get the pieces out. If getting the lock set free of the molded plastic was any indication, this was not going to end well.

"Want some help?"

"I'll get it."

He handed me a knife.

Once I used that, the plastic gave way and yielded several parts. "Thanks."

He showed me where to unscrew the old parts from the door, and how to insert the new ones with the new screws from the package.

My mind went places it shouldn't have when he told me to put the male part into the female part, but once I got past that, the rest of the installation went quickly.

"Now, try the keys before you shut the door."

I did, and they both worked. I closed and locked the door with a sense of accomplishment.

The project had only required the screwdriver and the knife.

I picked up the packaging and the old parts to take back. "What's the hammer for?"

He held up the tool. "Wolf spiders hunt at night."

~

ZACK

SOMEHOW DOUG'S SWEET SISTER HAD BECOME AN ARGUMENTATIVE LITTLE MONSTER. The bad part was I found it refreshing, and even alluring.

She wasn't afraid to talk back to me. I'd pressed her buttons, and she'd come right back for more, completely unlike any previous women in my life—except for my sisters, of course. They had, on occasion, relished giving me shit about one thing or another.

But outside of family members, my family name had always set the dynamic off kilter. I towered over all the women I dated, and I could karate chop a board in half, but that wasn't it. The physical differences didn't intimidate them so much as turn them on. It was the money and position that set us apart. Until now, I hadn't found a woman who had the self-confidence to take me on.

My sisters had conflicting ways of looking at it. Serena had always said I was such a good catch that none of them wanted to risk losing me. Her way of explaining it certainly massaged my ego, but it didn't always ring true.

Kelly, on the other hand, thought I attracted deferential women. She hadn't said it in so many words, but she'd implied that maybe that was the kind of woman I was attracted to as well. Of the two, I preferred Serena's analysis.

Did I choose women who were deferential to me? I didn't think so, but Kelly's question deserved serious consideration—not tonight, but sometime.

Brittney had brought this all suddenly into contrast. Perhaps it's because we'd grown up together in a way, with all the time Doug and I had spent together with her hanging around in the background. Could that have her seeing me as a stand-in for a brother? That would be awkward. I got a hard-on just thinking about her, and that didn't fit the brother prototype.

Back upstairs at my house after dessert, Brittney had busied herself in the guestroom, and I pulled out my laptop to email Doug. He was an Osprey pilot stationed at Marine Corps Air Station Futenma in Okinawa, and emails worked better than texts for communicating. He deserved to know Brittney was safe.

Doug-
     I thought you should know that Brittney came back to LA. It turns out the house she inherited from your grandmother is right next to the one I'm rehabbing (who knew). The house is a mess and uninhabitable until it gets fixed up (the copper thieves hit it). She's staying with me in the meantime, and I'm taking care of getting the house ship-shape for her, so no need to worry. I'll keep her safe for you.
     Keep the safety on, and the shiny side up.
     -ZB

I promised to keep Brittney safe, and that was paramount, but I also had to worry how I would keep myself safe from her. My cock stood at attention as I closed my eyes and saw that body again, the one I'd wanted to touch and to hold for the longest time, the one that drew me in with every glance.

Now that she was mere feet away, this was going to be sheer torture, but I'd brought it on myself. I could have sent her to room with my sister Serena maybe, but that wouldn't have worked, because she'd be over here trying to fix the house by herself and probably fucking it up—or even worse, getting hurt in the process.

No, I was doing the right thing, the only thing that made sense. I had to get her house up to snuff, and make sure it was done right. If I let it get screwed up somehow, Doug would hold me accountable, and he'd shoot me if anything bad happened to his twin sister.

I blew off the idea of resuming floor work tonight because it was too noisy. Everything related to this house would have to take a backseat to working next door. I got up to brush my teeth and turn in for an early night.

When I opened the door, she was there at the sink, peering into the mirror. "Am I in your way?" She wore a night shirt barely long enough to cover her ass.

"Not at all. I'll wait till you're done." I retreated to the hallway and closed the door.

She opened it right back up. "Come in. You forget Doug and I had to share a bathroom growing up. It's no big deal."

This house was suddenly a lot smaller. In my haste to do the remodel, this was the only functioning bathroom, outside of the half bath downstairs. I hadn't contemplated guests.

I followed her back into the bathroom, which had seemed larger yesterday. I added toothpaste to my brush and started on my teeth. In the mirror, I caught sight of her nipples poking against the thin fabric of her shirt and almost lost my mind. I closed my eyes as I continued brushing. I willed my cock to ignore the sight I'd taken in—unsuccessfully. I rinsed quickly and escaped to my room. Mind over matter was one thing, but mind over hormones was a completely different ballgame, and I was currently losing.

A while later, I heard her finish up, and I snuck back into the bathroom.

Once back in my room, I heard a knock against the wall between our rooms.

"Good night, Zack, and thank you," she called through the wall.

"Good night, Sunshine."

For the longest time, I lay awake in bed. All I could think about was Brittney. Brittney at dinner, Brittney in the car, Brittney over ice cream, and Brittney with pokey nipples in that night shirt. That led to imagining Brittney without the shirt. What would her tits look like? What would they feel like? What would she feel like wrapped around me. What would she taste like? Would she whimper, or yelp, or scream? How would she look when she came? How good would it feel to fuck her brains out?

She was going to be the death of me.

*Remember Rule Number One,* I mentally reminded myself. *She's Doug's sister, for Christ's sake. Hands off the sister. Hands fucking off the sister. No fucking the sister. No imagining fucking the sister either.*

Doug's sexy sister.

And she was more than sexy. She was smart, dedicated, and compassionate, not to mention tough.

I knew from Doug how she was almost single-handedly putting Samantha through school. Everything she'd done, she'd done for family.

Those were values I could relate to and admire. In that respect, we were cut from the same cloth.

Then I came back to sexy and those pokey nipples under the night shirt. Those legs, and those wonderful tits.

*Doug's incredibly sexy sister.*

Tomorrow I had to get busy fixing her house to get her the hell out from under my roof, before she ended up under me and I did something we would both regret.

BRITTNEY

I COULDN'T GET TO SLEEP. THOUGHTS OF THE DAMAGE TO MY HOUSE KEPT INTRUDING. Then the fucked-up situation with Dr. Fosback, which meant I wouldn't have anything beyond bar work for a while, depressed me. Managing Samantha's tuition was looking harder by the minute. Pretty soon, I was going to have to come clean with her that I just couldn't make it work, even with no rent to pay.

But until then, I would put off destroying my sister's dreams and just work harder at finding a way to make them come true. That strategy had worked before. Each time I'd managed to pull a rabbit out of the hat at the last moment and make it work for her. She deserved every ounce of effort I had before I gave up, and that's exactly what she was going to get.

I might be able to get another credit card, or increase the limits on my current ones. There had to be alternatives. There always were.

I put those thoughts out of my head, rolled over, and thought about Zack. Annoying, bossy Zack had brought a smile to my face and calmed my inner fears. Just spelling his name in my head had finally soothed me enough to slip off into the refuge of sleep.

# CHAPTER 13

*BRITTNEY*

THURSDAY MORNING THE SOUND OF THE TOILET FLUSHING WOKE ME. LIGHT CURLED around the edges of the shades.

Fuck, I was late. I had to have breakfast ready for him. It was part of my job now, and I never failed at my jobs. I slid out of bed, found my sweatpants, and pulled them on. Shoving my feet in my slippers, I rushed down to the kitchen.

I located an old box of pancake mix in the rearranged pantry. I didn't bother checking the expiration date. It would do for this morning. The back of the box called for milk and eggs, and I had those, so we were off to the races.

I mixed up the batter, added blueberries, heated a skillet on the stove, and in short order had a stack of mostly presentable pancakes warming in the oven.

Mango slices on the plates, OJ in the glasses, and I was ready, but something was missing—napkins. I searched and couldn't find any. Paper towels would have to do till I got back to the store.

My phone rang. Pulling it from my pocket, I was greeted by Samantha's cheery face on the screen.

She didn't even wait for me to say hello before she started her harangue. "Why didn't you tell me you moved to Grams's house?"

I sat. "I haven't had a chance to call you yet. And it was your idea anyway."

"And were you gonna tell me you're living with Zack?"

It was as if she was spying on me.

"I'm not *living* with him," I corrected. Technically, I guess she was right, but she'd made it sound like the *other* kind of living with a guy.

343

The sound of Zack's footsteps coming down the stairs filled the small kitchen. Without any carpets and minimal furniture downstairs, sounds carried.

Zack appeared at the kitchen doorway. "I have to get an early start on work. I'll see you this afternoon."

"I can hear him," Samantha said through the phone.

"No, you don't. Not without your breakfast," I told Zack, a hand on my hip.

My sister was instantly in my ear. "You tell him, girl."

"Call you back later," I told her. Not waiting for an answer, I hit the end call button and laid the phone down.

"Sorry, I don't have time," Zack said.

"Bullshit." I walked over and tugged him toward the table. "Remember our deal? My job is to make your breakfast. Your job is to eat it."

His eyes locked with mine for a moment—a test of wills.

"And smile," I added. I didn't blink.

He huffed loudly and sat, handing me another victory. "Now who's being demanding?"

"It was your idea, as I recall." I went to the oven and retrieved the plate of pancakes. "I did my part. Now you do yours."

His eyes softened, and a smile appeared that actually looked real.

I split the stack of pancakes between our plates and took a seat across from him.

Without another word, he dug into the food. "I really have to go," he said between mouthfuls.

The pace at which he was devouring it and the hint of a grin every time he looked up told me all I needed to know. He might be grumbling, but the complaints were fake.

"Tell me what we need to get," I asked him.

"Pardon?"

"To fix the house. I can go get materials, but I have no idea what we need."

He thought for a second. "I think we should start with the plumbing."

That was certainly a sentiment I could agree with—working toilets were top of the list.

"Why don't you call me when you get to Home Depot, and I'll help you figure out what to buy. It's a little complicated for me to put into a list right now. Like I said, I gotta get in to work."

I held out my hand. "I'll need some money." I wasn't about to be bashful about this.

He sat up, fished his wallet out of his back pocket, and set some bills on the table. Five Benjamins. Who the hell has a wallet full of hundred-dollar bills? That certainly put a point on the contrast between us. He got hundred-dollar bills out of the ATM when the rest of us settled for a twenty or two.

I gathered up the money. "Thank you. I'll need some for food too."

He released another bill onto the table. "Will that do?"

I scooped it up. "For a start."

He speared some more mango. "Like I said, I'm paying."

In a few minutes he was finished with his breakfast and stood.

"And your OJ," I reminded him, pointing to the half full glass.

"Demanding, aren't we?"

I pasted on my best smile. "It's my job to cook for you, remember?"

After finishing the glass, he waved his goodbye and was out the door in a flash, apparently worried I might make him eat another despicable fruit if he dallied for even a moment.

I cleaned up and loaded the dishwasher before dialing Samantha back.

She answered quickly. "So give me the skinny, and don't leave out any of the dirty details."

"It's pretty simple, really. Sometime after Grams died, the house got sort of trashed."

"What do you mean *sort of trashed*?" she demanded.

I took a breath. "They ripped out some of the wiring and plumbing. The place was pretty filthy on the inside too. Local kids have been using it as an after-school hangout and party place."

"That sucks."

"It took me a few trash bags just to gather up all the fast food wrappers and shit that they'd left lying around."

"How'd they get in?" she asked.

"They broke in through the back and took out the deadbolt so they could come and go as they pleased."

"That's all well and good, but I want to know what the deal is with Zack."

Of course she did. Gossip was her fuel. She couldn't pass the tabloids on the checkout aisle without buying one. Samantha had always been up on which movie star was breaking up with or dating somebody new, on pretty much a daily basis.

"Who told you? I just got here." It had been two nights ago, why quibble?

"I had to find out from Doug. He got an email from Zack. Somehow I got left out of the loop here, and I'm your sister, for God's sake. When you move in with a guy, I should be the first to know, not the last."

"I didn't *move in* with him."

Not exactly true, and I felt a pang of guilt that I hadn't called yesterday like I should have. Dinner with Zack and finding out about the damage to the house had thrown me.

"So tell me about Zack," she prompted again.

"Nothing to tell. He's just letting me stay at his place while we fix up Grams's house—our house—and make it livable."

"I heard that."

"What?"

"You said we," she threw back at me.

"Yeah, so? He's going to help me fix things."

"And his place, is it a penthouse? How far can you see?"

"It's the house next door—another old Victorian that hasn't been torn down and replaced yet."

"That sounds cozy. So have you…" She let the naughty implication hang in the air.

"No way," I said firmly.

Not that I hadn't thought about it, but I'd just gotten back to town. I wasn't a first-date girl. Holy shit. Was I calling dinner a date?

Her voice brought me back to the present. "I don't believe you."

"Believe what you want. He's just letting me crash here," I shot back.

"Have it your way. I wouldn't mind living with Zack. He's a hunk, and Zachary is a really strong name." The visual of Samantha coming on to Zack made me squirm.

I squeezed my legs together. I hadn't peed before making breakfast because Zack had been in the bathroom—naked probably. "Don't you have schoolwork to concentrate on or something?"

"Well, if you want to know, I think getting away from Benji was the right thing to do. But you can't always run from your problems."

"I'm not running. Moving into Grams's house saves money in the long run. It just made sense."

"Maybe I can come out at Christmas and see what you've done with the place."

"Maybe," I answered with as much conviction as I could muster. The way the finances were stacking up, it wasn't going to be even remotely possible. Assuming I got this semester paid for, the next tuition bill would be due right around Christmas. "Look, Sam, I gotta go."

We hung up, and I went upstairs. I should have skipped the coffee.

I'd moved to get my pants down too fast. I sat without bothering to look.

"Shit."

He'd left the toilet seat up, and I ended up on the dirty rim before I knew it. *Yuck.*

I wiped myself off, put the seat down, and swore at him under my breath. *Guys.*

# CHAPTER 14

*Zack*

The elevator door opened on the familiar top floor of our building.

Wendy was at her desk as usual. "You look chipper." She smirked. "How was your dinner?"

"Just fine, thank you. What do we have this morning?"

She shot me one of her tell-me-more looks. "And?"

Wendy was uncharacteristically curious this morning.

"Nothing to tell."

"Right." Her disbelief was obvious. "Stanton is having a bigger fit than normal today, and your dad stopped by." She handed me a few message slips. "These you can take care of later."

I walked into my office, turned on my computer, and sat down to take a look out the window while it powered up. Stanton could wait. The view was different this morning—more colorful, I decided after a moment. The wind had probably done a job on the smog.

Breakfast had been an interesting experience. Breakfast that didn't start in a wrapper and finish in a microwave was a new concept, at least recently. Brittney was determined to make me change my diet, and I was going to have fun resisting. I didn't care for the mango, but otherwise, fresh had its advantages.

I closed my eyes, and the scene came back to me. The pouty lips and the cute snarl as she told me to finish my OJ. And those eyes. Eyes that could convey fire. I wondered what they looked like when she came. Did they go wide and wondrous or slam shut?

Turning back to my desk, the monitor had come alive, and I logged in. Checking my watch, I pulled up the emails Stanton had sent overnight before picking up the phone to dial London.

The call was routine, with nothing very important to discuss, as it turned out.

Just as I was ready to hang up, he added, "I also wanted to go over the preparation for your visit next week."

My planned trip to London had completely slipped my mind. Brittney's arrival had crowded out other less-important items, and this was one.

"If you send me your presentation, we could go over it," Stanton offered.

I hadn't actually started working on it. "Maybe later. I'm a little busy this morning."

"We only have tomorrow left," he complained.

"That's all we need. We can go over it tomorrow." I didn't need him telling me what to do and how to prioritize things.

"But if we need to make changes..."

"Tell you what, if I need to go over anything today, I'll call you at home. Otherwise we'll talk tomorrow morning."

He got off the line with only a minor grumble. My call to Rome followed, which as always, went rather smoothly by comparison.

After finishing with the European calls, I noticed a return email from Doug and opened the message.

Zack-

Great to hear you're taking care of Brit. I know that can be pretty much a full-time job. Sorry to hear about the condition of the house - that sucks big time.

I need you to keep a close eye on Brit because she can get herself into trouble pretty easily. She has a tendency to fall for the wrong kind of guy. Her latest mistake was some asshole she hooked up with after I left - a real piece of work to hear Sam tell it. Brit was afraid to tell me all the details about how bad he was. Probably afraid I'd break the guy's legs when I rotate back to the US.

So do me a favor. Keep a close eye on her and check out anybody she dates. I don't want her getting involved with another loser. I've got enough blood on my hands already.

Thanks,

Doug

I composed a quick reply.

Doug-

I got it covered. She's full of sass, but I'll keep her under control somehow. No getting involved with any losers—I'm on board with that. I've got your back.

-ZB

348

Like it or not, I was Brittney's official guardian now—and I did like it. I owed it to Doug to keep her under control. Her ex sounded worse than she'd let on.

It was later than normal when I rounded up the coffees and returned to Wendy's desk with her mocha.

"Are you going to tell me, or am I going to have to call Serena?"

Her threat to call my sister was a serious one—an intervention I didn't need right now.

I took the guest chair on the side of her desk. "Brittney is my friend Doug's sister."

Her silent stare demanded I continue.

"She moved back from San Jose, and she's staying with me while I fix her house up."

Her head cocked slightly. "Staying with you?"

"Till I get her house fixed." I stood. "Could you please ask Kaden to come see me?"

She lifted her phone, and I took my coffee into the office. That was as much as I was willing to share this morning, and it was pretty much all there was to tell anyway.

I pulled up the customer-visit summaries Stanton had sent a few weeks ago and printed them out.

Kaden Peralta showed up a few minutes later. "Yeah, boss?"

He was the perennially eager type.

"Is your passport up to date?"

Only the briefest look of confusion crossed his face before it was replaced with a grin. "Sure. Where are we going?"

"How do you feel about London?" I asked this only as a courtesy. I was sending him regardless.

"I like London. I mean, I haven't been, but I'd like to go someday."

The exposure would be good for him.

I turned, pulled the sheets from the printer, and offered them to him. "Have a seat."

He accepted the papers and started to scan them.

"I was supposed to make these customer visits next week, but something has come up, and I need you to fill in for me."

"Sure thing. You're not coming along?"

"No, this is a solo assignment."

"Okay." Just the slightest quiver in his voice indicated nervousness.

"You'll do fine. Go over these and give Stanton in London a call later this morning with any questions you have. And plan on reviewing your slides with him first thing tomorrow morning. Wendy can give you copies of the correspondence, and ask her to book you a flight for Monday."

He looked at me expectantly, but I didn't have any more for him.

I sat back. "Well, go ahead. You need the slides ready by tomorrow morning."

349

He left with a spring in his step. I could hear the excitement in his voice as he talked with Wendy about flights.

I was still responding to emails when Brittney's call arrived. I closed my eyes, and the mere sound of her voice lifted my mood.

"I'm here at Home Depot. Now, what do I need to get?" she asked.

"Thank you for breakfast," I said first. I hadn't told her over the table this morning the way I should have.

"Thank you for the roof over my head. We're even."

"Let me give you a list of things from plumbing." I then proceeded to list the pipe and the dozens of fittings and supplies we would need to start rebuilding the piping in her house.

"I don't know if this will all fit in my car."

"The pipe is in ten-foot sections, so it'll have to hang out the window. That's what everybody does. The guys there will be happy to help you."

I had no doubt of that. The guys would fall all over themselves to help a pretty girl like her.

~

*Brittney*

"I think I've got it all," I told Zack after I wrote down the items he'd listed for me.

"Don't forget grade L," he reiterated. He'd said twice that the pipe needed to be grade L, not grade M.

After we hung up, I found Marvin in plumbing who was happy to help me, the clueless woman, find the dozens of fittings Zack had given me, as well as the proper grade of pipe.

"Grade L is the thicker, better one," he told me, something Zack hadn't explained.

I had a shopping cart full of stuff, including the torch, solder, and flux to make the joints.

"I'll bring the pipe up front for you, but first you should get a few items your boyfriend didn't list."

"Go ahead." I didn't correct the boyfriend comment.

He walked back up the aisle. "You'll need one of these flame protectors, and just in case, get two plant sprayer bottles from the garden center."

"What for?"

"You'll be soldering up against the wood of the house. This mat keeps it from catching fire, and the squirt bottles are just in case."

This suddenly sounded a lot more dangerous, like burn-my-house-down dangerous.

I took the black pad and wheeled my way to the garden center for squirt bottles. I got three.

With a dozen lengths of pipe hanging out the window, I drove home carefully, unloaded, and followed that with a trip to the supermarket.

With my chores done, I grabbed an apple and a paper towel, and started the drive to the Rusty Bucket to meet with Max. After finishing the apple, I wrapped the core in the paper towel and dialed my sister back.

Samantha didn't pick up, so I left a quick message.

After parking, I realized I'd forgotten to let Lillian know I'd arrived safely. I couldn't decide if I wanted anyone to have Grams's address, so I settled on a simple text.

ME: In LA safe and sound – talk tomorrow – thanks for everything

When I stepped through the familiar door, the Rusty Bucket was getting ready to open for lunch. I didn't recognize any of the servers readying the place as I made my way to the back. Since I seemed to know where I was going, none of them paid me any heed. I found Max in his office with Maria, so far the only one I recognized from before. I waited in the hallway.

He turned from his desk, and his eyes lit up. "Brittney Spear, as I live and breathe. You're a sight for sore eyes." He got up and gave me a quick hug. "Maria, I'll get with you later."

As she left, Maria shot me a scowl, clearly unhappy that Max was prioritizing me above her. She'd started just before I left, and had never been particularly friendly.

I'd need to apologize to her later and not start off on the wrong foot. It was my fault for not standing farther down the hall, out of sight.

"Come on in," he bellowed.

Max Stover was a bear of a man size-wise, but a real pussycat with the employees. On occasion, when an argument between pool players got heated, Max would read them the riot act, and I'd never seen anyone foolish enough to take him on when he did that.

"I'm back in town, and I was hoping you might be able to fit me into the schedule a little bit."

He stroked his chin before answering. "You in town for long?"

Given my sudden departure last time, his reticence wasn't surprising.

"Yeah, Grams left her house to me and Sam, and I'm moving in, permanent-like."

He returned to his chair. "Take a load off." He motioned for me to sit as well, which I did. "We've got a full crew right now."

My heart stopped with his words.

"But for you, I'm sure I can free up a few shifts, if you're okay with days."

My heart restarted. "Thanks. I'll take whatever you've got. Days is fine." I would have preferred nights because the day crowd was sparse and didn't tip as well as evening customers, but beggars couldn't be choosers. "A lot of new faces out there."

Max chuckled. "Yeah, turnover in this business always sucks. Almost everyone from your old days is gone. Now it's return-to-Max time. Maria there and Celeste both came back about a month ago, and now you. Go figure. Next thing you know, Lisa will be knocking on my door."

I knew better than that, and Max probably did too. Lisa had given birth to triplets, and I doubted she had the time.

He opened a drawer, pulled out forms, and handed them over. They were the familiar I-9 and W-4, but thankfully no application.

"Sorry you have to fill these out again, but the government is really a stickler these days on paperwork."

"No problem." I had the forms filled out in a few minutes, and after he photocopied my ID, I was ready to rejoin the workforce.

Max cocked his head as he viewed the copy. "Married?" He'd caught the name change.

I settled on a truthful statement. "Not now."

He checked his schedule. "You can start with lunch next Thursday. I'll figure out more after that. Drop the forms off with Maria. She's helping out with the paperwork."

I gave him my best smile. I'd hoped for something sooner, but at least it was a start. "Thanks, Max."

"Grab yourself a shirt on the way out. You know where they are."

"Will do, and thanks again." I excused myself and took two black shirts with *The Rusty Bucket* emblazoned on them from the stack on my way.

Maria accepted the papers from me once I found her.

"We need two forms of ID."

I handed over the copy of my driver's license. "My papers are being shipped down from San Jose. I'll bring them by in a few days."

She didn't look happy. "We need two. I can't file the form without it."

Max walked by. "Problem?"

"She doesn't have two forms of ID," Maria answered. She was being a pain in the ass.

I looked meekly toward Max. "It's in my stuff being shipped."

Max shrugged. "A week or two doesn't matter." He turned to Maria. "Get her signed up, and we'll fill that in later."

Maria forced a half-smile. "Welcome back. Be sure to read this." She handed me Max's little blue pamphlet of employee rules. "And the shirt limit is two."

I separated the shirts to show her what I had. "Only two."

She hadn't been overly friendly the short time I'd known her before I left, but now I could move her from the unsure column to the bitchy one.

A quick glance inside the pamphlet showed it hadn't changed.

Once outside, I fist pumped the air—my first success. I was back on the payroll at one place at least. Now I had to get my house livable and find some more work until Dr. Fosback came through for me.

The depth of my plight had just been made clear by Maria. The Bucket and Dr. Fosback were willing to let me slide on the two-ID requirement, at least for a while. But trying to land another gig was clearly out of the question until Lillian sent my desk stuff.

The drive back home was quick in the light mid-day traffic.

Zack had given me the code to open his garage, and I found the extension cords exactly where he'd said they'd be. I ran the electric cord over the fence to my house so I could continue cleaning up the inside with his vacuum.

I hadn't gotten very far when Samantha called. "Now I want to hear the real skinny on you and the Zack man. And let me remind you, Zachary is a super-duper name. Lots of good qualities, but you already know that."

That was as good a vote of confidence as Samantha ever gave.

I didn't start by asking if *opinionated* and *bossy* were qualities on her list.

"I told you already. Our house isn't ready to be lived in yet." I needed to stop referring to the house as Grams's; it was now mine and Samantha's.

"And you're making him meals?"

"Well, I need to pitch in a little."

"And the sleeping arrangements?" she asked.

"I'm in a separate room. Now, where is all this coming from anyway? Zack and I have been friends forever."

"Uh-huh. I remember how he used to look at you when you weren't looking, and it wasn't a friend look."

That couldn't be true. "Get outta here. There was never anything going on, and you know it."

"And the very first thing you do when you get back to LA is look up Zack and play house with him?"

"It wasn't like that at all."

"Then tell me how it is."

"You're impossible. If you must know, when I got to the house, the lights wouldn't come on. I was checking upstairs, and I heard a noise and a voice. Well, it turned out it was Zack. I pepper-sprayed him, and he turned it on me."

I had to work hard to keep from laughing at this part.

"You pepper-sprayed each other?"

"Kinda stupid, huh? But yes. His house is right next door, and he thought I was a prowler or something. Anyway, that's how I bumped into him, and I'm staying at his house while he helps me get our place fixed."

"So you're really not jumping his bones?"

"No way."

"And he isn't trying to date you?"

"No, we went to dinner is all."

"You liar, that's a date."

"It was not."

"Did you pay?"

I didn't answer the incriminating question.

"See? It was a date. I'll stop giving you a hard time once you admit it. I'm happy for you. He's a great guy."

Zack was a great guy, and by her standards, it had been a date, even if he hadn't meant it to be.

"I gotta go," I told her.

"I'm rooting for you, Brit. You need to stop falling for jerks like Benji and go after one of the good ones like Zack—someone who'll treat you right."

She had a point that Zack was one of the good ones—one of the really good ones, just not for me.

After we hung up, I went back to running the vacuum.

Had I always fallen for turds? Benji was in that category for sure. Better than Sully, but only by a little. He was definitely not a keeper in anybody's book. Why couldn't I have seen it earlier with either of them? With Sully, I'd thought him also being a twin would give us something special in common. I couldn't have been more wrong.

I didn't like the implication that I had a defect in my guy radar. Either that, or I wanted to be unhappy, which didn't make any sense.

Did I do this to myself on purpose? Was I twisted?

I shook off the thought, but only after I realized I was going over the same section of carpet with the vacuum again and again.

# CHAPTER 15

*Zack*

It was half past four when Kayden knocked at my open office door. "I've got the first pass of the presentations ready to review."

I wasn't in the mood. "I don't need to review them. Go over them with Stanton in the morning. That should be good enough."

He cocked his head. "You sure? It'll only take a minute."

I'd always reviewed his presentations—until today.

Getting a head start on fixing Brittany's house was higher up on my agenda than a marketing presentation. "I've got confidence in you, Kayden."

He beamed ear to ear as he left.

I gathered my things, turned off my computer, and locked my office.

"You're leaving early," Wendy said, stating the obvious.

"I've got important things to get done tonight."

*Done* was a bit of an overstatement. All I expected to do was get started. I backed toward the elevator.

"Don't let her keep you up late," Wendy called after me, trying to get under my skin.

I stopped and pointed a finger at her. I made a zip-your-lips-closed motion across my mouth. I didn't need the gossip mill getting hold of this.

She mimicked the motion herself and gave me a thumbs up to go with her knowing smile.

*Right. Don't let her keep me up late.*

The drive home was annoying in the traffic, which was heavier than I was accustomed to because of the time of day. My legs were jittery with frustration when I pulled into the garage. Brittany had left the door open.

I picked up my briefcase, closed my valuable car in the garage, and bounded up the back steps of my house. Inside I found the kitchen empty, and I called Brittney's name up the stairs. No response came back. She had to be next door.

I grabbed a Coke from the fridge before heading upstairs to change.

The door to her room was open, so I glanced in. Just the sight of her things on hangers comforted me. Somehow I'd had a fear that I might come upstairs and find her gone, similar to the way she'd disappeared those many years ago. No notice, no visit, no explanation—*poof* and she was gone, without even a call afterward.

I'd never understood it back then, and I didn't want a repeat. Someday when she was ready, I'd ask her to explain things to me, and hope she would be willing.

Doug had clammed up when I tried to get it out of him. He'd said it was something for her to explain when she was ready, if she ever was. He'd insisted I drop it and never ask again. Whatever it had been, must have been traumatic.

After putting on working clothes, I made my way over to her house. The front door was open, and inside the change was dramatic. A lot of effort had obviously gone into cleaning the place. It was no longer a filthy, dusty, abandoned, teenager hangout.

"Brit?" I called.

A vacuum was running upstairs, so I followed the sound to find my Brittany.

Her back was to me as she ran the machine back and forth over the floor and carpet runner.

"Brit," I said as I tapped on her shoulder.

She jumped with a start and turned around. "Don't you know better than to sneak up on someone like that?" she shouted over the noise of the vacuum.

She switched the noisemaker off and scowled at me.

I raised my hands in mock surrender. "I wasn't sneaking. It's not my fault you didn't hear me."

Her face softened.

"You made a lot of progress today. The downstairs looks great."

"It's a start. This place was a mess."

"I got off early so we could get started on fixing your plumbing. Let's take a look at what you brought back from the store."

She started for the stairs, and I followed. "I put it all out back."

When we reached the backyard, I found all the things she'd purchased arranged in nice neat stacks. I pulled open the cellar doors.

She pulled an apple from a paper bag and held it out to me. "You can start on this."

I didn't take it. "I don't eat apples."

"Why not? Everybody eats apples."

"The skin gets caught in my teeth."

She pushed it at me again. "Don't be a baby. I cook, you eat."

"This isn't cooking."

She gave me an I-can't-believe-you-just-said-that look.

I gave in, accepted the apple, and bit into it. "Undo that extension cord you have for the vacuum. We're gonna need it down here."

"Can't I keep cleaning while you do this stuff?"

"It will go a lot faster if we have two pairs of hands."

"But the spiders…"

"Do you want running water or not?"

I brought a set of work lights from next door while she got the extension cord from the house. In a few minutes, we had light on the situation in the basement.

The damage was worse than I'd realized. The thieves had made a complete mess of the place, and I might not have had her get enough materials to finish the job.

She helped by retrieving the parts I needed one by one, and also by holding things in place as I rebuilt the water system underneath the house. A few hours later, we called it quits for the night, having made good progress.

## BRITTNEY

By the time we called off the plumbing project for the night, my stomach had been objecting for over an hour.

"What's on the menu for dinner?" Zack asked.

Luckily I'd thought ahead and spared us a microwaved monstrosity of some sort. "Mushroom chicken bake."

It had been the simplest thing I could think of on short notice that didn't need looking after—two chicken breasts, some rice, and a can of cream of mushroom soup over the whole thing. It was waiting for us in the oven.

"If you cooked it, I'm sure it will be good."

Compliments on my cooking were a welcome change.

After washing up, I served the piping hot concoction to my equally hot plumber, friend, neighbor, housemate, roommate, or whatever he was. Samantha was right, he was one hot package of a man.

"Better let it cool."

I settled on housemate as being the closest to accurate, but roommate sounded enticing.

I added pear slices to the plates for a serving of fruit.

He wasn't willing to wait for the meal to cool, and resorted to blowing on it one forkful at a time to start eating.

I followed suit. "So how was your day today?"

Only after the words escaped did I realize how much I sounded like a housewife asking about her husband's day at work.

His eyes narrowed slightly as he continued chewing.

"Never mind," I added.

He swallowed and thought for a moment. "A boring day at the office. Except that I forgot I was scheduled to fly to London on Monday."

"You're leaving?"

The thought of being alone without my house ready to live in scared me for some reason. I'd always been independent, but relying on Zack felt suddenly natural. I raised a bite of chicken to hide behind and blew on it. I hoped the steam from the food hid my disappointment.

"No. I canceled." He took another bite of dinner.

I let out a relieved breath.

He swallowed and added, "I'm sending another guy instead. He needs the experience. It'll be good for him."

I bet he was a good manager, but I realized we'd only talked about my life in San Jose, and I didn't know enough about what he did at the family company.

"I'd rather stay here," he added with a slight upturn of the corners of his mouth that had me hoping to be the reason he wanted to stay. His eyes locked with mine.

My phone rang. I ignored it.

"Aren't you going to get that?" he asked, his eyes still boring into mine.

Breaking the moment wasn't what I wanted.

He cocked his head as his question lingered in the air. His eyes left mine, and the moment dissolved.

I pulled the phone out of my pocket. It was Lillian. "Hi, Lil, were you able to get into the apartment okay?"

"Yeah, and we have your clothes. Where should we send them?" she asked.

"You can send them to a friend of mine." I gave her Zack's address for the boxes.

Zack took another bite and watched me.

"About the couch..." she said.

"Yeah?'

"Randy thinks it's a little big for our place, but we would like the desk, the table, and the chairs, if that's okay?"

"Sure, anything and everything you want."

"You sure you don't want any of it?" she asked.

"Absolutely."

I couldn't afford to get it here, and there was already plenty of furniture in the house. Grams's stuff was better than the particleboard crap I'd accumulated up north.

"About the desk. You said you wanted me to mail the stuff in it, but it's empty."

My stomach knotted at the words. I needed my birth certificate and name change papers for work. "What do you mean empty?"

"Exactly that. Not even a paper clip. And…" She hesitated ominously. "The manager mentioned that Benji had already been by."

"That little slimeball," I hissed.

"The manager said he had a key."

I swore under my breath.

Benji had given me back the key to my place, but had probably made a copy, and I'd been too stupid and too poor to have the lock changed.

I thanked her for the heads up and for sending my things.

Now Benji had fucked me again. He had my birth certificate, all my papers, my tax returns, my name change paperwork, everything.

"Randy will put the stuff in at UPS this weekend," Lillian said, breaking the silence.

"Thanks, Lil, that's a great help," I said before we hung up.

Zack's eyes were dangerously cold.

~

ZACK

SHE PUT THE PHONE DOWN WITH A DEJECTED LOOK. IT HADN'T BEEN GOOD NEWS FROM the bit I'd heard on this end.

"Problem?" I asked.

"Just Lillian, a friend from San Jose. She's sending the rest of my things."

Brittney wasn't going to offer the answers willingly.

"I got that part, but who's the slimeball?"

She twirled her fork in the food before answering. "My ex. He's a creeper." She didn't meet my eyes.

"So what did he do now?"

The call had clearly upset her.

"How long have you been working on this house?"

"Don't try to change the subject, Sunshine."

She played with her food as she conjured up an answer. "He came by my old apartment." After a moment she decided to add, "He must have kept a key. He got into the place and took some stuff, from what Lillian could tell."

"Tell me his name. I'll pay him a visit and get your stuff back."

I knew how to handle creeps like this.

Her eyes went wide. "No way. Promise me you won't."

I gave in for the moment. "For now... We need to get your house ready first, I guess."

"Yeah, the house comes first. But thanks for offering."

Her smile said she'd gotten the message that I could fix this for her. It might take her time to come to grips with it, however.

We both went back to eating our late dinner.

After a moment I tried again. "I still want to know his name."

She sipped her water. "Tell me what marketing is like." She was intent on getting away from the subject.

"Nothing much to tell, really."

She kept up the questioning about my job through the rest of dinner. Every time I diverted back to her history or the creep, she returned the conversation to my work.

"And the London trip?" she asked.

"Customer visits. We have two big contracts pending, and the local sales guys can only take it so far. In the end, the customer wants to meet with someone from headquarters. They know we have more leeway to negotiate than the field sales guy. So we visit, give them the final little price cut, and everybody's happy. They get to report to their bosses that they called us in and got a better deal, a win-win."

"Why not let your London salesman give them the better deal? Then no one has to make the trip."

"Because a sales guy will fold like a wet noodle and give almost every customer the lowest price in record time. It would make their job easier, but it would be a price race to the bottom. This way the customer has to work at it to get a lower price, so it's more satisfying for them. And more profitable for us."

"Too much psychology for me. I'll stick to cleaning teeth," she replied.

"At least my customers are happy to see me."

She giggled. "True enough. Mine aren't happy till they're on the way out the door."

I pushed my plate forward.

"You're not done till you finish your pears," she told me with a scowl.

Busted. I'd hoped to get away with the single slice I'd eaten first. It was okay, but not worth repeating.

"I'm watching," she said.

She was cute in this argumentative mode.

"Not without some topping," I told her.

She marched to the fridge and brought back the chocolate syrup.

"That'll do." I took the bottle from her and squirted a bit on. I made a face as I chewed the next piece and swallowed.

"If you keep acting like a baby, I'll feed you stewed prunes tomorrow."

"Prunes are for old people." I forked up the rest of the pears and chocolate. It was actually quite good, not that I would admit it to her.

I scraped up the last bit of chocolate sauce and licked the fork. "Satisfied?"

"That wasn't so hard, now was it?"

I didn't want to lie, so I kept quiet. I forced a frown to answer her.

# CHAPTER 16

*BRITTNEY*

HE FINALLY FINISHED HIS FRUIT, ALBEIT WITH CHOCOLATE SAUCE, AND TOOK BOTH OUR plates to the sink. I followed with the glasses. As he rinsed the silverware, he stretched his shoulders with a grunt.

I set the glasses on the counter and took a chance. I put my hands on his shoulders and kneaded.

"Stiff?" His muscles were tight knots under my fingers.

"Oh, that feels good." The sigh that accompanied his words told the story.

"It should. I'm a trained medical professional."

I continued while he finished rinsing and loaded the dishes into the dishwasher.

He braced against the counter, his back to me. "Keep it up."

I did for a minute, but this position wouldn't do. "Get on the couch."

I pointed into the old dining room he'd outfitted with a couch and a TV, a typical guy move—television over all else.

I followed him there, and he plopped face down on the sofa.

I straddled his back and started at his shoulders, working my way slowly down his back, rubbing and kneading over his clothes. I was afraid if I worked on his bare skin, I wouldn't stop at stripping off his shirt.

The groans kept coming as I moved from spot to spot, over his broad shoulders toward his lower back and the tight ass right in front of me. The man was all muscle—tight and knotted muscle, but slowly loosening under my touch.

"Ohhh, keep that up," he groaned as I leaned into my work.

"Is this helping?"

"You have no idea."

I scooted lower, over his thighs, to work his lower back.

He lifted up and gathered his shirt at his armpits.

Suddenly faced with touching skin, I hesitated.

"Don't stop," he mumbled into the couch cushion.

I took a breath to steel myself and started again at his lower back, working my way up. I didn't know if he felt it, but the warmth of his skin under my hands was way above body temperature. Closing my eyes worked better to control my feelings as I alternated kneading with my fingers and grinding the heel of my hand or my knuckles into the tight knots.

Little grunts escaped him when I leaned in especially hard.

"Keep it up," he urged.

Slowly I could feel progress. Denying what I wanted was silly, so I opened my eyes and watched my hand work over his skin. My temperature edged up too. If I closed my eyes now, I'd just be imagining other areas I wanted to get my hands on.

He surprised me by struggling out of his shirt when I got back up to his shoulders.

I leaned forward and worked my way out his arms to his deltoids, then back to his shoulders and down his back again. I leaned hard on his lower back, mightily tempted to travel even lower. As I worked my fingers back up to his shoulders, I leaned over. With my breasts brushing his back, I whispered into his ear. "Enjoying this?" The light pine scent of his hair tickled my nostrils.

"You bet."

I straightened up and instantly missed the contact of my chest with his back.

"Your turn," he announced and started to wiggle out from under me.

I couldn't have kept him pinned there if I'd wanted to. I scrambled off, straightened my shirt, and then lay down when he stood. I went face down into the cushions, and he straddled my thighs, anchoring me in place with his weight.

He started on my lower back and worked his way up slowly. He was much gentler with me than I'd been with him.

"You can press harder. I won't break." Heat spread through me with the feel of his touch. This was even better than the reverse.

He pressed harder, but was still careful not to hurt me.

"Is that all you got, big guy?"

The challenge got him to really press in—almost, but not quite, too hard. He pulled the hem of my shirt, and I lifted myself, letting it ride up to my shoulders and off my arms.

The chill of the room made the heat of his touch even more enticing against my skin. I reached back and unhooked my bra.

He worked up and down with rhythmic kneading.

I slowly melted into the cushions under the combination of pain, relief, and excitement from his touch. I moaned, encouraging him. Closing my eyes, I envisioned myself turning over and enjoying a front rub of a gentler, more sensual kind.

"Had enough?" he asked.

"Not nearly." I was willing to be selfish right now as I luxuriated under his strong hands, just imagining all the things I'd like them to be doing a little later.

He kept it up a few more wonderful minutes before climbing off. "All done. Time for dessert." He reached for his shirt and pulled it back on, hiding what I wanted to watch.

I located my bra straps and re-hooked myself before sitting up.

He glanced at me, then quickly away as he ventured back into the kitchen.

I sat up, found my shirt, and followed him without putting it on.

Opening the freezer he asked, "Ice cream again?"

I put my shirt down and pulled bowls from the cupboard. "Only if we add fruit."

His eyes raked the length of me, and I didn't miss them stopping at my chest.

I brought the bowls to the table.

"Put your shirt back on," he said.

"I'm hot." The goosebumps on my skin said otherwise, but the heat in my core agreed.

He took my shirt from the counter and threw it in my direction.

"You're being bossy again."

He stayed turned toward the wall, avoiding looking at me the way I could tell he wanted to. "And you're being obstinate. Now behave yourself and get dressed before I spank you."

I huffed. "If it makes you happy." I pulled the shirt on.

"It's what's right."

He didn't say it was what made him happy, and the distinction was clear.

ZACK

UNBELIEVABLE.

The girl was trying to drive me insane. Walking into the kitchen in only her bra and claiming to be too hot? I turned away as she finally pulled her shirt back on. I blinked hard, but I couldn't get the sight out of my brain—her wonderful tits overflowing the cups of her bra, and red lace no less? That sight was going to haunt me all night.

*Un-fucking-believable.*

The feel of her skin under my fingers had been hot and soft, just as I'd imagined and dreamed of last night.

I sliced the strawberries slowly onto a plate, trying to regain my composure. "I've got the berries if you can get the chocolate sauce out of the fridge."

"Are we putting chocolate on everything?" she asked.

"Everything but pizza."

"You're twisted."

"That's what my sisters say." I put the knife in the sink, brought the strawberry slices to the table, and slid some into each bowl before sitting.

She sat and passed me the Hershey's sauce without adding any to her bowl.

"Sure you don't want any?"

"I'm good."

"That you are. Really good," I said before I caught myself. "I meant a good masseuse." I stretched my shoulders. "That helped a lot."

Her mouth turned up in a smile hot enough to melt my ice cream. "You too. Thanks. You can give me a rubdown any time."

I looked quickly down at my bowl and took a spoonful. When I looked back up, she was eyeing me over her spoon.

"What's the deal with this ex of yours?" I asked. "What did he take?"

The question wiped the smile off her face.

"Why does it matter?"

I put my spoon down and reached across to hold her hand.

She looked up, but didn't pull away.

"Because it's a problem for you, and I want to help."

She didn't open up.

"You're my roommate, and I care." I let go of her hand. "So tell me, what's his problem?" I spooned another bite of ice cream. "I'll promise to eat my fruit."

Her shoulders relaxed. "He's just a creep."

I swallowed. "You said that."

"Lillian said my desk was empty. He took everything."

"Anything valuable?"

"And she said according to the manager, he had a key."

I tried again. "What did he take?"

She shook her head. "I thought I was going crazy. Every once in a while something would be off just a little, not quite where it normally was, and I couldn't remember moving it—like my clock. I always had it pointed at the couch."

This implication was ominous. "You think he was sneaking into your place?"

"I don't know for sure, but it would explain things." She spooned a bite of ice cream into her mouth.

I waited.

"I kept papers in my desk. Bills, my tax returns, pay stubs, stuff like that, and my birth certificate." She stopped. A second later, her fist slammed down on the table. "Fuck. Everything was in there. I shouldn't have left so quickly. I just got my clothes, and I forgot about everything else. I can't sign up for work without a second form of ID."

A dejected look came over her.

"What's his name?"

"No. I can't have you get involved."

"I can help."

Her gaze locked with mine. "No."

I gave up for now. Doug would know the name. She didn't need to tell me.

"What else did he do? Did he ever hurt you?"

She shook her head again. "No, not like that." She was holding back, but twenty questions wasn't going to pry it out of her tonight. It would come in time, perhaps when she trusted me more.

I ate the last of my strawberry slices. "Look, I finished my fruit, like I promised."

That garnered a faint smile from her before her eyes settled on her bowl. Her face twisted into a scowl, and her mind seemed to drift off somewhere dark.

"Sunshine?"

"Yeah?" she answered weakly before looking up.

"I'm here for you. Anything you need."

This time she was the one who reached her hand across, and I took it. "Thanks, Zack. That means a lot."

"Anything you want, it's yours."

"Really?"

"Anything," I repeated.

"Can I save that wish for later?" she asked as she squeezed my hand.

"Absolutely." I squeezed her hand back. "But there's one thing I won't do for you."

She released my hand, stood, and picked up both our bowls. "What's that?"

"I won't eat a pomegranate." Some people loved the seeds, but I couldn't see the allure. I hated the things.

She laughed and took our bowls to the sink. "Okay, I can work around that, but everything else is fair game, is that right?"

"Sure." I joined her at the sink and started the dishwasher after we finished loading it.

"Maybe I'll have you give me a foot rub," she mused as I turned off the light and we started for the stairs, "in the bathtub."

I didn't dare go for that bait, and immediately regretted not setting some limits on my promise.

# CHAPTER 17

*BRITTNEY*

FRIDAY MORNING I WOKE MORE RESTED THAN I'D BEEN IN QUITE A WHILE, WITH lingering memories of a dream. A dream of me and Zack by the pool.

It hadn't just been the backrub that relaxed me, because truth be told, it was the backrub that had gotten me excited—excited for the possibilities in the future.

I'd had my hands on Zack, and he'd had his hands on me, hand to bare skin. He certainly hadn't been touching me where I yearned for it, but progress was progress—baby steps.

In my dream, he'd offered to rub sunscreen on my back, and when he finished that, he'd asked me to turn over and done my stomach and shoulders as well. The good part had been when he'd moved down to my legs and up my thighs, right up to my bikini bottoms, inside my thighs, oh so tantalizingly close to where I yearned for him to touch me. Then I'd awoken, and realized how far from reality the dream had taken me.

Zack was already in the shower when I got up, so I went downstairs to start breakfast. My previous shopping trip had only been a few items, so the choices were limited for this morning's meal. I chopped up the tomato and onion before grating cheese for omelet filling. I would've preferred more ingredients, but this would get us started.

I heard him coming down the stairs before I saw him as I started to cook.

"Morning, Sunshine," he said with a rich voice that lifted my spirits.

"I hope you like omelets."

"Does it really matter? The deal was you cook, and I eat."

"Of course it matters. I want to make things you like."

"Then yes, omelets are just fine—unless you're putting fruit in mine."

I shook my head. "No, the fruit's on the side." I loaded the omelets onto the plates and carried them to the table.

He stared at the kiwi like it would jump up and bite him. "This isn't fruit."

"It's not pomegranate, so you can eat it."

"Apples and oranges are fruit. This is something else. It's got fur."

"Stop being a pussy and eat it."

The grumbles continued, and he took the tiniest slice of the green delight.

I got up, strolled around behind his chair, and started to knead his shoulders. "Eat it, and you get another backrub tonight."

He sliced off another even smaller piece of kiwi and mumbled, "Why can't we stick to real American fruit instead of this imported shit? You said you were going to feed me things I liked."

I slapped the top of his head lightly. "I asked what you liked, but fruit is part of the bargain. And what country do you think this comes from, anyway?" I went back to working his shoulders.

He snorted. "New Zealand. Where else, with a name like that?" He poked at what remained of the kiwi but didn't cut into it.

"These are from here in California, so shut up and eat it."

He huffed and cut off another piece, followed by a bigger piece and then the last. "Only 'cuz you promised a backrub."

I finished his shoulders with another few tight squeezes and backed away. "Thanks."

He got up and carried his plate to the sink.

"What can I do while you're at work to move things along?"

"You mean next door?"

I nodded.

He ran fingers through his hair. "Nothing until I get back. We have to finish soldering those pipes before you can call DWP again."

"What about the electric?" I asked.

"What about it? Trust me, you want running water first."

"But can't I do anything on the wiring? There has to be something I can do instead of sitting around."

He took a deep breath in and out. "Okay, follow me."

I followed him to the other room.

He rummaged through a tool bag and handed me a green instrument with wires attached. "This is a multimeter. Turn it to twenty here on the scale to turn it on."

I nodded. "Got it."

"Down at Home Depot, tell the guy in electrical that you need to set up a circuit trace with this."

"Circuit trace," I repeated.

"He'll give you a little box with batteries and two leads with alligator clips. Go under the house and attach those clips one by one to the white and black wires of each of the cut-off wires under the house. Then you go upstairs and plug the multimeter into each of the electrical outlets in the house and write down the results. We need a map of what's connected to what."

I nodded. "Got it, a map." I thought I understood well enough. And I appreciated being useful in putting my house back together.

"A map. That's your job." He checked his watch. "I gotta go." For a second he stared at me, and it felt like he might make a move to hug me before he left. But the moment passed, and he turned to go.

"See ya," I said as he retreated upstairs.

I began on the dishes, and in a flash he'd collected his bag from upstairs and was out the door. The house was quiet when I shut off the water and closed the dishwasher. I missed him already.

Upstairs, as I stepped into the tub for my shower, I remembered last night.

He'd promised me a wish. I could have anything. "*Anything you want, it's yours,*" he'd said.

*A foot rub in the bathtub—naked.*

That had gotten to him, and it wasn't such a bad idea for a wish after all.

I soaped up, and when my hands ran over my shoulders, I closed my eyes, remembering last night.

I kept my eyes closed, my hands kneading my shoulders. Everything melted away, and I imagined being face down on the couch, his hands on my bare skin, leaving trails of sparks with every movement. Why hadn't I rolled over to face him and asked for more? Because I'm a dumbshit, that's why.

The warm water rolled down me, and I added more soap.

The door squeaked open.

I shrieked from fright.

"It's just me," Zack said.

My hands instinctively went to cover myself. "Shit, you scared me." I could make out his form at the door through the shower curtain, which wasn't much protection.

"I forgot to tell you something. Before you do anything, unscrew all the fuses in the fuse box—all of them."

I regained my breath. "Uh, okay."

"Sorry. Didn't mean to scare you, but I forgot about the fuses, and I didn't want you to get hurt. Oh, and I left money for you downstairs."

He didn't want me to get hurt—the words resonated in my brain for a few seconds.

"Zack…"

I considered my next move, my next request. If this were a romance novel, I'd ask him to soap up my back or maybe join me—*definitely throw open the shower curtain and ask him to join me.* I lowered my hands to my sides. If I could make out his form through the curtain, certainly he could see what I'd done.

"Yeah?" he answered.

I chickened out. What if he said no? This wasn't a book, and I wasn't brave. "Thanks."

When he closed the door, I could have kicked myself. That had been the perfect opportunity to find out how last night's dream might have played out, and I'd let it get away.

I was glad he cared enough to come back and tell me about the fuses so I didn't end up a crispy critter under the house after touching a live wire. That's why he'd come back, of course—not to see me naked in the shower and take up where we'd left off last night.

He'd left so easily, he obviously wasn't as eager to see me naked as I was to undress for him.

I took the soap, closed my eyes, and let my hands run over my breasts. What would his hands on me have felt like?

*Heavenly* was the answer that came to me as I let my imagination run a little too wild.

Next time, I wouldn't be such a chickenshit.

~

Zᴀᴄᴋ

Dʀɪᴠɪɴɢ ɪɴ, I ᴄᴏᴜʟᴅɴ'ᴛ ɢᴇᴛ ᴛʜᴇ ɪᴍᴀɢᴇ ᴏꜰ ɴᴀᴋᴇᴅ Bʀɪᴛᴛɴᴇʏ ᴏᴜᴛ ᴏꜰ ᴍʏ ʜᴇᴀᴅ. Sᴜʀᴇ, there'd been a shower curtain between us, but her form was easy to see. Although she'd initially covered herself, once she dropped her hands, it had been difficult to leave. She obviously thought the curtain was more opaque than it was.

I'd wanted to pull the curtain aside and show her the way I felt, but common sense had prevailed. My imagination was playing tricks on me, tricks on us. She hadn't meant anything by it.

Fuck it. That had to be it. Then there was Doug—he'd kill me for even imagining Brittney was interested in me. That was a whole other can of worms, and an even bigger reason to get my imagination under control.

As I parked and shut down the engine, I made a mental note to Google ways to curb this imagination of mine. There had to be exercises for it—ones that didn't involve cold showers. I hated cold showers.

Upstairs, Wendy handed me the normal urgent message from Stanton, and two others that had come up late yesterday after I'd left.

I laid them on my desk and fired up my computer.

370

"What's your poison this morning?" I asked as I picked up her coffee mug on my way to the machine.

"Caffeine is good this morning. The more the better." That wasn't an unusual request for a Friday.

When I returned with the two steaming mugs, Wendy nodded toward my door. "Your dad is waiting," she whispered.

After entering, I closed the door.

Dad didn't often stop by first thing.

"Morning," I offered.

He didn't wait for me to get seated. "I got a complaint early this morning from Mario that you were blowing off next week's customer visits in London."

Stanton could be such an ass.

Mario Shepard was his boss, the worldwide VP of sales, and he'd obviously complained to him to get my decision on next week's meetings overturned. The sales guys were all wimps, afraid to take me on directly. Logic wasn't always their strong suit, but I responded better to that than common bitching.

"I didn't blow them off. I'm just sending Kaden Peralta in my place."

He shifted in his seat. "Why the change?"

The twenty questions had started, but that was better than the alternative of being directly countermanded, which was always a possibility with Dad.

"He needs the experience. It'll be good for him."

He stroked the end of his goatee. "But as I hear it, the customers are expecting to see the marketing VP, not a flunky." *Flunky* wasn't a term in my father's vocabulary. It had obviously come from the sales team.

I took a breath. "He's not a flunky, and he'll have full authority to negotiate the deals."

"You trust him?" he asked.

"Yes. Do you trust me to make the call?"

That backed him off a bit. "Of course. It's just unlike you to avoid a meeting with customers. I'm surprised is all."

"I'm busy next week, and Peralta needs the experience, so it's a good solution."

He leaned forward. The tick in his jaw was the one he got when he'd found a thread he wanted to pull on until he unraveled a mystery. "Busy?"

"I need to help a friend."

"Go on," he urged. "It sounds important."

It was important to me, but on a personal level that I didn't care to discuss.

"It is."

He stroked his goatee for a moment, seeming to mull whether to take another run at me.

"I'll tell Mario to move the meetings out three weeks," he announced, "so you have the time you need here first. And when you go to London, take young

Peralta with you. I agree that it's good for these guys to get overseas customer experience."

With that, Dad had devised a solution to the problem meant to keep us all happy, or at least equally unhappy—no losers in the deal. He had a knack for that kind of thing. It actually was a tack I should have considered yesterday with Stanton, but hadn't.

"Works for me. Should I talk to Mario about it?"

"Nah, his office is on my way back. I'll let him know what you proposed, and I'm sure he'll like it. And don't worry about young Stanton. If Mario likes it, he won't be an obstacle."

That Stanton wouldn't bitch if it came from his boss was a given. It was interesting that Dad was trying to give me credit for the compromise he'd cooked up —one I should have thought of myself yesterday. Perhaps that was the lesson he was teaching me today. With Dad there was almost always a lesson, if we were smart enough to notice it.

He leaned on his cane, got up, and made his way to the door before turning back toward me. "Your friend, who is she?"

His powers of deduction hadn't slowed one bit. He'd guessed my issue without even asking.

"Brittney. Doug Spear's sister."

His eyes lit up for a second. "Good man that Spear boy. Joined the Marines, didn't he?"

Dad had been a Marine himself, and anyone who joined the corps had his instant respect.

"Yup, deployed to Okinawa right now."

"Good for him. One more thing…"

I waited for the other shoe to drop.

"Why don't you bring her along this weekend? I'd like to meet her again. It's been a long time."

The Habitat day had slipped my mind somehow. A house-building day with Habitat for Humanity was a family ritual multiple times a year. It *had* been a long time since Brittney had left town, and none of us had seen her since then.

"I will. I think she'd enjoy it."

Brittney had seemed enthusiastic last night when we were working together to redo her plumbing, not to mention her desire to keep the project moving forward today, and I hoped that would carry over to our Habitat construction event. Nothing like a day in the sun, cutting wood, banging nails, and watching a house come together in record time with dozens of busy bodies working on the project.

Dad nodded and turned for the door.

Bringing Brittney to the Habitat project would mean a delay in getting her house fixed, but it couldn't be avoided. The barbecues and these construction weekends were the only times I really got to see the rest of the family now that we were all grown and out of the house. Family attendance at these events was virtually one hundred percent, and I hadn't missed one in years.

And there was always Katie Knowlton's apple pie.

Bill Covington's sister had married Nick Knowlton from high school. Nick had gotten into a fight with Bill's brother Patrick back in those days. Patrick had gotten his nose rearranged, but in the end it was Nick who got kicked out of school. Years later, Nick dating his sister had been hard for Bill to swallow early on, but now that they were married, all was good.

I followed after Dad and stopped at Wendy's desk. "We need to cancel Kaden's bookings for the London trip. Have him stop in, and I'll explain it to him."

"He was really looking forward to it."

"Just a timing change. Let me explain it to him." To keep morale up, it needed to seem like our idea rather than a complaint from Stanton.

# CHAPTER 18

*BRITTNEY*

THIS ELECTRICAL WORK WAS HARDER THAN IT LOOKED, BUT I WAS MAKING REAL progress. And keeping busy was a damn sight better than sitting around waiting for Zack to get back.

It had taken me three trips to the store to get what I needed. The first to get the box Zack had told me about so I could trace the wiring. A second to get a ladder, and a third to get a tool called a wire stripper so I could actually clamp onto the ends of the wires—he'd forgotten to mention that part.

I'd also had to make a dozen trips from the cellar to upstairs already, and I wasn't even half done.

The thieves had made a complete mess of everything, and I was cursing them for the millionth time when my phone rang. I pulled the noisy device from my pocket.

Zack's name lit up the screen. "How's it going?" he asked.

"It's going." I set the wire stripper I'd been using on the shelf of the ladder and moved down to the bottom rung where I felt more comfortable.

"You sound tired. You don't have to finish it all today, you know."

I wasn't about to let this beat me. "I'm getting there." I checked the time on the phone. "I'll call it a day in a little while. I still need to go grocery shopping before dinner. What would you like?"

"Let's do steak on the grill out back. Does that work for you?"

"It's a plan. What cut do you like?"

"Let's go with filet."

I would have chosen filet mignon as well. "You got it."

"See you tonight, Sunshine."

I sighed. I could listen to that nickname all day long.

It dropped right in front of me.

"Shit," I yelled.

I freaked and fell backwards off the ladder.

My phone clattered to the ground.

The spider was a monster—at least it looked that way to me. Probably one of those wolf spiders Zack had mentioned.

I got up, never taking my eyes off the beast as he continued lowering toward the floor. I shifted sideways, and with a quick movement retrieved my phone.

"Brit? Brit? You okay? What happened?" Zack was saying into the phone.

My heart pounded. "A fucking spider."

"Step on him and show him who's boss."

I could barely breathe. "I can't. He's still in the air."

"Wave your hand above him and break the thread, then step on him when he hits the ground."

Easy for him to say.

"No way. You get him. I'm done for today. I'm not getting anywhere near that thing." I didn't add that I knew some spiders could jump—I'd seen it on *Animal Planet*—and I wasn't going to be his next meal if I let him get to the ground.

"Suit yourself, but sooner or later you've got to learn to whack your own spiders."

I walked the long way around the beast toward the exit. "Later sounds good."

We hung up after he tried two more times to talk me into doing battle with the creature. Now I was going to need a flyswatter as well before I ventured down here again—something I could use at a safe distance. How far could they jump? I didn't remember.

I needed time anyway to clean up and go shopping for dinner, so I brushed off and locked up the house. I closed the cellar doors on Wolfie, the wolf spider.

The store was only a short drive away, and when the last item in my basket passed over the scanner and beeped, I inserted my Visa card in the reader.

The cashier was loading my items into a paper bag when the card reader beeped at me three times with the message *DECLINED*. The cashier's frown meant he knew what three beeps meant—another deadbeat customer.

He stopped filling my bag. "Perhaps another card."

That wasn't an option. I knew I didn't have enough on the MasterCard. I'd maxed it out with the first portion of Samantha's tuition. The Visa had been the one with headroom. Something was drastically wrong in Cardville. I checked my wallet for cash as I replaced the card. The total on the register was more than I had.

"I'll have to cut this down a little," I admitted with the heat of embarrassment burning my cheeks.

He reloaded the items in my basket, and I left the checkout line for the back of the store.

Checking my choices, it became clear I couldn't afford the steaks. I took them back to the meat section and substituted them for a package of two small pork chops. Then I put the steak sauce back on the shelf, along with the pineapple. My mental calculation said I'd make it out with a dollar to spare.

For my second attempt at checking out, I chose a different line, and I still had two dollar bills to my name when I walked to the parking lot.

Once I was in the safety and privacy of my car, I pulled my phone out and dialed the 800 number on the back of my Visa card. After keying in my account number and zip code, the mechanical lady proceeded to tell me the bad news according to Visa's computer.

A cold stone formed in my stomach with the balance the mechanical voice read out, and I could hardly breathe after she announced I had no remaining credit.

*This can't be happening.*

I punched zero a dozen times to get transferred to a talking human, not that there was much humanity in the way they treated me. Every month I paid them a king's ransom in interest, and now they'd just cut me off.

"Your call is important to us. Please stay on the line for the next available agent," the mechanical lady said.

The hold music started, and the same bullshit line about how important my call was got repeated every three or four minutes.

I pulled an apple from the shopping bag. The apple was gone before I finally heard the line ring to some support desk somewhere in the world.

"Thank you for holding. May I have the account number you are calling about?" the actual human lady on the phone said.

I read the long number off my card for the second time and gave her my name, billing address, and mother's maiden name. I expected her to ask me my birth weight and sixth grade English teacher's name as well.

"How may I help you?" she finally asked.

I took a calming breath. "I got declined in the store just now, and I'm trying to figure out what's going on."

"First I'll need to verify one more piece of information. Can you please give me your four-digit PIN code."

I gave her the four numbers.

"Very good. That's a match. It's just a precaution to keep unauthorized individuals from accessing your information."

"Thanks, I know," I responded.

"Let me see. Just a moment please. There are quite a few transactions and notes here."

"Yes. I see the declined transaction this afternoon. Miss Clark, it seems you've simply exhausted the limit on this card. If you'd like, you can give me your checking account information and we can make a payment today that will free up some room."

I huffed. "That can't be. There was several thousand left on my last bill."

"Just one sec," she said again. "Yes, that's correct, but all the purchases you made on the new card we sent have used up your available balance."

I hadn't used this card except once for gas. "What purchases? And what new card?"

"You called and ordered another card with the name Benjamin Sykes, and we overnighted it."

My blood started to boil. "I did no such thing," I said loudly. I'd cut up Benji's old card a long time ago, and no way was he getting another one.

"Miss, calm down."

"You're telling me to calm down? He's not authorized to have a card."

"Miss Clark, as we just went through, only authorized users with the proper PIN code can access the account. And a replacement card is no exception."

"When?" I spat.

"Two days ago. On Wednesday."

I slammed my hand against the wheel. "And the purchases?" Now my hand hurt as much as my head.

"They were yesterday and today. Two at Best Buy, two at Target, one at Game Stop, and one at Walmart, from what we have processed so far."

"I didn't authorize those purchases, so we have to reverse the transactions."

She sighed over the line. "Miss, I'd like to help you, but if you gave him the PIN code, that authorized him to get a replacement card and make those purchases. You'll have to take it up with him."

The tears started to flow. I sobbed. "But he stole it. I didn't give it to him."

"Miss, if you have a police report, that would be something we could start with. You can mail it to the dispute address on the website."

"I don't have a report." I shook my head. "We need to shut down the account then."

"What I can do for you is invalidate the current cards and issue new ones to you, but you will still have to pay down the balance to be able to use them. You're currently two hundred and thirty-one dollars over your limit."

It might as well have been a thousand dollars. I didn't have that kind of money.

I told her to go ahead and mail me a new card at my new address here.

"One more thing, miss," she said.

This whole conversation had exhausted me. "Yes?"

"I would suggest changing your PIN to start with."

I should have thought of that.

"If there's nothing else, I'll transfer you so you can do that. The computer will ask you to key it in twice, and then it'll be done."

"Thank you," I said.

377

This wasn't her fault. That asshole Benji had gotten into my desk and was still fucking with my life even though he was more than three hundred miles away.

*Fucking Benji.*

She transferred me, and I went through the process, cutting Benji out of my credit card life. Again.

I never should have given him a card in the first place, but I'd fixed that by taking it back and cutting it up, or so I'd thought.

Two fucking dollars in my wallet and no credit cards—I couldn't be more broke if I tried.

With my vision blurred by tears, I didn't dare drive yet. I laid my head against the steering wheel and let them flow.

# CHAPTER 19

*Zack*

Hours later I was still smiling about my phone call with Brittney. Once I'd confirmed she wasn't hurt, I'd found it pretty amusing to think of her hightailing it out of the cellar because of a spider. I stood and stretched my shoulders, which were still sore from all the overhead work under her house yesterday. I smiled as I contemplated another rubdown.

I finished what was left of my afternoon coffee and wandered out to Wendy's desk.

"Let's call off the social media review." It was scheduled for later this afternoon, and any excuse to skip it was good enough for me.

She looked up. "Spider problem, or girl problem?"

"Wendy, were you listening?"

She tilted her head. "The door was open, and you were pretty loud." She smirked and lifted her pen to her chin. "Would you like me to call a pest guy for you?"

I turned. "No thanks. Just cancel the social media meeting."

"Lucky girl," she said under her breath as I closed the door behind me.

*Was I that obvious?*

I got busy with the purchase requisitions I needed to finish before I could call it a day. I'd put these off yesterday, but another day's delay wasn't called for.

An hour and a half later, after three minor emergencies and an interminable stack of purchase reqs, I was ready to leave. I still had a half dozen customer deal sheets to go over, but those could wait, so I stuffed them in my briefcase for weekend review and locked up.

"Give her my regards," Wendy said as I turned the key.

"I will."

"Do I get to meet her?" she asked as I started for the elevator.

"If you come to the Habitat project on Sunday," I told her as I stopped and turned around.

"I'll pass on that." She laughed. "I'd probably nail my foot to the floor."

"You're always welcome." I waved and turned back toward the elevator.

The ride home was uneventful, but that didn't keep me from getting more and more tense as I got closer. I'd been looking forward to getting back home to see Brittney since the moment I left this morning. That girl did something to me I couldn't explain, but something I was quite happy for.

Turning into my driveway, I found the garage open behind the house. I pulled the car up to the tennis ball I'd hung from a string, turned off the engine, and set the brake. The space was short by modern standards—long enough to get the Shelby in there, but not by a lot.

I bounded up the stairs to the back porch and entered through the kitchen. The room was empty, with no sign that Brittney had started dinner yet.

I should have called and given her warning.

Opening the fridge, I pulled out two cans of beer before changing my mind and opting for a bottle of wine.

I found her on the couch in the old dining room I'd set up for TV. "Hey there. Like to start with some wine?" I held out the glass for her.

She looked up with red, watery eyes.

I set the two glasses down on the coffee table and sat beside her. "What's wrong, Sunshine?"

"Everything."

Her answer didn't give me a lot to work with. I sat back, forced past my inhibitions, and put my arm around her. "Tell me."

She didn't resist my touch. "I couldn't get you the steaks for tonight. I'm sorry." She sobbed.

My arm around behind her felt more natural than I'd expected. Exciting, but natural.

～

BRITTNEY

ZACH'S ARM FELT SO WARM AND COMFORTING, EXACTLY WHAT I NEEDED RIGHT NOW.

"No worries, Brit. I should've left more money this morning."

"It's not your fault. It's mine." I sobbed again. "I've let Samantha down."

That was the true end result of this.

His fingers traced a circle on my shoulder as he kept me close and waited for more of an explanation. "I'm here for you."

I blinked back more tears as I realized the meaning of his words. He truly was the one I could count on, and he always had been. Until I left.

"If you're not ready yet, it's okay."

How could anyone be so understanding?

"There are things I didn't tell you." I hesitated, not knowing really where to start, and how to explain everything.

"I've got all night."

I sniffed. "This afternoon at the grocery store, my card got declined. And when I called the company, they said I was over my limit. But I shouldn't have been. Remember I got a call from Lillian saying some stuff was taken from my apartment in San Jose?"

"Yeah."

"Well, it was my ex, like I told you, and he's been busy with the stuff he took."

He stiffened, and the fingers that had been tracing circles on my skin stilled.

"He called the credit card company, and they issued him a card for my account." I sobbed. "And he used it again and again until my account was at the limit."

"Sunshine, I can help." His fingers resumed their gentle movement on my shoulder, a calming touch.

I snuggled closer. "It's all my fault."

"It's not your fault."

"Yes, it is. I shouldn't have left that stuff. I wasn't thinking."

"I told you, it's not your fault."

I couldn't accept that. "I'm failing Sam because I was stupid. And now she's not going to be able to finish. And she has interviews lined up. I've screwed it all up."

"Say that one more time, and I'm gonna have to spank you," he said firmly.

I pulled away. "I'm not a kid anymore."

"Then stop acting like one." He let me go as his gaze held mine. "It's not your fault."

"Of course you wouldn't understand," I spat. "You've got all the money in the world. What would you know about being broke?"

"I know a lot about making mistakes. I've made my fair share. You have to stop blaming yourself."

"I'm the one who screwed up. It's my fault."

In a flash he grabbed my arm and yanked me over.

I ended up over his knee.

"You really want to get yourself spanked?"

"Hey." I struggled, but it was no use against his strength. "Let me go."

"It's not your fault that your stupid ex-boyfriend—what's his name?"

I squirmed to no avail. "Benji."

"So, you're telling me it's your fault Benji is a thief?"

"Well, no."

"Benji's an asshole and a thief. Your life's in the shitter. All that means is it's time for you to pull up your big girl panties and get to work fixing it."

I struggled again and pushed at his leg, but he still held me down. "Are you going to let me up?"

"Are you going to behave and stop blaming yourself?"

"But I'm flat broke. I can't afford Sam's tuition. Fuck, I couldn't even afford tonight's dinner. I don't have a job, and without the papers from my desk I can't get one. I need a second ID. And the house I thought I had isn't even livable. Everything is so fucked up."

He sighed. "That wasn't the question."

"What was the question again?"

"Are you gonna behave yourself, stop dwelling on the past, and start moving forward?"

I didn't really see a choice. "Sure."

He started to tickle me.

I couldn't keep from laughing. "Hey, stop that. You said you'd let me up." I squirmed.

He relented and let me go.

I retreated to the other end of the couch. "You…you…"

I couldn't form a sentence. It was then that I realized just how easily he'd taken me from a downer pity party to laughing. I stopped complaining and folded my arms.

He shifted to face me. "I can help you, but only if you're willing to help yourself."

I couldn't figure out where he was going with this. "I can't accept your money."

"Clean out your ears, girl. I said I would help you. I didn't say I was giving you money."

"Big help you are. Money is what I need right now."

"Bullshit. The only thing you need is self-confidence." He stood and held out his hand. "Come with me." His tone was a demand, not an offer.

He hadn't heard a thing I'd said about my maxed-out credit cards and no job. That was the very definition of needing money before anything else. Sometimes the rich were so clueless about the real world.

At the risk of getting spanked, I sat still. "Where?"

"Sunshine, can't you stop arguing for once and just come along? I'm gonna show you that you have a lot more options than you think you do. A lot more of everything…except confidence, that is." He held out his hand.

I huffed, but stood anyway. It was a better idea to play along with him than argue while he was in this delusional state.

When I didn't take his hand, he turned and walked into the kitchen toward the back door.

I followed. "Where are we going?" I asked again.

He stopped and turned to face me. "Pick a piece of fruit. I'll eat it if it'll get you to be quiet for a moment and just come with me. I have something to show you."

I almost stomped my foot in frustration, but caught myself. I pulled an apple from the grocery bag still sitting on the counter and tossed it to him.

He caught it, took a bite, and opened the back door.

I followed him down the steps, through the backyard gate to my house, and up the back steps. We entered through the kitchen.

He put down the half-eaten apple and turned on the light in his phone.

I did the same and followed him into the dining room.

He shone the light on a small framed sketch on the wall. "What do you see?"

This was by far the stupidest question tonight. "It's probably something one of us did in art class for school."

I could see a smile appear on his face in the dim light. "You know what I see? I see money."

"No way."

"And this. What do you see?" He shifted to a small landscape painting on the opposite wall. Another stupid question.

"A painting." It wasn't large and didn't even look that good.

"So many people don't recognize value when they see it. The artist is Andrew Wyeth."

"Doesn't ring a bell," I told him.

He smiled again. "It's not a very large one, but it would probably fetch fifty to a hundred K at auction."

I stepped back, not sure I'd heard him correctly. "Fifty grand? As in dollars?" The number stunned me.

"That's right. Your grandmother collected really nice things. Right now they all look like shit because everything is so filthy. But clean them up and you've got a lot of valuable art in this house, and very nice antiques as well. What you called the kid's sketch…" He motioned to the other wall. "A small Picasso probably worth about five K, but you could unload it for three in a day at any one of the galleries around here."

I had to steady myself against a chair. Right now I'd kill for a few thousand dollars. "I had no idea."

"Do we agree now that things are not as dire as you thought?"

"I guess."

He switched off his phone's light, pocketed the device, and took me in his arms.

The comfort of his embrace was what I'd wanted earlier. At least I had it now, and it was better than I could've imagined. His body heat filtered through the clothing and into my heart.

"Sunshine," he said, pulling me tight.

I nestled my head into his shoulder, and his protective arms around me soothed away my worry. "Yeah?" I muttered.

He whispered in my ear. "I'll listen to all your troubles. I want you to tell me everything. Don't hold back; I'm here to listen—but only so long as you agree to not blame yourself. Got it?"

I nodded into his shoulder. "You're being bossy again."

"It's for your own good. You have to get it off your chest." He lifted my chin up with a finger. "Let me help you."

I looked up into his warm eyes and nodded. "Okay."

He let me go, took my hand, and led me back toward the door.

Immediately I wanted to be in his arms again, have him rub my back and let my fears melt away.

"But first you can cook that dinner you promised me," he said as he walked ahead of me.

I had to rush to keep up, he was in such a hurry. "Are pork chops okay? I couldn't afford the filet."

He opened the back door and ushered me through. "Any meal with you will be wonderful."

"Don't forget the rest of your apple," I reminded him.

"I still hate apples." He grimaced, but went back and rescued the apple before locking the door behind us. He took a loud bite for my benefit.

"Don't give me that look. You're the one who offered to eat it."

He shook his head and started down the steps. He'd gone from being bratty to saying the nicest things, and I liked this side of him better. I had to figure out where the switch was to get him to be like this more often.

Back at his house, he lit the grill on the back porch and started the meat.

Inside I prepared the Rice-A-Roni I'd gotten to go with it. While the mushrooms sautéed on the stove, I sliced up two pears for our fruit.

He located candles in a cupboard, lit them, and brought the wine from the other room.

When the food was finished, I sat down to candles, wine, fresh-cooked dinner, and Zack across from me. It wasn't as fancy as the dinner he'd taken me to at Cardinelli's, but it struck me as even more romantic. Maybe it was because we were alone, or maybe it was the look in his eyes as he took bites of the food I'd prepared and smiled at me. I knew we were just two people rooming together in a house and sharing dinner chores, but it felt more intimate than that.

He hadn't said a word beyond *"Bon appétit."*

When I finished cutting another piece of meat, I looked up to catch him smiling. The look was something beyond friendly.

"What?" I asked as I put my fork down to wipe my face with my napkin. "Did I spill?"

"No, it's nothing," he answered. "I was just admiring your smile."

Heat rose in my cheeks. "Stop it. You're trying to embarrass me."

"No, it was a sincere compliment, but if you want, I'll think of something nasty to say instead." His words only increased my self-consciousness.

"You're weird, but compliment away if you must. I'm just not used to hearing any."

I didn't dare admit how good it felt.

"You obviously don't hang around with the right kind of people," he said.

Maybe not. Whatever it was, he made me happy. This afternoon I'd been staring into the abyss, and this evening he'd brought me back from the edge to the equivalent of a sunny meadow. I had no way to know for sure, but I had faith that with Zack's help, my tomorrows would improve.

"Benji was a complete shit," I blurted.

Zack looked up. "Well sure, with a name like that anybody would be. I feel sorry for the guy already."

"Yeah, that's what Sam told me too. She knew he was a loser as soon as she heard his name."

"I'm with her. I've never met the guy, and I already don't like him."

"Trust me. If you met him, there's no way your impression would improve."

"You mentioned you left in a hurry..."

The statement was simple, but my answer couldn't be.

"Things sort of came to a head all of a sudden on Tuesday."

He scooped up a bite of rice and continued to eat, waiting for me to put my thoughts together.

"He came to my work and started to make a scene in the reception area. It got so bad he scared off some patients. That's when Dr. Call decided she'd had enough, and the only way she could get rid of him was to get rid of me, so she let me go."

Zack's brow furrowed. "You mean to say the little shithead got you fired?" The anger in his voice was obvious.

"Technically Dr. Call suspended me," I corrected. "But he cost me my job." I took a sip of water before continuing. "The real kicker was when I got home."

Zack stopped chewing and looked on expectantly.

"He'd gone to town on my door and the wall outside my apartment with a can of spray paint."

"He tagged you?"

I nodded in disgust. "Yeah, and I got evicted from my apartment."

"That sure qualifies as a shitty day. Now I'm gonna kill him for sure."

I cut another piece of meat, because the statement spoke for itself. "That's why I was in such a hurry to get away from there and come down here."

He reached his hand across the table.

I reached the rest of the way to take it, and the sparks ignited as soon as I did.

"I'm sorry that happened to you. You deserve better."

The emotion in his eyes warmed me through and through.

# CHAPTER 20

*Zack*

On Saturday, we'd made progress on her house, but between missing fittings that required trips to the store and difficulty reaching some of the connections, I hadn't gotten it finished.

I could have worked later into the night, but I'd lacked the motivation. I told myself I was going slow to be careful, but could it have been that I didn't want Brittney to leave my house and move into hers?

Today was Sunday, Habitat day, and we'd gotten up early.

I forced down the kiwi she made me eat for the second day in a row. I'd requested oranges instead, but it fell on deaf ears.

She packed a ton of fruit for the day after I told her the size of the group we'd be lunching with. She hefted the grocery bag, and I hurried her out the door.

"It pays to be early to these things," I told her as I locked the door behind us.

"Why is that?"

"Then we get our pick of jobs. This being your first weekend at one of these, I want us doing the right kind of thing."

"Why does that matter?" she asked.

"It matters to me. I don't want you up on the roof."

I was responsible for her safety today, and not that we had many accidents at these things, but I didn't need to hear from Doug later that I shouldn't have let her handle something dangerous—like a hammer.

"Think I can't handle it?"

"That's not the point," I shot back as I opened the garage.

"And what is the point?"

I popped the trunk while searching for a way out of this argument. "I don't want to explain to your brother that you fell off the roof avoiding a spider."

We packed up the trunk with the food she'd gotten, along with the extra shirts, hats, and sunscreen I'd brought out.

Her brow furrowed as she contemplated my answer. "Spiders?"

"They like to sun themselves on roofs."

"I don't believe you. You said they were in the basement. I saw one there."

I cocked my head. "That doesn't keep them from wanting to sun on the roof. If you want, I'll catch one for you. They make good barbecue."

"Get outta here."

"Just sayin'."

"Okay. No roof work."

I opened the door for her, and she slid in.

She buckled up, and I jogged around.

The engine started like a charm. I backed out onto the street and turned north.

"Why did you choose this car? You could've gotten yourself something nice, like a Ferrari," she said.

I glanced over and caught her grin.

She was goading me.

"Newer is not always better. I guess I just like some of the older classics. The new cars are all automatic this and automatic that, electronic this, electronic that, with a ton of extras—power seats, fancy turbochargers, GPS, and heated cup holders.

"This car, however..." I patted the steering wheel. "...is simple. Nothing but pure, unadulterated horsepower. In its day, it was the ultimate car for turning gasoline into noise, tire smoke, and speed. A simple machine with a simple mission—going fast as fuck."

She considered for a moment before stating, "You seem to like old things."

"I appreciate the classics. My house, and yours for that matter, were built by craftsmen. They have character. This car is the same. It's one-hundred-percent character. It doesn't pretend to be something it's not. It's about noise, fury, and speed."

"A man's car," she said.

I wasn't about to argue with that. "I'm not apologizing. If you're saying it's not a sissy car, I'll agree."

I turned onto the freeway onramp, and as we came to the merge, I saw a truck coming up fast in the right lane. I downshifted, popped the clutch, and with a squeal of the tires, we were up to speed and in front of him in seconds. It was a pity we didn't have an autobahn here to let me open it up.

Glancing over, I caught Brittney gripping the door, but also grinning ear to ear. She liked speed too.

I put it in fourth, and we settled down for the long drive over the hill.

"I wasn't interested in cars growing up, like you guys were, but this car is certainly growing on me," she offered. "When can I drive it?"

"The tenth of never," I answered. I'd never let anybody drive this car. "You don't even know how to drive a stick."

"Yes, I do. My first Corolla was a stick."

"Trust me, this is nothing like a Corolla."

She crossed her arms. "This is nothing but a stupid old Mustang with fancy paint and a snake on the carpet." She rubbed her foot on the cobra stitched into the floor mats.

My blood boiled momentarily, but that's exactly what she wanted. "For your information, this is a real GT500 upgraded to a Super Snake, with the old engine swapped out for a racing 427—the same engine that won the twenty-four hours of Le Mans for Ford and took the crown away from Ferrari." I clenched my hands on the wheel and loosened them, reminding myself to calm down.

"When do I get to drive it?"

"Like I said, the tenth of never."

This wasn't the car to learn on. Just like you didn't learn to ride a horse by jumping on a thoroughbred.

She changed the subject. "Where exactly are we going?"

"Over the hill to the valley. Habitat is building a house in Van Nuys."

We motored on and were over the hill and down into the San Fernando Valley relatively quickly in the light Sunday-morning traffic.

I'd checked the address before leaving and navigated off the freeway and through several turns until we arrived at the right street. The build site was obvious, with dozens of people milling around out front. I had to park down at the far end of the block. I jumped out, and Brittney wisely stayed in her seat until I opened the door for her.

"More people than I expected," she noted.

"I hope we got here early enough." I led her through the crowd to a table where they were handing out gloves and hardhats. Bill Covington and his wife, Lauren, were behind the table. Lauren had their son strapped to her in a front baby carrier.

Bill looked up from the paper he was consulting. "Hey, Zack, glad you could make it." His eyes flashed to Brittney with just a hint of recognition. "And your friend," he added.

I shook Bill's hand. "You might remember Brittney Spear from Brentmoor." I urged her forward.

Bill pointed at her. "Yeah, I thought I recognized you." He put his arm around his wife and baby. "This is my wife, Lauren."

Lauren offered her hand. "You wouldn't by any chance be related to—"

Brittney cut her off. "No such luck, and I can't sing worth a damn."

"It's a pleasure, Brittney. Any friend of Zack's is a friend of ours."

"How old is he?" Brittney maneuvered to get a better look at the baby.

"This is Wendell, ten months."

Brittney cooed to the little guy. "He's cute."

"Named after Bill's father," Lauren added.

I glanced over the crowd. "Dad around?" I asked Bill.

Bill, who was busy greeting the next person in line, pointed to the back. "At the plan table, I think."

"Glad to have you with us. Just don't forget to keep your sunscreen up to date," Lauren warned Brittney with a smile.

I picked up two hard hats and dragged Brittney away from Lauren and the baby.

"Got it—sunscreen," Brittney said as we left.

Dad was easy to spot at the plan table in the middle of what would soon become a house.

"Good morning," he called as we approached. "Zachary, I see you convinced her to join us."

"Couldn't possibly keep me away," Brittney responded.

"I don't know if you remember me," Dad said.

Brittney put on one of her winning smiles. "I couldn't possibly forget you, Mr. Benson."

"Lloyd, please. We're all family here," he said. He opened his arms for a quick hug, which she accepted.

"Tell your brother *Semper Fi* for me next time you talk to him," Dad said.

Brittney nodded. "Sure thing."

"Dad, you got something nice and easy for us for her first weekend?" I asked.

He picked up his clipboard and scanned it. "Want to start with electrical drilling?"

I didn't like the sound of that. "How about electrical boxes? Is that available?"

"Dennis is already down for that, but I'm sure you can convince him to give it up for the right price."

No price would be too high this morning.

"Glad to have you with us. Don't forget to keep your sunscreen freshened up," Dad warned Brittney as I pulled her toward my older brother.

"Yep. Sunscreen," she answered.

Dad pointed to his head. "Hard hats too," he reminded us.

I gave Brittney one of the yellow plastic hats and donned the other myself.

Dennis looked up as we approached. "Dad said you were bringing a girl today, but I had no idea it would be anybody as pretty as Doug's sister here. Brittney, isn't it?"

She blushed. "Thanks. Flattery is gladly accepted. You should teach your brother that trick."

I ignored the dig. "Hey, Dennis, since this is Brittney's first time, can we swap with you and take the electrical boxes?"

"What do you have to swap? I'm not doing roofing again."

"Electrical pass-throughs," I answered.

"And follow you two around all day?" He stroked his chin for a second, obviously giving me a hard time. "I guess, but just because it's her."

"Thanks, Dennis," I told him.

"I'm doing it for her and Doug, not for you," he said.

He was always busting my balls.

He handed me the electrical plan sheet. "You'll need this."

"And the tape measure," I told him.

Dennis unclipped a tape measure from his belt and handed it to Brittney.

"Try to keep up," I told him as I took Brittney to the supplies in back.

I located the cardboard boxes with the blue single- and double-gang electrical boxes and handed the one with the triples to my helper. After grabbing a hammer and a pencil, we were ready to start.

"We'll start at the front door and work our way around. Just follow me."

She followed me to the front of the house, where I checked the plan for the door swing and switch position. I held out my hand. "Tape measure."

She gave it to me.

I pulled it out and locked it with enough tape to measure forty-four inches.

"Okay. This is what we do: At each of these locations on the plan, we're going to nail in one of these blue boxes for the switches and outlets. For switches, we measure forty-four inches up from the floor and mark it with a pencil. Then we nail the box there so the bottom lines up with the mark. For outlets, the measurement is twelve inches, except in the kitchen and bathroom. We'll figure those out later. Got it?"

"Twelve and forty-four. Got it. But which size box goes where?"

I pointed on the plan sheet. "This is a single-gang box, this denotes a double, and this here is a triple. So, what size do we put here beside the front door?"

She checked the paper. "A three?"

I nodded. "You're a natural. So make your mark."

I picked a triple out of our supplies while she measured. Lining up with the mark on the stud, I banged in the nails attached to the box, and we had one complete.

"One down, and a hundred to go." It wasn't that many, but it would feel like it soon enough.

We were more than halfway through when Phil Patterson came by.

"My God, I thought I recognized you," Phil said as he got a look at Brittney's face. He pointed to himself. "Phil Patterson. We went to Brentmoor together. It's Brittney, isn't it? Brittney Spear?"

"It's Clark now, Phil. But yeah, good to see you too."

It almost got by me—almost. She said her name was now Clark.

Had she gotten married?

She wasn't wearing a ring.

There was definitely something I didn't know. Why hadn't she told me?

"Zack, I need four singles for the attic space. Can you spare 'em?" Phil asked.

"Huh?" I was still processing Brittney's married name.

"I need singles for up in the attic," he repeated.

I offered him the one I was holding. "Sure. Whatever."

Phil took the boxes and left.

Brittney tapped me on the shoulder. "This one's ready. The plan says a single."

I picked another single from the box and started to bang the nails into the stud when I missed and hit the box instead. The box cracked. I pulled the nail and threw the broken plastic to the side.

"Careful. Do you want to switch for a while?" Brittney asked.

"No, I got it. I just think I'm ready for lunch."

We made our way around the room, more slowly now, and still stayed ahead of Dennis drilling holes in the studs for the wires to pass through.

It wouldn't be long before Dad sounded the lunch horn.

*Married? What the hell is with that?*

# CHAPTER 21

*BRITTNEY*

I RECOGNIZED ZACK'S SISTER, SERENA, AS SHE WALKED UP.

After a quick hello, she asked, "Hey Zack can I borrow Brittney?"

Zack shrugged and checked his watch.. "Sure."

Serena tapped me on the shoulder. "How about you join me for the sandwich run?"

I stood. "Sure."

"And no forgetting my meatball again, Serena," Lloyd called as we walked by him.

After we were out of earshot, Serena said, "I'm trying to get him to eat healthier, but it's not working. He insists on having a meatball sub even though he knows it's bad for him."

"Men can be like that."

"Don't I know it." She pushed the button on her key fob, and the Escalade ahead of us unlocked.

We got in and started down the street.

"Subway is just around the corner. I called in the order early, so it should be ready for us." She smiled in my direction. "I'm really glad you could join us, Brittney."

"Me too. This is a lot of fun. You guys do it often?"

She turned left at the stop sign. "Not quite every month but pretty regularly. Sometimes a weekend is called off because of rain in the winter."

"That sounds like quite a lot."

"The community's been so good to us. This is our way of giving back a little. And, it's always good to get out in the sunshine and do a little honest work instead of sitting behind a desk. The most important thing, I think, is that it gets us together as a family."

I appreciated the sentiment—family was important. It was the one thing we could always rely on.

The Subway was just a few blocks away, as she'd said. It took a large bag to hold all the sandwiches she'd ordered, and another bag for the chips. We loaded ourselves and our stash back into her car.

We stopped at another stop sign, and she looked over. "When did you get back to town?"

"Just this week."

After turning on the street she asked, "Where are you staying?"

"With Zack," I said, not wanting to elaborate.

"That's good. He's a good guy."

Of course his sister couldn't say much else. I would always say the same about Doug.

Zack was waiting on the sidewalk in front of the construction site when we parked and got out.

A loud horn blast startled me.

I looked behind me to find Zack's father in the middle of the project holding an air horn above his head. He gave it another long honk.

Serena opened the back to retrieve the bags. "That means lunch."

Zack took my hand. "Now you get to meet the rest of the crew."

"Crew?" I asked.

"Yeah, a mixture of Bensons and Covingtons. We're pretty much all out here every time we have one of these things, at least those of us who are in town."

"I need to get the fruit from the car," I reminded him. He probably hoped I would forget.

"Right. Almost forgot," Zack said.

"Go ahead, I got these," Serena told us.

I pulled Zack down the street toward his car. The sun was high in the sky, so we retrieved the hats as well as the bag of fruit.

"We may not need all this," he said. "I'm sure Katie brought fruit with her too."

"Katie?" I asked. I thought I'd seen Katie Covington wandering around earlier. "Katie Covington?"

Zack handed me the bag. "Yes, but it's Knowlton now."

"You mean Knowlton as in Nick?"

"Yeah, she married him over her brother's objections. But now Nick's one of us, just a part of the family—a nice guy once you get past the rough exterior he puts up. And, he's a professor now at UCLA."

That floored me, because the Nick Knowlton I'd known in high school had been all about motorcycles and skipping class, not exactly the type to become a university professor.

"Are we talking about the same Nick?" I asked as we walked back toward the house.

"The same. See that bike over there?" He pointed at the Harley across the street. "He and Katie rode up on that."

When we reached them, Zack introduced me to the group, and I waved around the circle. The Covingtons were Bill, Lauren, Katie, and her husband, Nick. The Benson crew included Zack's father, his brothers Dennis and Josh, and his sister Serena. His brother Vincent lived in Boston now, and his other sister Kelly was in Europe today. Phil Patterson, who'd introduced himself earlier, and a Winston somebody rounded out the group.

With a cap that read Patterson Construction, Phil was the only pro among us.

I'd seen many of them at one point or another years ago, but they were all so grown up now.

When Serena set down the bags, everybody was in a hurry grabbing for their favorite sandwiches. I noticed Serena pull one of the meatball subs and hide it behind her back. Zack snatched the other one.

Frustrated after looking through the sandwiches that remained, Lloyd glared at Serena. "I warned you," he said with a pointed finger.

She produced the sandwich from behind her back. "I was just messing with you, Dad."

He wagged his finger again. "Do that one more time, young lady, and you'll regret it."

I doubted that his bite was as bad as his bark. It was easy to see he loved his children.

Everyone dug into the subs and chips.

Serena had ordered more sandwiches than people, which came in handy when most of the guys, including Zack, checked the bags and grabbed a second. Physical labor like this amped up the appetite.

Lauren, who was sitting to my right, leaned over and nodded toward Zack. "You two could get a little away time up at the cabin, if you like."

Zack was talking with Phil and not paying attention.

"Cabin?" I asked.

"Bill and I have a cabin in the mountains. We don't get much free time to go up, so it's available to family and friends. Very romantic." She winked. She seemed to have me and Zack pegged as a couple.

"Thanks for the offer," I said, not venturing to correct her impression of our situation.

When the sandwiches were mostly devoured, I brought out my bag and offered fresh fruit around.

Everyone except Zack was a taker. "I'll wait for Katie's fruit, thanks," he told me.

Katie turned and brought out two boxes from behind her. "I brought two today, both apple."

"Now that's my kind of fruit," Zack said as Katie opened the boxes to reveal gorgeous pies.

She'd also brought paper plates and plastic forks.

I shoved an orange at Zack. "No, you don't. Not until you finish this."

"You tell him, girl," Serena said.

A comment I didn't need.

Zack scowled, but started to peel the orange. "You know you can walk home, if you like."

The group became quiet.

"Just kidding," he said, realizing his comment hadn't gone over well. "Thanks, Sunshine." He smiled, and the group's banter resumed as they attacked the apple pies.

Her baby had been fussing a bit when Lauren stood. "It's his lunchtime too." She took her chair over by the fence.

"He's a cutie," Serena said softly to me.

I glanced over to where Lauren was starting to nurse her son. "Sure is." I couldn't help but smile.

After Zack finished his orange, he and I shared a large piece of pie.

"Thank you," I whispered into his ear between bites.

He shrugged.

"Who's turn is it for clean up?" Lloyd asked the group.

Serena raised her hand. "I think it's me."

"I nominate the new girl to help," Zack said.

He was probably getting me back for insisting on the orange.

I stood. "Sure, I'll help you, Serena."

The group slowly dispersed, and Serena and I were left alone with the aftermath.

Mr. Benson sounded his horn, and the other volunteers started getting back to the business of house building.

"I'm really glad you two got together," she said as we were picking up.

Before I could correct her, she continued, "He's had a crush on you since the seventh grade—a crush like you wouldn't believe. My room was next to his at home, and the walls aren't as soundproof as they should be. I heard him say your name in his sleep more than once—not that I would ever tell him, but it's the truth. That's half the reason I think it never worked out with any of the other girls."

I couldn't believe what I was hearing.

She smiled again. "Secretly, I think he was always waiting for it to work out with you."

This was a revelation. A surprise to top all surprises.

I contemplated an answer but didn't have one. "We're not—"

She interrupted me. "I get that you're not super serious yet. I just think it's good you got together. He deserves someone like you. I always thought you two would make a good couple." She tied the top to the garbage bag she'd filled. "And I was right. You're cute together."

"We're not seeing each other," I said, setting her straight.

She giggled. "Okay. If that's the way you want to play it, I'll go along. My brothers can be pretty secretive, not wanting people to know who they're going out with."

She didn't get it, but I'd said enough already. I didn't correct her again.

As we carried the full garbage bags to the dumpster by the street, her words haunted me. "*He's had a crush on you since seventh grade.*" Earth to Serena, that can't possibly have been the situation.

I knew the truth. I was just his best friend's sister, so maybe it had looked from the outside like he was coming over to our house to see me.

I tossed my bag over the edge. "Doug was his best friend."

"Guys can be so transparent sometimes. He likes Doug, but even if Doug really pissed him off, he was never going to stop going by to see you."

The implication was eye-opening. I still had a chance with Zack.

*Still* wasn't the right word. *Now*, I had a chance with Zack. I hadn't been imagining what I felt between us.

"Today is the happiest he's looked in a month," Serena added as we walked back to the construction site. She winked.

That wink hinted at the possibilities I had with Zack. That wink meant that as his sister, she knew things—things other girls wouldn't know. Sibling bonds allowed truths that otherwise got distorted or hidden. I knew that well enough myself, with Doug and Samantha.

"I'm glad he got over that best friend's sister crap. Guys can be so stupid about shit like that—the bro code, you know, hands off your best friend's sister, that kind of shit. Doesn't make any sense to me. You like him, he likes you, you're adults. Where's the harm? Doug should be proud you've got a boyfriend as cool as his best friend. Well, that's just me. Anyway, I'm glad he got over that shit and finally got smart enough to get together with you."

She went to the back of the house, and I went inside to work with Zack.

He looked my direction as I walked up, but then averted his eyes without a smile.

The bro code? Could that be the problem?

# CHAPTER 22

*BRITTNEY*

ALL AFTERNOON ZACK HADN'T SAID MORE THAN TWO WORDS THAT DIDN'T RELATE TO
the stupid electrical boxes, followed by the plates we hammered on the studs at
the height of the pass-through holes.

The drive back over the hill from the valley had been equally quiet. Now we
were almost home, and I wasn't sure what to do.

I didn't know where to start to make it better. "I'm sorry I embarrassed you."

He looked straight ahead. "What?"

"The orange. I didn't mean to embarrass you in front of your family and
friends."

"Forget it" was his only reply.

I needed more than that, but he wasn't opening up. I waited, but still got
nothing. I continued to watch him, looking for the slightest glance in my direction, the slightest opening.

We drove in silence for another few miles.

"I'm sorry," I said.

He looked over this time. There was something unreadable in his eyes. "I said
it's not a problem."

"Then what is it?"

He took a long, deep breath. "Do you have anything important to tell me?"

I did not see that coming. "No."

He took the off-ramp toward our neighborhood. "Then why are we talking?"

"Because I want to apologize."

"You did."

I crossed my arms, looked straight ahead, and managed to restrain myself from stomping my feet. I felt like hitting him, he was being so obstinate. "What is your problem?"

"I don't have a problem. I just don't like being lied to."

I jerked my head to look at him. I hadn't lied to him, and I couldn't think of what would have given him that idea. "I haven't lied to you."

He turned right onto Snakewood. "Right. Your last name isn't Spear anymore, it's Clark, and you're running away from this Benji character. Did you forget to mention he's your husband?" He pulled into the driveway around the house.

"I'm not married, and he's not my husband," I shouted as he stopped the car.

"Right, ex-husband then."

"You wouldn't understand." I unbuckled and bolted from the car. I started toward the back gate between the houses.

He shut down the engine and got out. "Where are you going?"

I turned around and yelled back. "I'm going to get the art out of the house before someone steals it."

"Do you want help?" he called.

I walked through the gate and slammed it shut, letting that be my answer. Call me a liar, will you? I'd been called a lot of things, but never that. I may not have explained everything, but I hadn't lied.

I stomped up the stairs and unlocked the back kitchen door.

"Stop running away," Zack said from behind me.

I ignored him and went inside.

Out of habit I flipped the light switch, and of course nothing happened. No electricity. For a moment I'd forgotten how fucked up things were.

I took the Picasso gently down from the wall and placed it on the table before going into the other room to get the more expensive painting.

That's when I saw it.

A brick in the middle of the floor amid broken glass from the front window.

I couldn't breathe. I leaned over, hands on my knees, trying to compose myself. Everything in my life was falling apart. The tears started and I crumpled to the floor.

# CHAPTER 23

*Zack*

Brittney was in one piss-poor mood. She'd slammed the gate in the fence between our properties so hard it rattled. A few more jolts like that to the old wood, and it would fall apart.

I followed her into her house, but she wasn't in the kitchen. It wasn't until I looked through the doorway toward the front of the house that I saw her kneeling on the floor, sobbing.

I rushed to her and knelt beside her, putting my arm around her shoulder. Shattered glass sparkled over the floor, and a brick lay in the middle of the mess.

"Are you okay?"

She shook her head and continued to sob. "Why is everything going wrong?"

I cradled her in my arms. "I'll take care of this, Sunshine."

Her sobbing slowed. She sniffed and wiped her nose with her sleeve. "I don't deserve this."

"Of course you don't," I assured her. "Let's get you back to the other house." I got to my feet and pulled her up.

She wiped under an eye. "Okay."

I pulled her toward the kitchen.

"But the pictures."

"I'll come back and collect them."

She stopped arguing and came down the back stairs with me. She shivered lightly as I held her and we made our way back through the gate and up the back steps into my house.

I deposited her on one of the kitchen chairs. "Stay here while I get the pictures."

She opened her mouth as if to protest, but closed it and nodded instead. *Good girl.*

Back in the other house, I carefully removed the precious artwork from the walls, piece by piece, and placed each on the table or leaning against the chairs. It took three trips to bring them all to my place, and then I made a trip back to see what I could do about the broken front window.

The brick had two rubber bands around it, and when I turned it over, I found a note secured to the projectile. It was written in red ink.

**I WANT WHAT'S MINE - LEAVE IT UNDER THE FLOWER POT AND THAT WILL BE THE END OF IT**

I folded the note and stuffed it in my wallet.

Only a small section of multi-pane window had been broken out, and that would be easy to replace. For a temporary fix, I returned to the kitchen for the roll of duct tape I'd left there earlier. A few strips over the opening, and I had it closed off enough to keep the insects out.

"You're going to get yours, you little fucker," I said after the last piece of tape was in place.

That little Piss Boy was one asshole I was going to teach a lesson he would never forget. The fucking pain in the ass was going to learn the hard way not to mess with me or my friends. And no fucking way was I putting his phone under the flower pot—not in a million years. I had a better idea.

Walking back to check on Brittney, I smiled as I envisioned him opening the surprise I had planned for him. Adding surveillance cameras to the house was also going on my to-do list, to catch the little weasel on tape in case he tried another stunt like this. There was no telling how stupid he was, no guarantee he'd learn his lesson quickly.

The deadbolt on my kitchen door locked with a pleasing click as I closed it behind me. I set one last picture down in the other room and returned to Brittney.

Her eyes were moist, and she still trembled. "Thank you."

I held her eyes with mine. "Have I ever lied to you?"

She shook her head.

"You have to believe me. You're safe here with me. I'm going to fix this."

She blinked back a tear, and the slightest hint of a smile appeared.

I took the other chair. "Now, I need an honest answer to a few simple questions, Ms. Clark."

She looked up with teary eyes.

"Are you going to do what I ask you to do?"

She gave me a shrug and a nod.

"Yes?"

She sighed. "What choice do I have?"

It seemed like the best I was going to get this evening.

Pushing out the chair, I rose. "None. To start with, don't go over there without me."

She drew in a breath and bit her bottom lip, but the argument I expected didn't come.

I took her hand and pulled her up. "Go sit down, and I'll get the wine." I pointed her toward the couch. "White or red?" I asked.

"Jack," she replied.

"You're getting wine. You don't need anything stronger right now."

She shook her head. "Easy for you to say."

I walked after her. "Come here, Sunshine." I opened my arms and took her into a hug.

She still shook. "Zack, I'm scared." She gripped me tightly.

I rubbed her back and kissed the top of her head. "I won't let anything happen to you. Now sit down while I get the wine. And then you can explain what's going on."

She didn't let go of me.

I ran my fingers through her hair. "Please," I added.

She did as I asked and slumped at the end of the couch.

"The question stands, white or red?"

"White, if I have to, but I really want Jack."

I poured us each a large glass of sauvignon blanc and returned to her.

I offered her the glass. "And I said no."

She accepted the wine. "Can't you be a little less...bossy?" She threw back a large gulp of the wine.

I sipped mine. "Can't you be a little less...argumentative?"

"I guess," she answered.

I shifted the glass to my other hand so I could pull her up next to me. "To less bossy and less argumentative." I offered my glass to hers.

She clinked with me. "Sure."

I took another sip. "I think you have something to explain."

She took another large gulp. "I guess. But I didn't lie to you."

"I'm sorry I said that. I was a little angry that you hadn't told me you'd gotten married. It's sort of a big deal. And telling Doug to keep it from me—that was just mean."

I didn't tell her how much it hurt to know she hadn't wanted to include me in that part of her life.

"That's because I didn't get married," she shot back.

"I'm listening."

She drained the rest of her glass and handed it to me.

I put it on the coffee table.

"I'll take a refill," she said.

"Not yet. Not till we finish here."

She took in a breath through gritted teeth. "But I want—"

I interrupted her with a finger to her lips. "Calm down, Sunshine. Less argumentative, remember?"

A grimace appeared. "But…"

I raised a finger. "Come here." I moved my hand from her shoulder to her neck and pulled her face to within inches of mine. "I'm here for you."

I pulled her the rest of the way.

She closed her eyes.

I brushed her lips with mine, not daring for more of a kiss, lest I get carried away.

She sighed.

"Tell me everything." I moved just a few inches away. "Slowly," I added.

Her eyes opened, tinged with wetness.

I moved back, away from the danger of being that close.

She took a breath and ran her fingers through her hair. "You don't know the story of why I left, do you?"

"I wasn't around, but Doug said you broke up with that guy Todd."

"That was the story he was supposed to tell you."

This was getting ominous. The secret she'd withheld wasn't a small one.

I took another small sip and waited for the other shoe to drop.

"I left because I testified against a guy, and it wasn't safe here."

"Go on," I urged.

"Todd's brother, Rick, had the bright idea to rip off this house. It turns out the house belonged to a drug dealer—Delgado was his name. Anyway, somehow he figured out who did it, and he killed Rick. I saw it, but for the longest time I refused to say anything to the cops."

"You were scared. That's understandable."

"It was six months later when Detective Swenson convinced me to testify. The trial was moved to Bakersfield, so nobody around here knew about it. It was only a two-day trip and then back here."

She took another deep breath. "A few weeks after the trial was over, Todd won this trip to Mexico—four days in Acapulco, some kind of contest prize. I didn't want to go. You know, Montezuma's revenge and all, but he wasn't going to let it go to waste, so he went alone." She sniffed. "He never came back."

"You mean…"

"He checked into the hotel and never checked out. *Missing* is what the Mexican police said."

I pulled her closer. "I'm sorry for you."

"When I went to the police here, they said the contest company didn't exist. I left that night. I just packed a bag and drove. Delgado killed him, and he meant to kill me too. He would have if I'd gone on the Mexico trip."

"Is that why the name change?"

"I ended up in Arkansas, changed my name to Clark while I was there, and eventually moved to San Jose. I didn't ever intend to come back here. Most people don't know my name was ever Spear. If I meet somebody who knew before, they assume I got married, and I'm not going to say no and explain—that kind of defeats the purpose. I can't have my old name talked about."

I put the glass down. "Until stupid Benji wrecked things."

She nodded. "Fucking Benji. If it hadn't been for him, I'd still be safe in San Jose with my old job."

I leaned in to kiss her temple. "But then you wouldn't have come back into my life."

Her smile grew. "There is that."

"What happened to Delgado?"

"He got twenty-five to life for Rick's murder, so he's still locked up."

I reached for my glass again and took another swallow. "I'm sorry I thought you lied to me."

"I'm sorry I didn't tell you. I should have said something before. Can I have my Jack now?"

I rose from the couch and took both our glasses. "Pick something relaxing to watch on TV. I'm ordering pizza for dinner."

"I can cook," she offered.

"No. You relax. I got this."

"But we need some fruit."

I located the pizza shop number on my phone. "I'll make it Hawaiian then. Pineapple will be our fruit tonight."

"But that's not enough."

I hit dial on the phone and pointed my free finger at her. "No arguments, remember?"

She looked ready to throw back another comment, but restrained herself and picked up the remote.

I listened to ringing on the phone. "You can feed me two kiwis in the morning to make up for it."

After ordering, I settled into the couch again.

"Sorry about the window. That brick was meant as a message for me."

Her head cocked to the side. "What do you mean?"

"Turns out there was a love note on the brick from the neighborhood juvenile delinquent. Piss Boy, I call him."

A slight smile came to her face. "Interesting name."

"He seems to be the head of the pack of kids that were using your house as a hangout. The last time I confronted him and kicked them out, he wet his pants. I don't know his real name, so Piss Boy it is."

"Were those the kids you took the phones from?"

404

"Yup. And he seems to think throwing a brick through your window is going to get me to give him back his phone."

"But you're not?"

"Not tonight."

She pushed me in the shoulder. "You forgot to fill the wine glasses, dummy."

# CHAPTER 24

*BRITTNEY*

ZACK HAD BEEN A GOOD LISTENER, AND IT FELT GOOD TO FINALLY TELL HIM WHAT had happened, why I couldn't come back or get in touch these past few years.

I flicked on the TV as instructed and searched through the listings. I chose *Sweet Home Alabama*, a light rom-com. I had no idea if it was the kind of thing that suited Zack, but he'd told me to pick.

He returned with the wine glasses.

I examined mine. It was less than half full, but his was the same. "Kind of miserly with the wine tonight."

"I don't want you getting ahead of me, and I plan to keep my wits about me this evening."

"Do you think he'll throw another brick tonight?"

"Nah."

The movie started.

"Come on, not a chick flick," Zack complained as he reached for the remote.

I kept it out of reach. "I did what you said. You told me to pick, so shut up and watch. You might even like it."

"Fat chance."

"'Live with your choices,' you told me. Are you gonna tell me you don't like Reese Witherspoon?"

"She's kinda hot," he admitted.

I felt a pang of something I wasn't used to feeling when he called her hot. I couldn't be jealous of an actress on the flat screen—that didn't make any sense. I was just upset he didn't share my taste in movies, wasn't I?

"But it's still a chick flick," he whined.

I stopped talking and settled in next to him.

When the doorbell rang, I paused the movie.

Zack returned with our aromatic dinner, and I restarted the film while we ate.

He shoved away his plate after demolishing a huge part of the pizza. His arm came protectively around me, and his warmth gave me the first peace I'd felt in a long time.

Relying on someone else wasn't in my nature, but Zack was worth an exception. The more I thought about it, the more it made sense. Zack was the one I could depend on—he always had been. He was big and strong in more than just a physical way. He had strength of character, and he stood behind his words.

I snuck a peek up at him.

"What?" he asked.

I stretched up to kiss his cheek. "Thank you."

He merely gave a man-grunt in return, a reminder that I was cuddled up next to the other half of the species—the half that didn't verbalize emotions. The half that would complain about watching a love story, but instantly pick up his gun and charge into the fray to protect me.

I blinked back a tear and snuggled closer to my protector.

As the movie went on, we both got to laughing at the funny parts, as Melanie worked herself deeper and deeper into a hole with the two men in her life.

For a guy who didn't want to watch a movie like this, Zack seemed to be enjoying it—not that he would admit such a thing.

He had taken to stroking my shoulder and arm with lazy, slow movements that relaxed and excited me at the same time. Back in the day, we'd watched plenty of movies together, the three of us, but never like this. This was different, in a comfortable, cozy way.

The warmth of his body soaked through the fabric separating us and made its way to my chest, where my heart interpreted it as a need to beat faster.

My hand slipped from my leg to his thigh, not entirely unintentionally. My fingers began a slow circle, which he didn't resist. I had trouble concentrating on the plot of the movie as this afternoon's conversation with Serena kept replaying in my head. "*He's had a crush on you since the seventh grade.*"

I couldn't get those words to stop repeating in my ears.

"Sunshine?" he said.

"Yeah?"

"This isn't half bad," he murmured.

"I promise not to tell anyone you said that."

He chuckled. "You better not."

"You want to know something?" I asked.

"Sure."

"I kinda like being here with you."

There, I'd gone out on a limb and admitted it.

"That's the wine talking," he said.

I sighed and pulled my hand back. He meant the rebuff in a humorous way, but it still hurt.

A minute later, he gave me a quick squeeze with his arm. "Me too," he added.

Two words had never been more welcome. What I hadn't admitted to Serena, of course, was that I'd had a crush on Zack since even before the seventh grade. These might not be the ideal circumstances, but I dared to hope his feelings hadn't changed in the years I'd been away. A lot had happened, though.

We'd just been kids back then. How would it work if the adult versions of us played out our younger fantasies?

The wine was taking its toll on my bladder, so I excused myself to pee. In the untangling process, my breast rubbed against his arm, and the sensation had me wondering how it would have felt without the clothing between us. My nipples tightened.

Checking myself in the mirror before returning, I made a choice. I ditched the bra and chose a scoop-neck T-shirt. I liked what I saw in the mirror after the change.

When I walked in, he was leaving a message on the phone. His eyes lingered long enough on my chest to tell me he'd caught the difference, and the look on his face was approval, and maybe a little more.

"Telling Wendy I won't be in tomorrow."

"Why not?"

He grinned. "Fixing your house is more important."

"Underwires suck." I answered the question inherent in his raised eyebrow as his eyes came to my chest again.

It was a useful enough lie. I retook my seat next to him and snuggled closer as his arm draped behind me again.

His eyes were on the screen every time I checked.

The movie was almost over. "Did you ever wonder what would have happened if—"

I didn't get a chance to finish the question.

"Stop it," he insisted.

I pulled away. I hadn't even decided how to ask about us before he'd interrupted me. "Stop what?"

"You're always worrying about the past. You can't change or fix that. It's a waste of time, and all it does is drain the energy you need to move forward. Take stock of the situation, and make today's choices to move toward the future you want. Deal with the present. It's the only thing you can affect. Focus your energy forward, not back. You have to learn that. Whatever happened, happened. It's not your fault. Benji was a bad choice. Get over it and make better choices in the future."

He didn't get me at all.

I stared him down. "I wasn't talking about Benji."

"It doesn't matter. Dwelling on past events that can't be changed doesn't help anybody."

I sighed and sat back. I couldn't possibly talk to him while he was in this frame of mind. "You're impossible."

"I'm pragmatic."

I moved closer. "Can we stop arguing and just enjoy the movie?"

"Come here, Sunshine." He opened his arms to me, and I moved to snuggle up next to my infuriating protector.

I purred contentedly, hoping nonverbal would work better than verbal with him.

He kissed the top of my head and pulled me closer. "I'm all about making you happy, Sunshine."

So long as he didn't have to talk to me, he should have said.

*Guys.*

I felt like kissing him, but I also felt like punching him. How could I be attracted to somebody so exasperatingly bossy and know-it-all? Mom had once told me, *"the heart wants what the heart wants,"* and now I got it. No amount of self-deceiving logic was going to change how I felt. I knew he was annoyingly sure of himself, bossy, and argumentative—and at the same time irresistible.

Why does the moth fly into the flame and burn itself? Because it's a moth, silly.

I shifted closer. The tingles signaled clearly that the attraction hadn't dulled from my perspective. I was the moth, and he was my flame.

What I couldn't tell for sure was how he felt. He smiled at me, and he said nice things at least some of the time, but then the roadblocks would go up. The warning signs flashed, and he would distance himself.

The movie was nearing the wedding scene, where Melanie would be forced to walk down the aisle to marry the guy from New York—and also tie herself to the mother-in-law from hell. Logically, she should marry the guy. She was a clothing designer back in New York, and he was a fit, in spite of his mother.

I moved my hand back to Zack's thigh, and his hand resumed its motions on my shoulder.

When the scene started to play out, however, I wasn't rooting for her to go through with it. The audience knew what Melanie hadn't realized yet, and in the end, she didn't marry him.

Zack fist-pumped the air. "Yeah."

The wicked mother-in-law had just gotten what she deserved, and Melanie set out in the rain to find the down-home Alabama guy.

I saw the parallel. Melanie finally chose the one she'd known from long ago, regardless of how infuriating he'd been recently. She got it. She understood the bond they had, and she had to choose him regardless of the consequences, regardless of his stubbornness, regardless of the distance.

I needed to do the same. I inched my hand toward Zack's crotch. I could let my actions replace words.

He looked over and pushed my hand away. "Careful there."

"Why?"

"You know why."

I shifted to lay my head in his lap and look up at him. "I'm old enough."

I could feel the surge of his cock under me.

He bit his lip. "You're Doug's sister." There it was. The bro code had reared its ugly head, just as Serena thought it might.

"So?" I needed to get him to talk about it.

He pushed my shoulder. "Sit up."

I fought it successfully and rolled my head toward the TV. "I want to finish the movie first."

He huffed, but stopped struggling.

"I want to." I didn't say what. I thought it was evident enough.

"No, you don't. You're a nice girl, and I don't do nice. And besides, you're Doug's sister."

I pulled the hem of my shirt up, so his hand at my side was now on bare skin. The feel of his touch was electric. I turned to my back to look up at him, and his hand slid to my stomach.

I snaked a hand behind his neck and pulled him down toward me. "You're talking too much."

His mouth moved closer, and he started to say something, but the words didn't come.

I knew what I wanted. "You told me to make my choices in the present for the future I want, and this is my choice." I pulled at his wrist and drew his hand to my breast as I pulled myself up to meet his lips.

I opened to his tongue, and the walls between us crashed down.

He took control of the kiss. His tongue searched out mine, stroking me, teasing me, claiming me, and igniting my blood as fireworks exploded behind my eyelids. He tasted of wine and pleasure and need. He fondled my breast and tweaked my nipple before moving to the other one.

I melded my mouth to his. Heat pooled between my thighs as his erection grew beneath me. He smelled of pine and maleness. I'd been kissed by boys before, but never like this. This was a new experience. A man. A man with a hint of animal.

*Things are going so fast.*

It didn't matter. This had been my choice. I had no regrets. I'd wanted this— and more—for longer than I could remember. I twined my fingers in his hair as I held on for dear life. My heart thundered against my ribcage as I relished the heat of his hand on my breasts, the rod of his desire underneath me, the scrape of his stubble on my cheek. The smell of his hair. The taste of passion on his tongue.

Time slowed, and the world melted away as I grew more drunk from his kiss than the wine. It didn't matter that Doug wouldn't approve… Nothing mattered, so long as Zack and I held each other.

When he broke the kiss, I whimpered a bit, or maybe I imagined it. Things were fuzzy as passion clouded my brain.

*Why did I wait so long? Why had we waited?*

He pulled at my shirt.

I lifted, and it came off.

His eyes feasted on my breasts, and his smile widened. "You have marvelous tits."

I pulled at his shirt. "How come I'm the only one getting naked here?"

He stood and removed his shirt, followed by the rest of my clothes. "My God, you're more beautiful naked than I ever imagined."

I felt oddly proud. The heat of a blush rose in my cheeks as I held my arms out to him and laid down on the couch.

He joined me, and we were finally skin to skin—at least partially. He'd kept his jeans on.

His mouth claimed mine again as a finger parted my folds and traveled the length of my soaked slit, teasing my entrance. He circled and stroked my clit as I rubbed his cock through his jeans.

I arched my hips to get more pressure, but he withdrew and continued to circle and tease, making me wetter by the minute.

He broke the kiss and turned his attention to my breasts. He continued to caress and lick and suck at my nipples as a finger entered me, moving slowly in and out and around, farther and farther. His thumb found my clit again. He alternated kissing and sucking my nipples with blowing softly. The cool air brought shivers to my wet skin. A second long finger joined the first as he stretched me and continued circling my clit with his thumb.

He let go of his lip-lock on my nipple. "You need to come for me, Sunshine."

I pressed into his hand, finally getting more pressure as he worked his thumb over and around my swollen bud, bringing me closer and closer to the edge. I clawed at his back and tried to pull him closer, but his mouth stayed focused on my breasts. He kissed my chest, moving occasionally to my collarbone and my neck, nibbling at my ear.

I tried to pull on his belt buckle. "I want you inside me."

He pulled my hand away. "I won't last if we do that. You need to come first, baby." He pulled my chest to his as he sucked and bit lightly on my earlobe, his breath loud in my ear. He increased his pressure and tempo on my sensitive nub as he pushed me up the pleasure slope.

The peak came quickly. I gasped for air, my pussy clenching on his fingers, my body spasming as he held me tight. Waves of pleasure crashed over me as lights flashed against my closed eyelids and blood rushed in my ears. I was helpless against the onslaught of my climax and the tremors in my core, an orgasm unlike any I'd experienced before.

In college, guys had wanted to get a finger inside me and squeeze my breasts on the way to getting into my pants, but they were certainly all clitoral-knowledge challenged. Zack had left them in the dust.

As I came down from my high and regained muscle control, I tugged at his belt again. "Please."

∾

*Zack*

She had made delicious little yelping sounds as she came on my hand.

I wasn't going to be able to hold out much longer. Any manual foreplay from her and I'd end up coming in my pants like a teenager.

I stood and quickly dispensed with my jeans and boxer briefs.

She reached for me and grasped my length while I searched for the condom in my pocket. She wouldn't let go, and the feel of her hand was almost too much.

I located the packet and tore it open.

She held out her hand. "Let me."

I handed it over and stood in front of her.

The sweet torture of her rolling the latex down almost undid me before we'd started. The heat of her touch was something else.

I pulled her off the couch and positioned her kneeling toward it with her head on the cushion. As I got behind her, she spread her knees and reached back to guide me in.

I started with small strokes. "You're so fucking wonderfully tight."

She moaned and rocked back into me.

I pushed in farther and leaned forward to let my finger find its target. I began to circle and press her engorged clit, yielding more moans and groans. As I pushed in all the way, I stilled a bit before resuming little thrusts, just slow enough that I could hold off while I worked her toward the edge again.

Her breathing became more erratic as she came closer to the end of her rope. She met my increasing thrusts, rocking hard back into me as I upped the tempo.

Her yelps began again as she spasmed around me.

I rammed home over and over, deeper and stronger. The pressure behind my balls built to overload, and with a sudden tensing, I came inside her, pulling her hips hard into mine.

She moaned contentedly and shifted forward to lean on the couch.

I shifted with her and collapsed on her back.

"We shouldn't have waited so long," she mumbled into the cushion.

412

"Yeah" was the only answer I could manage.

I agreed. This was too long in coming.

Spent, I untangled myself from her and went to discard the condom in the trash.

She was still breathing heavily when I returned. She gave a little squeak as I picked her up and carried her upstairs. I set her down on the bed, her bed.

She got up to use the bathroom, and I followed when she was done.

When I returned to my room, she was there. I didn't complain. Instead, I turned off the light and settled in next to her.

She draped an arm over me, her warm tits pressed up against my side. "Thank you."

"For what?"

I couldn't tell if she meant the orgasms or letting her into my bed.

"For not pushing me away, and for being here for me."

I stroked her hair. "Get some sleep, Sunshine."

My thoughts were swimming, and I didn't have a better answer for her.

I had to follow my own advice now and not look back. I may have made a disastrous choice when I kissed Brittney, but there was no turning back and no undoing it—and absolutely no sense in second guessing. I didn't do second guessing.

I stroked her back, and the softness of her skin brought me back to the problem: She was soft, vulnerable, and fragile.

She needed protection. That was the imperative, and I was the one to provide it. There was so much I wanted to provide her that I didn't know where to start.

Doug was going to be pissed when he found out, and probably want to kill me. Hell, I'd told him to stay away from my sister Kelly.

"What are you thinking about?"

"What I'm going to tell Doug."

Her hand moved to stroke my hair. "He'll understand."

"The fuck he will."

She was quiet for a moment. "Let me tell him."

I touched her nose with mine. "No way. I fight my own battles."

"It's just—"

I cut her off. "I said no."

She snorted. "You're doing it again."

I pulled her close. I didn't want to argue right now. "Sorry. Please let me handle it."

"Okay. It's your funeral."

I laughed. "That's what I'm afraid of."

She didn't bring it up again, and before long her breathing slowed to the steady rhythm of sleep.

As I lay with Brittney next to me, I couldn't believe how lucky I'd gotten. The girl I'd always wished for had come back to me.

I'd broken Rule Number One, and now Rule Number Two came into play: If you break Rule Number One, leave the country for your own safety.

My own dictates said I couldn't second guess my past decisions. All I could do was make a plan for the future and execute it. I had to decide what kind of man I would be tomorrow.

Before today, the logical choice would have been to end it with her tomorrow and stay true to my best friend. That man would've called this a mistake, a lapse in judgment, a lapse of self control. That man would've been contrite about his mistake.

But that was the weakling's way, not the brave way. For all my father's faults, he raised me to be brave enough to stand up for what I believed, and I believed Brittney was worth the hard choice. I'd always wanted her, and now that she wanted me—nothing else mattered.

Sleep overtook me as I envisioned a day when I didn't have to deny how I felt about her. I was going to make tomorrow that day. Screw Rule Number Two. I wasn't backing down, and I wasn't running. Brittney was mine, and Doug or no Doug, I wasn't giving her up.

Tomorrow was going to be a great day.

She deserved a great day.

# CHAPTER 25

*BRITTNEY*

LIGHT STREAMED IN AROUND THE CURTAINS AS I BLINKED MY EYES OPEN. I SMILED AS I took in the sight in front of me. Inches from my face, Zack's deep blue eyes stared into mine.

"Morning, sleepyhead." He shifted forward to place a kiss on my nose.

I pulled my arm over him and moved us closer together, pressing my breasts to his warmth, wanting more than just a kiss on my nose.

He obliged with a kiss reminiscent of last night.

Our evening was coming back to me now as my skin melted into his—an evening that had started off so terribly and ended so wonderfully.

He broke the kiss.

My hand traced its way down his side to his abdomen and finally to my prize. I found his morning wood, warm and hard.

He pulled back. "We don't have time for that this morning."

I tugged harder on his cock, trying to get him to come back. "Why not?"

"We're burning daylight. We have a lot to do today." He wrested my hand loose and rose from the bed, his cock standing at attention.

Last night I'd known he was big, but in the morning light I could see he was packing the grande burrito.

"What are you staring at?"

I giggled. "My new toy. I'm going to have to give it a name."

"We're not doing any stupid naming."

"I'll think of something." I shifted the sheet down to uncover my breasts. "Are you sure you don't have a little time?"

He wasn't biting. He turned to leave. "I'll shower first."

I had a better idea. I followed him.

After he was in the shower, I pulled the curtain aside and joined him.

He didn't complain. Instead his smile grew and he grabbed the soap to help me with my breasts—a definite tit man.

If his cock was my new toy, my boobs were his.

I took the soap from him and lathered up my hands before grabbing for him. "Your turn to come for me."

"We don't have time for this," he complained again.

"You'll just have to concentrate and be quick."

He gritted his teeth, barely holding back a complaint, but turned his back to the water and braced himself against the wall.

Several minutes of massaging, stroking, and playing with his cock and balls yielded the stiffening of his muscles that said he was getting close. I took some more soap and applied both hands to the job of making him lose the control he was so proud of.

I continued to work him, bringing one hand up and over the crown, squeezing as my hand slipped over the end followed by the other, and again and again, until...

He groaned, his legs shook, and a spurt hit the wall, followed by another, and another.

He panted, grunted, and pulled me to him for a kiss. "I'll get you later."

I knew he meant it too.

After that we got serious about washing and shampooing.

The sight of the water running down his muscled chest was too tempting. I traced the underside of his pecs and the groove that led to his belly button.

He retaliated by hefting my breasts in his hands. "Stop that, or you'll regret it."

"I doubt that."

He reached around and swatted my ass. "I'll spank you so hard you won't be able to sit."

"What if I like it?" I shot back.

He took my shoulders and turned me back toward the water. "Cut it out. We have a tight schedule."

"Yes, boss." I skipped the conditioner and quickly took a razor to my legs after he climbed out to shave at the sink.

I rinsed the razor and turned off the water. "What's the big hurry anyway?"

"We're going to San Diego."

I climbed out. "Not me. I've got more cleaning to do next door."

"I said *we're* going," he corrected.

I grabbed my towel. "And I said no thanks."

416

He turned and growled. "You are coming with me. Your cleaning can wait. Now stop arguing."

"What are you going to do? Grab me by the hair and drag me there?"

"If that's what it takes, yes. But you're a smart-enough girl to come willingly."

He said smart enough, but what he probably meant was pliable enough.

Still, I gave up. This wasn't worth the argument. "I have work on Thursday," I reminded him.

"I'll have you back in time."

Then I saw something I hadn't seen before, and a pang of jealousy overtook me. "Who's Deb?"

"Huh?"

I wrapped the towel around me and pointed at his ankle tattoo: **DEB**. "Your tattoo."

"Deborah Ellen Benson, my cousin who was kidnapped."

I shrank a few inches. "I thought it was... never mind."

He turned from the mirror to look at me. "I know what you thought, Sunshine." He grinned.

"I'm sorry. I'd forgotten about her." The tattoo looked fairly new, and the childhood abduction had been so long ago it hadn't registered.

He rinsed the razor under the water. "The tattoos were Dennis's idea. We all decided to get them a few years ago." He went back to shaving.

"Did they ever find her?" I didn't mean the question to be cruel, but I couldn't recall the details.

He shook his head. "No. The kidnapper died in a gunfight with the cops." He shivered.

I could tell this was hard for him, so I changed the topic. "Why San Diego?"

He ignored me. "The ransom note said she was buried with enough air for two days. With the kidnapper dead, the FBI stopped looking after two weeks. Dad and Uncle Seth paid to have investigators continue the search, but they ran out of leads. So, no, we never did find her. The tattoos are so we don't forget."

He took a deep breath and pulled the razor down his cheek.

I repeated, "Why San Diego?"

He made a stroke with the razor under his chin. "I decided I know what your problem is."

"I don't have a problem, except maybe you."

He ignored me. "Your happiness reservoir is empty. I need to help you fill it."

"You're nuts. I have things to do here."

He splashed to rinse off his face. "Those can wait."

"You're trying to tell me what to do again. I don't like it."

He patted his face dry and faced me. "Trust me on this, Sunshine."

I huffed, but gave up arguing, at least in the nude.

"Pack things for a few days, and don't forget a swimsuit, the skimpier the better."

I snapped my towel at his butt as he left the bathroom. I missed.

After the door closed behind him, I got busy drying my hair. I smiled. The idea that he was worried about my happiness was growing on me. No guy had ever suggested he and I take time to fill my happiness tank, and the idea was kinda cute.

Maybe he was right. I'd been running from one disaster to another, always in less than the best of moods, and that hadn't been good for my disposition. I wasn't working yet, despite my best efforts, so when was I going to have another chance like this?

I cracked open the door and yelled one more time, "Why San Diego?"

He yelled back from his room, "Why not?"

I didn't have an answer to that, so I wrapped the towel around myself and went to my room to dress and pack.

Pulling on a sweatshirt over my jeans, T-shirt, and Reeboks, I packed a few changes of clothes, and a string bikini I was sure would meet his definition of skimpy.

Zack knocked on the open door frame. "And bring something for a nice dinner out as well," he said with a devilish grin. "I'll meet you downstairs."

I didn't have a lot of choices, but I located a short red dress that would do and threw a pair of heels in the suitcase before zipping it up. I decided against bringing the heart-shaped pendant.

Lugging my suitcase downstairs, I found Zack pouring coffee into two travel mugs.

He checked his watch. "Time to go."

"Let's at least have breakfast first," I suggested.

He shook his head. "No time. You get the best of McDonald's on the way. Let's go."

"You take the suitcases, and I'll be right behind you."

He shrugged and lugged both suitcases out the door and down to the garage.

I heard the garage open as I went to gather the fruit. I knew what he was doing by rushing me, and I wouldn't give up that easily. I opened the backpack and added apples, peaches, and kiwis, along with bowls, napkins, forks, a knife, and a small cutting board for my lap. An extra plastic bag for garbage and I was ready to go. Slinging the backpack and my purse over my shoulder, I brought the coffee mugs outside, set them down, locked up, and joined Zack by the idling car.

We climbed in, and I set the backpack at my feet. The coffee mug had to go between my seat and the door. This car was built before cupholders were the rage.

As Zack pulled onto the street and turned toward the freeway, a kid on the far sidewalk flipped us off.

I turned to look back at him as we passed. "What's his problem?"

"That's Piss Boy, your local brick thrower."

I was tempted to tell Zack to back up so I could give the punk a piece of my mind, but I held my tongue. Today was for filling my happy tank, not the opposite.

After a few minutes Zack found a McDonald's with a drive-thru on this side of the 405 freeway, and we loaded up with three egg McMuffins, two hash browns, and two orange juices between us. The mouth-watering smells of grilled fast food filled the car.

I opened the wrapper for Zack so he could eat one-handed as he drove. My breakfast sandwich was warm, gooey, and tasty. The hash brown was crispy and perfect when dipped in ketchup.

Zack glanced over from behind his aviator sunglasses. "What's in the back-pack?" He handed me the now-empty wrapper from his second McMuffin.

I retrieved his hash brown from the paper bag. "It's a little something for later," I answered over the rumble of the engine.

He'd been right that this car was all go and no frills, but I was enjoying it. The occasional thumbs up from other Mustang drivers we passed showed that car aficionados on the road knew our ride was something special. The traffic was heavy but moving—the advantage of a late start.

When we passed Long Beach, I opened the backpack to pull out my supplies: cutting board, knife, and a bowl for the cut fruit. I started to peel the first kiwi.

"Hey, stop that. No food mess in the car," Zack complained as soon as he saw the dreaded fruit.

I kept peeling. "You thought you'd avoid fruit by eating on the road. I'm wise to you, buster."

"Stop. You can't make a mess in my car."

"You promised to eat your fruit. It's your fault for trying to pull a fast one."

"I said no."

I finished peeling the first kiwi and started slicing. "Stop whining like a baby. This isn't going to hurt you. And last night you promised to eat two this morning."

"I just want to keep the car clean."

"Bull-pucky. Now suck it up and grow a pair." I picked up a slice and leaned over to get it to his mouth.

He frowned for a moment before giving up and taking it.

We continued down the road, him objecting, and me feeding him slice after slice until he finished two of the delicious green fruits he despised.

I'd won this round.

"I've also got peaches, if you'd like one of those," I offered.

He *tsk*ed. "Maybe tomorrow."

He downshifted and roared around the slower car in front of us to end the conversation.

After slicing and eating one of the peaches myself, I wiped off the board and knife before storing things away for the rest of the drive.

Past Irvine, the endless urban expanse of the Los Angeles area gave way to hills and countryside. Passing Dana Point, the freeway joined the coastline for the rest of the journey to San Diego.

"Going to tell me where we're going?" I asked twice.

Each time the response was the same. "You'll see when we get there."

I gave up and settled in my seat.

Zack rolled down his window, and I followed suit. The noise of the engine and the wind whipping my hair around was invigorating. I guessed this was halfway to the experience of riding a motorcycle.

I was looking out the window at the ocean when his hand found my thigh, and the tingles started again.

"Are we having fun yet?" he asked.

I intertwined my fingers with his. "Uh-huh."

When I looked over, warmth radiated from his smile.

The drive took more than two hours, but we made it to San Diego. Zack took the exit to the Coronado Bridge, and halfway over, I had a guess about where he was taking me.

In high school, Samantha, Doug, and I had once planned a weekend trip with our neighbors, the Waltrips, to the Hotel Del Coronado, but it had been called off when Mr. Waltrip's business trip was rescheduled. It had been a heartbreaker for us, and we never got another chance that summer.

We grew up, life intervened, and I'd forgotten about it until now.

I wasn't positive, so I didn't voice my guess, but when the iconic red cupola of the hotel came into view and Zack turned into the parking lot, I could barely hold myself back.

"You remembered."

"How could I forget? It was all you talked about for a month straight."

He had that part right. We had looked forward to it forever.

We parked and unloaded the suitcases.

Wanting to memorialize this visit with photos, I opened my purse to get my phone. It wasn't there. "Fuck. I left my phone on the charger at the house."

My swearing got his attention. "You're not allowed to be upset, Sunshine. Besides, you won't need a phone down here."

"But I want a picture," I complained.

I sounded like a spoiled little kid.

He pulled his phone from his pocket. "Here, use mine."

"Thanks." I accepted the phone. We could transfer the pictures later. "What's the code to unlock it?"

He put his hands in his pockets. "0-4-0-4."

I started to type the numbers in. "My birthday?"

"I changed it this morning," he said with a grin.

The gesture sent a tingle down my spine and tugged a smile out of me even though I resisted. I unlocked it and took a shot of the hotel, then moved to get one with him *and* the hotel.

As soon as I finished, he started rolling his bag toward the building.

I floated after him with my suitcase trailing behind as we made our way to check-in.

We were expected, and when Zack pulled out his black Amex card, the desk clerk's smile went up two notches.

A bellhop arrived, and we followed as he pushed the luggage trolley to the north end of the property. When he stopped and Zack opened the door, I couldn't believe it. This wasn't a common hotel room. This was a beach villa suite, complete with multiple rooms and a kitchenette. The living room and patio bordered the beach and faced the ocean waves across the sand. Staying with Zack at his rundown old Victorian, and riding in his fifty-year-old car, I'd forgotten how different our backgrounds were. I stayed at Motel 6 or a Holiday Inn. He booked ocean-view villas when he traveled. The rich were different, after all.

Zack tipped the bellhop and closed the door.

"Like it?" He walked up behind me and kneaded my shoulders.

I fell back into him. "What's not to like? But you didn't need to splurge like this. A regular room would have been fine."

His arms came down to wrap me up. "Nonsense. I want to spoil you, Sunshine."

"Well, you succeeded."

He released me. "I'm not done yet. You'll need sunscreen and a hat. Let's go."

I collapsed onto the couch. "Can't we just relax here for a while?"

"Humor me." He extended his hand.

I took it, and he pulled me up.

"I need to use the bathroom first," I told him.

He pulled out his phone and dialed. "Hey, Phil. I need a little help... Hold on just a sec." He took the phone from his face and waved me toward the bathroom. "I'll wait," he told me. "Yeah. Do you have some time this weekend?" he said into the phone as he walked out to the patio.

I closed the bathroom door behind me and stopped. It took me a moment to figure out it wasn't a second toilet, but a bidet in front of me. I skipped the opportunity for a tush wash and used the one I knew how to work. How did you dry off afterward anyway?

# CHAPTER 26

*Zack*

It took a little coaxing to get Brittney out of the villa and on the road again.

But the drive to SeaWorld was a short one, and once we got inside, the smile on her face as she watched the porpoise and sea lion shows was priceless. Getting splashed by the orcas because we sat in the first row had been part of my plan, and she screeched like a little kid—a sure sign she was having fun.

Happiness was today's goal, and places like this always delivered.

We stopped for a lunch of hot dogs and fries.

Brittney sipped her soda while we waited for the food. "You forgot to leave the phone for the kid you hate so much."

I pulled out my phone. "I'll have Phil leave him something."

"You're not giving back the phone?"

"Absolutely not. I told him he had to write me a letter of apology to get it back, and those are still the rules. But I am going to give him something that's gonna make his day."

She looked at me apprehensively. "Just give it back and be done with it."

"You can't appease bullies that way. He needs to be taught a lesson in a language he'll understand."

I dialed Phil Patterson, hoping he had what I needed.

"Hey, I'm just getting things together for that project," Phil said as he answered. "And we missed you at the Ironhorse yesterday."

I winced. In my anger with Brittney, I'd skipped the normal restaurant stop on the way back from the Habitat site, and I'd let the guys down.

"Sorry about that. We had to rush home," I explained.

"Right," he said dismissively.

"Anyway, the reason I'm calling is I was wondering if you have one of those pirate packages left?"

He laughed. "I've got two. You prefer skunk or fart?" he asked.

"Skunk, if you can spare it."

"I thought you might like that one," Phil said. "No problemo."

"Could you do me a favor and drop it by the house? I need it put under the planter on the porch of the house to the right of mine."

"Got it. Porch planter. Who the fuck's this for?"

"A guy who threw a brick through my friend Brittney's window."

"Friend, huh? She's hot. I bet I know what kind of friend."

I didn't acknowledge his inherent question.

"Well?"

I stayed silent.

"I get it. She's fucking there with you."

"Uh-huh."

"Does she have a sister?" A typical Phil question.

"Yes, but I'm not your dating service. The package?"

"Sure. I'll get it placed this afternoon."

"Thanks, bud."

"If you want to thank me, introduce me to her sister."

We hung up, and I shook my head. Phil still didn't get that he needed to clean up his act, because under the rough exterior and bad language, he was a nice guy.

Brittney's eyes narrowed. "What was that about?"

I sat down across from her. "Phil had a problem a while back with porch pirates making off with his Amazon deliveries."

She nodded. "That sucks."

"So he made up a couple dummy packages. I'm getting the one with skunk oil. When Piss Boy opens it up, he and the room he's in are going to get sprayed, and it'll take forever to get the smell out."

Brittney giggled. Even she thought that was funny.

"After that, he's guaranteed not to mess with us again." I joined her laughing at the mental image.

She shook her head. "Don't you think that's a little extreme?"

"You don't think a brick through a window is extreme?"

She tilted her head. "I guess."

"It was your window, by the way," I pointed out.

She put her soda down. "Damn straight. I'm liking the idea more and more.

But wouldn't it still be easier just to give back the phone, or talk to his parents or something?"

"You don't give in to bullies. That just encourages them. I'm going to fix this for you so it stays fixed."

I should have said I'd fix it for both of us. Piss Boy was becoming a pain in the ass, and I didn't relish a brick through my window either.

Our food was ready, so I retrieved it from the counter.

Brittney quietly people-watched as we started in on the food.

My phone dinged with a text message.

WENDY: Your father is looking for you

Dad could wait.

Brittney cocked her head.

I put the phone down and ignored her unasked question.

She nodded toward the phone. "You sure you don't need to take care of that?"

"Today is about happy, right?"

She picked up a fry and dipped it in the ketchup. "Sure is."

"That means it can wait."

My phone rang, proving me wrong. Dad's name lit up the screen.

Brittney leaned forward to look. "You need to take that."

Part of me wanted to throw it in the bushes for interrupting my day with my girl. Just thinking the phrase *my girl* was odd. Brittney had always been Doug's sister, and that definition couldn't allow her to be anything else. What a difference a few days could make.

"Go ahead," Brittney said, breaking my trance.

I picked up my electronic tether to the real world and accepted the call. "Hi, Dad."

Brittney smiled and blew me a kiss, approving of my decision. She was the adult here.

"Zachary, Wendy tells me you're not coming in for a few days. What's the problem?"

"No problem, Dad. I'm out for a few days taking care of something for a friend."

"I see... Well, how long will you be? The Bartolo deal is going sideways, and Mario thinks it needs your attention. Can you make it in tomorrow?"

The problems changed day to day, and week to week, but the theme was always the same. Mario always threatened that if I didn't help him out, the deal might drift away to the competition. The job was like a treadmill: a lot of activity, but the next day we were in the same place. When I finished my rotations through the divisions and got to join Dad at the top of the pyramid, that's when it would get easier.

"No. I'll be out longer than that. I'll call in and get it taken care of." My brother Josh would be my first call. Mario wouldn't dare tell Dad Josh wasn't a good enough replacement.

"That sounds good. And my regards to Brittney."

He was no dummy.

"Thanks, Dad. I'll be back in as soon as I can."

Brittney was frowning when I looked up. "Is there a problem at work?"

"Dad says hi."

She glared, demanding an answer to her question.

"There's always a problem. It's nothing new."

"And your father wants you back?"

"That's also nothing new."

She stood. "We should go. I don't want to get you in trouble."

I pointed to her chair. "Sit down."

She put her hands on her hips, threatening to talk back. Obstinate Brittney had replaced my happy Sunshine.

"Sit," I repeated, pointing again to the chair.

She took her seat again, albeit reluctantly.

I leaned forward. "Sunshine, this is where I want to be. I'm prioritizing my time. You come first. They can do without me for a few days. The only thing I'm doing today is filling up your happy reservoir, get it?"

Her mouth formed a thin, flat line. "Got it."

I gave her a thumbs up. "Good. Because being with you today is what makes me happy too."

BRITTNEY

I WAS SURE I'D HEARD HIM CORRECTLY. FIRST HE'D TOLD HIS FATHER HE WAS HELPING a friend. Then he told me he was prioritizing his time, and I came first. *I came first* —the thought went through me with a warmth I wasn't accustomed to.

Zack was telling his father to shove it, although politely, and I was more important than his work, his family's company, his duty to his father, his duty to his family—the same duty he'd told me was paramount.

I watched as a family walking by stopped in front of us. Two middle-school-aged kids squabbled with their father about which ride to go on next. Dad was threatening to cut the day short. Mom wasn't amused, and Dad wasn't wearing his happy face when she sided with the kids. The children went running ahead, and the parents followed, no longer holding hands.

Suddenly I didn't relish being the cause of family friction between Zack and his father. "I want to go back home."

Zack looked up, surprised. "What?"

"I've had enough today. I'm tired."

His eyes narrowed. "Work will be fine. Trust me."

"I'm done. Let's go home."

"Dad understands my choice, and in his day, he made the same one."

"But I don't want to get between you and your father."

A grin replaced his stare. He'd guessed right. He reached across to take my hand. There was almost a literal spark as he touched me.

"Sunshine, it's cute that you're concerned, but don't be. Dad is always pushing, and I'm always pushing back. He's trying to teach me to watch all the details, and I'm trying to teach him it's the long-term plan that matters, not the day to day."

"And you think arguing is good?"

"He respects me for not rolling over. He's making progress teaching me what he wants me to learn, and surprisingly, I'm making progress getting him to see my perspective. He's already changed."

"I don't want it to be my fault that you argue."

He squeezed my hand. "Stop with the fault already. Nothing we do is your fault. Nothing anybody does is your fault."

It was the same thing he'd been saying, but it didn't make it true.

"I only want to be here with you," he added.

I could see the sincerity in his eyes, and I needed to be happy about that and block out my negative thoughts.

I sighed. "Me too. What do you want to do this afternoon?"

He let go of my hand, and an evil grin appeared. "There's not enough privacy here for what I want to do."

I giggled as heat rose within me, and I wished we were in a more private place right now. But that could wait.

"I meant here." I nodded toward the center of the park.

Zach insisted I pick, so we saw the sea lions again and went on some more rides before spending an hour just walking hand in hand along the paths. Everything he did made me feel special: the way he hugged me, kidded with me, held my hand. The way he'd asked about my time in Arkansas and truly listened, which was more than I could say for any of the guys I'd met since coming back to California.

By the end of the afternoon, I'd had enough fun and more than enough sun for the day.

We made our way back to the car, and I got another loud, wind-in-the-hair ride back to the hotel.

I decided his car wasn't old—it was special, and riding in it with Zack was a special gift.

# CHAPTER 27

*Zack*

I OPENED THE DOOR TO THE SUITE AND USHERED MY GIRL INSIDE.

After the door closed, she wrapped her arms around my neck. "It's private here…"

Her suggestion hung seductively in the air.

I unwrapped her arms from me. As much as I wanted to, we didn't have time. "We have a dinner reservation, and you have to get ready."

She grabbed my waist and brought herself close again. Her breasts rubbed against me as she fingered my collar. "We could order room service."

The offer was tempting.

I took her shoulders and pushed her away. "I'm taking you to a proper dinner, and I intend to show you off."

She walked toward the bedroom. "Then you're right. I'll need some time to get presentable."

I shucked my shirt off on the way to the bathroom and started the water in the shower.

She joined me after stuffing her hair inside a shower cap.

I took the time to soap her down thoroughly, paying appropriate attention to all the areas I intended to worship later this evening. I pulled a towel off the rack to dry off.

Being naked with her in the shower had led to the predictable situation that prevented me from getting my dick in my pants. It took several minutes in the other room, away from Brittney's nakedness, to deflate me enough to pull my

427

slacks on properly. A clean button down shirt and a blazer was all I needed to be ready. Women took more time. Checking my watch, I hoped she wouldn't spend too much time—I hated being late.

While I waited, I pulled out my phone and dialed my brother Josh.

"Hey, Zack. I hear you're out with your new girl."

News certainly traveled fast.

"That's sort of why I'm calling. I need a few days off to help her with some things, and Dad called today."

"Let me guess, he thinks you need to be at work?"

"Naturally," I replied. "He said the Bartolo deal is going sideways. You think you could spare the time to get involved and help me out?"

"I would if I could, but I'm in Atlanta today and Rome tomorrow."

That certainly put a hole in my plan.

"I'll be back next week, if that helps," he added.

"I'll let you know. Thanks anyway. Have a great trip."

"Good luck with Dad."

Without Josh around, I'd have to figure out some other strategy for Bartolo...

I scrolled through my phone contacts, trying to come up with a better idea than me going back to work and leaving Brittney alone.

After what seemed like an eternity—but was probably only fifteen minutes—I poked my head around the corner to check on Brittney's progress.

She was a sight to behold, a beauty packaged in a tight red dress with a skirt short enough to get everybody's attention. She was leaning over the counter working on her makeup.

I approached quietly.

She jerked. "Hey. Don't sneak up on a girl doing her eyes."

I raised my hands in surrender. "Sorry. I didn't think it was such a big deal."

"You try stabbing your eye with a mascara brush and see how you like it."

Appropriately admonished, I retreated back to the living room. "I'll wait out here till you're ready."

"Good plan," she called through the doorway.

**BRITTNEY**

AFTER I JUMPED AND MADE A MESS OF MY MASCARA, IT TOOK A FEW EXTRA MINUTES before I finally finished. Turning sideways to check myself in the mirror, I decided I looked pretty damn good if I sucked in my tummy a little. I'd hoped to be able to skip the bra, but the fabric was too thin and my nipples were a little too pokey for a fashionable dinner, so I'd grabbed my Victoria's Secret special push-up bra.

It had been a long time since I'd gotten dressed up to go out to dinner, and it felt good to be rocking a tight, short skirt. Plus, the bra was doing its thing. All I had to do was avoid tripping in these heels. I only wobbled a little as I strode into the living room.

Zack's eyes said it all as he looked me up and down. It was the look of hunger every girl hoped to get in a dress like this.

"You look fantastic, Sunshine."

"Thank you. I hope the restaurant's not far, 'cuz these shoes aren't made for walking."

That was no understatement.

"It's in the main building."

"I think I can handle that."

"Good, because I'm not letting you take those off tonight."

He chuckled, and I felt a rush of heat to my core.

"Promises, promises," I replied as I went back to retrieve the matching purse I'd brought.

I quickly dumped out the contents of my larger purse and fumbled through for what I wanted. I stopped at the pink envelope that was meant to remind me to be a better person. As penance for what I'd done, I always carried it with me, and this wouldn't be an exception. I folded it, put it in tonight's purse, and added lipstick, tissues, and my wallet.

"Now I'm ready," I announced on my return.

Zack held the door open for me.

The main building wasn't that far, but I almost wished we'd called a golf cart or something. These shoes looked great, but they were sheer torture after a hundred yards.

The restaurant was busy, with a large group waiting to be seated.

Zack introduced himself at the desk and discreetly passed a bill to the hostess. We were shown to a perfect table at the edge of the patio, facing the beach so we would have a wonderful view of the sunset later.

Zack held out my chair, and I sat, eager to get the weight off my poor feet.

Our waitress arrived, attired in a white shirt, a gray vest, and bow tie—another reminder that we weren't at Denny's. "May I start you off with something to drink this evening?"

After the briefest perusal of the wine list, Zack made a selection. "Chardonnay okay with you?" he asked.

I nodded. "Sure." If it came in glass with a real cork, it was better than I was used to.

"A bottle of the Trefethen chardonnay, please."

She smiled and left us to enjoy the bread and water.

Zack held the bread basket for me to pick.

I made a selection and broke off a piece. "You said you need to switch departments at the company. How does that work?"

He opted for the heel end. "Nothing much to tell. I get told to move, and I do."

"And that's it?"

"That's it."

"Did you ever consider working any place other than for your father?"

He chewed his bread for a moment. "Not really. It's my responsibility, and I want to do it."

"And all of you join up, just like that?"

"Not all of us. Vincent left to go work in Boston for Bill Covington. Dennis was at the company for a while, but he spun off a section, and that's where he is now."

He wasn't volunteering much.

"So you could too?"

Our waitress returned with the wine, which she had Zack taste.

I took the time to pick my dinner from the menu. The lamb shank looked good. It came with toasted saffron pasta pearls, olives, rainbow chard, and gremolata salad, whatever that was.

The waitress left after pouring us each a glass of wine.

I prodded my date. "You were saying?"

He twirled his glass and took a sip. "That was his choice. I owe it to Dad and the rest of the family to stick around. It's important to me. No... make that imperative. I'm the oldest son in the company now, and running it will fall to me some day. The family legacy will be my responsibility. It's who I am, I guess."

"And you don't get a choice?"

He looked over his wine glass at me. "Like I said, it's my responsibility, and I want to do the right thing." He sipped his wine without a hint of discontent on his face.

"And the department switching?"

"Dad wants us to get involved in the business. And that means that we rotate through different responsibilities in the company. He thinks it's essential to know how everybody does their jobs if you're going to be their boss. Before marketing, I worked procurement, and I'm scheduled to move to finance next."

Our waitress stopped by to take our orders.

I asked for the lamb shank I'd been liking. I was too embarrassed to ask what gremolata was—I'd settle for being surprised.

Zack predictably chose the filet mignon.

I handed my menu to the waitress as she left. "How do the other people at the company feel about you moving around like that?"

"What do you mean?"

"Do they feel okay working for a guy who just flits in and out of departments?"

"I don't flit."

"You know what I mean."

He thought for a moment. "I don't know. I never thought about it. It's a family company. That's just the way it works."

I wasn't surprised the question hadn't occurred to him.

He ate a piece of bread in silence.

"I think you're really lucky to be so sure of your destiny," I said after a moment.

He didn't say anything in response.

I took a sip of my wine during the pregnant pause.

He peered into his glass, then looked up. "I guess you're right, but I'm not going to apologize for being born a Benson."

After more reflective silence, the waitress brought our dinners.

I took a bite of my lamb—delicious.

He cut a piece of steak. "How do you like being a hygienist?"

"I like it, and it pays the bills—that is, when I can get enough hours."

"I know you're waiting for an opening at the office here, but is that a problem?" he asked.

"It was with my dentist in San Jose."

"Why?"

"Money. She didn't give any of us enough hours. I think she didn't want to pay benefits. Actually, I'm sure it's because she didn't want to pay us benefits."

"That sucks."

"No kidding."

"What was the hardest part of that job?"

"Knowing that nobody who was coming in wanted to be there with me. Patients are always happier when they leave than when they arrive. And it's not because they've enjoyed my company. It's because it's over, and they don't have to endure me any longer."

"It can't be that bad."

"The good part is knowing I'm helping people be healthier. Did you know poor oral health and heart disease are correlated?"

"I've heard that."

"So, in addition to helping people to keep their teeth, I might be helping them stay heart healthy. At least that's what the literature says."

"You should be proud."

"I am."

He lifted his wine glass, took a sip, and put it down with a grin and an odd look in his eyes as he stared at me.

"What did I say?"

"Nothing. It's the way you look."

I checked quickly that I hadn't spilled on myself. "What?"

"I don't think you could look any more beautiful."

Heat erupted in my cheeks. I took a quick sip to cool myself down as the unexpected compliment washed over me.

"How's your steak?" I asked as I looked down to fork another piece of lamb.

"Pretty good." He stared at me over his glass again. "But it's the view here that's really the best." His eyes didn't leave me for the beach.

Now we were getting into three-alarm territory with his compliments.

His phone rang. He flipped it to silent and sent the caller to voicemail before setting it down on the table. "Now, where were we?"

"You were telling me how much you liked your dinner."

"I thought I was referring to dessert." His grin grew as his gaze held me. The eyes of the hunter appeared, and I was his prey.

His phone vibrated on the table again.

"You better get that."

He sighed and flipped the phone over before showing me who was calling. My brother.

~

Zack

"Hey, Doug. How are ya?" I said in greeting.

I checked my watch. Okinawa was sixteen hours ahead, so it was midmorning tomorrow there.

"Fine. Just fine, but I'm worried about Brit. I've been calling, and she's not picking up her phone. She always answers."

He was speaking so fast I couldn't get a word in edgewise.

"I need you to check on her to make sure she's okay."

"She's around."

Brittney's eyes went wide, and she shook her head, warning me off in a way I didn't understand.

"Can I talk to her?" he asked.

"Sure. Let me find her," I answered. I waited a few seconds before handing her the phone. "Doug's calling."

"Hi," Brittney answered. "I'm fine… The battery died… Yeah, I'll get it fixed… No… Why would you say that?" She looked exasperated. "No. There's nobody, and if there was, it wouldn't be any of your business anyway… He wants to talk to you." She handed me back the phone.

"You gotta watch after her for me," Doug said.

"I'll keep her safe."

"More than that," he insisted. "The last time she acted like this, she'd just hooked up with that Benji creep."

"I don't understand," I said.

"I'm not there to protect her, and I need you to fill in for me."

"I'll keep her out of danger."

432

"That's not what I mean. She's got terrible taste in men, or it's just bad luck following her around. She moves to a new town, and she hooks up with the first creep she meets."

He didn't realize he was talking to the creep right now.

"You gotta find out who this guy is, 'cuz I'm gonna kill him when I get some leave."

"Well, maybe you're wrong."

"I'm not wrong. I've got a sense about this. You gotta find this guy."

"Sure. I'll keep my eyes open."

"She's my sister, and I swear I'm gonna kill the guy. Promise me no guy will get his hands on her."

"I got ya covered, Doug. She'll be safe."

"I knew I could trust you, Zack. See ya soon."

"Yeah, soon." I hung up the phone.

What the fuck was I going to do now? I'd just lied to my best friend, and slept with his sister.

My future held one hell of a fight, or maybe a coffin.

# CHAPTER 28

*BRITTNEY*

WHEN ZACK HUNG UP, HE HAD TURNED PALE.

"What's the problem?" I asked.

"He thinks you're in a vulnerable time."

"It's none of his business. I'm not a little kid."

He took the last of his broccoli on his fork. "He's just looking out for you."

"What does he know?"

My brother could damn well keep his nose out of my business.

Our waitress came by and asked to take our empty plates.

I sent a wink his way. "It's early. Maybe we could go dancing."

He shook his head, obviously less than enthused. "Nah. Maybe another time."

His countenance carried another message—maybe never.

"How about drinks at the bar then?"

That suggestion didn't get any better reception. My brother's call had certainly put a damper on things.

The waitress returned. "Can I interest you in dessert, or perhaps coffee or an after-dinner drink?"

Zack waved her off. "I think we're done." He refused the menu.

I held my hand out. "I'll take a look at that."

She gave me the maroon tablet.

I sucked briefly on the tip of my thumb. "I think I'd like something to suck.

Would you happen to have any popsicles?" I licked my lips while looking straight at Zack.

"No, I'm sorry. But we do have a nice sherbet."

I perused the choices. "I think the pistachio crème brûlée looks good." I glared at Zack. "And I think my date would like something sour. What would you recommend?"

She looked at me, perplexed.

Zack broke the silence. "I'll take one of those as well, please."

The waitress retrieved the menu and hustled off.

"Something sour? What has gotten into you?"

"I just thought it would match your mood."

"Now, hold on. Who says I'm in a bad mood? I have a lot to think about."

"Yeah, so much that you don't know what you want to do or not do anymore."

He shrugged.

I stood. "Well, I know what I want."

"Calm down and sit," he commanded.

"I need to use the ladies room." I snatched my purse and marched off.

I was washing up when two other ladies came in, chatting up a storm.

I unzipped my dress, removed my bra, and re-zipped.

Their chatting stopped.

I smiled at them. "I'm hot." I pulled my panties down and stepped out of them. My bra and panties went into my purse. I checked the mirror before I left the speechless pair. Their look was just what I was after. I was going to get his mind off of the call with Doug and back on us. Fuck the bro code.

As I walked back with an exaggerated bounce, it was obvious Zack noticed the double-barrel salute from my nipples.

A wicked grin returned to his face. Mission accomplished—at least partly.

I rounded the table and leaned over to whisper in his ear. "Hold these for me, will you?"

I dropped my panties in his lap before returning to my chair. After taking my seat, I leaned forward. "You may not know for sure what you want, but I do."

Our desserts arrived and were as delicious as they looked.

I stared into his eyes and deliberately licked my lips before every bite I sucked off my spoon.

His eyes got wider by the minute, and I could only imagine what his pants would look like when he stood.

He dropped a few large bills on the table, and we were instantly on our way back to the villa.

With his arm around me, he urged me faster than the damned heels wanted to take me.

I'd touched a match to the fuse, and I was about to reap the whirlwind.

He threw open the door and pulled me inside, where the pace instantly slowed.

He kicked the door closed and backed me into the bedroom. "Stand still and don't say a word."

I froze in place. My eyes slowly acclimated to the partial darkness. Moonlight through the window provided the only illumination.

He walked around me.

I shivered with anticipation as he traced a finger over my collarbone, my shoulder, my back, and returned to just under my neck.

I lifted my hands to bring his face to mine, but he pushed them down. "Still."

He walked behind me and inched my zipper down.

Returning to my front, he slid the dress off my shoulders.

"Zack," I whispered as it slipped to the floor.

A finger to my lips reminded me of his previous command. He didn't want me to talk. This wasn't a time for words. It was a time for touching, a time for hands and lips and tongues.

He knelt and lifted one of my feet and then the other, recovering the dress and tossing it aside.

"My God, Sunshine. You're fucking beautiful," he said in a raspy voice coated in lust.

I couldn't control the blush that overtook me—not that it was visible in the moonlight. He'd said it before, but tonight the conviction in his voice conveyed more than the words. The passion in his eyes sent the true message.

He moved closer, and my nipples scraped against him.

He had commanded my silence, and I didn't have the words for him anyway. All I could do was show him. I circled one hand around the nape of his neck and speared his hair with the other, pulling myself up. I kissed him like it was our last night together.

As I covered his mouth, my tongue began the dance with his. We exchanged breath and a hunger for each other. He tasted of pistachio dessert, lust, and need.

He gave me back all that I offered and more as his hands found my back and my ass, pulling me against him. I didn't care that I could barely breathe. I was in his arms and he in mine.

I broke the kiss and pushed away enough to reach his belt. I fumbled as I tried to undo the thing while he removed his shirt. Finally it loosened, and I was able to pull the zipper down. I wasted no time hooking my fingers into his underwear and pulling them and his pants down to his ankles, freeing his cock.

He pulled me back onto the bed on top of him, heels and all.

I straddled him as I rubbed my soaked slit along the length of his cock. I leaned over, my eyes conveying my wordless wishes to him as my breasts rubbed against his chest.

When I sat up, he kneaded my breasts and tweaked my nipples, sending shocks through me.

I moved down and took him in my mouth to get him to come for me. To get him to give in to me. To get him to give up control. To taste him.

"Not tonight, Sunshine." He pulled me up and rolled us over.

Pinned below him, I clawed at his back. I was his to have as he wished, but I wanted him inside me. He hovered there on arms extended at my sides, his eyes taking me in, pulling me in.

"You are so fucking beautiful," he repeated.

I felt tears building as his emotions shone in his eyes.

I worked my hands over his torso, his arms, his neck, feeling the bunched muscles as his eyes continued to dance over me.

He left me for a moment and came back with a condom, which he handed me.

I tore open the packet and rolled the latex slowly down his length. His eyes widened and his breath hitched with every stroke. I spread my legs to welcome him. Slowly, he positioned himself at my entrance and pushed in.

I pulled my knees up and grabbed my ankles. "I kept them on like you asked."

The sensation as he entered me was pure bliss. He began to thrust, and the sensation grew exponentially. If this was high-heel sex, sign me up.

We fit so perfectly and he filled me so fully, it was as if his cock had been made for me and me for him.

When he was inside me, whether gliding in and out, thrusting in and out, or pounding in and out—it didn't matter. The way he made me feel was nothing I had ever expected to experience.

With every thrust, I clenched more tightly around him. He brought me closer and closer to the cliff, building pressure within me as sensations crashed over me. The tension within me built to a crescendo. But I didn't want to come, because I didn't want it to end.

I held off my orgasm as long as I could. All I wanted was to stay like this, joined with Zack. I wrapped my legs behind him and pulled him in with my heels.

I rocked into him, giving him all I could, all I had. I was his completely. I needed to be his, to stay his forever.

With several more hard thrusts, Zack reached his limit and exploded inside me. He thrust harder and deeper, pushing me over the cliff into a soul-shattering orgasm as we screamed out each other's names.

I unclamped my legs, and he collapsed on top of me, panting, sweating, and kissing my neck.

"You're beautiful," he said over and over.

My pulse banged in my ears, and the pounding of our hearts against each other's chests overtook my thoughts.

437

I had given him all I had, offered it for him to take, and I would do it again and again.

As our jagged breathing slowed and the pulsating of his cock inside me dissipated, he rolled off me to the side.

I nestled up against him, my arm over his chest, my head on his shoulder, sensing the beat of his heart—the heart I wanted so much to win.

He got up to dispose of the condom.

I shed my heels and spooned with Zack, his hand cupping my breast, claiming me. Sleep came quickly.

# CHAPTER 29

*BRITTNEY*

ON WEDNESDAY AFTERNOON I LAID BACK ON THE BED AND CLOSED MY EYES WHILE Zack was off settling the bill.

Our time in San Diego replayed in my mind. He'd taken me to SeaWorld with the magnificent and funny seal and sea lion shows. I'd gotten to feed and pet a dolphin—and had the fish-smelling hand from the bait for an hour to prove it. We'd gone on roller coasters, wandered, and just hung out. He'd taken me to the zoo, where a morning of watching the animals had been relaxing, except when we got to the African penguin pool and leopard sharks were in the water. The signs assured us that the sharks and penguins got along well together. Who knew?

They had a bird that ate bees by catching them mid-flight and removing the stinger before swallowing. The baboons were too loud for my taste, but the panda bears were the opposite—three-hundred-pound versions of a kid's fluffy stuffed animal. The Komodo dragons were scary. Just knowing they occasionally attacked people put them on my *avoid* list.

Zack had also taken me jet skiing in the bay for an afternoon. He'd offered to get me surfing lessons as well, but that could wait until next time. I'd voted for relaxing by the pool instead.

It didn't matter if it was the ritzy hotel restaurant or the local burger stand, wherever Zack took me to eat, I was across from the most handsome and attentive man in town.

He had gone all-out to provide a mixture of fun and relaxing escapes from the day-to-day grind of LA. The one time I'd brought up my house and the work to be done, he'd set me straight that San Diego was not the place to discuss anything having to do with LA and my situation. We were on a vacation from reality he'd told me, and it had been far, far from reality.

In the real world, responsibilities, money issues, even doing the laundry needed to be dealt with. Ignoring them wouldn't make them go away. But those had been the ground rules for our days in San Diego, and the problems had receded temporarily from my consciousness, replaced with smiles, giggles, and the best company a girl could wish for.

Zack had brought me from the darkness of despair at my situation to the sunny side of future possibilities. He'd insisted I just needed to figure out a plan for the future instead of looking back at the failures in my past.

He opened the door and pulled me back to the present. "Ready to go?"

"Yeah." I got up from the bed slowly.

"We can stay, if you want."

"No, it's fine. I've got work tomorrow."

I followed Zack to the car and let him open the door for me as he liked to do —ever the gentleman.

"Back to the real world," he said.

I took one last look at this magical place. The bright red cupola might be merely an audacious hotel roof, but to me it now anchored memories of two wonderfully happy days. Me, Zack, and San Diego. Sunshine, smiles, and laughs. But he was right. Our few days in fantasyland were over, and now I was taking a ride back to my world of no money, no house, no job, and no future. A two-hour trip from carefree to reality, courtesy of Zack's ferocious Snake.

Zack laid his phone on the carpeted transmission tunnel behind the shift lever.

"When do I get to drive the Snake?"

"The tenth of never."

"You said that last time," I noted.

He started up the big engine without answering me.

I found a hair-band in my pocket and pulled my hair back into a ponytail. I didn't need the tangles.

"I like it better down," he informed me.

"You're not the one who has to comb out the knots."

"I will when we get back." He stared at me, not putting the car in gear.

"What?"

His eyes shifted to my lap.

"Oops." I grappled with the seat belt halves and shoulder belts. This was one thing that was difficult about the Snake.

He was still staring at me when I finished.

I rolled down my window. "I'm ready."

"Down, please," he said.

"Fine. But I'm holding you to that promise about the combing." I pulled the band free and shook out my hair.

He peered over his shoulder and put the car in reverse. "Thank you."

I smiled to myself, remembering the *Animal Planet* show on gorillas. They groomed one another as a sign of affection, and now my bossy, gruff Neanderthal was offering me the same treatment. In some ways, we weren't that removed from the primates.

It was a beautiful sunny day as we motored north, even if I didn't get a turn driving.

"How's your tank?" he asked as we passed La Jolla.

It took me a second to get his drift. "Almost full."

He had done a masterful job refilling my "happiness reservoir," as he'd put it. "How come almost?"

"Because you won't let me drive the Snake," I quipped.

"Then you'll have to settle for almost."

He was in full Neanderthal mode. *Me drive, you ride* was only one step removed from *me hunt, you cook.* I was riding, and I'd been assigned the cooking duties too.

I looked over at my driver, my protector, my happiness coordinator, and yes, my lover. I laid a hand on his shoulder. "Thank you."

"For what?" His hand came from the steering wheel, his fingers lacing with mine.

"For giving me these days."

"I promised to fill your happiness reservoir, and I keep my promises."

"And for being you," I added.

He glanced over. "You sure about that?"

"I'm sure, because I know you're going to let me drive."

He disentangled his hand from mine with a laugh. "Fat chance."

"I'm sure."

I wasn't going to give up trying. Sooner or later I'd catch him in a moment of weakness. And until then, I was still happy he was the way he was.

Before long we left the shoreline and climbed into the hills, then quickly descended again into the urban sprawl of the LA Basin.

We made good time in spite of the late-day traffic and passed the LAX exit without hitting any serious slowdowns.

I decided to try his technique of visualizing a better future for myself. I closed my eyes, ignored the wind whipping my hair in my face, and thought about what I wanted most. I wanted a phone call from Dr. Fosback saying I could start tomorrow. And I would get four days a week, and I was getting a raise.

That would put me in a happy place, a place where I could envision paying for Samantha's school. A place where I could start to pay down the awful debt Benji had saddled me with. A calm warmth filled me as I visualized that call.

My phone rang, yanking me from the dream.

I opened my eyes and blinked several times as I tried to swipe the hair from my eyes and locate the ringing phone.

I found it and answered. "Hello?"

"Hi," a surprised voice said. "This is Phil Patterson. Is Zack around?"

I took the phone away from my ear momentarily. I'd answered Zack's phone. He'd gotten the call, not me.

"Hi, this is Brittney. We met Sunday at the Habitat house. Zack's driving right now. Can I give him a message?"

"Brittney—I remember. Tell him the first stage is done."

"Got it. Anything else?"

"No, that's it. Thanks."

"I'll tell him."

Zack looked over. "Tell me what?"

"That was Phil Patterson. He said the first stage is done. I hope that means something to you."

He smirked. "It sure does."

"What's so funny?"

"Nothing," he answered. "I'm just happy about the news."

"Which is?"

"Later."

He clearly didn't intend to be more forthcoming. In Zack-speak, *later* could be shorthand for *never*. Like his statement that maybe later he'd eat his fruit? Translation: don't get your hopes up, girl.

I settled into my seat, closed my eyes, and went back to visualizing the call I wanted from Dr. Fosback to put my life in order. It had worked once to get the phone to ring—wrong call, but a call nonetheless. I concentrated, but I only heard wind noise and the thundering engine. No phone. I checked my purse for my phone to make sure it wasn't on silent.

*Fuck.*

I'd totally forgotten I'd left it at the house, which is why Doug had been unable to reach me before he called Zack the other night.

Zack's pleasant holiday had completely erased my brain. I'd been using his phone for pictures the whole time.

Zack slowed for the exit, and we left the freeway for the surface streets.

"Can we work on the water pipes after we get back?" I asked.

I liked being with Zack, but I desperately wanted to make the house that was supposed to be mine and Samantha's livable. I wanted to stake a claim to some space I could call my own.

"No," he said brusquely.

442

I recoiled at the word. "But we have daylight, and I want to."

"No," he repeated.

"But this is supposed to be one of my happy days," I complained.

"Exactly."

He made the final turn onto Snakewood. This time the street was empty—no one giving us a middle-finger salute.

I folded my arms.

He turned into his driveway and slowly drove to the back. "I have a surprise for you."

"Sure. But I'd rather make progress on the house."

"If you're going to have a poor attitude, I won't tell you."

"I'm listening."

"I had Phil work on the house while we were away. He got the water fixed and turned on today."

"Really?" I undid the seatbelt and lunged for my boyfriend, wrapping him in a hug.

He put a finger to my nose. "Yes. Really."

I opened my door. "The first thing I'm doing is flushing those horrid toilets." I jumped out of the car.

"Hey," he called.

I'd forgotten to wait for him to open my door. "Sorry, I was in a hurry."

He exited his side. "I'll get the bags inside. You go check it out."

I bounded through the gate and up the steps, before I realized I'd been in such a hurry, I'd left my purse with my keys on the floor of the car.

I retraced my steps, with the keys this time, unlocked the back door, and entered the kitchen. I turned on the sink, and water sputtered out. I left it on and turned to go to the downstairs bath.

My heart stopped, and I shrieked.

A dead rat with a knife through it lay impaled on the cutting board.

The note was in dark red letters.

**NOT FUNNY BITCH**
   **GIVE ME THE KEY**

I turned and lunged for the door.

It couldn't be him.

~

Zack

. . .

I HAULED THE SUITCASES INSIDE AND GRABBED A COKE BEFORE LEAVING TO GO SEE MY happy girl in her house with running water.

I'd started up the back stairs when I heard her scream. I rushed the final few steps.

She came barreling through the door and straight into me. My Coke went flying, and she almost bowled me over.

I grabbed her and held her tight. "What's wrong?"

Instead of pulling away and running, she gripped me tightly and planted her face in my shoulder.

"I've got you," I reassured her, stroking her back.

She shivered before she managed a few words. "We have to go back to the other house."

Her words didn't make any sense.

"What the hell's wrong?"

She sobbed. "It's him."

I pried her loose from me. "Stay right behind me," I commanded. If there was someone in the house, I was dealing with this now. With one hand holding hers, I slowly opened the kitchen door and looked inside before entering, dragging her with me.

Inside, the scene was horrific. A rat had been stabbed dead in the middle of the kitchen table. When I got closer, I saw the note.

**NOT FUNNY BITCH**
    **GIVE ME THE KEY**

My first thought went to Piss Boy and his crew, but the note didn't make any sense. He wanted his phone, not a key.

She was crying again.

The blood pooled by the rodent was still wet. The message writer could still be in the house.

I turned off the water running in the sink and backed her out the door. I closed it behind us. "I like your idea of going to the other house."

With an arm around her, I led her back to the gate and inside my house through the back kitchen door.

I deposited her in one of the kitchen chairs. "Stay here and lock the door after me. I'm gonna go check it out, but I want you to stay inside."

She nodded.

I hurried to the drawer with my gun safe, opened it, and pulled out my Sig Sauer. If the pistol was good enough for the Secret Service, it was good enough for me. And if he had a knife, I wanted a gun—a real one this time.

As I passed back through the kitchen, Brittney's eyes widened at the sight of my weapon.

"Just in case," I assured her.

As I descended the stairs again, I heard her latch the deadbolt as I'd told her. *Good girl.*

I took off the safety before I reached her house and mentally prepared myself for Piss Boy, or whoever else I might find.

Going through each of the rooms one by one, I confirmed the house was empty. With the flashlight on my phone I did the same for the cellar. I didn't put the safety back on until that was complete.

If this was that ex-whatever she'd run from in San Jose, he was dangerous. Why hadn't she told me?

When I returned, I found her with a suitcase.

"I can't stay now that he found me." She sniffed.

Fuck that shit. I planted myself in front of her. "You are not leaving."

"You don't understand. It's not safe for me here. I've gotta go."

I pointed to the kitchen table. "Sit."

"Stop telling me what to do," she yelled.

I grabbed her arm and yanked her to the table. "I said sit."

She fussed, but complied after a moment.

"Out there is where you're not safe. Here with me, you are. Running from this problem, whatever it is, won't solve it. I'll help you, but confronting the problem is the only way to fix it."

"But…"

"But nothing," I yelled. "I'm not fucking letting anything happen to you, and if that means tying you to the fucking bed so you can't leave, then so be it. I said you're staying. End of discussion."

She stared at the table, no longer arguing, but not accepting the inevitable either.

I took the other chair. "Now you need to tell me what's going on."

She looked up with teary eyes.

I locked eyes with her. "You have to trust me."

She nodded.

"You're safe here with me. I won't let anything happen to you."

She blinked back the tears, and the slightest hint of a smile appeared.

"Are you going to tell me what's going on?"

She gave me a shrug and a nod.

I took her hand and pulled her up. "Go sit down, and I'll get the wine." I pointed her toward the couch. "White or red?" I asked.

"How about stronger? I'll take that Jack now."

"Wine, until we talk."

She shook her head. "Easy for you to say."

I walked after her and took her into a hug.

She was shaking.

I rubbed her back and kissed the top of her head. "You need to explain what that note means. Now, go sit down."

She did as I asked and took a seat on the couch.

I poured us each a large glass of wine, and returned to her.

"When do I get the whiskey?"

Pulling the gun out of my waistband, I placed it on the coffee table, sat beside her, and offered her the glass. "Start with this."

She accepted the wine and quickly drained half the glass.

"Did Benji whoever leave you that present?"

"No... At least I don't think so."

I waited for her to continue.

She drained the rest of her glass and handed it to me.

I put it on the coffee table.

"I'll take a second," she said.

"Not yet. Not till we finish here. You know who wrote the note, don't you?"

"Maybe."

"You said you had to leave now that he found you. Who is he?"

"One of Delgado's people."

"What does a key have to do with anything?"

"Delgado is after me, and if I stay, I'll just put you in danger."

I nodded toward the gun. "But I can fight back."

Her explanation hadn't completed the picture, though.

"What about the note?"

"Todd told me he and Rick had hidden the money Rick stole somewhere, and only they knew where the key was. I never saw a key, and he never told me where one was, but I always figured they got the key or location or whatever from him before they killed him in Mexico. I mean, it would be sort of stupid not to, right?"

"These guys are not always the brightest bulbs in the pack."

"It has to be one of Delgado's guys, because he's still in prison."

"Are you sure?" I asked.

"He got twenty-five to life."

"How would they know you moved back?"

She shook her head again. "I don't know. Maybe somebody saw me?"

"But you haven't been in town a week yet. Could it be this Benji asshole? Did he ever know about the key?"

She thought for a moment. "I got talkative one night. More than a little. I was pretty drunk. I must have said more than I should have, because the next day he said it sounded scary. I don't remember what I said, but he never asked me about a key."

I reached for my glass again and took another swallow.

"I'm sorry I kept it from you," she said. "Can I have my whiskey now?"

I rose from the couch and took both our glasses. "Just relax for a minute, okay? We're doing pizza and a movie again tonight."

"And Jack?" she suggested.

"No. Better than Jack."

After ordering the pizza, I poured us each a glass of the hard stuff. "I think you'll like it."

She took a sip and nodded. "This is smooth. Glenfiddich?"

"Macallan. Now I have a call to make to get us some help."

"Help?"

"Protection for you. The professional kind."

She opened her mouth to object, but seemed to think better of it and instead took another swig of her scotch.

I went to the kitchen and called Bob Hanson of Hanson Security.

"Hey, Zack. What can I do for you? It's sort of late."

I started slowly. "You provided some security for the Covingtons a while back, is that right?"

"Yeah. Quite a clusterfuck for a few days. This crazy lady and her brother were after the lot of them—burned down a house, torched a car, and tried to abduct Emma. We got in late, handling protection and surveillance. The two perps are cooling their heels in prison on arson and attempted kidnapping raps right now. They won't be a threat for a while. And then they had another brother out east. Screwball family, if you ask me. What's your interest?"

"I have a friend who needs protection for a while till we can figure out her situation."

"Tell me a little about it," he said.

"When we got back today, we found a disturbing message in her kitchen."

"What kind of message?"

"A rat knifed to the table and a note."

Hanson's voice filled with concern. "Zack, that's serious."

"I get that. That's why I'm calling. Can you spare somebody?"

"Sure. I'll pull Winston off his surveillance first thing and send him over. I take it the protectee is a woman?"

Having Winston was good news, as ex-FBI, he was a solid guy. I'd met him at the Habitat weekends, and the Covingtons liked him.

"Yeah. My girlfriend." It felt odd to refer to Brittney that way without asking her, but it was how I felt this morning.

"Then Constance will head the team. She's ex-Secret Service, and with women it helps if one of the team is also female, if you know what I mean."

"I hear ya."

"Give me your location, and I'll have them there in the morning, unless you think we need to start tonight?"

"No, the morning works."

"One more thing—are you packin'?"

"Yeah, a Sig."

"Have you been to the range lately?"

"Why?"

447

"If Constance and Winston aren't comfortable with your abilities, we take your gun for the duration. Those are the rules. Can you live with that?"

"Do I have a choice?"

"No," he said flatly.

I gave him my address and returned to Brittney.

She needed additional alcohol and a movie tonight to calm down.

# CHAPTER 30

*ZACK*

BRITTNEY WAS SNORING LIGHTLY, FACING ME, WHEN I WOKE THE NEXT MORNING.

For a few minutes I lay there quietly watching my woman, my perfect woman. The woman who had finally come back to me, back where she belonged. Just the words *my woman* felt so right. She always had been the one for me.

It had taken a long time and a fair amount of alcohol for her to finally fall asleep after finding the sick present in the kitchen next door.

She deserved to sleep late, so instead of kissing her awake the way I yearned to do, I slipped slowly out of bed. I palmed my Sig from the nightstand before softly closing the door behind me.

My sweet Sunshine deserved happiness and safety, not the torment the note writer had brought to her. Last night hadn't been the end I'd envisioned to our San Diego outing. It made clear why she'd left with no notice years ago. Whoever these guys were, *scary* and *unhinged* only began to describe them.

Downstairs I made a quick tour of the house, checking windows and doors before I stuck the gun at the small of my back and started breakfast. In no time, I had two plates of scrambled eggs, English muffins, and even bowls of apricots in a nod to her need for fruit at every meal. At least with apricots, I didn't have to worry about the seeds getting caught in my teeth.

I was checking my phone for messages when she padded in, wrapped in my bathrobe. "Hey. Breakfast is my job."

I pulled the plates of eggs from the oven. "You looked like you needed the sleep."

She rubbed at her eyes. "I guess I did."

Adding the English muffins to the plates, I brought them over. "Are apricots okay for morning fruit?"

She sat. "Who are you and what did you do with my boyfriend?"

The boyfriend comment surprised me, but I tried not to let it show. It was a definite step up from brother's friend, and not one I was going to refuse. "Can't I make my girlfriend breakfast for once?"

The smile she wore went up several notches. She liked her new status as much as I liked mine.

I poured cranberry juice for both of us. "Coffee?"

She nodded. "And Advil."

I located the Advil bottle in the cupboard and poured two mugs of coffee. "You should have slowed down on the scotch."

"That was seriously good stuff. What did you say it was?"

I handed her the painkillers. "Macallan." I didn't add that it was aged eighteen years and cost over two-fifty a bottle.

After swallowing the pills, she ate slowly, mostly pushing the food around on her plate and sipping her coffee.

"It'll be okay, Sunshine. I promise."

She sighed. "I'm scared, Zack, and I don't want to drag you into this mess."

"We went through this last night. I'm not letting you leave. We are dealing with this together.'

Her eyes lifted from her plate, and a smile emerged. "Thank you."

It had taken a long time last night to get her to see I wouldn't back down on this.

"But they're dangerous," she said.

I pulled my gun from behind my back and laid it on the table. "So am I."

She gave up the argument and went back to her plate. Eventually she finished her apricots, but barely touched the eggs. She pushed the plate away. "I'm not very hungry."

I didn't tell her to finish the way she would have told me. "I'll keep it warm if you want it after your shower."

She stood. "A shower sounds like a good idea." She came around the table to me.

I stood and took my girlfriend into my arms.

"Thank you for breakfast," she said.

I kissed her and sent her upstairs. "Anything for you, Sunshine. Anything."

∽

*BRITTNEY*

. . .

Before going back downstairs, I had a call to make.

"Why haven't you been answering my calls?" Benji complained when he answered.

"I blocked you because you've been an ass."

"I need to see you."

"I want my papers back. I know you took them."

"Tell me where you are, and I'll bring them over."

That's one thing I *wasn't* doing. "Give them to Lillian at the Pig."

"No. I said I'd bring them over. We still have to talk."

I had to hold back to keep from yelling. "Give them to Lillian, or I'm calling the cops."

"I want to talk to you." He was just a broken record at this point.

Benji wouldn't have been able to lie like that if he knew where I'd moved. I felt confident now that he hadn't been the one to write the note.

I hung up and went downstairs. Zack was scrubbing dishes at the sink.

"Could you go next door with me?" I asked.

He put the pan off to the side. "Sure. We can go after you meet your protection detail."

"I'm not sitting around locked up with a bunch of goons with guns. I told you I have to go to work. I can't afford to lose this job."

"Give it a chance. This is for your safety."

The determination in his eyes meant he'd gone into full stubborn mode.

"It's not fair that I don't get a say," I shot back.

"Fine," he said, surprising me. "Meet them before you make up your mind though." He turned back to the dishes.

A half hour later, the doorbell rang while I was upstairs. Peering out the window, I located two black SUVs parked on the street: the goon squad. I went downstairs. Like Zack said, it wasn't fair to tell them to leave before meeting them.

At the base of the stairs, I was surprised by what I found. One of them was the hulking, buzz cut guy from the Habitat project the other day—Winston, if I remembered correctly. The surprise was his partner, a short woman with a bob haircut in a leather flight jacket. He looked like the dumb gun jockey I'd expected. She did not.

The big guy extended his hand. "Winston Evers, Brittney. I didn't expect we'd meet again so soon. By the way, thanks for the apple on Sunday."

My hand disappeared in his massive one as we shook. "At least somebody around here likes fruit." I shot a sideways glance to Zack.

The woman extended her hand. "Constance Collier."

I took her hand and received a surprisingly firm handshake. "Brittney Clark."

"Constance is ex-Secret Service," Winston noted.

Constance smiled.

A few moments of awkward silence ensued before I asked, "So, Winston, how do we get started with this?"

He turned to Constance. "What do you say, boss lady?"

A blush rose in my cheeks for making such a stupid assumption.

"Let's start with assessing the threat," she said. "Mr. Benson, you said there was a note?"

"Zack," he corrected her. "Yes, it's next door."

"Winston, why don't you and Zack go check it out," Constance suggested.

I waited until the door closed and the boys were outside before I spoke. "I'm sorry. I didn't mean to—"

Constance waved her hand dismissively. "Not an issue. I'm used to it."

"Coffee?" I offered.

"Water will be fine."

I led her into the kitchen and poured water from the fridge for her and an orange juice for me.

She accepted the glass and took a sip.

I twisted my glass. "Secret Service? Were you ever assigned to him?"

"No, not the president. I was on the First Lady's detail. Boring as hell."

"Really?" I wouldn't have guessed that.

"Protection detail is barely supposed to be seen, and certainly never heard." She stifled a laugh. "I was on that detail so long, I was afraid I'd forget how to talk."

"And this is better?"

"Tons," she said before taking another sip. "Better pay, better hours, and better partners—like Winston, top notch."

I could see we were going to get along fine.

The men came back in from next door.

Winston showed Constance some photos on his phone. "Pretty standard gang threat."

I cringed, recalling the sight from last night. "Normal?" I obviously led a sheltered life.

"I didn't mean this is normal so much as it's something we see a lot," Constance explained. "It's meant as intimidation."

"Mark me down as properly intimidated," I answered.

Winston pocketed the phone. "What key is the note referring to?"

I look to Zack for confirmation, and he nodded. "That's the problem. I don't know. It has to be related to a key they thought Todd told me about. But I never knew where to find any key."

"You think you know who left this?" Constance asked.

"You better start at the beginning," Zack told me.

I swallowed. "I testified in a murder trial that put a guy away—Luis Delgado. He's in prison, so I can only guess this is someone associated with him."

Winston put his hand up to interrupt me. "Can you spell that?"

I did so slowly.

"Go ahead," Constance urged me.

I told them about my ex-boyfriend Todd's brother getting murdered, then Todd disappearing in Mexico, and the messages about a key.

"And there's no way this could be anybody else, any other key they're referring to?" Constance asked.

"It's the only key that makes sense," I answered.

Constance turned. "Did anyone else know about this key? Did you tell anyone?"

I thought back. "Just the detective on the case, Detective Swenson."

"Who is he with?" Constance asked.

"LAPD," I told her. Then I remembered one other person. "I also told Benji one night."

Winston looked up from his computer. "Who is he?"

"Ex-boyfriend in San Jose."

"Recent?" he asked.

I nodded.

Winston hovered over his keyboard. "Last name?"

I looked to Zack for a moment.

He mock covered his ears.

"Sykes, S-Y-K-E-S," I told Winston.

He typed into his laptop.

Constance looked up from her notepad. "If you were to guess, who would you think did this?"

"I'm guessing one of Delgado's friends or relatives," I responded. "He got sent away for twenty-five to life, so it can't be him, and Benji doesn't make sense. I didn't even tell him I moved here."

Winston stood. "That's not quite true."

"What's not true?" Zack asked as he moved to see what Winston had on his screen.

"Luis Delgado was released from prison ten days ago. The conviction was overturned on bad jury instructions."

I shivered. I'd stopped checking the detective's emails long ago, and I didn't pay much attention to the news.

"He's one ugly son of a bitch," Zack said as Winston turned the screen so we would all see it.

The mug shot made Delgado look even more menacing than I remembered.

"At least he'll be easy to spot," Constance said.

The picture showed tattooed red teardrops under each eye, as well as the red star tattoo on his forehead. Those are what had made my testimony so damning at his trial. With those markings, there wasn't any guesswork involved in my identification, and that had been clear to the jury.

"So if we go on the assumption that this is Delgado, what do we know?" she asked Winston.

"We know he is risk averse," Winston offered. "Luring your boyfriend down to Mexico instead of confronting him here was a smart move. The closure rate on homicides in Mexico is extremely low. Also, leaving you a message when you weren't home means he's afraid to confront you directly."

"Afraid of me?" I asked.

"More like afraid of circumstances he can't control," Winston said.

"I agree with Winston," Constance added. "He's taking the low-risk approach in each case. That's good for us. Because it means he's not likely to make a crazy-ass move straight at you the way some gangbangers might."

"I don't see how that helps," I admitted.

"It means he's not going to try to come through us to get to you. He'll be looking for an opportunity where you're not protected."

"Wait—for how long?"

"That's not something we can answer right now," Constance said.

"I've got a question," Zack said. "How did he know she was here? She only arrived a week and a half ago."

Constance shook her head. "Brittney, who knew you were planning this move?"

"Nobody knew ahead of time. I left on the spur of the moment."

"And who have you told since you arrived?"

"Only my brother and my sister," I said.

"And since you've been here?" Constance asked.

"I've only been to Dr. Fosback's office, the Rusty Bucket, and the grocery store —and Home Depot to get some supplies. That's it," I answered.

"Winston, that's your assignment for this morning," Constance told him.

"What assignment?" Zack asked.

"Check out the employees," Winston answered.

"You can do that?" Zack asked.

"If anybody can, he can," Constance assured us.

I checked my watch. "I need to get ready for work."

"No, you don't," Zack said.

"I'll go with her," Constance said. "It'll be fine."

Zack backed down.

I went upstairs to change and get ready.

~

"WANT ME TO TAG ALONG? I DON'T ORDER MUCH, BUT I'M A GOOD TIPPER," ZACK asked as I picked up my purse.

I kissed him on my way to the door. "Thanks for the offer, but no."

I left the house with Constance just a step behind me. I would finally be

454

getting back to work and earning my own way. As I approached my car, Constance unlocked the closer black SUV with her key fob.

"I'll drive," she said.

I wasn't in the mood to argue this minor point. But she wasn't going to be following me around at work. "Do you know where it is?"

"Sure do. I've been there once or twice. I like the place." She didn't strike me as our normal clientele, but maybe off the clock she was more laid back.

"How does this work?" I asked. "You can't just shadow me."

She looked over, smiling for the first time. "It's nothing like that. I'll hang out where I can watch the entrance. There's only one entrance, right?"

"Yeah. Just one entrance off the street. The fire exit in the back is alarmed. A drunk crashes through it about once every two weeks, but that's only near closing. The lunch crowd is better behaved."

"What about the kitchen? I assume there's a back door for deliveries."

"There is, but Max is super strict about keeping it locked. It doesn't even have a handle on the outside, and deliveries are early in the morning, except for the beer distributor. He comes in the afternoon."

"Sounds simple enough," she said, turning down the main drag. "Delgado should be easy to spot."

"No kidding. With those tattoos, you can see the guy a block away."

"Is there anyone else I need to watch for?"

"Not that I know of," I told her.

She pulled into the Bucket's parking lot and stopped the SUV. She extracted a pendant on a gold chain and handed it to me. "Wear this around your neck. If anything happens and you need me, press the center stone and I'll be right there. Try it now."

I examined the pendant—cheap costume jewelry—located the central stone, and pressed it.

Her phone chirped.

I put the alarm jewelry around my neck. "Cool."

"Only if there's trouble," she warned me.

"Understood."

I climbed down from the truck and walked toward the door.

"I'll be in as soon as I check the back. Remember, I'm invisible."

As soon as I opened the door, Max called out to me. "There's my girl." He strode over and handed me a menu. "The menu's changed a little. You should check it out."

I took it. "I thought I'd be behind the bar."

His brow crunched up. "You said you wanted the first thing that came up, and this is it. Celeste has the bar today, and you've got section three."

"Sure, section three. That's great." Section three was nearest the pool tables, and always the slowest—a beer here and there, and nachos or poppers once in a while. The real lunch eaters usually took tables closer to the door.

After a few minutes memorizing the menu changes, I noticed Constance take a table near the side wall with a good view of the front door. Not once in the several times I looked over did I see her glance in my direction. They probably had classes in watching without being noticed at the Secret Service. Occasionally I saw her looking at what looked like a Kindle in front of her.

I was being fucking guarded by the Secret Service, was that ever a trip.

On my first trip to the bar, Celeste ignored me for a minute, and when she arrived, her scowl was icy. She'd probably heard the exchange with Max and thought I was trying to ace her out of tending bar.

"Welcome back," she finally said.

"Thanks. It's good to be back."

Lunch wasn't as slow as I remembered from before, and a few of my tables ordered more than just appetizers.

Maria stopped me by the kitchen entrance. "Why have you been checking out my tables all shift?"

I stepped back with the plates I was balancing. "What do you mean?" I instantly knew she was talking about my frequent glances in Constance's direction.

"Stick to your own section," she warned me. A moment later, she said something to Max.

As I returned from delivering food, Max's voice stopped me in my tracks.

"This ain't Starbucks. If you wanna read all day, go get a coffee or whatever." It was Max, telling Constance to take a hike.

I turned, and my mouth must have dropped as Constance rose and left without a word.

Max marched back to the kitchen and motioned for me to follow.

The kitchen door swung closed behind me.

Max had his hands on his hips. "Who is that lady you been watchin' all shift?"

"What?"

"The book reader who thinks this is a fucking Starbucks or something."

Maria and our cook, Paul, stopped what they were doing to catch the fireworks.

"My protection," I said in a low voice.

"Protection from what?"

"My ex," I whispered.

Max's expression softened, and he put a hand on my shoulder.

"Brittney, I'm all the protection you need. If'n he comes in here, you tell me, and I'll take care of it, permanent like."

I nodded. "Thanks, Max."

Maria pushed past me to the door.

Max looked me in the eye. "I take care of my own. Now get back out there, and don't worry about nothin'."

Max left first, and I followed.

As I left, I could see Maria huddling with Celeste. Celeste wasn't wearing a happy face.

*Fucking great.*

Now everybody was going to know my business.

# CHAPTER 31

*Brittney*
*(Three Weeks Later)*

For a little over three weeks already, I'd been "under protection," as Zack called it. Three weeks that felt like three years, and I was plenty tired of it. So far every time I asked if they'd tracked down Delgado, the answer had been no, maybe tomorrow.

We'd spent much of the day working on Zack's floors. It was hard work, but since it was Sunday, I had him here with me. Tomorrow he'd be off to work, and I'd be cooped up with my protection detail until my shift at the Bucket.

For now, I was cuddled up next to Zack on the couch. He had picked tonight's movie, so we weren't watching what he would call a chick flick. It was a thriller called *Paycheck* with Ben Affleck and Uma Thurman. I hadn't seen it before, and it got a little intense, at least for me. But when the end came, the good guy beat the bad guy, and the girl got her man.

Zack's arm around me pulled me tighter. "That wasn't so bad, was it?"

"A little scary for my taste. I thought for sure the bullet would hit him."

He kissed the top of my head. "But it didn't because he learned the lesson."

"What lesson would that be, oh wise one?"

"His future wasn't preordained the way it looked. He focused on a split-second change to the present when he was on the bridge to affect his future. That saved him, and the world."

The movie had indeed been about that, and I'd totally missed it. It was a variation of what he'd told me half a dozen times. I obviously wasn't a good enough student.

I looked up at him. "I got a different lesson from it."

"Yeah?"

"We should invent a shot like the one he had to erase memories, and use it on the bad ones."

He stopped being my pillow, stood, and pulled my hand. "Up."

"Why?"

"I said up." He pulled again.

It wasn't worth the argument, so I stood.

A second later, he'd picked me up and was carrying me to the stairs. "Your problem is you need more good memories to outweigh the bad ones."

I hung on his neck. "Really?"

He started up the stairs with me. "I aim to fix that."

I giggled as wetness pooled between my thighs.

He kicked the door closed behind him, and I had only the light from the full moon to see the grin that had eaten his face. He deposited me on the edge of the bed one second, and was yanking at my top the next. In short order he had me naked, with unmistakable lust in his eyes as he stood over me. The eyes of the predator were back.

I worked his belt while he pulled off his shirt, and with only a short struggle to free his erection, he soon stepped out of the clothes, his nakedness matching mine.

He pulled me to him, and the kiss he laid on me was worthy of his earlier promise to make tonight a wonderful memory. His strong arms clamped me against him as we traded breath and our tongues dueled for position. The pine scent of his hair tickled my nostrils, and the raspberry on his tongue was a reminder of his efforts to please my fruit obsession. The thickness of his arousal between us was a promise of what was to come.

He settled us down on the bed, our mouths still devouring each other with a hunger that wouldn't stop. He pushed my legs apart, and his fingers traced my folds as his kisses moved to the sensitive skin of my neck.

"You're going to come for me, Sunshine."

With one hand I grabbed his hair, with the other, I grasped his cock. "No. If tonight is my memory, I get what I want."

His finger slid forward to my clit, and his attack began. "I know this is what you want."

He got better every night at teasing me with just the right pressure, just the right circling, just the right rubbing, or sucking to drive me instantly crazy. He wasn't wrong that his ministrations were something I wanted, but only *one* thing. I wanted more.

I worked my hand on his cock, pulling, squeezing, and twisting. "That's not all I want."

His fingers continued to send electric shocks through me with every touch. "You'll get that too," he whispered as a finger entered me and exited.

I let go of his cock, pushed his shoulder over, and moved to straddle him.

"You want to be on top?"

I rubbed my wet folds over his length. "That's part of it." I leaned forward, placing a hand on either side of his head. I placed a gentle kiss on his lips. "But that's not all."

As I straightened up and slid forward and back over his cock, his hands came to my breasts, and his other talent came into play as he held them, fondled them, and circled the nipples playfully, teasingly.

I lowered a bit, and he brought his head up to take first one nipple and then the other into his mouth.

His breathing hitched just a bit every time I slid myself forward and over the tip of his cock.

He stretched to reach for the nightstand.

I tugged on his arm. "If it's my night, I should get to write the script."

He relented and his hand came back to my breast.

I leaned forward, my face an inch from his. "You said I could have a wish."

"Uh-huh."

I kissed him again lightly before whispering, "I'm on the pill. Can you guess my wish?"

His smile grew. "I'm clean. It's your script."

I lifted up and positioned his cock with my hand. "Me too." I pushed down just a little and lifted up, teasing his tip several times before his hands went to my hips and urged me lower.

He gasped as I slid down, taking much, but not all of him. "You're torturing me, baby."

I pushed down, taking him to the root. "My script."

He thrust up into me. I leaned forward to give his mouth access to my breasts. The sensations grew with each successive thrust as we glided against each other.

He pushed up into me. "Oh baby, you're so fucking good."

I rocked down on him again and again, my nerves firing harder each time he filled me to the end. I wanted to keep it up, to keep feeling him inside me, filling me as he was meant to, but the tension was building, and I wouldn't be able to keep my orgasm at bay for long.

The tension in his muscles and the gasps that came with each thrust said the same was true for him.

I clenched more tightly around him and pinched his nipples as he pulled me down hard with each push. I couldn't catch a breath as he picked up the tempo, and without warning, the waves of my climax rolled over me. I was over the edge into a sea of bliss as the spasms took over.

He tensed and pushed one last time with a groan and came undone himself, emptying inside me.

As I melted into exhausted limpness, I fell forward onto my man, panting to catch my breath and feeling the rapid beat of his heart beneath mine—the heart I hoped I'd won. I could still feel the pulsing of his cock within me.

He ran his fingers through my hair and kissed my ear. "I told you, you just need to add good memories to push the bad ones to the back."

"You won't leave me, will you?" My question escaped my lips before I could stop it.

He gave me a squeeze. "Of course not. I'll protect you always."

I kissed him. I wanted to stay like this, connected man to woman for as long as I could, and he let me.

He stroked my back and my hair as I listened to his heartbeat.

Eventually, I slid off to his side, and he got up.

I instantly missed his presence.

He returned with a warm washcloth for me to clean up and climbed back into bed.

I nestled against the man who had claimed me as his and promised to always protect me. Nothing could have warmed me more. I fell asleep as contented as I had ever been.

# CHAPTER 32

*Zack*

Monday morning, I woke with my woman snoring softly in bed beside me, where she belonged.

I slipped out of bed and out of the room as quietly as I could, taking my clothes to dress in the bathroom. Brittney deserved to sleep in after all the pressure she'd been under these last few weeks.

Once downstairs, I found Winston already up, in front of his laptop with a steaming cup of coffee in hand, as always.

He raised his mug. "Hey, boss."

"Anything new?"

"Maybe. I heard from a contact in Sacramento that he might have something for me later today."

I knew better than to get my hopes up. This was probably the fortieth lead, all of which had yielded zilch so far on Delgado.

"You should know this protection is getting on her nerves," I said.

"It can be tough. She just has to be patient."

I sprayed oil on the frypan. "She joked about giving you guys the slip to get some private time."

He put his cup down. "You better talk to her. That's not something to joke about."

I opened the fridge to get eggs. "I did, but you guys should be aware."

"Thanks. I'll let Constance know."

I added the eggs and dry ingredients to my bowl and had the batter whipped up quickly.

I got the other ingredients sliced and the pan heated by the time Brittney made it downstairs in her robe.

"Hey, that's my job," she said when she realized what I was doing at the stove. "Sit down."

"No, that's my job."

I turned and pointed my spatula at the table, where Winston was closing his laptop and preparing to leave. "Sit. I'm doing breakfast this morning."

Winston stood.

"And you stay," I told the big guy.

He sat back down with a slight eye-roll.

Brittney fussed for a second, but decided against further argument and took her seat. "What are we having?"

I flipped the last crepe in the pan. "You'll see in a moment." I pulsed the blender a few times for the topping.

A minute later I had two folded crepes on each plate and brought them over.

"Looks good," Brittney said, raising her fork.

I rushed back for the blender. "Hold on, I'm not done yet." I poured the raspberry sauce over each crepe. "Now it's ready."

Brittney took a bite with a smile. "Delicious," she proclaimed. "And with fruit. I've converted you."

"I wouldn't go that far," I replied. I dug into mine and was proud of the result, even if I'd have to floss after to get the seeds out of my teeth.

Winston sipped his coffee. "This is good. I vote we let him cook."

Brittney shot him a questioning glance.

"Once a week," he added.

The warmth of Brittney's smile as I looked over to her made even cooking something fruity for breakfast worth it.

She blew me a kiss when Winston wasn't looking.

I pursed my lips in a kiss in return.

"I got an email this morning from Benji," Brittney announced.

That got both my and Winston's attention.

"And?" I asked. Nothing good ever came from her interacting with that jerk.

"I called him because I still need my papers back."

"You shouldn't have done that," I told her.

Her fork hit the plate with a clank, and her glare could have frozen a steaming cup of coffee. "Hold on a minute. You're the one who told me to take actions in the present to create the future I want. Well, I need those papers, so instead of waiting around, I did something, and I'm not second guessing it."

Winston leaned back from the table to avoid being between me and Hurricane Brittney.

I put my hands up. "Okay. No second guessing. So what happened?"

She calmed down and lifted her fork again. "I told him to bring them all here this weekend, but then the asshole said the drive was too far and I should buy him tickets on Southwest. Do you believe that?"

"You didn't agree to that?" I asked.

"Of course not."

"Did you give him the address?" Winston asked.

"No. I'm not stupid. I told him we'd meet at the Bucket."

That was a relief, the last thing we needed was him knowing where she lived.

"I don't think that's wise," I said. "How about if I take you to San Jose this weekend and we do the exchange there?"

"No way. I'm not having you get arrested for assault. You have no idea how underhanded he can be. He'll fall down and claim you hit him. He'd stab himself and claim it was you. He's a looney toon."

I was about to argue the point, but Winston beat me to it. "I'll go with you instead. How about that?"

Her head tilted as she considered the offer. "That'll work." She smiled as she took another bite of her crepe.

"I'm coming too," I announced.

Winston shot me a disapproving eyeroll. "Constance and I are probably better suited to handle this than you are, boss man. And it would be safer that way for Brittney, which is our top priority, right?"

I nodded, unable to argue with his logic. "I'm coming, but I'll stay in the car. How's that?"

Winston stated the obvious. "It's Constance's call. She's the lead."

I didn't have a fallback position for that. Hanson had made it clear from day one that Constance called the shots.

When Brittney left to take a shower, I gathered up the dishes.

"Thanks for nothing," I said.

"Take your argument to Constance. I'm just calling it as I see it, and frankly you can be a loose cannon. We don't need to add unpredictability to the situation. Brittney's safety is our primary concern, isn't it?"

"Of course it is." I returned to doing the dishes, appropriately admonished.

Winston went back to his laptop in the other room.

The morning sun shone brightly through the window of my kitchen—her kitchen now, the kitchen she'd re-arranged, as she had my whole life.

Her return had brought a clarity I'd been missing. She was the tornado that blew everything around, and when the pieces finally settled, things made more sense than they had before. Order had replaced disorder, and it was an improvement.

I reached into my pocket and rubbed the Lombardi coin on my keychain. It was time to have a difficult conversation with Dad.

# CHAPTER 33

*Zack*

That afternoon, I was back at the house, sanding the spindles on the staircase railing.

Dad hadn't been in the office, so I hadn't stayed long.

Constance had decreed that I shouldn't go along on the San Jose trip. "Too many variables," she'd said—shorthand for agreeing with Winston that I was likely to do something stupid.

Brittney had the dinner shift at the Bucket today, and she and Constance hadn't been gone an hour when I got up to deal with the fruit Brittney had made me promise to eat this afternoon: plums. I pulled three from the fruit basket to slice up between Winston and me.

I always saved the pits to show her, but there was no room to cheat anyway. Winston had finked on me the first time I'd tried to fudge how many apricots I'd eaten, and that had cost me with Brittney.

Fucking Winston was as honest as the day was long, and nothing I could offer him would sway that, so Brittney always double checked with him.

He thought it was funny, and had fully committed to helping Brittney reform me on the fruit angle.

After peeling and slicing, I brought the bowls to the table. "Fruit's up."

Winston closed his ever-present laptop and came over. "Looks good."

I didn't echo the sentiment, although this was getting easier.

Winston had gotten through half his bowl when his phone chimed. He checked the screen. "This might be something," he told me before dialing a

465

number. "Detective Wilmont, what's up? … That's great… Where does this come from?" He thanked the guy on the other end before hanging up and dialing another number.

He rose and grabbed his coat and gun, his phone clutched to his ear. "Constance, we got a lead on Delgado. I'm leaving to go check it out before it goes cold. You okay to hold down the fort for a day or two?… I'll be in touch."

"Where's the lead?" I asked after he hung up with Constance.

"Sacramento."

"That doesn't make sense. Didn't he always live here?"

He checked his weapon's clip, as he always did. "Not unusual. A lot of guys held at Folsom don't land far from the prison, at least at first. His conviction was thrown out, so since he's not on parole, he can live wherever he wants."

"How solid is our lead?" I used *our*, although my only part in this was to pay the bills.

"One of Wilmont's CIs said he knows where we can find Delgado, so I'll go check it out. Informants aren't always reliable, but you never know till you check." He loaded his laptop and charger into a backpack.

In a few minutes I was alone in the house, with a bowl and a half of sliced plums in front of me.

*BRITTNEY*

IT HAD BEEN SUPER HECTIC FOR A MONDAY EVENING AT THE BUCKET, AND IT WASN'T over yet. Eddie hadn't shown up to tend bar, and Max was filling in. I could do a better job than he was, but waiting tables didn't suit him.

Celeste emerged from the back, holding her stomach and carrying her purse. She headed for the door. She'd been scheduled to stay till closing.

Right on cue, Max waved me over to the bar from the table I'd just served. "You need to stay late. Celeste had to leave."

"Sure, no problem," I responded.

I needed all the work and tips I could get since Dr. Fosback still hadn't scheduled a start date for me.

"Good girl."

I pulled out my phone and typed a message to Constance first.

ME: Working late

Her response was immediate as always.

CONSTANCE: OK

Table twelve was motioning for their check, so I took care of that before texting Zack as well.

ME: working late be back when I can

His text didn't take any longer than Constance's had.

ZACK: Miss you

ME: Miss you more

ZACK: Miss you most

It was our standard back and forth. I'd tried to skip the more line and claim the most title a few times. That hadn't gone well. It was against some set of rules I wasn't allowed to challenge—no way, no how. I found it kind of cute the way I could force my man into his bossy mode. If I pushed the right buttons, he couldn't help himself.

His bossiness always came from a caring place though, and made me feel wanted and protected when it reared its head.

I just had to accept it as his way of showing he cared.

On my way to greet another table, my phone announced another text.

ZACK: Text when you leave

He hadn't added please, but I knew that's what he meant. Then he surprised me.

ZACK: Pls

I smiled as I put the phone away and took the table's drink orders.

I texted him back on my way to the bar.

ME: Wilco

Doug had taught me that bit of military lingo meaning *will comply*, and I knew Zack would appreciate it, because *comply* wasn't always in my dictionary.

"Two chardonnays, a Bud Light, and a whiskey sour," I told Max when he slid down in my direction.

"I hope we aren't interfering with your social life," he said sarcastically.

I straightened up. "You asked me to stay late, and I had to let people know." I wasn't in the mood to let Max push me around.

He poured the two glasses of wine. "Good enough." That was as close as he got to saying I was off the hook.

As Max poured the whiskey sour, I noticed Constance come in and make her way to the restrooms.

Max handed me the drink and started pouring the beer. He nodded toward Constance. "She could at least buy something."

I pulled a five out of my apron and slapped it on the counter. "Here. You're the one who told her she wasn't welcome."

He grumbled something unintelligible and pushed the money back at me. He'd just finished the beer when a commotion caught his attention by the pool tables. "Those fuckers again. I swear, I'm gonna break their faces."

I looked over, it was that idiot Chuck and his stupider wingman Todd. They'd managed an argument at least once a month or so when I worked here before, and apparently that hadn't changed.

Chuck yelled at an equally big guy in a cowboy hat and boots. Chuck knocked the guy's hat off, and the fight started.

Max hurried around the far end of the bar to break it up.

I grabbed some towels to wipe up the inevitable mess and walked in that direction.

Before I got there, Todd was on his ass, and Chuck was howling like a stuck pig.

Mr. Cowboy picked up his hat.

Constance had Chuck in an arm lock. "Now, you apologize to the man before I break your arm."

Todd stood and backed away.

Before Max could get there, Constance had made Chuck apologize, and Chuck and Todd were on their way to the door with her right behind.

I still had some beer to clean up, so I got busy.

Max made apologies to the two closest tables and offered them a round of drinks, which lightened everyone's mood.

When I made my way back to the bar a little later, Max pulled me aside. "What's her name?"

"Constance."

"Well, she's all right. Tell Constance tomorrow that she's welcome back in here anytime, even if she only buys an iced tea."

I smirked. "I'll tell her."

"And tell her thank you from me. The last time those two got into it with the cowboy, it cost me two chairs."

"I'd tell her that too, but I'm not allowed to text on duty."

"Don't be smart with me."

I slid into the kitchen and typed out my message. It was time to leave well enough alone.

ME: Max says thanks

Another immediate response followed.

CONSTANCE: no problem

She was the best.

I pocketed my phone and went back to my tables.

A half hour later, Maria came looking for me. "Max wants two more cases of beer from the back." Every night, Maria seemed to think I was the only one capable of carrying a box of beer bottles. It seemed to be her version of new-hire hazing, even though I had worked here for years before leaving.

"As soon as I fill this drink order."

She nodded and left for the kitchen while I visited the bar for margaritas and a beer.

Done with my tables for the moment, I went through the kitchen to the dark hallway with Max's office and the storeroom.

Maria unlocked the storeroom door for me. "He wants two boxes."

I went inside and flipped the switch. The light didn't come on. Max had told Joey to change it, and in typical Joey fashion, it wasn't done yet.

Behind me, the back loading door squeaked open.

After a few seconds of acclimating my eyes to the dim light, I located the beer boxes along the wall. A faint skunk scent wafted in the air.

Another skunk had gotten run over in the back alleyway or some dog had gotten sprayed.

I leaned over to pick up the top box.

A hand grabbed my hair, yanking me back, and another brought a cloth to my mouth. The cloth was wet and sickly sweet.

I tried to scream, but the cloth and a hand muffled my attempt.

I struggled against the hand holding the cloth over my mouth. It was large and rough, definitely a man.

Moments later my knees buckled.

The world went dark.

# CHAPTER 34

*Zack*

CONSTANCE'S NAME APPEARED ON MY PHONE AS ITS ANNOYING RING STARTED.

"Hey, Constance—"

She cut me off. "Do you know where Brittney is?"

I sat up. "With you at work, I thought." I checked my watch. It wasn't closing time yet. My mind started going in all the wrong directions.

"She skipped out. Did she tell you anything?"

My heart stopped. "Not a thing. Yesterday she was complaining about how confining this all was, but she seemed resigned to it when she left with you."

"Fuck. We need Winston. Her car is still here in the parking lot. The owner, Max, came out to tell me she went out the back door and didn't come back."

"How long ago?"

"From what I got from Max, less than an hour. He was pissed she skipped out on the tables."

"That doesn't sound like Brittney. No matter what, she would have seen to it somebody took care of the customers."

The pit in my stomach grew. Brittney took her job responsibilities seriously. She would never up and leave unless it was an emergency.

"She didn't call or text?"

I paced back and forth. "Not in a while. She said she'd text when she left work." That was another thing—Brittney had committed to text me, and she wouldn't blow me off like that. "What about the pendant?"

"That's what doesn't make sense. If she was forced to leave, the range on that is a mile or so. She would have had plenty of time to press the button."

I slammed my hand on the table. "What do we do now?"

"Her phone's off, so I can't get a location on her. I'll call Winston to see if he can get a bead on her with any surveillance cameras in the area."

"What can I do?"

"Just sit tight. If she just bugged out for some privacy, she'll probably call you, or show up, and you need to be there when she does."

"I will. Keep me up to date."

"Of course." She hung up.

I was sweaty, and my legs felt jittery. This wasn't fight or flight, this was fight *and* fight some more. Only I had no target to vent my anger on. Delgado was in Sacramento, maybe.

Scrolling through my phone, I located the app and tried to ping Brittney's phone's location. No luck, just as Constance had said. There was no current location data, only her last location at the Rusty Bucket.

Kicking the leg of the table earned me a sore toe, but no change in the app's ability to find her.

*What the fuck?*

Could she really have run off to get some peace and quiet like she'd threatened? The sour state of my stomach told the answer. I didn't believe that for one stinking minute. She was obstinate and impetuous, but leaving her car didn't make sense—that was a stupid move, and she wasn't stupid.

BRITTNEY

As I blinked my eyes open, a wave of nausea rolled over me. I closed them again.

The putrid smell of skunk was unmistakable.

The lurch of the floor bumped my head against the cold surface and hurt my hip.

My moan of pain and frustration didn't escape the tape over my mouth. All I managed was a loud hum.

I went to rub my eyes, but couldn't. My hands were tied together and connected somehow to my feet. My heart started to race.

The floor bounced again, and I blinked my eyes open a second time.

The sound, the movement, the dim light, the metal wall in front of me—I was being driven, in a van.

Slowly, I started to process my surroundings.

Maria lay on the floor facing me, bound in duct tape with her mouth taped as well. Her eyes bugged out, and she shook her head slightly, telling me not to—not to what?

I had no idea.

She lay between me and the driver.

The vehicle slowed to a stop and started again. A stoplight passed through the portion of the windshield I could see beyond Maria. It was still night, or nighttime again.

As we passed under a streetlight, I made out the driver, a man. The passenger seat was empty.

I craned my head to look behind me. The nausea that returned in force told me that was not a good idea. I was near the back of the work van. It was just the two of us in here.

My pendant. I tried, but couldn't pull my hands up high enough to reach it. I pulled up, but they pulled against my ankles, and I couldn't pull my feet up enough to reach.

I was such an idiot. Instead of struggling against the hand holding the cloth to my face, I should have reached for my pendant to signal Constance.

It was my fault we were in this situation. I should have gone for the pendant. Why hadn't I?

Constance would have flattened this asshole, or better yet, shot him in the head. Scratch that—in the nuts, then the head. That's what he deserved, whoever he was.

The driver started to whistle softly.

I knew that from somewhere, but where? I closed my eyes and concentrated. I knew that whistle.

My eyes jerked open with the realization.

Delgado.

The two days I'd spent at the trial, he'd whistled like that each time he was taken out of the courtroom.

Luis Delgado was the driver. This couldn't get any worse. First Todd, and now me and Maria.

A skunk hadn't gotten run over behind the restaurant—it had been him coming in through the back door. He'd gotten the skunk package Zack had meant for our local juvenile delinquent. Delgado had been behind the brick through my window. Somehow he'd known I'd come back to town only days after I'd arrived.

He turned his head back toward us.

I shut my eyes and played possum.

The van stopped and started again before I chanced another glance. There was no way I could stand and get to the door, much less open it or run if I got it open.

Controlling my breathing was becoming difficult, but with my mouth taped up, there were only so much air I could get in through my half-plugged nostrils.

Yelling for help was a non-starter with this stupid tape.

How long would it be before Constance noticed I wasn't in the Bucket anymore? How long had it already been? Neither of those questions had an answer. Where was he taking us?

If only I'd accepted Zack's offer to come tonight. What could I do?

My God, I needed Zack. There was so much I hadn't told him. So much I wanted to tell him.

If Zack was here, he'd have an idea. What would Zack do?

First thing, Zack would have been smart enough to hit the emergency pendant. Or maybe not—maybe Zack would have overpowered Delgado.

I closed my eyes, and for a moment I envisioned how the fight would've played out. Delgado would be a whimpering mess on the floor in a few seconds flat. I wanted to smile, but the tape prevented it.

Zack would have saved me. Zack would have kept me safe.

*Why are you wasting time, girl? Get it together. You have to rely on yourself right now. Zack's not here.*

I'd just wasted valuable time wishing for what I couldn't have instead of figuring out what to do. Zack would tell me to make a plan for the future. Visualize it, and make it happen.

I tried using my tongue to wet the tape near my lips to loosen it. But my saliva was no match for the industrial-grade tape. It wasn't loose enough for me to try to bite through either.

What did they do in the movies? They found something sharp to rub against to cut the rope or the tape.

He turned to look at us again, and I played comatose one more time, counting to ten in my head before venturing to crack an eyelid open.

As often as he was checking on me, there was no way I could move toward the back wall and feel for a sharp edge. Unconscious women stayed put, and that's what I was pretending to be. It was the safest course of action—or inaction —at the moment.

The chain on the emergency pendant settled down my shirt, out of reach. I used my chin against my neck to pull on the chain. It moved just a bit. Another scrunch move, and it slipped to where I couldn't reach it with my chin.

"I see you're awake," his evil voice came from the front.

*Fuck.*

I hadn't checked to be sure he was eyes-forward when I tried to the pull the chain.

"You bitches and I are going to have a nice, long talk. I want that key."

I shivered.

I didn't have the key. How could I give him what I didn't have?

I was fucked. We were fucked. Poor Maria. It was all my fault for not pressing the pendant.

473

# CHAPTER 35

*B*RITTNEY

THE VAN STOPPED.

I could see a roll-up door moving through the windshield.

Delgado drove us in after it finished opening. He turned the engine off and got out.

The sound of the mechanical door closing came through the van's walls, and the lights came on outside the van.

I closed my eyes, dreading what would come next. I'd tried to use my chin to pull the pendant within reach—without success.

The sound of the van's back door opening behind me got me to open my eyes.

With a forceful yank, he rolled me over to face the back.

He had a knife in one hand. "You and I are going to have a little talk." The darkness in his eyes was pure evil, and the grin as he spoke was a bad sign. He ripped the tape off my mouth.

I trembled.

People who said it was easy if you ripped it off all at once were definitely wrong. It felt like my skin had been ripped off.

"I don't know anything," I mumbled.

He laughed. "Then this is going to be a very long night. I want the key."

"But I don't have it."

He waved the knife slowly. "In prison, we had a debate about how many cuts the body could endure. *Mi amigos,* they thought one hundred. I told them two hundred at least. Maybe tonight I find out." He laughed again.

I tried to squirm away from him, but ended up against Maria behind me.

He brought the knife to my shoulder. "Hold still, or this will be worse." He cut me with a quick slice.

I screamed at the pain.

"Only one hundred and ninety-nine more to go." The evil laugh reappeared.

I was going to die in here, and nobody could help me. Zack, Constance, Winston—none of them knew where I was.

He grabbed for my purse, which I hadn't realized was by my feet, and turned it upside down on the metal floor. "Is it in here?"

I shook my head, but didn't speak.

He rummaged through the contents that had spilled out. After a minute, he was convinced the key wasn't in my purse.

I started to hyperventilate.

"Is it at your house?"

That was my one chance.

I shook my head vigorously.

"No? I don't believe you. The house it is." He'd taken the bait.

I could only hope Zack and Winston could help if he took me to the house.

Delgado tore off a fresh section of tape, and I was once again gagged.

My shoulder stung.

The van door slammed shut.

~

*Z*ACK

It had been a half hour since Constance's last call when the phone lit up with her name again.

"I've canvassed the nearby streets, the coffee shops, and the diner. There's no sign of her in the vicinity," Constance told me over the phone. "Is there anybody she could have gone to see?"

I wracked my brain. "None that come to mind. Her sister is still out east. I'll join you, and we can cover twice as much ground."

"Not a good idea. I've called my boss, and he has two other agents on the way to help me. You need to cover the house. She could return there to pick up clothes or something. You should wait and watch."

Her advice sounded rational. It assumed that Brittney had left on her own and was dodging her security, and probably me too.

"Okay," I answered reluctantly. I hated being inactive.

Ten minutes later, I left my spot in the front room and went back to the kitchen for something to drink.

I chose grapefruit juice. A small gesture toward what Brittney would have wanted seemed like the right thing to do.

After rinsing the glass in the sink, I flicked the kitchen light off to return to the front. That's when I noticed the dim kitchen light on next door at Brittney's house.

It hadn't been on before. She was back.

My heart leaped in my chest.

Movement—I caught movement I couldn't make out. Running to the switch, I doused the lights in the TV room so I could see next door more clearly, and she wouldn't be able to see me.

Two people. No, three.

Brittney, another woman, and a man.

The man turned my way.

The red star tattoo on his forehead was unmistakable—Delgado, and he was waving a gun and a knife in Brittney's face, then the other woman's.

My stomach soured.

If fucking Winston hadn't confiscated my gun, I'd be able to take him, but now I had to do it unarmed.

I rushed to my phone and redialed Constance. "He's here, and he has Brittney and another woman."

"Slow down, Zack." I heard the screech of tires over the phone. "I'm headed your way. Tell me what you see."

Breathlessly I recounted it. "Delgado is here. He's got Brittney in the kitchen with another woman. He has a gun, and he's waving a knife in their faces too."

Constance was cool under pressure. "I'll get LAPD SWAT there as soon as I can. Don't make a move. The most dangerous thing you could do is try to take him on by yourself. Leave this to the professionals. I have to hang up now to call the police. You keep an eye on what's happening from your house. Call me with any change." She clicked off.

No fucking way was I sitting still while that whack-job had my woman.

I ran my fingers through my hair.

*Need a plan.*

I ran back to my darkened kitchen.

They were all still in Brittney's kitchen at the back of the house. The front was dark. I grabbed a big carving knife from the knife block, then decided I needed something easier to wield and chose a six-inch chef's knife, one I'd sharpened this week.

My plan was idiotic—bringing a knife to a gun fight—but if I snuck in through the front of the house and got behind him before he saw me, I stood a chance. It was my only chance. The only chance we had, and doing nothing was not a plan, not an option.

476

I walked calmly toward my front door. "Control your breathing, dickhead. You have to sneak up on him," I said to the empty room.

I found my key to her house on my key ring. I was prepared. I opened my front door and found what I was *not* prepared for.

Piss Boy.

He backed away from the door and eyed the knife I was carrying. "Calm down, man. I brought the letter." He held up an envelope. "I just want my phone."

Change of plan. He was just what I needed. I slid the knife in my back pocket. "Cool. Your phone is next door."

"You said here," he complained.

"I left it next door," I told him. I pointed to Brittney's house. "I've only got a key to the back door. You go to the front door, and I'll go in through the back."

"Why don't I come with you?"

"Because I said so, that's why."

He huffed, but didn't argue again.

"You go to the front door and ring the doorbell in two minutes. Ring it twice then get off the porch. Got it?"

"Yeah, man."

"Doorbell, two minutes, then off the porch" I repeated as I passed him to descend the stairs.

"Whatever." He followed me down the steps.

We'd taken to locking the back gate between the properties, so I scurried down her drive and around the gray van that had to be Delgado's. Sliding silently to the back steps, I climbed them, skipping the creaky one. It was a short crawl across the porch to the back kitchen door. Two panes of its glass were broken. That had to be how he'd gotten in.

"I don't know where it is." I heard Brittney crying clearly through the broken door.

"I'm going to cut you again. Every time you give me a wrong answer," Delgado yelled.

Brittney screamed.

It was all I could do to hold back and not break in, but a gun against a knife wouldn't end well, and that wouldn't save Brittney.

I heard the doorbell ring.

"Who's that?" Delgado asked frantically.

"I don't know."

"Maybe it's your boyfriend, and he can join us. We'll have a little party, the four of us. Maybe you tell me when I start cutting *him*."

The doorbell rang again.

I heard footsteps and chanced a peek through the window.

Delgado was going to the front door as I'd hoped he would.

I silently turned the key in the deadbolt, just in case. Leaving the key in the door, I twisted the handle and pulled the door partly open.

Neither of the girls had noticed me yet. They both had their wrists duct-taped to the arms of the chairs, and their feet to the legs.

I clamped my hand over Brittney's mouth from behind. "Shhh." I turned her head to me and took my hand away. She had two short bloody cuts on her shoulder.

The other woman coughed.

I turned to her and put a finger to my lips to silence her.

I quickly cut Brittney's hands loose.

"You came," she mumbled with tears in her eyes.

My heart was pounding so hard I could barely hear her. "Shhh," I reminded her.

I could hear Delgado arguing with Piss Boy. "Get the fuck outta here."

I cut Brittney's legs loose. "Leave," I said quietly nodding toward the open door.

"Not without Maria." She had to choose the worst possible time to be obstinate.

"Not till I get the phone," Piss Boy yelled. "The guy said he'd give me back my phone."

I cut at the tape securing the woman's wrists.

She yelped in pain.

I'd been careful not to nick her, but I slowed my cutting just the same.

The front door slammed.

I pushed Brittney toward the door and shifted to Maria's legs.

Brittney didn't budge.

I'd gotten the second of Maria's legs loose when the shot rang out.

It splintered the floor in front of me.

Looking up, I found Delgado in the doorway, his gun pointed right at me. I had a knee down to reach Maria's ankle, and Delgado was too far away for me to lunge from this position and have a chance.

"The next one goes through your boyfriend," he yelled from the doorway.

# CHAPTER 36

*BRITTNEY*

DELGADO WAVED THE GUN TOWARD THE CORNER WITH THE PANTRY. "CLOSE THE door, and over to the corner, all of you."

Moving on jittery legs, I closed the door and followed the other two.

This was going from terrible to horrific in a hurry.

Zack had wanted me to save myself, but I couldn't leave him and Maria here with this monster.

Delgado moved back. "Slide the table over in front of the door."

Zack moved slowly, eyeing Delgado every second. He pushed the table to block our escape through the back door.

Delgado slid a chair toward the sink. "Now tape the fat one to the chair, and we can continue our little conversation."

Maria sneered at him, but moved to the chair and sat.

Zack lifted the roll of duct tape from the counter, keeping his eyes glued to Delgado.

"You are going to tell me where the key is," Delgado said, his dark eyes glaring. "I guarantee it." He trained the gun on me, then Zack, then back to me again.

"I think you should," Zack said, drawing Delgado's attention.

What the hell was he thinking? Zack knew I didn't have a clue; we'd talked about it.

Delgado smiled. Zack's comment pleased him as much as it tormented me. "Tape her to the chair." He waved his gun at Maria and Zack.

Zack started rolling the tape around Maria's wrist and the arm of the chair. "Tell him about the safe," he told me, nodding toward the pantry.

Delgado pivoted to me. "Yes, tell me about the safe, bitch. Where is it?" The amusement in his face went up a notch.

I looked to Zack. How could he be doing this?

He winked.

Confusion tinged my terror. I didn't get what Zack was up to, but he had something in mind.

"So where's the fucking safe?" Delgado asked again.

Zack nodded toward the pantry. "In there."

Delgado waved his gun, motioning me away. "Move."

I slid down the counter, looking toward Zack for a clue.

Delgado opened the pantry door, keeping his gun pointed in our direction.

Zack mouthed something I couldn't make out as Delgado turned away.

I shrugged. Not risking a word, I mouthed *what*? I still couldn't lip-read his indecipherable message.

Delgado opened the door wider and turned back to us. "Open it," he commanded.

My legs were shaking as I went to the pantry and knelt in front of the safe. Damned if I could remember the combination Grams had told us once.

"I don't remember the combination." I looked back to Zack for a clue as to what he meant to accomplish with this.

Delgado's evil grin returned. "You better." He pointed the black gun toward Zack's knees. "Or he won't ever walk again."

Zack's face showed a confidence I couldn't echo. He nodded toward the floor twice when Delgado looked back at me.

I turned back to the safe and started twirling the knob. Doing something was better than nothing.

Grams had told us the combination as little girls, and it had been a birthday, but I couldn't remember whose.

"Don't you remember? You waved it in my face the night you came back," Zack said from behind me.

I looked back. "What?"

Zack's eyes shifted to the floor. "You waved it around."

Big help he was. He was hallucinating.

Then I caught on.

He wanted me to stall.

I turned back to the black steel box.

"I'm not waiting forever," Delgado said.

I raised my arms. "Quiet," I yelled. "I need to think."

"Faster," Delgado spat.

A birthday, and it had a seven in it.

480

I ran through our birthdays, including Grams's and Gramps's. No sevens popped up.

Fuck, I was sure she'd said a birthday.

What other birthday could it be?

I moved a container of colored sprinkles out of the way. Red, white, and blue. The answer was simple. Our country's birthday—seven, four, seventy-six.

I spun the wheel four times to the right, stopping at seven, then back around to the four, and back toward seventy-six. As I did, I saw what Zack had been hinting about on the floor beside the safe.

I shifted right to conceal the can before twisting the knob the final bit to seventy-six. Praying silently that I'd gotten it right, I tried the handle, and it turned with a satisfying clunk, unlocking the door.

"I got it." I didn't open the steel door.

"Let me see," Delgado demanded.

I turned and palmed the can, hiding it behind me as I rose.

"Out of the way," he said, approaching, eager to see the interior of the safe.

I slid sideways and waited. When he got close, I stepped to the side, raised the can, and gave him a full dose of pepper spray, right in the eyes.

He squealed as his hands went to his face.

Zack charged from behind, slamming him against the pantry door, and the gun skittered across the floor.

The two men threw fists.

I lunged for the gun.

Zack fell back from a wicked punch.

Delgado, his eyes closed from the stinging spray, lunged in our direction, a knife in hand, flailing at the empty space between us.

I raised the gun and pulled the trigger.

The explosive recoil ripped the gun from my hand.

Delgado fell back.

Maria screamed and leaped up, dragging the chair by the arm taped to her wrist.

Zack pulled me to the far wall and cradled me in his arms. "You're okay." He kicked the gun away.

Maria pulled the knife from the floor and cut at the tape holding her to the chair.

"I thought you'd never figure it out," Zack said in my ear.

Maria finished cutting herself loose from the chair. With the knife still in her hand she screamed, "You killed my brother."

Her eyes were wild, and anger filled her face. She stooped to pick up the gun.

Zack shoved me out of the room toward the front. "Run."

I ran for the front room, and a shot rang out. Bits of plaster from the wall stung my face.

Zack was right behind me when Constance appeared in the doorway. She raised her gun at me, shifted right, and fired.

As I reached her, she pushed me and Zack to the side. "Get outside." She advanced toward Maria on the floor.

I looked back, and she kicked the gun Maria had been holding to the side before holstering her gun. "Call an ambulance."

She rolled Maria over and applied pressure to her shoulder.

"Delgado's in the kitchen," Zack told her.

"Get outside," she repeated.

I was so hyped up on adrenaline I couldn't tell how long it took for us to be swarmed by LAPD officers and paramedics. It seemed immediate, but it probably wasn't.

# CHAPTER 37

*Zack*

The first two paramedics rushed inside, and I grabbed the next one I saw for Brittney. "Here. Over here. She's bleeding."

The cops were everywhere. A guy in a suit jacket, probably a detective, gave directions to the uniforms.

Paramedics wheeled Delgado out on a gurney.

"I'm going to get you," he said through the oxygen mask. The look he gave us was pure evil.

If that day ever came, I wanted my Sig back from Winston. Delgado had been let out of prison once, so there was honestly no telling what might happen in the future, but I would be ready. We would be ready.

Brittney shivered in my arms—not from any cold, but from fear and the massive amount of adrenaline this horrific night had induced. After a few minutes the paramedic began cleaning and bandaging her shoulder.

"The cuts are clean," he told her. "If you get theER at the hospital to stitch you up tonight, I don't think the scars will be noticeable after a while."

"Thanks," she replied.

The guy in the suit came over after talking with Constance for a minute. He asked our names and introduced himself as Detective Ryan, handing me a business card.

"Miss Clark, I'm glad you're all right."

"Thanks," she answered.

"Sir. You were in the house when this happened?"

"Yeah."

"I'm going to need a statement. Could you please come with me for a moment?"

I didn't budge. "I'm not leaving her." "Sir, two people have been shot. You need to step over here, please."

Brittney patted my leg. "It's okay. Go."

Reluctantly, I rose and followed the detective.

I ran through the sequence of events while he took notes.

"Miss Collier told us she advised you to wait for us to arrive. Why didn't you?"

"It looked too risky. I thought I could get them out of there with a distraction."

"That didn't work out so well, did it?"

"Only because Maria alerted him while I was cutting her loose."

"How?" He checked his notes. "You didn't mention that earlier."

"Sorry. I probably went too fast. When I was cutting her loose, she yelled like I'd cut her. That brought Delgado back to the kitchen early."

"But you hadn't cut her?"

"No, but I didn't know it at the time. We didn't know she was his sister."

"You said that. And you put the local boy you sent to the front door in danger as well."

I nodded. I hadn't considered that in my rush to help Brittney.

"Tonight could have ended very badly for all involved because you didn't wait."

"I made my choice, and it's done. I did what I thought was best at the time. I'm not going to spend a lot of time second-guessing myself."

"That's your prerogative, Mr. Benson."

He asked a few more questions about details of my statement, and I answered them.

"One thing I still don't understand…" He closed his notebook. "Why do you think she didn't give him the key?"

"Because there is no key—at least not one Brittney knows anything about."

"That's obviously not what Mr. Delgado thinks. Guys like him are dangerous, but they kidnap people for a reason. He thinks there's a key, and he thinks she knows where it is."

I shrugged. "I can't help that."

~

*BRITTNEY*

ZACK RETURNED TO ME AFTER ANSWERING DETECTIVE RYAN'S QUESTIONS.

Shortly after that, Constance finished with another detective and came to sit with me, too.

"You should have hit the pendant," she said.

That was an ode to obviousness.

"I didn't have time," I lied. "He drugged me with something." Also, I hadn't been thinking clearly enough. I'd probably had time, but I didn't have the right instinct. I'd fucked up, pure and simple.

"Why was the other waitress chasing you with a gun?"

"Maria, that's her name, said Delgado was her brother."

Constance nodded. "That explains a lot."

"Will she be all right?"

"Looks that way to me. I only winged her. You two were in the way, and it was the best I could do under the circumstances. Delgado's injury doesn't look life threatening either. You guys did good."

The anger welled up in me, thinking about poor Todd and what Delgado had been about to do to us. "I wish I'd killed him."

"No. Trust me, you don't. It seems right in the moment, but it would haunt you for a long time."

Her words made sense. I shouldn't want to sink to his level. I still needed to cool off from the horror of tonight.

"Did you ever?" I asked.

She didn't respond. Her eyes told the story, though. She'd advised me about regret from personal experience.

I switched subjects. "I forgot to thank you."

"It's the job," she said, tilting her head. "But I appreciate it. Three years on the First Lady's detail, and that never happened."

"A situation like that?"

"No." She laid a hand on my arm and smiled. "A thank you."

I reflected for a moment on how that must have felt to her, giving up a normal life to keep somebody else safe, and not getting any gratitude in return. No wonder she left that job.

"I saw an open safe in the kitchen. Is that where the key was?" Constance asked, fishing for an explanation.

"There is no key. The safe was empty except for some old papers. It was just a diversion to get to the pepper spray."

"Not to worry." She smiled. "It's all over now except the nightmares. Delgado and his sister won't be seeing daylight for quite a while."

The nightmares comment didn't help. It had taken long enough to get past them after Todd's disappearance.

"Will they be out on bail?"

"Not a chance. Kidnapping and assault? No way."

Her confidence was reassuring. I didn't relish hiding again.

Detective Ryan came back, this time accompanied by Detective Swenson, who I'd dealt with years ago during Delgado's murder case.

"Miss, Detective Swenson will be taking your statement."

Zack didn't looked pleased to let me go.

I walked with Swenson, and we settled on the front room couch.

"I thought you left the country," he started.

"Well, I'm here now." I hadn't trusted anyone but my family with the truth, and I didn't care to go into that with him.

"Miss Spear, let's start by having you walk me through the events as you remember them."

"It's Clark now," I corrected him.

He took a note, obviously surprised.

"I changed it after the trial," I explained.

"I didn't know."

"Nobody did."

"Well, Delgado obviously did," he retorted.

I'd been thinking about this, and now it made sense. "He didn't either. I only came back to town a couple weeks ago, but I went back to work at my old restaurant."

"And?" he asked.

"Maria, his sister, took my application paperwork. She knew me from before, and the application had my new name and this address. I never knew she was his sister."

"When did you find that out?"

I huffed. "Tonight when she screamed that I'd shot her brother, and then came after us with a gun."

We went over the events of the night three times before he let me get back to Zack and Constance.

～

ZACK

THE EVENING DRAGGED ON. NOW THAT BRITTNEY AND I HAD BOTH BEEN QUESTIONED, I hoped we'd soon be free to go.

I wrapped her in a tight embrace. "You're still shaking."

"A little. But it's getting better. I've never been so scared."

"I've got you now, Sunshine."

She looked up at me, and her smile told the story before her words did. She nestled her head against my shoulder. "I know."

"You two can go now," Detective Ryan said as he approached.

Brittney disengaged herself from me. "Can I have my purse back?"

486

"Purse?" he asked.

"It was in the back of the van."

Ryan backed up. "I'll check to see if it's been processed yet." He moved down the driveway.

"I'll bet you could use a glass of wine," I told her.

"Make mine a bottle."

Detective Ryan returned with her purse and told us again that we could leave.

"Not so fast," Constance told us.

With what we owed her tonight, I wasn't arguing.

She jogged to her Denali and returned carrying a gun.

It took an okay from the detective for her to get past the cop at the sidewalk.

"They took my piece…evidence," she told us. "Now we can go."

"You don't need to babysit me anymore," Brittney complained.

Constance addressed me. "I've learned that often the most dangerous time is directly after an attack." I knew she was telling me because I was the one contracting them.

"Do you think Sacramento was a deliberate red herring?" I asked.

"That would be my guess," she replied.

Brittney wrung her hands.

None of this made me more comfortable, especially the thought that there could be someone else out there.

"I'll drive," Constance offered. "We still need to get you to the ER for those stitches."

THE ER VISIT HADN'T TAKEN LONG AT THIS TIME OF NIGHT, AND CONSTANCE HAD been with us the whole time. Brittney and I had each already downed a glass of wine and were on our second when Winston finally arrived back at the house.

He had aborted his trip to Sacramento after hearing about Brittney's disappearance.

His return gave Constance the right to pour herself a glass of wine, down it, and pour a second. "I gotta catch up to you guys," she explained.

Brittney scrolled through the movie choices after her second glass of wine.

"Stop," Constance called. "Go back two. Yeah, that one."

Brittney shot me a grin.

"Constance has earned the right to pick tonight," I told her.

Brittney nodded and punched the button. *Sweet Home Alabama* started up.

Constance settled into the couch. "Ever since *Legally Blonde*, I love her movies."

A minute later someone knocked on the door, and Winston rose to answer it —with his gun, of course.

"Winston, put that thing away." My sister Serena's voice sounded from the front of the house.

With loud footsteps, she hurried our way. "I heard what happened. Are you okay?" she asked Brittney.

Brittney leaned against me. "Thanks to these two. Just a few stitches is all."

Constance hoisted her glass. "The good guys won this one." She took a gulp.

Serena looked at me and laughed. "I heard it was the good gals. Brittney shot one, and Constance shot the other one." She pointed at me. "Saving your ass."

I shrugged. "What can I say? I surround myself with strong women."

Constance rose and took the chair. "Have a seat," she said to Serena.

Serena shoved my shoulder to get me to make room, and Brittney and I moved down.

I ended up with women on both sides of me.

Serena insisted on talking over the movie. "I wish you'd killed him. He deserves it after what he did to poor Jonas," she said.

This was the first time my cousin's name had come up in years.

Brittney looked as perplexed as I was.

"What do you mean?" I asked.

"Delgado was Jonas's dealer, sold him the stuff that killed him." Serena leaned forward to talk around me. "Jonas is, was, a cousin of ours. Died of an overdose. Not something the family talks about much."

"You sure Delgado was his dealer?" I asked.

"Absolutely. Didn't you know that?"

"Didn't pay attention, I guess," I said.

Jonas had steered himself down his own road of self destruction, and she was right, it wasn't a topic we dwelled on.

"It's a good thing she only clipped him," Constance interjected. "The guilt of actually shooting a man is not something you want to wish on her."

"I still say he deserves a bullet." Serena sat back. "I love this movie."

Ten minutes later, my sister elbowed me. "I came over to see that you were all right too."

I squeezed her shoulder. "Thanks."

She did care, and it meant a lot to me.

We had to pause the movie several times as the family grapevine activated and my phone rang. One by one my parents, brothers, and my other sister called to see how we were doing.

# CHAPTER 38

*BRITTNEY*

I WOKE TUESDAY MORNING WITH A MILD HEADACHE. I SHOULDN'T HAVE LET ZACK switch us to red wine. Or maybe it had been Constance who'd requested red—anyway, it had been a bad idea.

Last night had been a late one.

It had taken several glasses of wine and two movies to relax from the terror of the evening.

By three in the morning, I'd finally been calm enough to sleep.

Zack's side of the bed was empty. I dragged myself out to join him.

"Morning, sleepyhead," he said as I wandered into the kitchen. He pulled a plate with a stack of waffles from the oven. "Been keeping these warm for you."

"Thank you."

Winston was parked in what I called the TV room on the couch, hunched over his laptop.

Zack brought over bowls of sliced papaya without me having to bug him.

I took a seat. "Hey, Winston. Want to join us for breakfast?"

He waved me off. "Thanks, but I already ate."

"Where's Constance?"

Winston looked up from his computer. "She went to the police station—something about an extended interview about last night."

I put some of the papaya slices on my waffle and cut a bite, which I stuffed into my mouth. This morning was not about being a lady. The taste was heavenly.

Zack pointed his fork at me. "How's the shoulder?"

I stretched it. "Not bad. It's the keep-it-out-of-the-shower-for-a-few-days part that will bother me."

"You'll just have to let me give you a sponge bath."

I looked up to see the devilish grin I loved on him. "You won't have to twist my arm."

Serena appeared, wrapped in Zack's bathrobe. "I shouldn't have switched to red last night. It gives me a headache."

"Red is healthier for you than white," Zack countered.

I got up to pour her a glass of OJ. "I didn't realize you stayed over."

"I wasn't in any shape to drive."

"She's a lightweight," Zack added.

I handed her the glass of juice. "We have waffles and papaya, unless you want something else."

She slumped into a chair. "Sounds great, but I think I'll start with Advil."

My purse was still in here from last night. "Sure. Generic ibuprofen good enough?"

She nodded and drank some more juice.

I poured four tablets into my hand for her, and two more for me. I tried to swallow mine dry. That was a mistake. I raced for my juice glass before delivering the tablets to Serena.

Zack wolfed down his waffles. "I need to go into the office," he said between mouthfuls.

I had hoped for more alone time with him after last night, but office time was clearly becoming an issue with his father. A family-member boss was more understanding in some ways, but the leeway only extended so far.

Five minutes later, after a quick kiss, he was gone.

Serena leaned forward after the door closed. "Dad wants to talk to him about London. I think you'll like it there."

I jerked back. "What?"

She cocked her head. "Zack's next rotation."

Zack had mentioned that he was due to start his finance rotation at some point, but London had only come up as a trip he'd canceled weeks ago.

Serena forked a slice of papaya. "Dad told me he wants to move up the timing."

I waited for her to explain further.

She finished chewing. "I found it an amazing city when I was there. I think you will too."

The lump in my throat prevented me from swallowing the bite of waffle I'd taken. I finally got it down with a swig of juice.

Zack had kept this from me. Moving to another city was a big deal—another *country* constituted a gargantuan big deal, not the kind of thing you forgot.

After an awkward silence, Serena finished the last of her breakfast and took her plate to the sink. "I can stay longer if you want to talk."

"No, I'm fine."

"Okay. You've got my number. Maybe we could have lunch later this week."

"Sure," I answered.

I stood and brought my plate to the sink.

She gave me a hug and was off.

I went to wipe down the table. With Delgado and Maria in jail, I should have been feeling better than I was, but the London news hadn't thrilled me. I knew Zack had to do this rotation bit for his father, but my hygienist certification didn't extend to foreign countries. Being the hanger-on girlfriend waiting all day for my boyfriend to come home didn't appeal to me. And, that was even assuming he wanted me to come along. He hadn't told me about it. What did that say? Nothing good.

I was sick and tired of being told what to do, and the next command was going to be to uproot my life and go to England with him? Hell, I didn't even have a passport.

I washed a plate and moved it to the drying rack.

This discussion should include me, not just Zack and his father, shouldn't it?

As I went to place the glass in the drying rack, it slipped from my grasp, and as I lunged to catch it, I knocked my purse off the counter. I caught the glass, but the purse landed on the floor, its contents spilling across the hardwood. Like an idiot, I hadn't zipped it shut.

Kneeling, I gathered things and put them back into the bag one by one...until I got to the pink envelope—my penance envelope.

Whenever I wanted to torture myself, the contents of this envelope never failed. I unfolded the faded piece of paper within and read the names of the people I'd killed.

Twenty-seven in all. Twenty-seven people whose lives I'd cut short. Twenty-seven who would never see another sunrise, much less London. Twenty-seven sentences of damnation for me.

As imperfect as my life was, at least I was still alive.

This time as I read, I noticed something new. When I reached the thirteenth name, I burst into tears. I'd never known who it was until last night. His name had never been mentioned. I'd never considered that they could be related.

But the thirteenth name was Jonas Benson, Zack's cousin.

Karma could be incredibly cruel.

∽

*Zack*

. . .

491

THE LOOK ON WENDY'S FACE AS I APPROACHED SAID THIS WOULD NOT BE JUST another Tuesday morning at the office.

"I heard what happened." Her eyes searched my face. "Are you all right?"

"Now that it's over, yes."

"I already told Stanton you wouldn't be calling this morning."

"Thanks." That was one aggravation I didn't need today.

She stood and took our coffee mugs in the direction of the caffeine dispenser. "I'll get the coffee today. The usual?"

"Please."

I had only just settled into my seat and opened my email when Dad arrived and shut the door behind him.

"Sounds like a harrowing night."

"It was, but Brittney's safe now, and that's what matters."

He took a seat. "You can expect a call from your mother. She's as worried as sin about you."

I could tell Dad wasn't. As Bensons, we got up, dusted ourselves off, and moved on to the next challenge. That's what this had been in his mind—just another challenge.

"I'm glad you're safe. I was worried too," he added, forcing me to reevaluate his feelings for a second.

"Thanks, Dad. I've never been that scared."

"It's when our loved ones are in danger, that it's the worst."

"That's for certain."

He shifted in his chair. This visit hadn't been merely to see how I was doing. Typical Lloyd Benson. He would have rushed in instantly to help me last night, straight into gunfire if necessary. But today, that episode was over, and it was on to the next item of business. That was one thing he'd taught me well. Don't dwell on the past—look to the future and deal with it.

"You wanted to talk?" I asked.

He fidgeted, very unlike his usual self. "It's about London. Harold's controller there has just given his notice, and that's going to move up the timing of your move." He hadn't phrased it as a choice, because it clearly wasn't intended as one. The timing had just been decided for me.

"How soon?"

"A week, give or take. You can talk with Harold about the specifics."

One week wasn't tomorrow, but it was a lot less time than I'd counted on to break the news to Brittney.

He rose to leave, but stopped at the door. "Have you decided what you'll tell her?"

Somehow he knew I hadn't broached the subject with Brittney.

"Yes. I have."

He nodded and moved off down the hallway.

Wendy used Dad's departure as an opportunity to bring in my coffee.

I took a sip of the hot brew. "I need you to make me an appointment with Harry Winston."

Puzzlement crossed her face. "The name doesn't ring a bell."

"The jeweler."

She smiled as recognition lit her eyes. "Right away."

# CHAPTER 39

*Zack*

After turning onto Snakewood, I could see Winston up ahead carrying things. Getting closer, I realized he was carrying clothes and paintings from my house to Brittney's.

I pulled into my driveway and parked in front of the garage.

"Brit?" I called, letting myself in through the back.

I made my way to the front of my house.

Winston opened the door and came back in.

"What's going on?" I asked.

"She asked me to help move her things next door."

"Why?"

He shrugged. "That's above my pay grade. All I can tell you is she was crying, but it's not my place to pry. She's next door. Oh, and she fired us."

"Huh? She can't do that."

"She doesn't want protection anymore. And maybe you can talk to her about it, but we can't force her. Constance already left for a new assignment in Long Beach."

I bounded out the door and over to her house.

At the front door, I stopped. Instead of bursting in as I wanted to, I rang the bell.

A minute later footsteps approached the door, and she let me in. Her demeanor was cool, with downcast eyes.

"We have to talk," I said as I closed the door behind me.

I moved to get close enough to kiss her, but she backed off. A bad sign.

She put a hand on her hip. "Really? Do you have something you want to tell me?"

The tone and the attitude said I was walking into a buzz saw.

I pointed to her couch in the front room. "Sit down."

I regretted the wording, but not quickly enough.

"Stop telling me what to do. I'm sick of it."

"Sorry. I meant, can we please sit down?"

She crossed her arms over her chest. "I can talk standing up. And I'm sure it won't take long."

Everything about this exchange screamed danger. The buzz saw was ramping up.

I took a breath. "I got called into a meeting with my dad this morning."

She shifted her weight and huffed. "I bet he had something really important to tell you."

"Sort of. You remember I told you I was doing department rotations at the company, and the next one was in finance?"

She shifted to the other foot. "Sure, I remember. But somehow I don't remember you telling me it would be in London."

My mouth must have dropped.

"Don't look so surprised. Serena told me. She let the cat out of the bag because she thought you'd already told me, but it must have slipped your mind somehow. I'm sure it didn't seem that important to tell me you'd be leaving the country."

I moved toward her, but she backed away.

"It wasn't like that," I protested. This was going south in a hurry.

"Right. It never is when guys plan on leaving the girl."

"Stop that," I said loudly. "And listen."

"You can't come into my house and yell at me." She pointed to the door. "Get out."

"No."

"No? You've got some nerve."

I pulled the box out of my pocket.

"This is not going the way I wanted, but I'm not leaving until you answer my question."

Her eyes teared up at the sight of the jewelry box I held.

I opened the box. "I want you to marry me and come to London with me this Saturday."

She sniffed.

"Not necessarily in that order," I added.

Somehow I was screwing this up, and big time.

She didn't say anything.

I'd forgotten something important. I went down on one knee. "Brittney Clark, will you marry me?"

She sniffed again. "No."

*No?*

~

It was the most gorgeous princess-cut diamond I'd ever laid eyes on, and certainly ever would see.

But now everything was completely confused. He seemed sincere about wanting me to come with him to London this weekend, but he certainly hadn't given me much time or input on the decision. And then there was what I'd realized about my penance list.

I didn't even have a passport, but that wasn't the big problem.

How could I marry him after what I'd done?

It was the hardest thing for me to say, but I didn't have a choice other than telling him no.

He held out a hand. "I love you, Sunshine."

Sure, he said that now.

A typical guy move. They said it in high school when they tried to get inside your bra. They said it in college when they wanted to get in your pants.

He'd had opportunities before, and I'd longed for it. I would have welcomed it and cherished the words. But after realizing who the thirteenth name on that list belonged to, *I love you* was a phrase I couldn't bear to hear.

Zack wouldn't love me for long. Once he found out the truth, he couldn't. The feeling would still start with an L, but it would go from *love* to *loathing* and never change back. It couldn't after what I'd cost him.

The guillotine would come down on those feelings, and what we'd had, what we'd shared, would sink in the quicksand of hatred and regret. He could never forgive me. It would be better if he never knew. So as hard as it was, I repeated myself.

"I said NO. Now please leave."

His brow creased in confusion for a moment before it fell into disappointment, and he stood. He walked toward the door, but before he opened it, he looked back. "This discussion isn't over."

*Yes, it is.* I said the words mentally, unable to find the strength to utter them aloud. It was over—the discussion, the relationship, the future, all of it.

The door closed behind him, and with it all my hopes for a better future. Life sucked, and it was my fault. If only I hadn't run, if only I'd had the courage earlier. But this guilt would haunt me for the rest of my life.

I locked the door and walked into the kitchen. After opening a bottle of chablis, I grabbed a water glass. I needed a big sturdy cup for what I had planned. My tears flowed freely as I trudged up to my room. I chugged the first glass before falling onto my bed, a whimpering mess of a woman.

My phone rang.

I ignored it.

It went to voicemail. A rational conversation with anybody was out of the question right now. It was probably Zack anyway.

My entire life had come crashing down around me in less than a day.

My phone chimed with distinctive notes that meant my sister had sent me a text.

SAMANTHA: Please call

I realized my sister had been the call a minute ago, not Zack. But I still couldn't manage a conversation.

As hard as I tried, I couldn't outrun my past. Nothing could erase my sins, and all I could do now was deaden my senses enough to escape into sleep.

I turned off the phone and refilled my glass.

Another followed it a minute later.

# CHAPTER 40

*B*RITTNEY

I woke up Wednesday morning to knocking at the door, and the bell ringing over and over.

I stumbled to the stairs, but didn't descend them.

"Brittney, Sunshine, we need to talk." Zack's slurred voice came from outside the front door.

Talking to him would only make it worse, especially with him drunk. I couldn't even handle a sober Zack.

Silence was my only weapon at this point.

After a few more drunken tries, he gave up and left. At least I thought he left, but I didn't dare peek for fear he'd see me.

Avoidance was my strategy, but it wasn't working well enough.

How could I explain it to him? It would only cause him more pain, destroy any good memories of me he still held. Every time I tried to understand it myself, a buzzer sounded in my brain. A big red X flashed. Game over. Does not compute.

Living like this, next to him—with him constantly reminding me of my sins and me constantly reminding him of what could never be—would be a hell I couldn't endure. And it was one I shouldn't put him through.

Once again, despite what I might want, leaving was the only alternative. I had no choice. At least this time I had a way to finance it, thanks to Grams.

I left a quick message for Max that I wouldn't be in for a while, and that I'd call later. He deserved better, but right now I couldn't give him two weeks' notice.

I returned to my room to pack. I wouldn't need a lot. The rest of my things could wait here, including the boxes Lillian had sent from San Jose. I hadn't even unpacked those yet.

Two suitcases, a backpack, and a duffle later I had enough to do me for a month or so. Quickly checking the bathroom and my drawers, I came to my makeshift plastic jewelry bag and added that to the duffle.

Downstairs, I checked the windows before venturing out the back to load up my car. When I finished, I went back inside for the treasure that would finance my getaway. Pulling the painting down from the wall I'd just asked Winston to hang it on, I swaddled it in towels and tape to keep it safe.

The first gallery I stopped at thought I was joking, and I left when they decided my painting had to be stolen if I was in such a hurry to sell it.

The second wasn't much better. My grand plan was washing out. Showing up at galleries in my little shitmobile, looking like the out-of-work waitress I was, didn't get me anywhere.

At the third gallery, I tried a different tack.

The salesman's first response was the same as the others. "Madam, I think you might want to try an establishment closer to the beach."

Translation, some place that sold hundred-dollar prints to the masses, not a real art gallery. A place where the clientele wore shorts and sandals, not skirts and heels.

I looked down. I was in jeans and my black work shoes, definitely not the skirt and heels look.

The salesman looked bored.

I had one more card to play. "Mrs. Covington suggested this gallery, but if you don't have the wherewithal to evaluate my painting, perhaps I should try uptown."

"Mrs. Covington?"

I pulled Lauren Covington's card from my purse and handed it to him. "Yes. William Covington's wife. He's on the board of the museum, and I expected her suggestion would be a good one, but if she was mistaken—"

"Not at all." He interrupted before I finished the rest of my threat and handed back the card. "You should have mentioned you were referred by the Covingtons. Right this way, and we'll have a proper look at your piece."

He and an older man looked over the painting before bringing over a third.

A fair number of *oohs* and *aahs* passed between them as the towels were removed, and an under-the-breath mention of Bill Covington. After that, the older man went off to the corner to make a phone call.

After a few minutes they made an initial offer I knew was low, based on the research Zack had helped me with.

"Why don't we check the auction history for a moment first," I countered.

The older gent returned from his phone call and huddled with the other two for a moment.

"Perhaps eighty-five thousand would be a nice compromise," the old man suggested.

I waited for a few seconds, doing my best imitation of pensive before nodding. "That seems fair to me." It was actually on the high side of what Zack had estimated I might get for it.

A half hour later, the teller at my bank was calling the manager over to authorize an eighty-five-thousand-dollar deposit to my account, which probably showed an average balance a hundredth that size.

"This will require a five-day hold," the manager said.

"It's an in-state check," I pointed out. I handed him the gallery manager's card. "Please call Mr. Gundry to verify, if you wish."

One phone call and two minutes later, we settled on five hundred today and the remainder in three days. Bankers were the worst. I knew he wouldn't have treated Zack like this.

My gray envelope problem was finally behind me—goal accomplished. Samantha's schooling was safely secured, and my promise to Mom fulfilled.

The next step was up to Samantha. She'd do well. I was sure of it.

With money for gas and food, I had one stop remaining before I left town—the reason I had Lauren Covington's card in my purse.

I'd called this morning, and she'd graciously invited me to visit.

When I pulled into the circular drive off Wilshire, the massive black glass building seemed like it reached to the sky. I found a place to park and made my way to the door where—wouldn't you know it?—they had a doorman. In LA, nobody had doormen. That was a New York thing. In California we pumped our own gas and opened our own doors, but apparently not everybody.

The doorman's nametag read *Oliver*. "May I help you, miss?"

"I'm here to see Lauren Covington."

"And your name, miss?"

"Brittney. Brittney Clark."

He checked his clipboard. "Yes, Mrs. Covington is expecting you." He opened the large glass door for me. "Elevators are at the rear. Unit 2-2-1 on the twenty-second floor. It will be to your right as you exit the lift."

"Thank you, Oliver."

"My pleasure, Miss Brittney."

The large marble and stainless lobby would have put a good-sized bank to shame.

Inside the elevator, I pressed the button for twenty-two. The numbers didn't go any higher—no big surprise. My ears even popped on the way up.

Upstairs, Lauren had her door open, waiting for me.

Oliver had probably called ahead.

Little Wendell was on her hip. "Come on in. It's so good to see you again."

I passed through into the massive open space of their penthouse unit. "Thanks. You too."

"I heard about that horrific incident. That must have been terrible." Her eyes showed genuine concern.

"I'm trying to get past it," I told her.

I'd had my fill of talking about it. Reliving any of the time with Delgado was not something I cared to do.

She walked toward the kitchen. "Would you like anything to drink?"

I followed her. "Diet, if you have it." The kitchen was the size of my apartment.

"Diet Pepsi okay?"

"Perfect."

She pulled two cans from the massive refrigerator. And then a glass from the cupboard, followed by another. She dispensed ice from the door of the fridge. Everything was slowed by her having one arm around her baby.

Since I had two hands free, I popped the top and poured mine as well as hers.

She thanked me and added, "I hope Mr. Gundry treated you right." The call in the corner of the gallery must have been to her.

"Thank you. Yes, they were very helpful."

"A Wyeth is quite a nice painting to let go of."

I took a sip of my soda. "I need the money to pay for my sister's schooling."

"She's going to Wharton, I understand? That's an accomplishment to be proud of."

She was better informed than I'd expected, because I hadn't mentioned it at the Habitat weekend, that I could remember.

"We are."

She seemed to realize I was surprised. "Zack was bragging," she added. "That's how I knew."

"He has a big mouth."

"Mostly he was bragging about you. You have quite an admirer."

I felt the heat rise in my cheeks, even though I needed to stop caring what Zack said or did.

"You've got a keeper there. Zack's one of the good guys, through and through. A bit rough around the edges—sort of like my Bill—but sweet on the inside."

"He can be a little bossy."

She touched my arm and laughed. "Don't I know it. My Bill is the same sometimes. But trust me, it comes from the heart, and that's what matters."

Her laugh brought a big smile to her baby's face.

I was impressed by how every little while she'd tousle Wendell's hair, or bounce him on her hip.

"Would you like to hold him?"

I took in a breath. "I'm not sure. I've never…"

501

I'd never held anyone's baby before, although I'd admired them from a distance when one of the girls brought a child to work for a few minutes.

"Don't worry, he won't break." She hoisted him up. "Here."

I took him and situated him on my hip the way she had. "Are you sure?"

He didn't cry. Instead, he looked up at me and smiled.

"I could use the break, and he likes you."

The little guy grabbed at my shirt for a moment.

Lauren picked up her glass. "Want to go out on the patio?"

"Sure." I took a drink and followed her.

She snatched up a floppy sun hat on the way and plopped it on Wendell's head.

There was so much about being a mother I didn't know. I wouldn't have thought about the hat.

We sat outside, sipping our sodas as she asked and I answered her questions about Doug and Samantha, all while bouncing Wendell.

He was a happy baby, and I found myself wondering if my own would be as well behaved.

Talking with Lauren was easy, relaxing, comfortable.

Wendell was happy on my lap, looking around, but mostly at his mother.

"You said you were interested in using the lake cabin," she said after a while.

I hadn't wanted to bring it up right away and seem ungrateful: *give me the key —thank you—no, I can't stay—I have to go hide—bye.*

"Yes," I answered. "I need a little time away after everything that's happened."

"I think you'll find it's the perfect place to find peace. Did I tell you that's where Bill proposed to me?"

"No, you didn't."

"I'll tell you the story another day. I'm sure you and Zack will enjoy it."

I didn't tell her Zack wasn't coming. This didn't feel like the time. "Your description sounds lovely."

"It's the anti-LA, secluded and relaxing. I went there to escape and think." She laughed. "And I left having found love. The place is built for romance." Her eyes misted over. "I'll get you the key." She hurried off.

Wendell watched his mother leave, then fixed his gaze up at me and smiled and gurgled a happy sound.

I bounced him a bit while she was gone.

Lauren returned with the key and a slip of paper. "The address for Casa Nelson. The drive takes a little while. If you guys want to go today, you should leave soon."

I accepted the items. "Nelson?"

"We have such good memories from there, we didn't want to change a thing when we bought it, so we kept the old name," she explained.

I stood and balanced the baby on my hip. "Thank you so much."

502

Wendell grabbed for my breast this time.

"It's time for his next feeding. This part of a mother's job is never done." She giggled. She put her hands out, and I gave him up.

I thanked her again, and she told me we could stay up there as long as we wanted. I wondered if that would change when she found out Zack wasn't coming along.

I left the building with a baby-spittle mark on my shirt. I was now a certified baby handler, and happy to be one.

When I made it to the freeway, Siri told me to turn north, and I was on my way to the cabin and away from Zack.

Secluded and relaxing, she'd said. Just what I needed.

I woke the next morning to the sounds of birds outside. It had taken forever to get to sleep. Actually, it had taken me forever to get up and locate some wine so I could sleep.

I sipped my water and looked out through the cabin's full-length windows that faced the lake. I'd have to make a grocery run to get juice and fresh fruit. This morning water and oatmeal would have to do.

Lauren had said this place was relaxing, and I could see what she meant. The view of the lake, with gentle windswept waves lapping the shore and the mountains beyond, was very *un-LA*, as she had put it—simple country splendor of the kind we didn't see in the concrete jungle of the city. Birds flew by, and the occasional fish breached the surface to feed on unsuspecting insects. Nature on display.

I opened the sliding glass door to breathe in the fresh air. Closing my eyes for a moment, the warmth of the sun on my skin and the faint pine scent of the air had me remembering a kiss with Zack, except his body had provided the warmth and his hair the scent. Kissing him had always been wonderful.

I jerked my eyes open to banish the vision. I was here to forget Zack and get back to the old me, the pre-Zack me. The rational me that didn't believe in fairy tales. The me that understood how hard I had to work to get anywhere in life. The me that knew I deserved better than Benji, but the me that realized I would have to settle for a lot less than Zack.

Maybe somewhere in the middle of the alphabet, with someone like a Mark, or a Mason, or maybe a Matt, I could find better than Benji. Yes, an M-name wouldn't be as wimpy as Benji, or as bossy as Zack. Samantha would have an opinion on a good name to look for. It couldn't be any worse than the way I'd met men so far.

Someone knocked on the front door.

When I answered it, I stepped back a bit.

The old man had a shotgun under one arm and appraised me warily. "Good morning. The name's Sam Patterson. I'm two cabins up the lake. You friends of the Nelsons?" he asked.

He pointed down at the doormat that read Casa Nelson, same as the wooden sign above the door.

"No, Lauren Covington gave me a key." I fished out the house key to show him.

His demeanor immediately improved. "Good, 'cuz the Nelsons ain't lived here for years. I'm sort of the neighborhood watch on this part of the lake."

Apparently I'd passed his test. I nodded.

"Like to see that nobody's squattin' where they shouldn't be."

"Would you like to come in, Mr. Patterson?"

"That's very kind of ya, but maybe later. I got my rounds to make. You fish?" I shook my head. "No."

"Mighty good fishin' on this lake. I go out every day, if the weather allows."

He expounded on the joys of fishing for a few minutes, and explained that on occasion he also liked to walk the circumference of the lake. He excused himself after a while.

I closed the door.

Neighborhood watch with a shotgun. I was definitely not in LA anymore.

After my grocery run, I made myself a sandwich. I set out for a walk with a water, an apple, and two apricots in my backpack. Circling the lake sounded good.

# CHAPTER 41

*Z*ACK
*(Three days later)*

"W*HAT THE HELL DID YOU DO?*" S*ERENA SCREAMED AT ME, ANGERING THE FIRE ANTS* that had invaded my brain.

Just opening my eyes hurt. "Don't yell." I squinted, trying to sharpen the image in front of me. It was daytime, but that was all I could tell.

She held a mostly empty bottle of Jack. "You're a fucking imbecile."

I reached for the bottle, but missed and ended up on the floor. "Give me that."

"Winston, put him back on the couch."

*Winston?*

Suddenly, powerful hands lifted me and dumped me on the couch. It was Winston all right.

I held my head. The creatures in my skull didn't like being jostled. "Winston, what are you doing here?"

Serena answered for him. "I asked him to let me in. You haven't been to work and wouldn't answer the door or the phone. Dad said *'by whatever means necessary'*. Those were his words."

Winston chuckled and went to the kitchen.

Serena took the chair and scooted it to face me before sitting. "Tell me what the hell you did to her."

I shook my head. That was a bad idea. The fire ants hated being shaken. I put my hands to my temples to try to squeeze them out. "Did to who?"

Winston held out pills and a glass. "Here, swallow these."

505

I took them. But just my luck, it was orange juice.

"Brittney, of course. She went crying to Lauren and asked to use her cabin for a while to get away. I'm sure she meant away from you."

It was coming back to me...the terrible word she'd said.

NO.

I closed my eyes and lay down slowly. "How many days has it been?"

"Three. It's Friday. Now sit back up and answer the question."

"Stop telling me what to do."

Now I sounded like Brittney. I slowly righted myself to avoid being manhandled by Winston again.

"No fair ganging up on me."

Serena waved the bottle. "Judging by this bottle and the way you look, you need all the help you can get."

I started to stand. "Screw you. And Winston, I want my gun back."

He shoved me back down. "Not a chance. Not when you're like this."

I didn't know what he meant by *like this*, but I didn't care. The fire ants eating my brain prevented any real thought.

"Then get me a drink."

"No way," he shot back.

"What good are you?"

He smirked.

Right now it was a smirk I wanted to wipe off his face with a fist. Although I might have had a chance on a good day, I stood zero chance in this condition. One good hit from him would give a normal man a concussion.

Maybe that wasn't such a bad idea. A concussion might make the fire ants go away. Unconsciousness sounded better than the way I felt right now.

Serena got my attention by kicking my foot. "Tell us what happened. How did you fuck up so royally that she wants to leave?"

Putting the pieces together took a moment. "I asked her to come to London with me."

"And she didn't want to?" Serena asked.

"No. I don't think so."

"What do you mean you don't think so? How was she feeling about it before?"

I shrugged. "I dunno. I hadn't told her."

Serena kicked me again. "Why not, you dumbshit? You've known forever."

"I didn't know how to approach it, I guess."

"So you wait until just before you have to get on a plane to tell her? Smooth move, Romeo."

"I didn't know how."

"When you reiterated how much you love her, that must have helped, right?"

I slumped down and closed my eyes.

"Don't tell me you didn't tell her."

I shook my head.

"Not even once?" she asked.

I didn't want to admit how stupid I'd been.

Winston chimed in. "What did you expect? She's just a piece of ass to him."

"She is not," I shot back.

He continued. "Now that he's leaving, I think I'll have a taste of that honey."

I lunged for him and swung my fist.

He jerked sideways, and I missed. He grabbed my arm, swung me around, and pushed me back to land on the couch again.

I put my aching head in my hands and wiped my mouth. "I asked her to marry me."

Serena's mouth dropped. "And she said no?"

"Duh."

"That's a pretty big bomb to drop on a girl when you haven't even told her how you feel."

"Maybe I won't ask her out after all," Winston remarked.

I shot him a *shut up, asshole* look.

"And you're just taking no for an answer?"

"Hell, no." The memory was fuzzy. "I went back over, and she wouldn't even answer the door."

Stumble over is what I'd actually done. I lifted my elbow to check, and sure enough, the scrape from falling down on the way to her house was right where it should have been.

"Was her car there?"

I couldn't recall checking. "Dunno."

I also couldn't recall how many times I'd gone over. It seemed like more than once, but I couldn't be sure. There wasn't much I was sure of.

"That's because she hightailed it out of town, you idiot."

"What's her problem?" Winston asked Serena.

"What he said," I repeated.

Serena pointed at me. "How should I know? He obviously did something bad." She stood. "Better forget her and move on."

I sat up. "I don't want to."

The sudden movement angered the bugs eating at my brain. I hated that idea. Moving on was the worst idea ever. The time since Brittney's return had been the best of my life, even with the threat of Delgado hanging over us.

Serena laughed. "Then you better sober up and go after her before you lose her for good. Argue your case. Banish her doubts, or problems, or insecurities. And for God's sake, tell her how you feel."

"How is he going to do that if he doesn't know what her problem is?" Winston asked.

"Haven't you guys ever heard of talking about your feelings? People have been doing it forever. Well, obviously not guys like you two."

Winston stiffened at the slight, but I knew Serena meant the comment for me. I stood, instantly regretted it, and sat back down. "Where'd she go?"

"First things first," Serena said. "You stink. Winston, put him in the shower while I make us something to eat."

Winston shoved the juice glass at me. "Finish this first."

I did. This time I actually enjoyed the orange juice.

"Can you make it upstairs on your own?" he asked.

I stood. "I'm not a baby." In spite of my throbbing head and unsteady legs, I was not going to be carried upstairs.

"Good. Because I'm not wiping your ass for you." He laughed.

❧

AFTER BREAKFAST AND A SHOWER, I HAD FINALLY KICKED THE INTERVENTION DUO OUT of my house.

Now I was attacking the flooring demo project I'd abandoned when Brittney came into my life. I was back to what was comfortable: prying up laminate and contemplating how marvelous the old oak would look after it had been sanded and re-finished. I could think while I worked.

My phone rang, and I checked it. But it was Wendy.

"Sorry to call you at home, but you need to know that your father is worried because you're not in."

"I got that message already." Dad had called directly after Serena had failed to bring me back, and I'd told him not to expect me for another day or two. "I talked to him at lunchtime."

"Is there anything I can do to help?"

"No, thanks."

The only help I needed was figuring out what I could have done differently with Brittney.

Serena had said I needed to be more open about my feelings. A typical girl point of view, but probably right, in retrospect. Still, the timing hadn't felt right, hadn't been right.

Winston said I should have been clearer up front about my family responsibility to go to London—another good observation after the fact, but not the way it had seemed at the time.

After doing physical battle with another section of recalcitrant laminate, I threw down my pry bar, and it skidded across the floor.

"Fuck," I yelled at the empty room.

I was doing the thing I'd vowed never to do. I was dissecting the past instead of acting in the present to affect the future.

What was wrong with me?

Five minutes later, I cleaned up. The paper towel I'd used to dry my hands wouldn't fit in the overflowing bin under the sink.

508

I grabbed the trash bag and went out back.
I felt a quick pain in my side and a huge arm came around my neck.
I couldn't breathe.
I dropped the garbage and yanked at the arm.
I kicked behind me, but failed to connect.
"I'm gonna kill you," he said.

# CHAPTER 42

*BRITTNEY*

THE WALKS AROUND THE LAKE WERE LONG, BUT THEY HADN'T KEPT ME FROM thinking about Zack. I hoped he was doing better than I was.

For a moment, I wished he were here to enjoy the walk with me, the way we had in San Diego. It had only been a few weeks since then, but it seemed both recent and so long ago. Reminding myself that this was for the best didn't make it easier.

My memories of San Diego were vivid—the zoo, SeaWorld, jet skiing, and walking on the beach. It all put a smile on my lips and a spring in my step. Zack had put his busy life on hold at a moment's notice to refill my "happiness reservoir." And refill it he had. I hadn't felt so carefree and content in forever.

He could have spent money on me, bought me beautiful things and wonderfully expensive meals. He had done that last one a little, but even the hot dogs at SeaWorld had been a special meal with him across from me, smiling the whole time. Instead of things, he'd given me his time and attention and shown me how happy we could be doing simple stuff, so long as we did it together. He'd shown me how to block out the world and focus on us—just him and me and the activity at hand. No worries about my past or my future, only a concentration on the present.

He'd shown me that it was possible for a guy—no, make that a man, because Zack was certainly more man than anyone I'd ever been with—to show his love in ways that weren't verbal.

I was just realizing that now.

510

I'd been wrong the day I pushed him away to think that had been the first time he'd said he'd loved me. It had been the first time he'd verbalized it, but not the first time he'd shown it. His love was something I could see everywhere when I looked back on our time together. He'd said actions spoke louder than words, and in his case, the actions spelled love loud and clear. I'd just been too stupid to see it clearly until now. He'd made me feel appreciated, and cherished.

But these memories of him, of us, were also distant, because I now had to categorize them as my prior life—a place I couldn't go back to any more than I could re-enroll in high school. Zack couldn't be a part of my future without me ruining it for him, for us, when the truth came out. And the truth always came out in the end. My sins would destroy him, and I couldn't bear that thought.

I'd made the right choice to leave. Leaving was always the right choice.

I would have to content myself with the short time we'd had together, and the memories he'd given me.

After stopping on the opposite shore for my lunch, I continued the walk, mentally berating myself for the mistakes that had gotten me to this point.

Twenty-seven names, and number thirteen was the worst.

Nearing Casa Nelson, I kicked the sand at my feet. A man waved from a small fishing dinghy. It was Mr. Patterson again.

I waved back.

His fishing pole hung off the back of the little boat as he puttered out to do battle with a wily fish somewhere on the lake. His life was so simple compared to mine. Man against nature. Get up, go fish, check the neighborhood, fish again, wash, rinse, repeat. No drama, no regrets.

I finally reached Casa Nelson and decided tomorrow I would pack more fruit and do two laps of the lake. It was a long way around. But long was good. I needed the exercise to tire me so I could sleep.

Last night I'd resorted to several glasses of wine, as I had every evening since arriving. It worked for a few hours, but I woke each morning way before I should have, and I hadn't been able to get back to sleep.

Wine before bed was one thing, but downing a few glasses at three in the morning to get back to sleep was not something I could do long term.

Unlocking the back deck door, I went inside and looked around.

Lauren had called this place romantic, and I could see how it would be if you had someone to share it with. A middle-of-the-alphabet guy, less Benji and more Zack, that's who this space needed. That's what I needed.

*Fuck.* I'd left without having Winston and Constance help me get my papers back from fucking Benji. Another mistake I could add to my list.

A check of the pantry showed another trip to the market was in order, and not just for food. I was also down to my last bottle of wine.

My little car started with a whimper, dependable as always. I goosed the gas before putting it in reverse. The whine wasn't at all like the roar and rumble of the Snake. Maybe I needed to spend a little of the money from Grams's painting on a new car. Less Corolla and more Mustang, that was the ticket. But it wouldn't be cheap to get a car that was half the ride the Snake was, if that was even possible.

As I walked the aisles of the market, I checked out the guys as much as the produce. What I already knew to be true quickly became obvious. It would be easy to find a guy more masculine than Benji, but it wouldn't be easy finding one that tipped the manliness scale at half of Zack's reading.

I added a bag of mandarins to my cart.

This was going to be harder than just finding someone with a name that started with M—a lot harder.

I might have to settle for one third of a Zack, or maybe a quarter-Zack.

~

## ZACK

"How could you sleep with my sister behind my back?" Doug growled as he tightened the choke hold he had on me.

I struggled against the arm around my neck, but I couldn't get a word out. The Marines taught their people well.

"I should fucking kill you right now, but I think I'll make it slow and painful instead," he hissed.

I swung an elbow at him to no effect.

He loosened his arm just enough for me to get a few words out. "It wasn't like that."

"How could you? I trusted you to keep her safe, not ruin her."

"I asked her to m-marry me."

He loosened his grip. "What?"

I still couldn't get loose. "I want to marry her."

He let go and shoved me to the deck. "You better not be messing with me," he growled.

"Never."

His scowl softened. "You're serious?"

I got up and dusted myself off. "Damn straight."

He cocked his head. "Then why is she crying her head off to Sam? What the hell did you do to her?"

"The fuck if I know. I asked her to marry me, she said no, and then she split. She's *your* stupid twin sister. You tell me what her problem is."

He ran his hand through his hair. "I got no idea. I got the call from Sam that Brit was in a bad way, and she let slip that you two had been playing house. I took emergency leave and hot-footed it over here to kill you."

"I got that part." I grabbed the garbage bag and trotted down the stairs to dump it.

Doug followed. "You have to have done something."

I headed back to the kitchen door. "Come on inside."

He followed me up the stairs. "You better start at the beginning and tell me what's gone down. Because Sam said things are not good. You messed Brit up somehow."

I gave him the short history, leaving out the R-rated details, and at the end we were where we'd started: both of us clueless.

"I still don't like you sleeping with Brit without asking me."

I noticed that for Brittney he used *sleeping with* her, rather than *fucking* her, which would have been his wording for any other girl.

"And you would have said yes?"

He huffed. "Fuck no."

"That's why, shit-for-brains."

He drank some water. "I guess you're right. So what did you leave out? Why is she crying her fool head off?"

"Got me. I was going to go after her to find out."

He looked me in the eye. "Bad plan with her. You gotta know what's going on first."

"What? You going to go talk to her?"

"No, better than that. We call the one person she's already talked to: Sam."

It made sense to me. I knew my sisters would confide things to one another they wouldn't tell me.

Doug pulled out his phone and dialed. He put it on speaker while it rang.

"Hi, Doug," Samantha answered.

Doug started. "Sam, I've got Zack Benson here with me."

Silence.

"Okay," she said tentatively.

"I want to hear about what has Brit so upset."

Silence again.

"I don't think I can say."

Doug snarled. "Don't give me any of this secret sisterhood shit. This is Brit we're talking about. Zack wants to make it right, and frankly he's a thousand percent better than any of those other A-holes she's been seeing, so spill. What's her problem?"

"It's not for me to say," Samantha answered.

"Yes, it is," Doug told her. "This is Zack we're talking about. You gotta give him a chance to fix this."

"He should talk to her," Samantha said.

Doug's face was getting red now. "Stop giving me the runaround. She's my sister too, for God's sake. Tell me what's going on."

"You should call her," Samantha responded.

"I tried that. She won't answer," Doug said.

"That's because her phone is off, I think," Samantha said.

I raised my hand to stop Doug from making the situation any worse. His combative stance wasn't getting us anywhere.

"Samantha, I'd just like to talk to her and try to understand her problem so I can help fix it."

Samantha was quiet on the other end of the line for a moment. "It's the list of names."

I had no idea what that meant.

"I thought we were past that," Doug said. "She hasn't talked about that in years."

"She hasn't talked about it with you for years. That's because you get like this."

"Like what?" Doug demanded.

"Combative, just like you are now. You didn't listen to her, so she stopped talking to you about it."

I cut Doug off again. "Samantha, what is it about the list?" I asked calmly.

She sighed. "One of the names is your cousin. She hadn't connected the dots before because she'd never heard his name and didn't think he was related."

I leaned closer to the phone. "What does that mean? What is the deal with this list of names?"

"I have to go to work. Doug knows enough to fill you in."

"Thanks, Sam. Be safe," Doug answered.

"Always," she said before hanging up.

I turned to my friend. "List?"

His face showed a mixture of frustration and anger. "That fucking list again. I thought I'd gotten through to her and gotten her to ignore that, put it behind her."

"What is it?"

"A bunch of people... Let me back up. What do you know about Delgado?"

I wracked my brain for a second. "He was a drug dealer she testified against for a murder she witnessed. The guy later killed her boyfriend, Todd—at least she thinks he did—but they never found the body. And so now when he gets out, he comes after her for revenge, and some stupid key he thinks she has, but she doesn't know a thing about. That's about it."

"Well, that's not the whole story," he began. "At first she was too scared to testify against Delgado, so she ran off. Then this piece-of-shit detective laid the list on her. He claimed it was a list of drug ODs that were her fault because she'd held off coming forward to testify. And he told her the list would only grow and be on her conscience if she didn't agree to come to court."

"That's a pretty heavy burden to put on someone."

"No shit."

"So she blames herself for these ODs?"

514

"That's about the size of it. I thought I'd gotten her past this years ago. But obviously not. So if your cousin is on that list, she's sittin' there thinking she caused his OD."

Now at least I knew what the problem was. "Thanks, man. I owe you."

He punched me in the shoulder. "It's up to you to make this right. If you don't get her to marry you, we'll be right back where we started: you sleeping with my sister and not marrying her. That's fucking unacceptable."

"Got it."

"I'll spread-eagle you in the desert, pour honey on your naked ass, and wait for the ants to do their thing." He laughed.

He might be exaggerating, but because it was Doug, I couldn't be sure. "Thanks for that warning."

"Nothing like proper motivation." He stood. "I think I'll go ask Kelly on a date." It was just like him to turn it around so I got the point.

"Don't you fucking dare," I snarled.

"Just sayin', turnaround's fair. Hey, I haven't gotten any shut-eye since I got the call. You got a place I could rack out?"

"Sure. Upstairs, second room on the right."

He gave me a mock salute and headed for the stairs.

Now I had what I needed.

Brittney was going to learn the truth. She was meant to be mine, and I was going to have her.

No question about it.

∼

ZACK

DAD WAS AT HIS DESK WHEN I OPENED THE DOOR LATE THAT AFTERNOON.

"Zachary, I thought you were taking the day off."

I took the seat across from him. "Maybe more than that, actually."

"I see. Does this have to do with Brittney?"

The family grapevine was working overtime if he already knew, but of course he knew. He always knew.

"Yes. And I've made a decision."

He waited.

I steeled myself for the argument to come. "I'm not going to London."

He steepled his hands and nodded. "Very well."

*Very well?*

I'd expected a lecture on family obligations instead of acceptance.

"You think she's the one?"

He'd also heard about my proposal, apparently.

"I know it."

"Then go make your argument. She has a say in this too, you know."

"Yeah, that's the problem."

"Why is she reluctant, do you think?"

"It's complicated."

"Then you have your work cut out for you, I would say."

That was an understatement. Combating irrational fears was the hardest. I stood.

"I think you should call Phillip Patterson."

"Why?"

"His grandfather has a cabin quite near the Covington place."

Serena had told me where Brittney had gone. I shouldn't have been surprised that she'd told Dad as well.

"Thanks. I will, if I need to."

It was too late to make the drive today, so tonight I would plan. Tomorrow I was going after my woman.

# CHAPTER 43

*BRITTNEY*

THE NEXT MORNING I TURNED ON THE TV LONG ENOUGH TO CHECK THE DAY. IT WAS Saturday, the day Zack was scheduled to leave for London.

I opened the door to the deck and smelled the clean mountain air—not a hint of LA smog. The sky was a clear blue, a nice day for flying.

Zack would likely be on his way soon, if he wasn't already in the air. He certainly wouldn't be taking a red-eye. For the briefest second I tried to imagine Zack saying something with a British accent, but I knew he wouldn't. Zack knew who he was, and he didn't change. He wouldn't change for anyone or anything.

I could even remember a fight over his hair in high school. The baseball coach had threatened to kick him off the varsity team if he didn't cut his hair. Every other guy on the team complied, but not Zack. He'd said it was who he was, and he wouldn't change for the coach, or anyone. He got to watch the season from the stands.

No, Zack wouldn't adopt even a hint of the accent to blend in. He would proudly be labeled the Yank, and they could stuff it if they didn't like it.

I had to stifle a laugh. That was Zack all right, defiantly unchangeable. Except I had gotten him to budge on eating fruit—a small victory.

Mr. Patterson's outboard motor sputtered to life, and I stepped out on the deck with my glass of juice to wave. His little aluminum boat made a small wake on the still surface of the lake. The wind hadn't come up yet to create any waves. I watched as he headed to the end of the lake he swore was the home of the big one—the one he intended to land.

It was another warm day, and yesterday's exercise had helped me sleep a little longer before waking. Back inside, I put the juice down and got on the carpet to stretch my sore leg muscles. If one lap helped a little, two might be better. Two laps of the lake became today's agenda.

After a breakfast of pancakes, I started out. This time I brought more rations: several apples and apricots, plus sunscreen, water, and a towel to sit on while I took a break.

The first lap went pretty much like yesterday, except I found a porta-potty that was surprisingly un-gross at a house under construction on the other side of the lake.

I spent the hike trying and failing to think about things other than Zack. I would concentrate on how Samantha might be coping out east, and that would distract me for a few minutes. Worrying about Doug flying over the open ocean off Okinawa also worked for a few minutes, but my thoughts kept coming back to the same topic—the man that inhabited my mind and my heart, Zack.

Halfway around the second lap, I realized today's mistake. I hadn't put on the right socks for this trek, and I was rubbing a blister on my heel.

It had been hard leaving Zack behind, and it was going to take a long time to get over him. I tried to get excited about finding a Mike, or Matt, or some other half-Zack—a guy who wasn't half as bossy or half as annoying, but the prospect seemed bland, like pancakes without syrup or a topping.

Samantha's advice for getting over a guy—well, pretty much everybody's advice —was to move on to the next. If your cat died, you got another cat. If your boyfriend didn't work out, you traded him in for a different one. But I'd gotten a whiff of the loud life: the roar of the Snake on the freeway, wind whipping my hair, sitting next to a man with enough testosterone to power a freight train. And I'd liked it.

I hobbled the last leg of today's journey, wishing I'd added Band-Aids or tape to my backpack.

Even through my foot pain, my thoughts kept coming back to him. The car he drove epitomized Zack. It was loud, powerful, and didn't let anything stand in its way. It could power around any obstacle. And everyone knew, with just a glance, that it was one of a kind. He was one of a kind.

I rounded the final cove, and the roof of Casa Nelson came into view. I walked past Patterson's dock. His trusty little fishing dinghy was tied up along-side, waiting to take its owner on his evening trip.

I laughed. Patterson went out twice a day to land the big one, and I'd just thrown the big one back.

When I reached Casa Nelson, I turned up the path.

Zack stood on the deck, hands in his pockets, staring at me.

Without an avenue of escape, I had to face him. Again.

He took his hands out of his pockets as I hobbled the last few steps to the deck. "Hi, Sunshine."

"What are you doing here?"

It was a stupid question, but I didn't have anything else to say if I didn't want to cry.

"We need to talk."

I hobbled around him. "I told you already, we did."

He blocked my path.

I stood and stared up at him. I was out of words.

Concern splashed across his face. "You're hurt."

He couldn't know how right he was.

ZACK

I FOLLOWED HER INSIDE THE CABIN AND CLOSED THE DOOR. "DO YOU HAVE ANYTHING to drink?"

"You won't be here that long."

I merely smiled.

She cringed slightly as she realized the bite of her words.

She limped to the fridge. "What would you like?"

"Do you have any orange juice?"

She shot me a questioning look. "Of course." She poured two glasses and brought them over.

We sat on the couch.

I brought out my jewelry box again.

"Put that away," she said.

I set it on the coffee table.

"Away," she repeated.

I ignored the request. "I need to understand why you said no."

She took a deep breath. "Because I don't want to follow you to London."

I settled back in the couch. "Why not?"

"I have a career, and it's here. My certification wouldn't transfer there, and I don't want to just sit around all day."

"And that's the reason?"

She crossed her arms. "Yeah, pretty much."

Her body language said something entirely different. She was antsy. She was holding back, and I knew it. She was trapped by her lie.

Somehow I had to get her to open up about the list so we could talk through it and get it behind her. I might not even need to get Doug or Samantha in hot water...

I tried a different approach. "Good, because I'm not going to London."

Her eyes widened. "But you have to. You told me it was the next rotation you had to do."

She hadn't been prepared for that, which told me how far I had to go in getting her to understand the depth of my feelings.

"It was, but I've told Dad I'm not going. Staying here with you is more important."

"But it's your duty to your family. That's the most important thing. You told me so yourself."

Was she trying to convince me or herself?

"Brit, I want you to marry me and be my family, and that's more important. The family business will be fine without me, but I can't say the same about me without you."

"I can't marry you."

"Why not? You said you didn't want to go to London. Problem solved. We're not going to London."

She fidgeted, caught by her own deception, her own inability to be truthful.

The first step in getting her past her guilt had to be for her to admit it. She had to acknowledge it.

～

*Brittney*

This was getting worse, not better. I couldn't be with him and destroy him when he learned the truth. Having given up everything and then learning what I'd done would compound the hurt.

"I can't," I said curtly. I rose from the couch. "Want some more juice?"

I shuffled toward the fridge. Being this close to him was messing with my ability to stay rational. The effect he had on me was magnetic, and the closer I got, the stronger his pull. I knew if I allowed him to touch me, the attraction between us would be a black hole that devoured me whole, never letting me escape to a distance that could keep him safe.

He reached me in two strides. "You sit down, and I'll get it." His hand on my arm was light, but the electric feel of his skin on mine was as strong as before. Dangerously strong. Black-hole strong.

I stopped, my mouth frozen, unable to say anything until he let go of me. I nodded.

"Sprain your ankle?" he asked as he continued to the kitchen to pour us more juice.

I limped to the couch. "Blister."

He poured a glass. "Ouch. Take off your clothes, and I'll take care of you."

"What?"

"I said take off your shoes, and I'll take care of you."

My traitorous libido was playing tricks on me, changing his words to the ones it wanted to hear.

"No. I can do it myself."

"Stop arguing and take off your shoes." Bossy Zack was back.

"No," I repeated, playing with him.

"I'm going to spank you if you don't behave. Now take off your shoes so I can fix that."

I removed one shoe, then the other, followed by my socks.

He brought over the juice and handed me a glass. "Which foot is the problem?"

I lifted my left.

He took one look and scowled. "This is not good. Show me the other."

I did, and his verdict was swift.

"I'll be right back. Lie face down on the couch."

"Why?"

"Sunshine, can you stop arguing for one minute and just do what you're told?"

I laid down as instructed. At least we'd gotten away from the question posed by the jewelry box I stared at on the coffee table.

He left through the front door and returned with a first-aid kit. He went into the kitchen where he turned on the stove.

"What are you doing?"

"Sterilizing." He turned off the stove and returned, kneeling by the couch.

I watched as he tore open an antiseptic wipe. The moist pad felt cool on the skin of my heels.

He put tissues under my feet and took sharp tweezers from the table.

"Hold still."

I jerked my foot away. "You're not poking me with that thing."

"I said stay still. Now behave yourself. I know what I'm doing. Teeth are your thing, and blisters are mine."

I put my foot back down. "This isn't fair."

He held my ankle firmly. "Life's not fair."

I didn't look as he brought the sharp end of the tweezers down.

"That's one."

I'd only felt a slight tug.

"That's two," he said after he held the other down and repeated the puncture. "This may hurt a little." He squeezed first one heel then the other.

It did sting, but not badly.

"Are you done yet?"

"Not yet." He took Neosporin ointment from his kit and dabbed it on my heels. Band-Aids followed.

I closed my eyes as he unspooled and cut pieces of tape, which went over the bandages.

He lifted my feet, sat, and pulled them over his lap. The gross, wadded up tissues from squeezing the fluid out of my blisters landed on the coffee table. "Now we talk."

I tried to pull away, but he held me down.

"Stay still."

"Let me go."

"After we talk."

"You're not being fair." His idea of a position for talking was distorted.

"What did I just tell you about life?" he shot back.

I huffed and gave up. "Okay, then talk."

"You know what your problem is?"

I snorted. "Yeah, you."

He tickled my foot. "Be serious."

I laughed. "Stop that."

He did after a moment. "You're not honest enough."

"I am too." I tried to pull my feet away to sit up, but he wouldn't let me.

"You are not."

"How would you know?"

"I know lots of things. Tell me something you wish you'd told me earlier."

I couldn't go to the list, so I didn't respond.

"Okay, I'll start." He looked into my eyes. "I love you, Brittney Clark."

The words halted my breathing as they cut through me. "You're just saying that."

"I should have told you sooner."

"We haven't been dating long enough," I said.

"Now you're being stupid. I've known you almost my whole life, and I've loved you for years. Tell me you don't feel the same."

I couldn't lie to him about that. "We can't be together. It wouldn't work."

"Bullshit. We're great together."

We actually had been great. I'd spent all my time walking the lake regretting how great we were together.

"Doug would kill us if he knew."

"I don't think so. Let me handle him."

"So you'd be cool with him screwing Serena or Kelly?"

"Hell no. I'd kick his ass. But I would be okay with him marrying one of them, if it came down to that."

I was getting his drift, but I still worried how Doug would react.

"I told you something I regretted not telling you earlier. Now, your turn."

I couldn't come up with anything. "I like your car."

He tickled me again.

I struggled, but couldn't pull my foot loose.

"I'm serious," he said gruffly.

"It won't work out long-term between us."

"Why not?"

I was running out of options to avoid talking directly about my sins. "Because in the end, you'll hate me."

"Not possible."

"But you don't know what I've done."

"Remember, what you've done in the past is water under the bridge. It's what you do in the present to affect the future that matters."

"You could never forgive me," I blurted. "I killed people. I killed your cousin Jonas."

He shook his head. "You had nothing to do with that."

He didn't get it. My inaction had killed his cousin. "Yes, I did. If I hadn't been scared, he'd be alive today."

"You had nothing to do with it," he repeated.

"Let me up. I need to show you something. Then maybe you'll understand."

He let me get up, and I went to the counter.

I extracted my list from the pink envelope in my purse and brought it over. "This is a list of people that died because I didn't come forward to put Delgado away earlier." I shoved the paper at him. "Read the thirteenth name." I couldn't keep the tears at bay any longer.

He took the paper, folded it, pocketed it, and stood to hug me.

I cried into his shoulder as he stroked my back. "You didn't read it."

"I don't need to. You didn't kill any of the people on the list. Addicts chart their own self-destructive paths. Just as you are responsible for your own destiny, so were they."

"But I could have put Delgado away earlier," I argued.

"Think about this, Sunshine. If an addict moves to a new city, does he stop using because he can't meet with his dealer anymore? No. He finds a new dealer. If Delgado had gone away earlier, they all would have found other sources."

I pondered his logic for a moment.

"Now it's time for you to agree to marry me so I can teach you this every day, until you learn to forgive yourself. Their fates are not your responsibility."

"But he was your cousin."

"You didn't kill him," he said softly into my ear.

"I don't know if I believe that."

"Is that all that's keeping you from saying yes?"

"Isn't that enough?"

He squeezed me tighter and kissed the top of my head. "Is there anything else?"

"No. I just can't live with you knowing that, your whole family knowing that. I don't want you to resent me."

"Well, Sunshine, now you *have* to marry me, because you didn't have anything to do with this death. There's something else you don't know." He loosened his grip and pulled my chin up with a finger. "I have Jonas's suicide note. He killed himself."

My heart stopped for a beat. "What?"

"I said, you have to marry me now. Drugs were just the weapon he used. Jonas took his own life. It didn't have anything to do with you or Delgado. Like I said, if not him, it would have been some other dealer. Jonas's death is not on you."

I blinked back the tears. Tears of remorse for his cousin who'd decided to end his life, and tears of joy that I could remove a name from my list. "You can't just tell me to marry you, though."

"Stop being obstinate. I tried asking, and that didn't go very well," he shot back.

"Well, maybe you should try again."

He let me go, retrieved the box from the table, and took a knee. "Brittney Clark, will you marry me?"

I leaned over to take his face in my hands. "Yes," I said before I planted the kiss on him I'd been holding back.

He stood, lifted me off my feet, and spun me around before setting me down. "You need to see if this fits." He picked up the box and slid the ring onto my finger. "What do you think?"

"It's a little big."

"I can get it sized down for you."

I looked down on the perfect ring, given to me by my perfect man. "No, it fits, and it's gorgeous. It's just the stone is so big."

"Not as big as my love for you, Sunshine."

Lauren had been right. This cabin was built for romance.

He pulled me in for another kiss.

As we intertwined, I drank in his taste and the love I knew he had for me—the love he'd shown me in his own non-verbal, masculine way.

# CHAPTER 44

*BRITTNEY*

ZACK AND I HAD SPENT ANOTHER TWO GLORIOUS DAYS AT CASA NELSON, JUST THE two of us. We wore out the bed and the couch as he lavished attention on me several times a day.

We'd also spent time hiking the nearby trails and around the lake some more. Each time, Zack bandaged and taped my heels to protect them, and they were healing well, in spite of the extra walking.

We'd had old man Patterson over for dinner, and I'd learned the Phil Patterson I'd met at the Habitat weekend was his grandson.

This morning, after I finished checking that we'd left the place clean enough, I closed and locked the door. I kissed my finger, and pressed it to the door. "Thank you for the memories."

Zack stood by the Snake. "Two cars or one?"

For work, I'd need my own car. "Two. And tell me again why we can't stay another few days?"

He hadn't actually said, but I could hope he'd slip up and tell me now.

It didn't work. "You need to meet someone before he leaves town," he said.

Now I knew it was a man, but that wasn't much help.

I'd tried guessing, but gotten nowhere fast.

He got in and started the Snake. The rumble of its idle had me wishing I could ride with him, but that would have to wait till we got back.

The drive was long, but uneventful as my little car tried to keep up with the Snake. I really needed a better car.

He parked in front of his house, and I pulled in just behind him.

The kid he called Piss Boy and an adult were walking our way on the other side of the street. This time the boy didn't give the middle-finger salute.

"Mr. Benson?" I heard the man call as I got out.

Zack stopped and waited for them to cross the street.

I put my arm around Zack when I reached him.

"Mr. Benson, Tommy has something he'd like to give you."

Now we had a name other than Piss Boy.

Tommy offered Zack the folded paper. "I'm really sorry, and I apologize for using the house when I shouldn't have."

Zack smiled. "Very well, but it's this lady you should apologize to. It's her house."

The boy repeated himself, and I assured him it was okay now.

Zack extracted himself from my grasp, leaned into his car, and pulled a cell phone from the glove compartment. He handed it to Tommy.

After a moment the man, apparently the boy's father, said, "And?"

"Thanks, Mr. Benson," Tommy said.

Zack nodded.

The duo left, and Zack turned to me. "Do you think he learned the lesson?"

"Looks like it." I went to pull my bag from the trunk of my car.

Zack started toward the steps. "Doug," he exclaimed. "What are you doing here?"

I turned to see my brother come out the front door.

"Is it true?" His wavering stance said he'd been drinking, a lot. "Have you been shacking up with this A-hole?" he yelled.

I froze. "It's not like that," I protested.

Doug's judgment was the first thing that went when he got drunk, and dealing with him when he got like this was never easy.

"Looks like it to me," he said as he grabbed the railing for support and started down toward Zack.

"It is, and I'm proud of it," Zack said, standing his ground.

My heart stopped. "No," I yelled.

Doug lunged, and Zack grappled with him.

I ran to them.

"I'm gonna kill you," Doug grunted as he and Zack each threw a punch and missed.

Doug grabbed Zack, and they both went to the ground.

"Stop it. It's not like that," I yelled at my brother.

I had no chance of breaking up a fight between these two, and as drunk as Doug was, it could end badly.

Doug started laughing.

Zack joined him, and the wrestling stopped.

Zack got up first.

"Just messing with ya, sis," Doug said as he got to his knees.

"Yeah, he knows," Zack confessed, brushing himself off.

Doug got up. This time he wasn't wobbly. He'd faked being drunk.

I slapped him.

He pulled back. "What the fuck?"

"You gave me a heart attack. You should know better."

Doug laughed. "That's what you get for not talking to me about what's going on." He pointed at Zack. "I almost killed this fucker on Friday when I got back."

"He did," Zack chimed in.

"Well, I didn't think—" I said.

Doug grasped my shoulders. "You sure didn't think. You should have told me." He wrapped me in a bear hug. "Congratulations, by the way. You caught yourself a good one. You just should have let me know."

"Can I come out now?" It was Samantha's voice.

Doug released me, and Samantha hurried down the steps. It became her turn to give me a congratulatory hug.

"How'd you get here?" I asked. I could hardly believe it.

"Zack's dad sent a plane to pick me up. That's the way to fly, by the way. You gotta try it. Super cool."

I turned to my fiancé. "Is there anybody that doesn't know?"

He shrugged. "I thought it was good news. What can I say?"

"Do you have a date?" Samantha asked.

I looked at Zack, who didn't offer any suggestion. "We haven't figured that out yet."

"We're having a barbecue tonight," Samantha proclaimed.

"We are?" I asked.

"We are," Zack confirmed.

"I gotta catch a flight in the morning," Doug explained.

I cocked my head. "Who's we?"

"Family and friends," Zack replied.

Samantha grabbed my hand and pulled me toward the cars. "So you get to take me grocery shopping."

"Hold on," Zack called after us. "You'll need these." He tossed me his keys.

I caught them. Keys to the Snake. "Really?"

"Just be careful."

My eyes widened. "I will. And we'll park at the far end of the lot."

He waved.

"You told me I couldn't drive it, and now you're letting her?" Doug exclaimed.

Zack shrugged as I backed toward the car. "She's family. What can I say."

Samantha followed me. "What's so special about an old Mustang?"

"You'll see," I told her as I unlocked the Snake.

Doug was still grumbling.

Sam climbed in her side. "What's with these seatbelts?"

"Competition belts." I showed her how to buckle them, just as Zack had shown me.

I started the engine.

"It needs muffler work," she said.

I pulled out onto the street and pressed the gas. The engine roared, and the car charged ahead. The tires chirped as I shifted into second and let the clutch out too quickly. I hit the brakes to slow down to a reasonable speed.

Samantha grabbed the seat and braced herself. "Holy shit, what is this?"

"This is a '67 Shelby GT500." I patted the steering wheel and repeated Zack's explanation. "It's a simple car. Nothing but pure, unadulterated horse-power. In its day, it was the ultimate car for turning gasoline into noise, tire smoke, and speed. A simple machine with a simple mission—going fast as fuck."

Samantha laughed. "I think it's super cool he lets you drive it."

I didn't explain how happy this made me, since the original schedule for letting me drive had been the tenth of never.

～

ZACK

I WAS TURNING OVER THE LAST OF THE HAMBURGER PATTIES ON THE GRILL WHEN Brittney came up from behind.

She wrapped her arms around me. "How did you get all these people here without me knowing?"

I pulled her arms away. "Careful, I don't want you to get burned."

"Well, how?"

"I slipped old man Patterson a list when we had him over for dinner, and he passed it on to Phil."

"That's sneaky."

"I wanted it to be a surprise."

"It is, and it's great—especially that you brought Samantha out. It's been too long since I saw her."

Phil appeared. "How are the burgers coming? We're running low."

"A few more minutes."

He mumbled something I didn't catch before turning away.

Brittney kneaded my shoulders quickly. "I better get back to mingling, but I wanted to say thank you again for letting me drive the Snake."

"Thanks will be accepted later after everyone has left."

She giggled. "Do you have anything in particular in mind?"

"I'll think of something," I assured her.

528

She left, and Phil returned again, looking over my shoulder to examine the meat. "I got a plate, if you think they're ready."

I loaded up his plate. We'd cooked all the meat the girls had brought back. This was a hungry crowd. I followed Phil to the table and fixed myself a plate, making sure to snag a piece of Katie's apple pie before it was all gone.

Looking around the crowd, we were still several short of a full family gathering. Mom was still in Paris, my sister Kelly couldn't make today, and Vincent was in Boston.

Dad, Dennis, Serena, my fiancée, the Knowltons, the Covingtons, Phil, and Brittney's brother and sister were here—a ragtag group if ever there was one.

Dad was bending Doug's ear, no doubt talking Marine to Marine. The girls had congregated around Lauren and baby Wendell.

A half hour later, Constance came in carrying a cardboard box. Winston followed.

"We have a present for you," she told Brittney.

Brittney accepted the box and opened it. "My God, my papers." She gave Constance a hug. "How?"

"Winston and I managed a quick trip to San Jose."

Brittney pulled a check from the box. "And a check for the money he took? How did you get that out of him?"

Winston chuckled. "We told him we knew people who could put him on the terrorist watch list."

I couldn't hold back my laugh. That was a good line.

Throughout the evening, everyone made time to take me aside and congratulate me on the engagement, and my choice of bride.

I couldn't have agreed more.

Dad pried himself away from Doug long enough to approach me again about London. "You know, we can keep that position open for a while, so you two can decide if it's the right move for you as a couple."

I patted his shoulder. "Thanks, Dad. I'll talk with Brittney about it, but don't hold your breath."

"I really do think it would be a good opportunity for you, Zachary."

He wasn't one to give up easily.

Phil came from inside the house, a concerned look on his face. "Zack, there's cops at the front door that want to talk to you and your dad."

I started toward the house. "Okay."

"I wonder what they want," Dad said.

Phil followed us.

When we reached the door, we found two sheriff's deputies.

Dad moved past me. "Hi, Ward, what can we do for you?" He shook hands with the older man.

That's when I realized the older one wasn't a deputy. He was the head man, the sheriff himself.

"Lloyd, it seems we've got a situation," the sheriff started. He pointed to a black SUV at the curb with a suited couple standing by it, a man and a woman. "The FBI would like to interview you. I told them I wanted to talk to you first."

"Thanks for the heads up. What do they want?"

"It's about a bank robbery in Maryland, but Lloyd, you need to prepare yourself for a shock."

Dad waved them up. "Let's talk to them, then."

The sheriff looked relieved that he wasn't going to have a showdown of some sort.

The short woman introduced the pair, FBI Special Agents Parsons and Newson.

The woman, Parsons, addressed Dad, "Mr. Benson, there was an after-hours bank robbery two days ago in Bethesda, Maryland."

"Go ahead," Dad said. "How can we help?"

So far none of this made any sense. A bank robbery in Maryland couldn't have any connection to us.

"Sir," Parsons continued, "blood evidence collected at the scene came back a match to a missing person. The parents are deceased, and you are listed as the next of kin."

I dreaded her next words.

"The blood belongs to a Deborah Ellen Benson."

I felt faint. *My missing cousin?*

Dad gasped. "She's alive, then?"

Parsons took a breath. "It would appear she wasn't killed in the abduction as was believed at the time."

Dad wobbled a little, and I steadied him. "Get Dennis for me, Phillip," he said.

Phil rushed off.

"How certain are you?" Dad asked.

"It's a DNA match. We wouldn't be here if it wasn't."

Dennis came up at a run. "Phil said it's news about Debbie?"

Phil returned just after Dennis.

"We have evidence that she's alive," Parsons told him.

"And may be involved in a bank robbery," the other agent added, which earned him a stern look from Parsons.

Dad grasped my brother's shoulder. "Dennis, you're the oldest. You need to go out east and learn everything you can. Get back to me when you have something solid to report."

"Vincent's already in Boston. Why don't we call him?"

Dad's jaw ticked. "You're the oldest. It's your job."

Dad turned to me and Phil. "In the meantime, we have a party to get back to. Not a word of this to any of the others until we know more."

I started to object. "But—"

He cut me off. "Not a word to anyone—not a single, solitary word. Understood? That means you too, Phillip."

We all nodded. Dad's tone said he was serious, and there would be no changing his mind on the subject. A task had been assigned and rules stated—end of discussion.

This changed everything. We'd never known there was an accomplice in Debbie's kidnapping. But there must have been. How else could she still be alive?

Another thing bothered me as I pasted on a smile on the way back to my fiancée. *Why hadn't we gotten another ransom demand if she's been alive all this time?*

# EPILOGUE

THE REAL LOVER IS THE MAN WHO CAN
THRILL YOU BY KISSING YOUR FOREHEAD OR
SMILING INTO YOUR EYES OR JUST STARING
INTO SPACE. - MARILYN MONROE

*BRITTNEY*

I ROLLED OVER TO FACE ZACK.

He had worked hard yesterday getting the house ready for today's party. He was still asleep this morning, which was unusual for such an early riser. My fiancé's chest rose and fell with the rhythm of waves against the shore—slow and steady. *Steady* was a good word for him.

I'd learned I could count on him for anything, anything at all.

With the heavy comforter over us, I couldn't see if he was as hard and ready as usual, or if I would find him soft and warm for a change because he'd been so exhausted last night.

I grew wet as I contemplated my attack. If I needed to stiffen him up, that would be fun too.

Lying next to him, for the moment I contented myself with watching him sleep, wondering how I had been so lucky to find such a perfect man. It had taken returning to the town I'd vowed I would never set foot in again to find the one for me—the one who'd been in plain sight forever, the one I'd left behind.

When Benji had forced my move back, I'd cursed him for ruining my life, not realizing his craziness could lead to an outcome like this.

I slipped my hand down under the covers and slowly made my way to my target.

"Morning, sleepyhead," Zack said groggily as he opened his eyes.

I moved closer and brushed my lips against his. "Good morning. But today you're the sleepyhead."

532

My hand found its destination, and I knew the answer before I asked. "Would you like to?"

"Always, Sunshine."

I stroked his hard length with a light grip and moved down to cup his balls.

He reciprocated by pulling me closer for a kiss. Our tongues tangled, and we exchanged breath. He tried to roll toward me, but I let go of his balls and pushed his hip down firmly. This morning was my turn to be in charge.

Releasing him from the kiss, I moved down to bite his nipple lightly.

He tensed as I did.

I blew on the tender flesh and moved farther down. I gave his cock a long, slow lick from root to tip before taking him in my mouth. A few quick strokes, and he was well lubricated. It was sexy the way his cock jerked slightly as I blew cold air on the wet underside.

I climbed up over him and positioned myself over his super-hard cock.

He kneaded my breasts and thumbed my nipples with the circular motion that always sent tingles through me.

I held his cock and lowered myself slowly, a bit down and then back up, and a little more down, teasing him with my slow approach.

His gentle moans as I lowered myself and his gasps as I pulled up were my guide. I slowly took more of him with each stroke until I reached his root. I rocked into him, and he guided me up and down with his hands on my hips.

He moved to thumb my clit, but I pulled his hand away. Not once, but twice he tried.

"No," I said. "My rules today. You first." I shoved down fully, and his steely cock stretched me.

He was always making me come, and often twice before he did, but not this morning—it was my turn to set the rules. He relented and went back to guiding my hips with his hands, thrusting up into me as he pulled me down, each push seemingly deeper than the last.

I neared my climax and every cell of my body tensed as he thrust into my core. My nerve endings tingled with every lift off of him, but I held on. I had to. I had to make him come first today.

His breathing became shallower as he tensed up, nearing his limit.

I rocked down hard on him and reached behind me to grab his balls. I used the other hand to pinch his nipple as he came, gushing into me with a loud groan and a final deep push.

His legs shook and his cock continued to throb inside me as I ground down on him. He moved his thumb to my clit. His circling pressure quickly took me over the top with a shudder as he pulled me forward to kiss and nibble at my nipples. He truly was the clit whisperer.

I couldn't catch my breath as the spasms shook me and my body dissolved into climax.

He pulled me down farther to hug me tightly. "You can wake me up like this any morning you want, Sunshine."

The smile on his face in the dim morning light was all the reward I needed.

"I know what I'm going to call him," I said.

"What?"

I shifted my hips on his cock.

"Not that again."

"I think I like Lightning."

"Any name is a bad idea, if you ask me."

"You like Rebar better?"

He chuckled. "No way. Where are you getting these?"

"From *Sweet Home Alabama*. It was lightning that brought them back together again."

He pushed me up and cradled my breasts. "Then I get to name these."

"Like what?"

"I'll think of something."

I relaxed against his chest. This was always the best part, the ultimate closeness between husband and wife to-be: the perfect beginning to a new day in our life together.

~

*Brittney*

Serena held up a pink top from the closet. "What about this one?"

Zack's sisters were helping me play dress-up for the combination housewarming and engagement party we were hosting this afternoon.

Zack's mother had insisted on a proper engagement party with the whole family, and Zack hadn't wanted to do it until at least the downstairs of the house was ready.

This was girl bonding time, and my chance to learn the family episodes Zack didn't want to tell me.

I took the hanger from Serena.

Kelly silently shook her head when her sister looked the other way.

"And then there was the time he tried to drive the old VW bug, before he got his license," Kelly said.

Serena laughed. "It was parked in the driveway. Dad wouldn't let him drive until he got his permit, but Zack decided to get a little practice in before then. Bad idea."

"It was on a hill," Kelly added.

"Every time he tried to put it in gear, the engine died, and it slipped farther down the hill," Serena told me.

534

Kelly pulled a lower-cut peach top from the rack, trying to control her laughter. "It ended up half in the street, and when Dad got home, he grounded Zack for two weeks."

I joined the laughter and handed the pink shirt back to Serena, holding Kelly's peach suggestion up in front of me.

Serena nodded. "I like it."

I took it off the hanger. "I'll save that one. Do you have any other good stories?"

"A ton," Kelley replied.

I pulled off my T-shirt to try the top.

Serena was already looking through my limited jewelry choices. "What do you have that's gold to go with that?"

I didn't have much in the necklace department that was gold. I slipped into the top they'd picked out while she searched.

She pulled out Todd's heart-shaped pendant. "This would be good. I especially like the chain length."

She meant that it hung enticingly low.

"I'm not sure that's a good one," I told her, not eager to wear Todd's piece.

"Try it on," Kelly encouraged me. "And let's see."

I gave in, and Serena helped with the clasp.

"What does it say?" Kelly asked.

I'd inadvertently gotten it on backwards—the inscription was facing front. "It's a Klingon love poem."

Kelly peered closer. "Cool."

"What does it mean?" Serena asked.

Sheepishly I admitted, "I don't remember."

Actually, I'd never known. Todd had said it was a secret for later, and later had never come.

"We should get Winston or Nick to translate it," Kelly suggested. "They're both super Trekkies."

I undid the clasp to reverse the pendant so the engraving was on the back, and reconnected it.

"That's a good look," Serena said.

Kelly nodded. "Yup."

Checking the mirror, I agreed.

WHEN I GOT DOWNSTAIRS, ZACK'S PARENTS HAD JUST ARRIVED.

"I hear there's a party around here somewhere, but I don't see any food yet," Lloyd joked.

"Try the kitchen, Dad," Zack told him.

Lloyd made his way toward the back.

Zack's mother, Robin, smiled warmly at me. "You look lovely, Brittney."

I felt the heat rise in my cheeks. "Thank you."

"Please excuse Lloyd. Sometimes he has no manners. Now, I hear from Serena that you've gotten Zack to start eating fruit again."

"I'm going to go check on Dad," Zack said before he scurried off.

"Every day," I told her. "He still complains about the kiwis, but I'm working on that."

"It's the seeds, dear. He won't admit it, but he's deathly afraid of them ever since the infection."

Now I was learning something new.

"What infection was that?"

"When he was young, we had an awful time getting him to brush properly. Anyway, he got strawberry seeds caught under his gum line and got a terrible infection that almost cost him a tooth. After that he pretty much swore off fruit."

"Well, that explains a lot."

Lloyd returned with two wine glasses and handed one to Robin. "You have to come see what Zack and Brittney have done with the kitchen."

When I turned, the house was overflowing with all the guests Zack had invited: the Knowltons, the Covingtons, Phil, and the rest of the Benson family, even Vincent and his wife were out from Boston. Zack had also invited a few dozen coworkers from the company. Samantha had just arrived from Philadelphia, but Doug was still overseas.

Phil was running his hands over the mantle Zack had repaired and refinished. "You know, you do such good work, I might have to hire you."

"You couldn't afford me," Zack replied.

All the work Zack had put into fixing this fine house was now on beautiful display. He was proudest of the hardwood floors, the staircase, and all the intricate millwork. It had been a pain to strip the layers of paint, but the end result was worth it.

"And these floors," Phil went on. "So much nicer than the shit they put down today."

Zack beamed. "The previous owners had glued laminate over this whole place. Twice."

"Fucking idiots," Phil agreed. "What do you plan on doing next?"

Zack nodded toward my and Samantha's currently unoccupied house. "I'll be fixing that one next. After that, I don't know."

Zack and his father had called a truce on the London move, and Zack's next rotation would be here instead, with time off for the house restoration.

I tightened my arm around him. I was *so* looking forward to that project. He was teaching me the joy of restoring a house to its former glory.

I got up on my toes and whispered into Zack's ear. "I have something to tell you."

Phil backed away. "If you guys are getting all mushy, I'm outta here." He turned and left, shaking his head.

"What?" Zack asked.

"You were right all along."

He chuckled. "That's no surprise."

I punched his shoulder lightly. "Cut it out. I'm being serious." I pulled my pink envelope from my pocket and pushed it at him. "I want you to help me with this."

He had reminded me every day that none of these deaths were my fault. As we moved forward with our lives, I needed to put this behind me once and for all.

He took the envelope.

I grabbed a match from the mantle matchbox, struck it, and lit the corner of the envelope as he held it out. The expired match went in the fireplace.

I took the envelope from him and rotated it as the yellow flames curled around the edge and grew. Slowly the paper gave way to ash, erasing this guilt from my pre-Zack life. When most of the envelope had been consumed, I tossed it in the fireplace. I turned my back on the flaming paper, a relic from my previous life, and faced the man that represented my future.

"I'm done looking backwards."

He wrapped me in his powerful arms and kissed me. "I'm proud of you."

I was proud of me too. "Thank you for being you."

I was grateful he was persistent enough to teach me the lesson I needed.

The moment didn't last long. Serena arrived to drag me over to Katie and Nick. "Hey, Nick, we have a question for you. Who's better at Klingon, you or Winston?"

He shrugged. "Depends."

Serena moved behind me to undo the clasp of my pendant, and in a moment she had the inscription visible for him to read.

Nick pointed Katie toward the front room. "Hey, Precious, go get Winston. This one might be more than I can handle alone."

Katie returned with the burly agent in tow.

Winston examined the writing. "Klingon, you say?"

I nodded. "That's what I was told. And the number is the stardate of our first date."

Winston shook his head. "You were sold a bill of goods. This is gibberish, no Klingon here."

Nick nodded his concurrence. "Definitely not Klingon."

Zack wandered over.

Winston examined it again. "Not Romulan either. This is just a monkey banging on a typewriter."

My shoulders fell. Forever I'd thought it actually meant Todd cared for me, but this made no sense.

Zack put his arm around me. "Well, you were going to melt it down anyway, right?"

"Yeah."

"Hey," Nick exclaimed. "This isn't a stardate. The first section here is the routing code for a bank in Miami. I see it all the time in my work. That second number is the right length for an account number, so somewhere in the rest of this crap is what we need." He rubbed his hands together. "Winston, got your laptop handy?"

Winston turned for the door. "In the car. Be right back."

A minute later we were huddled behind Nick, watching him work on the laptop.

He tried several combinations of the words in the inscription, and suddenly he was into the account profile page on the bank's website.

I gasped.

Zack nudged me. "It's a retirement account, and you're listed as the beneficiary?"

"I see it. I just don't believe it." The account was Todd's, but it was the balance that struck me—over eight hundred thousand dollars.

Zack whispered in my ear. "This must be the key Delgado was after."

I nodded.

Nick turned around. "What are you going to do with all that money?"

Phil piped up. "I know a construction company that's looking for an investor."

I knew exactly what I would do. "I think I'll donate it to drug rehab non-profits in Jonas's name."

The money most likely had been earned off the backs of drug addicts, and I intended to give it back to them.

Zack gave me a kiss of appreciation. "That's a great idea, Sunshine."

"Before you do that," Winston said, "report it as found money to the sheriff. If nobody claims it in ninety days, it's yours."

"Do you think Delgado will go after it?" Zack asked.

"How's he going to know? It's not like they advertise it. And besides, he'd have to explain where it came from. To have a chance, he'd have to give up who he worked with, and that would be a death sentence on the inside."

The group disbanded from around the computer after a minute.

An hour later, Zack's parents called everyone together. "Time for a toast to the engaged couple," Lloyd said.

Zack's brothers filled glasses with champagne.

I had Zack on one side and his sister Kelly on the other.

When Dennis tried to add champagne to my orange juice, I pulled the glass away. "I can't."

Zack gave me a knowing smile.

Samantha shot me a sly look. "Can't?"

I nodded.

She leaned close to whisper, "Check with me before you pick a name."

Kelly grinned and whispered to Serena. She hadn't missed the meaning of my words either.

The toast was made, and my man lifted me into a congratulatory kiss to applause from the crowd.

He was mine, I was his, and soon it would be official.

"I love you, Sunshine," he whispered in my ear as he put me down.

Just like in the movie, I'd come back to the town I thought I'd left for good and found my true love, right here where he'd always been—waiting for me.

I'd had to find my way back here before he could show me the way forward.

He'd given me everything: true love, his name, confidence in my future—in our future, and before long, a child.

I stretched up to whisper in his ear. "Will you eat a pomegranate for me, then?"

He backed away. "No way."

Some things weren't going to change.

THE END

# NAILING THE BILLIONAIRE

# CHAPTER 1

*JENNIFER*

*I'LL MAKE HIM PAY FOR WHAT HE DID.*

My modified headlamp cast a dim glow on the recalcitrant lock.

The file needed to be back in place before it was missed. I had my copy, and when the news broke, this folder would attract attention.

I stretched my aching shoulders. The tensioner slipped out of the lock as I pulled the pick tool toward me.

*Fuck.*

After wiping my brow with my sleeve, I repositioned the tool at the bottom of the key slot to start picking the cylinder again—for the fourth time, or was it the fifth?

Normal file-cabinet locks wouldn't have been this hard, but the company hadn't gone with standard, hardware-store locks. These were a bitch, and the latex gloves I wore didn't help. The YouTubers made it look so much easier than it was.

The faint sound of a door opening down the corridor caught my attention.

I ducked low and quickly covered my light source with one hand before clicking it off with the other.

The door closed, and footsteps followed. They came closer, and then stopped for a few seconds before clomping my way.

Shimmying back to crouch behind a file cabinet with my bag, I worked to control my breathing, with limited success. The sound of my heart beating threatened to swamp the sounds from the corridor.

Every time this happened, I was more scared than the last. Getting caught in this file room would be something I could explain away during the workday, perhaps. But after-hours, with the lights off? No way. It would be out-of-the-company time for yours truly, and most likely off to jail as well. Worst of all, I would fail at my mission.

There were days when jail didn't sound so bad—it would be a lot less stressful—but that was just me kidding myself. I couldn't live with what that would do to Ramona and Billy. Who would look after them if I couldn't? Certainly not Uncle Victor. Although, the thought of Ramona and him in the same room was amusing. She'd be after him day and night about his drinking, and I'd bet on Ramona carrying the day. She didn't lose many arguments.

I halted a laugh halfway up my throat. Silence was paramount until I knew the footsteps were far enough away. It didn't matter how funny my daydreams got, I had to concentrate on tonight's task.

Eventually I judged it had been long enough and struggled to my feet again.

I wasn't tall, but these locks were positioned for people shorter than me. Rolling a chair in here was out of the question, and hunching over for an hour was going to make this a multi-Tylenol evening. *Advil*, I reminded myself. I planned on a glass of wine, and research said not to take Tylenol with alcohol.

I started again on the file cabinet.

Somebody needed to invent an easier way to do this. Movie characters were always past the lock in less than five seconds, but Hollywood didn't need to be accurate. *Suspension of disbelief*, they called it.

One of those actors should come in here and tackle this lock. That would show them what the real world was like. Just because the script says *and the lock opened* doesn't make it so.

Suddenly, the tension tool loosened as the cylinder returned. Another quarter turn and the plug popped toward me with a loud clunk. At least it was open, but this stupid cabinet was all kinds of trouble.

I froze and listened intently for half a minute.

I couldn't detect any sounds, so I slowly pulled out the squeaky bottom drawer. Pulling my notes from my pocket, I double-checked where I'd originally found the file, just to be sure. Then I pulled the folder out of my messenger bag and slid it back in the drawer, exactly where it had been two days ago.

I eased the drawer closed, pushed in the lock plug, and turned the cylinder with my tension tool to the locked position.

Success.

Removing the headlamp, I clicked it off before closing it in my bag. With the tools back in place, I quickly pocketed the leather case of my pick set. It was too tall to fit well, but I'd deal with that later.

I shouldered the bag and made my way to the door.

The hallway was quiet, so I slipped through the door and closed it behind me.

Moving quietly, I started left. I couldn't relax until I'd made it out without being spotted.

At the corner, I listened before peeking around to look down the long corridor.

I pulled my head back quickly.

The bigger of the two night guards was halfway down the hall and coming this way.

I shuffled back the way I'd come as silently as I could.

The first office door I tried was locked, and the same with the second. There wasn't any time to try to pick one, and the file room door had locked behind me.

The sound of the guard rattling a doorknob just past the corner left me no alternative. I pushed my way into the bathroom, grabbed the handle to keep the spring-loaded door closer from doing its thing, and gently shut the door behind me.

I turned.

*Shit.*

I'd ended up in the men's room. Tiptoeing to the far stall, I slid inside.

A cough outside the door got my heart racing. He was just outside. If he came in here, I was done.

The sound of the door opening sealed my decision. With my hands braced against the stall walls, I put one foot on the toilet seat and climbed up, hoping it wouldn't squeak when I put my other foot on the opposite side of the seat and crouched.

It didn't, but as I lifted my other foot, my pick set case came loose from my pocket and fell to the floor, the light sound masked by the loud closing of the door to the corridor.

I closed my eyes and unsuccessfully willed my heartbeat to slow. Slow, silent breaths were agonizing as my lungs burned for more air.

The footsteps made their way inside and were followed by a grunt and the sound of a zipper coming down.

I opened my eyes, and the sight of my pick set on the floor only compounded my terror.

More grunts preceded humming and the sound of the guard peeing in the urinal.

A bead of sweat threatened to fall into my eye, but I didn't dare move to wipe it away.

The sound of the stream stopped and started a few times before the humming was replaced by another grunt as the zipper sound announced he was done.

The sound of flushing followed, then the door thudding shut.

Thankfully he hadn't bothered to wash his hands. If he had, he might have noticed the pick set on the floor in the mirror.

Finally able to breathe again, I wiped my brow with my sleeve, stepped off the toilet seat, and tried to compose myself. After retrieving the pick set and pocketing the latex gloves, I pulled two tissues from the box by the sink to dry my sweaty hands.

Two minutes went by on my watch before I listened at the bathroom door and found the hallway quiet enough to slip out again.

My path to the stairwell exit required a left down the long hallway, a right at the end, and another jog right. The path was clear as I made the final turn, and I could finally relax as I shuffled softly down the concrete stairs to the garage level.

The back of the garage had a separate set of stairs to the street, and no surveillance cameras.

Once back in the safety of my car, I pulled out my iPad, composed an email, and sent it.

> To: HYDRA157
> From: Nemesis666
> The pony is back in the barn.

I twisted Mom's ring on my finger. "I'll get the proof for you."
The words dissipated in the empty car, but I was sure she could hear them.

# CHAPTER 2

*JENNIFER*
*(Four Days Later)*

As I added pins to secure my French twist Monday morning, I wondered if the bomb would drop today. It had been four long days since I'd put the file back in place. A girl could hope.

I turned my head left and right, and a quick mirror check showed my twist to be perfect. A professional woman always presents a professional image—a habit Mom had taught me.

I ventured out to make breakfast for myself and my sister, Ramona. This meant pouring the Raisin Bran.

My nephew, Billy, had already poured himself a bowl of Cocoa Puffs.

"Are you taking me to school today?" he asked.

"No, not today. Your mommy's taking you."

"Why?"

Ramona opened her door. "Because it's Monday, and it's my turn."

Billy spooned another mouthful of cereal, seeming content with the answer for a change.

Ramona joined us and dug into her cereal. "Anything planned for tonight?" she asked me.

I swallowed. "Nope."

She was clearly fishing for some sign of a third date with Simon, but he hadn't called again, at least not yet.

She gave up the quest, and ten minutes later, the two of them were out the door.

After the dishes, I gave in and sat down at my laptop.

It powered up, and I logged in to the bank's website.

I unfolded the bill I'd pulled from the drawer, and a double-check showed what I feared. My mouth dried. We'd skipped eating out, but with three mouths to feed, I didn't have enough to cover this today.

My pay wouldn't be direct-deposited until Friday. That meant this would be another late payment to deal with. The envelope went back in my purse, at the bottom this time.

Mom would have figured a way to make this all work, but I wasn't her.

Before I could close the computer, the new-email chime sounded, so I clicked on the icon. It was good news at last.

> To: Nemesis666
> From: HYDRA157
> The balloon is launched.
> Hope you can see it.

I grinned. I needed to hustle if I was going to see his reaction.

I deleted the message, closed the computer, and hefted my purse.

Mom would've been proud of the actions I was taking for our family. Ramona and Billy had a roof over their heads, and most importantly, I was avenging my stepfather, the only real dad I'd had.

My little car started with the typical fuss, another thing I needed to spend money on. Money I didn't have. It could use a good cleaning as well. I closed the window when I ended up behind a bus belching the black death of diesel fumes. The state told us we had to get our cars smog-checked every two years, but the city busses did whatever they wanted.

The traffic was heavy, but I made it to the Starbucks in time.

Inside, I ordered a tall mocha and took my preferred table. The coffee was expensive, but it couldn't be avoided. When hunting the rich, you had to go where they went.

Nursing my latte slowly, I turned on my tablet to read the news. Now all I had to do was wait for my target.

The table provided me a clear view of the place, but I had to get here extra early to snag it ahead of the two old ladies who seemed to think it had their names on it. It was important to get the chair facing the right direction.

I scrolled through the news on the tablet in front of me as if I were reading it. Each time the door opened, I glanced over.

So far he was a no-show.

My phone chirped that a text had arrived. I rummaged in my purse, hoping Ramona wasn't telling me she'd locked herself out again.

It wasn't that, but it was equally bad.

EB: Still thinking of U

My worse-than-useless ex-boyfriend couldn't get it through his thick skull that it was over. His now-occasional texts were like having a wasp land on you: swat it and invite a counterattack.

I'd tried responding negatively—that had made it worse. The last time I'd texted back that he should *bug off*, which had resulted in a string of sixty-seven more texts before he gave up. I'd counted.

I put the phone away and ignored him, just like last week.

At least he didn't come by at work. He'd tried that once, and the monster fit I'd thrown had so far prevented any re-occurrence.

Fireman Nick was in line now, with his daily list of a dozen beverages in hand, and my target usually beat him here. Checking my watch, I fretted that he might already have seen the article and decided to skip his mocha before work today. That would be disappointing, to say the least. I was perfectly positioned to see his response if he followed his normal routine.

I switched back to the *Times* website.

The story was third from the top, and probably would remain there all day. It would serve him right. I'd checked the print version already and knew the story was several column inches on the front page below the fold, and it continued on page three. It was guaranteed to get a reaction—and cost him a ton in the stock market.

*It couldn't happen to a more deserving monster.*

～

DENNIS

I WAS RUNNING LATER THAN USUAL AS I SHOVED MY PAPER UNDER MY ARM AND pushed through the door of my building out into the bright, early-morning sunshine.

*Bad idea.*

He stood directly in my path and shoved an envelope at me. "Dennis Benson, you've been served."

In retrospect, looking through the glass before I opened the door would have been a good idea. But I knew that wouldn't have accomplished anything other than putting off the inevitable.

If I'd ducked out the back, he would have tagged me at work, or back here in the evening. As distasteful as it was, there was no avoiding these legal arrows she sent my way.

My God, the woman could be vengeful. *Hell hath no fury*, they say, and that was understating it in this case. What a bitch.

I pocketed the envelope and set off on my morning walk to get my coffee. Rituals were good; rituals kept me grounded. I'd read that the first half hour of the day set one's mood for the rest of it, and a brisk walk followed by a delicious brew was my way of starting on the right foot.

The California sun on my face brightened my mood with every stride. Exercise and being outside, even if not in nature, was good for the mood and the soul. The smog wasn't as bad as yesterday, and the Santa Monica mountains were visible. Their winter shade of bright green had already given way to summer's duller colors. I tried to ignore the wretched envelope and take my mind back to walking the woods and the seashore, camping, and cooking over a campfire.

Back-to-basics activities brought us closer to nature and our roots as pioneers. The Benson family had been early settlers in California, and I was proud to be a fourth-generation Californian, not a recent transplant like so many of those I encountered.

Taking a deep breath, I pulled open the door and entered Starbucks.

The line wasn't long, but the fireman at the counter was reading from a list, and the last time I was behind him it had been quite a wait.

Looking around the tables, I saw a lot of regulars—including the cutie, my fantasy girl—plus three empty tables near the back. Mr. Infinite List ordering now wouldn't take a table, and with only two others ahead of me in line, at least I could catch a spot to relax this morning.

The envelope in my jacket pocket was a lead weight, but I refused to let *her* have that level of control over me. A good run is what I needed, something to get the endorphins flowing.

~

*Jennifer*

An increase in street noise announced the opening of the door to the coffee shop.

I glanced over, and there he was. Mr. Immaculate—tall, imposing, with steely gray eyes and a defined, sharp jaw any woman would find attractive, especially compared to the short, bald guy just behind him in line. Mr. Immaculate's sandy blond hair was annoyingly in place, his suit perfectly tailored to span his broad shoulders and taper to his trim waist. The perfection of the man annoyed me to no end.

At least being in line behind Fireman Nick would annoy him.

He scanned the room.

I looked away and turned to catch the blonde to my left eying him.

Blondie was just short of drooling. Her eyes raked his form as she twirled the ends of her hair, and the corners of her mouth turned up. She was probably imagining his touch. She licked her lips. She moved her right hand over her left, concealing her ring.

*Yuck.* She disgusted me.

*He* disgusted me, because I knew what he'd done.

Blondie probably thought he was Adonis in a suit.

I knew better.

The suit hid the red skin of the devil himself, and the perfect hair hid his horns. One day soon, I would strip away the spit and polish and nail him to the wall, for all to see him as he really was: ghastly, cruel, and with an ugly soul.

Mr. Immaculate had his newspaper under his arm and his chin up, seeming confident that today he would win whatever struggles he encountered.

*Think again.*

I averted my eyes when he glanced my way. Looking back, I caught a smile on his lips as he approached the barista at the register.

He'd probably been checking out Blondie.

Straining to hear, I caught "grande mocha extra shot." It was his standard order.

Sticking to the routine was good. Like every hunter, I knew the predictable prey was the easiest to get.

He tipped the barista with a dollar bill as he always did, a subterfuge of generosity meant to conceal his true character.

I hid behind my raised tablet and watched him while he waited for his order.

He didn't check the paper.

Blondie stood.

Baldy, who'd been in line behind my prey, came over and kissed her before going to wait for his coffee.

*Oops.*

When Mr. Immaculate's order was ready, he took it to a table in the corner and opened his newspaper. He read with cup in hand, taking short sips.

It took thirty seconds or so for his jaw to drop when he found the article.

The door opened again, and I glanced reflexively in that direction.

Martha and Mona had arrived. The M&M girls, they called themselves. They made their way to me.

Martha arrived first. "Good morning, Jennie. Thought we'd come early today to see if you had any luck yet with—"

"Shh," Mona said, interrupting her and cocking her head in Mr. Immaculate's direction.

Martha looked over and put her hand to her mouth as she sat.

Mona took a seat as well. "Thank you for saving our table for us."

"My pleasure," I said. Each time they joined me, I couldn't bring myself to refuse.

Martha leaned over the table to whisper, "Did you approach him yet?"

"Not yet," I whispered back.

Mona adjusted her chair to see him better. "I don't see what the big deal is. I'll go talk to him, if you won't."

I reached out to touch Mona's hand. "Please don't. It's something I need to do myself."

"I agree," Martha interjected. "We're too old to be playing matchmaker."

"Speak for yourself," Mona shot back. "I'm not old; I'm mature."

"You're a year older than me," Martha corrected her.

These two could go at it for an hour, each jabbing at the other in a light-hearted way.

Martha stood. "Do you want your regular?" she asked Mona.

"Yes, please, but less cinnamon this time," Mona replied.

After Martha left for the counter, Mona leaned my way. "You should let me wave him over, and you could introduce yourself."

I had to keep nixing her suggestions, because I couldn't tell them my true intentions. "Thank you, but no. I need to do this my way."

She let out a loud breath. "At this rate, you'll be my age before you meet a man."

"There's nothing wrong with your age," I assured her.

That earned a smile. "You're a dear."

I glanced toward Mr. Immaculate. He'd put his cup down. His eyes got wider as he turned to the remainder of the article on page three.

I smiled as his jaw clenched.

The story corroded the confident exterior of the man, and wild anger grew in his eyes. His hands balled into fists as he probably planned his revenge against the writer—something along the lines of a meeting in a dark alley where he could pulverize him. Or would he choose the anonymity of a bullet from long range? Right now he was the rhino you didn't want to be in front of.

Mona giggled. "I saw that."

"What?"

"You like what you see when you look at him."

She couldn't possibly comprehend what made me smile this morning.

Mr. Immaculate stood to leave. He folded up his paper, tossed his cup, and headed for the door. His countenance showed the combination of anger and frustration I'd hoped for. The door closed behind him.

Martha returned with their coffees, and I excused myself shortly after that.

This would not be the last unmasking of his misdeeds, I promised myself as I walked to work. One by one I would reveal the skeletons in his closet, and the world would finally see the real Dennis Benson. His fancy suit wouldn't fool anyone then.

He deserved it all and more for what he'd done to me; what he'd done to my family.

# CHAPTER 3

*DENNIS*

THE FLOORS DINGED BY AND THE RED NUMERALS INCREASED UNTIL THE uncomfortably hot compartment finally opened on the top floor.

I turned left toward my office, and my phone dinged with a text message. I stopped to check it.

DAD: We need to talk.

Dad was the only one I knew who bothered to make sure his punctuation was correct on a text message. Talking to him was not at the top of my list right now.

My assistant, Cindy, was away from her desk, and before I even reached my office, I could hear Jay Fisher, our CFO, and Larry Zerfoss, my strategic marketing guy, going at it about this morning's article. It would be the only thing talked about all day.

They were standing in my office, and they halted their argument mid-sentence when I entered.

I closed the door behind me and hung up my coat to cool off. "Morning."

"Did you see the *Times* this morning?" Larry asked.

I took my seat and put down the paper. "Just did."

"They make it sound like it's our fault," he complained.

I opened the paper. "I know."

Jay nodded.

"It's not fair, not fair at all," Larry continued. "This is going to tank us."

"What's the damage so far?" I asked.

Larry checked his phone. "Fourteen percent down and still dropping."

The stock market didn't like surprises or bad news, and this was both.

I turned to Jay. "Have you read it?"

He nodded. "Several times and—"

Larry interrupted. "We didn't even own the company when this was going on."

I put a hand up to stop him. "I know."

"Is there anything we can do legally?" I asked Jay.

His face telegraphed the answer. "No. I can't see anything factually wrong, and that means there's nothing to dispute." He turned to Larry. "Unless I'm missing something."

Larry took a breath. "It's just the way they present it—it makes us look like the guilty party here."

"It's America," Jay told him. "Spin is allowed. The First Amendment gives them freedom to print shit like this, twice a day if they want to."

Jay's answer was the same conclusion we'd come to after the previous article. We had no recourse with the paper.

I pointed to the byline. "Larry, where are we on finding out who Sigurd is?" Each of the articles had been penned by a *Sigurd*—no last name, or no first, whichever it was.

Dad had been the one to point out that Sigurd was a mythical Norse dragon slayer. Apparently, someone considered us their dragon.

"Nobody's talking, and we don't have any way to force them. The last article was submitted online through Romania, which is obviously a ruse."

Just like the last article, this one included details that had to have come from inside the company. We had a mole, and a destructive one at that.

"Better get your talking points sharpened up, then," I told him.

He held up a set of pink message slips. "I've got five analysts' calls and counting to return on this."

I stood. "Then get going. It's your job to turn this around."

He shook his head. "This isn't going to be easy."

"That's why we have you," I told him. "Just think of them as Eskimos you have to sell a refrigerator to."

The two left, with Larry still grumbling.

If we did have to sell refrigerators in Alaska, he was just the silver-tongued devil for the job.

I followed them out.

Cindy had returned to her desk. "Good morning."

I nodded. "Not from where I stand."

"Your father called."

"I know. I'll call him in a bit." He probably wanted to remind me of the mistake I'd made.

"And Melissa called as well," Cindy warned me.

"You might as well tell me I have a root canal scheduled today."

"I'm just the messenger," she shot back.

I withdrew into my office. The root canal message would have been better news than a call from my ex-wife. If I could ever have a do-over in life, that's one rash decision I wanted to unwind.

Her Bitchiness, Melissa, could chill for a while.

I dialed Dad after all.

"Dennis, thank you for calling back so quickly. I wanted to see how you're faring with this *Times* nonsense."

"Feeling a little persecuted," I admitted.

"Well, that's one of the problems with deciding to take your company public. You have others judging you all the time, and it's rarely fair."

There it was, the lecture about how I shouldn't have insisted on splitting off a portion into Vipersoft Corp. for me to run and financing it in the public markets.

"Dad, we've been over this."

"You always have the option of taking it private again and not having to deal with days like today."

Rehashing my decision to leave wouldn't do either of us any good. "That's not a discussion for today."

"And that's not why I called," he said. "I'm calling to see if there's anything I can do to help."

"Not unless you know a way to get the *Times* to stop picking on us."

He paused. "Dennis, is that who you think you have a problem with?"

"No. I know it's most likely the anonymous writer."

"That's the one you need to find. But in the meantime, this reminds me of your grandfather."

I sighed. I didn't need another down-home, don't-count-your-chickens-before-they-hatch kind of saying today.

"Your grandfather used to say you couldn't add anything to the lemonade to make it more sour, but you could always add sugar to make it sweeter."

"Thanks, Dad."

A lot of good that did.

"Sugar can sweeten the most bitter lemonade, if you have enough."

My brain kicked into gear, and I understood his message for a change. I had no idea why the great Lloyd Benson couldn't be more direct; it would have made life so much easier.

"Thanks, Dad. That's a good suggestion."

When I was sixteen, I'd been sure my generation was a lot smarter than our elders. Ever since then, I'd been getting reminders that we didn't know as much as we thought, and today was another one.

"Have a good rest of the day," he said. "And don't forget to ask for help if you need it."

We hung up.

*Ask for help?* That was his way of telling me I'd made a mistake by going off on my own, and he'd remind me of it forever if I went back to him for help. I'd handled tough situations before, and I'd handle this one. Sooner or later he'd get it through his thick skull that I wasn't a kid anymore.

I went to my jacket and pulled the awful envelope I'd been served out of the inside breast pocket. I was about to slice it open and get the bad news out of the way, when I stopped.

I put the letter face down on the desk. I'd had enough bad news for today. Picking up my phone, I was about to dial Dad back, when I decided against it. I didn't need validation. I knew what to do. The phone went face down on the envelope.

The phone and envelope made an odd pair. Melissa had given me the phone, a recent peace offering, and I'd avoided the urge to chuck it along with everything else that reminded me of her—that would have been giving in and letting her dictate my actions.

Keeping the phone had been my way of proving she couldn't control me or my mood. But the letter under the phone proved she wouldn't stop trying. Those were the Jekyll and Hyde sides of Melissa—today she'd chosen the evil Hyde. And she'd already consumed more of my time than she deserved.

I walked to the door and opened it.

Thankfully, Cindy was at her desk.

"I need Larry, Jay, and Bob, right now," I told her.

~

*JENNIFER*

I PASSED THROUGH THE LOBBY, AND EVERYTHING LOOKED AS IT HAD YESTERDAY.

The elevator disgorged passengers at several floors before reaching the fourteenth, where I got off. Turning right into finance, I could see and hear the hum of gossip as people stopped at each other's cubicles to share what they'd heard, or read, or just guessed at.

I unlocked the drawers in my cubicle and dropped my purse in the bottom one after taking out my phone and putting it on the charger. A dead phone was a useless phone, and mine was losing charge faster these days. I needed to take it in for a battery replacement when I got the time—if I ever got the time. Time and money always seemed to be in short supply for me.

I pushed the power button, and my computer slowly came to life.

"Did you see the news?" Vanessa asked breathlessly from behind me.

I turned. "No, what news?"

"You have to check the *Times* website."

"Is it good? We're due for some good coverage about now."

"This is the opposite. You gotta read it."

"Okay." I turned back to my monitor and logged in. "We're having the worst luck with those guys." I selected the browser and navigated to the *Times* site.

The story was still third from the top. "Oh my God," I said as I read the words I knew so well. I put my hand to my mouth. "Oh my God," I repeated.

"It's terrible."

I kept my hand over my mouth to hide the smile that grew as I read. The article took the Bensons and this company down a notch. They deserved that, and much more.

I composed myself. "Is this true?"

"I don't know for sure, but Leo thinks it is."

Leo had been here the longest, and everyone approached him as if he held all knowledge related to the company.

Vanessa left, and I busied myself with work.

Three other people stopped by throughout the morning to see what I thought of the news. Each time I expressed horror and said it probably wasn't true, or that I hoped for all our sakes it wasn't.

This story had amped up the company gossip mill even more than the last one.

My cell buzzed. It was my sister, Ramona.

"I might have to stay late," she started.

"I can't talk right now," I answered. "Things are kinda busy here."

"I'll text you if I have to stay."

"Sure. No problem," I said.

We hung up, and I went back to the spreadsheet torture in front of me.

Vanessa wandered by a little later. "Sixteen percent," she muttered before she made a throat-slashing motion across her neck and left.

The upside was that the stock slide was hitting my target, Dennis Benson, where it hurt the most, and it couldn't happen to a more deserving toad.

Emailing Hydra, the one person I could share this with, was also off the table. No emails from work—that had been a firm rule from the beginning. I couldn't share the reaction until I got home, another reason to hope this day went quickly. While I attacked my spreadsheets, I had to keep my glee to myself. Nobody here could know I was the source behind these damaging news stories.

*Fuck you, Dennis Benson.* Someday I'd be able to speak those words to his face. That would be a good day. No, that would be a great day. Vengeance would finally be mine.

I checked the stock price again. Down eighteen percent.

As Shakespeare wrote, "Revenge should have no bounds." And I had only just begun.

# CHAPTER 4

*Dennis*

Bob Shapiro, our COO, was the first of the three to arrive. "Sort of an ugly day today with that *Times* story."

"Yeah," I agreed. "That's what this is about."

He took a seat. "You know I wasn't even here when that stuff happened," he said.

"Nobody's blaming you, Bob. Just wait until the others get here."

He checked his phone. "Can I buy today? Or am I locked out?"

That was probably the one question I *hadn't* expected. Today nobody seemed to want our stock. "Not with what I'm about to tell you. Why?"

"The company's on sale; I just thought I'd add a few shares. When hamburger goes on sale, everybody stocks up. People just don't react rationally to a stock going on sale."

"Yeah, well, I hope to take it off sale, so given what I'm about to tell you, you're locked out."

His impulse had been a good one. Baron Rothschild had become immensely wealthy buying when fear was prevalent, and his belief that "the time to buy is when there is blood in the streets" was still taught in business schools today. The MBA weenies, however, never took it to heart. They all followed the crowd down the path of panic, which only amplified the fear.

When the previous two Sigurd articles had come out, I'd taken the opportunities to buy a significant chunk of company stock and come out way ahead so far. Hamburger had been on sale those days. The difference today was that I had a counterattack, and knowing that, I couldn't take advantage of the situation and buy.

Bob settled in, and I gave him a quick overview of my plan.

A wide smile grew on his face. This was going to be a good day for him.

Jay walked in a minute later.

Larry was the last. He looked askance at Bob. The two had never seen much use for the other.

"I have Citibank calling in a half hour," Larry announced. "Can't this wait, whatever it is?" He didn't bother to move past the doorway.

I pointed at the empty chair. "Have a seat, and close the door." I looked between them. "Ever heard the saying, you can't make lemonade more sour, but you can make it sweeter?"

All I got were blank stares and shaking heads. Apparently, we were all from the wrong generation.

"Well, we're going to add sugar to today's lemonade." I turned to Jay. "What are the projection ranges for the brake division spin-off to our net?"

Jay rubbed his chin. "You mean to our bottom line?"

I nodded. "Exactly."

He shifted in his seat, apparently unsure if I was setting him up. "They're not final, but twenty-two to thirty-cents positive."

"Good. We're announcing the spin-off today."

Bob smiled, the other two went slack jawed.

"But we're not ready," Jay complained. "The plans Bob and I put together are only preliminary."

"They're final now," I told him. "Larry, we're announcing the spin-off, and use thirty cents as the projected effect."

Larry's face went from confusion to elation as he absorbed this new ammunition to counter the article's negativity. "When can I use this?"

Jay was the only unhappy one of the group. "We should always go with a middle-of-the-road projection, and thirty cents is an optimistic upper limit."

I shrugged. "Then you and Bob need to figure out how to make it happen."

Bob was all smiles. "We'll make it happen."

He would be going with the spin-off and have his own show to run for a change. It was a serious step up for his career. I could count on Bob to push this through in record time.

Jay was the one with hard work to do based on my pronouncement, and his furrowed brow showed his apprehension. "This is awfully short notice."

"That's it," I told them. "Let's get cracking."

The other two left, but Jay dawdled. He shut the door. "Can we talk about this a minute?"

"Sure."

"This isn't going to be easy," he cautioned.

"It never is, but we have all quarter to make it work."

"A lot more goes into a transaction like this than you realize. Bob needs a finance and marketing staff set up right away to handle things on his end, not to mention HR."

I nodded. "Yeah, we'll have to power through it. Today we need sugar to add to the lemonade."

"Are you absolutely certain you don't want to take a few days to discuss it? We can always add your sugar to the news cycle next week. Sometimes unintended consequences crop up in things like this."

"I'm sure."

"This can only be done if Bob and I have the authority to make the hard decisions on personnel and such without other departments coming to you to complain and muck up the plans."

"That won't be a problem," I assured him.

After he left, I turned to my best thinking position: facing the window without a desk or papers or a computer crowding me. Jay was right—caution could be useful at times, but this wasn't one of them.

The market had been down significantly already, and these things had a tendency to snowball out of control if left untended. We were under attack by Sigurd, whoever he was, and giving him a chance to get another blow in before we reacted to this one didn't fit my style.

The benefit of splitting off from the family company was that I got to set the rules and make my own decisions, right or wrong. And I knew this one was right. Hell, leaving Benson Corp. hadn't even cut me off from Dad's advice.

The only difference was that this morning Dad had *suggested* what he thought I should do instead of telling me, and that was a thousand-percent improvement.

JENNIFER

VANESSA STOPPED BY AFTER LUNCH. "WE HAVE AN ALL-HANDS FINANCE MEETING AT three."

"What about?"

"No idea," she said as she moved on to pass the word.

It was a typical big-company move. We'd had one after the last bomb hit the papers, too. Departmental meetings would rally the troops, explain the company's biased point of view, and rescue morale from the abyss it was falling into.

Most of the people I worked with had drunk the Kool-Aid at the last meeting and come out happier than when they'd gone in.

This time I had a plan. I'd made a list of what I expected the PR points from management would be, and I had a few embarrassing questions to pose regarding the facts of the article—nothing that would put me in the enemy camp, just clarification questions that were guaranteed to give them fits and raise a good number of queries from the audience.

I reviewed my questions before the meeting time. I just had to wait for the question-and-answer portion that would follow the rah-rah bullshit speech our boss, Jay Fisher, certainly had planned. I knew his background. He'd come out of public accounting, worked his way up at Benson Corp., and become the CFO here under Dennis Benson when Vipersoft was spun-out. Facts and numbers were king with him. His reputation was his stock in trade. He wouldn't sully it by continuing to spout the company line when the facts were on my side. Fisher was the perfect foil. His answers, or non-answers, would show everybody there how heartless Benson had been.

I left for lunch with my question list in my purse. Last time I'd made the mistake of forgetting it, and I'd failed to ask my two most killer questions. The rush of adrenaline from challenging Fisher had made me nervous and had cost me my best opportunity to score points. I wasn't letting that happen today.

At street level, I removed the lanyard displaying my company badge. Advertising that I worked for the soon-to-be universally hated Vipersoft wasn't wise.

After two blocks, that same odd itch at the back of my neck bothered me. I turned, but didn't see anybody following me. My late-night hide and seek in our building had made me paranoid.

I walked an extra few blocks to avoid any company people and chose Tina's Tacos as the recipient of my meager lunch spending today. Several nice tables near the window were available, so I got in line and made my mental choice from the overhead menu.

The tables filled up quickly, as none of the people in front of me chose take-out. By the time I collected my change, the only table left was in the back corner next to the restrooms, right behind two suit-types I didn't recognize.

As I munched my two tacos, I overheard talk of local companies, and the lingo of stock traders drifted my way. They weren't quiet about it either. The taller one was arguing the bullish case for Intel, and not getting far convincing the shorter one. They reminded me of a lot of my classmates at biz school—all numbers and no concept of the people and products behind the real world of the companies. To them, a company was a stock symbol with a number attached and no more. They didn't make money by producing anything. The stock market was just a casino to them, and if they could beat the other suckers by hearing gossip first, they'd call that an honest day's work.

I ignored them and read over my third question again and again, until I could visualize the words if I closed my eyes.

Q3: The paper said thirty-three deaths have been attributed to defects in our products so far. How many do you think the total will rise to by the end of the year?

That should get the room buzzing. It was a killer question, but maybe it could be shortened somehow…

Tall Guy changed the subject. "Did you see that latest from Gumpert? He thinks Cartwright is going to take down Vipersoft."

I stopped chewing to listen to their conversation. I'd seen negative comments in the press from Carson Cartwright about our company, but hadn't paid them much heed. If this guy could damage the company, I was all for it. He might even warrant reaching out to anonymously to provide data. I'd helped Hydra; why not another aligned interest?

Tall Guy switched topics again, and I went back to my questions after losing interest. Unfortunately they were loud. Harleys revving their engines on the street would be less distracting than the jabbering of those two.

I finished my lunch quickly, and back on the street, my phone chirped with a text.

RAMONA: I have to stay late can you pick up Billy pls pls pls

I moved to the building side of the sidewalk, stopped, and typed my reply.

ME: Sure

This would work out well, because I didn't want to stay late today anyway.

∿

THE AFTERNOON STARTED SLOWLY AS I TRUDGED THROUGH MY WORK AND AVOIDED the groups gathering to gossip about the afternoon's all-hands department meeting.

I took the long way to the break room for some tea. Fisher and several others were huddled in a conference room going over something, and they were still at it two hours later when I went by again.

The sight of them still in there lightened my step on the way back to my cubicle. It evidently took a long time to figure out enough lies to explain away the misdeeds.

When the appointed time came, we assembled, and I took a position near the back. When I asked my questions, my voice would carry over the crowd, and everyone would hear. Last time, I'd been near the front, and I'd found out afterward that the people in the back couldn't hear me.

It was a few minutes after three when Fisher stopped exchanging pleasantries with the people up front and the group quieted to hear him speak.

"I know it's been a rollercoaster day for everyone, and I'll be brief," he said.

Rollercoaster, my ass. The market was already closed, and the stock had finished down twenty-two percent. Rollercoasters go up and down to end up back where they started. This had been a one-way trip down.

He cleared his throat. "I have a rather large announcement to make. The company has been exploring a reorganization transaction for some time."

Murmurs began in the crowd. *Reorganization* was usually a codeword for layoffs—*downsizing* in corporate jargon.

The article's effect had been even more than I'd anticipated if they were downsizing already to save the company.

"The management has decided that the best way to enhance shareholder value is to spin off the automotive brake division as a standalone business."

A number of heads in front of me cocked to the side. They were as confused as I was.

*A spin-off?*

"This is going to be a very rapid transition. The production people will be moving, naturally, but this will also affect support departments such as ours."

People looked at each other with questioning faces. Nobody had seen this coming, apparently.

If it had been on the company grapevine, Vanessa would have told me. She was as plugged in as anybody could be.

"As a result, several of us will be transferring with Bob to the new company." That brought a few gasps.

"Don't worry, those of you who are moving on will be getting what I think are rather substantial stock-option packages for the inconvenience."

With that, the mood of the group improved. Stock options were a favorite topic in finance. They weren't worth anything in the short run, but could be quite valuable years in the future.

"As I said, this will be a rapid transaction. The people going with new organization will be…"

He started listing names, and the seventh and last name was a surprise.

"And Jennifer Hanley."

My heart skipped a beat. Without so much as a discussion, I was being shuttled off to a new company.

"If you seven could join me in the conference room after this, I'll fill you in. HR has your new packages to go over as well."

A hand went up.

"Yes?" Fisher said.

"Who will be running the new company?"

"Bob Shapiro will be going over as the new CEO."

Shapiro was the current COO, second in command, so that made sense, and he seemed like a nice-enough guy.

This was all too much to process.

"When will this be announced?" someone else asked.

"It was put on the wire just as we started this meeting," Fisher answered.

Another hand went up, and Fisher pointed to Vanessa.

"Can any of the rest of us apply to go with them?"

"Not at this time, but when they have openings in the future, I'm sure we'll be kept in the loop."

"Who will be running finance?" asked one of the other conscripts assigned to leave.

"Mark Timlin will be the CFO," Fisher answered.

After that there were one or two other questions I didn't follow. My head was spinning.

The group dispersed, and I wandered into the conference room on autopilot to hear my fate. The condemned walking herself to the guillotine, that was me.

Changing companies screwed up my entire plan. I'd lose access to the records I needed in this building. I wouldn't be able to complete my revenge.

Fucking Benson had found a way to thwart me.

This couldn't be happening. *Poof.* All my plans had gone up in smoke.

# CHAPTER 5

*DENNIS*

JAY FISHER WAS BACK AT MY DOOR BEFORE THE DAY WAS OUT. "GOT A MINUTE?"

"Sure."

He closed the door behind him and took a chair. "This isn't going to be easy."

"It never is, but like I told you this morning, we have all quarter to make it work."

"A lot more goes into a transaction than you realize. Bob needs a finance staff right away to handle things on his end."

I nodded. "Yeah."

He took a breath and peered at me over his glasses. "This is going to affect you as well. Remember, your acquisition analyst, Mark, was my pick for Bob's CFO."

"And I said I'd support that. I'll find a replacement." Mark Timlin deserved the promotion opportunity.

The hint of a smile on Jay's face telegraphed a *gotcha* line coming. "Well, he needs to move right away. He's meeting right now with his new team. He has to hit the ground running if this is going to get done."

I wasn't prepared for that. I'd planned on having a few months to locate someone to fill his shoes. "I need him for a few months part time, then."

"You didn't ask me ahead of time about the ramifications of this decision. This is one of those ramifications. You can call Larry and pull back the announcement, or lose Mark starting tomorrow. We don't have time to find another qualified CFO candidate for Bob, and you can't do the spin-off without a CFO in place. If this isn't done right, the SEC will come down on us like a ton of bricks, and it won't be pretty."

I took a breath, but didn't see any alternative. "We go ahead. You can have Mark. And, Jay, I'm sorry I didn't prep you ahead of time on this."

He stood. "Water under the bridge." He stopped at the door. "By the way, who gave you that lemonade-and-sugar quote? Was it Lloyd?"

"Yup, Dad's full of them."

He reached for the door. "That he is."

"Just a minute, Jay."

He turned. "Yes?"

I was still the boss here, and that gave me some prerogatives. "I need someone to fill in for a month while I interview replacements."

"I'll have Denise in HR get someone for you from the temp agency I use."

"I have a better idea. Send me somebody qualified from your group, and *you* get a temp to fill in."

"Yes, sir." He shook his head and left.

After the door closed behind him, I turned to the window and chuckled. This would cost him a good guy. He wouldn't dare send me a turd.

Jay had insisted on teaching me a lesson about being rash, and I'd just taught him a lesson about how shit had a tendency to run down hill, which in this case was his direction.

Dad's suggestion hadn't been a bad one, but Jay had just pointed out— without rubbing my nose in it too much—that I'd made a rookie move. I could have taken a day or two to make this decision, and not huddling with him and others had just caused my first unintended consequence and bitten me in the ass. And the day wasn't over yet. The decision might cost me more in the future than I'd stopped to anticipate. Something more middle-of-the-road—between Larry's instant-action philosophy and Jay's conservatism—might have been better. A thought for next time.

I looked out over the expanse of the LA area. My office was this high up because I was willing to take risks, and sometimes those came with costs.

∽

*JENNIFER*

THE OTHER SIX WHOSE NAMES HAD BEEN CALLED TO GO WITH THE SPIN-OFF WERE already in the conference room when I shuffled in—happy faces on all of them as they mumbled about stock options. This greedy group had no other questions apparently, like where we would be working.

I returned their smiles as I contemplated the abundant empty space on the lower floors of this building. The company had been trying to lease that out. The possibility that I might keep a badge that gained access to this building brightened my outlook. My vengeance could stay on track.

Fisher introduced Mark Timlin, the CEO's acquisitions analyst, as our new boss and left the room.

Timlin took a seat at the head of the table. "Look around. This merry group will comprise the nucleus of the finance team we're taking over to Hydrocom—that'll be the name of our new company. Jay has told me wonderful things about all of you, and I look forward to helping you staff our team for success."

It was just my luck to end up working for someone who had spent the last two years at the right hand of the devil himself.

He was energetic in his description of the opportunities for all of us with the new venture. As the new CFO, it made sense that he would be.

I concentrated on the wood grain of the table in front of me as he went on too long for my taste about how excited he was.

He then went around the table, getting names from those he didn't know and telling us our new positions.

"Jennifer, you'll be the new General Ledger Supervisor," he said when he got to me.

My mouth might have dropped open, but with the fog in my brain I wasn't sure. It sounded like he'd said *supervisor*.

"You'll have two open reqs, one for a senior accountant, and a junior as soon as you can recruit candidates," he continued.

He had meant it when he said *supervisor*.

I nodded. Minions working for me was a serious step up career-wise. And a supervisor position had to mean more money—a promotion.

A godsend.

After Mark moved on to the next person, Ernesto leaned over. "Congrats. You deserve it."

The praise sent a tingle sent up my spine. Ernesto was right. I did deserve it. I'd worked hard here—not because I was devoted to the company, but because that was the way I was wired. Giving a hundred percent was the way I'd been raised, and there wasn't any alternative.

"Thanks," I whispered back.

"Now, HR has new packages to go over with each of you downstairs before you leave for the day. Also, we'll be moving into our new digs in Pasadena over the weekend." He slid a pile of papers down the table, and we each grabbed one. "That's the address of our offices starting next week."

Pasadena was not too far, but it would add more than an extra half-hour each way for me and half the people in the room. So much for keeping my access to this building.

Ernesto grinned. Pasadena wasn't far from his home in the valley—a win for him.

I couldn't help but slump in my seat. An extra hour-plus of daily commute torture in my car was going to be one cost of the promotion. The other would be an end to my quest for revenge on Benson, and that was the worst of all.

A series of meaningless questions from the others followed as I concentrated on the paper in front of me. Without access to this building, I'd never be able to feed Hydra the material that would make Dennis Benson pay. And who knew how many other families would have to pay the price in the coming years if he wasn't brought down.

"Any more questions?" Mark asked.

I had one I couldn't ask.

"Very well then, welcome aboard. HR is expecting you downstairs. And we'll start off right back here tomorrow morning at seven-thirty." He stood, and the happy group followed him out.

"Jenn, you okay?" Ernesto asked as we passed through the door.

"Oh, sure. I'm just thinking about the commute is all."

"Yeah, that can be a drag, but you made supervisor."

He and I took the second elevator down to HR.

A half hour later, I sat across the table from an HR specialist with a written compensation letter in front of me.

"The salary increase will be fourteen thousand a year," she said.

I could hardly believe it as I read along. Over a thousand a month extra gross pay would go a long way toward making life livable for all of us. Between my student debt and helping with Ramona's schooling, I'd been getting further behind on my credit cards every month.

"The option package is twenty thousand shares vested over four years," she added.

That was huge as well. I'd only been awarded two thousand when I started.

Everybody in finance knew how valuable the options could be over time. Nobody in her right mind would pass on a deal like this, despite the extra commute.

I sat back. "How long do I have to consider this?"

Her brow shot up. "It's quite an opportunity, Jennifer. I can check, but as I understand it, these transfers are mandatory."

"What if I don't want to drive all the way to Pasadena?"

"If you're not satisfied, I suggest you talk to Mark. He might be willing to sweeten it a bit. But I'll tell you right now, this is quite generous." She shrugged.

I'd obviously thrown an unexpected wrench in the works by not jumping at the opportunity.

"Mark?" I asked.

"Yes. I'd start there. We weren't given much time to work on these, so I'm sorry if it's not what you were expecting."

She didn't get it. She was talking money, and I was thinking of not going at all.

"I just don't make decisions like this on the spur of the moment."

568

"We were told to have you sign this afternoon."

She was obviously not the one to be having this discussion with.

"I'll go talk to Mark, then, and be back later."

She didn't seem thrilled that I'd messed up the schedule.

I excused myself and stood by the elevator, rereading the paper.

Ernesto passed by me, all smiles. "See ya tomorrow, Jenn."

I waved and decided to press the *up* button on the elevator. Only one person in our department was likely to be able to override this, and it wasn't Mark.

Jay Fisher was in his office when I approached. It was just after five, and his assistant, Margie, no longer guarded the door.

He waved me inside. "Jennifer, come on in."

I closed the door after me.

His brow lowered at my attempt at privacy. "Is everything all right?"

"I wanted to talk about the move."

He nodded and looked over his glasses at me. "Okay?"

I took a seat opposite him and folded my hands, unsure how to put it. "I'm not sure going with Hydrocom is the right thing for me."

He steepled his hands and leaned forward. "I see. It's a promotion, and frankly, Jennifer, I think you're ready."

I couldn't possibly explain my real motivations. "I'd like to stay here with this team."

He sat back. "But your position here becomes redundant with the move." *Redundant* was a nice way of saying my job was going away.

"I understand. I'm open to changing areas, but I'd like to stay here with you, rather than go with them."

"Do you have some particular issue with Mark or someone else in the group?"

That was my opening.

"Well, there was this… I'd rather not say."

He seemed to be buying it. "If you stay, are you up for a challenge?"

"Yes. Certainly."

He took a deep breath. "The hours may not be what you're used to, and your new role can be a little demanding at times."

"Not a problem," I assured him. I needed something, anything that would let me stay in this building.

"I only have one place I can put you right now, and it will be difficult but like I said, I think you're ready."

I waited.

"You'd be replacing Mark, working for Mr. Benson on acquisitions."

In spite of my efforts, my face must have fallen. Working for the devil himself was never part of the plan. "Is there anything else I could move into? Maybe Vanessa could do the acquisitions work."

The corners of his mouth turned up. He thought that was as unlikely a solution as I knew it to be. "Jennifer, think about it overnight, and let me know tomorrow. Those are your two choices." His eyes held mine.

"Would there be a raise involved with the acquisitions position?"

His head tilted. "It's not a supervisory position, but perhaps I could suggest some adjustment. That's really a discussion you'd need to have with Mr. Benson at the end of your probationary period."

Three months to find out would be an eternity working for the devil.

I tried to keep eye contact and discern if there was any way I could get another alternative out of him with more pleading. I settled on *no*. "Thank you. I'll think about it."

"They're both good opportunities," he said as I left.

I thanked him again and headed to my desk. I didn't have a lot of time before I needed to retrieve Billy from daycare.

Before I turned off my computer, I checked the stock price for the dose of good news I needed after these meetings. The stock had closed down twenty-two percent, but I couldn't believe my eyes. The after-hours quote was up five percent. The spin-off headlines had overpowered the *Times* article.

I'd had such high hopes for today, and now I was faced with two awful choices. Benson had pulled a rabbit out of a hat and dodged the news bullet.

How was that possible?

I stopped on the floor for HR on the way down.

Her door was closed. I'd have to get with her in the morning and explain my discussion with our CFO.

# CHAPTER 6

*JENNIFER*

Ramona helped me clean up the dinner dishes. "What are you moping about?"

My eyes darted to Billy. "Later." He was still finishing the last of the broccoli his mother had insisted he eat.

The television news was on, and it was something about a little girl gone missing this afternoon on her way back from school. An Amber Alert had been issued.

Ramona rushed to get the remote and changed the channel. "That's depressing."

Billy left his plate and went to the couch.

"Hey, little guy. Let's see your homework first," his mother told him.

"I did it already," he said as he picked up the DVR controller.

"Then I want to see it already," she said.

He gave in more easily than usual and brought it to the table from his backpack. "It was spelling, which is easy."

Ramona checked the paper and nodded. "Good job, little guy."

Billy stiffened at the comment. "I told you I did it. And I'm not little. Jeremy is little."

Jeremy was another kid in his class, and Billy had it right that Jeremy was tiny for a seven-year-old.

"You'll always be my little guy," Ramona said as she tousled his hair. "Why don't you go into the bedroom to watch so I can talk to your auntie Jenn."

"Okay." He got up, but stopped at the hallway. "When do I get my own room?" He'd lodged the complaint before, but it was becoming more frequent.

"When we can afford it. Not just yet," Ramona answered.

Financially, things were tight, even with this two-bedroom place, and when we'd last looked, getting a place with a room for him would have meant a neighborhood neither of us felt comfortable with, and Billy wouldn't have been able to stay at his current school either.

He shrugged, retreated to their bedroom, and closed the door behind him.

Ramona shut the dishwasher after loading the last dish. "I know pretty soon sleeping in the same room as Mom is going to be a giant embarrassment for him, but it's scary out there, and I feel safe here."

True to form, she hadn't addressed the crimp it put in *her* life to not have a room of her own, but rather how it affected her *little guy.*

"He won't stay this age forever, you know."

She shrugged. "Doesn't make it any easier." She walked to the couch and sat. "So what's the big news you couldn't tell me?"

I brought my glass of water and also took a seat on the couch. "Did you see the news today?"

"No, did you and your sick accomplice put out another hit piece?"

Ramona hadn't embraced my desire for revenge against Dennis Benson and his family.

I smiled. "This morning." I felt for Mom's ring on my finger.

She shook her head. "This isn't healthy. You know there's a name for what you're doing, and it's not a pretty one."

"I'm avenging Mom and Dad," I shot back.

"No, you're getting pleasure from hurting someone else, and that's not right. Two wrongs don't make a right, and none of this will bring him back." She'd long ago made her opinion of my crusade clear. "And Mom killed herself."

"It was Dad's accident that caused her drinking."

Mom had taken to the bottle and driven drunk, going off the road into a telephone pole. At least she hadn't taken anyone else with her.

Ramona huffed. "It was her drinking that killed her."

"And that was because of Dad's accident."

Ramona shook her finger at me. "She was a drinker before, and you know it."

She had me there, because Dad had always been on her about it, and his persistence had kept it to a minimum.

It wasn't worth the argument. I'd given up trying to convince Ramona to see it my way. "That's not what I wanted to talk about."

She glared across the space between us. She wasn't giving up. "When is enough going to be enough?"

It wasn't a question I'd spent much time thinking about. "I don't know yet."

"Then you're just doing it for spite."

"Can we drop it? I have a problem."

She waited for me to explain.

"The company is shifting me to a new job. Actually, it's sort of a choice between two jobs."

She sat up. "That sounds interesting."

I put my water down. "This afternoon they told seven of us that we were leaving the company with a spin-off."

"Those things happen, I guess. Does that mean we have to move?"

I ignored the question to start with. "If I go with that one, it's a promotion to supervisor."

She stood and gave me a high five as she passed me on her way to the kitchen. "That deserves a toast. I knew sooner or later they'd see how hard you work."

Her pride warmed me. She was the most supportive sister anyone could ask for.

She opened the fridge and pulled out the bottle of cheap red wine we'd used for cooking yesterday.

"If I went with them, it would be a raise and stock options."

She unscrewed the cap and pulled down two glasses. "How much of a raise?"

I sat up. "Fourteen thousand."

"Fourteen? That's fucking fantastic." She put down the bottle and screwed the cap back on. "That calls for the good stuff."

I agreed.

She pulled our special bottle of cabernet from the back of the cabinet.

"No! That one's for when you graduate." We'd been saving it.

She started to unwrap the foil over the cork. It was our only bottle of wine that wasn't screw top.

"We can get another," she said.

Giving in, I located the corkscrew in the drawer. "And, I'd get two minions working for me."

She handed me the bottle. "That's a real supervisor job, then. Next thing you know, you'll be a manager."

I worked the corkscrew into the cork, pushed down the levers, and pulled it free. "Let's not get ahead of ourselves."

She held out a glass for me to pour. "What's the other opportunity?"

"Working for the CEO."

She pulled the glass back. "You mean *him*?"

I took the other glass from the counter and poured. "The one and only."

She put her glass forward, and I poured.

"To you, sis." She raised her glass.

I raised mine as well. "Thanks."

We both sipped.

The wine wasn't as sweet as what we usually had, but then I had no experience with good wine—and it hadn't been chilled either. The wine snobs all had cellars or separate wine coolers, didn't they? It had to make a difference.

Ramona followed me back to the couch. "It sounds like the second one is also a step up."

I sat and nodded. "It probably is, but I would have to work with him, and I don't know if I could stomach that."

"Have you ever considered that you could be wrong about him?"

I ignored her comment. She wasn't going to dissuade me from my goal. "And, I'm not sure there's much of a raise involved." There certainly wasn't a bird in the hand the way there was if I went with the group to Pasadena. Knowing Benson, he'd probably delight in not giving me a raise, especially if he knew my lineage.

But he probably didn't. He was likely cold enough to not remember the names of the people he'd hurt. *Don't know* went along with *don't care* in my experience.

"Are you sure about that? You said they were both promotions."

I finished the sip of wine I'd taken before answering. "Not one hundred percent, but if I stay here it's not a supervisory position."

I still thought this wine wasn't worth the price, but then, was a Ferrari that cost ten times as much as a Chevy ten times the car?

With the likelihood that I would ever own a Ferrari at dead zero, that was a question I'd never know the answer to. They did look good though.

"What are you smiling about?" Ramona asked, pulling me from my internal deliberations.

"Nothing. Just wondering if we could afford a three bedroom after my raise."

"Fourteen K sounds good enough to me."

I nodded. Even after taxes, it should allow us to get Billy his own room.

She worked the remote. "Sandra Bullock okay?" She'd stopped on *Two Weeks Notice*.

"Sure."

The movie was funny, and I couldn't help but compare it to my situation. The heroine ended up working for the guy she didn't like and didn't have anything in common with. He betrayed her for corporate greed. Then the movie took a weird turn and he reformed for her—so unrealistic in the real world. In real life, the bad guys got away with it most of the time, got caught some of the time, and never turned over a new leaf.

My phone chirped that a text had arrived.

EB: Call when u have time

Ramona shot me a quizzical look, so I pointed the screen her way. She rolled her eyes. "Screw that."

I turned the phone off. Ed didn't deserve my time.

At the end of the movie, the rich guy made a joke about how small Sandra's parents' apartment was. That brought me back to the choice I had to make.

Ramona and Billy deserved a bigger place with separate bedrooms. The Pasadena option made the most sense, even though I'd have to give up my access to the files that held Vipersoft's dirty laundry.

I could handle the commute; giving up justice for Dad was the hard part.

When the movie ended and Ramona and Billy had gone to bed, I poured myself another glass of wine to contemplate my decision.

# CHAPTER 7

*DENNIS*

TUESDAY MORNING I WOKE EARLY. ACTUALLY, I'D BEEN SO NERVOUS ABOUT THIS morning's market opening that I kept waking and checking the clock.

I gave up and dressed for a run when my latest clock check showed five thirty. I made a long loop of it, but was still back with plenty of time to shower before the market opened at six thirty Pacific Time. This was one of those times where it helped that the New York types were lazy and didn't start work till nine thirty their time.

I finished my cantaloupe and toast and had my laptop open to the trading software I used.

Promptly at six thirty, the trades for Vipersoft started scrolling down the screen. They were all green, and the little daily chart gapped up from yesterday's terrible close. It had already crossed above where it had been before the *Times* story.

"Yeah," I yelled to the empty house. "Take that, you asshole."

Sigurd's latest attempt to torpedo me had failed.

Dad's advice had been spot on, and I'd won this battle. We still didn't have a clue who was behind this, but secrets like that didn't withstand the test of time.

The first rule of secrets was not to tell anyone. Keep the secret to yourself, and you only had yourself to blame if it was discovered. But since Sigurd clearly had an accomplice, the circle of those in the know was already beyond one, and a slip up was just a matter of time.

Melissa's envelope from yesterday sat next to my computer where I'd left it

576

last night. I picked it up, but decided to let it rest unopened again today. Why give her the satisfaction of annoying me? My lawyer could give me the short version later after he'd digested it and had a plan for how to deal with her.

As if she had surveillance in my house, my cell burst to life with her ugly mug on the screen.

I hit the decline button, and the face disappeared. The picture of her wasn't actually ugly; it was just that I had seen through the facade.

Beneath the pretty face, embellished with too much makeup, was an ugly soul, one intent on inflicting pain and misery. She also had less common sense than a squirrel. She had insisted more than once that we give it another try, but that would be like pissing into the wind—after all the effort I'd come out even worse than before I started.

It had been my fault for rushing into the wedding, but maybe more time wouldn't have changed the outcome. She was, or had been, an actress, after all. And her performance had been good enough to fool me.

The phone beeped, and the screen showed she'd left a voicemail.

I navigated to the voicemail page and deleted the message without listening to it. I'd had enough aggravation yesterday to last me a month.

THIS MORNING, I SKIPPED MY NORMAL STOP AT STARBUCKS AND WENT DIRECTLY TO work.

The elevator doors opened, and I was ready for a better day than yesterday.

When I opened the door to Mahogany Row, as some called it, Cindy was already at her desk.

Her smile was even perkier than usual. "I thought today might be a busy one," she said, answering my unasked question. She handed me several pink message slips. "They started calling early."

"Thanks, Cin." All three messages were from analysts. I handed them back. "Larry can handle these. He'll enjoy it."

The analysts were always trying to get past Larry and talk directly to me, hoping to get something beyond the standard info dump he gave all the analysts access to. They were looking for an angle, an advantage over the next guy.

She held one slip up. "All except Gumpert. He was mad yesterday that he hadn't gotten a heads up."

"He deserves Larry."

Inside my office, I spotted a cup of coffee already on my desk.

"Thanks for the coffee," I called.

"I figured you could use it," Cindy replied from my door. "Also, Jay was already by this morning."

After his attempt to lecture me yesterday on being rash, I would look forward to pointing out how well the spin-off strategy had worked at turning around our stock price.

I powered up my computer and clicked on the stock price bookmark. Up another two percent.

Yes, it would be a good discussion.

I took off my jacket and hung it on the antique coat rack in the corner, a gift from my brother Zack, who was into antiques. Even the car he drove was old.

"Hey, Cin, would you mind fetching Jay for me? I'd like to have that chat."

She agreed and was off. If she called, there was a chance he'd be busy. When she went personally, she never failed to return with him in tow.

Jay had worked directly for my dad back at the family company. He'd never said as much, but I wondered if he didn't think working here for me represented a step down for him.

My desk phone rang, and I answered it.

"Glad I caught you," Michael Gumpert said when I picked up.

"Morning, Michael. I'm on my way to a meeting." It wouldn't be wise to hang up on him the way I wanted to.

"Dennis, I won't take much of your time. I wanted to ask for your take on the revised EPS projections Larry is handing out. They seem a bit aggressive to me given the current climate."

The question was a trap.

Things had moved so fast yesterday that I hadn't gotten a copy of the notes Larry had written up for his analyst calls. But I couldn't say I didn't know exactly what Larry was feeding the analyst community—that would be suicide.

"I don't have anything to add to Larry's comments," I said.

"I get that, Dennis. I do. I was just looking for your take on the aggressiveness of the numbers."

Another trap. He would use any tilt I offered in his forecasts. If I were optimistic, he'd set a high bar of expectations, and the market would punish us if we missed. If I didn't show confidence, he'd move them down right away in a surprise move, the other analysts would follow, and the market would punish us.

Managing their expectations had to be done slowly, not the day after a major announcement, and he knew that.

"The numbers he gave you are our numbers. There's been no change."

"And the bottom-line benefit next quarter of the Hydrocom spin-off?"

"Michael, I'm late for my meeting. Get with Larry on your questions. He'll be happy to help you."

"I'm going to have to move down my forecasts, then."

His threat might not be an idle one, but it was for Larry to handle.

"And also, do you have any rebuttal to Cartwright's comments yesterday afternoon about the spin-off?"

I didn't pay attention to Cartwright's barbs anymore. He could go fuck himself. I took a moment to control my anger. "No, I don't have any comment. Bye, Michael." I hung up on him.

Not the best way to curry favor with the financial community, but he was supposed to be calling Larry, not me.

Besides, Gumpert was an arrogant ass and needed to be taken down a notch or two. He carried around a handkerchief embroidered with his family coat of arms, as if that should mean something in this day and age.

Cartwright was another thorn in my side. With a history of attacking companies such as ours—and extorting them—he was a financial low-life. His plan of attack followed a standard path. He'd publicly attack a company while buying stock and increasing his position. If the company became vulnerable enough, he'd demand seats on the board to "help" them.

That's when his targets often paid him off to go away, and where he made most of his money. Wall Street had even invented the term *greenmail* for this approach. Occasionally he'd go further in his attacks and attempt to gain control of the board.

I had to wonder if this was payback for the run-in I'd had with his son, Adam, years ago. Regardless, I had no intention of paying the blood-sucking scum.

∼

*JENNIFER*

MY ALARM MADE THE FATAL MISTAKE OF BUZZING AT ME FROM THE NIGHTSTAND.

It took me two tries to whack it hard enough to get the devilish thing to shut up. The noise it made hitting the floor didn't sound good. One of these days it wouldn't survive the abuse.

Ramona had suggested I use my phone, but I was deathly afraid I'd break it the way I had my last two alarm clocks. At less than twenty bucks, they were expendable, and my phone wasn't.

I rolled out of bed having gotten almost no real sleep last night. But I needed to get up. Tuesday was my day to use the bathroom first.

The warm water of the shower slowly rinsed the grogginess out of my brain.

It should have been a soothing night after seeing Dennis Benson take the beating he deserved. Instead, *my* world had taken the beating, and my sleep had suffered.

It was so unfair that Benson had found a way to thwart me. He'd come out on top and put me in the position of having to choose between Dad and Ramona.

How would Ramona feel if I stayed at Vipersoft and cost us the income we needed? She and Billy would suffer the most.

How would I feel putting them through that?

She'd never supported my revenge project, and this would turn her even more against me. I'd tried to reason with her about it, but there was no bridging the gap of our views on the subject.

Usually I found the shower a calming place to think through a problem, but today I climbed out no more sure of my path forward than when I'd entered. If anything, I was more mixed up.

Billy was already eating his cereal, Cocoa Puffs again, by the time I finished dressing and got out to the kitchen.

"It's Tuesday today," he announced.

I poured a glass of grapefruit juice for myself. "That's right. Want some juice?"

"It's hamburger day." His tone was more dejected than excited. He didn't answer my juice question.

His school served burgers at lunch on Tuesdays like clockwork. One of the parents owned a local burger place and sold patties at a discount to the school.

"If you want, I can make you a sandwich instead." I poured him a small glass of juice.

"No, I want a cheeseburger, but last week they only had ones without cheese left, and I didn't want the pickle either."

I brought the glasses over. "You were late?"

"Yeah, a little, but they know I always want a cheeseburger and no pickle."

I sat opposite him and drank from my juice. "Sometimes the early bird gets the worm."

He pushed his cereal around in his bowl. "Mommy told me not to complain."

"She's right about that. You don't want to be labeled as a complainer. You could always take the pickle off and get almost what you wanted."

He gulped down the juice I'd poured him. His cereal didn't merit the same attention.

"It's your turn," he said.

I stood to get some cereal for myself. "For what?"

"It's Tuesday. You take me to school, and Mommy said we could have pizza night tonight."

I checked the time on the microwave.

*Shit.*

This would mean no breakfast for me today. "Get your backpack. We have to go." I quickly moved the ball of pizza dough I'd made last week from the freezer to the refrigerator.

Ramona hadn't shown her face yet. If I'd wanted to switch, I should've arranged it with her last night.

I hustled him out and we made the drive to school. Unfortunately, work was in the opposite direction.

*Take off the pickle.* I needed to talk to the man who could change the options— the man who could take off the pickle. That was the solution to my problem.

Billy exited the car with a quick goodbye. I didn't pull away from the curb until I saw him make it safely inside the school.

I needed the new position with the big raise *and* to negotiate access back into the Vipersoft building. With seven people moving over, that had to leave holes somewhere in finance that I could help with after hours or on weekends, thereby keeping my badge with access to the building. Part-time weekend work would also ease my access to the file rooms.

I made a U-turn at the light, and the sun broke through the clouds—a definite omen that things were improving.

My skills were broad enough that there had to be something I could help with at headquarters—something between take it or leave it. I refined my sales pitch to Fisher as I drove in to work.

# CHAPTER 8

*JENNIFER*

THE GROUP WAITING FOR THE ELEVATORS AS I ENTERED THE LOBBY WAS LARGER THAN usual.

Ben sat at his normal station behind the desk. As I approached, he tilted his head toward the crowd. "One of the elevators is down for maintenance."

I nodded. "Thanks."

I shuffled closer with each opening of the polished stainless doors, but I didn't make it on until the third filling of the little car.

Sweat was already threatening to soak my blouse when the door closed and it instantly got warmer. Packed between marketing people complaining about not being chosen to go with the spin-off, I counted the floors as the doors opened and disgorged a person or two at each stop.

Getting off at the finance floor, I dropped my purse at my desk before making my way to the conference room.

Through the glass I saw the meeting had already begun. I smoothed down my skirt and opened the door.

Mark looked up. His forehead creased. "I'll be with you in a minute, Jennifer."

I stopped. It was as if he knew I wanted to talk to him about doing after-hours work back here.

"Outside," he added.

I retreated to the hallway, but not before noticing the group had increased by one since yesterday.

Vanessa sat on the far side of the table, concentrating on the paper in front of her.

I silently rehearsed the lines I'd come up with in the car.

Mark came out and closed the door behind him. "Let's talk in number three."

I followed him into the adjoining empty conference room.

He didn't sit, so neither did I.

"You didn't sign your paperwork yesterday afternoon the way I asked you all to."

My shoulders slumped. "I went back, but they'd closed the office early." I backed up a bit. This wasn't the conversation I'd envisioned. This was all wrong.

"Everyone else managed to, and Jay told me you had misgivings about joining us based on the commute."

My throat went instantly dry. *Those two have already talked this morning?* "I can make the commute work." I couldn't start with my new boss thinking I didn't appreciate the opportunity. How often would I get a chance like this?

He held up a hand to stop me. "Vanessa expressed an interest yesterday in joining Hydrocom." He took a breath. "So she will be filling the general ledger supervisor role."

"But—"

"I have a meeting to get back to. You can apply for a transfer in the future if you like, when you're more certain of your situation." He left, and the door closed behind him.

Tears threatened, and my knees wobbled. The room became cold, and I slumped into the closest chair. I'd totally screwed this up. I'd let Ramona and Billy down. Vanessa had aced me out of my chance at the raise we needed.

After a few minutes, I took a deep breath and sat up straight. My current job was being eliminated, and I needed to work. The only thing left to do was to put on my brave front and face the music. What alternative did I have? Short answer, none.

After a stop in the ladies room to check my eyes, I turned right toward Fisher's office.

His assistant, Margie, appraised me with cold eyes as I walked up. She helped his productivity by protecting his time, as she saw it. Nobody got past her without an appointment.

I stopped and prepared to argue my case, but was cut off with a hand gesture. "He asked for you to join him in Mr. Benson's office." She checked her watch. "That was four minutes ago."

"Thank you," I said as I turned for the elevator.

"You should take your purse," she said.

I reversed course and gathered my purse before heading once more for the elevator that would transport me to my doom.

The door closed, and a line from *Alice in Wonderland* popped into my brain: "*Off with her head!*" That's exactly how it would go if Benson got an inkling of how I felt about him. I practiced the smile I planned to hide behind. It didn't look half bad in the polished stainless of the elevator door.

As I entered the executive offices, I heard voices and stopped short of the door with Dennis Benson's nameplate beside it.

"I need a guy with an MBA, and experience," Benson said.

"No, you don't. I have someone who can provide the support you need," Fisher said from inside the office.

"Are you deliberately trying to jam me up for moving fast on the spin-off?"

"I just said these kinds of trade-offs wouldn't have been necessary if we'd taken the time to plan properly."

"We had to move quickly. You know that."

"If you want to go outside, you can start interviewing next week to fill Mark's position. It shouldn't take longer than a month or two."

My God, they were arguing about me. Not only did I not want to work for the devil; he didn't want me either. Suddenly the prospect of losing this job too became a real possibility, and then where would I be? Unemployed, on top of all the other things I stood to lose.

I smoothed my skirt, took a deep, composing breath, knocked on the door frame, and then moved into the open door.

"There you are," Fisher said.

"Dennis, I'd like you to meet Jennifer Hanley."

I pasted on my fake, I-don't-hate-you smile and entered the devil's lair.

∼

## Dennis

She walked into my office.

*Jennifer Hanley*—now I had a name to go with the face, the body, the fantasies.

"I think she'll be just what you need," Jay said with a sly grin.

Could he know what he'd just done to me?

My mind raced. I caught myself before my jaw dropped very far. I hadn't been expecting a girl, much less this girl—my Starbucks girl. Jay stood and made his way to the door. "I'll be downstairs if you need me," he said as he left, leaving her behind.

I composed myself and rounded the desk to shake her extended hand.

It was warm and soft as I'd always imagined, but with a firm grip—a grip I'd imagine every time I closed my eyes in the shower to stroke myself.

She looked down at our joined hands before I realized I'd held hers too long, enjoying the warmth, the electric touch I'd imagined for months.

I let her go. "Please take a seat, Jennifer." Returning to my chair, I scooted close to the desk, a position that hid my stirring cock. "Where did you get your MBA?"

She looked down. "I have a BS in Accounting and Business Administration from Pepperdine, not an MBA."

I noticed the rise and fall of her chest as she talked. No way was having her just down the hall going to work.

This was totally fucked up. Her working under me couldn't possibly end well. She didn't have an MBA, and she was the face I saw every morning as I closed my eyes and jerked off—the one keeping me sane during my enforced period of abstinence leading up to the court date with Melissa.

"Mr. Benson?" she asked.

Her voice pulled me back to the moment. "Dennis, please." I tried in vain to look away from those luscious lips I wanted on my dick every morning when I woke up, but looking any lower would probably break my zipper.

She shifted in her seat. "How should we start? Would you like to explain the position I'm going to be in?"

I had barely enough working brain cells to keep from explaining ten different positions I'd like her to assume.

Her face had softened from the distressed, forced smile of a minute ago to something more neutral. She might have overheard my complaints to Jay.

I cleared my throat. "Just a second."

I buzzed Cindy to come in. I had to get this girl out of here and make a plan, any plan.

I'd meant what I'd told Jay, even before I knew he'd picked this girl to saddle me with. Now my concerns were tripled at least. Working this close to her could, or most likely *would*, lead to something that would unravel everything with Melissa.

She was supposed to be an after-Melissa treat, not a fuck-up-the-negotiation indulgence. The plan had always been to pursue her after the Melissa legal skirmish was done.

Cindy opened the door and popped her head in with her usual speed. "Yes?"

"Jennifer here will be taking over Mark's position. Would you please get her situated in the office?"

"Sure thing," Cindy responded with a smile. "Jennifer you said?" She extended her hand.

Jennifer stood and greeted Cindy. "Yes, Jennifer Hanley from downstairs in finance."

"Oh," I added. "Get her the Talbot paperwork. Jennifer, get up to speed on them for the two o'clock meeting."

"Of course," Jennifer responded as they left, and Cindy thankfully closed the door.

I'd made the decision to send her back to Jay's floor the moment I laid eyes on her. He needed to be taught a lesson about messing with me this way, but to make it sink in, she had to help me by screwing up in a documented fashion.

~

ALTHOUGH HE'D ACTED AS IF HE DIDN'T KNOW ME, A HINT OF RECOGNITION HAD flashed across Dennis Benson's face when we met. What were the chances that he knew me and what I was up to? Could this be a scheme to fire me and later paint me as a disgruntled former employee? My mind raced a thousand miles a minute.

Cindy led the way. "Don't let his gruff exterior scare you. He's a softie underneath."

Easy for her to say. He hadn't ruined her life.

I followed, checking my hand for all five fingers. I'd survived my first encounter with him.

"I'm sure he keeps plenty of things hidden," I said, attempting a light tone. "How long have you worked for him?"

She stopped at the final office door on the row. "Long enough to know where the bodies are buried."

"You'll have to tell me some day."

She smiled. "We should do lunch soon."

She didn't realize how literally I meant what I'd said.

She handed me a key. "The key to this office. I hope you find it comfortable, and I'm sure you'll enjoy working for Dennis."

That last part I couldn't agree with.

I used the key and opened the dark wooden door. My mouth must have dropped. It was smaller than Benson's office—or rather Dennis's—but not by a lot. It was easily as large as Fisher's, and he was the CFO, for Christ's sake.

"Are you sure this is the one?" I asked.

"Dennis doesn't believe in squabbling over rank, so the offices of all the people reporting to him are the same size."

The statement made sense, but at the same time it didn't. I was a lowly analyst, just out of business school with no staff, and my office was two floors above Fisher's *and* the same size?

The view out the window was magnificent, looking over the city and toward the Pacific beyond. I wasn't in real-ville anymore, that much was certain. Ramona wasn't going to believe this.

"Nice view, huh?" Cindy remarked.

"I was just thinking that." I ventured in and felt the polished mahogany of the desk, another step up from cubicle-land.

"I'll get you the Talbot paperwork," she said. "Take an inventory, and let me know if you need anything else."

"Sure."

"Your system login should be the same, but with upgraded access. Give me your cell number, and I'll send you all the office contacts."

I wrote the number down for her. "Thanks. I'll need a few minutes to get my bearings. And where will the meeting be?"

She pointed toward where we'd come from. "The boardroom. Second door past Dennis's office."

It was odd to hear her call him Dennis, as if he were just another guy, a normal occupant of this floor, instead of the creature from hell I knew him to be. How would she feel about him when the truth was revealed?

She left me alone in the space that was now *my* office.

I opened one of the short lateral files, which was mahogany like everything else in sight. The top drawer was sparsely filled, and its files were alphabetized. The second-drawer files were numerically coded—the same system as in the file rooms I'd burgled.

The numeric coding made it impossible to find something unless you knew the code it has been stored under, and only Hydra had access to that information somehow. But even he had been wrong twice and sent me after files that didn't seem helpful in bringing down Benson.

As promised, my phone chirped with Cindy's message, which contained a bunch of office and cell numbers. I added them to my contacts.

A few minutes later, Cindy reappeared with an armload of papers. "This is everything on Talbot—at least everything I could find." She set them down on the small, circular conference table near the door.

I had an office with a couch, a meeting table, a monster desk, and a view to kill for. What a life.

The sheer height of the stack Cindy had arranged changed my perspective quickly.

"Two o'clock? Is that right?" I asked.

"That's right. It's the final meeting to sign, as I understand it."

"Sign?"

"Didn't he tell you? We're purchasing a Talbot division. It's been in the works for a few months now."

I sighed. "By two o'clock?"

"If you want to tell him you need more time, you better do it right away. The Talbot team is flying in from Oregon."

I followed her down to Mr. Benson's, *Dennis's,* office. I had to remember to use his first name if I wanted to fit in.

I knocked, and he called for me to enter.

He looked up as I stopped just inside the door. "Yes?"

"The Talbot files are massive. What would you like me to concentrate on for this afternoon?"

His brow knit as if that was a stupid question. "The entire file, of course. This is the final meeting with them. We should be signed by tonight."

"It's just that it's so—"

He put up a hand to stop me. "Should I get someone else?"

I pasted on a smile, finally understanding the game. "Not at all. I'll be ready."

This was his way of getting me to fire myself because he and Fisher had some power play going on, and I was the pawn.

"Good. I'm counting on you, Jennifer." He looked down at his desk, a non-verbal cue that our discussion was done.

I departed and closed the door behind me.

Cindy raised an eyebrow, but didn't say anything.

I merely smiled in return. Internally, I called bullshit on him being a softie.

Being unprepared for the meeting was one way to point out my inadequacy, but I didn't plan on playing along. I would not be the pawn in their tug-of-war.

I returned to my office and shut the door to concentrate.

The term sheet and contract papers were in the first folder I opened. Five hours to go to finish this stack and attend a corporate merger closing meeting. It was worse than cramming for finals.

By noon, I'd made good progress and dialed Cindy to inquire about lunch.

She offered help. "I'll order for you. Chinese, Thai, pizza, or a sandwich?"

I chose Chinese.

# CHAPTER 9

*DENNIS*

I SAT IN THE BOOTH AT THE BACK OF THE RESTAURANT. LARRY HAD AGREED TO MEET for lunch, but as always, he was late.

I'd ordered his usual and changed mine up as I tended to do. I couldn't see getting the same thing every time.

He called it controlling the variables; I called it boring.

Finally he slid in across from me. "I see you let Mark get away from you. Who's the new girl?"

I took a sip of my hot tea. "Jennifer. Jennifer Hanley."

"She's cute."

"Give me a break. Jay stole Mark and sent her up in his place. This is Jay trying to teach me a lesson."

"What kind of lesson?"

"He thinks I should have gotten the group together to decide the Hydrocom spin-off instead of just announcing it."

"He's right. You should have."

"I thought at least you'd back me up."

"Shoot the messenger, why don't ya? I agree with Jay on this one."

"We needed good news, so I pulled the trigger and moved up the spin-off. Big deal. We were doing it at the end of the year anyway."

"Asking for help from the group isn't a sign of weakness."

I'd heard that lecture before.

"Anyway, she's got no experience and no MBA," I lamented.

"Maybe she's better than you think."

The waiter interrupted with our plates.

My kung pao chicken smelled delicious.

The broccoli beef on his plate was the same as always: boring.

Larry spooned some rice onto his plate and offered it to me. "Give her some time and see how she does."

"I don't have the time to find out. I'm going to see to it that she hates the job and wants to move back downstairs."

Larry thought about that for another few bites. "How?"

"Easy. I'll be the impossible boss."

He shrugged. "Not like it's hard for you."

JENNIFER

It was a few minutes before two when I closed the final folder of the Talbot paperwork tower Cindy had brought me. My brain swam with numbers, contracts, and a million details.

How had he ever expected me to absorb all this in one day and go into the meeting prepared? I knew he hadn't. He counted on me not finishing, not being prepared, and not knowing what was in these. He expected me to make a fool of myself and prove I wasn't ready. He expected a quick exit from Mahogany Row for me.

I felt the smooth, cool, real-wood surface of the table I sat at and looked over my shoulder at the cityscape out my window—my top-floor office window.

Screw him. He wasn't getting an easy win today.

I pushed away the carton of Chinese I'd barely had time to touch. Twisting the top off my Diet Coke bottle, I wet my parched mouth with two gulps. A quick time check showed I had just enough time for a trip to the bathroom before the meeting.

The restroom door seemed heavier than the one downstairs, but that was probably my imagination. Inside, I almost dropped my purse. The difference was stark. The sinks were set into a granite counter, and the stalls weren't the standard beige, airport-style metal structures found on my floor. Here, solid-wood partitions provided the elegant privacy top-floor ladies deserved while they peed. Everything about life on the top floor was evidently different.

After washing up and refreshing my lip gloss, I was ready to learn what a signing meeting was all about.

As I approached, four men were standing about between Cindy's desk and the conference room door, which was open—the Talbot team, apparently.

I ducked into my office to grab a pad of paper and my phone. It had a good calculator and was better than doing things in my head.

I put on my brave face and approached the group. I stopped at Cindy's desk, unsure if I should introduce myself.

The oldest among them looked at me. "Honey, I'll take a coffee. Two sugars."

I froze.

"Gentlemen, you can set up in the conference room," Cindy said. "Mr. Benson will join you as soon as he's off the phone."

The group followed Mr. Coffee through the door.

"I'll get it," Cindy said to me. "Wait for Dennis and go in with him. It may be a few minutes." She headed off to the coffee room. I'd stumbled upon it on my way to the bathroom.

Glancing at her desk, I noticed neither of Dennis's phone lines were lit.

I laid my things down, my phone on top, and headed back for my Diet Coke in case I needed the caffeine. After finishing most of the bottle and releasing a quick burp, I was back at Cindy's desk.

She pointed at my phone. "You got a message while you were gone."

The phone was face up with the awful text on the screen.

EB: We should talk

I shook my head. "My ex. I wish he would stop texting." I picked up the phone, cleared the screen, and put it on silent.

Cindy shrugged. "Surely he'll give up after a while."

It was another several minutes before Dennis emerged from his office. A forced smile crossed his face as he saw me. At least it wasn't a frown.

"You ready?"

I nodded. "As ready as I'm going to be."

He closed his office door and stepped toward the room with our guests.

I put my arm out. "Stop." The word escaped before I could come up with a nicer one. I stepped in front of him and reached up to straighten his tie.

His eyes met mine, and the smile was no longer forced. "Thank you."

"I want you looking your best." My brain-word filter was malfunctioning this afternoon. I'd meant to say *we*, not *I*.

He turned for the door. "Your job is not to grill them, but let me know if they say anything that's off."

I followed him and closed the door behind us. *Don't grill them?* That should be no problem. I'd just been thrown in the deep end without a life preserver.

The group of four stood and one by one started introducing themselves and shaking hands with Dennis.

I came next.

Mr. Coffee was the first to reach me. He extended his hands, a business card in one and the other open to shake. "James Talbot the third."

I accepted his card and shook with him. "Jennifer Hanley. Sorry, I don't have a card yet. I'm new."

His hand fell away quickly. "Are you by any chance related to Senator Hanley?"

"Sadly, no."

"You look like her. You must get that a lot." It was the first time I'd ever been compared to the senator. The comparison made me smile. The old man was a top-notch bullshitter.

"Not often enough." I smiled.

The name-handshake-business card exchange, minus my card, repeated three more times with the others. Sweaty Palms was their CFO, Baldy their marketing VP, and Beak Nose their general counsel.

I collected their cards while still clutching my legal pad, phone, and pen in one hand.

Dennis had his hands free. He'd pre-placed his notepad and pen on the table before they arrived, claiming his seat: one chair down from the head of the table and on the side facing the window.

I obviously had things to learn about the power dynamics of these meetings.

I took my seat to the right of Dennis after he sat.

The Talbot group had helped themselves to refreshments from the drink cart Cindy must've supplied—all except Talbot himself, who waited for the coffee he'd ordered from me.

The others had chosen Pellegrinos.

I retrieved a fresh Diet Coke bottle and unscrewed the lid. Before I sat, I noticed my faux pas. They'd all poured their drinks into glass tumblers.

I retrieved a glass from the cart and took my seat, feeling like a child at the adults' table.

Then I noticed Dennis didn't have a glass either and took a sip directly from his plastic bottle.

I also took note that Dennis was also coatless, versus suits for the opposing side.

I definitely had yet to understand the dynamics.

Dennis and Talbot were saying something about the weather when Cindy entered and placed a coffee cup on a saucer in front of Talbot.

He nodded, without a verbal thank you to her. Jerk.

Before she left, another of our team came in and went through the handshake ritual with the other side.

I learned he was Pembroke, our general counsel.

He took a seat next to me. "Syd," he whispered, sliding me his card.

I leaned and whispered back, "Jennifer." I arranged my cards in front of me in the order of their seating.

"Shall we get started?" Talbot asked.

"Let's," Dennis responded. The pad in front of him was blank. He lifted the top sheet to read from the next page. "My note says you were going to give us a quarter update."

I glanced sideways. The page he read from was also blank.

Sweaty Palms gave Talbot a sideways glance.

"I don't remember that," Beak Nose said.

Dennis lifted his Coke. "Let's start there anyway."

Sweaty Palms shuffled through his pile of papers, pulled out a folder, and opened his laptop to start the presentation..

Syd got up and flipped a switch on the wall that brought down a screen from the ceiling, and then adjusted the vertical blinds on the far wall to darken the room a bit.

Sweaty Palms started talking to the first slide.

"Can we get a copy of that for Jennifer?" Dennis asked.

Sweaty Palms glanced at Talbot, who nodded before he pulled out a stapled set.

I rose and thanked him before reclaiming my seat. Following along, the numbers were similar, but not the same as what I'd seen, but without the folder in front of me, I couldn't be certain. I fidgeted, but decided not to leave to get the folder.

Then Dennis started asking me if I had any questions for Sweaty Palms after every few sentences their CFO got out.

Each time, I was question-less, and now my palms were sweaty as well.

Dennis was testing me, and I was failing at my new job.

By the fourth page of Sweaty Palms's presentation, Dennis had given up asking me and had taken to grilling Baldy and Sweaty Palms himself about projections down the line.

Turning back to the second page, something had seemed odd at the time, but I hadn't connected the dots.

I opened my phone's calculator and had the answer in a few seconds. I raised my hand like a schoolgirl asking a question.

Talbot started talking over Baldy about the new product line and ignored me.

"Excuse me," I inserted at a pause in their conversation. "I want to go back to the receivables for a moment."

Talbot dismissed me with a wave. "We're past that. George, let's hit the next slide."

"George, let's not," Dennis said in a tone that froze the man at the projector. "I'd like to see the receivables again."

Talbot sent me a sneer.

Sweaty Palms complied and went back to the receivables page.

"The footnote on the bad-debts reserve seems to have been left off of my copy," I said. "Could you slide that up so we can see it?"

Talbot huffed. "Are we going to go backwards and get into footnotes here? I thought this was going to be a signing meeting."

"George, slide that up, please," Dennis said.

He did. The footnote was at the bottom of the slide, but omitted from my printed copy.

I read it out loud. "Subject to revision. How big a revision?"

Sweaty Palms looked to Talbot for guidance but got none. "Double digit millions." The blood drained from his face.

"Can you be more specific?" I asked.

"Eighty-ish," was his reply. The man looked like he wanted to melt into the carpet.

I had him on the ropes. "Eighty what?"

"Eighty-nine."

"It'll be resolved before the end of the quarter," Talbot said loudly. "Right, Malcolm?"

Baldy was a deer caught in the headlights. "Sure. It's just a small disagreement in China."

Dennis turned to me. "Does that answer your question?"

I swallowed hard and hoped my memory was good enough. "George, if it doesn't get resolved, doesn't that put you in violation of your bank-debt covenants?"

Sweaty Palms turned even whiter than before, but didn't answer.

"Does it?" I asked Talbot.

"Technically, but I don't like your insinuation," he answered.

Dennis stood. "Syd, you can hold down the fort. Jenn, a word." He grabbed his note pad and walked to the door.

I gathered my things and followed. I'd found the flaw in their numbers Dennis wanted me to find.

Talbot's mouth hung open as I closed the door behind us.

Dennis went to his office door and motioned for me to follow him, which I did.

"Shut it," he said.

I did.

He walked behind his desk. "I should fire you right now. That's a two-month negotiation you just blew up. I wanted that division, and now you've insulted the hell out of old man Talbot."

I sat and shrunk into the chair, my mouth instantly parched. "You weren't clear about what you expected of me. I'm sorry. I thought you wanted me to point out discrepancies."

"You don't get it. We're past that stage. We were supposed to exchange pleasantries and sign today. You just made us look like assholes."

"They're the ones who were hiding something."

"Everyone is hiding something," he shot back.

He didn't know how true that statement was.

"We need to close this deal today. We don't have any time left before the end of the quarter."

My heart was pounding so hard his words barely registered. "Can we slow down a second and talk about what they hid?"

"Are you trying to blow up months of work, or are you just stupid?"

"You told me to flag anything they said that was off. That's what I did."

He ignored me. "I knew you were too junior. You don't get it. This acquisition is already baked into this quarter's numbers. We need to close."

I stated the obvious. "You were going to fire me today no matter what. You've already made up your mind."

I was clearly a goner. No promotion, no raise, and now no job. The conversation I'd overheard made it pretty clear what this was. It hadn't mattered how prepared I was, if I'd asked too few questions or too many—either way the outcome had been predetermined: a quick chewing out and a summary execution.

He didn't deny it. "You've got ten minutes. Go back in there. Apologize, kiss ass, suck dick, or whatever you have to do, just fix the damage. We have to sign today."

His tone was not joking. Suck Talbot's dick? I almost puked at the thought. Wobbly legs carried me to the door.

"Ten minutes," he repeated.

My blood boiled as I closed the door to his office behind me.

The cocksucker had ruined my family, and now I'd be forced to leave the company with *my* reputation in tatters instead of his.

The unfairness of it was staggering. The rich made the rules, and the rules determined the outcome—an outcome that always favored them over the rest of us.

# CHAPTER 10

*Dennis*

I waited a minute after Jennifer left to cool down before calling Jay.

"How did the Talbot closing go?" he asked.

"You went too far this time, Jay. Saddling me with a rookie may have blown up the whole deal."

"Slow down a second. What happened?"

I worked to control my breathing. "I took her into the meeting, and she blew the thing up with some questions about their accounting."

"Then it's on you," he said.

"Fuck that. She screwed the pooch."

"You shouldn't have been in such a hurry to take someone new into a meeting like that, then. I warned you. Slow down. If you hadn't moved so aggressively on the Hydrocom spin-off, you wouldn't be in this predicament."

"Let's not go there again," I said.

"Lloyd wouldn't have made that mistake."

Another thing I didn't need today was a father-son comparison.

"Get me somebody better for tomorrow."

"I don't have anybody better."

I had the retort for that. "Find someone by tomorrow, or you come up and do the job yourself."

"Let's talk in the morning when you've had a chance to cool off." He hung up.

I didn't call back and berate him because I didn't need the blood-pressure spike.

I couldn't fantasize about my Starbucks girl anymore, the Talbot transaction was going sideways, and I was on the verge of pushing Jay too far. Everything about today sucked.

I wanted to rewind to two days ago where I could jerk off to visions of Jennifer, I hadn't gotten the latest nastygram from Melissa, Sigurd hadn't written another hit piece, and Talbot was within my grasp.

This week sucked big time.

~

*Jennifer*

After closing the door to Dennis's office, I leaned back against the wall to catch my breath. He'd chewed me a new one, and I didn't deserve it. It was so unfair.

Cindy wasn't at her desk, so I could stand here and contemplate the path he'd laid out: kiss ass and suck dick. My God, the man was crude, but above all *mean*. It didn't matter to him how demeaning it was—or whether they were cheating him—so long as he got his stupid deal.

It only made my blood boil hotter to think of how he'd ravaged my family and was now killing my career. At the next job, they'd want a reference from here, and there was no way I was getting a good one after pissing off the CEO.

I felt for Mom's ring on my finger and counted to ten in my head before I opened the conference room door. If I was leaving, it wouldn't be with my tail between my legs. The parting shot would be mine.

The conversation stopped, and all eyes went to me when I closed the door behind me and moved to the beverage cart.

"When is Dennis joining us again?" Talbot asked.

I unscrewed the top of a second Diet Coke and downed two swallows, this time directly from the bottle, before answering him. "He's not."

Talbot's eyes widened. "Pardon?"

The other suits were speechless, and even Syd's brow knit with confusion.

I retook my seat. "He put me in charge of this negotiation."

"That's absurd," Talbot said with a huff.

"Do you have a problem with a woman being in charge, James?" I asked. "Because I'm the one you're talking with now, not Dennis. If you don't like it, you're free to leave."

He didn't budge, at least not yet. "Now you remind me of his father."

I fixed Talbot with my coldest stare and ignored the comment. "He told me to handle it, and I am. End of story."

597

Syd looked like he might have a heart attack any second.

If Benson thought I was screwing up his negotiation, he had no idea how bad I could make it for him. I would gladly fuck him over with these idiots.

"You four are the ones who waltzed in here trying to hide material information."

Sweaty Palms and Baldy cringed. Only Beak Nose held his head high. Lawyers had no compunctions about trying to cheat. I'd learned that years ago.

I took the agreement Talbot had pushed our way earlier and slid it back to him. "You tried to cheat. We're not signing this. You insulted me. You insulted my boss, and our entire organization."

"But…" was all Talbot had to say for himself.

I stood and walked out.

Fuck them. Fuck Benson, fuck 'em all. Benson wanted this deal, and I'd just nuked for him. Take that asshole.

I passed Cindy on the way to my office. "I'm going home," I told her.

"Are you okay?"

I turned. "I don't get paid enough to put up with this shit." I spun and continued to the temporary sanctuary of my office.

After closing the door behind me, I let out the yell I'd been holding in. "Fuck!" It was the most coherent thing I could manage. It summed up my whole horrible day.

Take that, *Dennis fucking Benson*. I'm not kissing anybody's ass, and there goes your precious little deal.

Collapsing into the chair behind my desk-for-a-day, my eyes closed with the weight of my failure. I would have to be satisfied with torching the deal, along with his relationship with Talbot. It was all that could be salvaged out of this miserable day.

Tomorrow I'd have no job, no paycheck, and no entry back into this building to get the files to take down Benson once and for all.

He had no idea I was his personal nemesis, but somehow he'd dodged the bad news bullet *and* gotten rid of me, all in two days. The man had some super-lucky charm.

As my eyes reopened, I took one last look around the sumptuous office. "I guess you win."

He'd won, I'd lost, and it was time to find another job. The rent would still be due.

How long would it take to get on unemployment? That was something I didn't know.

The karma of this was all wrong, dead wrong.

A knock sounded at the door.

"Come in."

It was old man Talbot.

I straightened up, and hid my surprise. "What can I do for you James?"

"We'd, like… I'd like another chance to talk this through." The man was fresh out of bravado.

"Okay, I'll join you in a minute."

He shut the door, and I gathered up my nerve.

The deal was harder than a cockroach to kill, but where there was a will, there was a way, and I sure as hell had the will.

I'd make sure Benson and Talbot didn't talk to each other for a fucking year.

# CHAPTER 11

*DENNIS*

I'd been mentally swearing at my bad luck this week for ten minutes when the knock came.

Cindy popped her head in. "They're ready for you now."

That meant Jennifer had finished kissing ass enough for me to try to recover the deal.

Later I would have to apologize to Jay. He'd been right that I should have known better than to take a rookie into a meeting like that. I'd eat the crow I deserved for jumping down his throat earlier.

"You better give her a raise before you lose her," Cindy said as I passed by.

"Right." No way was that happening. It didn't matter how distasteful apologizing to Talbot had been.

As I entered, Syd was sliding paperwork across to Talbot. "I made the changes we agreed on, and we're ready now," he said.

I had no idea what changes Syd had agreed to, but right now closing the deal was the imperative.

Syd was too smart to give away the store.

Talbot finished initialing all the pages and signed on the back page of the first copy before sliding it over to me. He started on the second copy.

I took my seat and started initialing as if I knew what was going on. Never let them see you sweat, Dad had taught me. Letting them see me as indecisive or uninformed was also not in the cards.

Talbot finished the second copy just before I completed the first and slid it down to Syd.

The second copy went to their lawyer after I signed the last page.

Their entire entourage stood, looking happy to escape the room Jennifer had turned into an insult party.

I shook each of their hands on the way out.

Talbot was the last.

I pumped his hand. "I apologize for her rudeness."

"She's quite a spitfire, that Hanley girl. Reminds me of doing business with your father." He patted me on the back, and in a few seconds Cindy was showing them out.

Syd closed the door as I gathered my pad and special signing pen. His grin was ear to ear. "I'm sure glad you chose her."

I spun my pen on the table. "Huh?"

"She's packing a set of brass ones. I've never seen anything like it."

I wasn't following him, but the rule about them not seeing me confused was still in effect.

"When she told him she had full authority and since she didn't like the deal, it was off. She walked out. Their side had a heart attack. Talbot had to go chasing after her himself. Then she told him you wouldn't sign unless they took double the accounting slip-up off the price, and then she walked out a second time. Talbot folded like a wet napkin, and I had Cindy make the changes to the contract. You two concocted one hell of a plan, and she executed it like she's been doing this for years. That was the best good cop-bad cop routine I've ever seen."

"Pretty good, huh?" was all I could say at this point.

Syd thought I was in on it, and I wasn't bursting that bubble today.

He shook his head. "She had them shitting in their drawers. All I can say is I wouldn't want to get on her bad side. Ballsiest move I ever saw."

Syd took the signed contract and left me alone in the conference room with the door open to figure out what the fuck had just happened.

I was watching my pen spin on the polished surface of the table when Cindy walked in.

"You should call."

"Call who?" I looked up and corrected myself. "Excuse me, call whom?"

"Jennifer. Syd told me what happened while I was typing up the contract changes. She didn't deserve what you said to her."

"You heard that?"

"You were pretty loud."

"Where'd she go?"

"She wasn't a happy camper. She left. And I quote, '*I don't get paid enough to put up with this shit.*'"

"That bad, huh?"

"Worse. She's a nice girl, and that thing you told her to do. I won't repeat the words, well… If you don't fix it with her, don't be surprised to find salt in your morning coffee."

Cindy wouldn't have any problem making my life miserable, and maybe I had been a little too graphic.

"For an entire year," she added.

I nodded. "Can you get me her cell number?"

She put a sticky note on the table and waited.

This new girl was a lot more capable and complicated than I'd guessed.

Now I owed Jay an even bigger apology.

I dialed the number on the sticky note. It rang twice, and then my phone died. The apple logo appeared on the screen again as it restarted.

"I gotta get this fixed." I turned the screen to face Cindy. The damned phone did this once a week and wanted to reset itself.

"We have a guy down in IT that's a real whiz with those. I could give it to him."

I checked my watch. I was already running late for my dinner meeting. "Not tonight." I handed her back the sticky note. "This will have to wait till the morning. Text her and have her meet me at Starbucks first thing."

"Which one?"

"The regular. She'll know which one."

~

*Jennifer*

I MIGHT BE UNEMPLOYED NOW, BUT I'D FINALLY GOTTEN BENSON WHERE IT HURT—IN his wallet. I'd shoved Talbot's underhandedness in the old man's face, sure it would screw the deal and have him walking out.

It would have served both those snakes right. Talbot had tried to pull a fast one, and well, Benson deserved to have what was important to him taken away, and today that was the Talbot deal.

Then Talbot had backed down, and I gave him one right between the eyes. I'd upped the stakes and walked out a second time. With that, Talbot was sure to never return Benson's calls again. With two torpedoes like that, the deal was going down.

*Take that, you arrogant jerks. Both of you.*

I would have preferred to keep my job and the ability to hurt Benson some more, but at least I'd gotten a good parting shot in and screwed his plans. That would cost him in the stock market when he had to admit the Talbot transaction wasn't happening.

My phone rang on the car seat beside me.

Glancing over, the screen showed it was Dennis. I ignored it, and the ringing stopped. I reached over to turn it off.

Eventually I reached our apartment and let myself in.

"You're home early," Ramona said.

"Yeah." I didn't elaborate.

"What's wrong? First day as supervisor not go well?"

I shrugged and went to change out of my work clothes, particularly these diabolical heels.

"I'm just trying to help," she said before I closed the door behind me.

I sat on the edge of the bed and unbuckled my shoes. It felt good to curl my toes in the carpet. The feeling grounded me. The soft carpeting protected me from the cold floor the way the walls protected me from the meanness of the world. This was my safe space. Dad's picture was on my dresser alongside pictures of the rest of my family, as if he were still with us.

Ramona yelled from the other room. "I'm going to pick up Billy."

"Okay," I yelled back.

She meant well, and I'd have to level with her tonight about the situation. I laid back on the bed and closed my eyes.

I'd have to move to the backup plan.

Vipersoft contracted with an outside cleaning crew, and I knew their routine. In time I'd find a way onto their crew and gain access to the building again. It would take time, but good things came to those with patience and persistence—two qualities I possessed.

I opened my eyes. It was time to stop whining, get changed, and start dinner.

Once in my sandals, shorts, and T-shirt, I started pulling together the ingredients for tonight's dinner. Billy expected homemade pizza.

By the time Ramona returned with him, I'd preheated the pizza stone in the oven, rolled out the crust, and we were ready for toppings.

Cooking for the three of us was good therapy. It got my mind off my work, or lack thereof, and back to the basics in life: food and family.

Billy put down his backpack. "Mommy said you get to be the boss."

I shot Ramona a you-shouldn't-have look.

"What? I'm proud of you," she said.

"Salami or hot dog slices on your pizza?" I asked.

"Salami and no olives. I don't want olives."

Ramona shot him a scowl. "Yes on the olives. They're good for you."

He'd been getting really picky about his eating lately.

"But I don't like them."

Ramona didn't back down. "Then you can have green soup tonight, and Auntie Jenn and I will have the pizza."

His shoulders slumped. "Okay. But I don't like olives."

The split pea soup she'd threatened was at the absolute bottom of Billy's food list.

I added the toppings, including the black olive slices Ramona liked, and slid the pie into the oven.

Billy had already turned on the TV when Ramona wandered my way and braced herself against the counter.

"What happened?" She plugged one charging cable into her phone, and the other into mine, which I'd left on the counter.

I slid sideways to get the plates. "Huh?"

"You can't hide your bad mood behind a pizza."

She was probably right about that. The cooking was only a temporary distraction. "Work didn't go very well. I didn't get the supervisor job."

"How come? You said they offered it to you yesterday."

I pulled napkins from the counter. "I screwed up by asking about staying, and the new CFO decided he wanted somebody more committed to the new company."

"I'm sorry. Something better will come along soon. I'm sure of it."

She should have been mad, knowing I'd screwed up the raise that would have allowed us to move, but she didn't focus on that. Ramona was the most supportive sister a girl could ask for.

"There's more," I added, preparing to tell her that instead of getting a promotion, I was about to get fired.

My phone chirped the arrival of a text when it powered up.

Ramona picked up my phone. "Who's Cindy?"

"Assistant to the big boss. Why?"

"She says you have a meeting tomorrow morning." She held up the phone for me to read.

Cindy: Meeting at Starbucks at 7:30

"What's that about?" Ramona asked.

My gut tightened. "Probably my exit interview. I screwed up pretty badly today."

She took silverware to the table. "I doubt that."

"Trust me, it was worse than anything you could imagine."

Cindy's text must have been sent earlier while my phone was off. I composed the most polite reply I could come up with and sent it.

ME: Not feeling well might not be in tomorrow

The timer went off, and I extracted the pizza.

Ramona had the cutting wheel ready, and we had it sliced on our plates in minutes.

I'd only taken a few bites when my phone chirped again.

Ramona quickly lunged for it and handed it to me with a smile.

"Probably not as bad as you thought, huh?" Ramona asked.

Billy chowed down on his pizza, picking the olives off when he didn't think Ramona was looking. He slid them under an uneaten slice.

I texted back.

ME: Which Starbucks

Her reply was immediate.

Cindy: Your normal one

How the hell could she know where my normal Starbucks was?

I didn't bother asking that question, or the more important one of what the meeting was for. I didn't know her well, but I had to trust her.

Ramona grabbed for my phone as soon as I set it down. "It's good news. I can feel it."

Her feelings always went to the positive, and it was pretty much a coin flip whether she was right or not. She gave up on interrogating me.

It was just as well. I could tell her about my need to find a new job tomorrow after my exit interview.

A few minutes later, Billy pushed his chair back and picked up his plate. "I've got homework to do."

He was halfway to the sink before Ramona finished chewing enough to say, "No you don't, little guy. Come back here and eat your olives."

She hadn't missed his trick.

He slouched back to the table. "I don't like them."

"And I don't like paying for food you don't eat. They're good for you. They have a special oil that's healthy."

After retaking his seat, it took Billy a full ten minutes to push them around on his plate and eventually force them down. He made a face for his mother's benefit with every one.

"That wasn't so bad, was it?" Ramona asked.

I knew the answer before Billy mouthed it.

"Yuck. I don't want pizza again if we have to have olives."

"Then you can have green soup next time," Ramona replied.

He didn't say anything, which promised a repeat on next week's pizza night.

As I watched these confrontations grow, I wondered how I would handle them with my children.

Ramona had a difficult situation raising Billy by herself, but it was certainly better than when her ex, Stanley, had been around.

An unintended pregnancy followed by marrying the jerk hadn't left Ramona with a lot of options. Loser couldn't be spelled in big enough letters to describe Stanley.

She'd thought she could marry him and fix him, but from day one, I'd known the odds of that were less than zero.

My sister's positive attitude often had its redeeming qualities, but it had led her to stick with a bad situation for too long—way too long.

# CHAPTER 12

*JENNIFER*

I STOOD UNDER THE HOT WATER LONGER THAN USUAL THE NEXT MORNING, BECAUSE I was still groggy from lack of sleep.

I'd stayed up late after Ramona and I had finished the movie, perusing the online job listings for accounting types like me. There had been several openings that might work, but each one had a large salary range listed, which extended quite a bit below what I was making now, and only a little above.

That didn't bode well for finding a better-paying position.

One listing had been in Pomona, and that was even farther than the Hydrocom location I hadn't liked.

Once I went to bed, I'd tossed and turned, wondering how I was going to get out of this mess. It seemed I hadn't gotten to sleep until just before my infernal alarm clock had demanded I get up.

I made it to Starbucks a few minutes before seven-thirty. Even if I only worked at Vipersoft another few minutes, I would be on time for this meeting. I was a professional, and a professional was always on time.

A quick scan of the tables didn't reveal Cindy anywhere. The M&M girls were already in our usual spot, but they hadn't gotten their coffees yet.

"There you are," Mona exclaimed.

"Hi." I pulled out the chair facing the door, so I could see Cindy when she showed up.

"This is a treat," Martha told me.

I almost fell over when Dennis Benson appeared, tray in hand with four cups.

"Cinnamon latte for you," he said, putting the first cup in front of Mona. He proceeded to pass out the other drinks. He gave me a mocha—same as his, except for the extra shot, thankfully.

"He was just about to tell us what you did yesterday," Martha said.

I looked at Dennis, expecting wrath to show in his eyes, but all I got back from him was a smile.

He finished his sip. "Why don't you tell them?" He raised his cup to me.

I'd been ambushed. "I don't think I should."

Dennis put his mocha down. "We had this very important meeting yesterday." The girls leaned in to hear.

He pointed at me. "The other side tried to gloss over a very large issue, money-wise, but Jennifer caught it and threw it back in their faces."

"Not very nicely," I added.

"True," Dennis said. "So I took her aside and instructed her to apologize so we could sign the deal as it was."

I slid down in my chair.

"But," he continued, "she had a different idea."

"What was that?" Mona asked.

Dennis looked to me for an answer.

It couldn't get much worse, so I told them. "I told them we weren't doing a deal with a group like them."

"You tell 'em, girl," Martha chimed in.

Martha crossed herself. "That's what my Marty—God bless his soul—would always say. To win the negotiation, you have to be willing to walk away."

Her husband had been a salesman at a car dealership forever.

I picked up my drink and sipped to keep from talking.

"You know what happened?" Dennis asked.

The girls didn't offer a guess. They didn't understand that I'd screwed the whole thing up.

Dennis's eyes held mine captive, perhaps daring me to admit my failure in front of my friends?

I waited for the *you're fired* sentence to arrive.

He grinned. "She demanded better terms, they agreed, and that's what we signed. This lady here talked them down one hundred and seventy-eight million dollars in a few minutes." His smile brightened even more. "That's why she's getting a raise today."

I choked on my coffee. "What?" I asked through a coughing fit.

He reached across to touch my hand. "Jay told me you turned down a raise for the chance to work with me, and after yesterday, you certainly deserve one."

His touch sent an uncomfortable tingle up my arm. My brain was misfiring. I blinked hard.

He was still here, his fingers over mine.

I pulled away and lifted my coffee to my lips to hide my speechlessness.

"You're my kind of boss," Mona said.

Dennis gave her a warm smile. "I try."

My heart had almost returned to a normal pace, but my head was spinning. I had attempted twice yesterday to screw up his deal with Talbot, and somehow I'd only made it better. Why on Earth would Talbot have gone for that? Everything was working out backwards. I was helping Benson instead of taking him down.

On top of that, now I had to continue working with him, though it was good to still be employed. Then his words registered—I was getting a raise.

"How much?" I asked.

He stood. "We'll talk about it at the office. I'm going to run along now. You girls have a wonderful day."

"Can't you stay just a little while?" Mona asked.

"Sorry, not today," he replied. "Jennifer, I'll see you at work."

His words were more command than prediction. He was off in a flash, despite another plea from Mona to stay.

"I think he likes you," Martha said.

"And you didn't tell us you'd already met him," Mona said.

"I hadn't, not until yesterday."

Martha twisted her cup. "You made quite the impression on your first day."

"It didn't work out the way I expected," I told them.

An understatement by a mile.

I scooted my chair back. "I need to get going. I don't want to be late."

Martha pointed to the table. "Sit back down. You should stay a while and make him wait. That always works better with men."

"I agree," Mona said. "You don't want to seem too eager. Right now you have that man right where you want him."

Martha giggled. "Not quite where I'd want him."

"You're not helping," Mona shot back.

Martha pointed her finger a Mona. "Just because you're too old to get any action doesn't mean I can't dream."

Mona put her chin up. "And who had the most recent date?"

I stayed quiet; they could go like this for an hour.

"But that was Harold, and you had to ask him. That doesn't count," Martha said.

Mona huffed. "It does too, but we should be concentrating on Jennifer's dilemma."

"What dilemma?" I asked.

"Whether you should wait for him to ask you out, or if you ask him," Mona replied.

"He doesn't want to go out with me," I said.

Martha giggled. "Are you blind? I saw the way he looked at you. That man's engine is revving for you, sweetie."

At her age, she shouldn't be smoking whatever was giving her these delusions.

"No way," I protested. "He's just feeling bad that I showed him up." I sipped my mocha.

For sure, and he had to atone for what I'd caught him saying to Fisher yesterday about wanting somebody more senior.

"I'm with Martha," Mona said. "Mark my words, you're sharing a meal, and soon. It's in his eyes. I remember the first time I saw that look in Marty's eyes." She sighed loudly. "Things certainly got more complicated after that—complicated in a good way."

These two didn't understand what I knew about Benson, about his true character and how incompatible we were. "He's not my type."

Mona shook her head. "And that's why you watch for him every morning? You're so transparent, Jenn. Don't think for a minute I didn't see your reaction when he touched your hand."

"And the way your face lights up every time he comes in," Martha added. "You can't hide that from us, you know."

"You have it all wrong," I said.

"Tell me you don't think he's good looking," Mona demanded.

"I'd say yes to him in a flash," Martha said.

"I wasn't asking you," Mona said. "Your definition of the right man is any man with a pulse."

"At least I didn't go out with Harold," Martha replied. "Now, Jennie, answer the question. Hot or not?"

I shook my head. "That's not it."

"Hot or not?" Martha repeated.

I took in a breath. "Okay, I admit he's kinda good looking."

That was putting it mildly. Dennis was movie-star handsome—tall, with an athletic build, and richer than sin. He was every girl's dream, and he would be mine if he weren't a monster underneath.

Mona gasped. "You're not... Are you gay?"

I laughed. "That's not it. I just know he's not right for me."

Martha shook her head. "You hadn't even spoken to him before yesterday. You can't possibly know that."

"Now that I've met him, I know we're not a good fit," I replied.

"Trust me. I speak from experience," Mona said. "If he's a tight fit, that's even better." She laughed.

Martha laughed as well. "You're incorrigible. I can't take you anywhere."

"Well, it's true," Mona said.

I stood. "It's time for me to go to work."

Mona lifted her cup. "Till next time. Go get that raise."

"I intend to," I told her.

"Not so fast, honey," Martha said. "You should negotiate a bigger raise. Don't take his first offer."

"Yeah, hold out for more," Mona agreed.

"And walk slow," Martha added. "Make him wait."

After saying goodbye and depositing my cup in the trash, I left them to bicker between themselves.

A little while later I caught myself walking quickly down the sidewalk and slowed my pace.

He could wait.

~

## DENNIS

I'D REACHED FOR JENNIFER'S HAND OUT OF INSTINCT, AND IT HAD BEEN A MISTAKE. Only sheer force of will had kept me from jerking mine back like a frightened kid. I'd left the Starbucks as quickly as I could after that, lest I drool or babble incoherently and make a complete fool of myself.

All the way to work, my hand had tingled as I walked—from the spark of touching Jennifer. I'd wiped it on my trousers, but I couldn't rid myself of the feeling. It was as if she wore some damned skin cream laced with pheromones, and the chemicals had leached into my skin.

The woman was beautiful, but there was much more to her than that. The shock of hearing Syd's description of her closing the Talbot deal, followed by old man Talbot's comments had solidified that she was not the meek junior accountant I'd taken her for. All night, I'd played back my scolding of her and realized how wrong I'd been. I was rarely wrong, and never a hundred and seventy-eight fucking million wrong—never. She was a puzzle wrapped in an enigma, she was.

And a force of nature. Jennifer had saved me triple-digit millions yesterday, and today she'd given me a jolt like she was wired with electricity.

I stopped outside our building to take a few calming breaths.

Upstairs, when I opened the door to the executive area, Jay was seated by Cindy's desk, chatting.

I could hear Larry on the speakerphone in his office.

"Am I putting salt in your coffee today?" Cindy asked.

I passed Jay, who cocked a brow.

"No. I expect her in later," I responded.

Jay rose from his chair. "I want to hear the real story about Talbot."

Cindy tilted her head. "He doesn't believe me."

I opened my office door. "I don't know why not."

"Well?" Jay asked.

611

I entered and waved him in as well. "We closed the deal on better terms than expected."

He followed. "I won't believe it until I see it in black and white."

I picked up the signed contract on my desk and handed it to him. "By the way, I owe you an apology."

He accepted the papers and sat. "Cindy, could you come in here, please?"

She appeared at the door.

"Would you repeat that?" Jay asked me. "I want it on the record."

I shook my head. "I owe Jay an apology for underestimating Jennifer, and you can write that down for him."

"I could make a plaque, if you want," she said to Jay, before addressing me. "But I would say you're apologizing to the wrong person."

She was right. The apology needed to go to Jennifer.

Jay ignored her comment.

Cindy retreated to her station.

Jay sucked in a breath when he got to the critical page in the contract. "I told you she would do fine. Where do you think she learned negotiating?"

I leafed through my messages. "No idea. Maybe her father is a used-car salesman." I meant it as a joke, but realized I knew absolutely nothing about her beyond her name—and that she'd worked in Jay's department before yesterday.

"Maybe." He finished and stood, taking the contract with him. "I'll get this back to you after I make a copy."

I waved him off and picked up the phone to return the first of my calls for the morning.

A half hour later, I spied Jennifer through my open door, walking by on the way to her office.

She didn't look in my direction.

~

*JENNIFER*

I WALKED INTO WORK WITH A SPRING IN MY STEP THAT HAD BEEN MISSING FOR FAR TOO long.

Once on Mahogany Row, I carefully avoided looking toward Dennis's office as I passed Cindy and moved to my office.

Cindy followed me a few seconds later. "How did it go?"

I unlocked my door and slid inside. "Fine, I guess."

It had been two days of contradictions, with everything happening the opposite of the way it was supposed to.

"Did he do right by you?"

I shrugged. "I don't know yet. There were other people at the table. He said we'd talk when I got in."

"Well, then go on in and ask."

I didn't feel comfortable about this. It was too surreal to be reality. "Is this your doing?"

"Absolutely not. You're the one who pulled the rabbit out of the hat."

That praise got a smile out of me.

She lingered by the door. "He tests people when they're new, and you passed. He tried to call you after you left."

"I know. My phone was dead." Not true, but that was my story.

"He told me he'd decided to give you a raise, but you'd already left. Pretty good for your first day, I'd say."

My smile grew. By her measure, I had done well, even if it was by accident. And a boss that showed he appreciated me—that was a new feeling. "Yeah. It didn't go quite as I'd expected."

"It never does. Go down there and get the good news. You deserve it." The sound of a phone ringing pulled her away.

I touched up my lip gloss before marching the few steps to Dennis's office.

He was on the phone. "Sure, Dad, I won't forget." His voice didn't carry any of the harshness I'd heard from him yesterday, but then it shouldn't when he was talking with his family. He noticed me and held up a finger to indicate a delay.

I wondered what he wasn't supposed to forget, but then I was always too curious about Dennis, and for all the wrong reasons. I leaned against the wall, and it occurred to me that in all my plotting to take him down, not once had I considered that he had a family.

To me he had always been the devil, the cause of pain in *my* family. But he had a family too, and I hadn't considered the effects my actions might have on them. However, he hadn't either a few years ago.

He hung up and urged me in. "Close the door."

As I walked in to take a seat, I caught him scanning me—and not just my face.

For a moment, his eyes held mine with a laser-like focus.

I returned his gaze without a blink. "You said we should talk."

*Surreal* wasn't a good enough word for this situation. Yesterday I'd helped the man who killed my stepfather, and now he'd expect me to thank him for a raise. That wasn't happening.

# CHAPTER 13

*DENNIS*

WHEN I HUNG UP AND MOTIONED HER IN, I COULDN'T HELP BUT SEE A DIFFERENT GIRL than the one I'd met yesterday.

She didn't break eye contact—very interesting.

"You said we should talk." She returned my gaze with intensity.

I motioned to the chair. "Have a seat."

"Is that an order?"

Attitude radiated off her like waves of heat.

"An offer."

"I'd rather stand."

I finally looked down and opened the folder in front of me. "Jennifer, I want to start with an apology."

That was not something I said lightly. Dad had taught us to be careful, because apologies could be turned against us as a sign of weakness. But this merited an exception to his rule.

The smile left her face. "Yes, you do. Before you met me, you decided I wasn't who you wanted for this job, and you set me up for failure." Her tone conveyed even more anger than the words.

I shifted in my seat. I'd never had to sit and take backtalk of any kind from an employee before—hell, from anyone outside the family. If an employee had ever felt this strongly, they hadn't had the guts to say it to my face.

*Spitfire* was the word Talbot had used, and this was a firsthand taste of what he meant.

614

"You're a bastard," she continued. "You didn't tell me what you expected of me, and then berated me for not knowing what you wanted. It wasn't fair."

I leaned forward. "You are right. I was entirely wrong about you and your capabilities. I treated you poorly, and for that I'm sorry."

Her eyes thawed.

My words had hit home. "I'm not used to being this wrong, and I'm… I'm not very good at apologizing, but I'm truly sorry."

Her eyes narrowed, but only momentarily before her face softened to a smile. "You do suck at it, but apology accepted."

I let out the breath I'd been holding and took in the sight of her.

She broke the silence. "Cindy said you decided yesterday afternoon that you wanted to review my compensation."

I'd have to thank Cindy later. It was just like her to change things around and give me more credit than I deserved.

I looked down at the personnel-change form I hadn't filled out yet. "I'm giving you a fifteen-thousand-dollar raise, effective immediately."

Her head cocked as if she was calculating. "Did you call me in here to insult me again?"

The words set me back. I'd never had someone react badly to getting a raise. "No. Not at all." This girl had me completely off balance.

"I was offered fourteen to move to the Pasadena job, and you're offering me fifteen? That's insulting." She huffed and turned.

I should have checked what Mark had had planned for her at Hydrocom before this discussion. I made a quick correction. "You've got it all wrong, Jennifer. I meant fifteen on top of the fourteen they offered." I'd had no idea about the Pasadena job, but surely this would rescue the situation.

She turned back and this time decided to take the seat I'd offered, crossing her legs slowly.

My mind was playing tricks on me this morning. Everything she did looked like slow motion in a movie.

A stray hair fell forward across her cheek.

I wanted to tuck it behind her ear.

As if she'd read my thoughts, she swiped it to the side with a slow finger. "That will be acceptable, on one condition."

"Yes?"

"You make it retroactive to the first of the month."

The request seemed inconsequential compared to her bargaining power at this point.

"Done."

"Thank you, Mr. Benson."

We'd moved back a step from Dennis to Mr. Benson.

"Dennis," I corrected her.

"Very well, Dennis. What do you have for me to do today?"

615

I couldn't give her any of the lewd answers that came instantly to mind. "Familiarize yourself with the Stoner transaction."

My cell phone rang. Bill Covington's name appeared on the screen.

She stood. "Anything else?"

"No, that's it to start with."

I realized I'd just had a taste of the treatment she'd given Talbot yesterday. She knew she had the leverage, and she'd used it to get a better deal. This morning she'd had the leverage on me, but that would change.

She stood and turned to leave.

I reached for the phone while admiring her ass. My cock stirred at the sight of her hips swaying. I blinked back the mental image of that ass bouncing on my cock. I would grab those hips and give her a ride she wouldn't forget. I blinked and the image of me spearing her burned itself into my brain.

She reached the door and looked back, breaking my mental image of her naked. Her mouth twitched, and she bit her lower lip. Could she feel it too?

I cast my eyes down and answered the phone.

JENNIFER

I TURNED AT THE DOOR AND CAUGHT HIM LOOKING. I SMILED AS I LEFT.

He'd averted his eyes, but he'd definitely been checking me out. He'd studiously stayed focused on my face during our talk, our negotiation—but then I'd turned my back.

*Men.*

"Sure, Bill, I haven't forgotten. I'll be there early Friday," I heard him say into the phone. It was the second time I'd heard him promise not to forget.

The man had a weakness after all. The master of the universe was forgetful.

I reached Cindy's desk. "Thank you," I said softly.

She looked up from her typing. "Did it go well?"

"Satisfactory, I'd say."

I didn't need her to know how over-the-top happy I was about the outcome. The M&M girls had been right about rejecting his first offer, and it had netted me a raise that definitely put a three-bedroom place in our future.

"That's good, because sometimes he can be a little clueless about how tight money is for the rest of us."

"He wants me to look over the Stoner deal. Where do I find those files?"

"I'll get them for you in a moment—as soon as I'm done with this one thing for Larry." She pointed to the notes she was working from.

I backed away toward the restroom. This morning's coffee was getting to me. "I'll be in my office."

Cindy nodded, still typing away.

Ten minutes later, I was at my desk, and I turned to face the view of the city and the ocean beyond. Things had changed so much from last week, my life was unrecognizable. I had a top-floor, window office, and I was working for the CEO after a twenty-nine-thousand-dollar raise—two things that would burnish my resume when I left for greener pastures, even if I did have to work for *him* in the meantime.

Karma had taken an odd few turns this week, but I'd come out in a better position to wreak my vengeance. I could more easily get the files for Hydra that he'd assured me would take down my nemesis, and I had a position that would keep people from questioning my access to any part of the facility, or any file I wanted. Long term, that was the definition of success.

Later, I would quietly slip off to another company, my mission accomplished, and restart my life—a normal life, happy in the knowledge I'd righted a wrong, justice had prevailed, and the guilty party had been punished, even if not through the legal system.

In the end, nobody except Hydra and my sister would know of my involvement in Benson's destruction.

Cindy arrived with an armload of files. "This is the first batch."

"There's more?"

She set the files down on my circular table. "This is about a third of it."

I wondered if this could be another test, but discarded that idea. "Where do I start?"

She stopped at the door. "You got me. That's why we pay you the big bucks."

This was going to take forever, but I moved to the table and sat. The first file I opened was from a year ago.

When Cindy returned I asked, "How long has this been in the works?"

"About a year." She set down a second stack of files bigger than the first.

"Do they normally take that long?"

She thought for a moment. "No. This is probably the longest. Three months or so is more normal. I'll get you the last stack."

"This is going to take forever," I lamented. "When are we meeting with them?"

"I'll check, but two weeks or so, I think."

I started my notes as I paged through the first document.

By eleven, I was going batty with the Stoner files. This job was going to bore me to death if I spent all day, every day with crap like this.

After a trip to the bathroom, I stopped by Cindy's desk for a chat. "Did Mark spend all day, every day reading files?"

"Not every day."

That was little consolation.

# CHAPTER 14

*Jennifer*

FRIDAY MORNING, AFTER READING BORING MATERIAL ON STONER FOR THE UMPTEENTH hour, I had three questions for Dennis about this purchase: why, why, and another why. The company didn't seem to fit at all with what we were doing. Not that we couldn't branch out a little, but livestock feed, with an emphasis on poultry, didn't move the excitement meter for me.

I'd tried to get a minute with him yesterday, but he'd put me off.

Larry poked his head into my office. "Having fun yet?"

My eyes were going blurry, so his interruption was a welcome one. I waved my hand over the stack of papers. "Tell me why we're talking to Stoner about livestock feed. I don't get it."

Larry leaned against the door jamb. "He's a good friend of Dennis's dad. I guess he doesn't want to make him feel bad by telling him to shove it."

"Was Talbot also one of his dad's friends?"

"Yeah, but that one made sense. Especially after you knocked the price down."

"Thanks." Things were a little clearer now.

"Any time." Larry waved and wandered off.

I gathered up the relevant files. Dennis wasn't going to avoid me any longer. He needed to tell me if he was serious about this or not.

When I made my way down the hall, I found Dennis's office empty.

Before I could ask Cindy where he'd gone, her phone rang. "Uh-huh. How many? I'm not sure my car will hold all that. Just a sec." She removed the phone from her ear. "Jenn, do you have a car?"

I nodded. "Not much of one, but it runs."

"Could you spare some time to help me with a delivery?"

"Of course."

She got back on the phone. "Jenn and I will leave right now." She hung up. "That was Dennis. At least he's in a better mood today. Whatever he had for dinner last night, he needs more of it."

I met her at the elevator with my purse. "What are we delivering?"

The doors opened, and we entered.

She pressed the button for the parking level. "Chickens. You know where Costco is?"

"Yeah, one of my favorites." Having to watch pennies meant things like breakfast cereal in bulk. If it wasn't at Costco, sometimes it wasn't on the menu.

The numbers clicked down, and the doors opened onto the parking garage.

"I'll meet you there. We need to pick up some food for Dennis," she said as she walked to a small four-door.

It seemed big enough for most people's Costco runs, so I wasn't sure why she needed me.

The drive to Costco wasn't a long one.

Cindy was waiting with one of those flatbed push carts when I walked up. "We'll need a second cart."

I followed her in with another flatbed. Mine had a wheel problem that made it want to veer left.

She walked quickly to the meat department at the back of the store, where she started loading rotisserie chickens onto her cart.

I grabbed one. "How many do we need?"

"Fifty."

"Fifty?" I repeated.

"Let's make it sixty to be on the safe side."

I piled the warm plastic containers on my cart. Thirty chickens was going to to be a serious stacking project on this sucker. I stopped after I counted the thirtieth and hoped they wouldn't all tumble off halfway to the register. That would make one hell of a mess.

"Why so many?" I asked.

"A lot of mouths to feed." She counted the stack on her cart. "I've got thirty. How about you?"

"Same."

She started off to the registers.

I pushed my squeaky cart behind her, careful to go slow enough not to lose one of the birds off the top.

The cashier counted the containers and rang us up like it was no big deal that we'd wiped out nearly their entire supply of pre-cooked chickens.

"Who is this for?"

She paid with her credit card. "Dennis. We're going to meet him on Laurel. Do you know where that is?"

"Pretty much. Where on Laurel?"

"Near the south end. You can follow me."

We split up at the door. After loading the birds and backing out, I found her idling by the front of the store, waiting for me.

The traffic-signal gods were merciful, and I didn't lose her on the way to Laurel Street. I still hadn't gotten an explanation of who we were feeding, and on the drive over, nothing rational came to mind.

When we reached Saint Helena's, Cindy signaled and turned into the parking lot. The sign outside explained that they served food to the poor and homeless here. A soup kitchen, you might call it, but today we were providing chicken.

Dennis was outside waiting for us.

The bazillionaire was donating food to a soup kitchen.

The thought made me smile. It was a nice gesture—better and more personal than just sending a check.

A good deed from a bad man was still a good deed.

～

*JENNIFER*

A LARGE GROUP WAS GATHERED BY THE FRONT DOOR.

I followed Cindy, who parked by the side door.

Dennis waved over several guys after we stopped, and they grabbed armfuls of chickens and took them inside.

"How many did you get?" Dennis asked Cindy.

"Sixty."

He gave her a thumbs up. "Good call. The crowd looks bigger than normal."

Moments later, the original helpers were back for more birds, along with a few more helping hands.

I waited quietly by my car as it was being unloaded, unsure what to do next.

Dennis said goodbye to Cindy and walked my way. "Want to stay and help?"

The question was a simple one. My answer was the hard part.

Staying with him made me uneasy, but leaving would mark me as a jerk. "Sure."

He pointed back toward the front. "Park in the lot, and then meet me inside."

I closed up my car and moved it to the parking lot. The question of how to get inside loomed. The front door had a line of people slowly entering, and I didn't want to look like I was cutting in, so I walked around to the side door where the chickens and Dennis had disappeared.

The aromas of warm food hit me the second I passed through the door. Our dozens of chickens were now stacked behind the counter, and in front of me were several people—including Dennis—serving delicious-smelling plates.

He looked back and noticed me. His hands were full. A jerk of his head asked me to join him. "Wanna help slice?"

When I reached where he was serving, the immensity of the operation hit me. "Sure."

"Gloves are on the table."

I donned a pair and realized I'd been wrong about Dennis. He wasn't just donating the food, he was donating his time as well. I'd always thought the rich massaged their guilty consciences by writing checks at the end of the year to a charity here and a charity there. This was a different level of giving. I hadn't suspected this aspect of Dennis Benson at all.

"White or dark?" he asked the next woman in line.

"A little of both," she answered.

He cut the last of the useful meat off the carcass he was working.

I retrieved another for him from the stack on the counter, and one for myself.

He slipped the finished one into the garbage. "Thanks."

"White or dark?" I asked the man in front of me.

"White. I like breasts."

There was no hint of an insinuating smirk. He just preferred chicken breast meat to drumsticks or thighs.

The hall had filled with people at tables, eating away.

The two servers to my right, a man and a woman, both in suits, were also doling out chicken.

Farther down the line, ladies offered mashed potatoes, green beans, and peas. At the very last station, a lady was serving brownies and reminding each guest that the limit was one, which she enforced, regardless of the diner's protests. By and large, the group was better mannered than the clientele at some restaurants.

To my left, it sounded like the peas weren't faring as well as the green beans.

Several times Dennis's shoulder brushed mine, and each time I succeeded in controlling the gasp that threatened to overcome me. I was going all high school just working next to the man, even without conversation or emotion-filled glances. Just a guy and a girl standing next to each other serving food.

It should have been easy. The touches were innocent enough, but his touch transferred electricity each time.

I looked up and decided his profile would have been one a Greek sculptor might have chosen.

"White, please," the slight old lady in front of me said, jerking me back to reality.

"Sure. I've got extra dark meat, if you'd like some of that as well."

"Extra?" she asked.

"Sure."

She nodded vigorously as I added more to her plate.

The exchange brought out what we were doing here. This wasn't bonus food, or a social outing, this was food they wouldn't otherwise get to eat. Food they probably couldn't afford.

The group ranged from the obviously homeless to those who seemed merely down on their luck. They were young and old, a few with young children, but not many.

"Thanks," she said as she moved down the line.

My next customer asked for dark meat, preferably a drumstick. He was in luck. All the people here today were in luck, thanks to Cindy.

If she hadn't decided on the extra ten chickens, we would have run out before serving the final person in a line, a middle-aged man in an old army jacket.

Dennis helped him. "Joe, have a little extra, if you want it."

He knew the man's name.

Joe's jacket had *Mason* stitched on the name tag. His eyes darted around, and he wiped his hands on his jeans more than once.

"Sure, but white meat only. I don't eat the greasy stuff."

Dennis cut off some extra for him. "Take care now, Joe."

"Thanks, Mr. B."

Not only did Dennis know Joe's name, but Dennis had been here often enough for Joe to know his name as well.

Joe limped down to the mashed potatoes.

"That's a wrap," said the guy in the suit to my right.

"Joe is always our last customer," Dennis explained.

"Is he always late?"

Dennis continued to carve his bird. "No, but he waits for everyone else to go first." That painted Joe in a different light. "Would you do me the honor of lunching with me?"

His question meant Martha's prediction of sharing a meal with him had come true.

I didn't have to think twice. "Sure."

He sliced more from the chicken he was working on. "White or dark?" he asked me, just as he had all of his guests.

There was more dark left on his bird. "Dark will be fine."

"Good, because I'm a breast man myself." He smiled as he looked up.

No doubt there was a double meaning to his statement.

I stifled my laugh, but couldn't resist poking him. "I would have taken you for a leg man."

He moved the chicken slices onto a plate for me. "It's a close call at times, but I find the breast…" His tongue darted out to wet his upper lip. "…more succulent."

The wickedness of his smile sent a tingle through me. I couldn't believe I was standing here trading sexual innuendos with him. I took my plate and walked down the counter to add mashed potatoes and green beans. The thought of a man's tongue, his tongue, on my nipples sent heat to my core.

Farther down the counter, the brownie plate was almost empty.

He plucked two brownies from the plate, and placed one on each of our plates. "Unless you don't like chocolate."

I smiled back at him. "Who doesn't like chocolate?"

He picked up his plate and motioned toward the tables.

I moved out of the way. "You saved yourself two? I thought one was the rule."

He led the way toward an empty table. "The second was for you."

He nodded at several of the people we passed as they acknowledged him as "Mr. B."

I took a seat on the bench across from him.

He was already chewing a bite of his brownie. The man and woman who'd been serving next to him walked our way. The way the man guided the woman with a hand at her back made it obvious they were a couple, and a gorgeous one at that.

When he got closer, and with his apron now off, it was easy to tell his suit wasn't off the rack.

"Thanks for the help, Dennis," he said. "Lauren and I are going to head out."

Dennis looked back and stood. "Any time. I'd like you to meet Jennifer Hanley. Jennifer, this is Bill Covington and his lovely wife, Lauren. She's the brains of the pair."

The name rang a bell, but I didn't immediately place it.

Bill scowled in response to Dennis's ribbing, but only briefly. He extended his hand, which I stood and shook with my mouth still full of food.

Lauren's broad smile showed how much she appreciated Dennis's compliment, even at her husband's expense.

She offered her hand as well. "Be careful with this one. He's a silver-tongued devil."

"Nice to meet you both, and thank you for the warning."

They were gone with a quick wave.

Only then did I place the name. "I visited UCLA, and there were Covington buildings there. Are they related to—"

Dennis nodded. "His grandfather."

I'd pictured bazillionaires lunching on exotic dishes with unpronounceable French names over white linen tablecloths, washing it all down with bottles of wine that cost a month's rent while discussing their Mediterranean yachting plans for the summer. Instead I sat across from one—on a wobbly folding chair with no padding—eating the same food we'd just served the homeless on a worn wooden table. Then there were the Covingtons, husband and wife both taking the time to volunteer here.

The producers of *Lifestyles of the Rich and Famous* weren't about to be filming this scene.

I took a sip of my water. "Do you help out here often?"

He had to finish chewing before answering. "Roughly every two weeks, but Wednesday Bill called to say they expected to be short staffed." He motioned to the retreating Covingtons. "It's one of the ways we give back to the community that has given us so much."

"And he, they, come down here often?"

"About the same frequency, and his restaurant brings leftover food every morning as well. But today that got gobbled up before you arrived. It always does. It's an incentive to be early."

The Covingtons brought food every day? That was a shocker.

A man's voice boomed from behind me. "Thank you for the chickens. They were a great help."

Dennis waved. "My pleasure, Father Dan."

I looked over as Father Dan sat with a couple behind us.

I turned back to my lunch partner. "Do you always bring food with you?"

Dennis shook his head. "No. The Carmelos' truck broke down. They were scheduled to bring turkey. I was just helping out." He shrugged as if it was normal to wipe out Costco's chicken supply to feed a few hundred people on a moment's notice.

He stabbed another bite of meat. "You look surprised."

I closed my mouth, realizing it had fallen open. "It's just…"

He waved his fork at me. "You're prejudiced. I get it."

"About what?"

"You don't like rich people. It's typical, but I'm proud of my family, and I'm not going to apologize for being born a Benson."

"How can I not like them when I don't know any?"

He pointed at one of the other men who'd been serving with us. "If it's okay for Stan to volunteer here, why can't I?"

I looked at Stan without an answer for him.

He looked like a retired…well, anybody, in faded jeans and polo with a slight rip on the sleeve.

"Stan," he continued, "has done a lot of things in his life. He was a waiter, a painter, a handyman, a hardware store clerk, and you know what he would tell you?"

I shook my head.

"He told me once that he never got hired by a poor person. He always worked for someone richer than himself. My family employs tens of thousands of people. That's how many families we support. I'm not apologizing."

I'd gotten myself into a hole here. "I'm sorry. I didn't mean—"

"You probably think people with money drink expensive wine with every meal."

*Can he read my thoughts?*

"I do not. I just thought you were…too busy for this."

He sighed. "We should never be too busy to care."

He finally put the chicken he'd been waving at me in his mouth to chew.

I felt ashamed and wished we'd stuck to the back and forth about breast meat and legs.

He finished chewing. "Since we're on the subject of applying labels to people and misjudging them, I want to apologize again for underestimating you because you don't have an MBA."

"I understand."

"It wasn't fair of me, and we haven't gotten much time together since you started, but I want to say I'm very happy to have you working for me."

"Well…" For a moment my revenge-focused brain didn't know what to do with this information, but then I managed a heartfelt smile. "Thanks, I'm glad you think I'm doing a good job."

I meant it, and I hoped to get off the topic of my surprise at his generosity and caring. It wasn't a comfortable conversation.

He swallowed and pointed his fork at me. "And I look forward to having you under me for a long time." A wicked grin grew over his face.

I blushed at the dirty innuendo.

Confusion gripped my rational brain. He was the devil who deserved my vengeance, after all. The death, the pain he'd caused had been real, and it couldn't be papered over with a few dozen chickens. None of this brought my dad back.

But the primitive, cavewoman side of my brain sent heat to my core as it signaled its desire. I had to blink back the image of his face over mine with the ceiling in the background—or would it be outdoors with the sky in the background? I averted my eyes to my plate and forked some green beans.

Had he meant it the way I'd taken it? I couldn't tell, as his face quickly went back to the passive mask he often wore. I could hope though, couldn't I? But why would I *want* to hope?

It was wrong to be attracted to him, one side said. *I don't care. I want to feel good and be wanted*, the other side replied. I should've known better than to dance with the devil.

I crossed my legs. The cavewoman was winning this argument. When I looked up, we locked eyes. I hadn't verbally responded to him.

As a smile tugged at the corners of his lips, I could sense my eyes had betrayed me and telegraphed my desire.

My phone chose that moment to come alive and chirp on the table.

Turning it over, I found what I didn't need.

EB: We really need to talk

I put the phone back down.

Dennis glanced at the phone, which still displayed the message. "It's okay if you need to answer that."

"No way. It's my ex. He doesn't know when to give up."

"Tell me who EB is, and I'm sure I can convince him."

I ignored the offer, flipped the phone over, and looked away. "Do they serve here every day?"

Dennis's impassive face returned. "Six days a week. On Sunday Father Dan is busy with some other things."

The moment had passed. He was back in boss mode.

Our meal concluded as he gave me a quick history of Father Dan's mission to feed the poor in this part of town.

He stood and took his plate and glass with him.

I followed to add mine to the dirty dish stack. Somebody had a monumental task this afternoon.

He touched my shoulder. "Thank you for helping."

The shock of the touch unwired my brain for a second. "It was my pleasure."

"See you back at the office," he said before turning for the door.

Father Dan intercepted me. "Jennifer, isn't it?"

I nodded.

"Thank you for helping us today. It makes a world of difference to those we feed here to have the support of caring people such as yourself."

"You do good work here. It was my pleasure."

As I walked to my car, his thanks gave me an internal warmth I hadn't felt in a long time. I'd spent much of the last months and years worried about Ramona, Billy, and myself, without stopping to realize we were luckier than some. We had food to eat and a roof over our heads, even if it was only a two-bedroom apartment.

As I drove back to the building, I had trouble making sense of today's experience.

Yesterday I'd known Dennis Benson to have an evil heart, bent on profit over safety, but this episode completely muddled my image.

*We should never be too busy to care,*" he'd said. The simple sentence tugged at my heart strings in a way that made me tear up. He'd shown me *two* sides of himself I hadn't seen before, and they didn't fit my previous view at all. The puzzle of Dennis Benson was no longer as simple as a devil hiding behind a suit.

Although I knew beyond a doubt he was guilty in Dad's death, the man had compassion for others that I couldn't square with that knowledge. He also had pride in his family and himself for what they contributed to the community. I'd have to leave that part of the equation in the enigma column for now. This was more than I could handle today.

Then there was the sheer animal magnetism when he looked at me. It was a pull I couldn't deny. It was a force I couldn't wish away.

Last week, my objective had been clear. Now Dennis Benson was messing with my ordered view of the world, and nothing made sense.

# CHAPTER 15

*JENNIFER*
*(Two Weeks Later)*

I'D BEEN WORKING UPSTAIRS WITH DENNIS FOR JUST OVER TWO WEEKS NOW. IT HAD been odd at first to call him Dennis instead of Mr. Benson—or the devil, as I'd always named him before—but the day at Saint Helena's had changed that.

Since then, I'd seen more instances of the man who was giving enough to volunteer at a soup kitchen, more of the boss who cared about his employees, and none of who I'd thought he was. When I looked at him, I was seeing more suit and less devil every day.

This morning, my before-breakfast email check revealed my first message from Hydra in weeks. Not that previous communications had been frequent, but I hadn't gotten any feedback from him after the disastrous day Dennis's spin-off announcement had nullified our "bad news balloon," as Hydra liked to call them. I'd expected a reaction of some kind, given how shitty I'd felt about Dennis escaping the wrath of the market that day. Hydra had to have been pissed as well, but his radio silence had been deafening.

> To: Nemesis666
> From: HYDRA157
> Number 89461 is next.
> It may have moved upstairs.

As usual, the message was businesslike and to the point. I'd asked once before how he knew what file numbers I should get, and been told merely that he had his sources. Clearly I wasn't the only one in the company in league with Hydra. Someone else had to have access to the file number cross-reference—it was the only way to find these.

The fact that I'd gotten another file number from Hydra should have cheered me up. But now that I'd met the man and knew him as *Dennis*, this morning's message hadn't had its normal effect on my mood. Had I gotten too close? Was my judgment impaired, or getting clearer? My two views of him didn't mesh, and my hold on the truth was getting murkier by the day.

Nevertheless, I needed to focus on the task at hand. I'd promised Mom I'd get the proof. I wouldn't let her down, and for that I had to follow Hydra's instructions and not ask questions. My vow to her to make him pay was a promise I had to keep. I might not enjoy it the way I'd thought I would, but it had to be done.

I'd been clear about my motivations, and Hydra had been clear that I would have to wait until I'd retrieved all the files he was interested in. It wasn't a surprise, since once I had what I wanted, we both knew I could blow off Hydra and stop my high-risk, nighttime sneaking around.

I would need to pull this file one night this week. The quicker I got what he needed, the quicker I would get what I wanted.

My attempt at creating a problem for Dennis had failed so spectacularly that I clearly needed to leave the bad news to Hydra. And I had a part to play in that— small, but essential.

I wrote the file number on a Post-it note, folded it, and stashed it in my wallet before heading off to work. A month ago, I would have been eager to get the file. Today, it was an obligation.

I'd helped Dennis with the Zarniger transaction last week and earned a bonus, in addition to the gigantic raise he'd given me. His interest in my analysis of the Zarniger deal had led to a change in our strategy when they came to visit. His adopting my view had done more to build my self esteem than even the day I'd graduated from Pepperdine.

It was an odd feeling to be appreciating his comments, even his praise, given what I knew he'd done. But I'd decided right now good news was welcome from any front, even from him.

Ramona had been getting more excited by the day, and she planned to start the hunt for a suitable three-bedroom this weekend. She and Billy deserved rooms of their own.

My drive into work was uneventful, and uneventful was good. Overall, life had improved. I could see financial daylight for us, and my new normal with less stress was a welcome change.

Upstairs, when I passed through the door leading to Mahogany Row, I didn't feel the apprehension I had those first few days. The unease of entering the devil's lair had been replaced by a feeling of calm. This was a safe place, a place I belonged, more importantly, a place I'd earned.

At first, the denizens of these offices had been standoffish, but Dennis's public praise for my efforts in the Talbot and Zarniger transactions had changed that. These people worked on a higher floor than others in the company, but they weren't the stuck-up jerks I'd expected. Even Larry was nice.

At eleven, I gathered up my notes on the huge Stoner purchase and made my way to Dennis's office for our scheduled meeting.

Dennis waved to me and motioned to the small conference table while he continued a phone call.

I closed the door behind me and took my normal seat facing the window—a seat that allowed me to watch him at his desk while also viewing the ocean.

He finished up his call and joined me at the table. "Where should we start?"

"I've done a quick analysis of their last three years of financials, if you want to start there."

"Sure. That sounds…" He stopped mid-sentence. His eyes went to the door.

A woman walked in without so much as a rap on the door frame.

I knew the face instantly from my research on my target.

Her choice of a dress—more appropriate for going to the opera than anything work-related—was almost laughable. She wore it well, but a plunging neckline of obviously braless cleavage and a thigh-high slit didn't fit in the office environment.

She gave me a flit of her hand as if she were shooing away a bug. "You can go. We'd like privacy."

I had no desire to make her acquaintance and stood.

Dennis stood as well, and his hand on my arm was a command to stay instead. As much as I wanted to get the hell out of here, I was the pawn in this war of wills, and I was Dennis's pawn.

"Dennis, we need to talk." She cast a glance my way. "In private."

"Melissa, this is Jennifer Hanley. Jennifer, Melissa."

"A pleasure," I said, offering my hand.

She huffed, shaking off the introduction as if it were beneath her to respond in kind. "Melissa Benson, his wife."

I pulled my hand back when she didn't accept the offer to shake.

Dennis stiffened. "Ex-wife."

I waited for the inevitable verbal artillery barrage.

If break-ups were on a continuum from cordial to murderous, the papers had categorized theirs as one step short of bloodshed, and the legal aftermath still raged, with her claiming he'd misrepresented the situation and hidden assets. Her demands for more were still ongoing, I'd gathered from the news sites.

Her glare at me was cold enough to freeze a cup of coffee. "Dennis, I said *in private.*"

Dennis moved his gaze to the table. "I'm in a meeting, Melissa. If you want to talk, make an appointment with Cindy on your way out." He made a point of not looking at her. "For next month."

She ignored the put-off. "I'm on the organizing committee for the museum fundraiser, and think you and I should go to your father's gala together. It's what he would want." Her voice had a fake sweetness so syrupy it would have attracted flies if we'd been outside.

Dennis's jaw clenched. "Not in a million years."

The insult bounced right off her. "Don't be impetuous, Dennis. You know that's your weakness. We should both do it for Lloyd. We did it last year."

The woman's eyes were cold as death. It was abundantly clear why she was now the *ex* Mrs. Benson. She was the kind of bitch who deserved to be kicked out of the female category for giving the rest of us a bad reputation.

Maybe I couldn't screw up Dennis's life today, but it sure seemed this woman could.

I knew his father, Lloyd Benson, was the chairman of the museum, but she was insinuating a deeper backstory than that.

Dennis shifted, clearly off balance with this woman. "And last year was the last time. I'll be taking someone else this year." His jaw twitched.

She rolled her eyes. "Don't be silly. You're married to this job—you always have been—and I checked the seating chart. You're not going with anyone."

Perhaps *witch* was a better description for her.

"You're going with me," she concluded.

Dennis didn't say anything. He wasn't a good liar, and she seemed to know it.

Melissa was here to create trouble, and if she was trying to ruin his bank account, and I was out to ruin his reputation, we were aligned, in an odd way. I didn't like her, but we had the same end goal.

The witch advanced a step.

Dennis was quiet, seeming to search for an answer.

She'd unnerved the great Dennis Benson, not an easy feat.

I saw my opportunity to strike a blow and took it. "*I'm* going with him."

I slid close to Dennis and put my arm around his waist. An even-more pissed off ex-wife would certainly screw up Dennis's day. Mom would have been proud of me.

I chalked the icy stare I got from her up as a win. She was steaming mad, the kind of mad that would make her dangerous if there were sharp objects handy.

Dennis snaked a hand around my waist and moved me closer yet. When he looked down at me, his smile was oddly warm and appreciative.

I didn't flinch. Instead I upped the ante against his ex. I welded myself to his side. "Isn't that right, Denny?"

Melissa's face went red with fury.

Dennis looked down at me. "And I'm so glad you said yes, Angel." He gave me a squeeze.

Calling me Angel? I hadn't seen that coming. But it was my signal to smile up at him.

"I'm so looking forward to it." I turned to her. "I've heard so much about it, but this will be my first time."

Her Witchiness huffed audibly. "I don't believe it for a second."

Dennis spun me toward him, and his mouth came down to mine in a kiss clearly meant as payback for his ex.

He pulled me close, my breasts pillowed firmly against the hardness of his chest. A hand behind my head held me in place.

His tongue sought entrance, and suddenly this was anything but acting.

My eyes slammed shut, and my heart thundered in my chest as his hand fell to my ass and squeezed. He tasted like coffee, desire, and *passion*. As his tongue swept over mine, I breathed in the woodsy scent of his hair or his aftershave—I couldn't tell which, and it didn't matter. All rational thought halted.

Logically, I should have pushed the ogre away, but logic wasn't in charge any longer. All that mattered was that I'd tasted the predator, the king of the jungle, and my body wanted more. It needed more. Hormones, instinct, and desire won the day.

My fingers speared through his hair, and I pulled myself up to meet his passion.

His hand moved to my breast, stroking the underside through my clothes, before a thumb smoothed over the pebbled nipple straining to puncture my bra and meet his touch.

The witch huffed.

The door slammed.

He didn't stop. For what seemed like an eternity, he held me there, kissing me, caressing me, like we belonged together, like I belonged to him. And for this moment, I did.

He shifted, and the unmistakable bar of his erection pushed against me. This embrace wasn't fake for him either. His reaction couldn't be hidden.

I surrendered entirely to my animal brain. The instructions it sent to my tongue, my mouth, and my hands said to pull him close and not let him get away. In my core, I wanted him to desire me as much as my body desired his.

In the end, I didn't pull away. He did.

Catching my breath, I smoothed my clothes and looked to the space Her Witchiness had vacated at some point. "She's gone."

Dennis smoothed the hair I'd messed up. "Good riddance."

"Is she always like that?"

"You caught her on a good day." His hand went into his pocket, probably in an effort to hide the bulge in his trousers—it didn't work. "Will you accompany me to the museum fundraiser?"

It wasn't clear if that was an actual question or a rhetorical one at this point.

"Please," he added.

I took a deep breath and willed my logical brain to save me from myself. My tongue darted out to trace my still-tingling upper lip. "Will it piss her off?"

He chuckled. "Incredibly." It was the answer I'd hoped for—the witch would be working extra hard to destroy him now.

But of course I'd already made up my mind. "I'd love to." Going to the party with him was sure to frost her ass even more. Fantastic kisser or not, he needed to pay. My family deserved to be avenged.

He shifted nervously. "Thank you for that. I wasn't prepared for the question." He looked away. "We should get back to Stoner later."

With my rational brain back in charge, I agreed. I was hot, aroused, and completely unable to concentrate in my current state. Hormones could be such a bitch. After another deep, calming breath, I walked to the door and turned. "Later, Denny."

His eyes narrowed at my audacity, before the smirk he tried to hide showed itself. "Later, Angel."

I closed the door behind me and rested against it for a second.

Cindy rolled her eyes with a chuckle. "A piece of work, isn't she?"

"You heard that?"

"Hard not to."

"Not somebody I want to spend any time with."

Melissa and I might both be working against Dennis, but that didn't mean I had to like her.

Cindy went back to her computer, and I headed to my office.

After I closed the door behind me, I took the seat and swiveled to face the ocean.

The man had scrambled my brain. Rational Jennifer knew he was dangerous, unpredictable, and exactly what I didn't need. Emotional me, hormonal me, said he was exactly what I wanted—dangerous, predatory, the king of the jungle and all he surveyed. His kiss had been everything I hadn't experienced before—sensual in a new and different way I couldn't put a name to. Not a boy's kiss, not even a man's kiss, something more animal than that, primal even.

The ancient cavewoman genes in me had reacted to him as the caveman I instinctively craved—the biggest, baddest one around, the one who would keep me safe.

My tongue still tingled with the aftereffects. I closed my eyes, and a smile overcame me. Our brief touches while volunteering in the lunch line a few weeks ago had hinted at what the kiss had proven. Dennis was my kryptonite. There was no denying it. I'd melted in his arms, completely at his mercy.

I told myself I'd impulsively claimed to be his date to piss off his ex. If she was trouble for him, our goals were aligned, and I expected an angry Melissa would cause him extra-serious grief. But I don't think that was the whole truth.

What the hell was wrong with me? Which was reality and which was illusion? Had I snuggled close to him and accepted the kiss merely to piss her off, or because of the magnetic attraction he held for me?

And for him, what part of it was play acting to piss her off? Any of it, or all of it?

*He called me Angel.*

I could live with that. In time, he would learn I was an avenging angel.

# CHAPTER 16

*DENNIS*

MELISSA'S VISIT HAD COME OUT OF THE BLUE, AND CLAIMING TO HAVE ARRANGED TO go to Dad's museum fundraiser with Jennifer had gotten rid of her.

But that had undone a lot of work, on my part. I'd been careful to avoid any improper contact with Jennifer since our visit to Saint Helena's.

She'd been temptingly close that day, and just brushing against her had almost stirred me to act on my fantasies. I'd considered asking her to join me for dinner more than once since then, but I'd pulled back each time. I couldn't risk it.

Melissa's motion to modify our divorce decree had been assigned to Judge White. My lawyer, Birkman, had been complaining about that turn of events ever since.

Judge White had married into money, and after her husband dumped her for a younger trophy wife, she'd become the most husband-unfriendly judge in the district.

Birkman had warned me that any hint I was involved with another woman, even now, would allow Melissa's side to play to the judge's prejudices and hurt me in the end. I would be painted as the rich guy trading the poor first wife in for a newer model, and the result could be very expensive.

As a result, I'd not even been on a date in a long while. I'd hooked up with a woman in Vegas, but that hardly counted as a date.

When Jennifer had claimed to be going to the gala with me, the shock had served its purpose of getting Melissa the hell out of my office. But what I hadn't counted on was the reaction I got from Jennifer, or my reaction to her when I'd upped the ante with a kiss.

She'd more than played along. Her kiss had consumed me and taken me down a road not recently traveled. A road called desire, where logic didn't register, where impulses took over, and I did what felt right. Kissing her felt right. The heat of her against me had made it difficult to avoid stripping her on the spot once Melissa stormed out.

It hadn't been smart. It hadn't been logical, but now that it was done, it felt natural. It felt right. Denying that it felt good—better than good, *great*—wouldn't be honest. I still felt her as I ran a finger over my bottom lip. Her peach scent lingered with me. *Great* might not even be a strong enough word.

But now I had to deal with the consequences of being impulsive once again. If I called Melissa right away and apologized, I could probably avoid the court fallout of what I'd just done. I considered that for a moment. I would have to tell Jennifer I wasn't taking her after all *and* endure the evening with Melissa.

How long would Melissa hold it over me? Probably forever.

Jennifer had already saved me a hundred and seventy-eight million on Talbot alone. And she was still doing great work.

*Screw Melissa.*

I was taking Jennifer to the fundraiser. If I was going to piss off Melissa, I was doing it right. The Talbot savings had already paid for it, but beyond that, it's what I wanted. I was done letting Melissa ruin so much as one more day of my life.

A knock sounded at the door, and Larry popped his head in. "Got a sec?"

Larry didn't often waste my time, so I motioned him in. "Sure."

He closed the door behind him. "It's about Gumpert."

Gumpert was always asking for a little something extra. "What's he want now?"

Larry leaned on the chair back instead of taking a seat. "He's really pissed about the spin-off."

"He's the one who wanted to paint the news story that day as a death knell." I'd overstated it a bit, but Gumpert had gone out on his own limb on that one.

"Rumor is he lost half a mill."

"The stock was up the next day. All he had to do was not panic."

"It's worse than that. He shorted us in the afternoon, and he thinks you stiffed him on purpose by not giving him a hint."

I shook my head. "All I did was refuse to give him anything we weren't giving everyone else. He's a twerp."

Larry cocked his head. "A very powerful twerp. I'm giving you a heads up that he's out to get us. It's personal for him now, so I wouldn't advise talking to him at all. And don't be surprised when he writes a hit piece on us next quarter."

I wasn't sure what Larry wanted me to do with this information. "Do you want me to call him and try to square it?"

Larry's eyes widened—I'd guessed wrong. "No way. I think it's beyond repair. This is just the price of being publicly traded."

Yep, I knew it was one of the big trade offs, probably the biggest. "It just burns me that these guys get to critique us, when most of them couldn't run a profitable lemonade stand."

Larry straightened up, ready to leave. "Life's not fair. Anyway, you've been warned."

This visit had been to put a stake in the ground for the future when Gumpert caused trouble. Larry didn't want me blaming him.

"Got it. Give me a heads up if you see it coming."

He waved a salute as he backed toward the door. "Will do."

Life certainly wasn't fair, and not all shit ran downhill either. The Melissa and Gumpert vendettas weren't problems I could delegate away.

*JENNIFER*

AS I TURNED ON TO MY STREET, I CHECKED MY REARVIEW MIRROR, BUT I DIDN'T SEE the gray car I thought had followed me. Paranoia was a bitch.

Upstairs, I busied myself with dinner to control my urge to tell my sister everything. It had been such a confusing whirlwind of a day. I downed a glass of wine while cooking to calm myself.

"And whose canary did you swallow?" Ramona finally asked me after we'd eaten.

I closed and started the dishwasher, then crossed the room to settle on the couch, smiling wordlessly.

Billy was at the kitchen table doing his homework. "Eww. That's gross. Jeremy ate a salamander once. Do the feathers tickle?"

"It's just a saying that means she looks like she's hiding something," his mother explained.

"Oh." He went back to his paper.

I didn't think the discussion was Billy-appropriate. "Maybe you should finish your homework in the bedroom."

"I like it out here."

I had another idea. "You'll like it better in the bedroom. We're going to talk about kissing boys."

That got him moving. "Eww."

Ramona let the door close before continuing her interrogation. "I knew you were holding something back at dinner."

I couldn't keep this from her. "He kissed me."

"Who exactly is *he*?"

"Dennis."

"But you hate that guy."

I nodded. "It happened so fast." It had been fast and surprising—wonderful and terrifying all at the same time.

"And you let him?"

I gave her the whole story about his haughty ex and how it had started as a fake kiss to piss her off but ended up so much more.

"So I gave her another reason to hate the guy and put him through the ringer," I concluded.

Ramona had been slack-jawed the entire time. "He's using you to piss off his ex."

"That's the point. She wants to ruin him, and so do I. Getting her more pissed off will damage him in the long run."

"That's sick."

"I know, but that's not all. He asked me to go with him to the museum fundraiser."

"But that's still using you to rub her nose in it."

"I said yes."

"I didn't ask what you said. Don't you get how this looks?"

"You weren't there."

"This is seriously screwed up. A few weeks ago you would have been shopping for cyanide-laced lipstick, and now you want his and hers bottles of lube?"

I knew she was kidding, but I had no idea how to answer. "It was just a kiss."

"Three seconds?"

I shook my head.

"How long then?"

"I don't remember."

"Was it good?"

I couldn't hide the grin. "Yes."

"See? You want him."

"Aren't you the one always telling me he might not be as bad as I think?"

"I always thought your obsession with getting back at him wasn't healthy, but that's not the same as instantly switching to wanting him in your bed."

"You're getting a little ahead of yourself."

She scoffed. "You know how guys think. He's gotten you to first base, and he'll be looking to round the bases and score pretty quickly. And besides, you've got horny written all over you."

I ignored the horny comment—not that she was wrong, but it wasn't the point. "You weren't there."

She shook her head. "I would have stopped you. I know you've had a dry spell. Hell, we both have, but wouldn't it make more sense to hook up with a guy you don't want to kill?"

"But I'm using him too."

"Are we back to poisoned lipstick now?"

"No, but getting close to him will give me better access to the company's files."

"So the poisoned lipstick comes later, *after* the bottles of his and hers lube."

"You're not helping."

"Only because you don't want to hear how fucked up this sounds. You have to make a choice. You can't be both lover and destroyer. You need to choose now."

I settled back and closed my eyes. I had to admit that how it felt and how it sounded were completely opposite. "I guess."

Ramona clicked on the DVR. "I don't want to see you get hurt. In the end you have to decide if he's your enemy or your love interest. He can't be both. You have to put him in one category and bury the other. You can't let it pull you apart."

I mulled that for a moment. I didn't have to decide tonight, but eventually it would come to that, and she had it right. I would have to decide.

She scrolled through the movie selections. "Hey, go spend time with him, and in the end you might decide you were wrong about him all along. But you have to figure it out before you round the bases." She punched a button to check out a movie's description.

I'd hoped talking to her would help me make sense of the situation, but it hadn't. I knew what I knew, and I knew how I felt, and the two were polar opposites.

Ramona wasn't done with me yet. "You know, the biggest problem I have with this obsession of yours is that you can't really hate a person you don't know. So go full Mata Hari on him and decide if you still hate the guy later. Just understand going in that you're using him for sex and dump him." She clicked on another movie. "My God, I can't believe I just said that."

Billy didn't have a father because she'd realized too late that Trevor had only been "using her for sex," as she put it.

Perhaps the latest file Hydra had pointed me toward would provide clarity about who Dennis really was. In the meantime, color me both horny and confused.

The one thing I'd learned today was that Dennis Benson was dangerous in the extreme. He could be impulsive and demanding, a combination that could get me in over my head before I knew it—a tornado that could sweep me up in a vortex beyond my control.

Ramona started the movie, but I couldn't concentrate.

My thoughts kept coming back to the kiss. I hadn't read the kiss wrong, but what if my sister was right and he was only using me to spite Melissa? That was okay, wasn't it? It would make his life harder, and that was a good result.

Mom had always told me to trust my gut, but how did that translate to a situation like this? Was Ramona right that I was too horny to understand how I really felt about him? It *had* been a long dry spell; too long. Perhaps a drink from that well would clear things up. Even if it didn't, it would quench a thirst. And boy, was I thirsty for that man.

Just the thought of what it might be like sent a tingle to my lady parts.

Ramona looked over. "You all right?"

I squeezed my legs together. "I will be."

He could use me for his purpose, and I could use him for mine. We'd both get what we wanted.

I smiled. That would be fair.

### DENNIS

I stood outside Cascada Azul at dinnertime waiting for my sister, who was late as always.

Serena and I got together about once a month for dinner, and she'd scheduled this one at her favorite Mexican restaurant.

Cascada Azul wasn't a hole in the wall, but it wasn't elegant either. The family-run restaurant had a loyal following and was as packed as usual.

I'd already told the hostess we wanted a booth in the back and was waiting for my name to be called.

The young hostess opened the door. "Dennis, party of two."

I raised my hand and followed her inside. "My sister will be along in just a bit."

She smiled, grabbed two menus, and started toward the rear. She stopped at a booth very near the back, as I'd requested.

I accepted the menu and pressed a bill into her hand, getting a warm smile in return. I'd only been seated long enough to receive the bowl of chips and the tray of bean dip and salsa when Serena waved from the front. I waved back and stood.

She rushed over and gave me a hug. "Dennis, sorry I'm late."

I'd long ago given up trying to get her to be on time. "No worries. You're looking good."

"Why, thank you. It's the Pilates."

Our waitress arrived to take our drink orders.

I chose my standard Luna Azul margarita on the rocks, no salt, and Serena asked for the same, only frozen. The blue curacao made it look similar to my favorite drink, a blue Hawaii.

Serena started in as soon as the waitress left. "I heard you got a visit from Maleficent today."

That had been Serena-speak for Melissa since shortly after we got married, and it fit.

I knew where she'd gotten the heads up, but I asked anyway. "Who told you that?"

She scooped a chip in the bean dip. "You know Cindy keeps me up to date. What did *she* want?"

She'd probably also gotten that from Cindy.

"She wanted to talk about the museum gala."

"Dad should kick her off the committee, if you ask me. She's just never-ending trouble."

I felt the same way, but it wasn't an argument worth having with Dad just yet. "That's Dad's cross to bear. Take it up with him." To help smooth over the divorce, Dad had promised to let Melissa stay on the committee. It had been another of her off-the-wall demands when we ended things.

It wasn't in writing, but Dad felt he had to honor it, even if Melissa never kept any of her promises.

Serena waved her chip at me. "Go on."

"Nothing much to tell. She wanted me to attend with her. I said no."

She continued to fish. "And what else?"

"Nothing else."

"I heard she blew her top, Mount Vesuvius style, so you must have said more than that."

"I told her I already had a date."

"Who?"

This is where it could get tricky. "Someone from the office."

"Really?"

Our waitress appeared to take our orders, chicken tacos for me and the enchilada suprema for Serena.

After the waitress left, Serena came at me nine different ways, trying to get more out of me, but all I gave up about Jennifer was her name.

I didn't mention the off-the-charts kiss, her incredible body, the fantastic smarts, or those green eyes that looked right through me—none of it.

I smiled, recalling the feel of her warm, soft tit under my hand, and the way she'd gasped when I'd squeezed her ass. It hadn't been a gasp of protest, rather a gasp of desire, of hunger for more.

Jennifer wanted more, and today I didn't give a shit about how it affected the legal negotiations with Melissa.

Serena eyed me as she finished chewing another chip. "I saw that."

I could play innocent with the best of them. "What?"

"That smirk." She pointed her finger at me. "You just thought of something you're holding back, and it made you smile. Now give."

"It was nothing. I liked the sound of the door slamming behind Melissa is all."

Serena set her drink down. "Liar."

Our dinners arrived. We got off the Jennifer-Melissa-fundraiser topic after I started probing Serena about her dating life.

She could dish it out, but she couldn't take it.

The rest of the meal was more sedate after we both abandoned the topics the other didn't want to discuss.

# CHAPTER 17

*JENNIFER*
*(Four Days Later)*

MY ALARM CLOCK SCREAMED WAY TOO EARLY.

It stopped its diabolical racket when it hit the floor.

It was another Monday morning, and I dragged myself out of bed. I'd stayed up late last night to make another after-hours trip to the file rooms at work. It hadn't taken long to locate the file folder for Hydra. I still had to drop it off, but that could wait.

This file had contained a thumb drive in addition to papers. I'd made a copy of its contents to peruse later. The memos inside didn't look like anything important, but I wasn't privy to Hydra's full plan.

The hot water of the shower slowly cleared the cobwebs from my brain.

Things with Dennis had been completely businesslike in the days since that kiss. He'd taken to calling me Jenn on occasion instead of Jennifer, and I suppose that was something, but he hadn't used the Angel moniker again. In fact, he hadn't alluded to it in any way, as if it hadn't happened.

I hadn't been thinking of it as a kiss, but *The Kiss*. Maybe it hadn't been as spectacular for him as it was for me. But he'd grabbed my ass and cradled my breast with a passion that had surprised me.

Maybe I was supposed to reciprocate and squeeze his butt, or rub him through his pants. Guys liked that, didn't they? But we'd been standing in his office, for God's sake—with an audience for at least part of our performance.

By the time I finished with the conditioner, I'd replayed the scene a dozen times, and I had to turn the water temperature down to keep from overheating.

Had I misread him? Had it only been a good acting job to piss off his ex?

I could have sworn it was real.

Getting out of the shower, I banished thoughts of Dennis and busied myself with my morning routine. I hurried and decided on a stop at Starbucks for a breakfast sandwich, instead of cereal here.

The M&M girls were at our usual table.

Martha saw me first and waved as I ordered.

As I approached with my sandwich and mocha, Mona pulled out a chair for me. "We haven't seen you for a while. Welcome back."

I told them the truth. "Work's been pretty hectic on the days I don't have to take Billy to school."

Martha twisted her cup. "Did you get a good raise?"

I nodded. "Sure did."

Martha smirked. "And did you hold out for more?"

"Yes, and it worked."

Martha nudged Mona. "I told you he was a good man."

Mona protested, "I never said he wasn't."

Martha lifted her cup. "Did my prediction come true yet?"

A blush rose in my face. I wasn't about to tell them everything. "Actually, yes. We did have lunch together, if Saint Helena's counts."

Mona cocked her head. "Mr. Moneybags couldn't splurge and buy you a meal himself?"

I smiled as I recalled my surprise as well. "That's not it. He was serving. Well, that and he supplied the chickens. I helped." I took a bite of my breakfast sandwich.

Martha looked back to me. "That's a good start. What's next? Dinner?"

I should have been prepared for the twenty questions. I hadn't seen them since the kiss. "He's taking me to a museum fundraiser." I followed it up with another bite.

Martha smiled.

Mona's mouth dropped open "That's pretty highbrow, like going to the MET in New York. What have you picked to wear?"

I was still chewing. Like an idiot, I hadn't considered the question until she asked it. "I dunno," I mumbled.

Martha added to the bad news. "That's a do-your-hair, mani-pedi kind of event, not something you just dash some lipstick on for."

I was way behind the power curve in getting ready for this. But I wouldn't give Melissa the pleasure of seeing me looking like the poor girl I was, as if I'd just moved out of a double-wide.

"I'll have to work on that."

Martha reached over to touch my arm. "You'll do just fine. Let us know if you need any advice. Mona here used to go to that."

She perked up. "My Harold took me. The highlight of my year."

This was sounding more and more ominous. I took one last bite of my breakfast and stood. "I gotta get to work."

We exchanged goodbyes, and outside, I turned toward work with more questions about this weekend than answers.

Upstairs, I made it to my office and a search of the internet came back with terrifying news: dozens of images of ladies that looked like they were dressed for the red carpet.

I'd thought this would be a simple dinner at a hotel ballroom, eating rubber chicken with men in suits and women in nice dresses, not men in tuxes and ladies in gowns.

Now I was totally screwed. There was no way anything in my wardrobe qualified as nice enough for this event. My best dress looked like it came from Goodwill compared to the pictures here.

I'd have to tell Ramona we were putting off the apartment search for a month or so. Buying something for this would use up the money I'd been saving for our first, last, and security deposit on the new place.

It was either that or tell Dennis I couldn't go, after all.

I'd been a complete idiot to agree to the invitation without thinking through the ramifications. But it had been too tempting to refuse, and now I was trapped. I didn't even know where to shop for something like this.

# CHAPTER 18

*DENNIS*

IT WAS A NEW WEEK, AND I'D FINISHED OFF THE LAST ONE WITHOUT MAKING A FOOL
of myself with Jennifer after the kiss to shut down Melissa.

It had taken all of my self control to not ask her to dinner—a dinner I would
certainly have wanted to take further, with her as the dessert.

Just the thought made my dick swell. But that was dangerous.

We'd had sandwiches brought in for a few lunch meetings with just the two
of us in my office. That had been tempting enough.

It had been impossible to tell how she'd felt about the kiss. She hadn't
brought it up, or even hinted at it since, and I hadn't either.

*Professional* had been the watchword. No hand holding, no touching, and
absolutely no kissing. I'd shortened her name to Jenn, but I hadn't slipped up
and called her Angel again. The name fit her, though. She had been nothing but
good luck since she'd started upstairs.

Cindy appeared at my open door, came in, and closed it behind her.

"You've created a problem," she said.

"What did I do now?"

"You asked Jennifer to go with you this weekend to your father's fundraiser
for the museum."

She'd actually invited herself, but Cindy didn't need to know that. "Yes?"

"She doesn't have anything to wear. She's too proud to mention it, but I don't
think you understand how big a problem it can be for someone in her financial
situation."

This had been the first I'd heard of money problems for Jennifer.

"Thanks for letting me know." I picked up my phone and dialed Jennifer's extension. "Come down here. We have to go out."

"Where? What should I bring?" she asked.

"Nothing. Just make it quick." I hung up before she could ask another question.

Cindy opened the door. "Thank you."

"I'll take care of it. Please ask Karl to bring the car around."

She gave me a thumbs up.

Jennifer arrived a moment later.

~

*JENNIFER*

CINDY WINKED AT ME AS I WALKED UP.

When I got to his office, Dennis was slipping into his jacket.

"I thought we were meeting at three," I said.

"Change of plans. We're going out."

I couldn't keep my mouth shut. "Where?"

He didn't answer, just moved past me toward the elevator.

I hurried behind him.

The man was a perpetual-motion machine, never taking a break. When one task was complete, he immediately moved to the next.

After the elevator door closed, I tried again. "Where to?"

"You'll see."

I gave up trying to crack the shell. I shifted away. In the enclosed space, his scent reminded me of the kiss, the kiss I couldn't forget if I wanted to. I'd decided it had been an act on his part, since he'd not mentioned it and had studiously avoided getting anywhere near my personal space.

Downstairs on the street, he opened the door to a waiting town car.

I stood back. "This is yours?"

"The company's." He was all short answers today. He held the door for me.

I slid in and across to the other side, which I found out was a mistake when he rounded the back of the car and opened the street-side door to let himself in.

I slid back to the right. "Sorry."

He closed the door. "Apologies for the short notice, Karl."

Somehow it didn't strike me as odd that this particular billionaire apologized to his driver.

The driver nodded. "Anytime, sir." He pulled us out into traffic.

I decided against asking a third time about our destination and tried another tack. "Who are we meeting with?"

Dennis smiled. "Some very nice people. I think you'll like them."

He was enjoying this little game.

If he was going to be mum, I could be too.

We didn't speak for the rest of the trip.

Karl navigated to Santa Monica Boulevard, and I watched the buildings go by for a few minutes. I settled back in the seat, closed my eyes, and enjoyed the new-car scent of fine leather.

Karl finally pulled to the curb on a side street.

Dennis opened his door, and I followed his lead by opening mine. "Don't you move." He rushed around and held the door for me. "A gentleman holds the door for a lady."

I couldn't tell what had gotten into him, but it was cute. "I'm not always a lady." I accepted his hand climbing out, and instantly regretted it. That same electricity flowed between us that had scrambled my brain before.

He poked his head in the door. "Karl, I'll buzz you when we're done."

*Done with what?* I didn't bother to ask. Instead I looked around to get my bearings. The storefront said Bulgari, and the street sign on the pole read fucking *Rodeo Drive*. My mouth dropped. I hadn't recognized it because everybody knew you had to have a dozen zeros on your bank account to shop here, so I'd never even driven by.

I jumped at Dennis's touch. He had put a brain-fog-inducing hand to the small of my back.

"Let's start across the street."

Thankfully he removed his hand as I started to walk.

We crossed the street, and he guided me into the Vera Wang store on the other side.

I thought it was time to ask again. "What are we doing here?"

"I want you to look gorgeous when you walk into the gala."

I stopped.

"That came out wrong," he corrected himself. "You're gorgeous, and I want you to be wearing a dress worthy of you."

I wasn't comfortable with this. "I'm not your prize pony, you know." The objection escaped before I had a chance to play it in my head and hear how bitchy it sounded.

He locked eyes with me. "The party is my treat, and that includes the dress."

Some little birdie had been singing.

I'd confided in Cindy that the dress was going to be a problem. I hadn't meant it to pressure him. "You don't have to do that."

A saleslady started toward us.

He shrugged. "But I want to. You'll be representing the company, and we need to make the best impression possible."

That was almost a rational reason.

I only had a second to object before the saleslady glommed on to us. "But—"

He raised a finger to silence me the way he sometimes did. "Please, this is important to me."

The perceptive saleslady backed away to give us privacy.

I blew out a breath. "Okay. Because you asked nicely."

This was surreal. I was arguing with a guy who wanted to shower me with gifts. Why? Anybody else and I would have been falling all over myself to agree. But I'd trained myself that whatever Dennis wanted, I wanted the opposite.

"And shoes?" I asked.

"Shoes, handbag, the whole enchilada."

I was such an idiot. This was every girl's dream come true. A fully paid shopping trip to Rodeo Drive, and here I was arguing because it was him, and everything he wanted I seemed to end up resisting on principle. I should've been happy spending his money, the more the better.

The saleslady judged that it was finally safe to approach. "And what can I help you find today?"

Dennis took charge. "The lady is going to the museum gala this weekend, and we'd like to find a nice dress for the occasion."

Her smile moved up a few notches as she turned to me. "The gala. How nice. I'm sure we can find something you'll like." She motioned toward the rear of the store. "Let's see what we can find for you. My name's Kayla, by the way." She started off.

I followed her. "Jennifer."

"Lovely. Now, are we thinking a special color? I think a black would be particularly striking on you, and very appropriate for a function like that."

I looked back. "I wouldn't know. I've never been."

Dennis had taken a seat.

She walked on. "Neither have I, but we can always hope."

Kayla showed me several things, and one by one I tried them on.

A few didn't work well enough for me in the mirror, but two did, and I walked out to show Dennis.

It was my own little fashion show, walking and turning, but neither of them earned the glint in his eye I was looking for.

If I had volunteered for this as a way to make his life miserable by pissing off Melissa, I was going to do it right. The dress was going to be mouth-wateringly sexy. If it got Dennis's eyes to pop out, it would elicit the reaction I was aiming for from his ex: full-on, red-faced, homicidal anger.

I'd seen it in her eyes at the office. She'd stared daggers of jealousy at me. Turning my back on the crazy lady at the party would be dangerous.

Kayla wasn't happy when we decided to go a few doors down to the next store, but I wasn't settling for anything less than Dennis's eyes bulging when I came out of the dressing room.

He was patient, but his smile wavered when we walked out of a third store without a dress.

I'd had several more brain-fog incidents where he put a hand to my back to guide me into a store or down the street. Each time he touched me, the sensation was like the first time—an electric jolt that shook me to my core, a jolt I didn't want to admit meant something. My subconscious, my irrational animal brain, didn't understand the kind of man he was.

I'd avoided jumping, but only barely. One of these times, I was going to yelp like a little girl and embarrass us both. Twice I'd been about to object, but my animal brain had shut down my vocal cords.

I discarded the thought that he was being anything more than gentlemanly—that had to explain it. He couldn't help himself. Insisting on opening doors for me, always walking on the street side, he was just following the gentleman's code he'd been taught.

His words pulled me back to the present. "Should we try in here?"

"Sure."

On cue, he held the door open for me.

We were quickly met by Veronica, and he again explained my quest for a dress to wear this weekend.

I followed Veronica back to the racks while Dennis waited up front.

She pulled out several selections that were lukewarm at best. "These would be fitting for the museum event."

I looked them over briefly. "Not quite right."

She tilted her head in Dennis's direction. "You don't think he'd like these?"

*Like* wasn't the word I was going for. "He might, but I don't want him to *like* it, I want him to love it, or better yet, be shocked by it."

She moved down a rack. "Then this might be what you're looking for." She pulled out a bright red number.

I emerged from the dressing room. "How do I keep this from falling too open?" The neckline plunged almost to my navel.

"We have tape for that. Everybody uses it on the red carpet. I mean, if they didn't, they wouldn't be able to televise it, now would they?"

I turned around for her.

"You'll also need to go down the street to La Perla for something to wear under that." She pointed to where my panties were showing through the more than thigh-high slit. "They can also match this color for you."

I wiggled and pulled my underwear down to step out of them. I didn't want them ruining the effect when I showed this to Dennis.

～

DENNIS

HOW WOMEN COULD SPEND ALL DAY LOOKING FOR A SINGLE DRESS WAS BEYOND ME.

We were at the fourth store, and I'd approved of everything she'd come out modeling. But after each one, she'd said it didn't feel right, whatever that meant.

Each of them had looked beautiful on her, but that was to be expected. Jennifer was a beautiful girl. She could make a T-shirt and jeans look sexy.

She appeared from around the corner. "What do you think of this one?" She twirled in front of me.

My mouth dropped.

She wore a bright red gown with a deep V front showing off her marvelous braless cleavage, and a slit that came almost to her waist, revealing a complete leg with each step, barely hiding what I guessed was her naked pussy. Each time she moved, my eyes darted to her thigh, hoping for a glimpse, but I was denied —just barely.

"Well?" she asked, breaking my stare.

I fumbled for the right word. "Breathtaking."

"You think so?"

"Absolutely. Every man in the room will be wondering..." I stopped myself and rephrased. "...how I got so lucky to have you as my date."

She would cast a spell on every pair of eyes in the room.

"You're going to make me blush."

"It'll just make the dress look better on you."

That extra line did draw a blush out of her, and it was cuter than I'd expected.

This latest saleslady was hovering, waiting on the verdict.

I stood and offered her my credit card. "We'll take it."

We had spent hours and only selected one thing so far.

When Jennifer came back, changed into her work clothes, all I could think of was how magnificently sexy she'd looked in that dress. My eyes drifted to her chest, imagining the luscious cleavage that had been on display, and that slit— my God that slit was like a pulse of aphrodisiac with each step, displaying her leg and all that skin.

I offered to carry the garment bag. "Shoes next?"

She tilted her head. "Among other things." She winked. "Just a few more stops, I promise."

Thankfully she knew where she wanted to go for shoes, and we accomplished that with only a single stop.

Next up was a handbag. The surprise after that was a visit to La Perla for lingerie.

I opened the door for her. "I hope you'll be modeling for me again?"

"Not a chance."

I didn't hide my disappointment well.

"I promise I won't be long." She held out her hand. "Card?"

I surrendered my black Amex card one more time and was relegated to wait by the front while she and one of the sales staff wandered off.

As additional female customers entered the store, I garnered a sideways glance from each that seemed to wonder if I was a pervert or just a guy too stupid to know this was a designated testosterone-free zone—no Y chromosomes allowed.

Jennifer reappeared with her purchase concealed in a bag.

"What'd you get?"

"I'm not telling." The vixen had me at her mercy.

# CHAPTER 19

*JENNIFER*

SATURDAY EVENING HAD FINALLY ARRIVED: THE BIG NIGHT.

The doorbell rang.

I glanced at the clock.

He was a half hour early.

Ramona closed the fridge. "Want me to get it?"

"Thanks. I'm almost ready." I closed the bathroom door to finish my eyes.

I could hear them in the other room.

"They're beautiful," Ramona said.

She introduced herself and offered him coffee while I touched up my eyeshadow.

The rest of the conversation was too muted for me to make out.

Moments later, there was a knock at the bathroom door. "Your boss man is here," Billy yelled.

"I know. I'll be right out."

When I opened the door, there Dennis was. I knew the man could wear the hell out of a suit, but the tuxedo took it to the next level. He looked like he'd walked straight off the set of a Bond movie.

He held out a bouquet to me.

I took the gorgeous red roses. "They're beautiful." I held them strategically to hide my cleavage. Now that I was wearing the dress for real, the neckline seemed even more daring than it had in the store. I'd expected it to make me feel empowered, but *vulnerable* better described my current state of mind. What the neckline didn't show was pretty evident behind the thin material. My nipples were hard and pokey.

"Not half as beautiful as you."

I contained my laugh at the corny comment. I was going as his arm candy, in an effort to unnerve his ex, nothing more.

"Stop that. There's no audience here." The words sounded harsher than I'd meant them.

His smile turned to a scowl, telling me I'd once again been too sassy—that was becoming a constant problem for me.

His mouth opened, then closed, as he apparently decided to keep his thoughts to himself.

Ramona came from around the counter. "Let me put those in some water for you." Ever the peacekeeper, she defused the argument.

I relinquished the bouquet, and his eyes went to my plunging neckline and back to my face with an approving smile. "You *do* look gorgeous this evening." His tone conveyed the don't-contradict-me message even louder than the words.

I tried not to squirm under his stare. "Should we get going?"

He swung his arm toward the door. "The lady's carriage awaits."

Billy scurried to open the door.

Dennis followed. "Thank you, Billy."

Ramona grabbed my arm. "Should I wait up?" she whispered.

I silently shook my head. I had no idea how late this would go.

Downstairs, Dennis held the door open for me as I exited the building.

At the curb, his driver, Karl, waited by the town car.

My neighbor, Mrs. Butterfield, stopped short and stared as I gathered up the long dress and slid into the car. Her glare made it obvious what she thought of my attire, and it wasn't complimentary.

Dennis climbed in the other side and closed the door. "Don't you dare do that again."

I jerked back. "What?"

"Refuse an honest compliment."

The man was impossible. "I didn't mean—"

"Yes, you did," he said, cutting me off. "A lady graciously accepts a compliment."

"I already told you I'm not a lady."

He pointed a finger. "That won't work with me. I won't tolerate anyone denigrating you. Not even you. Now, let's try this again. Angel, you look gorgeous this evening."

*Angel* disarmed me. "Thank you."

He fished into a bag on the floor and produced a small box. "These are for you."

I froze in place. It wasn't just any box. It was a small blue box with the initials HW on it. It was a fucking Harry Winston jewelry box.

"Go ahead, open it."

I took the box and after another nod from him, I opened it. Earrings with brilliant green emeralds and a pendant with a matching stone on a simple, white-gold chain sparkled in the late-day sunlight.

This was too much. "But I can't."

"What did I just finish telling you about arguments? These match your eyes perfectly."

This was completely over the top. Naturally the man shopped at the same place as the Prince of Wales and Hollywood elites.

I looked at him again. "Are you sure?"

"Have you ever known me to say something I didn't mean?"

I didn't answer, but started to remove the simple gold dangles I'd chosen for tonight. I swapped them out for the gemstone earrings.

He helped me with the necklace clasp, and then gave an approving smile. "They look good on you."

Paying attention to my training, I replied simply. "Thank you."

Dennis explained what to expect at this party. It sounded boring—a silent auction, dinner, and a bunch of old stiffs gaining social credibility by donating to a worthy local institution.

I took a guess. "And how many of these people are trying to curry favor with your father?"

Dennis took in a breath. "That's a crass way of putting it. But it's the way things work. Between Dad, Bill Covington, and the other board members, the attendees have a lot of interrelated interests."

I understood. "This is a rich people's mutual-admiration-society meeting—normal people need not apply."

His glare was cold. "It's not like that. Do you think the city is better off with or without a fine art museum?"

I hadn't meant to get into an argument, so I kept my mouth shut for a change.

"It's a simple question."

Art wasn't my thing, but I'd been to the museum once on a school field trip, and I had enjoyed it.

"With a museum, of course," I said.

"Dad insists on not charging admission, so he holds events like this to raise the money to keep it running. Normal people, as you call them, don't have money to spare for a cause like this. The people he invites do. At the end of the night, they feel better after having donated to the museum and getting the side benefit of rubbing shoulders with the other guests. In exchange, the city gets to keep its museum. Everybody wins."

Once again my smart mouth had gotten me into trouble. "I'm sorry. I didn't mean it was a bad thing."

"Sure you did. You let your prejudice show through. You think rich people should be punished for having money."

"No, I don't. I just…" I didn't know how to finish the sentence without getting deeper into trouble. I couldn't very well explain that I thought being rich let him get away with things normal people would go to jail for.

He reached over to take my hand. "Sorry for going off on you like that, Angel. I guess I'm a little sensitive."

∼

WHEN WE ARRIVED, KARL STOPPED OUTSIDE THE MUSEUM ENTRANCE TO LET US OUT.

Once inside, I found Dennis's description hadn't prepared me for what awaited us. Walking through the museum's doors was like stepping onto a Disney fairytale set. *Wow* was the only description that came to mind.

I walked alongside Dennis past multiple ice sculptures, colorful bunting, and tall floral arrangements lining the entrance hall—an explosion of opulence in complete contrast to the drab exterior of the building.

Past that, waiters in white waistcoats weaved through the crowd, carrying silver platters of bubbly and hors d'oeuvres. We passed a fountain of liquid chocolate. Avoiding a stop to taste it was a supreme effort in self-control.

Dennis snatched two glasses of champagne for us as I followed him to the easels displaying the seating charts.

So far I hadn't seen any sign of Her Craziness, Melissa.

Dennis motioned toward a doorway to the side. "Let's check out the silent auction."

I nodded. "Sure."

On the way, he introduced me to his younger brother Josh and his sister Serena. In both cases he introduced me as his date.

I wanted to explain that we worked together, but thought better of it. After a quick, amiable chat, he dragged me into the other room with the auction items.

Tables stretched the length of the space, covered with expensive items for people to bid on, with proceeds going to the museum. Dennis put his name down on a week for two in Hawaii with a ridiculously high bid.

"Cindy said you don't take vacations."

He shrugged. "I don't."

I'd scoped out Hawaiian vacations—not that I could afford one, but internet browsing was free. "You know it doesn't cost that much, don't you?"

"It's for a good cause."

He intended to win this one. Apparently rich guys like him didn't mess around when they wanted something. I couldn't have afforded to bid on anything we had seen yet except an ugly chess set that hadn't gotten any bids.

"Why bid on something you're not going to use?"

"Hey, what's with the twenty questions?"

Appropriately chastised, I kept quiet as I followed him on a complete circuit of the tables.

In the end, he only bid on the Hawaii trip.

When dinner was called, we sat at a table with his sister and some others from work. Cindy was here with her husband, a nice guy who worked as a mechanic at the local Toyota dealership, as well as my old boss, Mr. Fisher, and his wife.

Just as I took my seat, I caught a glimpse of Melissa at a table on the far side of the room. She was looking the other way.

Larry, the marketing guy with the loud mouth, hadn't brought a date and took the seat on the other side of me before I could get Serena's attention to sit there.

She took the chair on the other side of Larry.

I expected Larry to chat me up, and he didn't disappoint.

"I'm glad you came," he said. "We haven't had much of a chance to talk."

I'd gathered from the other girls at lunch that Larry was a player and readied myself for the come-on lines.

"Dennis has kept me pretty busy," I said.

"Do you like dogs?"

I'd anticipated a more direct come-on. "Sure, who doesn't? But I can't have one in my apartment." I caught his quick look down my dress and was thankful the tape was holding. The unease of feeling naked caused a momentary shiver.

The dog question turned out to be just a delay. "How about lunch next week? I know a killer Thai place down the street." He shifted his chair an inch closer.

I sucked in a breath. "Thanks, but I generally like to eat in."

"My treat. I'd like to hear how you got old man Talbot to drop his drawers so quickly the other week. I'd been telling Dennis he was soft on the price, but he didn't listen."

"I really didn't do much."

He leaned even closer. "Still, I think you did great for being so new at this. Maybe we could spend a little time, and I could give you a few pointers. You could give me some dog advice."

I knew his kind, and there was only one pointy thing he wanted to give me. I nodded wordlessly as I sipped my water as noncommittally as possible.

"I see you didn't come with a date either."

His comments were becoming more obvious.

Dennis leaned forward before I could say anything. "She's *my* date."

The alpha lion had spoken.

His words shut Larry down like a blast of cold water from a fire hose. "I was just telling Jennifer how good a job she did with Talbot."

Dennis ignored him and went back to talking with Jay Fisher on the other side.

I listened to their conversation for a moment, and when I looked back, Serena was asking Larry to switch places with her so we could talk.

I didn't know if she was rescuing me from Larry, or wanting to size up Dennis's date, but in the end, I didn't care.

When dinner arrived, the choices were chicken or salmon.

Mrs. Fisher had received a plate of chicken and was having trouble cutting it. When the waiter got to me, I settled on salmon.

The conversations slowed a little as we ate, and Cindy, Serena, and I found common ground discussing Serena's passion for her vegetable garden.

She forked a tomato from the salad. "These are like cardboard compared to what comes out of my garden. Why can't they give us ones with some taste?"

I didn't have an answer for that, and we turned to the subject of rose pruning.

Serena struck me as very grounded for a rich girl, but then I remembered Dennis's comment about my rich-people prejudice. Maybe he had a point.

Larry seemed more likable after he mentioned his difficulty house training the puppy he'd recently gotten. "Binky just doesn't get it. I've followed what the book says, but it's not working."

I felt sorry for the poor mutt already. Not even a dog deserved a name like that. Asking how he chose that name got me a grumbled answer having something to do with Tina, who had left the critter with him two weeks ago and hadn't returned.

After hearing that, I felt sorry for Larry. But not sorry enough to have lunch with him.

"Try the training pads," I suggested.

"I've tried those, but he sleeps on them and pees on the carpet."

That garnered a muffled laugh from Cindy.

"The scent may not be right for him," I offered. "Wipe some of his piddle on the pad, so he thinks he's gone there before. That should work."

Larry shook his head. "The package says they're already scented like that."

Dennis got in on the action. "You should know better than to believe all the marketing bullshit on a package."

Larry looked crestfallen.

"What kind of dog is he?" Serena asked.

He lowered his voice. "Chinese crested."

I stifled a laugh. "Not your choice, I'm guessing." I'd seen pictures of the breed. They were hairless except around the head—definitely not a man's dog.

He shook his head and mumbled something less than complimentary about Tina.

Serena and I commiserated with him. Even Larry didn't deserve the likes of Tina.

An older man had been stopping at the tables to our left, seeming to be making the rounds. He resembled Colonel Sanders with his white hair, goatee, and cane.

"How are we doing at this table?" he asked as he arrived at our table. His tone was jovial.

Dennis spoke up first. "Great, Dad."

So this was the patriarch of the Benson family, Lloyd Benson himself.

He greeted each of the guests around the table by name, and then got to me. "You must be the great negotiator Dennis has told me about. Jennifer, isn't it?"

The man was charming and obviously good with names.

"I don't know about the great part. Pleasure to meet you, Mr. Benson."

He rounded the table to our side. "I want to shake your hand, young lady. Jimmy has needed to be taken down a few pegs for quite a while now."

Jimmy had to be James Talbot the third.

Lloyd extended his hand and gave mine a firm shake. "Good for you."

I couldn't help but like the friendly old man, even if he was a Benson.

Dennis interjected. "He certainly left with his tail between his legs."

The elder Benson laughed. "I'm sure he'll deny it next time I see him."

Without realizing it, I'd gotten myself in the middle of a pissing contest between two powerful families.

"Well, thank you all for coming and supporting our museum," Lloyd said. "Have a wonderful evening." With that he was off to the next table, once again greeting most of the guests there by name.

The waiters soon cleared our dinners, and the desserts arrived.

Cindy's husband was busy giving Larry housebreaking tips.

"He even peed on the top of my poker table," Larry complained.

That merited a round of laughs from all of us.

"The green felt probably looked like grass to him," Mrs. Fisher offered.

Larry shook his head. "Outside he refuses to go on the grass and pees on the concrete instead."

Dennis had an interesting question. "Where is he now?"

"Since he likes cement so much, he's in the garage till I get back."

The waiters were still clearing our dessert plates when the emcee took the stage. The crowd hushed with his announcement that the silent auction winners were about to be revealed.

Larry won a case of nice wine and jogged up to get his prize slip to a round of applause.

Fisher and his wife won a weekend trip to Las Vegas, which surprised me. Financial types were not usually gamblers, but maybe they were going for the shows.

And Dennis won the Hawaii trip he'd bid an outrageous sum for.

They reached the end of the auction, and music began playing through the loud speakers.

Dennis stood and held a hand out to me. "Dance?"

The question took me by surprise. I'd figured this was a dinner and boring conversation function, maybe with some awards or something.

He cocked his head. "Well?"

"Go ahead," Cindy urged.

I put my napkin on the table and stood to accept his hand, which quickly moved to my back to guide me to the open area rapidly filling with couples dancing—slow, intimate dancing. The heat of his touch was doing its brain-fog thing again.

I put my hands on his shoulders as we started to sway to the music.

He pulled me in. First our thighs touched, and then my chest met his.

I didn't push away.

The heat was unmistakable, a dangerous heat that threatened to weld me to him.

His mouth brushed by my ear. "Thank you for coming."

I looked up into his eyes. "Thank you for asking me."

How a week had changed everything. When I'd blurted out that I was his date, I'd meant to antagonize his ex-wife and cause him trouble. Tonight though, it didn't matter if I was using him, or he was using me. It felt good to be in his arms, and I was going to enjoy it.

His hand slipped lower on my back and pulled me tighter against him. The warmth of his chest against mine, the heat of his breath against my ear made my cares drift away.

Right now I wanted this, and I definitely deserved it. Thinking could wait until tomorrow. The how and the why weren't important tonight, just the who and the where.

I closed my eyes. Him, me, the music and the motion on this dance floor. Nothing else mattered.

# CHAPTER 20

*DENNIS*

HER WARMTH AGAINST ME AS WE SLOW DANCED WAS AN ELIXIR I NEEDED MORE OF. The scent of peaches in her hair reminded me of the whiff I'd gotten during that kiss in my office, and I smiled to myself as I played the memory over again.

Having noticed her at Starbucks, I'd wondered what she might feel like in my arms, but I'd never imagined it could be as intoxicating as this.

After the thrashing from the latest article by Sigurd and the harried spin-off workaround, a night like tonight was a welcome break. Family, friends, music, and a warm woman in my arms brought back to me what I had been denying myself for too long.

She looked up at me with soft eyes. "What are you thinking about?"

The question caught me off guard. "Nothing in particular."

"You're not a good liar, Denny." It was the first time she'd used that nickname since the day of our kiss.

I went with at least a partial truth. "Nothing, really. I was noticing the peach fragrance in your hair."

"You're deflecting. I can hear the gears turning."

I gave in. "I was thinking how nice it is to be here with you." Saying the words to her didn't feel as awkward as I'd expected, even though it was our first date.

*Our first date.* The words rattled around my head for a second. My subconscious was clearly voting for more time with her.

She stretched up and kissed my neck. "Me too."

I pulled her in tighter for a few steps and took a chance. "We should do this again."

Everything about her intrigued me. It wasn't just her surprising ability at work to see things from a different perspective, but also her simple grace with the people at the table.

She was a complete package of looks, brains, and class, with modesty to match, plus an extra helping of sass.

As we danced, I was certain of one thing. I had my arms around a woman I didn't want to let go of.

The song stopped and another started, and another followed that. Each song was a suitable slow dance for us, or a waltz for the few couples feeling more formal about their dancing.

Dad wasn't a fan of anything that engendered fast dancing at his gala event. He didn't think it was dignified, and tonight, with Jennifer in my arms, I agreed wholeheartedly.

Nothing that put distance between us was getting my vote, especially with the condition in my pants.

As the music went on, she melted more comfortably against me, if that was possible.

She had to notice my stiff cock pressing against her with every step, but she didn't push away, and she didn't show any alarm. If anything, her steps seemed intended to rub against me, or perhaps it was my imagination, or just the height difference.

The latest song ended and she pulled back, nodding toward a door leading to the courtyard. "Want to go cool off for a bit?"

I released her. "Sure." Backing away, I shoved a hand in my pocket to hide the bulge in my pants as I led her toward the courtyard at the center of the building.

It was chilly outside, and she wrapped an arm around me.

I reciprocated and pulled her around the back of the fountain where we would be shielded from those in the room we'd just left. Literal dancing had been fine, but I was done dancing around what was or wasn't between us. Stopping on the far side, I turned her toward me.

She let out the slightest gasp as I took her face in my hands and moved my head to within inches of hers. The light coming up from the water played on her face, a face that held not concern, but a question.

I hoped my question was the same. "Jenn, did I tell you how lovely you look tonight?'

"Four times."

She'd counted.

"I want..." The words halted as I searched for the right ones.

She wrapped a hand behind my neck, lifting up and closing the distance between us. Her lips did the talking as she took mine, and we resumed where we had left off in my office.

Arms intertwined, hands roamed, and the taste and feel of her mouth and tongue against mine was what I'd craved for days. We were on the same wavelength. I wanted her, and she wanted me.

She broke the kiss and put her hand on my chest. "What did you want to ask?" she said breathlessly.

It took me a second to organize my words, lest I tell her straight out I wanted to fuck her senseless tonight. "I want to take you on a date."

She giggled. "I think this qualifies."

"Then another date, just the two of us."

Her smile widened, transmitting her answer. "I'd like that." She lifted up to meet my lips again.

As we re-engaged our lip lock, her hand squeezed my butt, sending a clear signal of where this was heading later.

My fingers made their way to the slit in her dress and slid up her thigh, looking for the answer to the question that had haunted me since first seeing this dress. *Was she or wasn't she?*

The loud clack of heels on the cement and the yell came from behind her.

"Get the hell away from him, you slut." It was the unmistakable shriek of an angry Melissa.

Jennifer broke the kiss with alarm.

I guided her behind me, shielding her from the hellion that was my ex-wife on the war path.

Melissa's nonsensical yelling continued as she approached. "He's mine."

"Get a grip. We're divorced," I yelled back, holding Jennifer behind me. "Get the hell out of here before I have you thrown out."

"You wouldn't dare."

I stepped forward with a finger pointed at her. "It would be my pleasure." I pulled out my phone. "Are you going to make me call security?"

She hissed and fumed before backing away. "I'll ruin you both." She spun around and clacked off toward the doorway.

I didn't turn back to Jennifer until the door closed behind Melissa.

My girl was shivering. "She scares me."

The feeling was understandable, this being her first and hopefully last encounter with Melissa's hysterics.

"Don't let her get to you. That's what she wants. We should go inside where it's warmer."

Jennifer shook her head. "Not until we know she's gone. I don't need a repeat with everybody around."

"I'll tell security to not let her back in, and I'll bring more champagne so we can plan that date."

The mention of a date brought back her smile, and I gave her a peck of a kiss before marching inside.

The original three bartenders had dwindled down to one, and there was an uncharacteristic line. Eventually I received two flutes of bubbly and made my way to the front.

It was manned by Gus, one of the museum security guards and an LAPD cop. He looked up as I approached. "You shouldn't have. We can't drink on duty."

"Sorry, Gus, not for you."

The cop controlled his laugh.

I hadn't seen Melissa anywhere inside, or in the hallway leading here. "My ex-wife, Melissa Benson, is not to be readmitted under any circumstances."

Gus cocked a brow. "You got it, Mr. Benson, but I didn't see her leave yet."

*Shit.*

This was my father's party, but I made an executive decision. "Then radio the other guys to look for her and escort her out."

He pulled out his radio as I headed back to the tables.

My jacket was at our table, and I'd bring that out to Jennifer with the bubbly. Gus's guys could deal with Melissa.

∾

*JENNIFER*

I'D MELTED INTO HIS ARMS FROM THE FIRST DANCE. THE SONGS WEREN'T MY FAVORITE, but I had no complaints as he'd held me. I'd molded my body closer to his with each song, feeling the hard strength of his muscles beneath the fabric as he moved.

And that wasn't all that was hard. His reaction to me may have been easier to notice than the liquid heat pooled between my legs, but it was no more real than the arousal I felt enveloped in his arms.

Every shift of his weight brought me closer to demanding he take me someplace private. His suggestion of another date had my mind going to all kinds of naughty places.

All of that had made me forget the original plan for tonight—until his ex appeared, with all her full-throated anger.

Mission accomplished on that front, but oddly, it didn't give me the satisfaction I'd anticipated.

I held my arms tight around me to stay warm while I waited.

The man had thoroughly messed with my brain. I was having trouble meshing my previous view of him as the devil in a suit with the man who'd danced tenderly with me. My cavewoman brain wanted to be naked with him as clearly as he wanted me. The dress was meant to have that effect, and now that it had—and the ex had gotten angry—I could call off the charade and go back to hating him.

But it wasn't a charade, was it? Not once in the days I'd worked with him had

I seen even an inkling of the deviousness, the cruelty, the inhumanity I knew he'd been responsible for. What did that mean? Why was he so different? Had he changed? Or had he been something other than I believed all along?

The push came from nowhere.

With a splash, I tumbled over the edge and into the frigid water of the fountain.

The shock of the cold stunned me. I pushed up from the rough bottom and swept the hair out of my eyes. "What the fuck?"

The angry, red face of Melissa Benson screamed at me. "I'll ruin you both. I promise."

# CHAPTER 21

*DENNIS*

I WALKED BEHIND ONE OF THE GUARDS WITH THE CHAMPAGNE FLUTES. HE OPENED THE door for me just as I heard Melissa scream again.

"I'll ruin you both. I promise."

She saw us and ran the other way.

"Stop," the guard yelled as he gave chase.

I couldn't see Jennifer anywhere, but splashing in the water got my attention. It was her.

"My God, what happened?"

"Your psycho ex happened, that's what."

I put the glasses down and slid over the edge, finding my footing in the cold water and splashing my way to my girl.

"Here." I helped her up, and she hobbled with me to the edge.

I heard her dress rip as she struggled to get her leg over the edge.

"Fuck." She held on to me and luckily didn't fall again.

I followed her out and wrapped my coat around her. Pulling out my phone, I told Karl to meet us out front right away.

"Come with me," I urged.

She shivered, and her teeth were starting to chatter.

As we approached the door she asked, "Is there another way?"

"No. This is the only way."

She was clearly embarrassed to walk through the crowd like this, but it couldn't be helped, and she needed to get warm.

I hurried her through as quickly as I could, grabbing her clutch as I passed the table. She'd lost a shoe in the water and was hobbling on one heel.

Karl was out front, and I got her into the backseat.

"Home. Quickly," I told him.

"Yes, sir." He gunned the engine and we sped off.

The water had chilled my lower legs to the bone, and it had been much worse for Jennifer.

I held her tight and rubbed. "We'll get you warmed up in no time, Angel."

She was quiet, save the shivering sounds she made.

Karl had cranked up the heat, but it wasn't enough to thaw either of us.

We arrived at my house in short order, and Karl sprinted to the door. He had a key for when he had to get things for me, and he'd unlocked the door by the time I got there carrying my frozen girl.

"Thanks, Karl. You can lock up and call it a night."

"You sure?"

I nodded. "I got it from here." If I was going to do anything, it was take care of Jennifer.

I heard the deadbolt click behind us as I carried her to the master, dripping all the way.

She still hadn't said anything beyond mumbling a few times that she was cold.

I set the shower to lukewarm, carried her in, and set her on her feet.

We were both in the spray, still clothed with water running off us.

I pulled one of her hands to the wall to brace her. "Can you stand?"

Her dress hung open, revealing her tits. She nodded.

I knelt to pull off her remaining high heel.

Once it was off, she was more stable.

I raised the temperature and turned her slowly in the spray.

The water running off of her began to warm as she thawed.

~

*JENNIFER*

I KEPT MY EYES CLOSED AND MY ARMS WRAPPED TIGHTLY AROUND ME, LETTING THE water run over my body. The shivers slowed. I knew the water was only warm, but at first it had felt scalding hot against my cold skin and was only now bearable.

Dennis kept me rotating in the spray, and the water running down to my feet was no longer icy cold. He adjusted the temperature up again.

I opened my eyes to the marble wall of the shower and turned to face him. The water had made the white shirt of his tux sheer and plastered it to his chest.

The chiseled physique hidden behind his daily suit was finally on display. The ridges and valleys of his muscled form warmed me as much as the water. I glanced up to see the smile he wore, having caught me checking him out.

"You're ruining your tux," I said.

Without a doubt the expensively tailored tux he'd worn tonight was dry clean only.

He laughed. "It'll match your dress."

I looked down. The dress was ruined all right, and my boob was hanging out. The tape was no match for the water.

I covered up and wrapped my arms around him. "Why did she do that?"

He turned us so the water ran down my back. "There's no accounting for crazy."

"What did she mean, she'll ruin you?"

"She said *us*."

I waited for an answer.

"I don't care. She's not worth the effort of thinking about. Getting caught up in her mind game is a losing proposition."

Having experienced her rage up close, I wasn't so sure ignoring her was a wise idea.

I'd accomplished my original goal of getting her mad at him, but I hadn't anticipated that her anger would be directed so squarely at *me*. A scowl, a mean comment or two I had been prepared for, but not being attacked like this. She was crazy in a dangerous, unpredictable way.

He rubbed my back, and the brain fog started up again.

"Thawing out?" he asked.

I nodded against his chest—his rock-hard, muscled-like-Apollo chest. "Uh-huh, thank you." It was the most intelligible thing I could manage as I hugged him. I looked up. "We didn't get our last dance."

He started to sway me side to side, without turning as we would have on the dance floor. "This will have to do."

The muffled sound of a phone ringing began. It was coming from his pants pocket. Apparently, he could afford a waterproof phone—mine would have been history in this shower.

One arm let me go as he fished for it.

I didn't want the moment to end. "Let it go," I urged him.

He brought the phone up to eye level. "I can't. It's family." He answered the call. "What?... Slow down. I can't understand a thing you're saying. He turned and opened the door to the shower, leaving me alone under the warm water.

I adjusted the temperature up a bit more.

His voice was agitated. "Where again?... I'm on my way." He put the phone on the counter and rejoined me, lifting my head with a hand to my chin. "I have to go. There's been an accident."

The words chilled me, as if the water had turned cold once more. "Who?"

"My brother. Now listen. You stay here. You can sleep in the room across the hall. Don't you dare leave. I'll talk to you in the morning."

"I can come with you." I knew it was a stupid suggestion as soon as I said it, but I didn't want to be alone.

"No way," he growled. "You're safe here. Don't you dare leave, Angel. Now promise me you'll stay."

I nodded. His calling me *Angel* sealed it.

The next minute he was gone, and I was alone. Ending the evening at his place wasn't supposed to be like this.

Eventually I got out, dried off, and located clothes in the room across the hall —women's clothes. When I found my clutch and phone, I sent a text to Ramona.

ME: Staying out will call tomorrow

It only took her a minute to respond.

RAMONA: Good for you I'm envious

Wait until I told her how tonight had gone.

∼

*Dennis*

I PULLED ON DRY CLOTHES AND SHOES AND WAS OUT THE DOOR AND IN MY JAGUAR IN record time. The cat's engine growled as I sped down the street and almost didn't make the turn at the end. I chastised myself out loud in the empty car.

"Slow the fuck down. One accident tonight is more than enough."

Serena had called, and all I could understand between her sobs was that Josh had gotten into an accident and had been taken to UCLA Medical Center.

The decision to tell Jennifer to stay had been an easy one. After Melissa's meltdown, I wasn't taking any chances. Jennifer would stay under my protection until I understood why my ex had become so unhinged and literally dangerous. It also could have been an act, a small part in some elaborate play of hers that was beyond me to understand. With Melissa, there was no telling. Logic was not her strong suit.

I slowed for the red light, and gunned the car through the intersection when I didn't see any cross traffic. In daytime traffic, it would have taken at least a half hour, but this time of night it would be quicker. The next red light was not so forgiving, with steady traffic from the right.

Following the signs to the hospital's emergency entrance, I parked, grabbed my phone, and ran for the door.

"Where are you?" I asked when my sister picked up.

"Fourth floor ICU, four-four-three-one."

"I'll be up in a sec."

At the elevator bank, it took forever for a car to arrive. But it did, and the door finally opened on the fourth floor. I only got held up at the nurses' station for a minute, pulling my license out of my soaked wallet.

When I found the room, I stopped.

"What happened?" I asked as I entered.

Josh was in the bed with a bandage on his head, attached to IVs and wires galore.

Serena and a nurse were on one side, with Dad and Bill Covington closest to me on the other.

My father urged me into the hallway and away from the door before speaking. "He got pretty banged up in the roll-over. The doctors are reviewing the MRI now and deciding if he'll need surgery."

The word *surgery* when we were talking about a head wound was alarming. "What happened? I told him he shouldn't be driving that pickup of his."

Pickups, especially raised 4X4s like his, were notoriously easy to roll.

Dad shook his head. "He was driving the Jaguar."

"The Jag? That doesn't make sense." Josh's Jaguar was an F-type, same as mine, even the same year. The car had a seriously low center of gravity and was nearly impossible to roll.

"Nevertheless, that's the information we have now. I called young William in to get a little leverage with the hospital."

With three buildings on campus named after Bill's grandfather, the Covingtons had more pull here than the governor.

"He has their neurosurgeon on the way in now, just in case," my father added.

"When can we talk to him?"

"That's for the doctors to decide. He's sedated right now."

I still wanted something to do. "So what's the plan?"

"Nothing much for us to do but wait."

Dad went back into the room, and Serena came out, with a question on her lips.

"That was quite the spectacle Melissa put on."

"No shit. I don't know what got into her."

"Of course you do."

"Do not."

"Do too." She argued as if we were still little kids.

"Then tell me."

"She saw the same thing the rest of us did. I could see it in your eyes. You never once looked at Melissa with the eyes you have for Jennifer."

I couldn't believe I was hearing this. "Huh?"

"Don't *huh* me. I saw you two dancing. It was pretty erotic for two people with their clothes still on."

Dancing with Jennifer had been hot as hell, but I wasn't admitting that to my sister. "She's a good dancer."

"Where is she, by the way?"

I hadn't expected that question. "Back at my place."

"See?"

"It was closer than her apartment, and I needed to get her warmed up before she froze to death. And then you called."

"Uh-huh." She poked a finger in my chest. "I like her, so go slow and don't screw this up is all I have to say."

That was a lie. There was no way she wouldn't bring this up again.

"I like her too."

"Duh." She turned and reopened the door to Josh's room.

I followed her inside. I hated waiting, but there was nothing else to do at this point.

*How the hell did he roll the Jag?*

# CHAPTER 22

*JENNIFER*

I PRIED MY EYES OPEN ON SUNDAY MORNING, AND THE FIRST THING I COULD MAKE out was the empty wine glass on the nightstand. It brought last night back to me.

The room Dennis had pointed me to across the hall from his was a second master with its own huge bathroom. I'd located a T-shirt and sweats in the dresser and, with a towel wrapped around my wet hair, quickly toured a few of the rooms in the house. I'd steered clear of his bedroom after leaving the shower he'd thawed me in.

Everything about this house was on a scale I'd only seen in pictures, and the kitchen was immense. I had a thing for checking out kitchens in the magazines, wondering what it would be like to have one as nice. His had many of those beat.

I'd waited up for Dennis and located a bottle of wine in the fridge. It had become my companion for the evening when he didn't return. I'd tried to wash away the memory of the evening's shitty conclusion with at least a glass or two too many.

Eventually, the soft bed had beckoned, and I gave up the vigil, hoping his brother was all right, but knowing in my bones that Dennis's absence meant things were the opposite of good. The wine and soft, million-thread-count sheets had brought slumber quickly.

Padding to the bathroom, my tongue now felt fur-coated from the wine. Dennis had a nice setup for guests here, including a fresh, plastic-wrapped tooth-brush, toothpaste, and mouthwash.

Wearing the Dodgers T-shirt I'd slept in, I looked like death warmed over in the mirror. Sleeping on slightly damp hair would do that.

A metallic clank sounded down the hall, and I stilled myself to listen. Nothing.

I ventured to the door, and when I cracked it open, the faint aroma of coffee tickled my nostrils.

Somebody was here.

Quickly, I retrieved the fluffy bathrobe from the bathroom before venturing out. He'd probably hired a cook to make him breakfast, and the poor lady didn't know he wasn't here.

When I rounded the corner to the kitchen, I found him with his back to me, working at the stove.

Dennis turned. "Sleep okay?" He didn't have a cook after all.

I nodded and walked his way. "Uh-huh. How's your brother?"

He pointed to the breakfast bar attached to the island. "Coffee's on the counter. Cocoa powder is on the end, if you want."

I wrapped my fingers around the hot cup of java. "Thank you. How's your brother?"

"Josh gave us quite a scare last night, but according to the experts, he'll be okay in the long run. He has a tube in his skull to monitor the inter-cranial pressure."

I shivered at his description. It sounded pretty damned serious to me. "But he'll be okay?"

"Nothing broken. A nasty bump to the head, but he's already driving the nurses crazy. Good thing he has the thick Benson skull."

I spooned some of the cocoa he offered into my coffee and stirred. "What happened?"

He turned off the stove and brought the two frypans over to the counter. "He was driving home and had an accident is all we know. I'll find out more later."

"That smells wonderful." It looked it as well.

"Omelets." He slid them one at a time onto plates.

"When did you get back?"

"About four."

"You should have woken me."

"After last night, you deserved the rest." He lifted the empty wine bottle I'd left on the counter. "And after emptying this, I probably couldn't have woken you if I'd tried."

I broke eye contact. "I didn't drink the whole thing."

"Did you pour the rest down the sink?"

I shrugged, unwilling to lie.

He picked up the plates and walked toward the table in the nook.

I followed with my coffee mug.

The news was playing softly on a TV mounted on the wall.

He set the plates down and held out a chair for me before taking a seat himself. "I want to apologize for the way Melissa acted last night."

"It's not your fault."

"Sure it is. It wouldn't have happened if I hadn't invited you."

"You forget, I sort of invited myself."

"It's still on me."

"I had a wonderful time, up until—"

"The eruption," he offered.

"Yeah. How did you ever..." I stopped before making a complete ass of myself.

He knew exactly where I'd been going. "Marry her?"

I nodded.

"She was an actress before we married, and she was obviously good enough to fool me. It's my fault, really."

"How so?"

"I was in a hurry. Dad was pressuring me, and I gave in."

"That doesn't seem like you."

"I know better now, but at the time, let's just say I wanted to get him off my back. We've patched things up now, but it was what made me leave the family company."

I digested that for a while as we ate. "Did you love her?"

He stared into his coffee cup before answering. "That's a hard one."

"I'm sorry. It's none of my business."

"No." He reached to put his hand over mine. "It's one of the things I like about you. You're frank, and you push me out of my comfort zone."

"I didn't mean to pry." That was the polite thing to say, but I remained curious about how a guy who seemed so level headed and was rich and good looking enough to have his pick of women would end up with such a wicked one.

He pulled his hand back, and I missed the feel of his touch.

"Yes, you did," he said.

The news flashed to the story of the death of Randy Bethman, with a picture of his young wife, Virginia—very young, very pretty Virginia. Black Widow of the Palisades, they'd nicknamed her.

I pointed my fork at the screen. "I hope they fry her ass."

He looked up and followed the commentary for a moment. "Why would you say that?"

"Just look at her. Forty years younger—of course the trophy wife did it."

"You always jump to conclusions like that?"

"It's pretty obvious." The news had published enough details for anybody to see it. "He was poisoned, and she inherits a fortune. She did it for sure. She got tired of waiting for him to croak and hurried things along. I'd bet on it."

"If I ever go to trial, I'd hate to have someone like you on the jury."

"What does that mean?"

"You're ready to convict the woman based on a few things you heard, without having all the facts. You don't know she did it. Neither you nor I can possibly know that."

"You think she didn't?"

"I'm saying jumping to conclusions about someone's character without knowing all the facts is wrong. Why does she deserve less benefit of the doubt than you or me?"

"I..." I was at a loss for what to say after he put it like that.

"Wouldn't you want the benefit of the doubt? I know I sure would."

"I guess you're right." Clearly I wouldn't want to be judged as hastily as I'd judged her.

As I ate the rest of the breakfast Dennis had generously cooked me, I couldn't get past the question he'd just raised without knowing it. *Had I possibly judged him too hastily as well?*

The last memo I'd seen hadn't been conclusive. Instead it had opened another question—one I didn't have the answer to. I definitely didn't have all the facts.

Mom had convinced me years ago that Dennis was responsible, and I'd been working under that assumption ever since, looking for the information that would prove it.

Would I want someone judging me and later only looking for evidence to back up the accusation?

As I looked up from my plate, I realized the man in front of me hadn't exhibited any of the traits I'd suspected him of. The opposite was more true.

Mom had always said he was responsible like it was a fact, but was it? Since I'd started working for Dennis, nothing I'd seen or heard had corroborated what my mother and I had been certain he was guilty of.

He wanted the benefit of the doubt, he said. I'd been denying him that by judging him without compelling evidence—without any evidence, it turns out.

What if I was wrong? The thought chilled me.

I'd passed on information that clearly hurt Dennis, and would continue to. What if he wasn't guilty of killing my stepfather after all?

What kind of person did that make me? Was I the one who should be punished?

He caught me staring at him. "Hey, I shouldn't have jumped on you like that. I'm sorry."

"No, you were right." I smiled up at him. "I don't know all the facts."

He couldn't know that I was talking about more than the TV news story. I was convinced now that those other memos held the key.

"What's bothering you, Angel?"

It unnerved me to hear him call me that again. I liked it, but whereas I'd thought he might change his opinion once he learned I was an avenging angel, now I worried I might be a malevolent demon in an angel's disguise.

I decided he deserved an honest answer. "Pondering my future."

He laughed. "Angel, you have a very bright future ahead of you, starting with another date after this last one didn't end so well."

I was tempted. "I really have some thinking to do." A lot of thinking was more like it.

The file I'd retrieved for Hydra gnawed at me. If I passed it on as I had the others, wasn't I passing judgment before the evidence was in? Or was this another hormone vs. neuron battle? This had been so much easier before all this gray invaded my black-and-white view of this man.

He wasn't giving up so easily. "I know just the place. It's where I go when I have to sort things out."

"But—"

"No arguing. You're coming with me."

"I don't have anything to wear."

"There's plenty to choose from upstairs."

"I don't want to wear any of your ex's clothes, thank you very much."

"None of it is Melissa's."

"Then not any of your ex-girlfriends' stuff either."

"It's all my sister's."

"Oh." Once again I'd jumped to a conclusion without any facts.

"Kelly stays with me when she comes out. You two are about the same height."

He didn't seem to realize more than height went into fitting into another woman's clothes.

I stood and picked up my plate.

"Leave it," he said. "I'll clean up while you get dressed."

I put the plate down and retreated toward the bedroom.

"Shorts," he called after me.

Once the door closed behind me, I sent another text to Ramona.

ME: Out with Dennis don't know when I'll be back

She'd want all the details, and I didn't have time for the half hour Ramona would hold me on the phone if I called. I was picking out a top when my phone chirped with her reply.

RAMONA: I warned you about having too much fun

I couldn't decide on the right response to that, so I didn't respond at all.

# CHAPTER 23

*JENNIFER*


I SLID INTO THE SEAT OF HIS SLEEK CAR. "WHERE ARE WE GOING?"

He gave the same answer as the last four times I'd asked. "A place I like to go to decompress. I think you'll like it."

The Jaguar had the smell and look of luxury with supple leather on the seats, and even the dash. The sound when we started out was not obnoxiously loud, but had the throaty exhaust melody of a powerful motor.

I gazed out the window, watching LA go by as we made good progress in the light weekend traffic.

Eventually he turned west on Venice Boulevard, and our destination became clearer. In three miles on this course, we would run out of roadway and be facing the Pacific Ocean.

I'd been wondering, but he hadn't offered any more information about his brother, so I asked. "What happened with Josh last night?"

"All we were told is that he had a single-car accident and rolled the vehicle."

"Was he drunk, you think?"

"Dad asked the same thing. Point zero two—not even close to the limit. It's all strange. He's not the type to drive too fast and lose control. We'll know more later when we get the accident report."

"But you said he'll be okay, right?"

"I called this morning, and the news is better. He'll be plenty sore, and he's under observation because of the head wound and the fact that he lost consciousness, but I think so. They just have a protocol to follow."

He turned left onto Speedway, the last road paralleling the beach, and in a few blocks, he stopped. A push of the opener button, and a garage door rolled up.

The houses in this area were narrow. We climbed the stairs to the main living area above.

The home was very open, with a parquet wood floor and a full-width window on the beach end of the house.

He ushered me through a sliding glass door to the patio, which boasted a marvelous view of the wide sand of Venice Beach.

"What would you like to drink?" he asked.

"Soda is fine, or just water."

"In life you have to make choices, so which is it?"

"Water, then."

While he fetched the glasses, I sat on the comfortable couch and surveyed the scene: people walking just below us on the Ocean Front Walk, couples on the sand, a guard tower that looked straight out of *Baywatch* to the right toward the Muscle Beach outdoor gym, and the fishing pier off to my left.

He'd said we had to make choices in life, and he was absolutely right. I had to choose the woman I would be—the cocksure one of a few weeks ago that knew in her bones how evil he was, or the woman he challenged me to be, the one who would demand evidence to evaluate before pronouncing judgment on him. Life had been simpler before his challenge, and I didn't know if I could do it, even if I wanted to. Mom had been so sure. For years, I'd believed my duty was to be the avenging angel.

He appeared from behind and handed me a glass of ice water. "Deep in thought, I see. Anything I can help with?"

"No, just enjoying the view."

"Close your eyes."

"Why?"

"Stop asking silly questions for once. Just close your eyes."

I relented and did as he asked.

"What do you hear?"

Kids had been bicycling by a second ago. "Kids."

"And?"

The muffled voices of people walking by caught my attention. "People talking."

"Behind that."

The noise of the teenagers slowly receded. I smiled as I realized the answer. "The waves."

"Very good. Now focus on that and relax."

I lay back and focused to bring the ocean sounds forward out of the background. The soothing, rhythmic sound became easier to pick out as I stayed still.

"Now synchronize your breathing with the waves."

I had trouble with that because the waves were slower than I wanted to take breaths. "I can't. It's too slow."

"Take deeper breaths. You can do it."

I opened my eyes to confront him, but his were closed. I sat back again. "If it's so easy, you do it."

"I do it every time I come out here. I think you're scared to try, scared to learn."

I wasn't scared of anything. "Shut up. Give me a minute." I took in a deep breath and concentrated on listening. Deep breath in, deep breath out, deep breath in, deep breath out. Eventually, I got the hang of it.

"Now," he said. "Ask your question."

"What question? I don't have a question."

"Sure you do."

I didn't argue further, and instead did as he asked. Deep breath in, deep breath out. *Which woman am I?* Deep breath in, deep breath out. *Which woman do I want to be?* Deep breath in, deep breath out.

It didn't take long for the answer to become clear. Deep breath in, deep breath out. I never shied away from a challenge, and I couldn't live with myself if I settled for less than I could accomplish.

He would get what he wanted. I would accept the challenge he hadn't realized he'd set for me and give him the benefit of the doubt. I'd demand evidence.

"I heard that," he said.

I still had my eyes closed, but I could envision him pointing an accusatory finger at me. "You heard what?"

"You got the answer. It works every time."

"But I didn't even have a question."

"Yes, you did. Now what was it?"

I fumbled for a way out of this. "Okay, I was deciding if I should let you kiss me again."

He laughed. "That's not a real question."

"How can you say that?"

"Because you already knew the answer was yes."

"If you don't like my question, what was yours?"

"I can't say. Mine is X-rated." His words sent heat to my core.

I sat up, opened my eyes, and threw the aptly named throw pillow at him. "I am wearing underwear, if that was your question."

We had gone from some yoga-style relaxation technique to talk that brought me back to all the things I'd like to explore with him if he wasn't really the devil in a suit.

He laughed again. "No, that was last night's question. And what was the answer, by the way?"

"I'm hungry."

"Now who's deflecting?"

"Do you have anything to eat here, or do we have to go out?"

He stood and grabbed my hand. "Stand up and close your eyes."

I gave in and stood. "Not again."

His arms encircled me. "Keep your eyes closed."

He pulled me close and my chest pillowed against his, bringing back vivid memories of last night on the dance floor, last night before the fountain.

His breath was hot against my ear. "Now tell me honestly. Do you want to kiss me again?"

The heat of his body against mine would allow only one answer. I nodded.

He released me without the kiss I'd requested. "See? I was right."

I huffed. "And you're a tease."

"I wasn't the one wearing the waist-high slit last night."

"Thigh high," I corrected him.

He pulled me back into the house. "We're going for a walk. Trust me. Later, I won't be teasing you."

The naughty implications melted my panties on the spot. "Those are dangerous words, mister."

"Better be careful. You have no idea how dangerous I can make things. Now, let's get going."

"What if I like dangerous?" The statement escaped my mouth before I realized how un-Jennifer I'd suddenly become.

The smirk he wore grew to a smile. "I'm going to remember you said that. Let's get a move on, Angel."

There it was again. *Angel.* The word that sent a tingle through me every time.

*DENNIS*

I TOOK HER HAND AND LED HER OUTSIDE.

The woman was an enigma—smart, talented, a little sassy, and a lot sexier than she gave herself credit for.

We walked the path along the edge of the beach toward my favorite taco stand in this part of town. Her head was on a swivel, taking in the sights, all with an excited smile pasted on her face.

I squeezed her hand. "Ever been down here before?"

"No." She looked away. "I've only been to the beach at Santa Monica once."

"Only once? If you live in LA, you have to come to the beach more often than that. Here you get away from the endless city. Half the horizon has no people and no buildings."

She shrugged. "It is nice."

Perhaps I was happier to be with her than she was with me. That was a disturbing thought.

Something had bothered her this morning that she wouldn't talk about, but true to form, the beach-breathing technique I'd long practiced had helped her deal with whatever it was. I'd seen it in her face as she'd silently matched her breaths to the ocean waves. It had given her a moment of calm.

In time, I hoped she'd trust me enough to open up. "Have you lived with your sister's family long?"

Her smile dimmed. "Since Mom died. It's just the three of us now: me, my sister, and Billy."

"What happened to Billy's father?"

"He didn't stick around long. Ramona's raising Billy herself."

My heart went out to them. "That must be hard." With what my father meant to me, I couldn't imagine a boy growing up without one. It would leave a huge hole, and the workload for Jennifer's sister had to be tough without the father around to help.

We kept walking.

Jennifer didn't elaborate, and I didn't pry.

Taco Bandito was just opening up when we arrived.

I knew how she liked her coffee from Starbucks, but I had no idea what food she preferred. "I forgot to ask if Mexican is okay."

"Sure." She perused the menu for a second. "Are the chicken tacos any good?"

"Everything is good. Just take it easy on the salsa."

While I ordered for us, she took the drinks to a table under an umbrella.

I joined her with the chips and salsa.

She absentmindedly twisted the silver ring on her finger.

I pointed to her hand. "You do that a lot."

She pulled her hand away. "Sorry."

"It's special to you, isn't it?"

She looked down at the ring with a smile. "It was the first ring my stepdad gave my mother."

"That is special."

She tilted her head and nodded. "It's so I don't forget them." Her eyes misted over with the memory.

The sentiment was one I understood.

I grabbed a chip. "Freshest chips on the beach."

She was ready to dip a chip in the red salsa when I warned her. "You'll want to stick to the green."

"Really?"

"You won't be able to handle the red."

"Is that so?"

"I can see it in your eyes. You're scared."

She heaped the red on her chip and took the whole thing in her mouth.

I stuck to the green and waited for the fireworks. I'd just learned something interesting about her—she couldn't resist a dare.

In less than a minute, beads of sweat had formed on her forehead, and she sucked down half her Coke.

I waved my next chip at her. "I warned you."

"It's not that bad." She switched to the green after that. Three chips later she said, "It is hard for her."

I was glad she'd decided to open up about her sister and nephew. "How old is he?"

"Seven, and he's a good kid. I help out, and with the two of us, we make it work."

Our order was up, and I went to retrieve the plates.

She took a small sip of her almost-depleted Coke. "I wanted to thank you for the raise."

"You already did."

"We've been wanting to move into a larger place for a while. Billy's getting a little old to sleep in his mother's room."

In my quick visit, I hadn't guessed that her apartment was that small. "Have you found a place yet?"

"Not yet. Ramona's doing the scouting. I'm pretty flexible. The most important thing is for her to be happy with it."

I asked, and she continued to tell me about her sister and nephew. I soaked it all up. Her dedication to her family struck a chord with me.

None of her sentences began with *I*. Everything was *we*, and sometimes *they*. Her attachment to them seemed almost maternal. She'd stepped up to replace her mother in providing for her sister and nephew.

She asked about my family, which took longer, running through my two brothers, two sisters, and their whereabouts.

I pushed my empty plate to the side. "You mentioned your mother passed a little while back. What about your father? Is he able to help at all?"

Her expression told me instantly I'd stepped in it. "My stepdad died just before she did. An industrial accident."

"I'm sorry to hear that."

I didn't have anything better to say to comfort her. My friend Bill Covington had lost both his parents, his mother long ago and his father recently. It had taken a toll on him.

She lifted a chip from the basket, scooped up a large helping of the red salsa, and offered it to me. "You made me eat one."

There it was again, her change of subject. This was another taboo topic.

I wasn't going to push the conversation. Her expression when I'd brought up her stepfather had been more anger than remorse. He'd obviously wronged her somehow.

There was a story hidden there, and I wasn't trusted enough yet to share it. Perhaps someday I would be. She wasn't one to grant trust quickly, it seemed, but I could be patient.

I wouldn't back down from a challenge either, and I had enough of my Coke left, so I accepted the chip and put on a brave face while it scorched my mouth.

# CHAPTER 24

*JENNIFER*

DENNIS DIDN'T HESITATE. "ANYTHING FOR YOU."

He took the chip and shoved it into his mouth, chewing loudly. He swallowed and opened his mouth, taking a deep breath and blowing out before finishing his Coke and chugging half his water glass.

I loaded up another chip and held it up to him.

He didn't flinch and ate the second just as quickly, washing it down with more water. The sweat on his brow showed he wasn't immune to the heat.

"Did I pass the test?" he asked.

I nodded with a giggle. Mom had told me one of the indicators of a guy's interest was how much of your bad cooking he'd put up with. I got goosebumps realizing Dennis's interest in me matched mine in him.

"Can we go back now?" I asked.

He took his tray to the trash, and I followed with mine.

A seagull cawed loudly as it flew by, looking right at me with accusatory eyes.

I cringed.

"You cold, Angel?"

"I'm fine," I lied.

I wasn't fine, and even the bird knew it.

Now I'd lied to Dennis.

I hadn't meant to, but when he asked if I'd been here before I couldn't share that Dad and I had once ridden bikes on the beach path near here all the way to

Marina Del Ray. That had been the last weekend I'd shared with Dad before the accident.

We'd laughed, raced a bit, stopped for food, laughed some more, and had a great afternoon. It was the way I wanted to remember him: carefree, happy, and alive. Then he was gone.

Instead of walking back south, Dennis pulled me along to the north.

"Hey, that's the wrong way."

The gull cawed again and swooped toward us.

Dennis was stronger than me, and the tug-of-war was no contest. He stopped, and I was instantly in his arms, shielded from the angry bird.

I didn't fight him. Instead I relished the contact, the safety of his embrace.

I knew he hadn't meant to hurt me by asking about Dad, but that didn't make the questions any easier. They were normal questions about family, siblings, parents, and history, but it was a history I couldn't share with him.

He still had a full complement of family members. He couldn't understand the anguish of losing one, much less two.

It was hard to talk about, like the loose sand was harder to walk on than the cement of the path we'd taken here.

He rubbed my back. "I'm not done with you yet, Angel."

"But I thought—"

"No. You didn't think. You assumed. You know what they say about the word *assume*?"

"Yeah, it makes an ass out of you and me."

Today seemed to be one big lesson in not drawing premature conclusions.

"I told you I was taking you somewhere to relax so you would forget what's bothering you."

"And we did. On your patio. Remember? Your silly wave listening."

"On a scale of one to ten, how relaxed are you?"

I didn't have an answer for that, so I chose the safe middle ground. "Five."

"That won't do." He started off again and pulled me along.

It was getting more crowded along the boardwalk. The little shops had rolled up their doors and were hawking their sunglasses, T-shirts, hats, and all manner of things.

He stopped at a skate and bike rental booth. "Can you skate?"

"It's been a long time."

He pulled me up to the counter. "Then it's time again."

They handed me roller blades and pads.

When he took off his shoes, I noticed something.

"Who was the lucky girl?" I pointed to the name tattooed on his ankle: DEB. I laughed. "Do you have Melissa hidden somewhere else?"

He didn't join my laugh, and for a second I feared I'd overstepped a hidden boundary.

"I'm sorry. I didn't mean to pry." Another lie of sorts, but a white one.

"Deborah Ellen Benson, my cousin. She was kidnapped as a child. And… well, the kidnapper died in a shootout with the cops. We didn't get her back, and we never even found her body… We all got these a few years ago."

"I'm sorry."

"We don't talk about her. It's too painful." He smoothed a finger over the letters and blinked back the hint of a tear. "But she's not forgotten."

The sentiment was one of the sweetest things I'd heard a man say in a long time.

"I'm sorry," I repeated. Delving into the particulars seemed over the line, so I didn't ask any of my morbid questions. I placed a hand on his knee, and for a few moments, his pain and mine were linked. We'd both suffered tragedy and loss.

"Thank you. " He patted my hand and sniffed in a breath. "Enough of that. Today is for new memories, not reliving old ones."

We laced up and strapped on our pads in awkward silence.

He'd given me a peek behind his shell, and I'd learned another thing about Dennis I hadn't suspected.

He slapped on a smile. "Ready to go?"

He had me start out ahead of him, presumably so he could pick up the pieces and administer first aid when I fell.

After a few hundred yards, it all started coming back to me, and I didn't feel like such a klutz anymore.

We zoomed up north past the Santa Monica Pier and kept going.

It was a beautiful southern California day with a light, cool breeze off the water—nothing but sunshine and the smell of the ocean.

"How much farther?" I asked.

He pulled ahead of me, turned, and started skating backwards. "To the end."

"Where is that?"

He smiled. "You'll see."

I pointed ahead. "Bicycles."

He flipped to skating forward in time to dodge the two-wheeled menaces. Some of the kids either didn't appreciate the rules of the road, or merely didn't have good control, but we routinely had to dodge them.

We were almost to Malibu when the path ended at a parking lot up against the hills of the Pacific Palisades.

As we returned, we passed numerous bikini babes of the kind you saw all over TV—girls skating the path in barely there swimsuits. Yet every time I checked, Dennis's eyes were either on me or looking out for the next hazard on the path. This was the kind of attention I could get used to.

We made a pit stop at the Santa Monica Pier, and I almost asked if we could go on one of the rides, but I chickened out. Dennis was calling the shots, and I was along for the ride.

He bought us waters and handed me one.

After several good slugs, I put the cap back on my bottle. "Why did we have to go so far?"

"I'll tell you when we get back to the house." He had me lead and insisted on skating behind me.

I preferred it when he chose whether to dodge left or right, meeting others on the pathway. "Why can't you go first?"

"I could, but I like the view from back here better."

I laughed. I knew he didn't mean the ocean or the beach.

We skated on, and two more attempts to get him to answer my question were for naught.

Back at the rental shop, we returned the roller blades and retrieved our shoes. I sidled up next to him as we walked back. "Are you going to tell me now?"

"I said when we get back to the house. You have to learn patience, girl."

Today everything was a lesson. "Denny, you're being annoying."

"I'm being consistent, Angel."

I didn't have a comeback to that, so I put my arm around him. This had been fun, and not something I would have thought of.

His arm came over my shoulder, pulled me tight, and he adjusted his stride to match mine.

I glanced toward him.

He smiled back.

All I saw beyond him was the expanse of the ocean—no buildings, no people, just the two of us, sunshine, and warm sand. Being with him had lightened my mood to match the brightness and warmth of the day.

*Dennis*

Back at the house, I followed her up the stairs to the main level. The way her ass looked in those shorts from down here almost had me drooling.

Once upstairs, she turned and asked again. "Why did we have to go so far?"

I put down my water bottle. "Did you finally stop thinking about what it was that bothered you this morning?"

She lolled her head back. "Yeah."

"That's why. I wanted your full attention."

Her eyes narrowed. "For what?"

I cupped her head in my hands. "For this." I brought her in for the kiss I'd promised earlier—the kiss we should have gotten to last night. The kiss I'd waited patiently for.

She didn't waste any time meeting me. Her lips tasted salty from the exercise. At work she dressed demurely, but as soon as I had her in my arms, the passion beneath her cool exterior came out. Her hands clawed at me, pulling her soft form closer.

My cock went hard in an instant. She wasn't holding back, and we were going to take this where it could have gone, where it *should* have gone last night —just without the sexy red dress.

Our tongues sought connection and began the sensual dance of learning one another.

She was hot against me as I searched to feel the hardness of a nipple under my thumb.

She squeezed my butt, and I gave her back the same as she ground herself against my erection, making it difficult to hold back from ripping her clothes off.

I pulled back and broke the kiss. "I need an honest answer."

She looked up at me and blinked. "Yeah?"

I needed her to commit now or back away before we started. "I'm not a nice guy."

"So you say."

"No. I'm dangerous. We need to stop now if you're not ready for that."

She pulled away.

I'd misjudged her.

# CHAPTER 25

*JENNIFER*

YESTERDAY I WOULD HAVE BACKED AWAY FROM DANGEROUS. YESTERDAY I WOULD have run.

I pushed back out of his hug.

His face fell.

Today I probably should as well. But the rebel in me had another idea. I pulled my shirt over my head.

"Bring it on." I launched myself into his arms and back into the kiss. I speared my fingers into his hair. As his hands found my ass and lifted me, I wrapped my legs around him.

He might be the devil, he might be dangerous—and I'd been warned—but this afternoon I didn't care. I'd tried safe before and ended up with boring too many times.

Our tongues dueled as he kissed me with a fervor equal to mine. He smelled of spice, manliness. We traded breath and desire like wild animals. He lifted me up and down, rubbing against his hardness as he carried me into the kitchen. Guys had kissed me before, but never like this. This was a real kiss, even better than the one in his office. A kiss with a man, not a boy. I'd had no idea a kiss could convey such passion. His mouth branded me, with intensity and pure, panty-melting lust.

I had never done anything remotely like this. I'd never even gotten beyond second base with a guy on the first date, and here I was shucking off my shirt and attacking him. A week ago—hell, two days ago—I would have stopped and run, but today I was going to taste the wild side of life.

In an instant he'd unhooked my bra with a practiced, single-handed motion and pulled it away as I untangled my arms.

The feel of my breasts against his muscled chest was heavenly, and the heat in my core built to an intolerable level.

He set me down and pulled off his shirt. Then he undid my shorts, pulling them to the floor. With one hand on my shoulder, he slid the other down through my curls.

"Last chance to change your mind."

I gasped as a finger traced my drenched slit and entered my slick heat. It was decision time, but I wasn't going back to boring.

"More," I told him. I was ready to mingle sweat. I reached for his belt.

"No," he told me sternly. He removed his finger and stepped back. "Lose the panties and the shoes."

I pulled them down and removed my shoes, while he took his off as well, though he kept his pants on.

"Stand still," he said.

If anything, the bulge behind his zipper had grown. His hands cradled the weight of my breasts.

Hot tingles shot through me as his thumbs traced lazy circles around my nipples. I remained frozen in place as he pulled his hands away and stood back to look me over.

"Now turn around."

I did. Guessing what would come next, I spread my legs and leaned over, placing my hands on the counter.

"All the way around."

I'd guessed wrong. I turned further until I faced him again.

He looked me up and down with unmistakable heat in his eyes. "Again."

Instead I moved toward him.

He pushed me back. "Again." His voice was firm, commanding, and building a naughty heat within me. My pussy sizzled with anticipation. This was unlike anything I had experienced before. The raw power of his voice and the animal look in his eyes demanded obedience.

I'd been told who was in charge here. I turned a slow circle for him, like the gazelle turning for the lion.

His eyes left my body to lock with my eyes. "Angel."

I trembled, waiting for the next words. My nipples were hard with excitement, and my thighs slick with anticipation. All my nerves tingled with impatience for his touch.

"You're beautiful." He pulled me to him, and his mouth devoured mine again.

I laced my fingers through his hair and pulled myself up.

His hands roamed my body, leaving trails of hot sparks everywhere they went.

I rubbed myself against the bulge in his jeans, trying to coax him to show me. Another try at his belt ended up with the same admonition. I wasn't in charge here.

He lifted me suddenly and sat me up on the edge of the counter. A wicked smile came to his face as he took in the sight of my spread pussy.

I was completely open to him. The lights were on, and I wasn't prepared for this. Modesty pulled my legs closed, but he pushed them apart.

He went to a knee.

I gasped as his face approached my crotch. I'd never asked for it, and only one guy had gone down on me before. That had lasted a half a minute before he asked how he'd done. Maybe honesty hadn't been the best policy that day.

Dennis put his mouth to my pussy, and his tongue traced the length of my folds, parting my soaked lips, teasing my entrance. His stubble scraped my thighs as he moved in. His tongue circled my clit several times before he sucked on my little bud.

As his hands went to my breasts, all I could do was run my fingers through his hair as his tongue worked my clit. My legs opened to him as his magic mouth sent sensations crashing over me, in crescendo after crescendo.

I'd had no idea what I was missing. Every stroke of his tongue, every little suck took me by surprise. My nerve endings lit on fire in a way I hadn't experienced before.

His tongue alternately circled my opening and moved up to my clit, stabbing, stroking, and sucking in a delicious torture.

I widened my thighs and pulled at his hair. I needed him closer, harder—just more. Waves of pleasure rolled over me in ever-increasing strength. I had never been this high off the ground as my blood boiled and my eyelids clamped shut.

Every fiber in my body tensed as he drove me closer to the cliff and finally over into the spasms of my climax. My back arched, and my legs shook. I pulled at his hair, threatening to suffocate him against my throbbing pussy. Instead he pulled back, and a thumb pressed hard against my clit, intensifying the final throes of my release.

I had fingered myself to climax plenty of times, but he had shown me the better kind of orgasm. Catching my breath, I opened my eyes to find his belt unbuckled and him shoving down his jeans.

His cock sprang loose and rose against his stomach. He stepped out of his jeans. Dennis was a tall guy, and I should have expected big, but his long, thick, beautiful rod was more than I'd guessed at. I was about to be tested.

I grasped it and pulled.

He groaned a wonderful sound of pleasure. Pulling away, he grabbed the jeans, took a condom from his pocket, and handed it to me.

When I had trouble opening the packet, he tore it with his teeth and handed the little disk back.

He took a finger and wiped the bead of pre-cum off his tip. He put the finger to my lips.

My eyes went wide as I sucked—salty, naughty, forbidden, dangerous.

After he pulled the finger away, I fumbled with the latex.

He put a gentle hand on mine. "This side."

*Duh.* I didn't have any experience with this. Other guys had never wasted any time and had always rolled the rubbers down themselves. The sounds Dennis made as I rolled it down his length were well worth the wait.

He moved between my legs and began to enter me, stretching my walls, as it had been a while—too long a while.

I bit my lip as he pushed in.

His eyes locked with mine. "Hurt?" He pulled back.

"No," I lied. I didn't want to stop now.

He obviously didn't believe me as he pushed in slowly and slid out again, a little farther each time.

I took in a breath. "Keep going. I want you. Don't stop."

I needed to give him back what he'd just given me, and I knew I could do this. I wanted this. I wanted him. Wrapping my heels behind him, I pulled him to me and let the pressure build.

With a final push he filled me to the limit.

The small flash of pain was quickly overtaken by layers of pleasure as he began to thrust.

I kept my legs behind him, pulling him in with each push and rocking into him.

He groaned. "You are so fucking good, so fucking tight, baby."

My words surprised me. "Then fuck me."

And he did, bouncing against me at a furious pace. The animal in him took hold. There was no holding back now.

Clawing at his shoulders, I pulled him in to kiss me and rocked my hips with his rhythm.

He held my hips, pounded into me and bit my neck. The animal in his eyes matched his actions. Dennis showed me sex on a different, more primal level—rough, urgent, intense.

I gave him back rough as I clawed at him.

Without warning, his thumb went between us and pressed my clit with each thrust.

I lost my battle trying to control the sensations, to drag it out longer. My nerves were on fire as the tension grew and the spasm of ecstasy overtook me again.

He rubbed harder. "That's it, baby. Let yourself go."

My walls clenched around him, and in a few more thrusts I felt him tense up as his orgasm followed mine. I used my legs to clamp him deep within me.

He stayed deep, his cock throbbing, as his mouth met mine for another breathless kiss.

We were both panting too raggedly to maintain the kiss, and he wrapped his arms around me, pulling my breasts to him. His fingers softly rubbed my back as I came down off my high.

I nestled my head on his shoulder, relishing the last throbs of his cock deep inside me. If this was the dangerous life, I was signing up. The post-climax pressure between my legs didn't trail off quickly as it always had before.

He pulled out and lifted me down off the counter, urging me toward the bathroom. "Shower time."

I followed him on wobbly legs, enjoying the view. The red streaks of my scratches on his back contrasted with the white below the tan line of his tight ass.

After disposing of the condom, he turned on the water and pulled me into the shower with him. What followed was the opposite of the sex. His hands soaped me slowly, softly, caressing all my skin from head to toe. Dangerous had morphed into gentle, even soothing.

I did the same for him, enjoying the response I got as I washed his balls and cock. He cuddled with me, rocking me in the water in a motion that recalled our dancing before his awful ex had shown up.

"You okay, Angel?"

I nodded into his shoulder. "More than okay." I hugged him tighter.

He laid his chin on top of my head. "Good."

My pussy still throbbed, reminding me that sex with Dennis was like the potato chip commercial. Even if I'd wanted to, it would be impossible to stop at just once. I'd denied myself too long, but no longer.

The girls at Starbucks who hid behind their lattes and secretly drooled over him had no idea how good it felt to be in his arms.

Jennifer wasn't in Kansas anymore, and she liked it.

# CHAPTER 26

*Dennis*

On Monday morning, my dick still tingled as I rode the elevator up to the top floor. I smiled recalling my session with Jennifer in the shower this morning. We'd stayed at the beach house until this morning, and the time we'd spent together had recharged my batteries. It had been way too long since I'd felt this good, and it was all because of Jennifer.

I'd dropped her off at her place on my way in, and I knew she'd be in the office before long.

That would present the next problem. How good would I be at keeping my hands off her in the office, and keeping my feelings under wraps?

Melissa had been an excellent actress—seeming to care when she didn't. I needed to pull off the reverse with Jennifer. Studied ambivalence was the goal.

When I opened the door to the executive area, Cindy spoke before I could ask why my door was already open.

"Your father is waiting."

Since when did Dad come over here unannounced? His usual routine was to summon me to his building.

I walked into my office. "Good morning, Dad."

"Not so good, I'm afraid. Please close the door."

His words were ominous. It took a lot to rattle the great Lloyd Benson.

I closed the door and took my seat behind the desk.

He slid a folder across the desk to me. "The report on Josh's crash."

I took the folder and opened it. "What's the conclusion about the accident?"

"It wasn't an accident."

That stopped me cold. I looked up. "What does that mean?"

"It means the crash wasn't Josh's fault. Keep reading."

I read down the page. Most of it was physical descriptions of the location, a diagram, and most importantly Josh's blood alcohol, which thankfully was a quarter of the legal limit. It would have been terrible if this had been caused by his drinking at Dad's fundraiser.

The second page contained the kicker. "Two bullet entry holes were located on the right rear quarter panel of the subject vehicle and one in the passenger side door."

My jaw dropped. "Three bullet holes?"

Dad nodded. "Keep going."

The next paragraph had another surprise. "Subject vehicle's right rear tire was deflated, and additional holes consistent with bullet entry and exit were located on the outer and inner sidewalls of that tire. Two bullets were recovered from the vehicle interior."

The report concluded that the rollover of the car down the embankment was due to the loss of air in the rear tire and subsequent loss of control.

I looked up after finishing. "It was deliberate?"

"Not much doubt about that. You don't fire multiple shots at a car by accident."

"Do they have any leads?"

"Not yet. Josh couldn't be much help. All he knew was he had just passed a black car when it happened."

I ventured a guess. "Road rage?"

"That is possible, but there are other theories."

"Who would want to hurt Josh?"

It didn't make sense. Josh was mild mannered compared to me, and he hadn't been in much of a position to piss anybody off.

"Nobody comes to mind." Dad rubbed at his goatee. The zinger was coming. "He drives the same car as you."

His implication floored me. "You think the bullets were meant for me?"

"You have had a rather nasty public fight with that Cartwright fellow."

I'd called Carson Cartwright a few choice names, but that was all.

I shook my head. "That's a financial spat. Resorting to violence doesn't seem his style. He's a boardroom bully, not a street fighter."

"How can you be certain? The man is a snake."

Dad had expressed his opinion of Cartwright before. The man called himself an activist investor, but he didn't care about any investors beyond himself. *Extortionist* fit better as his title.

I just couldn't be sure. "Is that what you think?"

Dad shrugged. "Do you have a better suspect? I'm here because it makes more sense than Josh being targeted, and I want you to promise me you'll be careful."

"I will."

This was the first time since college I could remember my father asking me to promise anything, and saying yes was a no-brainer. Later I'd have to figure out what being more careful entailed. Carrying a gun seemed extreme.

I closed the folder and slid it his way.

He stood. "You can keep that, and I'm putting the Hanson team on this to see if they can come up with anything more. As far as the police are concerned, I'm afraid that folder is all that we're likely to get."

Cartwright targeting me still struck me as absurd, but I didn't have anything better to offer.

He stopped at the door. "Can I tell your mother you'll be careful?" He had to be very worried to pull that trick out.

"Absolutely."

After he left, I turned to face the window. Somewhere out there was Josh's attacker. I quickly discarded the idea of verifying Cartwright's whereabouts Saturday night after I realized Dad could be on the right track. I hadn't met Cartwright, but I doubted he was personally brave enough to carry out what had happened to Josh. But I couldn't rule out his hiring somebody. That scenario upped the odds that Dad was right.

~

*JENNIFER*

DENNIS HAD DROPPED ME OFF AT HOME EARLY THIS MORNING.

Ramona was herding her son toward the door when I came in.

Billy rushed to hug my legs. "I missed you."

I hugged him back. "And I missed you too."

Ramona arched a brow. "You look tired. You'll have to tell me all about it later."

I shot her my best evil eye. "Later."

She opened the door. "Come on, we gotta get you to school."

Billy let go of me, and in a moment I was alone.

The apartment looked different, a little more drab, like my life before this weekend—plain vanilla, safe and drab instead of dangerous and interesting. Brushing aside the useless thoughts, I hurried to get ready for work—the work where I'd be back with Dennis, but with everybody else around we be required to abstain from any public displays of affection.

I hadn't talked to him about avoiding PDA—a pretty big oversight. But I decided our weekend would be my little secret until we talked, although *little* didn't describe it very well. Spending the weekend with the CEO sounded wrong. Had it been merely a hookup, or time with my new boyfriend?

I started changing and smiled as the word rolled around in my head. *Boyfriend* sounded good. We hadn't discussed anything. Was I getting ahead of myself by assuming we'd get together again? I mean it had only been a weekend.

By the time I was ready to leave, I'd talked myself out of *boyfriend*, but still didn't like *hookup*.

Why was I overanalyzing this? It was what it was—fun, interesting, exciting, and soothing at the same time. It wouldn't be right to categorize it yet. It had been something completely outside my previous experience—not just the sex, but the way he talked to me, and the way he looked at me.

Out of habit I checked my email. I smiled when I didn't find anything from Hydra.

I closed and locked the door and started counting.

One hundred and three, when I reached my parking space. I had a habit of counting the steps to my car in the morning as a way of clearing my mind for the day ahead. It was always one hundred and nine or ten.

It had only been a day, and already things were different.

*Jennifer has gone from Kansas to Oz.*

~

I MIGHT HAVE TAKEN FEWER STEPS TO MY CAR, BUT THE ELEVATOR WAS JUST AS SLOW and just as hot this morning on its trip to the top floor.

Once inside my office, I busied myself. Ignoring the temptation to wander down to Dennis's office was like staring at a piece of chocolate cake just out of reach after a long fast. The strain interfered with my concentration, and I ended up having to reread sections of the report I was studying. My legs were covering more ground this morning, but my eyes weren't.

After an hour I'd reached my limit with the endless Stoner documents and turned to face the expansive window. The coastline lay in the distance.

Closing my eyes, I recalled Dennis's technique and took a deep breath in followed by a slow deep breath out. How would I handle this work situation? Deep breath in, deep breath out. *How do I handle it?* Deep breath in, deep breath out.

When it came to me, I opened my eyes and stood, refreshed and relaxed—another Dennis Benson benefit. The coffee machine beckoned, and that was an urge I didn't need to put off.

When I turned the corner to the coffee room, there he was. We were on the same wavelength coffee-wise.

"Good morning, Mr. Benson."

He turned with a creased brow. "What did I do to go back to Mr. Benson?" The hint of a grin escaped to tell me he was messing with me.

"Sorry, boss. Good morning, Dennis." The room was empty save us, but that could change at a moment's notice, so I didn't add anything about the weekend.

His grin increased as his eyes traveled over me.

I couldn't hold back my return smile at his appreciation of what he saw. "We should talk."

His smile disappeared. His words came out curt and business-like. "I can't fit you in until the end of the day."

I nodded. I'd meant now, but I'd been put in my place, and coldly, officially. This was work, and here he was king.

As he passed, I turned to find Larry behind me. I hadn't heard him approach. I moved to the machine, and it started concocting my java as soon as I punched it in.

Larry came up to the counter and rinsed out his cup. "Exciting night at the museum, huh?"

I watched the coffee pour. "I could have done without the swim."

He sucked in a breath. "She's a real piece of work."

I was tempted to correct him to *piece of shit*, but this was the office. "That's one way of putting it. What is her deal, anyway? I didn't do anything to deserve that."

Larry might know some of the history that Dennis hadn't been willing to share.

"You know that saying *hell hath no fury*? It was written with her in mind."

"But how dare she? We only met once."

"Who knows? I'd be careful around her. She's capable of pretty much anything."

He made her sound like a complete psycho.

I pulled my steaming cup from under the spout. "What happened between them?"

He put his empty where mine had been. "Dennis married her in sort of a hurry. I warned him, but his father was pressuring him. This was while he was at his dad's company, and his father had the idea that Dennis wouldn't be mature enough to follow in his footsteps until he was a family man, so to speak." He put air quotes around that last part. "Dennis has never been good at reading women, and he fell for Melissa's act." Larry punched in his coffee preference.

I waited for more.

"She's a social climber, wanted Dennis's name and money, and when he put his foot down on the spending side, she threatened divorce. I guess she didn't expect him to take her up on it. You notice she didn't go back to her maiden name, Melissa Kaltehande."

I joined him in a chuckle at the name, which sounded like German for cold hands. Cold heart was more like it.

"If they dislike each other so much, why is she still on the board?"

I'd chickened out on asking Dennis this directly. Letting her stay on the board only gave her another way to cause trouble for him.

"Part of the divorce. It was a trade-off for him to retain more shares, and she doesn't have enough support on the board to cause any serious problems. I wouldn't have done it, but it was his call."

I sipped from my cup and waited, hoping for the next juicy detail.

"She's been hassling him ever since with the courts, demanding a redo on the divorce settlement. She'll never be satisfied, if you ask me."

I liked this version of Larry better than gala-night Larry. Perhaps all it took was Dennis setting him straight, or for him to be sober.

"Wasn't she an actress before?"

He pulled his finished cup from the machine. "She was on a series for three years, but she only got that job because Daddy was the show runner. Daddy's retired from the business now, and I heard she developed such a reputation as a diva that she's not likely to get another gig as good as that one."

"Dennis called her crazy."

"No. She's crazy like a fox. She'll act crazy or nice, depending on what it is she wants. She's a manipulator, and with someone as logical as Dennis, crazy works for her because it gets under his skin."

I sipped again from my cup. "I'll go with total bitch."

A nod was his only response. "You and Dennis looked pretty cozy out there on the dance floor."

I had to nip this in the bud. "Dennis's idea. He wanted to act that way to piss her off."

"It worked." Larry's expression indicated he bought my line.

"Yeah, more than I expected." This topic wasn't a good one to linger on. "How's the dog?"

He added sugar to his cup. "We'll see about tonight, but yesterday no mistakes, thanks to your advice about the mats. I owe you one. He was driving me crazy."

"I'll keep my fingers crossed for you and Binky." I stirred my cup and walked toward the door with a much better feeling about Larry this morning, especially his devotion to Dennis. Once again there was a chance I'd jumped to a premature conclusion.

I turned around before I reached the door. "Hey, I know this is going to sound sort of stupid…"

He chuckled. "Go ahead. I majored in stupid."

"I need to find some files for the Stoner deal, but the filing system is so confusing here with all the numbers. How do I navigate it to find something specific?"

He nodded. "I know what you mean. Each of us has an index for our department, but if you need something broader, talk to Cindy. She can set you up with a company-wide index."

That company-wide index must be what Hydra had.

"Thanks. I'll do that."

Back in my office, I tried to stay awake while taking notes on the endless Stoner documents. The ringing of my cell provided a break. The screen had a name from long ago—Suzanne from college, a person I hadn't heard from since graduation.

I answered hesitantly. "Hello?"

"Jennifer. It's Suzanne Murtog from Pepperdine."

"Hi, Suzanne. I remember. How have you been?"

"Good. I'm new—well, not new in town, really *back* in town, and I wanted to see if we could get together at lunch to catch up."

The request seemed a bit odd in that we hadn't been very close at school.

"Sure." I needed a break from the monotony of my reading, and all my work friends had relocated to the Pasadena Hydrocom building.

"You're at Vipersoft, right? I've got an interview in a building near there tomorrow. How about eleven thirty tomorrow at the Panera Bread near you?"

I agreed, and we ended the call. Lunch out would be a welcome change, and with my raise, I could finally afford it without feeling guilty. Plus, I deserved it.

# CHAPTER 27

*DENNIS*

IN THE COFFEE ROOM, JENNIFER HAD ASKED TO TALK, AND I'D ALMOST LET SOMETHING slip before I noticed Larry.

I'd put her off until later, but now I had second thoughts.

After a half hour, she passed by.

I left my office to follow. When she reached a spot outside the small conference room, I called to her.

"Jennifer, got a sec?" I nodded toward the conference room door.

Her initially flustered look quickly relaxed. "Sure."

I opened the door. The room's vertical blinds were partially drawn.

She followed me in and closed the door.

I pulled the blinds the rest of the way.

She turned. "What can I do for you?"

I approached without a word.

She backed away, stopping at the door.

I put a hand on the wood at either side of her. I kept my voice low. "You said you wanted to talk." I was mere inches from her and could feel her body heat.

The color of a blush rose in her cheeks. "I had a good time this weekend."

"That was the idea. I did too." I didn't add that it had been the best time in what seemed like forever.

Her breath was halting. "We need to…to talk about how we're going to handle it."

I cocked an eyebrow. "It's pretty simple. I'll pull down my zipper, and you can handle it any way you want." Her peachy scent invaded my nostrils, and it took all my will power to not move closer.

She giggled. "This is serious. How are we going to handle the situation here at work?"

"I'll lock my office door before I take you over my desk. Is that good enough?"

She pushed against my chest. "Cut it out. This is serious."

"I was being serious. You drive me crazy, and you are definitely getting introduced to my desk."

"People will talk. Larry's already suspicious."

"Let them." My cock was getting all kinds of ideas, just talking about this, and I inched closer, anxious to feel her body against mine.

She stomped her foot. "You might not care, but I do. People will think I got the job because I was...you know..."

Her mood was a sweet angry that made her even more irresistible.

"What? Banging the boss?"

"Yeah. If you were a gentleman, you would understand."

That hurt because I was a gentleman, at least I liked to think so. "I understand. Hush, hush, nobody knows. I can be very discreet."

"And no special favors. You can't act too nice to me, or they'll get ideas."

"Right, mean boss it is. I can be mean."

"Be serious."

"I am," I lied.

Being mean to her was the furthest thing from my mind. She was going to get the best version of me, not the worst. I couldn't resist any longer and closed the distance until I could feel her tits against my chest, with just the fabric between us.

She looked up. "You're making this hard."

My lips were an inch from hers. "I've been hard ever since the door closed."

She took a long, slow breath. "We can't be alone in the office. You can't be making eyes at me, and I have to stay at my place during the week."

"Those are harsh rules."

"You have to agree. This is important."

"I will on one condition."

She closed her eyes. "What?"

I brushed her lips with mine. "You remember you have a date with my desk at some point." I backed away.

Her chest was heaving as I put my hands in my pockets to conceal what she'd done to me.

I left the room first, and she followed, turning the other direction.

I knew two things. First, it was going to be hard in more ways than one to be near her at work and not be able to touch her. And second, I was absolutely having her over my desk at some point. That would be my reward for behaving myself for the time being.

Larry came around the corner in my direction. "Dennis," he called.

I raised a hand and ducked into the men's room and then into a stall. It would take the effects of my dirty talk with Jennifer a few minutes to wear off, and I wasn't jabbering with Larry in the hallway in my current condition.

The bathroom door opened.

"Dennis, Jay and I need a word with you." Larry had followed me in here.

"I'm busy. Can't it wait a minute?"

"Sure thing. We'll be in your office."

The door closed, and I willed my dick to deflate by visualizing the ocean waves. Unfortunately, my imagination drifted to seeing Jennifer sitting beside me, with her eyes closed, listening to the waves, and me staring at her erect nipples. Blood flowed back to where I didn't want it, and it took another few minutes till I got myself under control. Maybe mean boss wouldn't have this problem. If I stayed horny boss, I would have to sit behind my desk most of the day.

When I returned, the duo had taken up residence in my office, as Larry had warned.

Jay was the first to speak as I sat. "There's been a development."

I nodded and waited. Development in Jay-speak could mean anything.

Larry let the cat out of the bag. "Cartwright filed a 13D this morning."

That wasn't good news. They'd only have to file that with the SEC if they'd accumulated a sizable position in the company stock.

"How much?" I asked Jay.

Jay opened his folder. "Nine percent, actually a little over. About half of it on the down day of the news story last week."

I didn't correct him. It hadn't been a news story, more like a hit piece. "They were already at five before that and we didn't know?"

Larry jumped in. "Not quite."

Jay adjusted his glasses. "They're not required to file until they hit five percent, and it looks like they stayed just under that until last week."

"When did they start buying?" I asked.

Jay turned the page. "About a month before that. Almost all on the day of the prior article from our good friend Sigurd."

I slammed my hand on the desk. "Are they coordinating with that asshole?"

Larry cocked his head. "Wouldn't surprise me."

Jay was more cautious. "We don't know that. Cartwright has a reputation for buying on dips. It could be coincidence because those were the weak days for the stock."

Weak didn't begin to describe it. They were blood-letting days, painful days.

Larry faced Jay. "And what are the odds that they buy on the absolute lowest days of the year?"

Jay's eyes narrowed. "I didn't say it proves anything either way. Until we know who Sigurd is, we don't know anything for sure."

It was a true enough statement, but it ignored the odds.

Larry wasn't giving in. "I say Sigurd works for Cartwright."

"Fine," Jay agreed. "Now all you have to do is prove it."

I had another worry. "What does it say about intentions?"

The SEC required filers to be frank about their intentions for holding a major stock position.

Jay turned another page. "I'll read it for you. Due to the incompetent marketing efforts of the company recently, the filer will be…"

Larry's eyes bulged.

Jay continued. "Working with management to locate better talent—"

Larry lunged for Jay's folder. "It doesn't say that."

Jay held the papers out of Larry's reach and continued. "Better talent with which to staff the marketing function of the company."

I laughed.

"That's not funny," Larry complained.

Jay joined my laugh. "Sure it is."

I pointed a finger at Jay. "Enough of that. What does it really say?"

Jay had trouble controlling his laughter. "It…it says the position is for financial gain while they engage in discussions with the company's management and evaluate the company's status."

Larry shook his head. "That doesn't mean squat."

"Exactly," Jay concurred. "It's a place holder that they can and will change later to say they want changes from us and they're going to challenge the board, or whatever their tactic becomes."

I raised a finger. "It says one more thing. We can expect a visit from them."

"Should we prepare anything?" Larry asked. "Or call them?"

I shook my head. "No way. We give them nothing. We shouldn't make any assumptions about what they want, and certainly none about what we're going to give them, if anything. And, if fucking Cartwright wants to talk, it'll be on my schedule, not his."

Jay tilted his head. "I don't know. I wouldn't antagonize him, if I were you."

I shot back. "Bullshit. Being nice to him wouldn't change a thing. He's a thug and a bully. What he deserves is a swift kick in the nuts."

They departed, and after a few minutes, I pulled out the very first communication I'd gotten from Carson Cartwright, by certified mail no less. It had seemed innocuous enough on the surface. He'd offered his services as a *consultant* to help me maximize shareholder value and went on to list his many accomplishments.

It went back in the drawer, and I cursed myself for not taking steps earlier to fend him off. The letter was his first step in eventually making a case to the shareholders that he was their savior. In failing to avail myself of his advice, I was ignoring the shareholders' interests, yada yada yada.

He'd followed it up with multiple public comments about us, and me in particular. He'd even managed to get quoted in more than one of Gumpert's commentaries. The shtick was an old and well-worn one, and it sometimes played well if the stock suffered setbacks, as we had with the damned Sigurd articles.

He had to be tied into it somehow. There had to be a link.

I wasn't going to leave this to Dad any longer. I strode to the door and opened it. "Cin, get Baird up here pronto."

She lifted her phone and nodded.

A few minutes later Ed Baird, our head of security, was in my office, notepad in hand. "What do you need?"

"You know we've had leaks from the company that ended up in the paper."

He nodded. "I'm still looking for any links to that Sigurd character or the paper."

I raised a finger. "There's been a new development."

He leaned forward.

"I think this is all tied into the Cartwright group, Carson Cartwright in particular."

"You think he wrote the articles? The hedge fund guy? You think he's behind all this?"

I sucked in a breath. "It's possible, but it's more likely he got the info from someone here and paid somebody to write them. So I want you to change tacks and stop trying to find links to the paper. Instead look for anybody here with a connection to Carson Cartwright or his firm."

He wrote on his pad. "You still think it's somebody inside."

"That's what I want to find out."

He rose. "We'll get started right away."

"And Ed, overtime's no issue on this. Whatever resources you need."

"You got it." He closed the door behind him.

Fucking Carson Cartwright. The more I thought about it, the more sense Dad's analysis made. Cartwright's demands had started as a distraction, become an annoyance, then an irritant, and lately a threat. Last month, Jay had pointed out the possibility of a proxy fight materializing. His contacts in the financial community had mentioned rumors of just such potential. Still, a physical attack seemed out of bounds for corporate-raider types. The attack on Josh didn't fit.

~

AFTER LUNCH, I WAS IN MY DOORWAY TALKING SCHEDULING ITEMS WITH CINDY WHEN Jennifer walked up.

"Do you have time to go over some things?" she asked.

"No," I barked.

She blinked, and the drop in her countenance was immediate. "How about later?"

I gave her another firm answer. "No."

Jennifer spun and slunk back toward her office.

I caught sight of Cindy's questioning expression. "What?"

She pointed at her calendar. "You have time after three."

I put a hand in my pocket. "I need that time to think."

She picked up her pen. "Let me write that down. Three o'clock: time to think about how to be more considerate. Now, how long do you think that will take?"

I turned back into my office and closed the door firmly.

Mean boss wasn't as easy as it sounded.

# CHAPTER 28

*JENNIFER*
*(Three Days Later)*

IT HAD BEEN THREE DAYS SINCE OUR CONFERENCE ROOM CONFRONTATION—THREE difficult days.

The week had been hectic, with Dennis calling meetings on the Cartwright group left and right.

I'd been assigned to look over everything we had assembled on them. The stack was enormous, given all the SEC reports they'd filed.

Meanwhile, I'd received the master index from Cindy to find the memos I'd been waiting all this time to uncover about Dad's accident, but I hadn't gotten the courage to retrieve them yet. Now that the truth was within my grasp, it frightened me. Dad's death had led to a month of nightmare-filled nights I dreaded reliving.

I also hadn't sent Hydra the information he'd been after. The no-man's land of limbo was where I was stuck. If the memos exonerated Dennis, I'd betrayed him and the company. If the memos proved him guilty, I'd slept with Dad's killer. The situation was lose-lose for me, and procrastination had taken over. If I didn't know the truth yet, I couldn't convict myself of either sin.

Last weekend had shown Dennis Benson to be the opposite of what my picture of him had been based on Mom's accusations.

I exited my office for lunch, but retreated behind my door when I saw Dennis come out of Larry's office. The flush in my cheeks would've been too obvious. Lunch could wait.

WHEN I WAS READY TO CALL AN END TO THE DAY, DENNIS WAS STILL STUCK IN HIS office with Jay Fisher. I hadn't managed any alone time at all with him since the Monday Cartwright emergence broke.

My rule about avoiding each other at work had resulted in us both being horny and sharing a few late-night phone calls and text messages.

Dennis's demeanor at work had been the mean boss I'd suggested times about ten, and it bothered me more each day—a lot more.

It might be the hell I'd condemned myself to, but that didn't make me feel any better about it.

To brighten my mood, I pulled up last night's texts on my phone.

ME: How about Saturday breakfast on the beach?
    DENNIS: I know what I'm having
    ME: What?
    DENNIS: U
    ME: And what do I get?
    DENNIS: Do you like popsicles?
    ME: Depends
    DENNIS: On what?
    ME: Warm or cold
    DENNIS: Getting warmer right now
    ME: Will it be big enough to be filling?
    DENNIS: You can count on it
    ME: Can't wait
    DENNIS: Have to

The wait for the weekend was killing me. Since it looked like I wasn't getting any time with him today to go over work, I packed up to leave and locked my door behind me.

Cindy collected her purse as I approached and joined me in the elevator.

She punched the button for the garage. "Long day, huh?"

"I'm used to it." What I wasn't used to was the feeling of helplessness at the situation I'd created between Dennis and me.

"I'm worried that Dennis is going to burn out if he doesn't take a little time to relax."

I couldn't tell her how relaxing last weekend had been, and how I planned to relax him this weekend. "I'm sure he'll find the time sooner or later." The thought of the coming weekend sent a tingle up my spine.

"It better be sooner. I've had all the Mr. Grumpy I can take. He's wound so tight, he's going to snap."

The doors opened to the garage level.

She stepped out, but I made a different decision. "I just remembered I forgot a file I need for tonight."

I was responsible for Dennis's mood, and I planned to address it.

"Okay. See you tomorrow."

I waved as the elevator doors closed.

Back upstairs at Dennis's door, I listened for a few seconds.

Hearing no sounds of conversation, I let myself in and closed the door behind me.

He looked up from his papers. "I have to finish this response." He smiled, but then looked back to his desk and the smile faded.

I pulled the pins from my hair as I approached. "I'll let you work."

He flipped a page. "You shouldn't be in here."

Shaking out my hair, I walked around his desk, and put my purse on the corner. "It's my rule, so I'll break it if I want to."

He didn't look up. "Capricious, a little?"

"You keep working while I do what I came for."

I rolled his chair back, and he looked up at me, surprised.

When I knelt and reached for his zipper, surprise became delight.

His eyes went wide. "We can't be caught like this."

I quickly loosened the belt and zipper to pull out my prize. "Then you'll have to be quiet, won't you?"

He spread his legs and pulled the lever to lower his chair. "Did you know I've fantasized about this?"

I licked the tip of his cock. "I guessed." After undoing two buttons on my top, I took the quickly hardening rod in my mouth. I started the popsicle treatment I'd planned for the weekend just a little early.

He quickly grew under my hand, tongue, and lips. His light groans told me what he liked. He leaned forward to pinch the back of my bra strap through my top and undid the hooks.

I used both hands to stroke him and pull him to my lips. Circling my tongue around the tip and licking the underside pulled the best sounds out of him.

He stretched forward to put a hand down my shirt and knead my breast.

A knock sounded at the door.

My heart stopped.

*Shit.*

He pulled his hand away.

I scooted back under the desk, and he rolled his chair toward me as the door opened. He lowered my purse to the floor.

"We should go over this press release one more time."

It was Larry. His door had been closed, and I'd been wrong to assume he'd gone for the day.

"How about tomorrow?" Dennis asked.

I went back to work on him. The excitement of almost getting caught made me instantly wet.

"This needs to be on the wire at six in the morning. It has to be tonight."

Dennis's breath hitched as I circled his tip again and tickled the underside of his gorgeous cock.

"I trust you to handle it."

Larry didn't give up. "I really need your input to get this right."

I heard the shuffle of papers above me as I scraped my teeth lightly over him.

Larry tapped the desk. "You okay?"

"Sure. The timing just sucks."

I gave Dennis an extra hard pull and suck after he said that. I was rewarded by a tremor in his legs.

Dennis tried once more to get rid of him. "I'll look at it later and leave you my notes before I leave. How's that?"

"I can wait," Larry replied.

He wasn't going anywhere quickly.

This was going to be a contest. I held back a laugh. Could I get Dennis to come before he got rid of Larry? I went about the task of pulling, licking, and sucking, careful to stay quiet as they talked through the two paragraphs Larry wanted to go over.

Larry didn't say anything more about Dennis's obviously halting speech.

I was going to get lockjaw if this went on too long. I used my hands more, and the tenseness in Dennis's legs told me I almost had him at the end of his rope.

"Thanks. That helps," Larry said.

I heard him scoot his chair back.

"Next time find me earlier," Dennis said. "And lock the door on your way out. I have to finish something here, and I can't be interrupted."

Larry chuckled. "Sure." I heard the click as he turned the lock on the knob and closed the door.

Dennis pushed back and away from me. In an instant he had me out of my hiding place and on my feet.

"That was dangerous," he said softly.

"You promised me dangerous."

I looked down at his cock poking up at me and grabbed it to finish him.

He quickly undid the remaining buttons of my top. It and my bra ended up on the floor. His eyes turned feral as he palmed my breasts. "I promised you something else as well."

I yelped as he turned me around.

"Quiet."

My heart raced as he lifted my skirt, pulled down my panties, and pushed me over against the desk.

"I told you you'd get this."

I braced myself against the cold wood as I heard him rip open the packet. I lifted a shoe to free my ankle from the panties and looked back to see him struggling to roll the latex down his length. "Want me to help?"

"You be quiet."

I spread my legs for him and braced my hips against the desk. The wood was cool against the heat of my breasts. I'd lit the fuse, and he was about to explode.

His tip found my soaked entrance, and he didn't go slow this time.

I yelped again as he pushed in forcefully, seating himself fully in two thrusts, his hips flush to my ass.

He started to pump and grabbed my hair. "Is this what you want, dirty girl?"

"Yes, boss."

It's what I hadn't been able to admit, even to myself. I'd wanted this since the moment he mentioned it—naughty with a side of danger.

He let go of my hair, and one hand went to my breast as the other held my hip. He pounded into me like the king of the jungle he was.

I was done being the good girl. I wanted the dangerous he'd threatened, the dangerous he'd promised.

The slapping sounds of flesh on flesh grew louder as the feral animal in him took over.

Bigger and bigger waves of pleasure broke over me as he took it to the next level.

"Fuck me harder, boss. Harder."

My words added fuel to his fire, and his grunts became louder as he banged against me. Without notice, he pulled my hips back a few inches and his hand circled me to find my clit. "You want harder?"

The sudden pressure on my little nub took me higher, and I braced against the desk to match his thrusts and rock back into him.

He filled me fully, and his rubbing of my clit sent me over the edge as fire filled my veins and the spasms shook me.

I moaned. Only the clamp of his hand over my mouth kept me from screaming out his name.

My legs shook as all the cells in my body tensed.

With a final groan, his hand left my mouth and he pulled my hips back into him as he found his release deep inside me.

I locked my knees to stay standing. I was a boneless, sweaty heap leaning over the desk.

He leaned forward. His weight pressed me against the desk. "That's what you get for being naughty."

"I'm leaving," Larry yelled from beyond the door. "Don't stay too late."

Dennis didn't answer him, instead he kissed my neck. "It's been hard."

"Hard is good."

He slapped my butt lightly. "I don't want to be the mean boss anymore."

Those were the words I needed to hear—the words I'd hoped for.
"I missed you too."
Insisting on the mean boss had been my mistake.

# CHAPTER 29

*DENNIS*

I ROLLED OVER SATURDAY MORNING TO FIND JENNIFER STARING AT ME. "HAVE YOU been awake long?"

She stroked a few hairs behind my ear, her sweet smile filling her face. "No. Just enjoying it here and listening to the waves."

The window was cracked open, and the sound of the ocean beyond the beach was soft, but distinct.

I pulled her toward me. "Figure anything out?" I placed a kiss on her forehead.

She nodded, and her hand came behind my head. "Yeah. I don't like your mean boss impression anymore."

It was tough to carry off, but I'd tried hard. "I thought I was doing it perfectly."

"Maybe you were, but it's not you, and I shouldn't have asked for it."

"So what, then?"

Her fingers stroked my cheek. "Can't we just be like normal employees? Hide our feelings? Can you ignore me without being mean?"

"That might make it easier for people to figure out. Are you okay with that?"

"I guess?"

I kissed her again. "You need to be sure, Angel, because it's not something we can undo."

"I think I am."

"*Think* doesn't cut it. You are, or you aren't."

She took in a deep breath, as if she were preparing to step off a high cliff. "I am."

No doubt the statement was like jumping off into the unknown for her.

"That's good, because I wasn't sure how much longer I could keep up 'mean boss' without Cindy killing me."

Jennifer rolled over to go to the bathroom.

I watched her and realized I wasn't only fixated on the bob of her tits or the sway of her ass, but the whole woman. When she returned, I couldn't help but smile. It wasn't that I didn't enjoy the bounce of her tits as she approached, but she was more than the sum of her physical assets—more than her smile or her wit. In an impossibly short time, I'd come to appreciate so much about her. How had that happened?

She stopped. "What?"

"Just thinking."

"Don't wear yourself out." She picked up her panties from last night and pulled them on. "I have to go."

I swung out of bed. "What's the hurry?" I quickly enveloped her. I wasn't about to give up the heavenly feel of her warmth against my skin.

We rocked in each other's arms for a minute, and it calmed me.

She, apparently, wasn't eager to go either. "Ramona has a study group all day, and I have to watch Billy."

"Great. I'll watch him with you."

She snorted. "And hang out at my apartment?"

I pushed her back to look into her face and held her shoulders. "No way. Let's bring him here for a beach day."

Her brows furrowed. "You know he's only seven, right?"

I pulled her back into a hug. "I'm great with kids. I was one once."

I wandered into the bathroom to get ready.

She was fully dressed by the time I'd finished brushing my teeth.

"I don't think today is a good day," she said.

Her face wasn't the happy one she'd started the morning with.

I spit and rinsed the toothbrush. "What's wrong?"

She swayed a bit. "We haven't talked about…"

I waited for the clue. We had talked about a lot of things, but I didn't know what we'd missed. I passed her to get dressed for the drive.

"Ramona doesn't want…"

That didn't tell me enough to guess yet either. I pulled on a pair of shorts, waiting for the bomb to drop, whatever it was.

"She doesn't think it's good for a lot of men to go in and out of Billy's life."

That was the bomb. The unasked question—what was our future?

This had always been the beginning of the end of a relationship for me. When a girl got to asking about the future, I cut bait and found another, less-clingy one, and then another.

I turned, and the fear in her eyes petrified me. "Come here." I held my arms out and waited.

A second later, she plastered herself against me.

"I'm not asking for anything." Her words were muffled by my shoulder.

I stroked her back. This was make or break time, and for once I didn't feel like running. "I'm not going anywhere." I smoothed over her hair and kissed the top of her head. "Trust me."

"It's just that—"

"I know. Trust me, I know. Angel, you make me very happy, and I'm here for you."

Her voice was tinged with fear, but it was only half as scared as I felt.

In a typical snap judgment, I'd committed myself to uncharted territory, but I trusted my gut. She was different in ways I couldn't describe. She felt right in my arms, right by my side in bed, and right across the table at work. Somehow she was what I hadn't realized I needed.

I let go of her and located a shirt in the dresser.

She wiped her eyes. "Sure you don't mind?"

"It'll be fun."

That was one thing I could count on. Nephew or no nephew, I would enjoy the day with my girl.

*My girl* had a nice ring to it, I decided.

I laced up my Adidas and headed for the door. "Come along, woman. We don't want to be late."

Downstairs, she went around to the passenger side of her car, expecting me to drive that shit bucket of hers.

Instead, I opened the door to the Jag.

She looked confused. "There's three of us. We have to take my car."

"Trust me, he'd rather ride with me. You can follow."

She shook her head. "That's a waste."

I opened the garage door. I wasn't giving her a choice. It was no contest that a boy would rather ride in the Jag any day of the week over her car.

She opened the rear door of her car. "He needs his booster seat then."

A minute later the booster seat was strapped in. I revved the engine, the cat roared, and we were off.

∽

*JENNIFER*

THE DRIVE TO MY PLACE HADN'T TAKEN LONG IN SATURDAY TRAFFIC.

715

Ramona cocked her head when I told her what we had in mind. "The beach?" Her words were polite, but her scowl wasn't.

Billy jumped off the couch. "I wanna go to the beach."

Dennis stood with his hands in his pockets. "We won't let the sharks get him."

Ramona's huff said that wasn't the right approach. "I don't know."

Dennis looked up. "Or we could stay here and see if we can get marshmallows to stick to the ceiling."

"Do they really stick?" Billy asked.

Dennis tousled Billy's hair. "If you throw them hard enough."

Ramona finally got Dennis's sense of humor and smiled. "Maybe the beach would be better."

Billy had another idea. "Can we do both?"

Dennis tousled his hair. "We don't have time for both. Let's get your swim trunks."

They left us for a moment.

Ramona leaned close. "Is he always like that?"

"Only when he's nervous."

"You'll be careful, right?"

"Aren't I always?"

The boys returned before Ramona could answer, and we were off.

Dennis had been right. Billy's eyes lit up at the sight of the Jaguar, and the choice of riding with his aunt or the stranger with the hot sports car was no choice at all.

I lost sight of them twice as Dennis did his James Bond imitation and roared away from the stop lights.

When we arrived, Billy was wide eyed as he described the car to me. "It goes fast, and it roars like a lion, and it can go two hundred miles an hour, and..."

I didn't catch the rest as he ran up the stairs after Dennis. I was clearly the third wheel here. That feeling was rectified as soon as Dennis's arm came around my waist upstairs.

While Dennis took Billy out on the patio, I poured orange juice for the two adults and milk for Billy.

I carried the glasses outside.

Dennis put his finger to his lips. "Listen carefully. It's there," he said to Billy.

Billy had his eyes closed, getting Dennis's brand of meditation instructions.

"I don't want to listen." He opened his eyes.

Dennis took his glass from the tray I offered. "That's okay. You're probably not old enough yet."

Billy couldn't resist the challenge. "I am too."

"Then close your eyes and listen." Dennis didn't tell him to breathe to the tempo the way he'd done with me.

After about a minute, Billy's eyes popped open. "I heard it."

716

I held out his milk. "Good for you."

"I don't want milk."

Dennis fixed him with a glare. "A man doesn't talk to his aunt that way."

Billy slumped back. "But I don't want milk."

"Before we talk about that, a man would apologize."

Billy's nose turned up, but he got the message. "I'm sorry."

"Apology accepted."

Dennis wasn't done yet. "Now you can decide about the milk. Do you want to grow up to be big and strong or weak?"

Billy didn't bite on the question. "Joey says only sissies drink milk."

Dennis chuckled. "Joey is an idiot then. Do I look like a sissy to you? Do I?"

Billy shook his head.

Dennis held up his arm and flexed his impressive bicep. "I drank milk when I was your age, and all through high school too. It's important to do what's right instead of worrying about what other people think."

Billy reached for the glass and started to drink his milk so fast I thought he'd choke. Ramona's little guy was under Dennis's spell.

I took back Billy's glass. "What do you want for breakfast?"

Billy leaned back with a shrug.

"I'd like Cocoa Puffs," Dennis answered.

"Me too," Billy shouted.

I took the milk glass back inside and located the cereal for them. I wouldn't have guessed Dennis for a guy that ate kids' cereal, but there was a lot I didn't know about him. Granola would have suited me better, but I poured myself a bowl of the dark little balls as well.

The three of us ate on the patio while Dennis quizzed Billy about his school.

Dennis ate slowly and was the last to finish. "Should we start by skating, or swimming with the sharks?"

Neither of us answered right away.

I shot Dennis a disapproving glance. Hanging out was a better idea.

Dennis stood and grabbed his empty bowl. "Skating it is, then."

Billy followed Dennis's lead and brought his own bowl to the sink—another first. "But I don't know how."

"Today's a good day to learn." Dennis grabbed a hat.

Billy went first down the stairs, and I followed Dennis.

"Cocoa Puffs?" I asked.

"Chocolate is the food of the gods."

The man surprised me at every turn.

At the rental shop, I got outfitted with roller blades, and Dennis chose easier-to-balance roller skates for himself and Billy.

Billy also got the full pads, gloves, and helmet treatment.

Our shoes went into a backpack Dennis had brought along.

Dennis held Billy up between his legs for the first half mile or so, working

717

with him on balancing and understanding the basics of pushing off one foot onto the other.

At an open stretch, Dennis let him go. "Turn right. Lean right."

It was no use. The little guy went left, off the cement, and face planted in the sand. But he got up laughing.

After several more tries, my nephew got to where he could turn the right way and stay on the path if Dennis kept giving him a boost to keep going.

Dennis kept at it patiently, and by the time we got to Santa Monica, Billy didn't look elegant, but he stayed upright and was nothing but smiles and laughter. The pads had done their job, and he was still in one piece.

"Here's where we stop," Dennis announced.

Billy scowled. "But I'm not done yet."

The disapproving glare Dennis sent his way changed that instantly.

"Can we please do some more?" Billy asked.

Dennis had already chided him twice about talking back.

"Sure," Dennis answered. "Later. First we have some rides to check out."

Dennis sat on a bench to undo his skates, and we followed. The shoes came out of the backpack, and the skates went into a locker.

From there it was a series of rides and games, with Dennis challenging Billy every step of the way until we got to the rollercoaster. The cars only sat two across, so Dennis took Billy with him, and I slid into the seats behind them.

Starting at the first plunge, Billy screamed the whole time, but he kept his hands up in the air, mimicking Dennis.

When we got off, I was the weak-kneed one Dennis had to help.

"I want to go again," Billy announced.

He modified that as soon as he noticed Dennis's stern glance. "Can I please go again?"

Dennis checked his watch. "Maybe after lunch."

He offered me his hand, and with interlaced fingers, I strode to lunch linked to my man, Billy's new idol.

Billy turned up his nose at the suggestion of the Bubba Gump Shrimp Company, and we settled on Pier Burger. Leave it to Billy to insist on lunch at a burger joint and then order a hot dog, but that was his prerogative.

I went for the chicken sandwich, and Dennis was the only one of us to order their signature Pier Burger.

"How old are you, Billy?" Dennis asked.

Billy sipped his Coke. "I'll be eight in October."

"October, huh. Let me see..." Dennis rubbed his chin for a moment. "I guess that makes you old enough then."

"Old enough for what?"

"For a grown-up name."

"What's a grown-up name?"

Dennis poked the straw in his shake. "Let me guess. Your full name is William?"

Billy nodded and sucked on his drink.

"Billy is a kid's name. I think you're ready to be called Bill, unless you like William better."

Billy looked at his cup and turned it. "Mommy calls me William when she's mad."

"Then it should be Bill, unless you like Will better. That's another choice."

Our number was announced, and Dennis got up to retrieve the tray with our food. He returned and set the tray in the middle of the table.

"Have you decided?"

Billy shrugged.

"A man needs to know how to make decisions. Maybe you're not ready for this yet."

"I am too."

"Then which will it be?"

Billy straightened up. "Bill."

Dennis offered his hand across the table. "Pleasure to meet you, Bill. My name's Dennis."

Billy shook his hand with the widest smile I'd seen on him in a long time.

"What was your kid's name?" he asked.

"Growing up my name was Denny. I made them stop when I was about your age. I've been Dennis ever since."

Billy thought for a second before taking a bite of his hot dog.

I finished chewing the fry I'd snagged. "People used to call me Jenny."

Billy finished chewing and ignored my comment to ask Dennis, "And nobody calls you Denny anymore?"

"I only let one person call me that."

I choked on my drink, realizing who that was.

Dennis patted my back. "Are you okay, Angel?"

"Yeah." I coughed. "The fizz just tickled my throat."

"Just one person?" Billy asked.

"Just one."

Billy attacked his hot dog again before asking. "Why?"

"She's very special."

The room suddenly seemed ten degrees warmer.

AT THE END OF THE DAY, WHEN IT WAS TIME TO DRIVE BILLY BACK HOME, IT FELT SILLY to be taking two cars, but I didn't have the heart to deny Billy another ride in the Jaguar. And in the back of my mind, I doubted I would have won the argument with Dennis anyway.

With my nephew around, I'd had to be on my best behavior with Dennis all day. We'd held hands, walked the pier with his arm around me, laughed together, and even snuck a kiss when Billy was in the bathroom. But that was all. Being close to Dennis all day, yet having to keep my distance had made Jennifer an anxious girl—anxious to be alone with her man after the enforced separateness I'd insisted on at work, and now in front of my nephew.

The drive also gave me time to reflect on what I'd learned. In a few short hours I'd seen Billy develop more than I'd expected. Dennis had a way with my nephew that neither Ramona nor I could replicate, and it was more than Dennis's imposing physical stature. Billy had instantly looked to him for guidance and accepted it.

Dennis hadn't needed to offer Billy anything more than a play outlet or babysitting today, but he'd gone out of his way to fill the male-role-model void in my nephew's life. We'd even had lessons on manners that went better than I'd expected.

∾

RAMONA TURNED AS WE WALKED IN. "DID YOU HAVE A GOOD TIME, BILLY?"

My nephew didn't waste any time. "I want to be Bill."

"What does that mean?"

"My name is Bill."

"Of course, but you'll always be my little Billy."

"No, I'm Bill." He caught Dennis's disapproving glare and quickly corrected himself. "Please."

Ramona took in a breath. "Well then, Bill, want a soda?"

"Can I have milk?"

Ramona's mouth dropped. "Milk?"

"Yes." A second later he added. "Please."

Ramona's eyes popped as she looked to me for confirmation.

I tilted my head. "He grew up today, what can I say?"

She opened the fridge. "Are you guys available to watch him next weekend?"

I couldn't tell if my sister was being serious or not before Dennis answered in the affirmative, and we were locked in to another Saturday with our mini chaperone.

Dennis pressed a key into my hand. "I'm going to stop by the store for some steaks. I'll see you back at the beach house."

"Thanks again," Ramona added as Dennis headed for the door. "What do you say, Bill?"

Billy stopped playing with the TV remote. "Thank you."

"See you next weekend," Dennis said on his way out.

Ramona sidled up to me. "If he can get Billy to drink his milk, I like him."

"Bill," my nephew yelled from the couch.

"It's probably time," I told her.

She shrugged. "It's just that he's growing up so fast."

"I need to get some clothes and get going."

"Do I need to plan on taking him to school every day now?"

I placed a hand on my sister's shoulder. "It's just the weekends. I'll be here during the week."

I meant it, but her expression said she didn't believe it would stay that way.

# CHAPTER 30

*DENNIS*

MONDAY MORNING I SQUINTED INTO THE BRIGHT SUNLIGHT AS I DROVE EAST TOWARD the office. The lack of coastal overcast this early in the morning pointed to a warmer than usual day today. But even that couldn't match the heat Jennifer and I had created between the sheets this weekend.

It had started out slowly, but enjoyably, with Jennifer's nephew keeping us from devouring each other, and quickly progressed to red hot that night and all day yesterday.

The woman was a balm to my soul. In her arms, I could let go of my Cartwright obsession and unwind the tension that had built all week long.

Since I was in early, I made coffee for Cindy and put it on her desk. Back in my office, while the computer booted up, I watched the city come alive out my window.

Cartwright was out there somewhere, but it wouldn't be long before he showed himself and appeared on my doorstep for "the talk." It would start out innocently enough, but progress to the veiled threats he was so good at.

I'd read up on him, and last week I'd gotten the chance to debrief two of his previous victims. With a basic understanding of his modus operandi, I now figured he had a plant or two in the company feeding him information, and would soon be ready to make his next move.

"Do I have you to thank for the coffee?" It was Cindy from the doorway.

I spun my chair around. "The least I could do."

"Thank you. Did you have a good weekend?"

I couldn't hide the wide smile that came to my face. "Yes, thank you. What about you?"

"We survived a dinner with my mother-in-law."

"One of those dinners, huh?"

"I swear my husband must have been adopted. George isn't much of a complainer, but his mother... My yard needed sprucing up, the house wasn't properly decorated, the vegetables had too much salt, and... Well, it just went on and on."

"But you avoided bloodshed, I hope."

"Barely."

I hazarded a suggestion. "Next time she comes to town, meet her at a restaurant and give her something different to complain about."

Cindy's face perked up. "I like that idea. And maybe halfway through, you could call me with a work emergency."

I chuckled. "Happy to."

"I'm going to remember that." She backed away. "Glad to see you're in a better mood."

I turned back to the window to think. Better mood was right—much better mood. When I looked back over last week, I realized the weekend with Jennifer and her nephew had re-centered me. He was a great kid, and she was quite a woman.

∽

*JENNIFER*

MONDAY MORNING, AFTER RAMONA AND BILLY LEFT, I WAS ALONE TO PUT MY HAIR up and trade my weekend shorts for my work attire. I also had to prepare myself for another five days of avoiding non-essential interaction with Dennis—not looking his direction, not smiling as soon as I saw him, and not calling him Denny.

We'd had another wonderful weekend together at the beach. Once again we'd taken Billy off Ramona's hands Saturday, and enjoyed Sunday with just the two of us.

Walking the beach path south instead of north yesterday, Dennis had surprised me when we got to Marina Del Rey. He'd rented us kayaks.

I knew squat about paddling a kayak, and I had trouble keeping up with him for a while. That made splashing him all the more fun when he finally slowed down enough for me to catch him.

He'd introduced me to another thing I'd never experienced, and made our day nonstop fun. The fresh air, sunshine, and ocean water had invigorated me, and also worn me out by the end of the day. As expected, trading back rubs had led to more hands on skin in more places, which led to another night in his arms that I didn't want to ever forget.

My life had become two days of delight followed by five days of frustration before the next round of delight. It was the personal trial I'd have to endure for a while. Three months should do it, I figured. Then we could pretend we'd just started dating. Although that seemed like an awfully long time to keep this up.

I checked my computer before leaving, and found the message I'd dreaded.

> To:Nemesis666
> From: HYDRA157
> Still waiting. What is taking so long?

I sent a quick reply.

> To:HYDRA157
> From: Nemesis666
> Have not had the right opportunity.

Time was running out. Being around Dennis had melted my resolve, but I couldn't put it off any longer. Today I was going to have to read the memos and discover which sin I was guilty of. Then I'd know whether to drop off the file for Hydra.

∼

ONCE IN THE OFFICE, I PULLED UP THE COMPUTERIZED INDEX AND PERFORMED THE search I'd done last week regarding Dad's accident. The results came back with the same file number I'd memorized last week.

I stopped by Cindy's desk. "I need something out of File Storage B."

She opened a drawer and handed me the key. "Knock yourself out."

I accepted the key to my unknown future. "Thanks."

This retrieval was much simpler since it didn't involve a headlamp and my pick set. Back in my office, I opened the folder I'd pulled and found three memos in it. As I read down the first one, my feelings tangled in an unimaginable jumble.

I re-read it twice.

As a corporation, it is imperative that we accept full responsibility for the fire, not withstanding the accident report. Our position is clear. Allied Insurance is instructed to not dispute the company's liability in any proceeding, in any jurisdiction. Our official position is that the accident is due to management's failure to ensure a safe working environment—in particular the CEO's waiver of rules meant to forestall accidents of this nature and prevent outcomes such as these.

It was what I'd hoped to find months ago, but it was a gut punch today. Dennis and his company were responsible, and I had the evidence I'd promised Mom I would find.

I'd been sleeping with the enemy. Regardless of his intentions, Dennis was directly responsible, and I'd slept with the man. My stomach rioted.

My dash to the bathroom was almost not quick enough. I retched my breakfast into the sink. The woman already in the room practically ran out as I did. The waves came again and again.

After several dry heaves, they finally stopped. Looking up into the mirror, all I saw was a girl with *traitor* stamped on her forehead. Rinsing the disgusting taste of my own bile from my mouth didn't improve the picture in the mirror. I'd betrayed Mom and Dad. I was a failure for allowing attraction to cloud my judgment.

Cindy entered, probably alerted by the fleeing woman that I was ruining the place. "Are you okay?"

I managed a half-smile. "I shouldn't have had leftovers for breakfast."

"Can I get you anything?"

"No. Just give me a minute."

She departed, and I was alone again with my guilt.

After washing my face, I made it back to my office and closed the door. There were two more documents to finish reading to complete my promise to Mom. The whole truth regarding my stepfather is what I'd committed to.

The next document had an odd passage.

We are committed to the welfare of our employees and their families. I allowed our employee to work afterhours on a personal project. The accident report notwithstanding, I take full responsibility for the incident, and that is our final position.

The note was intended for the insurance company again and signed by Dennis. Another nail in his coffin.

The third document, the accident report Mom had said they'd refused to provide her, wasn't as legible, so I struggled reading it.

I stopped to reread the most important section.

The fire was triggered by Mr. Davis's failure to follow well-known safety protocols. Namely, the video clearly shows Mr. Davis cleaning the bicycle frame with acetone, placing the open acetone can on the welding table, and starting to weld the bicycle frame in close proximity to the open can of solvent in clear violation of prohibitions against any flammable liquids being outside their respective fireproof cabinets while welding is performed.

I swallowed hard and continued.

It is therefore the conclusion of this committee that the accident was caused by Mr. Davis's failure to follow safety protocols well known to him. A contributing factor was management's waiver allowing Mr. Davis to weld without a second employee in the room. This waiver, although it did not contribute to the fatality, allowed the fire to cause more damage to the facility than would otherwise have been the case.

Closing the documents, I dumped the folder in my drawer. I sat back and closed my eyes. This changed everything all over again. Dad had been at fault, not Dennis. Mom had been wrong. *"The fire was triggered by Mr. Davis's failure to follow well-known safety protocols."* The words stung.

After gathering my purse, I locked my office. I needed time alone to think.

"Going home?" Cindy asked as I passed her desk.

"Yeah."

"That's a good idea."

She had no idea why I felt so terrible.

Mom had been dead wrong about Dad's accident. If she'd known the truth, would she have drunk less and be alive today? There was no way to know, but the possibility haunted me.

As I punched the button for the garage level, I almost upchucked again, thinking of the damage I'd caused Dennis and the company.

≈

Dennis's call came an hour after I got home.

"Cindy said you weren't feeling well. Anything I can do?"

There was no right answer to that question.

"No. I just shouldn't have had the leftover shrimp," I lied.

What was one more lie on top of what I'd already done to hurt him?

I heard the sound of a door closing.

"I could come over tonight, if you feel like breaking our rules."

"That's sweet, but I'll be okay by tomorrow."

Another lie. I'd have to find a way to tell him, and that couldn't happen without a face to face—and without me owning up to what I'd done.

The worst part of all this kept gnawing at me.

Dad had been trying to fix my bike when it had happened.

# CHAPTER 31

*DENNIS*
*(Four Days Later)*

FINALLY IT WAS FRIDAY. THE WEEK WAS ALMOST OVER, AND TONIGHT I COULD RELAX across the dinner table from my girl.

Mid-morning, Ed Baird was at my door.

"Do you have a sec?" he asked. "I have something on that matter you asked me to look into."

I waved him in.

He closed the door behind him and brought a folder to my desk. "I think I found the conduit to Cartwright." He took a seat.

I leaned forward. This could turn out to be a much better week if we had a lead on Cartwright. "Go ahead."

"We spent a lot of time and effort on this last week."

"I'm sure you did. Now what did you find?" I'd save the back patting for later.

He pulled out a photo and laid it on my desk. The photo wasn't very good quality—actually it was pretty crappy.

I looked up from the picture. "What am I looking at?"

He pointed to the window of the restaurant. "These two women having lunch. One is a girl who works here, and she's meeting with a person from Cartwright's firm."

"Who?"

"The lady's name is Suzanne Murtog." He pulled out another picture. This one was clearer, of a woman going into a building.

"But I don't see her face."

"It's the same woman from the restaurant, I guarantee it. And Cartwright has an office on the fourteenth floor of that building."

"I meant who did she meet with?"

"Jennifer Hanley."

I quickly schooled my expression to hide the horror I felt. "Jennifer Hanley?"

"That's right. I followed her myself from our building to the restaurant."

I went back to the first picture. "I can't make her out through this window."

"Trust me. It's her on the left."

A few seconds later, I decided it could be her, but it wasn't a good enough picture or from the right angle to be sure. "You're sure?"

"Absolutely."

I sat back. It didn't make any sense. Jennifer didn't have a reason to meet with the Cartwright people. "There has to be some mistake."

He produced two printouts from the folder. "Here's a list of top employees at First Century, which is a Cartwright subsidiary."

Suzanne Murtog was highlighted on the page.

Another sheet landed on my desk. "And this is from their website." It had her name again and a head shot. "I can interrogate Hanley this afternoon."

I shook my head. "Not so fast."

"If you prefer, I'll loop Mr. Fisher in, and he could talk with her instead."

I wasn't going that route either. "No, thanks. Let me figure out what to do next. I'll be in touch."

Disappointment crossed his face. He surely had planned on some high-pressure interrogation to round out his investigation. Probably something straight out of a TV show—bright lights and lots of yelling.

He placed the folder on my desk. "I'll leave these with you." He stood.

"Good work, Ed. Thanks."

"It's what you pay me for. I'll keep digging on this."

A minute later I was alone with a pit in my stomach and questions that needed answers.

～

*JENNIFER*

WHEN I'D PASSED DENNIS IN THE HALLWAY JUST BEFORE LUNCH, I'D GOTTEN THE mean boss treatment again. He'd scowled and looked away as he went into his office—worse even than ignoring me.

After fuming over it for a few minutes, I sent him a text.

ME: Can we talk?

I also texted Cindy to tell her I wanted to talk to Dennis.

Ten minutes later, I called her. "Did you tell him I needed a few minutes?"

"He knows, but I'll tell him again when he comes out."

That meant he was alone in his office, so ignoring me had been deliberate.

I went back to my office and closed the door.

Over lunch down the street, I thought back to what I could have done. Staring out the window didn't make the answer appear. Neither did running my fingers up and down the condensation on my drink cup.

I almost puked as a dirty, sweaty construction guy passed by on the way to a booth behind me. His BO was terrible, but in my current emotional state, it didn't take much. I was a mess, and looking at my half-eaten sandwich only made it worse.

After lunch, I was specifically excluded from the meeting on the Cartwright response.

I couldn't have been imagining this. I was sure we'd agreed that there wasn't a need for the mean boss treatment anymore, so what had I missed?

If I'd said something, or done something, I couldn't put a finger on it. It wasn't like I'd forgotten his birthday. I didn't even know when it was. A brisk walk twice around the block didn't help.

By the end of the day, I'd had enough.

"Is he in there?" I asked Cindy.

"Yes, and I hope he stays there. Today started off so well, and then he nearly bit my head off at lunch time."

"Mean boss."

"Pardon?"

I grasped the door handle. "Oh, nothing." I opened the door, stepped inside, and closed it behind me.

He glanced at me only briefly before turning back to his computer. "Whatever it is, I don't have time."

Refusing to be intimidated, I walked up and took a seat across from him. "We agreed that mean boss was over."

There, I'd said it, and that should have been enough to jog his memory. It had only been last week.

"I don't have time," he repeated.

"And I don't deserve this." I sat and waited.

He typed on his keyboard, ignoring me.

"Why are you being like this again? You agreed to stop it."

He looked up with cold, piercing eyes. "That was when I thought I could trust you."

The comment froze me. "You...you can. You know that."

I'd thought he knew that. He should have known that.

729

He turned back to his monitor. "Is that so?"

The words dripped with disdain, another thing I didn't deserve.

Wracking my brain, I couldn't come up with anything that could have prompted this turnaround. "What did I do?"

"How about meeting with Cartwright?"

I cocked my head. I'd never heard anything so outrageous. "I've never even met the man."

"Not him. One of his henchmen, or should I say henchwomen?"

I straightened up. "I have no idea what the hell you're talking about."

Before I got to know him, I would have considered doing something like that, but now? No way.

"Yeah, right."

He surprised me by opening a manila folder on his desk and sliding a picture my direction. "And I suppose this isn't you?"

It was a blurry picture of the outside of Panera Bread.

I couldn't see myself in the picture anywhere. "And just which smudge is me?"

"Did you go there Tuesday afternoon?"

It took a few seconds to register. It seemed so long ago, but I put it together. "Yes," I admitted. "I was meeting a friend."

"And this is her, right?" He slid over another picture. This one was of a woman whose face you couldn't see. It could have been Suzanne. She was entering a nondescript building. "It could be, but what does that have to do with Cartwright?"

He slid another piece of paper in my direction. "Cartwright has offices in that building, and she works for him."

My mouth went dry.

The last piece of paper was a picture of Suzanne, labeled senior analyst, on a page of First Century employees.

"It says First Century."

"That's a Cartwright subsidiary."

I swallowed hard. "I had no idea. I went to undergrad with her. She just called up asking to meet for lunch. She said she was back in town and wanted to get reacquainted. She wanted me to pass her resume around."

"Security followed you to the meeting, so you can drop the innocent act."

The realization of what had transpired was like a gut punch.

Ed was fucking with me, and big time.

"If you got this from Ed Baird, you can't believe a word of it. He's just trying to screw with me...with us."

"Is that so?"

"You wanted to know who my ex-boyfriend, EB, was? EB is Ed Baird, head of security here."

That stopped him with his mouth agape.

I could see the wheels turning inside his head.

"Your ex-boyfriend?"

"That's right, and he's trying to jam me up and mess with us. She asked me to pass along her resume. I printed it out and took it down to HR, and I sent it over to Pasadena. Call them if you don't believe me."

He pondered silently. His eyes were no longer the fierce cold they'd been a minute ago, but we clearly weren't back to Denny and Angel either.

"I swear I had no idea she worked for Cartwright, and that was the only time I've seen her since college. She, Ed, and I all went to Pepperdine."

I hadn't seen the possible setup until I'd spoken the words.

Ed and I hadn't hooked up until after school, and I'd never considered him having a connection to Suzanne. But he could definitely be that sneaky. Had he set me up?

"Your ex-boyfriend?" he repeated.

I nodded. "Don't you see what's going on here? He's pulling a Melissa." I gave him a few seconds to process it all. "Who was it that said we should gather all the evidence before passing judgment?"

He rose, and in a few strides had circled the desk and pulled me to standing. "You're right. I'm sorry I was so easily taken in by it."

I looked into his eyes, which had warmed. "We're even, I guess. I used to think you were a jerk."

"I did sort of set you up with the Talbot meeting."

"Don't remind me or I might change my mind. Can we please drop the mean boss act now?"

His kiss was my answer. Things were going back to normal—whatever that was. We needed more time to get settled, established. Based on his reaction to this news, this weekend would be too early to tell him what I actually had done. I needed him to trust me more before I could apologize for how I'd hurt him. I needed to be sure he'd believe how truly sorry I was.

Leaving his office with a flush in my cheeks from the kiss, I realized I'd just been on the receiving end of a rush to judgment, and it sure sucked. I'd have to admit I'd done the same to him, and that wasn't going to be easy.

Leaving him behind was my other alternative, but he was too good to walk away from, and after what we'd shared, the guilt would eat at me anyway. I needed his forgiveness, and I had to find the right words to ask for it.

~

**Dennis**

The door closed behind her. I could still feel her on my lips, but the taste in my mouth was one of regret.

She'd called me on my shit this time, just as she had before. There was no doubt this woman was different in several ways, the most important of which was her honesty in dealing with me. She was a refreshing change.

I'd wronged her, and I intended to rectify that by showing her how I felt this weekend. The first step, however, was one I had to take at the office. I opened my door.

"Please ask Ed to come up," I told Cindy.

He arrived a few minutes later. "What can I do for you?" he asked as he closed the door behind him.

I asked him to take a seat, which he did.

"Is there anything else you want to tell me about Jennifer Hanley? Anything else I should know in relation to the report you gave me about her meeting with somebody from Cartwright?"

His eyes flashed fear. "I don't know what you mean."

I spoke slowly so there would be no misunderstanding. "Did you date her?"

He swallowed and nodded. "For a while."

"And you didn't think that was relevant?"

He sat up straighter. "No. What I gave you was factual. Did she say she didn't meet with the Murtog lady?"

I took in a breath. "No, but that's not the point. Have you been texting her since you...since you stopped seeing each other?"

He nodded. "Yes, but that has nothing to do—"

"Even though she asked you to stop?"

He didn't respond to that, but I knew the answer. It had everything to do with his accusation against Jennifer.

I pointed the door. "Next time you bring me something having to do with her, I want to be certain it doesn't have even a hint of your personal feelings attached to it. Are we clear?"

He stood. "Perfectly."

"Ed, I still want you putting a full-court press on this Cartwright thing. Just don't bring me anything half-baked."

He nodded. "Got it." He left without another word.

# CHAPTER 32

*JENNIFER*
*(Three Weeks Later)*

DENNIS AND I WALKED BACK ALONG THE BEACH PATH AFTER A LATE DINNER SUNDAY night. This was our fifth weekend together, and it seemed like so long ago that I'd been surprised by the kiss in his office meant to piss off Melissa.

All had been quiet on the Melissa front since the fountain incident, and Dennis thought perhaps that night had used up a month or two of her anger. He'd also confided in me that our relationship would likely cost him in his upcoming court battle with her.

That conversation had brought up conflicting emotions. I felt bad about hurting him in front of the judge, but nothing could have made me happier than knowing he felt I was worth it.

It had been an unreal journey from that day to here. I would have laughed at it as impossible if I'd read it in a magazine, but here I was, arm in arm with the master of all he surveyed. The king of the jungle had chosen me, claimed me, and showed me what happiness could be like.

The dreariness of my past life paled in comparison to my future. Weeks ago I would have laughed at the thought of a future that included Dennis, but now I couldn't imagine life without him. The only cloud on my horizon was the conversation I knew we needed to have about my past actions. So far, each weekend had been better than the last. That string would be broken when I came clean, as I knew I had to.

Monday we would be back at work, ignoring each other. And it would be another five days before we could express our feelings again on Friday night. Wednesday and Thursday had become the hardest days for me. Every time someone at work mentioned hump day, I had to control my urge to march into Dennis's office and hump him again. My one introduction to office sex over his desk had been beyond naughty and exciting.

I shivered, remembering the danger of it.

He tightened his arm around me. "What's up?"

"Nothing."

"Cold?"

"No, I just don't want this to end."

He stopped and turned me toward him. "This isn't ending. We're just beginning." His eyes held mine.

Even in the dim light, I could see the sincerity on his face. "I meant the weekend."

"Oh... Me, too. You know, we could take this to the next level and tell people."

I'd originally told myself three months of hiding our relationship would probably be enough, but after a month of this, I wasn't sure I could keep it up for another two.

He kissed my forehead. "You're not ready yet, are you?"

"No. Not quite." I did like the sound of the next level, though.

"I can wait. You know I'll do anything for you, Angel."

The name warmed me every time. "I know you think it's stupid. Can you forgive me for not being ready yet?"

"It's not stupid. It's how you feel, and I'd forgive you anything. You know that."

I smiled. I'd need that forgiving attitude when I got up the nerve to tell him what I'd done. And if I didn't get it, I wasn't sure what I'd do.

For now, we resumed our walk to the beach house.

Two more months of office secrecy loomed like an eternity.

∼

*Dennis*

My phone rang, and when I pulled it out, Serena's face graced the screen. I showed it to Jennifer before answering.

"Hi, Nina." She hated me reminding her of her childhood nickname.

"Can I come over? I need to talk."

The fact that my greeting hadn't gotten a response was not a good sign.

"I'm tied up right now. How about lunch tomorrow?"

"She's there, isn't she?"

I ignored her question. "What's the problem?"

"Yeah, tomorrow works. We need to talk about Cartwright."

"What about Cartwright?"

"Lunch then. Bye, and my regards to your girl."

"Bye." I ignored the comment about Jennifer—denying it wouldn't have helped. I put the phone away.

Jennifer looked up. "You can go talk to her if you need to. I'll be fine."

I pulled her along the path. "You're my priority tonight. She can wait till tomorrow."

"Want to talk about it?"

I shook my head. The mention of Cartwright had ruined my mood, and I needed a dose of my Angel.

～

JENNIFER

WE AMBLED DOWN THE PATH IN SILENCE.

"It's nothing," Dennis finally said. "Serena wants to talk about Cartwright, and nothing having to do with that family ever ends up being good news."

Cartwright had been a thorn in his side, and now it was affecting his sister somehow.

"Are you worried about the meeting?"

Cartwright had requested a meeting with Dennis, and so far he'd put them off.

"*Worried* isn't the right word."

"Nervous?"

"Yeah, that works. I have to fend him off, or a lot of people will pay the price."

As usual, Dennis was focused on the effect others would feel, not what it would cost him.

When we got back to the house, I went to get some wine. "White or red?"

He picked up the remote. "White."

"Sweet or dry?" That was as far as my wine knowledge went, although Dennis was teaching me a little more every week.

"Not sweet."

I pulled out a bottle of pinot grigio he'd promised wasn't sweet and unwrapped the foil top.

Dennis scrolled through movie choices. "What do you feel like?"

I put the lip of the bottle up to the wine opener and squeezed the grips to hold it. "Something light and funny."

We'd watched one of the Fast and Furious movies last night, and a change would be good. I pulled the handle forward, and in a quick move, the opener threaded the corkscrew in and pulled the cork out.

"How's *Miss Congeniality*?"

"Works for me." I poured the glasses and brought them over.

As I snuggled in next to my man, the movie started to play.

I clinked my glass to his. "To CC."

"Huh?"

"Conquering Cartwright."

He smiled, and we both drank heartily.

The movie started heavy on the comedy, but then added a little suspense, since nobody knew who the bad guy was.

Dennis laughed when Sandra screamed at the bikini wax scene.

I cringed. I'd been there and knew how painful it could be.

In the end, Sandra caught the bad guy and rescued the pageant. Every time I'd watched this before, I'd wished to be her, the heroine who saved the day.

"What is it?" Dennis asked.

"What?"

"You're off somewhere else. What's up?"

"Just thinking how wonderful you are."

He chuckled. "I'm not buying it, but the flattery is appreciated."

I brought my lips a mere inch from his. "I want to give you something, but there's a condition."

He rubbed his nose against mine in the way I loved. "What's the condition?"

I ran my hand up his inner thigh. "You have to do whatever I say." The agreement wouldn't come easily—giving up control was his biggest hang-up.

He swallowed hard. "Okay."

I pushed away. "Get undressed."

Glee wrote itself across his face.

I went to the kitchen and found the little chocolate pudding containers near the back of the fridge. Two and a spoon would do.

His clothes were in a pile at his feet when I returned. His member was hard and upright with anticipation.

My wetness matched his hardness. We were both ready. I pointed to the bedroom. "On the bed."

His cock bobbed as he walked, and I admired his tight, white ass all the way to the bedroom. He climbed onto the bed and sat up.

I put the pudding down and slowly pulled my shirt off.

His eyes glued to my chest as I reached behind me and undid the hooks of my bra. He scanned me, as if willing me to go faster.

I slowed down. Clamping my arms to my sides to hold the bra in place, I pulled the shoulder straps off one by one, then held it a few seconds before allowing the garment to fall away.

His eyes popped, as they always did.

My boobs were my secret weapon. The right jiggle—especially braless in the morning with my nipples showing through a T-shirt—never failed to command his attention.

I moved one of the puddings to the nightstand. "Lay back and interlace your fingers behind your head."

He hesitated before he did as I asked.

I brought a small spoonful of the pudding to his lips.

He sucked the spoon dry.

Setting it down, I slipped off my shorts. In just panties, I picked up the pudding and straddled his thighs.

The lion emerged in his eyes as my breasts bobbed in front of him.

He moved to cradle them when I waggled my shoulders.

I whacked his hand hard with the spoon.

"Ow."

"Behind your head. Denny needs to behave, or he won't get his treat."

His hands went back where they needed to be, but his eyes stayed glued to my breasts.

I dabbed a bit of the chocolate on one nipple and leaned forward to offer it to him.

He licked, and sucked, and licked.

It was heavenly, and I didn't know which of us was enjoying it more. It didn't matter. I scooted my pussy forward, over his hard length, with a single layer of soaked fabric between us.

I put some pudding on the other nipple and was treated to the same delicious sucking. We went back and forth until the first container was emptied.

Each time he strained up to reach a nipple, I pulled away until he behaved and let me offer myself to him at my own pace.

I climbed down and pulled my panties off before grabbing the second container. I dabbed a bit on his shaft. It sprang as I did.

"Hold still."

"I can't. It's cold."

"Don't be a baby." I moved to lick the pudding off.

His groans were like music to my ears as I added a little here and a little there, followed by slow licks of his throbbing cock.

"You're killing me, Angel."

"Baby." I applied the last spoonful and ever so slowly licked him clean. Putting aside the pudding container and spoon, I straddled him and leaned forward to rub my breasts over his chest.

He strained upward to meet me.

I pushed him down again.

I sat up and ran my slick slit the length of his cock. A wonderful jolt of pleasure ran through me as my clit slid over his tip.

The hitch in his breath showed he felt it too.

I ran myself up and down his length, coating him with my wetness, and pressing down firmly every time I reached the tip. Electricity shot through both of us.

The lust in his eyes and the smile that ate his face told me all I needed to know—this was nearly unbearable for him.

He was nearing the edge, yet still behaving.

I loved that I could drive him crazy like this, the same way he did me with his tongue.

I continued to work him, stopping and starting again, using his moans and breathing as my gauge of how much he could take. I leaned forward to offer him a nipple.

He rewarded me with a hard suck.

I offered the other breast. "You said you want to take it to the next level."

He nodded.

"I want to go bare."

His eyes widened at the prospect. "I'm clean, if that's what you're asking."

"Me too, and I'm on the pill."

In an instant, he'd rolled us over and was on top.

I'd unleashed the animal, and I was no longer in charge. The change suited me fine as he entered me, skin on skin. The primal beasts in each of us took over, and there was no controlling this, no slowing it down. That time had passed.

We quickly found our rhythm, and I couldn't hold off as I ground against him to get the clit pressure I sought. He speared me deeply. Each thrust sent shocks all the way to my toes.

"You feel so fucking good," he groaned, breaking his silence.

He worked me quickly to the edge.

The shocks of pleasure overloaded all my nerves. My blood sang, and I came with a vengeance, clamping around him.

He went stiff and followed me over the cliff with a loud groan.

The pulsing of his naked cock inside me without the latex was a special closeness. It soothed me as all my muscles went limp.

He collapsed on top of me, but quickly moved to the side, sparing me his full weight.

I rubbed his back and scratched his scalp as we slowly got back our breath. We fit together, and things couldn't have been better.

He stroked my hair. "That was terrific."

I stretched to kiss him. "Get me a washcloth, and we can do it again."

He slipped out and off me, and returned with a warm, wet washcloth for me. "Give me a little while to recover."

I cleaned myself and set the cloth aside. "What? No stamina?"

He lay down beside me. "Very funny."

I snuggled up to my man.

Before I drifted off to sleep after our second round, I thought back to tonight's movie.

Tonight I no longer wanted to be her.

Even though I couldn't save the day the way Sandra had, I realized I had something more important. I was here with a man who'd told me we were only at the beginning, a man who wanted to take things to the next level.

I had something that had eluded Sandra in the movie. She'd succeeded on the job, but I'd succeeded in a more important area.

Soon, Dennis's soft, rhythmic breathing indicated he'd passed into sleepy-land.

I definitely had something that had eluded Sandra. I had Dennis. He was a real man, and most importantly, he was my man, and he knew I was his.

Life couldn't get any better.

I still had to find a way to talk to Dennis about what I'd done, but that seemed so long ago now, and it could wait. Maybe next month I'd find the right words.

In a flash, I realized I might be able to have both. I couldn't defeat Cartwright for Dennis the way Sandra had saved the day, but I might be able to do something nobody else could. I might be able to unmask Hydra. That would make the talk easier, wouldn't it?

# CHAPTER 33

*JENNIFER*

MONDAY MORNING I TRUDGED UP THE STAIRS IN OUR APARTMENT BUILDING. GOING latex free had meant even more *exercise* and less sleep than before.

Sleeping at my place during the week meant I could catch up. The weekdays were for helping Ramona with Billy, but starting Friday night, Dennis and I could escape again to his beach house.

So far nobody at work had figured it out, that I could tell.

We'd fallen into a routine the last three weeks. No PDA, no lunches or dinners together—except for the occasional lunch meeting in a conference room with others present—and absolutely no mean boss.

He'd offered to have me join him at Saint Helena's again last week, but Cindy had invited me to lunch that day, so I declined.

It had been three weeks since Ed had tried to torpedo me with the accusation about the Suzanne meeting, or maybe he'd even set it up. Luckily he hadn't tried anything since, and I probably had Dennis to thank for that.

The one time I'd asked Dennis about it, I'd gotten nothing but a grunt.

Dennis had crazy Melissa, and I had vindictive Ed. But, now that Ed's texting had stopped, we might be down to only one ex who was a problem.

Larry had said he thought crazy Melissa was an act, but if so, she'd perfected it. I couldn't help but think about what she might be capable of, even though she hadn't shown her face in weeks.

Every time I'd thought I was ready to broach the subject of what I'd done with Dennis, I chickened out. I convinced myself I didn't have the right words, or the setting was wrong, or we didn't have enough time, or a million other reasons to put off the inevitable.

Procrastination, thy name is Jennifer.

My latest excuse was that I would track down Hydra first, and I had a plan for that, but I needed Ramona's help.

After briefly fumbling for my keys in the hallway, I opened the door.

Billy and Ramona were eating breakfast.

Ramona looked up, with excitement on her face. "Come take a look."

I put my heavy purse down. "What is it?"

She waved me over. "We got accepted for that place on Annapurna Drive."

Billy held up Ramona's phone. "And I get my own room." Billy swiped to a picture of a bedroom when I made it to the table. "This one is mine."

The pictures were nice. The unit was clearly larger than this place.

"Which one is mine?" I asked.

Billy looked to his mother, who answered my question. "Your choice, of course."

"I think she should get the big one," Billy suggested.

His mother had a better idea. "Maybe she should get the smaller one, if she's going to be gone all the time."

I didn't have the energy for this right now. "Maybe so." In the end I knew Ramona would insist that I take the bigger one. She always had. "Well, I'm sure it's great."

"Wanna see the pool?" Billy asked.

I tousled his hair. "I have to get ready for work. You can show me tonight." I left the table for my room. "Can you help me with my hair?" I asked my sister.

"Sure." She followed me with a confused look.

I closed the door after her. "I need your help."

"Okay. What?"

"I want to tell Dennis about the...you know."

"Your sick, evil plan? You should have come clean weeks ago."

I didn't want to have the argument again. "I need your help catching Hydra."

"Your sick email buddy? I have no idea how to trace somebody on the internet."

I'd been thinking about this over the weekend. "No. I owe him a file. If I drop it off, can you watch the location on Saturday and get pictures of him for me when he picks it up?"

She sighed. "Okay. I'll see if we can move the study group to Sunday."

"Mommy, we have to go," Billy called from the other room.

I gave Ramona a hug. "Thanks a million."

She opened the door. "You know, none of this would have been necessary if you'd listened to me in the first place."

I nodded. She had a point, but arguing about my promise to Mom wouldn't get us anywhere.

"We have to put down a deposit today," she added, leaving my room. "Write down the details for me, and I'll send the money."

That needed to be job one today—making sure that apartment didn't get away from us.

While I was still getting ready, Ramona called from the door that they were leaving. "The deposit information is on the table."

I yelled back, "Have a great day."

Now, with a bigger apartment in sight and a plan for Hydra, things were really coming together.

After a final mirror check, I took the payment information Ramona had left and tucked it into my purse.

My laptop taunted me. I opened it and logged in to check my mail.

Hydra's message was dated Saturday.

> To: Nemesis666
> From: HYDRA157
> Stop stalling. Get me the file or you will regret it. Would you like me to publicize where I get my information?

Time had run out. I couldn't wait until the weekend, and I couldn't turn over the file I already had without Ramona in place. That would only be compounding my errors. I had to find a way to tell Dennis the truth.

~

*DENNIS*

SERENA FINISHED CHEWING. "I JUST HAVE TO SAY, SOMETIMES YOUR COOKING IS better than Mom's."

Lunch had been called off in favor of dinner tonight at my house. She wanted to chat about Dad, Josh, and Cartwright, and it had turned into a long discussion.

"It's just spaghetti and meatballs, for God's sake."

She raised her fork. "But you get the spices just right."

"You can't be in a hurry. You have to let the sauce marinate for a long time."

I'd seen Serena's attempts at anything with marinara sauce. They started with opening a bottle of sauce and ended with a microwave.

"Well, it's delicious, and thank you for listening to all my whining."

I put my wine glass down. "What else are big brothers for?"

Dad was still convinced that the Cartwright family had something to do with Josh's accident, and Serena worried it was turning into an unhealthy obsession.

I could understand her concern, but I didn't share it.

"I need your help," she said.

"Name it." She was family, and I'd do anything for family.

"I want you to teach me to cook chicken parmigiana."

I couldn't help but laugh.

"What's so funny?"

"Since when are you interested in cooking?" Of all my brothers and sisters, she was by far the worst cook. A tuna fish sandwich was a challenge for her.

"I need to make a special dinner."

I lifted an eyebrow. "For a special someone?"

She grimaced. "Are you gonna help me or not?"

It seemed we both had a special someone we were hiding.

"Sure. How about Thursday? Will that be soon enough?"

"Thursday would be great." She leaned her elbows on the table. "I have to say, you've been in an unusually good mood the last few weeks."

"What can I say? Things are going well at work." I didn't intend to explain that there was one person in particular responsible for that.

"What's her name?"

She often tried to catch me with a surprise question.

"Like I said—"

"Right. Things are good at work."

Last week she'd asked about Jennifer from the gala, and I'd explained our dancing close had been a dig at Melissa. Tonight I wasn't sure she was buying it anymore.

Serena pushed back and put her napkin on the table. "Thank you for this. I've got to get going."

Sometimes I had to hold her here for a while until she was safe to drive, but tonight she'd barely touched her wine.

"Stop in anytime."

"You know I'm going to find out."

I shrugged and walked her to the door. "By the way, who are you seeing right now? I want to let Dad know who to start a background check on."

Her scowl told me my question had hit the mark. She could dish it out, but she couldn't take it.

"Don't try that on me. You're just deflecting."

"So you are seeing somebody. I picked up a week-long trip for two to Hawaii at the fundraiser. It's yours if you tell me his name."

"We were talking about you." She turned to leave.

My question had gotten to her, and we both knew it. Tonight we would call it a draw.

I walked her to her car, held open the door, and got a quick hug.

She stood back and held my hand. "All joking aside, I'm here when you need an ear."

I tried to keep my expression neutral. "Thanks, but there's nothing to talk about."

Her smile and the tilt of her head told me I hadn't gotten neutral quite right. "When you're ready." She settled in to the seat. "I'll see you Thursday at six."

I nodded. "Six works." I closed the car door for her.

After seeing her off, I went back in to tend to the dishes.

"*When you're ready*," she'd said. I didn't know when that would be.

~

*JENNIFER*

AFTER THE MESSAGE THIS MORNING, IT WAS CLEAR I HAD TO CONFESS WHAT I'D DONE to Dennis, and it couldn't wait until Friday.

I'd gotten Subway for lunch and driven to the parking lot at Target to practice my speech. All afternoon I was a wreck, and I clearly couldn't put this off any longer.

After Dennis had been gone from the office for an hour, I finally got up the courage. Leaving the garage, I turned my car toward his house—the one he called the "big house." There was no turning back now.

When I reached Dennis's street, there was another car in his driveway, a pricey one. Someone else was visiting. I drove to the end of the cul-de-sac, turned around, and stopped two houses short of his across the street.

My legs shook as I turned off the motor. "I need to tell you something," I said out loud in the empty car. "I'm the mole."

My throat clenched. I'd thought this would be easier. I'd put it off, convincing myself that the more he got to know me, the less important it would seem. The shaking of my legs said otherwise.

His door opened, and he came out, walking a woman to the strange car.

She faced away from me. I couldn't recognize her from this distance. It was just someone visiting him. What was the big deal?

He held the door for her the way he did for me. He hugged her the way he did me. The instant pang of jealousy stabbed me in the heart, though I urged myself to calm down, get all the facts.

I rolled down my window but couldn't make out their words from this distance. The warm smile on his face, though, was one I knew well, and I'd thought it was reserved for me. Perhaps I was less special than I'd thought.

She backed out in her expensive car.

I hadn't expected this to be an easy conversation, but now I definitely wasn't ready. Seeing this other woman had scrambled my brain.

After her taillights disappeared around the corner, I started my shit bucket to leave. I was making comparisons? How pathetic. I pulled forward, and when I reached his house, I thought about turning in to his driveway, but chickened out. Barely able to breathe, I pulled over down the street.

I couldn't leave. I had to do this, but I couldn't do it. I was a complete mess. My head came down on the steering wheel. I didn't know the right words anymore.

A crow cawed at me from a tree branch. I couldn't understand the bird any more than Dennis would understand me right now.

# CHAPTER 34

HE OPENED THE DOOR. "JENNIFER. IT'S A WEEKDAY."

"Am I intruding?"

"Not at all. Come in." He held the door open. "Good thing you weren't ten minutes earlier. Serena just left."

His words were a relief as I entered. That I'd so misjudged the situation made me feel even worse. Why did I always jump so quickly toward the wrong conclusion?

"We have to talk," I told him.

"Sure." As soon as he closed the door, he took me into a hug, one I couldn't fully return.

With my face buried in his shoulder, I managed a few words. "I'm so sorry."

That only made him hug me tighter. He smoothed my hair with his hand. "Talk to me, Angel."

I wasn't so sure he'd be ready to hear what I had to say, because he didn't know the weighty baggage I brought with me. Baggage I'd tried to ignore for weeks now. I shivered at the realization that time might not have made this easier. As the tears came, I clung to him tighter.

I concentrated on what he'd just said. It might be the last time I heard him call me Angel, and I desperately wanted to hang on to that memory.

He pushed back far enough to lift up my chin. His eyes gazed into mine with warmth and caring. "Want to sit down?"

I nodded.

He tried to lead me to the couch, but I pulled him to the small breakfast table instead. He held my hands across the table as we sat.

I had no idea how to start. None of the words I'd practiced made sense to me now.

His kind eyes hadn't changed yet, because he didn't know my sins. "I told you, whatever it is, we can fix it. I meant that."

"I've been bad." I sounded like a child saying it that way, but I was feeling my way into this.

"That's nothing special. We've all done something bad at one time or another. But let's quantify bad. Did you kill a dozen people?"

That bit of nonsense coaxed a half-smile out of me. "No. It's not that bad."

"Then we can get past it, Angel."

I still doubted he'd want to call me that after I got this off my chest.

The warmth of his hands holding mine gave me the courage to go on. "You know the articles in the paper about the company?"

"Yeah, the ones in the *Times*?"

"They're my fault."

His grip on my hands tightened as he chuckled. "Don't be ridiculous. They're not anybody's fault. It's just some sicko who wants to torment me and everybody who works at the company."

"No, you don't understand. He got the information from me."

There. I'd said it.

His grip on me faltered as his mouth dropped open. "You what?"

The words spilled out in rapid fire. "I'm sorry. At the time, I didn't know you weren't responsible."

He let go of my hands. His words came out slowly and deliberately. "Slow down. You're not making any sense. Are you saying you provided the leaks to that Sigurd asshole?"

I nodded. "I'm sorry. I didn't know."

He sat back, and his eyes went wide with disbelief. "Why?"

"I didn't know," I repeated.

The room was suddenly cold.

The kindness in his eyes skipped through disbelief on their way to anger. "Didn't know he would write what he did? Didn't know it would hurt the company? Didn't know it would hurt me, and all the people you work with?"

The accusation that I'd wronged not just him but everybody at the company hung over me like a guillotine.

"I thought you killed my dad."

That set him back even farther in his chair as he cocked his head. "I don't go around killing people," he spat. "I don't even know your father. You're the only Hanley I've ever met."

"It's complicated. This was all before I knew you."

"And you thought it was okay to attack me because you didn't know me?

That's a stupid-ass thing to believe. Do you have any idea how many people's lives you've hurt?"

I felt even worse. "Do you remember Robert Davis?" I shivered, having to say Dad's name out loud.

His eyes narrowed for a second as he tried to recall. "Yes. But what does that have to do with you?"

"He was my stepfather."

He nodded as the memory registered. "He died in an accidental fire at the company. How could you possibly think I killed him?"

It sounded stupid now, but I had no choice. "My mother was sure it was your fault. You wouldn't let us see the accident report. I promised her I'd get to the bottom of it."

"And because you thought the company was responsible, you thought you'd take it out on all of us? That's stupid, and frankly, mean."

I deserved the criticism. "I'm here to apologize."

"Do you want to know what really happened? Or do you and your mother not care about the truth?" The words were tinged with anger.

"I know the truth now."

"I'm not sure you do. I spared your mother the knowledge that your stepfather caused his own death. And do you want to know why?"

He continued when I didn't say anything.

"I did that to maximize the insurance settlement she got. If it had been ruled his fault, your mother would have gotten almost nothing."

"We didn't know that."

He rubbed it in. "I didn't do it because I had to. I insisted on it because it was the decent thing to do for her." He shook his head. "How could you?"

I didn't have an answer. There was no way for me to repent for the sin I'd committed. "I judged you without the evidence, and that was wrong. I was wrong. I'm so sorry."

He stood. "I think you should leave."

I got up, pulled my employee badge from my pocket, and put it on the table. "I really am sorry."

"You think you can come in here say you're sorry for ruining my life and just walk away?"

I didn't understand the question. "I can't stay after what I've done."

"You can't leave the company until I say so."

"What?"

"I don't know what to think, other than I'm angry and you're stupid. I need time to process this. You stay at the company, and every time you pass someone in the hallway, think about what you've done to them, what you've cost them."

I backed away from the table.

"Take the badge with you," he ordered.

I picked it up and slunk to the door. "I didn't mean for this to happen. I'm sorry."

He shook his head, but didn't say anything.

I opened the door and closed it behind me as I walked away from the one good thing that had happened to me in years. Outside I was alone and cold. My legs were wobbly as I made my way to my car.

I hadn't known what to expect, and my stomach was about to turn itself inside out as I climbed into the driver's seat.

If this had been a movie, he would have come running out the door to tell me it would be all right. A quick glance at his door confirmed this was no movie, and a happily ever after wasn't in the cards for me.

I'd made a terrible mistake, and with that came consequences. Being told I still had to work among the people I'd wronged was a penance I hadn't seen coming. But then maybe Ramona had been right all along. My path here had been wrongheaded from the beginning, and I deserved whatever I got at this point.

My phone chirped. As I pulled it from my purse, I expected the text to be from Ramona, but it wasn't.

EB: We need to talk

Another problem I didn't need.

# CHAPTER 35

*DENNIS*

I HADN'T SLEPT HARDLY AT ALL LAST NIGHT, UNABLE TO GET MY MIND AROUND HOW Jennifer could have betrayed us all like that.

Tuesday at work was a blur. I couldn't concentrate, and by the end of the day I was glad to leave for my brother Zack's barbecue to meet his fiancée.

I arrived fashionably late.

Zack put a beer in my hand and introduced me to his lovely Brittney. She had been around when we were kids, and now that she'd come back to town, it hadn't taken long for things to heat up between the two.

I didn't expect to see either Kelly or Vincent, as they were both back east, Mom was still in Paris, but Dad and Serena were here, and Josh had made it too.

He'd been released from the hospital four days after the accident. Luckily, the brain swelling they'd worried about hadn't occurred, and he'd passed all his concussion protocols. His bruises had healed, and you couldn't even tell now that he'd been in that horrific accident.

Serena walked my way. "Where's your girl?"

"What girl?" I wasn't sure it would work with her, but I needed to keep the denial going. It was better than admitting I'd been taken in by a person trying to destroy me.

She cocked her head. "I know that look. You're trying to hide something, but it won't work."

"Yeah. You got me. I'm planning on penis-reduction surgery later in the week, but you have to keep that to yourself."

She laughed. "And disappoint half the women in LA?"

"It's so I won't hurt them."

"Very funny. You know I'm going to find out."

Bill Covington and his wife, Lauren, joined us, putting an end to Serena's interrogation.

I'd had only a short chance to catch up with the Covingtons when Dad corralled me to join him.

He re-introduced me to Doug, Brittney's brother, who had been one of Zack's friends from way back. Doug had joined the Marines and was on a short leave from Okinawa. Having been a Marine himself, Dad was enthralled with Doug's stories of his current life in the Corps.

Dad set his beer down. "Excuse me, I'm going to have another go at Zachary." He took his cane and strode toward my brother.

"What's that about?" Doug asked after Dad was out of earshot.

I lifted my bottle. "Zack hasn't escaped the family company yet, and Dad is trying to convince him to go to London for more training."

"I bet Zack can hold his own."

"We'll see. Dad can be a pretty irresistible force, if he wants to."

"I hear you got out of the family business, though."

"Yeah. It wasn't easy, but I like being my own boss."

"No orders from above, huh?"

"No direct orders, but I do work for the board, and the Wall Street bozos who take every opportunity to tell me what they think I'm doing wrong. It sucks."

Doug nodded.

"Not a one of them has run so much as a successful hot dog cart."

Doug swigged more beer.

I listened from a distance, and luckily for Zack, Dad didn't seem to be putting on the hard sell.

After a moment, Phil Patterson, another regular at our Habitat for Humanity weekends, came up and rescued Zack from Dad's clutches.

Not one to give up easily, Dad followed them into the house.

A few minutes later, Phil jogged up to us. "Dennis, you gotta fucking come to the front right now. There's news about Debbie."

I put my beer down and sprinted to the front door. Debbie was a name I hadn't heard in a very long time. We never spoke of her abduction and death.

When I reached the door, Zack and Dad were talking with a woman and a man in FBI windbreakers. Closer to the street were two sheriff's deputies.

"Phil said it's news about Debbie?" I asked breathlessly.

Phil arrived right behind me.

The short woman spoke. "We have evidence that she's alive."

"And may be involved in a bank robbery," the other agent added, which earned him a stern look from the woman.

Dad grabbed my shoulder. "Dennis, you're the oldest. You need to go out east and learn everything you can. Get back to me when you have something solid to report."

I had a better suggestion. "Vincent's already in Boston. Why don't we call him?"

Dad's jaw ticked. "You're the oldest. It's your job."

Clearly this was not up for debate. I was the oldest, and with that came responsibilities.

He turned to Zack and Phil. "In the meantime, we have a party to get back to. Not a word of this to any of the others until we know more."

Zack started to object. "But—"

Dad cut him off. "Not a word to anyone—not a single, solitary word. Understood? That means you too, Phillip."

We all nodded. Dad's tone said he was serious, and there would be no changing his mind. The decision had been made, a task had been assigned, and the rules stated—end of discussion.

In a blink, everything I'd known about Debbie's disappearance had changed. The kidnapper had died in a shootout with the authorities, and since his communications had said Debbie had less than a week of air, we'd all assumed the worst when she couldn't be located.

Dad and Uncle Seth had paid privately for a search after the FBI stopped looking, but nothing ever came of it.

We'd never known of an accomplice in Debbie's kidnapping. But if she was still alive, there had to have been one.

"We should leave Dennis to it," Dad announced as he herded the others back inside. "And I'm serious about keeping this under wraps."

I closed the door after them and spoke to the FBI agents. "I'm Dennis Benson. Debbie's my cousin. So tell me what we know."

"Special Agent Liz Parsons," the woman said, introducing herself. "And my partner, Special Agent Paul Newsom."

She offered her card.

Evidently the FBI didn't shake hands.

I accepted both agents' cards and stashed them in my pocket.

The man was obviously the junior partner here, as Parsons did the talking.

"When Deborah was abducted, her DNA was entered into the National Missing Persons Database. A search was initiated on a sample obtained in Maryland that generated a hit on Deborah's record today. The original agents on her case have retired, so we're now lead on her disappearance."

I noticed she'd switched from *abduction* to *disappearance*. "How sure are we it's her?"

"It was a total match. The sample is definitely hers."

I breathed a long sigh. After a lack of closure, this was welcome news. "You said something about a bank robbery. Was she injured?"

The agents looked at each other before Parsons continued. "She's a suspect."

"That's not possible."

Parsons held up her hand. "I understand it's a shock. But all we know at the moment is that DNA evidence collected at the scene of the robbery matches Deborah Benson."

"A shock? I told you, it's not possible she'd be involved in something like that," I argued. She was a Benson, and I knew she wouldn't have, couldn't have changed that much.

"Sir, don't get belligerent."

"Belligerent? First you guys shoot the kidnapper so we can't get her back, and now you want to accuse a helpless girl of bank robbery?"

I must have given off a dangerous vibe, because Agent Newsom braced, as if expecting me to lunge at him.

Parsons advanced on me instead. "Dennis, you need to calm down."

The switch from *sir* to *Dennis* surprised me.

"I worked with your sister-in-law Ashley in Boston, and I've met your brother Vince. I asked to be assigned to this case because I'm on your side here. This is a notification visit only. You know as much as we do at this point."

That changed my perception of the pint-sized agent, and put an item on my to-do list. I was calling Boston first thing to get the lowdown on this woman.

"The local field office in DC is working the robbery case, and that's all they've shared with us so far," Parsons said.

I took a breath and backed up, which got Newsom to relax.

"Okay, so who do I get in touch with out there?" I asked.

"We're handling the original kidnapping angle, so we'll visit DC and make a determination as soon as we can."

Shifting back to calling it a kidnapping was a step in the right direction.

"We'll see that you get introduced to the team out there, and you can discuss the bank case with them. Will that be acceptable?"

I was grateful for the Vince connection, because the federal government was now asking me if their plan was acceptable.

I nodded. "Of course."

"How soon can you get to DC?" she asked.

"Probably quicker than you can, with the company jet. I can provide transportation, if you like."

Parsons backed up. "Thanks, but we can't. Text your contact info to my number on the card, so we can connect with you in DC. We'll meet at the field office on Fourth Street Northwest."

Newsom's look said he wished they could have accepted the flight.

"Thank you." I waved as the duo departed toward their SUV and immediately texted my phone number to Parsons. I sent a second text to Newsom for good measure.

The deputies that had been at the curb then got into their vehicles as well. Apparently their time babysitting the agents was over.

Five minutes later, I made an excuse that I had to leave and wished Brittney and Zack the best. Dad had called his flight department, and his jet would be fueled and ready for the trip to DC by the time I got to the airport.

Serena caught me on the way out. "Still not going to admit it?"

"Shhh. Surgery's not till Friday."

Outside, I composed a text to Cindy.

ME: Not in the rest of the week - No calls - Jay is in charge until I return

That should allow me to concentrate on the only thing that mattered—Debbie. The next few days were not for multi-tasking.

Once in my car, I dialed Vince in Boston.

He picked up after a few rings. "Hey, big brother, what has you calling this late?"

"I need the skinny on an FBI agent who just visited us out here by the name of Liz Parsons, says she knows you and Ashley."

"Sure, I remember her. She worked with Ash before transferring to California."

"Can I trust her, and what kind of cooperation can I expect from her?"

"Hey, Ash," he yelled away from the phone. "Dennis wants to know if he can trust Liz Parsons, and will she cooperate with him?"

I heard the "*Hell yes*" part of Ashley's answer, but I didn't catch the rest.

Vince spoke into the phone again. "She'll call Liz tomorrow and make sure you get full cooperation. What's the case?"

"I can't say."

"Give me a break. You're not keeping it from me. Ash can find out in ten seconds."

"You have to promise to keep this to yourself. Just you and Ashley, nobody else—Dad's orders."

"Okay."

"I'm coming to check out evidence that Debbie is still alive."

He was silent for a second. "Deb?"

"Yeah. I can't say any more. I'll let you know when I have something solid."

"Holy shit. You can count on Ash to make sure the Bureau is cooperative."

"Please ask Ashley not to call. The whole thing is sensitive at this point. For the family's sake, this needs to stay under wraps."

"Okay, if that's the way you want to play it. Look, Liz owes us big time, and if you need anything from her and you want a little leverage, ask her if she remembers Kirk Willey."

"What about him?"

"Just mention the name. Like I said, she owes us. That should be enough to get you any help she can arrange, and she can be pretty damned resourceful."

"Thanks. I won't use it unless I have to."

We hung up after I refused again to tell him any more, and he assured me he'd keep Ashley under control.

My mind returned to the person I'd misjudged: Jennifer. My feelings were a jumbled mess, and I doubted tonight would be any better in terms of restful sleep.

Everything had gone to shit in the last month. Josh shot at, Melissa attacking, Cartwright after me, and now Jennifer undermining me. What had I done to deserve this hell?

Maybe finding Debbie would turn my luck around.

I noticed the text as I was boarding Dad's jet. It had come earlier, but I hadn't heard it at the party.

CINDY: Jay says the Cartwright Group wants to meet tomorrow afternoon.

One more thing I didn't need right now. I typed my response.

ME: No fucking way

I didn't hit the send arrow. Instead I retyped it.

ME: No meetings - No calls

The first version more clearly matched my mood, but I didn't need to take this out on Cindy.

Aboard Dad's jet, the seats were comfortable leather, and the glass of wine I helped myself to was perfectly chilled. But nothing about this trip felt right.

I was leaving town right when I needed to talk to Jennifer. I needed to sort this out. How could it work between us if I couldn't trust her?

After another sip of wine, I decided to focus on tomorrow instead of yesterday.

Finding evidence that Debbie was still alive after all these years created a slew of uncomfortable questions. Where had she been all this time?

If the kidnapping had been about ransom, why hadn't there been another demand after the first foiled attempt? The fact that there'd been a shootout with the FBI might have answered that, but these days kidnappers could demand untraceable Bitcoin payments and not risk being followed from a money drop. With our family's resources, they could have demanded a king's ransom, but they hadn't.

If this wasn't about money, had the original ransom been a diversion, or merely an added bonus to their goal of child abduction? That thought sent a chill down my spine.

What had Debbie had to endure all these years? Jaycee Dugard was the only long-term child kidnapping survivor that came to mind. Her ordeal had lasted 18 years. Elizabeth Smart had escaped after eighteen months, Jamye Closs had escaped after three months. But by far, the majority of child abductions that lasted over a month didn't end well.

Deb had only been five when they took her. Would she even recognize her own name at this point?

Then the specter of Patty Hearst raised its ugly head. Could Debbie have joined her kidnappers?

# CHAPTER 36

*DENNIS*

THE FLIGHT HAD BEEN MOSTLY TURBULENCE-FREE, AND THE RIDE INTO TOWN WAS A quick one in the darkness.

Yet when sunlight began filtering around the edges of the blackout curtains Wednesday morning, I'd only managed a bit of fitful sleep.

After showering, I went downstairs for an early breakfast. I needed something to keep me busy. My thoughts had bounced from what Jennifer had confessed Monday night to the Patty Hearst scenario as it related to Debbie, and back again. As the cycle repeated, I only felt worse.

Hearst had been raped and threatened with death. And yet she'd still gotten jail time for participating in a bank robbery with her captors. That didn't bode well for Debbie.

The text from Liz Parsons arrived while I was eating.

PARSONS: Noon meet at 601 4th St. NW ask for Boxer

I tapped out my response.

ME: I'll be there

If I had to wait till lunchtime to get started, I could hit the gym and burn off a little nervous energy while muddling through my feelings about Jennifer and what she'd done. When it rained it certainly poured.

I took a minute to call my sister Kelly.

"Hey, Dennis," she answered. "I hear from Serena you've got a new girl."

Just what I didn't need.

I ignored the jab. "I flew in last night for a customer meeting. Want to do dinner?"

Her hesitation was palpable. "Dinner?"

"Yeah, you know, food, wine, family."

"Sure." Her voice betrayed her.

"Is everything all right?"

"Sure. I've just got stuff going on."

Whatever stuff she had going on, I needed to hear about it.

"It's your town—you pick a place, and I'll call you later."

I gave her a brief Josh update, and we ended the call.

AFTER MY WORKOUT, I LEFT THE HOTEL FOR MY WALK TO THE FBI FIELD OFFICE, which wasn't far. A few blocks down Massachusetts Avenue and a right turn on 4th Street brought me to the building. Just like every other government building in town, it was built with granite, not the steel and glass that would've been common in California. They loved their granite here in DC. Even the curbs of the streets were granite blocks instead of the simple formed concrete we used on the west coast.

I took the right-hand doorway marked visitors, which led to the expected security check—much like going through the airport, except these guys all packed weapons.

Telling them I was here to see Boxer got me a reprimand for not calling him Special Agent. Apparently everybody in the FBI was a Special Agent.

I was escorted to a conference room on the fourth floor, where Parsons and Newsom were eating sandwiches.

Parsons looked up. She noticed me looking at their roller bags in the corner. "We didn't get a meal on the flight."

"I told you I'd beat you here."

She took the final bite of her sandwich and didn't respond.

Newsom pointed to a chair. "The DC team should be here in a moment."

I chose the seat next to Parsons.

A few minutes later, two more suits joined us.

The first one offered his card. "Special Agent Neil Boxer."

I accepted it and gave him mine. "Dennis Benson."

I recognized the second agent before he said a thing.

He offered his card. "Special Agent Adam Cartwright."

The same Adam Cartwright who had fought me many years ago—and the son of my current corporate enemy. My luck sucked.

We exchanged cards, and I pasted on a smile. "It's been a long time." I hadn't known or cared what had become of him after high school.

Adam nodded with cold eyes that said he hadn't forgotten. "It has."

The glance I got from Parsons indicated she'd noticed the frostiness. "Neil, why don't you run us through what you have?"

"Adam's lead on this," Boxer told her.

She shrugged.

Adam smugly opened up a laptop and with a few keystrokes, the monitor at the end of the table came alive. "Let's start with the outdoor feed."

The image wasn't as clear as they looked on TV shows, but we could see the street, people, and traffic.

Adam began to narrate. "Here's where they pull up."

He stopped the feed when a dark, older-model Chevy pulled to the curb. He ran it forward.

"Two suspects get out, and the driver remains." The two moved across the frame to the area of the door. "One vehicle, three robbers this time. Two go inside, and one drives. Next we go to the inside feeds."

The screen split into four viewing angles, and in the upper-right frame, the two from the car entered through the glass doors.

"Here we have a man and a woman. The woman is your vic," Adam continued. He moved the video forward a bit. "Here they pull out guns and start issuing commands."

In the next several frames, the customers all panicked and started getting down on the ground. There was no audio, but the video was clear. They were ordered to the floor.

"He fires one shot into the ceiling for effect, and the woman goes to the tellers to collect the cash."

On the video, the male robber waved his gun at the woman, motioning her to the line of tellers, and then trained it back on the customers.

"Hold it," Newsom said.

Adam halted the video.

Newsom pointed. "Why is the man masked and the woman not?"

Adam shrugged. "She's not smart enough, is my guess."

Parsons put a hand on my arm as a warning before I could protest.

Adam started the video again. "These three are amateurs, dangerous amateurs. The driver and the man have pulled off two other jobs nearby, but this is the first one where they bring her along." He pointed at Debbie on the screen. "She's our best lead so far to get this group. Let's go on and see the rest."

The video continued as the woman put the gun in her coat pocket, then stopped, probably surprised, and looked straight at the camera for a second before going down the line, collecting cash in a duffle bag. Her face was pale, and she reminded me of the way I remembered Debbie... But then she'd been five at the time, and her most notable characteristics had been the tiny birthmark on the back of her neck and the green in her eyes.

The quick video shot wasn't clear enough to determine the presence of either of those things.

The tellers appeared scared as they handed over the money, and some of the customers were squirming a bit on the floor.

He stopped the video again. "This is where it went wrong."

He restarted the video as the woman brought the bag back to the man. Then the man turned to his right and fired a shot. A teller dropped to the floor in a separate frame, and the others dove behind the counters.

He stopped the playback again.

"What's the teller's condition?" Parsons asked.

"Stable," Boxer replied.

"Good thing he was a terrible shot. We've been worried about exactly this, because the guy likes to shoot his gun," Adam added.

I hadn't seen anything to provoke the gunman, and all that ran through my head was the Patty Hearst scenario.

"Why did he shoot?" Newsom asked, echoing my question. "Get anything from the witness statements?"

Parsons leaned over to whisper. "This is not good."

I nodded. No matter how it had started, she had joined in the robbery, and when she was found, she'd be treated as the accomplice, not the victim, especially with a shooting involved. She hadn't pulled the trigger, but that wouldn't matter to the prosecutors. The circumstances were damning.

"Don't know. Maybe she said something, or moved too fast," Adam answered. "So that's the first screwup, and here's the second."

He restarted it and the pair left, the man followed by the woman.

"What did we miss?" Parsons asked.

Adam backed it up and went forward in slow motion. The man turned, and the woman leaned over a bit, then straightened and followed.

"See it?" He backed it up and restarted it.

On the second try, Parsons saw it. "She spit on the floor."

"That's right. Forensics pulled DNA from that spit, and that's when you got the call."

"Why did she do that?" Newsom asked.

Adam shrugged. "Don't know. Like I said, stupid. Once we catch her, we got a sure conviction on the robbery and attempted murder—thanks to DNA, because we got no prints at any of the scenes."

"The car?" Parsons asked.

Boxer shook his head. "Stolen plates, no defining decals, a dent in the right front is all we have to go on so far."

"Video of them casing it ahead of time?" Newsom asked.

Adam stiffened. "As hard as it is for you west coast whiz kids to believe, we do know what we're doing. We checked the old footage, back six weeks. So far nothing, but we're still working it. Like I said, amateurs. This is a new crew. They got a little money out of the heists, so they'll be back and shooting other people if we don't find them first. Sorry you had to make the trip out, but we've got it from here, and we'll let you know when we catch her."

He hadn't used the word *find*. Instead he'd said *catch*.

I couldn't believe he'd just dismissed us like that.

"Kidnapping takes priority," Newsom said.

"That was yesterday. Already ran it up to the AD. Because of the shots fired, the robbery takes priority, and we have the lead."

"Assistant Director," Parsons told me, explaining what AD meant.

"What do you have that can help us find her?" Adam asked.

"Nothing at all," Parsons answered. "Kidnapped at five years old. At the time it was presumed to be a single kidnapper who died after the ransom pickup. When no further communications came, the child was assumed deceased. Until now."

Boxer looked at me. "And no communications with the family since then?"

I shook my head. "Not a one."

Adam shut down the video. "Thank you for your time, then."

I couldn't believe that was it. There had to be more. "I'd like updates as you get more."

He scoffed. "I'll let you know when we catch her."

"She's my cousin, and a victim here," I complained.

He scowled. "She's a suspect. The victim is the lady in the hospital who took a bullet."

Parsons interceded. "She's both. The kidnapping is still open, and she's the victim in that. You can send me the updates, and I'll pass them along."

"Sure." Adam sighed.

"And," I added, "I'd like a hard copy of the frame where we see her face."

Parsons beat Adam to it. "Not a problem. I'm sure the family would like to see what she looks like after all these years."

Boxer frowned—even he thought Adam was being an ass.

Fifteen minutes later, Parsons, Newsom, and I were outside on the sidewalk.

Parsons stopped not far from the door. "Time to go home and wait. At least you got a picture."

"That's all? We don't get more? What about witnesses? They might be able to tell us something."

Newsom answered for her. "He got to the AD and got the lead assigned to him, so that's it. And, I heard he was a…"

Parson's scowl stopped him mid-sentence. "It doesn't matter."

I couldn't live with that. "What do you mean it doesn't matter?"

"Because they have the boots on the ground here. They get the credit if they find her, and the shit if they don't. All of that means…" She stopped while another local agent walked by. "That means they'll work hard on it, which is what we want. Boxer and Cartwright will work the team hard to find her, trace the car, track down sightings. Those are *his* leads right now. If he gets told to report to us, he'll drag his feet, resources will go to other cases, and we won't get anywhere."

She was short on height, but not on savvy. Her analysis was solid.

"Anyway," Newsom said. "You can call your friend Cartwright, and maybe he can give you a little insight."

I shook my head. I wasn't going into particulars. "He's not my friend. If I show up missing, he's the first one you should question."

Parsons chuckled. "Then it's a good thing you're not sticking around to annoy them." She cocked an eyebrow the way my sister did when she had a zinger. "And they missed the most important part."

Newsom asked the question for me. "What?"

She smiled. "When was the last time you spit on a marble floor inside?"

"Never," I answered.

Parsons nodded. "Exactly. She didn't have a mask, she looked straight into the camera, and then she spit on the floor after the guy turned his back. She wanted to be ID'd. Smart girl. This is still a kidnapping investigation."

That put an entirely different spin on today.

~

*JENNIFER*

WEDNESDAY, AFTER LEAVING WORK EARLY, I GOT THAT SAME ODD FEELING THAT I WAS being watched. Looking over my shoulder, I didn't see anyone or anything out of the ordinary. But nothing had felt right since the night I'd tried and failed to explain myself to Dennis. Every person I encountered in the company made me feel the same awkwardness. Did they suspect what I'd done? Were they watching me in order to catch me in the act?

Dennis had left town last night—that was all I could get out of Cindy today. She either didn't want to say any more, or really didn't know. I couldn't tell which.

After shucking my heels, I wandered to the cupboard and located the bottle of Jim Beam Ramona had hidden away. I poured the first glass. It was time to determine how many it took to deaden the guilt I felt.

My phone still held the latest text from Ed, which I'd ignored. He now represented another level of problem for me to deal with—eventually.

EB: I know what you have been doing - we need to talk

I deleted it.

It didn't matter anymore what Ed knew or didn't know. I'd told Dennis the awful truth, and no suspicion of Ed's could be worse than that. It didn't matter if he knew when I'd started seeing Dennis, or how often. That embarrassment didn't matter anymore.

Dennis's command to stay at work had seemed odd at first, but now I understood it. With every person I passed in the hall or saw in a conference room or the cafeteria, I was reminded of his question. *"What have they done to deserve the way you treated them?"* I'd not just failed them, I'd sabotaged them. Though meaning to strike at Dennis, I'd hit the company and all the employees. And, worst of all, their families.

A stinging gulp of the amber liquid took my mind off the problem for a second. But the sting was replaced by warmth in my stomach, and my mind returned to the darkness.

In the cafeteria at lunch, I'd overheard a conversation about how one person's plan to buy a house had to be put on hold. He'd planned to use his stock options for the down payment. There wasn't anything I could do to fix that. None of it was fixable. It had all been avoidable though, if only I'd listened to Ramona months ago when Hydra had first approached me.

Why hadn't I listened?

Why had I put my faith in Mom's anger instead?

It was so obvious, in retrospect. She'd lashed out in fury and despair, and I'd allowed myself to get swept up in it. For what? To accomplish what?

Vengeance that was misplaced, and worse than that, so misdirected that it affected innocent members of the company I worked for, my teammates?

The door opened as I took another gulp.

Ramona closed the door behind her. "You're home early."

Billy ran over to give me a hug.

I set the tumbler down. "How was school, Bill?"

After the hug he grinned. "I got an A on spelling today."

"That's great. Can you spell pizza?"

"T-A-S-T-Y."

"Perfect, and I'll only put half the olives on because you aced your test."

"No olives," he countered.

"Half," Ramona said. She gave me the stink eye for the bottle in front of me. Billy ran off.

"What's got you down in the dumps?"

I looked over to see that Billy was far enough away. "I fucked up."

I hadn't told her anything last night.

She'd been busy studying for a test, and if I'd started, we would have been up half the night. If that had affected her test, I would have been the cause of another disaster.

She joined me on the couch. "Let's hear it."

"First, how was the test?"

"Hard. Good thing I spent all last night studying. Eloise told me she didn't 'cuz she thought she had it down cold. Bad move."

Hearing that made me extra glad I'd held off.

"So what's got you into the hard stuff?" she asked.

I sniffed. "Dennis. I went to see him."

She waited silently for more.

I stared at the little liquid left in my tumbler. It didn't hold any answers. "I told him what I did."

She gasped and moved closer. "And it didn't go well, huh?"

"He told me to get out of his house."

She sighed. "You sort of knew that would happen."

"I thought it would be easier. I thought as we got closer, what I did before would be less important."

She put her arm around me. "So what happens now? Do you have to leave the company?"

She nicely didn't remind me that she'd warned me I couldn't have it both ways.

I gulped down the last of the bourbon. "He won't let me leave yet. He said I need to be around the people I hurt."

"Huh?"

"The other people that work at the company."

"Oh."

"I hadn't thought about how it would affect them. But at lunch..." I sniffled. "...I overheard someone saying he couldn't buy the house he wanted to because our stock was down. I never thought..." I didn't finish the sentence.

Ramona leaned forward to pour more bourbon into the glass, and then she took a sip. "That sucks."

I couldn't hold the tears back. "I really fucked up."

She handed me the glass.

I gulped some more down. It didn't alleviate the pain. "What do I do?"

"You finish the glass, and another if you want. Then you find a movie to take your mind off it, go to sleep, and in the morning you get back up and deal with life. One foot in front of the other. That's all any of us can do."

I nodded and sipped the drink. "He was the best thing that ever happened to me."

She held me. "Do you love him?"

I nodded. "So much it hurts."

"Then talk to him. Try to work it out."

"He's out of town."

"Talk to him when he gets back, then. He's got to be hurt by what you did. If you get a paper cut, you suck on your finger and go on a few seconds later. If you stub your toe, you curse and jump around on one foot for a minute or two before you can walk again. The time to get over something changes with how big the hurt is. You can't expect him to get over this in a few minutes."

"You think he'll ever forgive me?"

She took a deep breath. "That's something even he probably doesn't know yet."

I nodded.

She got up. "How about if I make the pizza and you find a movie?"

I scrolled through the choices and settled on the same movie I'd seen a while ago: *Two Weeks Notice*. At least in that one things had worked out in the end.

I was about to pour another glass when I decided it could wait until bedtime. I'd need all the help I could get finding sleep tonight.

~

DENNIS

"I DIDN'T EXPECT YOU BACK SO SOON," DAD SAID.

We sat in the Atlantic Aviation conference room at the airport. I'd left DC quickly after being told twice by Parsons that staying would only make things worse.

"The agents out there weren't going to let me stick around to look over their shoulders, and Kelly called off our dinner."

"I expected them to be more cooperative now that we've got a lead on Debbie. I could get young William's Uncle Garth involved."

I waved him off. "Let's hold off on the big guns until later. The local agents will keep me up to date, but the ones out there aren't worth pissing off—antagonizing right now."

Parsons had said they wouldn't give me the time of day, and pissing them off would only make it harder for her to get any cooperation out of them.

I believed her.

Dad held up the picture I'd brought, which was less than ten hours old. "This is Deborah?"

"No doubt about it. The DNA sample is definitely from her. Agent Parsons thinks she did it on purpose."

"Parsons…I know that name."

I filled in the blanks for him. "In Boston she worked with Ashley."

"Yes, I remember. I met her at Vincent's place. Short girl?"

"Yup."

"Smart cookie, that one." He stroked his goatee. "She thinks it was purposeful?"

I used the same line Parsons had. "When was the last time you spit on the floor inside a building?"

"I see."

"Parsons' thinking is that Debbie wanted to be identified. She spit when the other robber's back was turned."

"Good thing, then. Otherwise, we'd never have known."

"Exactly." I hoped Parsons was right, because I'd drunk the Kool-Aid and bought into her hypothesis. "It implies but doesn't prove she was coerced."

He lifted the picture again.

"You can keep that. I've got another."

"Let's keep this under wraps for now. The last thing we need is a Benson in the news as a bank robber."

"I had to tell Vincent and his wife."

His eyes narrowed. "Unfortunate. I'll have a talk with them. Nobody else, though. We have to keep this from getting out."

"There's one other problem. I bumped into Adam Cartwright. He's one of the agents on the case, so we're not going to get much cooperation."

Dad sucked in a breath. "That's not good. Bad apples popping up everywhere. And his father is circling you like the vulture he is." He stroked his goatee again. "I see why you didn't want to stay out there."

# CHAPTER 37

*Dennis*

After another night of fitful sleep, I was in the office early Thursday morning.

Cindy was nice enough to bring me a second cup of coffee. "Jay says he needs to talk to you about Cartwright."

"Okay, send him up."

"And there's another thing. You should talk with Jennifer."

I sat back in my chair and steepled my hands. "And why is that?"

She leaned on the desk. "She needs some cheering up."

I crossed my arms. "You can handle that. Buy her a donut or something."

She spun around and went to the door, closed it firmly, and turned toward me. "I think it's something you need to handle."

A week ago somebody mentioning I should handle Jennifer would've brought pleasant thoughts to mind, but not this morning.

"It's not my job to keep everybody around here happy. My job is to make sure we can earn enough that everybody keeps getting paid."

She advanced toward the desk. "I'm not blind, you know. It's an issue you need to address." Her implication was clear.

Jennifer and I thought we'd been coy enough that nobody caught on. But nobody didn't seem to include Cindy.

She sat down in the chair opposite me. "She asked me three times when you'd be back. I can read between the lines. With all she's done for you, for us, since coming upstairs, don't you think you owe it to the company to talk to her?"

I didn't answer.

She crossed her arms. "I can sit here all day until you say yes."

"Yes."

"Yes what?"

She was being a real hard ass today.

"Yes, I'll ask her what's bothering her. But what's bothering me right now is that my assistant won't let me get back to work."

She rose and headed toward the door. "Yes, boss." The sarcasm in her voice wasn't lost on me.

After the door closed behind her, I knew what I wanted to ask Jennifer. The one question that kept coming up: *How could you betray us all like that?* I'd spent hours and hours on the subject. It ate at me day and night. My stomach was so sour thinking about it, I'd been chewing Tums like they were candy.

I didn't get any more time to ponder what else to say to Jennifer.

Jay knocked and let himself in, closing the door behind him. "Cartwright's coming in at ten."

"I thought I left word that we weren't having a meeting yet?"

"He called yesterday afternoon to set it up, said he heard you were going to be back in town this morning."

Fucking Adam must've told him.

Jay leaned against the chair, not bothering to sit. "Who do you want to invite?"

I had an easy answer. "You, me, and Larry should do it."

He cocked his head. "What about Jennifer? She seemed pretty canny at reading Talbot and Zarniger."

"Fine. Her too." I didn't need another person asking me why I was avoiding Jennifer.

After he left, I kept my office door closed. I wasn't dealing with Cindy's suggestion before this meeting. Instead, I spent the time reviewing what we'd previously gotten from Cartwright.

∽

CARSON CARTWRIGHT STOOD AS I ENTERED THE CONFERENCE ROOM AND MADE A point of checking his watch. "Glad you could make time to see us on such short notice."

I was my usual intentional five minutes late. "Always a pleasure to meet our shareholders."

It was true in general, but not this time.

The corner of his mouth ticked up. "Adam sends his regards."

Obviously not everybody in the FBI was as tight-lipped as they liked to pretend, but at least we hadn't come to blows again in DC.

Cartwright was shorter than I'd guessed and considerably older looking than the pictures I'd seen. I'd had run-ins with his sons, but never met the father in person. Vanity had him using at least a ten-year-old photo on his website.

I shook hands with him, followed by the two people he'd brought with him, Lester and Swartzman.

I took a seat directly across from Cartwright, with Jay and Jennifer on one side of me and Larry and Syd on the other. "What can we do for you this morning?"

Cartwright sat up in his seat. "I'm here as a courtesy."

That was a crock. He was here to threaten us.

"Today we're filing a revised form 13." He let the implication hang in the air. They were increasing their holding of our stock.

I had his business card on the table in front of me and slowly turned it around, waiting for him to continue.

"We've increased our position to twenty-four percent of the outstanding shares."

The words almost knocked the air out of me. I twisted his business card around one more time, doing my best to appear unfazed. "I'm glad to hear you have such confidence in our future."

Lester held back a laugh, and Swartzman smirked.

Cartwright's expression, though, didn't shift one iota. "Also, we're amending the form to state that we intend to become active in advocating for better management of the company."

I twisted his card around one more time. "We're always open to suggestions."

Cartwright's eyes narrowed. "I'd like Lester, Swartzman, and myself to be invited to join the board."

He'd made his first move on the chessboard.

I sat back and looked to my right. "Syd, do we have any openings on the board currently?"

I'd be damned if I was going to put him on the board—or any of his goons. Letting the likes of him onto your board was akin to bringing a rattlesnake into your bed.

Syd cleared his throat. "No, Dennis, we don't. We're authorized for seven, and we're at the max."

Syd's statement didn't seem to faze Cartwright. "The three of us are quite experienced at corporate turnarounds."

I knew it was more like they were experienced at corporate dismemberments, but I held my tongue in that regard.

"As Syd said, we don't have any vacancies right now," I offered.

His hatchet man, Lester, spoke up. "Things might go more smoothly if we were invited to the board. The alternative could be a messy proxy fight."

I checked my watch. "If that's all, Carson, I have to get to another meeting.

Thank you for stopping by, and for showing such faith in our future by putting your money into the stock."

He shook his head. "I think you're making a mistake by not inviting us onto the board."

Bullshit. He just wanted to avoid the expense of a proxy battle, which would cost him as much in legal fees as it would us leading up to the showdown of the shareholder vote.

I stood. "Thank you again for stopping in." I turned for the door.

"One more thing you might want to consider," the old man said.

I turned back to face him.

"We've been recommended by one of your current board members."

I didn't see that coming. "Is that so?"

Quickly cycling through the list of board members in my head, I didn't find anyone stupid enough to want to deal with the likes of him.

A broad smile came over him. "Yes. Your wife, Melissa Benson."

He knew damn well she was my ex-wife.

"She never did have good judgment." I turned and left the room before he could say anything else.

∼

*Jennifer*

SINCE MONDAY NIGHT, DENNIS HAD MADE A POINT OF AVOIDING ME.

I was obviously still in my adult timeout. I was supposed to be off in the corner contemplating how I'd been a bad girl. The problem was, it was working.

When Cindy had come down to tell me I was expected in the conference room for a meeting with the Cartwright group at ten, I couldn't have been more surprised.

I'd expected to be frozen out of anything important.

Dennis hadn't spoken to me as he'd entered the meeting, but he hadn't said anything to Larry either, and those two always had some banter going on.

Watching the interaction between him and Carson Cartwright had been a bit like watching two prizefighters circling each other in the ring—taking little jabs, searching out weaknesses.

Dennis had mentioned he'd never met Carson Cartwright, but when his son Adam was mentioned, I'd caught the tick of recognition in Dennis's jaw. Some history I didn't understand lay beneath those words.

The Cartwright Group had delivered one hell of a surprise this morning. Accumulating almost one quarter of the company stock put them in a very strong position to argue for seats on the board—maybe not three, but at least one.

And their zinger at the end about having Melissa on their side had been another blow. That had instantly put another five percent of the company's voting power on their side and made them extremely dangerous.

I'd looked at Dennis multiple times during the meeting, but he hadn't taken his eyes off the Cartwright team, except to ask Syd a question.

When the meeting broke up, I'd headed to my office and turned to see Dennis inviting the other three to his office for discussion of what had just transpired.

The border of trust had been defined, and I was clearly on the outside.

An hour later, the guilt of what I'd done was back to eating me up, and nothing I did kept my thoughts from returning to all the times I'd ignored Ramona's warnings.

The walls of my office were empty and clean, save the few nail holes where the previous occupant had taken down pictures he'd hung. I'd told myself a dozen times that I'd personalize the space and hang some things. But I'd not followed through, perhaps because subconsciously I'd known from the beginning I didn't deserve this office, and my time here would come to an end quickly.

As I looked around, even the drab beige of the walls was cheerier than my mood, and their emptiness reflected the state of my heart.

Spending the weekends with Dennis had transported me to a happy place, but that had been a dream world, not the reality of the future that lay in front of me now. Melissa had shoved me into the cold water of the fountain, but that was nothing compared to the way karma had smacked me upside the head. For a few weekends, I'd tasted what life could be like, but that life was now out of reach.

The futility of staying was obvious. I didn't have a future here. Dennis would let me go from the company after whatever period of punishment he'd planned.

I couldn't live like this, and I couldn't cede control of my emotions to him that way. I was a grown woman, and it was time to take control of my own fucking pathetic future.

My pen hovered over the paper for a moment before I wrote the words. There truly was no alternative.

I resign, effective immediately.
Jennifer Hanley

Cindy's desk was empty as I passed by and placed the note face down on the surface.

~

*DENNIS*

.  .  .

expectantly as Jennifer walked back to her office.

I didn't follow her down there, because I still didn't know what to say.

I turned to Syd, Larry, and Jay. "Guys, want to join me for a postmortem?"
The three filed into my office, and I closed the door.

"What do you think?" I asked.

Jay was the first to speak. "I'd heard they were buying up shares, but to tell
you the truth, that's way more than I would've guessed."

"Twenty-four percent is almost critical mass," Syd added, "for your standard
proxy fight."

Larry shook his head. "It's worse than that if he has Melissa behind him."

Their words weren't cheering me up.

"Do you think he really does, or was that just a bluff?" Jay asked.

I shrugged. "Most likely a bluff, because there's nothing in it for her."

Larry looked at me like I was an idiot. "After the way she acted at the
museum party, it's pretty obvious she'd sign on if she thought it would hurt
you."

"But that's not in her best interest," I argued.

Larry pointed a finger at me. "Don't you get it? An angry woman doesn't
need to be a logical woman. And that's one angry woman."

Larry's words bugged me. Melissa had always been crazy, but behind it she'd
always had the goal of helping herself. If that had changed, I'd missed it. The
legal maneuvering on the divorce had always seemed to be aimed at increasing
her share of the pot.

"I'm with Larry," Jay said. "I doubt it was a bluff. If he hasn't approached her,
lying about having her support would only make it harder for him to get it in the
future if she found out."

Jay's logic seemed sound.

Syd's silent nodding made it three to one that Melissa had thrown in with
him, which made the situation that much worse.

"Thanks, guys. I need to figure out what to do next."

Larry and Syd left.

Jay stopped at the door. "You might want to have some group brainstorming
about how to proceed. You know, to get a broader perspective."

"Thanks, Jay."

That was one possibility.

When Jay departed, he was quickly replaced by Cindy at my door.

She waved a paper in her hand and wore a scowl that would drop a buffalo at
a hundred paces.

I braced for the storm.

"You promised to talk to her," she spat as she approached the desk.

"I didn't get a chance…yet. Send her down."

She threw the paper at me. "It's a little late for that."

The note said Jennifer was quitting, and my stomach clenched. "She can't just leave."

"Day late and a dollar short, I'd say." Cindy turned and left.

I pulled the roll of Tums from my pocket and popped another two in my mouth.

# CHAPTER 38

*DENNIS*

I WAS ON MY SECOND SCOTCH WHEN THE DOORBELL RANG.

Serena waltzed in with a bag in her arms as I opened the door. "Did you forget about our dinner date already?"

I had, but it wasn't a good idea to admit weakness with my sister.

I looked at my watch. "I guess I lost track of the time."

"And started early on the drinking, I see. What's wrong?"

"What do you mean?"

She wandered toward the kitchen, ignoring me for a moment before she turned. "You look like shit. I'd ask you if your dog died, but you don't have a dog."

"Things didn't go well at work today."

She started to unpack the grocery bag she'd brought. "I got all the ingredients they listed on a website. I hope I didn't forget anything. What do we do first?"

I'd completely forgotten that tonight was her cooking lesson. "Preheat the oven to four-fifty to start."

"How?"

"I don't believe—"

She hit my shoulder lightly. "I'm just kidding. You need to loosen up a little."

I lifted my scotch glass. "I am."

She set the upper oven to preheat.

"We need bags to flatten the chicken." I leaned over to get freezer bags from the drawer.

After I'd pulled two bags from their box, I found her pouring my drink down the sink. "Hey, that's expensive stuff."

She put the glass in the sink and turned to me. "Not while we're talking."

"We're not talking, we're cooking. Put a chicken breast in each of the bags and close them up."

She took the chicken out of the store package and loaded it in the bags.

I grabbed a mallet from the drawer and handed it to her. "Now you need to pound on it to flatten them down."

She handed the mallet back to me. "You do this part. You're the one that needs to get your frustrations out."

I glared at her as I pounded the chicken into submission. "We're tenderizing the pieces as well as making them thinner. Grab two of your eggs and mix them in a bowl."

"With what?"

"A fork will do."

I kept hammering the chicken while she did the eggs.

"You'll find flour in the pantry, did you bring breadcrumbs?" I asked her when she'd finished. "And we'll need four plates in a line."

She located the items and placed them on the island. "You want to tell me what's bothering you?"

I shook my head and continued pounding the chicken. "I'm fine."

"Bullshit. This is you screwed up. Drinking before dinner isn't you being fine."

She had that part right.

The chicken breasts had taken a good-enough beating. "Sprinkle some bread-crumbs on the second plate, carefully pour the eggs onto the third one, and put flour on the last one." I watched her a moment. "What's his name?"

She ignored me while she carefully poured the egg mixture. She looked up. "What's her name?"

I ignored her the way she'd ignored me. "Now you're gonna add a little Parmesan to the breadcrumbs and mix it up."

"How's this?"

"Looking good. Now, what are we doing for the sauce? You aren't planning to use that jar of Ragu are you?"

She nodded. "Baby steps."

"It's your dinner." I located a frying pan and put it on the stove. "Okay, take the breasts out of the bags, and you want to press each into the flour. Try to get it coated all over so it's dry to the touch."

She did fine with that step. "It's Jennifer, isn't it?"

I put a pot of water for the pasta on the stove. "Now take the first floured breast and put it into the egg mixture. Turn it over and move it to the bread-crumbs. Press it into the breadcrumbs on both sides so it's well coated and then put it on the empty plate."

She did a good job with the first one. "This gets all over your fingers."

"You can wash them off after you're done with the last piece of chicken."

It took her a few minutes to work both pieces through the process. While she washed up, I added some olive oil to the pan and turned on the stove.

"You can get rid of these extra plates, and there's a dish we can cook this in over there on the bottom shelf of that cupboard."

She cleaned up the plates and located the dish. "Why did she quit?"

The question startled me for a second, coming completely out of left field. "Who?"

"Jennifer, of course."

I sighed. "You've been talking to Cindy."

"You know she tells me everything."

"She obviously tells you too much. Wipe a little bit of olive oil on the bottom of the baking dish."

She grabbed a paper towel and did as I asked. "What happened between you two?"

The frying pan was heating up nicely. "What makes you think there's anything between us?"

"She's not stupid, you know."

I turned the gas down. "Cindy reads too many romance novels. She's imagining things."

Serena put her hand on her hip. "And was I imagining what I saw down by the Santa Monica Pier last weekend? You with her and that cute kid? Is he her son?"

There was no sense in denying it anymore. "Nephew."

"You guys looked like you were enjoying yourselves."

We certainly had been. Every weekend.

I pulled a spatula from the drawer and offered it to her. "Now you want to fry each of the pieces for two minutes on each side and then take them out."

She put the chicken in the pan all at once and stepped back from the spatter of the oil.

"Two minutes?" she asked.

I set the timer for two minutes. "Each side."

She flipped them when the time was up, and I reset the timer for her.

The second side finished.

"Okay, now bring the baking pan over and put the pieces in there. You can also take the frying pan off the heat."

She moved the pan with the chicken to the island. "What's next?"

I located my cheese grater. "Pour your marinara sauce over the chicken."

"Like this?"

"Not too much."

She stopped.

"Now I would sprinkle basil over the chicken pieces and then add parmesan

776

cheese. You can grate on some provolone or mozzarella, or both—whatever you feel like."

"I didn't bring any other cheese."

I opened the fridge to check. "I've got provolone you can use."

She slowly added the grated cheeses.

I set the timer for twenty minutes. "Now pop it in the oven, and in fifteen to twenty, dinner is ready."

She loaded the dish into the oven and closed it, beaming at her accomplishment. "That wasn't so hard."

"What pasta are you having with it?"

She pulled fettuccine from the bag. "These."

"Okay, you need to warm some of your sauce, and then the pasta goes in the water when the timer gets down to nine minutes."

"Nine minutes. Got it."

When the time was up, I helped her drain the pasta and serve the chicken parmigiana.

We took the plates to the table, and I opened a bottle of cabernet.

She cut into her chicken and forked a piece. "Now you can tell me what happened. And, just so you know, I'm not leaving until you do."

I'd had that threat from her before, and I knew she was serious.

"You know those nasty articles about the company?" I asked.

She nodded while she chewed.

"Jennifer was the source of the leak."

"She wrote those pieces?"

I sipped my wine between bites. "No, but she supplied the memos." Just mentioning it made my heart hurt.

"Why would she do that?"

"She thought I killed her father, actually her stepfather."

Her fork stopped mid-flight to her mouth. "What the fuck? Is she delusional?"

"No. He died in a welding accident at the company, though, and I had us take the blame so the family would get the full settlement."

She took the piece from her fork and chewed thoughtfully for a moment before sipping her wine. "And she didn't believe you?"

"No, that's not the problem. Don't you see? She attacked me personally as well as everybody at the company, and she did it on purpose. It wasn't an accident."

She stirred her pasta around a bit. "So Cindy was right. You're the problem."

I put my fork down. "*I am not*. I didn't do anything to hurt her. It's the other way around." I held her gaze.

She blinked first.

I went back to my dinner.

"And when are you going to get past this?"

"I'm not sure I can, knowing what she did."

She ate another few bites. "She lashed out at you because she thought you killed her stepfather. I can see that."

I heaped some fettuccine on top of my next piece of chicken.

"She did a bad thing, the wrong thing."

"Exactly," I mumbled with my mouth full.

"But she did it for a good reason, the right reason."

I'd had enough of this. "It wasn't a good reason. She was wrong. Her father violated safety rules put in place for his own protection, and that's what cost him his life."

"Don't you see? You said it yourself. She didn't know that. She did the wrong thing, but for the right reason. Tell me you haven't ever been guilty of that."

"I always try to do the right thing, and you know it."

"Right. Like with Adam Cartwright?"

That stopped me cold. "But..."

The vision of that day was a cold slap of reality.

"But nothing. That was you doing the wrong thing, but sure, you had the right reason," she said. "Tell me you don't wish you could take that day back."

I hung my head in shame. "I do."

I had often wished I could take that back, but it wasn't possible now—never had been possible. A torn ACL had ruined Adam's dream of an NFL career. An injury I'd caused had cost him his chance, and it had all been due to a lie I'd believed at the time.

"Don't you see the parallel?"

I wasn't giving her this easy a win. "Okay, it's a little similar."

"Bullshit. It's the same fucking thing."

"Stop it already. I get your point."

She continued anyway. "Doing the wrong thing for what you believe is the right reason—should you be punished your entire life for that?"

I didn't answer. I didn't need to. She knew where I stood on that. Adam had retaliated later, and it had cost me. The whole episode had cost us both.

"Answer me. Should you be punished forever for a mistake like that?"

"Of course not, but it's not the same."

She pushed her chair back. "Man up and do the right thing with Jennifer."

We were done here. I nodded. "Think you can remember how to do this for your dinner with Bill?"

"It's not Bill."

"Then John."

She stood and shook her head. "His name's Troy, but keep that to yourself."

She was giving me one win tonight.

I had a lot to think about.

# CHAPTER 39

*JENNIFER*

FRIDAY MORNING, I CHECKED THE MESSAGE ON MY PHONE AGAIN.

CINDY: Let's meet for coffee - Starbucks at 7:30?

I'd felt like putting all things Benson behind me and getting on with my life, but I'd agreed because Cindy had always been nice to me.

Last night had been the first night I'd gotten three hours of uninterrupted sleep all week. The decision to move on had been hard, but empowering in a way.

Ramona emerged from her room and closed the door behind her. "I say you're being a chicken."

"Good morning to you, too."

"You shouldn't give up so easily."

That was easy for her to say. She didn't have to look at the people at work and know the problems I'd created for all of them.

"You just don't want to lose your Saturday babysitter," I shot back.

She and Billy had definitely both benefited from having Dennis around.

"You've never been one to run from a fight. I still say you should go and give him a piece of your mind before you give up."

"It's different when I know I'm right, but this time I'm not. I told you, I've made up my mind. I'm moving on."

"To another Ed?"

"That's not fair."

There was no comparison between Ed and Dennis. They were one letter away from each other in the alphabet I guess, but they couldn't have been more different.

"Just saying, take a look at what you're walking away from." She turned and opened her door again. "Hey, Bill, time to get moving."

Her calling him Bill was another reminder of the impact Dennis had had.

Billy now did his homework before asking to turn on the television. And all it had taken was a comment from Dennis about it.

I found my purse. "I'll be back in a while."

~

THE M&M GIRLS WERE AT THEIR FAMILIAR TABLE.

"Got the day off?" Mona asked as I walked up.

"Something like that." I'd been so busy at work that I'd only been able to stop in to see them on Wednesdays since moving upstairs.

There were three cups on the table, and the extra one had my name on the side.

I sat at the chair with my cup. "This is nice of you. How'd you know I'd be by this morning?" I asked.

"It wasn't me," Martha said, nodding her head toward the corner. "It was him."

Dennis walked our way.

I froze in place. The fight-or-flight response got my heart racing, and the only alternative here was fight.

"Good morning, Angel."

The words slipped off his tongue almost as if he meant them.

I nodded. "Morning." I couldn't go so far as to say *good*.

Mona touched my shoulder. "Dennis told us how invaluable you've been at his company."

"And I told him he should have given you a bigger raise," Martha added.

Dennis nodded. "So I agreed."

That dropped my jaw to full fly-catcher mode. "But—"

"First," Dennis said, interrupting me. "I need you to be honest with these ladies about something."

The girls hung on his every word.

He sipped his mocha. "You see, ladies, Jennifer and I have been seeing each other for a while now, and hiding it from the people we work with."

I cringed. Where on Earth could he be going with this? Was he about to unleash some sort of twisted revenge?

He took my hand.

I pulled it back.

He held his hand out for me again.

Martha elbowed me, and I put my hand forward. The warmth of his touch welded me to him as it always had before.

He put his other hand over mine. "Jennifer, I don't want to hide our relationship anymore. I'm asking you to be my public girlfriend."

This was nowhere on any script I'd imagined. My eyes welled up.

Martha elbowed me again. "Well?"

"Please?" Dennis added. "I understand why you did what you did, and now I need your help at the company."

"Can you forgive me?" I managed.

"Of course. I love you, Angel."

Martha pushed on my shoulder and whispered, "This is where you kiss him, dear."

I leaned toward him, and our lips met in a simple but heartfelt kiss. The kiss I wanted to give him would have gotten us banned from the shop forever.

"If this place served liquor," Mona said. "I'd order us a round of champagne."

I liked the sentiment.

I broke the kiss to look into his eyes. "Just like that?"

"Just like that. You did what you did for an honorable reason, and someday I'll tell you about how I once did something even worse."

"I doubt it."

He pulled me up to stand. "We have to get to work, girl. We'll see you two next Friday."

"It's a date," Mona replied.

"I want to hear about the raise," Martha added.

Dennis pulled me toward the door. "Next time."

*Dennis*

WE WALKED WITH INTERTWINED FINGERS TOWARD WORK.

She looked up at me. "Thank you."

"Don't thank me. Thank Cindy and Serena."

"Huh?

"I'll tell you later."

She squeezed my hand. "I love you too."

She hadn't said it in the coffee shop, but it was certainly good to hear it now.

I let go of her hand and circled my arm around her as we walked. "Are you ready for this?" I adjusted my stride to hers.

"Not really. Are you?"

"Definitely. It's been harder than you can imagine ignoring you at work."

"Hard, huh?" She giggled, looking down at my crotch.

"Keep it up and you're getting another introduction to my desk."

"Promises, promises."

I slowed our pace as my cock hardened. "Stop that. I won't be able to walk into work like this."

"Just put your hands in your pockets like you always do." She smiled.

I pulled my hand back and did just that. By the time we reached the building, I had things under control.

After Cindy had set up the Starbucks meeting, getting my Angel back had been easier than I'd expected, although there was certainly the possibility I'd need to do some groveling later for the way I'd treated her.

Soon the elevator doors parted upstairs, and we walked into our new reality. Cindy was at her desk.

"Cin, let's get the large group together in the boardroom at nine."

She scribbled a note. "Sure."

I looked at Jennifer. "That means you too, Angel."

Cindy cocked an eyebrow, not missing what I'd said.

"And don't be late for dinner tonight," I added as I closed the door slowly.

Cindy was looking to Jennifer for an explanation. I listened at the door after it closed.

"You're staying, and it's not a secret anymore?" Cindy asked.

"Yes on both counts."

"Good, because frankly, he needs the help—and the attitude lift."

I walked to my desk. I didn't need to hear any more girl talk. *Go big or go home*, Dad always said. I'd made *us* public in a big way. The company grapevine would see to that.

Ten minutes later I walked out to Cindy's desk and handed her the envelope from the night at the museum.

She took it. "What's this?"

"A thank you for your help."

Her eyes lit up when she opened the envelope. "Hawaii?"

"You earned it." I turned for the door. If she hadn't been in contact with Serena, I'd probably still have my head up my ass.

❧

JENNIFER

AS I WALKED TO MY ONCE-AGAIN OFFICE, I WONDERED HOW MANY PEOPLE BEYOND Cindy had seen through our charade and guessed Dennis and I were seeing each other. It didn't matter, but it brought back the awkward feeling that I might be judged has having slept my way into this job, and I wouldn't even know it.

782

Yesterday every employee I'd passed had made me wonder if they knew what I'd done to hurt them. Today, I had to add the issue of whether they thought I'd slept my way to where I was. Agreeing to go public about us didn't feel as good as it'd sounded at Starbucks.

A little while later, I took a place at the far end of the long table as the group assembled in the boardroom.

Dennis had invited more department heads and managers than I'd seen him assemble before, and I didn't even know all their names.

Larry chose a seat next to me as the room filled, and the ambient noise of a dozen side conversations grew. Dennis was talking with Fisher.

"Let's get started," Dennis said.

The group instantly quieted, except for the young IT guy and his neighbor.

A few seconds later the two realized all eyes were on them and stopped.

Dennis surveyed the room. "Let me bring you up to date. An outside activist group called the Cartwright Group has taken a very substantial position in our stock, and they have visited us to say they're going to advocate for change in the company."

"Like what?" one person asked.

"They will say we're not running the company optimally for the shareholders, and they can do a better job. So expect that your employees are going to start seeing things either in the papers or in their mailboxes basically saying I'm a jerk."

That got a few giggles from the crowd.

"I'm a jerk, and they can do better," Dennis added.

"Why?" the same guy asked.

"This can likely play out one of two ways. Either they want to take over the company…"

The group grew restless at the statement.

"Or they'll end up blackmailing us into paying them to go away."

"Can they do that?" Paul, the guy from HR, asked.

"Yes and no. They'll be overt about it, but they'll imply that if we agree to purchase their stock back from them at a certain level, they'd sell and move on to their next target."

"Like hyenas," Larry added.

"What will this do to our stock options?" the IT guy asked.

Larry spoke up again. "In the previous companies they've gotten control of, they've ended up cutting stock options drastically. They view it as a way to save money."

"But the options are the main tool we have to attract people," Paul complained.

"I'm just telling you what they've done," Larry replied.

"They also have a history of advocating for significant staff reductions as a

783

way of boosting profitability," I added. I'd researched this pattern in several of their recent attacks on other companies.

"That's a fancy way of saying layoffs," Dennis said.

The group grew sullen. Layoffs was the last thing they wanted to hear.

"What are we going to do to fight back?" the young IT guy asked.

Dennis smiled. This was obviously the question he'd waited for. "We're going to fight them aggressively on two fronts. First..." He looked around the room. "You and your employees own eighteen percent of the company and have a significant say in how this plays out. HR will distribute talking points to you laying out our position, as well as the facts of what happened to the employees at Cartwright's last two targets. This should help you convince your people that the Cartwright Group is not the benevolent force for good they claim to be. If the majority of our employees vote with us, that will be a significant help. The other thing we'll be doing is visiting a few of our major shareholders to shore up their support."

"But what if that's not enough?" a woman asked.

"Then I'll be out of a job," Dennis answered. "And you'll be on your own in dealing with them."

The looks of horror on the faces around the room were clear. They didn't want Dennis leaving. After answering a smattering of other questions, he called an end to the meeting.

After the managers filed out, I followed Paul, Syd, Larry, and Fisher into Dennis's office.

Syd was the first to speak. "We need to be careful what we say to employees, or we could get in serious trouble with the Securities and Exchange Commission."

Dennis leaned against his desk. "Larry, you and Paul work up the most persuasive literature you can, but run it by Syd before we put it out."

Paul nodded.

"It has to be factual," Syd said. "It can't be your normal marketing bullshit."

"I know that," Larry shot back. "And it's not marketing bullshit. It's persuasion material."

"I don't care what we call it," Dennis said firmly. "Larry, it needs to be persuasive. And, Syd, it needs to not get us in trouble with the SEC. But I don't want to shy away from anything. We need to snuggle up close to the line, just not go over it."

Syd sighed, likely not happy about being pushed out of his comfort zone. He looked over at our HR guy again. "Paul, I also don't want it just sent around. You need to see that all our managers and supervisors are trained on it. When we're done, no employee in his right mind should even consider voting with those Cartwright assholes."

Dennis shifted his focus to Fisher. "Jay, you need to make a list today of major shareholders we should meet with. You, me, and Jennifer are going on a road trip to shore up their support."

Fisher nodded.

I raised my hand. "I have a suggestion." I felt stupid for putting my hand up as if I were still in school.

Dennis looked at me expectantly.

"I think we might contact some others who have had dealings with Cartwright and ask them to go along and support our position."

"Who did you have in mind?" Fisher asked.

"Hugh Stoner. He had a nasty encounter with them a few years ago. I think he'd be on our side."

Dennis nodded. "He's been friends with Dad forever. We can probably get him to help."

"Talbot is also not fond of Cartwright," Fisher said.

I didn't think that would fly. "I'm not sure they'd be receptive."

Dennis smiled. "Jennifer, you and Jay go talk to them. Old man Talbot likes you."

I shrugged. An assignment was an assignment, even if I disagreed with his assessment.

"One more thing. Jenn, could you stay a minute?"

I took a seat again, while the others filed out.

Dennis closed the door after them. "I have something else to tell you." He retook the seat behind his desk. "The trip I took?"

"Yeah?"

He sucked in a breath. "My cousin, Debbie, is alive."

"That's great. Where is she?" I had a million questions, but he stopped me.

"We can't talk about it to anybody yet. We don't know where she is, but we have DNA evidence that she's alive?"

"What about your family? You have to tell them."

He shook his head. "Dad and Vincent know, but we can't tell the others yet."

"Why not?" I waited for more. There had to be more.

"She was involved in a bank robbery, and we know she's alive. But we don't know any more than that yet. We won't know the answers until we find her."

I couldn't make sense of it. Child kidnap victim, and now an adult bank robber.

"I needed to tell you, but we can't talk about this. We can't let it get out until we know more."

I nodded. I didn't agree, but it was his family and his decision.

As I walked back to my office, the import of the conversation struck me. He'd confided in me a secret he wouldn't tell his brother or sisters.

# CHAPTER 40

*DENNIS*
*(Ten Days Later)*

IT WAS LUNCHTIME MONDAY, THE LAST DAY OF THE WHIRLWIND OF SHAREHOLDER meetings Jay had lined up for us.

Royce Capital had been the final shareholder on our New York list after our meeting at Barron Funds earlier this morning. After eleven of these meetings last week, I'd had enough. I hoped we were where we needed to be.

I followed the group out of the mutual fund building onto the busy midtown Manhattan sidewalk.

"Jay, how do you think that one went?" I asked.

He scooted farther from the door before answering. "He might have been on the fence before, but that guy doesn't like Cartwright, is my read. He should go with us."

"Hugh, what about you?

Hugh Stoner checked toward the door before speaking. "Just like the others. Once Jim told them Fidelity and Price were behind you, they had no choice."

James Talbot agreed. "Bunch of sheep, the whole lot of them. Not a single one with the balls to cut away from the crowd and make his own decision. I think you've got it sewn up now. They won't give Cartwright the time of day."

Jennifer's smile told me she agreed.

Finally we had the support we needed for Monday's meeting with Cartwright.

Hugh checked his watch. "I'm due to meet Millie for lunch. Jim, you want to join us?"

"If you're buying," Talbot replied in his typical fashion.

Jay's phone rang, and he stepped away to answer it.

I thanked Stoner and Talbot profusely and shook both their hands as they broke off. They'd been invaluable.

"I'll tell him," Jay said into his phone. "It's Cartwright. They're all here in town, and they want to meet to make an offer."

"Now?" I asked.

Jay nodded. "Yeah."

Jennifer nodded as well. "Doesn't hurt to listen."

"Okay," I said.

Jay asked where and then hung up. "Restaurant two blocks north."

"Did you tell them we were going to New York?" I asked him.

"No."

"It doesn't take a genius to figure out we'd be making the rounds where the money is," Syd noted.

But what were the odds that they'd picked a place to meet that close?

*Dennis*

Walking to the meeting, Jay and Jennifer agreed that this would most likely be the "greenmail" offer Cartwright was known for—pay him enough, and he would go away.

After asking for the Cartwright party at the reservation desk, we were escorted to a private room upstairs.

Carson Cartwright greeted us. "Glad we could meet on such short notice."

When the obligatory hand shaking was done, I took the seat across from Cartwright, and Jay chose the seat across from his weasel lawyer, Beasley.

Jennifer took the next chair down the rectangular table, which was devoid of place settings.

A meal was apparently not part of the plan.

"You said you had something to discuss?" I asked.

Cartwright nodded to Beasley.

The lawyer opened a folder in front of him and slid a single sheet of paper across to me, and a copy to Jay. "Sorry. I only brought two copies."

Jennifer leaned over to read Jay's.

This was an agreement to give them a single board seat—down from their previous demand of three—and also to buy back their shares at a thirty-percent premium over today's stock price.

It was simple corporate blackmail, as expected.

"It expires as soon as we walk out of this room," Cartwright said. "Otherwise we'll be at your offices tomorrow morning with our official proxy proposal. From there, the offers only get worse."

I wasn't rushing into anything without a discussion with my team. "Then we can talk tomorrow. I'm not entering into anything today."

Beasley shook his head. "That's too bad. I heard a rumor that someone suspected you had an SEC problem."

Jay's face reddened. "Our accounting is flawless."

Cartwright stood. "We're on a tight schedule here. We just finished with Barron Funds, and we're scheduled at Royce Capital now."

Jay glanced at me.

Beasley laughed. "Yeah, looking forward to hearing what lies you told them."

I held my tongue as the two slimeballs departed.

Jay waited for the door to close. "Those terms weren't bad, as a Cartwright deal goes. It sounds like they've been following us around, and that's going to make it harder if they're getting the last word in."

"Your point?" I asked.

"You should have taken the deal."

"I'm not rushing into something without consulting the team."

Jay moved to the door. "The gall of that asshole to suggest the SEC has a problem with our accounting."

# CHAPTER 41

*DENNIS*

IT WAS MONDAY MORNING BACK IN CALIFORNIA—MAKE OR BREAK TIME WITH Cartwright. Their group had arrived shortly before nine, and Cindy was getting them situated in the boardroom.

Jennifer had done her best to lift my mood all weekend. Another Saturday with her nephew had been a relaxing diversion, but seeing Cartwright in New York had been a complete surprise—a very unpleasant one. And how he could have managed to know our itinerary bugged me to no end.

Grabbing my lucky pen, I ventured out of my safe office and into the lion's den of the boardroom.

Cartwright pasted on a fake smile as we shook. "Good to see you again so soon, Dennis."

"Always a pleasure to talk with our shareholders," I offered.

"Yes, I'm sure it is. And so nice that in our corporate structures, the shareholders are the ultimate bosses, don't you think?"

Jay interceded before I could say something snarky. "We understood you had a proxy you wished to put forth?"

I took my seat, as did Cartwright.

His attack-dog lawyer, Beasley, passed us each a copy.

As I read, my blood started to boil.

Larry didn't hold back. "This is bull, and you know it."

Cartwright didn't flinch. "The company's charter allows us to submit this to a vote of the shareholders, and that's what we are requesting today."

"No way," Larry spat.

Syd put a hand on his shoulder. "Larry, they have the right."

"Not if it's full of lies like this," Larry said.

Beasley slid Larry a piece of paper. "I've circled the relevant section. The wording is at the shareholder's discretion." He looked proud of himself.

Jay reached over and slid it back to him. "We've met recently with most all of the major shareholders."

"We know," Cartwright said. "So have we."

Jay continued. "I'm confident they'll side with management on this."

The door opened, and Cindy came over to whisper in my ear. "Ed Baird has something he needs to talk to you about."

"Later," I told her.

"It can't wait."

I spun my pen on the tabletop and stood. "Excuse me for a moment."

Cartwright nodded with a smirk.

Once outside, I closed the door behind me and motioned for Ed to join me in my office.

He closed the door behind him.

"What is it that can't wait?" I demanded.

"The SEC is downstairs with a warrant, and *that* won't wait."

The words completely surprised me. "A warrant? For what?"

"Jennifer's office and computer." He hesitated. "And your computer."

∼

JENNIFER

I HADN'T HEARD WHAT CINDY HAD WHISPERED, BUT THIS WAS NOT THE MEETING TO pretend to be called out of.

The other side was quiet and, oddly, smiling at the delay.

Dennis rejoined us. "Syd and Jennifer, there's something that requires your attention."

I got up and followed Syd.

Cartwright's next line came before I reached the door. "After the SEC charges you two, I think the shareholders might rethink supporting the current management."

*The SEC charges who with what?* I wondered as I closed the door and faced Ed. It was our first face to face in a long time.

"What's going on?" Syd demanded.

Ed took a breath. "You need to go downstairs, sir. The SEC is here with a warrant."

"Is this a joke?"

"No, sir. And Miss Hanley, you need to stay here with me until they come up."

Syd took off for the elevator, muttering under his breath.

Ed whispered, "You should have talked to me before it got to this."

I led him away from Cindy's desk. "Got to what?"

"The SEC is here to seize your computer and the contents of your office."

My jaw dropped. *Why would the SEC be interested in me?*

The next few minutes were a jumble in my mind as agents of the government came upstairs with Syd and we watched them take Dennis's computer before moving on to my office. The goons boxed up everything in there. They only left me my purse and cell phone.

Syd didn't allow me to say anything or ask any questions.

I almost puked. The whole process was humiliating.

After Syd had a conversation with the head guy, he came over.

"Jennifer, you should go home and wait for me to call you. They're charging you and Dennis with insider trading," he said.

"That's ridiculous."

"They think they can prove you wrote those articles in the *Times* to push the stock down so Dennis could buy low. If you're contacted by the SEC, don't meet with them without me present."

His statement took a moment to sink in. I nodded, half in a trance.

"Do you understand?"

"No," I protested. "I don't understand a fucking thing about what is happening."

The only thing I knew was that what I'd done was somehow coming back to hurt Dennis even worse than before. I was at fault, because if I hadn't cooperated with Hydra, there wouldn't have been any articles, and these thugs wouldn't be here.

～

*DENNIS*

THE CARTWRIGHT MEETING ENDED SHORTLY AFTER THE SEC'S SURPRISE VISIT.

Cartwright's words rattled around in my head. "*After the SEC charges you two, I think the shareholders might rethink supporting the current management.*"

He'd known this was coming, and probably had a hand in it somehow.

Syd had handled the interaction with the feds, and had gotten on the phone with the SEC as well.

I called the group back into the boardroom as soon as Cartwright and his SEC accomplices were out of our hair.

"Cin, get Jennifer as well."

She shook her head. "Not here. Syd sent her home."

I turned to Syd. "Why?"

"Because their warrant focused on her. It's best if she stays out of the building until we understand the formal complaint, or we could have them back in here again tomorrow."

"I don't like it."

Syd stood his ground. "That's my legal advice, and the smart thing to do at this point."

I relented for the moment. "Let's get started." I ushered Syd back into the boardroom.

"Syd, what do we know from your guy at the SEC?"

He cleared his throat. "They got a tip—"

"What the fuck kind of tip?" I demanded.

"Let me finish. They got a tip that... They're investigating the likelihood that you've engaged in inside trading."

"That's stupid," I spat. "I file my form fours regularly." I'd filed with the SEC after every purchase, and I hadn't had any sales to report.

He took a slow breath. "They think you planted the stories in the *Times*, and then you took advantage of that to buy when the news tanked the stock."

"So, I'm guilty because I have confidence in the company, and I'm willing to invest when everybody else is running for the hills?"

Looking around the room, the entire group seemed to back away from engaging me in this debate.

"Well?" I asked Syd.

"It's worse than that. They think Jennifer wrote the stories under the Sigurd name at your direction."

Suddenly the situation looked a whole lot more complicated. Because Jennifer had confessed to me, I knew something the rest of the room didn't that made this SEC mess all the more dangerous. And I had no intention of sharing it with the group. In a long conversation, she'd come clean on her involvement with Sigurd —the person she knew as Hydra—and it was my call to forgive her for that. Nobody else needed to know, and I was keeping it that way.

Once again, only Syd was willing to speak up. "They expect to find evidence on Jennifer's computer or yours that will prove it."

"And when they don't?"

"Then it goes away," Syd answered.

Jay leaned forward. "It's not that simple, I'm afraid."

"Go ahead," I urged.

"This whole process will take way too long. It won't get settled before the proxy vote. Cartwright will use the news to his advantage, and he's right that a lot of our shareholders will move to his side with this stink hanging over you. This smells like a setup by Cartwright."

I prided myself in being able to keep a positive attitude, but this was too much. "So you think we're fucked?"

Jay's hesitation said it all. "Unless Larry has some rabbit to pull out of his hat, I don't see any way this plays, except to Cartwright's advantage."

Larry ignored the magic act comment. "He was probably hinting at a surprise coming during every meeting last week."

I nodded, agreeing with Larry. "It's what I would have done if I knew a bombshell was about to drop."

I let the group go and locked myself in my office.

Cartwright had been sneakier and smarter than I'd given him credit for, and now it was game, set, match.

He would win, and I would lose.

Everything had gone to shit, and I needed to talk to Jennifer, the one good thing in my life today. I tried to dial her, but my cell phone did its stupid reset thing again. I called out my open office door. "Cindy, I give up."

She appeared at the door. "What's the problem?"

I held up my phone. "You said we had a whiz kid in IT that could fix this thing?"

She walked in, hand out. "Yeah, I'll get it to Oleg."

"Is he the one who looks like he's fourteen?"

She took the phone from me. "That's the one. He's actually twenty-three, and he runs the group."

"Thanks."

I suddenly felt old having to get help from kids. The entire IT group looked like they belonged in high school. I dismissed the thought as wasted energy. I didn't need to be a phone genius to run the company. And maybe they weren't getting younger—maybe I was getting older.

"And, I need another fucking computer."

A scowl was my punishment for swearing at her.

"I'm sorry. Would you please ask IT to get me another computer so I can do my work?"

The scowl was replaced by her happy face. "Gladly."

I still needed to check on Jennifer. She'd been dragged into this mess as well. After closing my door, I dialed her number on my desk phone, but didn't get an answer. I didn't leave a message, face to face would be better.

The bottle of scotch in my credenza called to me, and I poured a glass.

The liquid burn did nothing to soothe me, so I put it down.

"I'm going for a walk," I told Cindy as I passed her desk.

With my phone in the shop, I was off my electronic leash and free to take as much time as I wanted.

Downstairs, I decided on a few quick laps of the block to get the blood flowing so I could think.

# CHAPTER 42

*JENNIFER*

I SAT IN MY CAR. MY LEGS SHOOK SO BADLY I WAS AFRAID TO START IT. I COULDN'T drive like this.

Charged by the SEC? Insider trading? That was crazy. I hadn't written the articles, and Dennis hadn't known anything about my part in their creation at the time. But there was no way to prove a negative. The accusation alone would taint both of us. I'd never get another accounting job, and he could lose the company. Even being investigated by the SEC would be a black mark that would follow us both around forever. My actions had wounded him much worse than before.

As hard as I tried, I couldn't stop the tears. It wasn't like I could go back to being a bank teller either. Not only had I likely ruined my relationship with the one good man I'd managed to find, but now my career future officially sucked. Perhaps I could enter the wonderful world of hospitality services, or food preparation.

Pulling a tissue from my purse, I wiped my eyes and summoned the courage to drive home. I wasn't ever coming back to a job like this. An SEC investigation would preclude any kind of corporate finance work. It had been my passion, and this would end it.

The hardest part would be having to tell my sister and Billy I'd let them down.

I'd been naïve to think Dennis could easily forgive me for the damage the articles had caused. And even though somehow he had found a way to do so, it

794

would be insane to expect his forgiveness for inadvertently bringing the SEC down on him, especially if he lost the company he'd created.

There was no coming back from this.

I drove slowly and reached home without getting in an accident.

Upstairs, I was pouring the first of my planned several dozen glasses of wine when my cell rang.

I'd already ignored a call from the company number, which was probably Syd with more bad news.

I pulled the last pin from my hair and shook it out before checking the phone. Cindy's name was on the screen.

I couldn't bring myself to ignore her the way I wanted to. "Hello?"

"How are you holding up?" she asked.

"I'm already one glass into a bottle of wine, if that tells you anything."

"I know this isn't any of my business...but he needs you."

"Who?" I asked stupidly.

"The man who's been pretending forever to not be in love with you."

The words hit me hard. She thought he still loved me.

I plopped down on the couch. "You think so?"

"I think you're smart enough to know the answer to that."

I nodded silently. I knew how I felt, and even if he'd only recently said it, every day we spent together he'd shown me his feelings in his kidding, his little gestures, and in the way he looked at me. It added up to what every girl wanted from a man.

From the first morning he took me to his beach house, it had been all about me—about expanding my happiness horizons. From the silly listening to the ocean routine to the fun new things he got me to try every weekend, it had been about pulling me out of my shell. And it had worked, without me ever being focused on it.

It had all fallen apart when he learned what I'd done, but I'd been lucky enough to get him back after that. This, though? This was ten times worse. I couldn't dare hope to be forgiven again.

"Jennifer," Cindy said, bringing me back to the present. "The guys think this is all Cartwright's doing, and they're talking about Dennis losing the company."

I blinked back the tears that threatened. "I'm so sorry." I couldn't bring myself to admit to her the part I'd played.

"Come back in and help."

"Syd told me to stay away until he called."

"Syd can fuck off."

I almost dropped the phone. I'd never heard a swear word of any kind out of Cindy's mouth, or even one allowed in her presence.

"Dennis needs you," she repeated. "I'll get your badge reactivated."

"But—"

"But nothing. Don't leave him to fight this alone."

Her words stung. But maybe I owed it to Dennis to fight, not just slink away in the shame of what I'd done. What kind of woman did that?

Not any kind I wanted to be.

"I'm on my way."

I put the wine glass down. I was done with self-pity.

We hung up, and I didn't take the time to put my hair back up before grabbing my purse on my way out.

We hadn't lost yet, and my one regret from this morning was not going back into the boardroom to personally kick Cartwright in the balls.

DENNIS

THREE LAPS TURNED INTO MORE THAN A DOZEN BEFORE I ENTERED THE BUILDING again.

After my long walk that went nowhere, the heat in the elevator was more uncomfortable than usual.

I opened the door to our executive area, *my* executive area. This was still my fucking company.

Cindy nodded toward my door. "I got you a surprise."

"Not sure I can stand any more surprises today."

She merely smiled back.

I opened the door, and Jennifer was in my chair.

"I'm here to help," she said.

Her hair was down, the way I enjoyed it on the weekends.

I closed the door behind me and opened my arms.

We met mid-room for the kiss I owed her. My eyes closed, our lips met, and the scent of peaches filled my nostrils, bringing me back to the first kiss we'd shared in this room: the piss-off-Melissa kiss that had started it all.

Jennifer broke the kiss too soon for me.

I stroked her long locks. "I like the hair."

She smiled and twisted the ends around her finger. "Syd told me to stay home."

"Syd can go fuck himself."

She giggled. "Cindy said the same thing."

"I'll have to give her a raise for expanding her vocabulary."

Cindy's distinctive knock sounded.

I took a step away from Jennifer. "Yes?"

Cindy poked her head in. "IT has the computer you wanted."

"Let's have it."

An IT tech wheeled in a cart with a computer, monitor, and a fresh printer to replace what had been taken.

Oleg, the department head, followed him in.

"Did you fix my phone yet?" I asked.

Oleg stopped. "Still working on that."

The tech lifted the computer off the cart, placed it where the old one had been, and started connecting things.

I stepped forward to see what he was doing. "How long will it take to get software loaded so I can get back to work?"

Oleg answered. "Already done. We back up all the machines every night, so this is an exact copy of your machine the way it was when you came in this morning. All you've lost is anything you did today."

A few seconds later, the tech powered up my machine. "You're all set to go."

I thanked them as they left and asked Cindy to reassemble the brain trust, this time in my office.

Syd eyed Jennifer as he walked in. "I don't think this is wise, Dennis."

"She stays," I told him.

He shrugged. "Your call."

"Where do we start?" Jay asked.

Larry spoke up first. "Did you do it?" he asked me.

The question was beyond stupid.

If I'd had something to throw, I would have. "What the fuck do you think?"

"I think you didn't." He turned to Jennifer. "Did you write those articles in the *Times*?"

Her answer was swift—and truthful as far as it went. "I did not."

Larry looked back at me. "That means we need to figure out how Cartwright is framing you."

An almost-smile appeared on Syd's face. "I agree with Larry."

"That's a first," Larry said.

"What was on your computer that would be incriminating?" Jay asked Jennifer.

She shrugged. "Nothing that I know of."

"There has to be something," he countered.

Syd pointed out the obvious. "We don't have the machine, so we're not going to know until they tell us."

"Not necessarily true," I told him.

That drew a befuddled look from Syd.

I picked up the office phone and dialed down to IT. "Oleg, get your butt back up to my office."

Jennifer gave me a knowing look.

"We can make a clone," I told the group. I explained how I'd just gotten a copy of my machine from this morning delivered.

Oleg entered, breathless from what must have been a sprint back upstairs. "Is something wrong with the computer?"

"No. I want you to make a clone of Miss Hanley's computer, just like you did mine. Then I want you to work with Syd here to comb through until we find it."

He looked puzzled. "What are we looking for?"

"I have no fucking idea. That's Syd's job. Syd, you and Oleg and his guys are to keep at it all night, if that's what it takes."

Syd sighed and stood. "We better get started, then."

"Okay, guys," I said. "We get back together as soon as they find something."

Larry came over before leaving. "What do I tell the analysts when they call? Cartwright is probably already on the phone with them."

I didn't have a good answer to that.

"Tell them to look forward to the other shoe dropping soon," Jennifer offered.

"What's the other shoe?"

"Our counterattack, but don't tell them that."

Larry nodded. "I like it."

"We still need to carry on with our normal business," Jay said, pointing to me. "And you owe me some time reviewing the inventory analysis before I finalize it."

An hour later, we were going over the inventory analysis downstairs in Jay's office when his phone rang.

He answered and handed it over to me. "It's Cindy for you."

"Yeah?"

"Ed is here, and he says he needs to see you right away."

"I'll be up in a few."

I left Jay's office, wondering what Ed had this time.

Upstairs, I found Ed at my door with Oleg, the IT prodigy. "What's going on?"

Ed nodded toward my office door instead of answering.

Security guys were always overly paranoid about talking in public.

Oleg followed me in and Ed brought up the rear, closing the door after him. "Oleg's guys found something on your phone you should be aware of."

I took my seat behind the desk. "Okay. What?"

Oleg spoke. "It's a piece of tracking software."

He still didn't look or sound over eighteen to me. "How long?"

Oleg shifted in his seat. "We can't say how long it has been on the phone, or how it got there."

"Given the Cartwright situation, they could be behind this," Ed suggested. "Monitoring your calls and your physical location."

"Son of a bitch. And you know it's Cartwright?"

Oleg shook his head. "We can't say yet. That will take some time."

"We can clean the malware off the phone," Ed offered.

Oleg concurred with a nod.

I thought for a moment. "Will they be able to tell?"

Ed looked to Oleg. "Yes. Definitely," he said.

That settled it for me. "I don't want them to suspect anything while you try to track it down. I'll get a new phone in the meantime. Thanks, guys."

Ed rose, and Oleg took the hint.

"One more thing," Ed said. "It'll have to be a new number. You have to leave the old number assigned to the old phone."

I rounded the desk and patted Oleg on the back. "Good work, and thanks guys. Keep working on Jennifer's computer."

～

Two hours later, Cindy handed me a new iPhone box and a clear case.

"Who gets your new number?" she asked.

"The senior staff. And send it to Dad, along with the rest of the family. That should do it for now." I opened the box. "You didn't." The phone was a godawful rose gold.

"You'll be stylish for a change."

I knew she'd picked the color on purpose to annoy me.

I put the ugly thing down.

At least now I knew how Cartwright had followed us on our shareholder visits.

～

*Jennifer*

Cindy called me back into Dennis's office around three.

The IT guy, Oleg, and Syd were already there.

Syd wore a sour face. "We found what they were after."

"What?" Dennis asked.

Syd handed Dennis several sheets of paper. "The private email you set up on the computer was hidden, but Oleg found it."

"What private email?" I asked.

Dennis was busy reading the sheets.

Oleg spoke up. "It wasn't that well hidden, and it contains—"

Syd interrupted him. "Jennifer, it's the emails you sent to the *Times* to publish."

My mouth went dry as I read the sheets with the articles I knew well, and each email said it had been sent by darkhorse666 to the *Times* shortly before the first two articles had been published, just like he said.

"This isn't me," I told them. "I didn't write these."

799

"They're on your computer, and they were sent to the paper. The dates match up with the stories."

I looked to Dennis, who hadn't said anything yet. "I swear I didn't write these."

Dennis read another page. "I don't see the latest one here."

"That's all we found," Oleg answered.

"How could you?" Syd said, looking squarely at me. He'd clearly already convicted me in his mind. "These are company trade secrets. You know sending these out to the paper is a federal offense."

"I told you I didn't write those."

"It's in black and white, perfectly clear to me," he shot back.

"It's not clear to me," Dennis said.

I blew out a relieved breath.

"Syd, you're not helping," Dennis added. He put the sheets down. "Oleg, could these have been placed on the computer by someone else?"

The computer guy cocked his head. "It's possible, but they would have had to access the machine directly. It's also possible that she clicked on some malware on the web that downloaded it."

"I don't go clicking around the web. I know better than that," I protested.

"I just said it's possible," Oleg explained.

Dennis steepled his hands. "And the SEC guys—would they be able to tell if that happened?"

"No. If I can't tell, they certainly can't. The most likely way for them to be there is that she wrote them."

"You keep your office locked, right?" Syd asked me.

I nodded. "Every night."

Dennis shook his head. "Hold on, Syd. Oleg, you told me you backup every day, right?"

"Three hundred sixty-five days a year."

"Then I want to know what day each of these documents appeared in our backups."

Oleg pulled out his phone and barked a few instructions to one of his guys. "Yes, day by day for each file in the darkhorse folder we found." He hung up. "It'll take a few minutes."

"Then we wait," Dennis said.

"Can I go?" Syd asked.

Dennis waved him away. "Sure."

I felt Syd's accusatory stare as he left the room.

The minutes ticked by slowly.

# CHAPTER 43

*DENNIS*

FINALLY OLEG'S PHONE RANG. "YEAH?...ARE YOU SURE?... THANKS. YEAH THAT'S IT for now, I think." He hung up. "They all showed up four weeks ago on the fifteenth. There's no trace of them before that."

I drew in a relieved breath. At least now I knew what Cartwright's plan had been and how he'd executed it—at least, almost all of it. "Thanks, Oleg. That's it for now."

Oleg seemed happy to get out of my office, and he closed the door.

"You believe me, don't you?" Jennifer asked.

"Of course I do, Angel."

She settled into her seat, seeming relieved.

"You told me what you did and didn't do, and I have to get to the bottom of this without giving the guys that piece of the puzzle."

"I can quit if I have to," she mumbled.

I rounded the desk. "Not on your life." I pulled her up to stand and took her into my arms.

"Wouldn't that make it easier?" she mumbled into my shoulder.

"No. We're in this together, you and me. What kind of boyfriend would I be if I let you do that?"

"A smart one, maybe."

I let go of her. "Bullshit. Now get going. Go work with Oleg. Show him what you do on the web, answer any questions he has. We have to figure out how they set us both up, and I have a call to make."

She turned for the door.

"And leave your hair like that," I added.

She turned. "It's more professional up."

"I could make it an order."

She shook her head and left.

I lifted the phone and dialed downstairs.

Ed answered. "Yes, boss?"

"Ed, we think somebody got access to Jennifer's computer on the fourteenth or fifteenth, and I need to know who."

"Does this have to do with those *Times* articles?"

"It does. It looks like someone planted something on her computer, and I need to know who."

"You don't think she was involved?"

I sighed, ignoring his question. "I need to know who got into her office. And I need to know today."

"We'll start on it right away."

～

*Jennifer*

I walked back from my second run to the coffee machine. Waiting in my empty office with nothing to do was the pits.

A security guy stood outside my door.

I ignored him and went inside.

Ed got up from a chair. "Jennifer."

I put my cup down on the credenza. "Ed, you agreed to stay away."

"You should have talked to me earlier, when I might have been able to help you."

"Get out. We don't have anything to talk about."

"You have to come with me to the boss's office."

"What?"

The guy at the door made a move to enter, but Ed put his hand up to stop him. "Please don't make this any more difficult than it already is. We need to talk to Mr. Benson."

The other guy had a Taser on his belt.

I grabbed my coffee. "Whatever."

Ed followed me as I walked to Dennis's office. I'd had more Ed than I could stand, but whatever trouble he was making, I needed Dennis to straighten it out.

The door was open, so I marched in and took a seat.

Dennis looked up and put his pen down.

Ed closed the door after him, with his goon on the outside. "I need to give you some information about Miss Hanley."

Now he was going all cop-formal on us.

Dennis nodded. "Go ahead."

"She's been passing information to the Cartwright people."

"I have not," I spat. "This is just because—"

"Jenn, let him finish," Dennis said.

I grabbed the arm of the chair to control my anger.

Ed continued. "In addition to the meeting with Suzanne Murtog last month—"

"I explained that," I interrupted.

Dennis's eyes fixed me in place. "Jenn."

"In addition, I have this photo of her dropping off a folder in a park." Ed handed a picture to Dennis.

My stomach turned over, because Ed had discovered my interactions with Hydra. I could have asked why the hell he'd been following me like the stalker he was, but that wouldn't solve anything.

"And these." Ed slid over more small photos to Dennis. "The Cartwright person picking up the package."

*Fuck.* Things weren't looking up, if he'd caught Hydra.

I put my hand out toward Dennis. "I want to see those."

"Just a moment. Ed, email me this one." He held up a picture of someone getting into a car.

Ed fiddled with his cell. "Sure."

*Dennis*

Ed's picture of the car arrived in my email. I opened it, and that clinched it. I recognized that car, and on my big monitor, I could make out the vanity license plate I knew all too well.

He'd caught Jennifer's Hydra, and it all made sense now.

Jennifer still had her hand out to see the pictures, but I ignored her.

"Thanks, Ed. I know who this is. I'll take it from here."

"But don't you think we should—"

I stopped him with a raised hand. "Like I said, I'll handle the next step. And good work. This is really good work."

Ed stood and puffed up like I'd awarded him a medal, which was fine, because he'd just given us a break. "Thank you."

He left, clearly not happy that I hadn't asked him to handcuff Jennifer or something equally active.

The door closed.

"Gimme," Jennifer complained.

I handed her the pictures of Hydra. Although none of them had a good shot of the face, I recognized the car. "Jenn, I know who it is."

"Who?"

I looked back at my screen to reread the license plate again.

TOTALWAR.

The plate did fit her. "Your swim coach."

*JENNIFER*

"Your ex-wife? Melissa?"

He turned his monitor so I could see. "That's her license plate."

The plate read TOTALWAR. Should have been *total bitch.*

"Then we have her."

Dennis sighed. "Now that we know she was behind the articles and not Cartwright, this confuses things. How did the emails end up on your computer, and how did Cartwright know to send the SEC looking for them?"

"Do they know each other?" I asked.

"Probably, but that doesn't prove a connection. And that doesn't fix our SEC problem, or the proxy timing with Cartwright."

"You could confront her."

"That won't work. A picture of her picking up a package? That doesn't tie her to Cartwright, or prove the emails on your computer were planted."

I slumped in my chair. He was right. "I could email her and ask for a meeting."

"She won't fall for that. Tell me how she contacted you."

I sat up. "She would email me at home at nemesis666 using her HYDRA157 account. Her messages were file numbers, and nothing more. I'd email back when I put copies in the park, and then when I'd replaced the file where I'd gotten it."

He stroked his chin. "Do you have a list of the file numbers?"

"The most recent ones are on a Post-it in my purse."

"Were they all used in the articles, or are there still some left to publish?"

"A few were business plans that didn't fit with the articles, but everything else got published." I cringed, remembering the damage I'd caused the company with those articles, and all of it unwarranted.

Dennis closed his eyes and nodded, then opened them again. "Syd was more helpful than he realized." He pulled out his wallet and rummaged through it.

~

*Dennis*

"I've got an idea," I told Jennifer. After pulling the card I was looking for from my wallet, I dialed the number.

"Parsons," she answered.

"Agent Parsons. This is Dennis Benson."

"Dennis, I don't have anything further for you on Deborah."

"That's not why I was calling. I want to report that I've been the victim of a federal crime."

"Go ahead."

"Trade secrets have been stolen from my company."

"That's not my area, but I can put you in touch with the section head who handles that."

"I really want you on the case."

"Like I said, it's not my area."

I pulled out my trump card. "Do you remember Kirk Willey?"

She was quiet for a second. "This must be very important to you. How can I help?"

I let out a relieved sigh. "We performed a sting. A woman who works here was contacted by email to steal trade secrets."

Jennifer sent me a quizzical look.

"And?" Parsons asked.

"She dropped them off, and we have photographs of the thief picking them up."

"If you know who it is, we can bring him in for questioning," she offered.

"Her, actually. But I have a different question. Is that enough to get a warrant for the thief's email? And if you do get a warrant, will she know?"

"To your first question, if you and your employee sign affidavits that she was approached by this person, and that she turned over papers this person knew were trade secrets, the answer is yes. And no, she won't know about the warrant, most likely. We serve the warrant on the internet provider, not the person."

"Great. I'd like to get started this afternoon."

# CHAPTER 44

*DENNIS*
*(Two Days Later)*

LATE WEDNESDAY MORNING, THE STOCK WAS TAKING ANOTHER NOSEDIVE. LARRY'S
wait-for-the-other-shoe-to-drop line wasn't working anymore with the analysts,
and Cartwright was trumpeting the SEC investigation every chance he got.
Gumpert had called my direct number three times already this morning.

Cindy had handled him with more courtesy than he deserved.

Jennifer checked her watch. "She's late."

"That's normal."

Cindy popped her head in the open door. "She's downstairs. Should I have
security bring her up?"

"Why don't *you* bring her up? That would be more hospitable. Set her up in
conference room three."

"The boardroom is free, if you want to use that."

I shook my head. "No. Three is perfect. She won't be staying long. Oh, and
have her seated facing the hallway."

Cindy left, muttering.

"You didn't tell her the plan?" Jennifer asked.

I tapped the folder. "Only you and Syd."

Syd had to know, so he could check that all the legal technicalities were
correct. He'd enjoyed the irony of the plan and wanted to sit in, but I'd said no.

A few minutes later, Cindy was back. "The two of them are ready for you."

I stood and followed Jennifer to the conference room.

Melissa's face turned an angry red when Jennifer and I entered. "What is she doing here?"

I pulled out my chair after Jennifer took her seat. "She's my representative."

Melissa's lawyer slid a card across to Jennifer. "Karen Jenkins, Jenkins and Schwartz."

Jennifer took the card, but didn't offer one in return. "Oh, I'm not a lawyer."

Confusion filled the lawyer's face. "We thought this was going to be a resolution meeting."

"*Surrender* was the word you used," Melissa said.

It *was* the wording I'd used. She just didn't realize I meant *her* surrender.

Cindy knocked and opened the door. "The FBI is here to see you, Dennis."

"Tell them I'll be a few minutes." I turned far enough to see Parsons and Newsom waiting in the hall, wearing the FBI windbreakers I'd requested.

I'd chosen this room so that with the vertical blinds open, Melissa could see them clearly.

She smirked. "In trouble with the SEC, I hear."

I opened the folder and slid across the stapled copies of the emails I'd brought. "Yesterday the FBI served a warrant on your internet provider and found these emails."

She pushed them away with barely a glance. "I don't know anything about these."

It was Jennifer's turn to speak, and she aimed her words at the attorney. "I was approached by your client to steal trade secrets from the company. I passed them to her through a dead drop at a nearby park."

Melissa attempted a calm demeanor, but her facade cracked. "Lies."

Jennifer slid over the pictures of Melissa and her car. "The company surveilled the drop site after I left, and these are photographs of you picking up the material."

"I brought this to the attention of the FBI, and with the emails here..." I pointed to the paper stack. "...which are all tied to your home IP address, that gives us enough to have you charged with multiple counts of trade secret theft. That's up to ten years per count."

Jenkins's eyes bugged out. She put down the pictures and started to leaf through the emails.

"She's the one who stole them," Melissa complained, pointing at Jennifer.

"She did it at my direction, in order to find out who the real culprit was."

"That's a lie," Melissa spat. "It was all her idea."

"I don't think you should say any more," her lawyer cautioned.

"That's not the story the emails tell," I told her. "It's all in black and white, and it doesn't look very good for you. You recruited her, and you're the one who wrote the *Times* articles."

Melissa's face couldn't have been any redder.

I pulled out the documents Syd had prepared and slid them to Jenkins.

"Either we come to an understanding, and you sign these, or I'm going to meet with those two agents, and we'll see you in court."

"But..." Melissa started to say.

I stood. "You have five minutes."

Jennifer followed me out of the room.

I winked at Parsons. "Can you two give me a few minutes?" I said loudly enough to be heard in the conference room. I herded Jennifer down the hall. "Do you think she'll go for it?"

"Of course. Did you see her eyes when you told her ten years per offense?"

# CHAPTER 45

*JENNIFER*

A HALF HOUR LATER, CINDY HAD FINISHED NOTARIZING THE PAPERS, AND DENNIS and I were free of Melissa—hopefully forever. One of the papers she and her lawyer had signed ended the post-divorce dispute with Dennis.

I walked into the boardroom, where the next meeting was set to start soon.

Cartwright was due, and Dennis's fate hung in the balance. The Melissa legal dust-up was minor compared to Cartwright's attack.

Syd sat in his usual chair near the end, reading some of the papers Melissa had signed, and grinning.

I waited until he'd finished the last one. "Are those good enough to get us off the hook with the SEC?"

"Probably, but the timing isn't likely to be soon enough for the proxy vote. Even then, dropping the charges is not the same as the SEC declaring you innocent. Cartwright can still point to the original charges and claim that the SEC is just perfecting the case before they refile it. The whole thing casts a shadow over the company."

Larry wandered in. "Somebody said Cartwright was coming in. Should I join you?"

"Sure. You might find it entertaining," I said.

"You should ask Dennis," Syd told him.

Larry decided he liked my invitation better than Syd's warning and grabbed a seat. "What's the topic?"

"I'm just here to take notes," Syd grumbled.

"Why is he in such a good mood?" Larry said, leaning my way.

"My mood will improve when I stop being served court papers," Syd shot back.

A minute later, Cartwright and his slimeball lawyer arrived.

We went through the pleasantries without Dennis, and we all selected something to drink.

I stuck to Diet Coke—Dennis style, without a glass.

Dennis walked in and closed the door behind him. "Thanks for meeting us on such short notice."

Cartwright pasted on a smile. "You said you wanted to discuss restructuring the company, and that's a subject dear to my heart."

I doubted he had a heart. If he did, it was about to skip a beat.

Dennis took his seat, unscrewed the lid to his Coke, and downed a slug.

I did the same, and the glare we got from Cartwright was priceless. I unlocked my phone, selected the text message page, and put it in my lap in case I lost the bet.

Dennis spun his pen on the tabletop in front of him. "My ex-wife, Melissa, resigned from the board this morning."

"I take it you're offering us that seat?" Cartwright asked gleefully.

"Under the right circumstances. So you don't misunderstand, let me go through this slowly."

Cartwright sat back.

"Syd?" Dennis asked. "Do you have those papers Melissa signed?"

"Right here."

"Can I get a copy?" Larry asked.

"Pass them across, would you, please?" Dennis said, opening the folder in front of him and ignoring Larry.

Syd passed them to the two visitors. "I didn't bring extras," he told Larry.

Swartzman started the fireworks. "What is this bullshit?"

"Notarized statements that implicate your client in the stock manipulation you accused us of," Syd answered. "You orchestrated the negative press and bought on the down days."

"That's total crap," Cartwright spat. He pushed his chair back and stood. "We're not sticking around to be insulted."

I pressed send on the text I had ready. I'd lost the bet that they would stick around at least a minute to hear what we had.

ME: Now

Swartzman pushed his copy of the papers back at Syd and got up.

The text had gone to Cindy, and she opened the door as instructed. "Dennis, the two FBI agents you had an appointment with are here."

Swartzman and Cartwright froze at the word *FBI*.

"Have them wait a few minutes, please," Dennis told Cindy.

She closed the door.

Dennis spun his pen. "They're here to collect the evidence I have of your criminal conspiracy with my ex-wife."

The blood drained from Cartwright's face.

This was where it would get fun.

"Now, do you want me to pass it along, or would you rather listen to my proposed alternative?"

Cartwright answered by taking his seat again.

Swartzman followed.

Syd broke a smile.

"Very good," Dennis said. "Syd, show them the agreements."

Syd slid over a second set of papers.

Cartwright's eyes bulged. "A ten-percent discount? That's ridiculous."

The first page was an agreement for them to convert their stock to company debt at a ten-percent discount from their purchase price.

"And you expect us to help you finance a going-private transaction?" Swartzman asked. "Is this a joke?"

"No, and for that you get one board seat."

"That's worthless in a private company," Cartwright said.

"You're the one who wanted on the board. I want to take the company private, and this way we both get what we want."

Only, it wasn't anything like what Cartwright wanted. Because once the company went private, he lost all leverage.

"The agents are waiting," Dennis reminded them.

"A twenty-five percent premium, and I'll consider it."

Dennis took a long slug of his Coke. "Jennifer, you can handle it from here." He stood to leave.

"The case won't stand up," Swartzman argued.

"Syd, you can bring the affidavits along in a few minutes."

Syd nodded, and the door closed behind Dennis.

Swartzman pointed at me. "Nice try, but the SEC found the emails on your computer already, and that implicates you, not us."

Cartwright nodded, and his smile reappeared.

Larry's smile faded.

It was time, so I opened the folder I'd brought. "You directly attacked me, and if it were up to me, we'd be talking to the FBI right now. But Dennis is a nice guy and insisted on giving you a chance to find a mutually beneficial resolution."

Cartwright huffed. "You have a losing hand, young lady."

I held up the first paper. "You haven't seen all our cards yet. I have here an affidavit from Melissa Benson stating that she sent you, Carson..." I pointed a finger at him. "An email containing the files that were to be planted on my computer."

The happiness melted from his face.

I held up the USB Suzanne had given me with the resume on it she'd asked me to print and distribute. "You then had those files transferred to this thumb drive."

Swartzman objected. "We did no such thing."

"You instructed your employee Suzanne Murtog to give it to me." I lifted the last paper. "I also have an outside analysis confirming that this USB contains malware that would transfer the files to any computer it's plugged in to. I attached it to mine on the day I met her."

Cartwright glanced at his lawyer and back to me.

"The analysis also shows that the files on my computer are identical to the ones on this USB drive, and also identical to the ones emailed to you by Melissa Benson. They appeared on my computer that same day I met with your employee. And yes, the FBI retrieved those emails of Ms. Benson's yesterday with a warrant, so there is no question of their authenticity."

Happy Larry spoke up. "I'd say that is game, set, match."

Syd nodded, now back in confident mode. He'd not known what I had up my sleeve.

Cartwright shifted in his seat. "We'll need some time to read these over and consider it."

Swartzman nodded his agreement.

I checked my watch. "You have sixty seconds before I send Syd to join Dennis with the FBI agents. Decide quickly."

Cartwright looked at his attorney, who shrugged and put pen to paper.

A minute later they were gone, and Larry and Syd were high-fiving it.

# EPILOGUE

## "LIFE IS A FLOWER OF WHICH LOVE IS THE HONEY." — VICTOR HUGO

*JENNIFER*

It was Saturday morning, and as usual, the bedroom window was cracked open at the beach house. The wind made the curtains billow slightly, letting in the morning light. This early, the only noises outside came from the surf in the distance.

I rolled toward Dennis.

He was fast asleep after our late-night bottles of celebratory champagne. The go-private transaction had closed yesterday, and the company was now out of Cartwright's or anyone else's reach. The king's throne was secure.

Lifting up to see the red numerals on the clock, I realized we didn't have much time this morning. We were due over at the big house early, to get it ready for all the employees he'd invited to celebrate with us this afternoon.

The magazines said a man's testosterone levels were highest in the morning, and I had no intention of letting that go to waste. I got wet just thinking about the prospect. Slipping beneath the comforter, I lay my head on his abdomen, grabbed for my prize, and started to stroke.

He was already erect, and growing harder.

"Morning, Angel," he said groggily.

That name still sent a tingle down my spine every time—especially now that I knew I wasn't destined to disappoint him by being the avenging angel.

"Morning. Does Little Denny want to play?"

"Always, but you know that name sucks."

"How 'bout Big Willy?"

He pulled me up from my cave under the covers. "That still needs work."

I kept stroking him. "You have two choices this morning."

"Who's being bossy today?"

"You said I could have a turn." I made that part up, but it was worth a try.

"When?"

I kissed him lightly. "Last night after your third or fourth glass."

"I don't remember it that way."

I pulled my hand away. "Are you going to renege on a promise?" I scooted to the side of the bed to get up.

He pulled me back to him. "Never, my love. What are my choices?"

I took his nipple in my teeth.

He tensed.

I released. "We could go out and do it under the lifeguard tower."

"In the daylight? No way."

"It's dangerous."

"It's that, and a good way to get arrested. That'll have to wait until really late at night."

The danger of it obviously excited him.

"Or I'm in charge. My rules." *Take that, Mr. Control Freak.*

"Today is your day, Angel. You can have anything you want."

I pushed him over onto his back and threw the covers off. Moving down south, I gave his cock a long, slow lick from root to tip before taking him in my mouth for a few quick strokes in and out. It was sexy the way his cock jerked slightly as I blew cold air on the wet underside, or tickled just below the tip.

I stroked his hard length with a light grip and moved down to cup his balls.

He pulled at my shoulders to get access to my breasts, but I resisted. "My rules."

I climbed up over him and positioned myself over his super-hard cock.

He reached for my breasts, kneaded them, and thumbed my nipples with the circular motion that always got to me.

I lowered myself onto him, a bit down and then back up, and a little more down, teasing him with my slow approach.

His eyes showed the lust I'd induced in him. Holding back and not taking charge was killing him.

His gentle moans as I lowered myself, and his gasps as I pulled up were my guide. I took more of him with each stroke until I reached his root. I rocked into him, and he guided me up and down with his hands on my hips.

He moved to thumb my clit, but I jerked his hand away. He tried again, and I pulled him away again.

I shoved down fully, and his steely cock stretched me. "My rules today. You come first."

He always made me come first, and often more than once, before he did. It was his superpower, but this morning I wanted things to be different.

He relented and resorted to guiding my hips with his hands. He thrust up into me with my every downstroke. Each thrust seemed deeper and more filling than the one before.

I neared my limit as every cell of my body tensed with the thrusts down. Every lift up had all my nerves on fire, but I held off. I had to. I had to make him come first today. With concentration, I could win. I knew I could.

He tensed, and his breathing became shallow and rapid as he neared his limit.

I rocked down hard on him. I reached behind to grab his balls and used my other hand to pinch his nipple. He came with a loud groan and a final deep push. He gushed into me as he held me down on him.

His legs shook, and his cock continued to throb inside me as I ground down on him. He moved his thumb to my clit, and this time I allowed it.

I'd won for once.

His circling pressure on my sensitive nub quickly took me over the top. I couldn't hold off any longer and came undone on a shudder.

I leaned forward on him. I couldn't catch my breath as the spasms shook me and my body dissolved in a heap.

He hugged me tightly. "Angel, I love you," he groaned into my ear.

"I love you, too."

A perfect smile filled his face as I lifted up off his chest to kiss him.

I relaxed down against him again. The pulses of his cock inside me slowly diminished. This was always the best part, the ultimate closeness between us, physically and emotionally linked to each other.

I rolled off of him and headed to the shower. I turned at the door. "How about Dickzilla?"

He huffed. "Keep trying, Angel."

◇

*Jennifer*

Dennis had hired Lusso's Catering for the event at the big house, and I felt like a bit of a fifth wheel instead of the hostess. The backyard was overflowing with people from the company.

Tony Lusso had taken over the huge kitchen, and he barked orders at his staff.

I quickly grabbed a can of the Bud from the fridge, which I'd stocked for Ramona's new squeeze, Ian.

He was fireman with the LAFD. Ramona had met him at her new job at Mercy Hospital, now that she'd graduated. He seemed nice, and because he was divorced with a six-year-old son, the two had a lot in common as single parents.

I located them out back by the pool, and handed the chilled beer to Ian. "You know we have other choices as well."

"It's Bud or nothing, and I have to stop drinking by three. I've got a shift tomorrow."

Ramona deserved a responsible guy after what she'd been through with Billy's father, and Ian definitely checked that box.

It also didn't hurt that when we'd gotten together a few times on the weekends, Ian had impressed Dennis as well.

Ian had been spending quite a bit of time at our new place, which had allowed me to spend more time at Dennis's.

Billy crouched down to feel the pool's temperature. "Can we go swimming later?"

"Bill, you have to ask Uncle Dennis," his mother replied.

Every time I heard Ramona use that nickname, I wished it were true. But after the disaster of his quick marriage to Melissa, I understood that *slow* was Dennis's watchword for relationships.

Ian's son tugged on his father's leg. "Can I be Ron? I don't like Ronnie anymore."

"You're not old enough yet," Billy told him proudly.

I left them to find my Denny.

As I searched for him, I was relieved that one face was missing in the crowd.

Ed had moved to another company. Dennis had written him a nice letter of recommendation, which he honestly deserved. We wouldn't be where we were today without his help nailing Melissa.

Fortunately, months ago he'd come to grips with the situation and picked up with a new girl. The texts had stopped permanently, and I'd come to realize that the later ones had been his way of trying to help me. After he'd realized what I'd been doing, he hadn't turned me in, but instead reached out to talk.

Eventually I located Dennis talking to his father.

Serena joined us.

"So you were behind that?" Dennis asked Lloyd.

"I knew you weren't going to ask *me* if you needed help, so I had Hugh approach you."

Dennis had finally told Hugh Stoner last month that we weren't interested in his livestock feed business.

Stoner had admitted it had been Lloyd's idea all along.

"That's underhanded," Dennis complained.

"It worked, didn't it?"

It had worked. We'd been in contact with Stoner for a long time, and he'd been there when Dennis needed help talking to shareholders.

Serena elbowed me and whispered, "He didn't suspect?"

I whispered back. "Not a clue."

"I told you Cartwright was a snake. He always has been," Lloyd said. "I still wish he'd gotten jail time. It's what he deserves." The animosity was palpable.

Dennis finished his sip of wine. "He's gone for good now."

"I wouldn't count on that. The Cartwrights are like a bad rash, always appearing at the worst times."

"But you were wrong about the attack on Josh being Cartwright's doing," Dennis noted.

We'd been informed that the police had made an arrest in another road rage incident where shots were fired, and the gun they found on the guy matched the bullets in Josh's car. Since they didn't have any other evidence, they couldn't prosecute him in Josh's incident, but they would get him on the current charge.

"There's a first for everything," Lloyd said. "I've been right about them all the rest of the times. Bad apples, the whole lot of them."

While they went back and forth on the Cartwright family, I asked Serena, "Is there a history I don't know about?"

She nodded. "Dad won't tell us the details. All we know is it's bad."

I filed that comment away for later.

Although Dennis's solution to getting rid of Cartwright didn't sit well with his father, it was a win-win, which was pure Dennis. We were done with both him and Melissa. And by taking the company private with Cartwright's forced help, Dennis no longer had to deal with the Wall Street types he despised.

To add irony to the situation, Dennis told me he'd given Gumpert's number to Melissa.

I hadn't understood why, until Dennis had said they had similar moral compasses, and he deserved her.

Having experienced Melissa, I wasn't sure anybody deserved her.

"Hey, Larry, get control of your dog," Dennis called out.

Serena and I cracked up.

Larry's little mutt Binky was dry-humping Dennis's leg.

The attractive brunette on Larry's arm raced over to fetch the little monster. "Binky, behave yourself." She picked him up and whisked him away.

Larry had decided to keep Binky after women started approaching him at the park to meet the hairless wonder.

Dennis and I'd had Larry and several of his ladies over for dinner, and so far this latest one, Sylvia, had lasted the longest.

After a fair amount of food and alcohol had been served, Dennis dragged me with him up to the deck. "Gather round," he yelled a few times.

Ramona and Ian joined us on the deck.

Larry whistled loudly to get everybody's attention, and Syd went inside to pull anyone else out.

Dennis had worked on a speech for this crowd of mostly Vipersoft employees, intended to tell them how he felt about the future of the company now that it had gone private. The speech emphasized the company's new ability to plan for the long term instead of the short. He'd been totally focused on how it would provide a more stable workplace for the employees.

I was proud of the job he'd done with it and expected it to go well.

Dennis pulled the folded sheets of his speech from his pocket. "Thank you all for coming. We officially completed the go-private transaction yesterday."

There were a few claps.

He still hadn't opened his notes yet. "I know the last half year or so has been a rough time for all of us, and I appreciate all your support in this process. I prepared a few words for you." He unfolded and held up the pages. "But I feel they are inadequate for the occasion."

He refolded the papers. "The reorganization we accomplished isn't yet complete."

He'd lost me, and judging by the faces in the crowd, most of them as well.

"Jennifer, Larry, and Syd have been a great help in this. But one thing remains incomplete that I need Jennifer's help with."

He was seriously off script.

I surveyed the crowd, and with everybody looking at me, my blush went to three alarms. I looked back at Dennis, and he was on one knee.

"Jennifer Susan Hanley," he began.

I couldn't believe my eyes.

Ramona had handed him a box—a fucking Harry Winston jewelry box.

He opened the case.

A gorgeous diamond solitaire sat in the blue velvet.

Tears of joy welled in my eyes. This was really happening.

"And this is not an opportunity for negotiation," he said.

The crowd laughed.

"Will you marry me?"

The crowd hushed.

"Yes," I squeaked. "Yes."

The applause started, and Dennis rose to kiss me. It was another one of those breathless kisses that made the noise of the gathering drop into the background, behind the thundering of my heart.

He released me, too soon, and slipped the ring onto my finger. We were official.

"You make me so happy," he said loudly.

We descended the deck into the throng of well-wishers, and Lusso's people were miraculously everywhere, passing out champagne.

After the congratulations died down, Dennis and I wandered the thinning crowd.

"I have one problem," I told Dennis as I waved my sister over.

Dennis held my hand. "The deal is done. No re-negotiation allowed, and no arguments."

"I still have to help out with Bill. She can't handle him alone."

"I heard that, and no you don't," Ramona said as she and Ian walked up.

Her boyfriend put his arm around her. "We're moving you out, and Ronnie and I are moving in."

Dennis squeezed my hand. "I asked your sister's permission first."

Ramona giggled. "It was sorta sweet. He was worried about Bill."

I snuggled up to my man. "How did I get so lucky?"

"I'm the lucky one," Dennis replied.

I knew I was truly the lucky one, but decided to live with his request for no arguments.

At least for today.

**THE END**